How to Read Chinese Prose in Chinese

HOW TO READ CHINESE LITERATURE

HOW TO READ CHINESE LITERATURE

ZONG-QI CAI, GENERAL EDITOR

YUAN XINGPEI, EDITORIAL BOARD DIRECTOR

How to Read Chinese Poetry: A Guided Anthology

(2008)

How to Read Chinese Poetry Workbook

(2012)

How to Read Chinese Poetry in Context:

Poetic Culture from Antiquity Through the Tang

(2017)

How to Read Chinese Prose: A Guided Anthology

(2022)

How to Read Chinese Prose in Chinese: A Course in Classical Chinese

(2022)

How to Read Chinese Drama: A Guided Anthology

(2022)

How to Read Chinese Prose in Chinese
A Course in Classical Chinese

Jie Cui, Yucai Liu, and Zong-qi Cai

Columbia University Press   New York

Columbia University Press wishes to express its appreciation for assistance given
by the Center for Language Education and Cooperation in the publication of this series.

Columbia University Press
Publishers Since 1893
New York   Chichester, West Sussex
cup.columbia.edu

Library of Congress Cataloging-in-Publication Data
Names: Cui, Jie (Chinese philologist) author. | Liu, Yucai, 1964– author. |
Cai, Zong-qi, 1955– author.
Title: How to read Chinese prose in Chinese : a course in classical Chinese
/ Jie Cui, Yucai Liu and Zong-qi Cai.
Description: New York : Columbia University Press, 2022. | Series: How to
read Chinese literature
Identifiers: LCCN 2021010090 (print) | LCCN 2021010091 (ebook) | ISBN
9780231202923 (hardback) | ISBN 9780231202930 (trade paperback) | ISBN
9780231554787 (ebook)
Subjects: LCSH: Chinese language—Readers. | Chinese language—Textbooks
for foreign speakers—English. | Chinese prose literature—History and
criticism. | LCGFT: Textbooks.
Classification: LCC PL1117 .H69 2022 (print) | LCC PL1117 (ebook) | DDC
495.186/421—dc23
LC record available at https://lccn.loc.gov/2021010090
LC ebook record available at https://lccn.loc.gov/2021010091

Columbia University Press books are printed on permanent and durable acid-free paper.
Printed in the United States of America

Cover design: Milenda Nan Ok Lee
Cover image: Susii © Shutterstock

目 錄

Contents

* This text is also featured, with English translation and commentary, in *How to Read Chinese Prose: A Guided Anthology* (New York: Columbia University Press, 2022).

Preface to the How to Read Chinese Literature Series

Welcome to the How to Read Chinese Literature series, a comprehensive collection of literary anthologies and language texts covering all the major genres of Chinese literature. The series will consist of ten volumes: five guided literary anthologies, one book on literary culture, and four language companions. Together, they will try to promote the teaching and learning of premodern Chinese poetry, fiction, drama, prose, and literary criticism.

In particular, the five guided anthologies offer innovative ways of overcoming some barriers that have long hindered the teaching and learning of Chinese literature. While fine scholarly monographs on Chinese literature abound, they are usually too specialized for classroom use. To make that scholarship more accessible, each guided anthology presents the highlights of scholarship on major genres and writers through commentary on individual texts as well as broad surveys.

Every reader of Chinese literature is aware of the gap between English translations and Chinese originals. Since most existing anthologies offer only an English translation, however, students often find it hard to see how diverse linguistic elements work together in the original. To remedy this, each guided anthology presents the Chinese text alongside an English translation, with detailed remarks on the intricate interplay of word, image, and sound in Chinese.

So far, scant attention has been given to the relation between sound and sense in English-language studies of Chinese literature. As a corrective, the poetry anthology explains in detail the prosodic conventions of all major poetic genres and marks the tonal patterning in regulated verse and *ci* poetry. Samples of reconstructed ancient and medieval pronunciation are also given to show how the poems were probably pronounced when first composed. For the poetry and prose anthologies, we offer a sound recording of selected texts, read in Mandarin. For the drama and fiction anthologies, video clips of traditional storytelling and dramatic performance will be provided free of charge online.

For decades the study of Chinese literature in the West was a purely intellectual and aesthetic exercise, completely divorced from language learning. To accommodate demand from an ever increasing number of Chinese language learners, we provide tone-marked romanizations for all poetry texts, usually accompanied by sound recording. For any text also featured in the accompanying language companion, cross-references allow the reader to quickly proceed to in-depth language study of the original.

Designed to work with the guided anthologies, the four language companions introduce classical Chinese to advanced beginners and above, teaching them how to appreciate Chinese literature in its original form. As stand-alone resources, these texts illustrate China's major literary genres and themes through a variety of examples.

Each language companion presents a select number of works in three different forms— Chinese, English, and tone-marked romanization—while providing comprehensive vocabulary notes and prose translations in modern Chinese. Subsequent comprehension questions and comments focus on the artistic aspect of the works, while exercises test readers' grasp of both classical and modern Chinese words, phrases, and syntax. An extensive glossary cross-references classical and modern Chinese usage, characters and compounds, and multiple character meanings. Sound recording is provided for each selected text in the poetry and prose companions. Along with other learning aids, a list of literary issues addressed throughout completes each volume.

To achieve a seamless integration of literary anthologies and language companions, we draw from the same corpus of canonical texts and employ an extensive network of cross-references. Moreover, by presenting the ten books as a coherent set, we aim to help readers cross the divide between literary genres and between literary and language learning, thereby achieving a kind of experience impossible with traditional approaches. Thanks to the innovative features described above, we hope the series will help to energize the learning and teaching of Chinese literature, language, and culture throughout the English-speaking world for decades to come.

Zong-qi Cai

A Note on How to Use This Book

Our goal with this book is twofold: to introduce major Chinese prose genres developed from antiquity to the early twentieth century and, at the same time, to systematically teach the essentials of classical Chinese.

As indicated by the addition of "in Chinese" to the title, this book serves as the Chinese language learner's version of *How to Read Chinese Prose: A Guided Anthology* (hereafter *HTRCProse*). We present forty-four prose texts (excerpts or complete texts) in the original over thirty-eight lessons, organized by genre into eight units. The sequence of these units reflects the successive emergence of eight major prose genres, while the four to six lessons in each unit showcase that genre's prominent achievements through different historical periods. Readers of this book will gain the same kind of exposure to the rich legacy of Chinese prose as *HTRCProse* readers, along with the additional insight that comes from approaching texts in their original language. Comprehension and appreciation of selected texts is aided by notes on their historical and cultural contexts as well as by commentaries on their unique artistic features, with extensive reference to more in-depth discussions in *HTRCProse*. These literary commentaries are generously provided by twelve *HTRCProse* contributors, all experts on individual prose genres. Famous, oft-quoted idioms and remarks are highlighted by shading and should be learned by heart.

As the subtitle suggests, this book is also—perhaps to many, primarily—a course text for classical Chinese. In each lesson, we provide copious vocabulary notes with modern Chinese equivalents for premodern words and phrases and sample sentences to illustrate their idiomatic usage.

In addition, we introduce one to seven major grammar points per lesson (in all but lessons 20, 25, 27, 34, and 38). A distinctive feature of our approach to classical Chinese grammar is the emphasis on helping readers recognize different grammatical functions performed by the same function word (*xuci* 虛詞). Multiple functions of major function words are clearly numbered (①②③ and so on) and are gradually introduced over a few lessons. Whenever a major function word appears in a text, we identify and explain its particular function in that text while alerting the reader to its other uses through our system of interlesson cross-references. For instance, in explaining the function word 夫 in lesson 8, we provide this interlesson reference to its other uses: "Three uses of 夫 are explained in this book. In addition to the use below, see 夫①② in L2 Grammar Note 4." Moreover, when a taught function word reappears in another text, we always list it in the vocabulary notes with a prompt where its use has been explained: for example, "See L2 Grammar Note 4 ①."

Another noteworthy feature is the keying of grammar explanations to the selected texts. We illustrate all grammar points with examples drawn almost exclusively from the current or previous lessons, aiming for a mutually enhancing effect between these aspects of study. To deepen comprehension of the texts and grammar points, we typically provide five sets of exercises in each lesson. In addition, "Unit Exercises" help readers review and synthesize what they've learned in a unit; the answers can be found in the back matter. After careful study of this rigorous presentation, readers should have a firm grasp of all the critical aspects of classical Chinese grammar, codified in "Essentials of Classical Chinese Grammar Taught" in the back matter.

Combining a prose anthology with a classical Chinese textbook under one cover was clearly a daunting task—and no doubt the reason it was never attempted before now. Perhaps the greatest challenge was to align these very different goals in a lesson sequence that simultaneously reflects the historical development of prose genres and provides a gradual, measured increase in language difficulty. To overcome this obstacle, we devised a translation approach: by providing modern Chinese translations alongside original texts, we believe we can make all texts, even the earliest ones, accessible.

Translation is done in simplified Chinese with basic vocabulary and should be readily comprehensible to second- and third-year students of Chinese.

We would advise readers to first read the simplified Chinese translation for content and then read the original text in traditional Chinese against the translation. A side benefit of this approach is that readers will boost their proficiency in recognizing traditional Chinese characters. As additional reading aids, we have provided tone-marked romanization and sound recordings for all lessons, accessible free of charge at **cup.columbia.edu/supplemental-materials-for-how-to-read-chinese-prose-in-chinese** (QR code given below), as well as copious vocabulary and culture notes.

Having benefited so much from the readers of the *How to Read Chinese Poetry* set, we wish to engage the readers of this book through social media. We encourage all interested readers to visit **facebook.com/HowtoReadChinesePoetryZongqiCai** and work together to form an active community of Chinese literature lovers. We will do our best to foster and maintain an informative dialogue on all matters concerning the series volumes and the teaching and learning of Chinese literature in general.

Finally, we would like to thank Jennifer Crewe, associate provost and director of Columbia University Press, for her enthusiastic support of the How to Read Chinese Literature series and Christine Dunbar for her editorial guidance. Our thanks to Christian Winting for assistance with clerical matters; to Zhao Bingbing and Cara Ryan for their meticulous copyediting of the Chinese and English parts of the book, respectively; and last but not least to *HTRCProse* contributors for their literary commentaries illuminating all the lessons.

Zong-qi Cai

 Sound files for all selected texts

Symbols, Abbreviations, and Typographical Usages

☞	A marker of reference or cross-reference.
① ② ③	An enumeration of a word's multiple grammatical functions.
MdnC	Modern Chinese.
L1	Lesson 1 in this book.
HTRCProse	Zong-qi Cai, ed., *How to Read Chinese Prose: A Guided Anthology*. New York: Columbia University Press, 2022.
<u>齊</u>，<u>曹劌</u>	An underline is added to a proper name for a person, a place, or a state.
之ₐ, 之_b, 之_c	Subscripts a, b, and c indicate different meanings or functions of a word that appears more than once in a text.
一鼓作氣	Shading is applied to all famous and oft-quoted phrases.
军队	A wavy underline is applied to a modern Chinese word given as a gloss to a classical Chinese word and used in the modern Chinese translation.
（这些东西）	Words and phrases added to smooth modern Chinese translations are put in parentheses.

Contributors Who Have Written Literary Analyses for This Book

AKD   Alexei Kamran Ditter, Associate Professor, Reed College

ML   Manling Luo, Associate Professor, Indiana University

PRG   Paul Goldin, Professor, University of Pennsylvania

RE   Ronald Egan, Confucius Institute Professor of Sinology, Stanford University

RHS   Rivi Handler-Spitz, Associate Professor, Macalester College

SC   Scott Cook, Tan Chin Tuan Professor, Yale-NUS College, National University of Singapore

SFL   Shuen-fu Lin, Emeritus Professor, University of Michigan at Ann Arbor

WHN   William Nienhauser, Halls-Bascom Emeritus Professor, University of Wisconsin at Madison

WL   Wai-yee Li, 1879 Professor, Harvard University

XL   Xinda Lian, Professor, Denison University

YW   Yugen Wang, Associate Professor, University of Oregon

ZC   Zong-qi Cai, Professor, Lingnan University of Hong Kong, University of Illinois at Urbana-Champaign

How to Read Chinese Prose in Chinese
A Course in Classical Chinese

第一課

《左傳》：曹劌論戰

"Cao Gui on Military Strategy," from *Zuo Tradition*

Introduction

Zuo Tradition 左傳 (*Zuǒzhuàn* 左传) is a year-by-year history of China covering the period from 722 BCE (the first year of Duke Yin of Lu 魯隱公) to 468 BCE (the twenty-seventh year of Duke Ai of Lu 魯哀公). Early Chinese sources claim that the author of this history was a relatively obscure associate of Confucius (551–479 BCE) named Zuo Qiuming. However, the text as we have it today took shape around the fourth century BCE, well after Zuo Qiuming would have lived. *Zuo Tradition* is traditionally regarded as a comprehensive commentary on the *Spring and Autumn Annals* 春秋 (*Chūnqiū*) and the definitive history of the Spring and Autumn period.

This excerpt tells of Cao Gui, a man not of noble lineage, who masterfully leads the Lu troops to defeat the stronger Qi army. His conversations with the Lu lord spell out two important factors for military victory: winning the people's trust and support and launching an attack at the best moment—when morale is ebbing for the enemy but still high among one's own troops. A translation of this text is given in *HTRCProse*, chapter 2, "Pre-Qin Historical Prose: *Zuo Tradition* (*Zuozhuan*)," C2.6.

Zuo Tradition is also regarded as a masterpiece of Chinese prose, known for its dramatic and anecdotal narration, vivid portrayal of historical figures, and terse, expressive language. The excerpted passage exemplifies these traits.

正文與簡體譯文 Text and Modern Chinese Translation

十年春，齊師伐我。¹ 公將戰。曹劌
shí nián chūn qí shī fá wǒ gōng jiāng zhàn cáo guì

請見。² 其鄉人曰：「肉食者謀之，又何間
qǐng jiàn qí xiāng rén yuē ròu shí zhě móu zhī yòu hé jiàn

焉？」³ 劌曰：「肉食者鄙，未能遠謀。」⁴
yān guì yuē ròu shí zhě bǐ wèi néng yuǎn móu

鲁庄公十年的春天，齐国的军队要攻打我鲁国。¹鲁庄公将要迎战。曹刿请求拜见鲁庄公。²他的乡人说："这是吃肉的人谋划的事情，你又为什么要参与到这件事情里面?"³曹刿说："吃肉的人目光短浅，不能够考虑长远。"⁴

1. 十年 or 魯莊公(鲁庄公)十年 the tenth year of Lord Zhuang of Lu, 684 BCE.
   齊 (齐) the Qi state.
   師 (师) *n.* troops. MdnC: 軍隊 (*jūn duì* 军队).

伐 *v.* to launch a punitive expedition against, attack. MdnC: 攻打 (*gōng dǎ*).

我 *pron.* I, me. Here it refers to the Lu state.

2. 公 refers to 魯莊 (鲁庄) 公 (ancestral name 姓, Jī 姬; given name 名, Tóng 同; r. 693–662 BCE) Lord Zhuang of Lu, the sixteenth king of the Lu state in the Spring and Autumn period.

曹劌 (刿) (fl. 684 BCE) a famous strategist of Lu in the Spring and Autumn period.

見 (见) *v.* to pay a formal visit. MdnC: 拜見 (*bài jiàn* 拜见).

3. 食 *v.* to eat. MdnC: 吃 (*chī*).

者 *auxiliary pron.* the one who…. MdnC: ……的人 (*de rén*). 肉食者 means "the people who eat meat." See Grammar Note 1 ①.

謀 (谋) *v.* to plan. MdnC: 謀劃 (*móu huà* 谋划).

之 *pron.* this, these things. MdnC: 這 (*zhè* 这). See Grammar Note 2 ①.

何 *interrogative particle.* why? MdnC: 爲什麼 (*wèi shén me* 为什么). See Grammar Note 3 ②.

間 (间 *jiàn*) *v.* to come in between, intervene. MdnC: 參與 (*cān yǔ* 参与).

焉 *pron.* in it, there. See Grammar Note 4 ①.

4. 鄙 *adj.* vulgar, limited. MdnC: 目光短淺 (*mù guāng duǎn qiǎn* 目光短浅).

乃入見，問何以戰。⁵公曰：「衣食所
nǎi rù jiàn　wèn hé yǐ zhàn　gōng yuē　yī shí suǒ

安，弗敢專也，必以分人。」⁶對曰：「小
ān　fú gǎn zhuān yě　bì yǐ fēn rén　duì yuē　xiǎo

惠未徧，民弗從也。」⁷公曰：「犧牲、玉
huì wèi biàn　mín fú cóng yě　gōng yuē　xī shēng yù

帛，弗敢加也。必以信。」⁸對曰：「小信
bó　fú gǎn jiā yě　bì yǐ xìn　duì yuē　xiǎo xìn

未孚，神弗福也。」⁹公曰：「小大之獄，
wèi fú　shén fú fú yě　gōng yuē　xiǎo dà zhī yù

雖不能察，必以情。」¹⁰對曰：「忠之屬
suī bù néng chá　bì yǐ qíng　duì yuē　zhōng zhī shǔ

也，可以一戰。戰，則請從。」¹¹
yě　kě yǐ yí zhàn　zhàn　zé qǐng cóng

于是曹刿入朝拜见鲁庄公，问鲁庄公凭什么跟齐军作战。⁵鲁庄公说："衣服食物这些安养的东西，不敢<u>独自享有</u>，一定会分给别人。"⁶曹刿回答说："这些小恩惠没有遍及老百姓，他们不会顺从您的。"⁷鲁庄公说："祭祀时的牺牲和玉帛，我不敢夸大这些祭品的数目，一定会用诚信来面对神灵。"⁸曹刿回答说："小的诚信不能让人信服，神灵未必会保佑您。"⁹鲁庄公说："大大小小的诉讼案，即使不能一一考察，也一定会根据实情来判断。"¹⁰曹刿回答说："这是忠于职守一类的，可以和齐军作战。如果作战，请允许我跟从您。"¹¹

5. 何 *interrogative pron.* what? See Grammar Note 3 ①.

以 *coverb.* by means of. See L2 Grammar Note 1 ②.

何以 by what? how? MdnC: 憑什麼 (*píng shén me* 凭什么). See Grammar Note 3 ③.

6. 所 *pron.* 所 stands for the object of the verb 安, that which. MdnC: ……的東西 (*de dōng xi* 的东西).

安 *v.* to secure, settle down. MdnC: 安養 (*ān yǎng* 安养).

弗 *adv.* no, not. MdnC: 不 (*bù*). See L4 Grammar Note 5.

專 (专) *v.* to monopolize. MdnC: 獨自享有 (*dú zì xiǎng yǒu* 独自享有).

以 *coverb.* to use. MdnC: 把 (*bǎ*). See L2 Grammar Note 1 ②.

分 (*fēn*) *v.* to distribute, assign. MdnC: 分給 (*fēn gěi* 分给).

7. 對 (对) *v.* to reply, answer. MdnC: 回答 (*huí dá*).

惠 *n.* favor. MdnC: 恩惠 (*ēn huì*).

徧 (遍) *adv.* all over, everywhere. MdnC: 遍及 (*biàn jí*).

從 (从) *v.* to follow, obey. MdnC: 順從 (*shùn cóng* 顺从).

8. 犧 (牺) 牲 *n.* sacrificial animals, including pigs, oxen, and sheep.

帛 *n.* silk, fabric. Here jade and silk 玉帛 refer to part of the sacrificial offerings.

加 *v.* to add, increase. Here it means "to exaggerate (*kuā dà* 夸大) the number of sacrificial offerings."

信 *n.* trustworthiness, honesty. MdnC: 誠信 (*chéng xìn* 诚信).

9. 孚 *v.* to have confidence in. MdnC: 信服 (*xìn fú*).

福 *n.* blessings. Here it is used as a verb, meaning "to bless" 保佑 (*bǎo yòu*).

10. 之 *particle.* a possessive marker. MdnC: 的 (*de*). See Grammar Note 2 ②.

獄 (狱) *n.* lawsuit. MdnC: 訴訟案 (*sù sòng àn* 诉讼案).

雖 (虽) *conj.* even though. MdnC: 即使 (*jí shǐ*). See L4 Grammar Note 6.

察 *v.* to investigate, examine. MdnC: 考察 (*kǎo chá*).

情 *n.* feeling, facts. MdnC: 實情 (*shí qíng* 实情).

11. 忠 *adj.* faithful, loyal. Here it connotes that Lord Zhuang of Lu was devoted to his duty 忠於職守 (*zhōng yú zhí shǒu* 忠于职守).

屬 (属) *n.* kind, type. MdnC: 類 (*lèi* 类).

從 (从) *v.* to follow. MdnC: 跟從 (*gēn cóng* 跟从).

公與之乘，戰于長勺。¹² 公將鼓之，
gōng yǔ zhī chéng zhàn yú cháng sháo　gōng jiāng gǔ zhī

劌曰：「未可。」¹³ 齊人三鼓。劌曰：「可
guì yuē　wèi kě　qí rén sān gǔ　guì yuē　kě

矣！」齊師敗績。¹⁴ 公將馳之。劌曰：「未
yǐ　qí shī bài jì　gōng jiāng chí zhī　guì yuē　wèi

可。」¹⁵ 下，視其轍，登，軾而望之，曰：
kě　xià　shì qí zhé　dēng　shì ér wàng zhī　yuē

「可矣！」¹⁶ 遂逐齊師。¹⁷
kě yǐ　suì zhú qí shī

鲁庄公和曹刿一同乘车，（带领鲁国军队与齐国军队）在长勺交战。¹² 鲁庄公要击鼓，曹刿说："不可以。"¹³ 齐国人击鼓三次。曹刿说："可以了。"齐军大败。¹⁴ 鲁庄公要驾车追赶齐军。曹刿说："不可以。"¹⁵ 下车查看地上齐军车轮留下的痕迹，又登上战车，扶着车前横板远望齐国军队，说："可以了。"¹⁶ 鲁国军队于是追击齐军。¹⁷

12. 之 *personal pron.* him. Here it refers to Cao Gui. See Grammar Note 2 ③.

乘 (*chéng*) *v.* to ride, take a ride on. MdnC: 乘坐 (*chéng zuò*).

長 (长) 勺 place name in present-day Laiwu 萊蕪, a city in Shandong Province.

13. 鼓 *n.* drum. Here it is used as a verb, meaning "to beat a drum." MdnC: 擊鼓 (*jī gǔ* 击鼓).

之 *particle.* an added syllable with no meaning. See Grammar Note 2 ④.

14. 績 (绩) *n.* achievement. 敗績 (败绩) means "to be defeated."

15. 馳 (驰) *v.* to gallop. Here it means "to run after" 追趕 (*zhuī gǎn* 追赶) the Qi army.

16. 轍 (辙) *n.* wheel tracks, wagon rut.

登 *v.* to climb up.

軾 (轼) *n.* the horizontal wooden bar on a chariot.

17. 遂 *conj.* then. MdnC: 於是 (*yú shì* 于是).

逐 *v.* to chase, pursue. MdnC: 追逐 (*zhuī zhú*).

既克，公問其故。[18] 對曰：「夫戰，勇
jì kè　gōng wèn qí gù　　duì yuē　fú zhàn　yǒng

氣也。一鼓作氣，再而衰，三而竭。彼竭
qì yě　　yì gǔ zuò qì　　zài ér shuāi　sān ér jié　bǐ jié

我盈，故克之。[19] 夫大國，難測也，懼有伏
wǒ yíng　gù kè zhī　　fú dà guó　nán cè yě　jù yǒu fú

焉。吾視其轍亂，望其旗靡，故逐之。[20]」
yān　　wú shì qí zhé luàn　wàng qí qí mǐ　gù zhú zhī

《春秋左傳正義》（《十三經注疏》），北京：中華書局 (2009), 3835–3836.

已经战胜了齐军,鲁庄公问曹刿原因。[18] 曹刿回答说:"战争,靠的是士气。第一次击鼓振作士气,第二次击鼓士气就衰落了,第三次击鼓士气就耗尽了。他们的士气耗尽了,我们的却很充沛,因此战胜他们。[19] 强大的国家,是很难预测的。我害怕他们在那里有埋伏。我看到他们车轮的痕迹乱了,望到他们的军旗倒下了,所以追逐他们。"[20]

18. 既 *adv.* already. See Grammar Note 5.

克 *v.* to defeat. MdnC: 戰勝 (*zhàn sheng* 战胜).

故 *n.* reason. MdnC: 原因 (*yuán yīn*).

19. 夫 (fú) *initial particle.* used to begin a statement. See L2 Grammar Note 4 ①.

氣 (气) *n.* air, breath, vital energy. MdnC: 士氣 (*shì qì* 士气).

作 *v.* to activate, start up. MdnC: 振作 (*zhèn zuò*).

再 *adv.* the second time, again.

衰 *v.* to decay, become weak. MdnC: 衰落 (*shuāi luò*).

竭 *v.* to exhaust. MdnC: 耗盡 (*hào jìn* 耗尽).

彼 *pron.* they. MdnC: 他們 (*tā men* 他们). See L14 Grammar Note 2 ①.

盈 *v.* to be filled with, be full of. MdnC: 充沛 (*chōng pèi*).

故 *conj.* therefore, for this reason. MdnC: 因此 (*yīn cǐ*).

20. 測 (测) *v.* to estimate, predict. MdnC: 預測 (*yù cè* 预测).

懼 (惧) *v.* to be afraid, fear. MdnC: 害怕 (*hài pà*).

伏 *v.* to lie hidden, lie in ambush. MdnC: 埋伏 (*mái fú*).

焉 *pron.* there. See Grammar Note 4 ①.

靡 (mǐ) *v.* to fall down. MdnC: 倒下 (*dǎo xià*).

語法注釋 Grammar Notes

1. 者 ① *auxiliary pron.* verb/verb phrase/adjective + 者. 者 functions here as an auxiliary pronoun, meaning "the one who" or "the one which." MdnC: ⋯⋯的 (*de*), ⋯⋯的人 (*de rén*), ⋯⋯的東西 (*de dōng xī* 的东西).

> 肉食者謀之，又何間焉？
>
> [吃肉的人谋划这件事情，你又为什么参与到这里面呢？]

See 者②③ in L4 Grammar Note 3, 者④ in L6 Grammar Note 8, 者⑤ in L7 Grammar Note 3, and 者⑥ in L8 Grammar Note 1.

2. 之 ① *demonstrative pron.* this, that, those, these. MdnC: 這 (*zhè* 这) ⋯⋯.

> 肉食者謀之，又何間焉？
>
> [吃肉的人谋划这件事情，你又为什么参与到这里面呢？]

② *particle.* a possessive marker. MdnC: 的 (*de*).

> 小大之獄，雖不能察，必以情。
>
> [大大小小的诉讼案，即使不能一一考察，也一定会根据实情来判断。]

③ *personal pron.* third-person pronoun: him, her, it, them. MdnC: 他 (*tā*), 她 (*tā*), 它 (*tā*), 他們 (*tā mén* 他们).

> 公與之乘。
>
> [鲁庄公和他（曹刿）一同乘车。]

④ *particle.* 之 is often used after a monosyllable intransitive verb or a time adverb to form a bisyllabic metric unit with no meaning in itself.

> 公將鼓之。
>
> [鲁庄公要击鼓。]

See 之⑤⑥ in L2 Grammar Note 2 and 之⑦ in L7 Grammar Note 2.

3. 何 ① *interrogative pron.* what? MdnC: 什麼 (*shén me* 什么).

> 乃入見，問何以戰？
>
> [曹刿于是拜见鲁庄公，问鲁庄公凭什么作战？]

② *interrogative particle.* for what reason? why? MdnC: 爲什麼 (*wèi shén me* 为什么).

> 肉食者謀之，又何間焉？
>
> [这是吃肉的人谋划的事情，你又为什么参与到这里面呢？]

③ 何以 is an inversion of the regular word order, 以何; its literary meaning is "by what?" or "how?" MdnC: 怎麼做 (*zěn me zuò* 怎么做), 憑什麼 (*píng shén me* 凭什么).

> 乃入見，問何以戰？
>
> [曹刿于是拜见鲁庄公，问鲁庄公凭什么作战？]

See 何④ in L4 Grammar Note 2 and 何如 in L6 Grammar Note 3 ④.

4. 焉 ① *demonstrative pron.* 焉 functions as an equivalent of 於之 (*yú zhī* 于之): 於 is a preposition, and 之 is a pronoun here, meaning "there," "here," or "in it."

> 肉食者謀之，又何間焉？
>
> [吃肉的人谋划的事情，你又为什么参与到里边？]
>
> 夫大國，難測也，懼有伏焉。
>
> [强大的国家，是很难预测的，我害怕他们在那里有埋伏。]

See 焉②③ in L2 Grammar Note 3, 焉④ in L5 Grammar Note 4, 焉⑤ in L6 Grammar Note 5, 焉⑥ in L12 Grammar Note 1, and 焉⑦ in L30 Grammar Note 3.

5. 既 *adv.* 既 shows that the action is done. MdnC: 已經 (*yǐ jīng* 已经).

> 既克，公問其故。
>
> [已经战胜了齐国，鲁庄公问曹刿原因。]

Literary Analysis

Who has the right to intervene in state affairs? This emerges as an important question in Chinese texts from roughly the fourth century BCE onward, when the aristocratic system based on hereditary power and privilege showed signs of strain and men of humbler origin could gain attention by offering expert advice. Most of the voices of authority in *Zuozhuan* still belong to nobles and ministers, but there are exceptions, like Confucius and his disciples and Cao Gui here. How does the dialogue form establish the dramatic balance of power between ruler and adviser in this passage? Cao Gui declares that the "meat-eaters" 肉食者 (i.e., the wellborn) are "limited" 鄙 (*bǐ*), a word whose root meaning refers to "the area beyond the boundaries of cities and settlements." Cao Gui thus turns a term designating spatial marginality into a value judgment implying short-sightedness and parochial perspectives. As a person living far from the center of power, he is literally at the margins (*bi*), but he suggests those in power are more truly marginal due to their limited understanding. Such wordplay is typical of *Zuo Tradition*.

The exchange between the Lu ruler and Cao Gui on the basis of engaging in battle raises important questions of political legitimacy. Is "political capital" to be sought in the dispensing of favors, assiduously held religious rituals, or impartial legal judgment? What would the modern equivalents, in different political systems, in our times be? Note that all three things imply reciprocity as the cornerstone of moral reasoning, and if the third wins out, it is because it is considered the most beneficial to the people. Cao Gui's political judgment prepares the reader for his success on the battlefield. His timing and caution remind us of early Chinese military writings. Why does Cao Gui initially withhold explanation? How do delay and suspense augment his authority?

👉 *HTRCProse*, chapter 2, "Pre-Qin Historical Prose: *Zuo Tradition (Zuozhuan)*," C2.6.

—WL

課後練習 Exercises

一 給加點字注音 Give the pinyin romanization for each dotted word.

1. 曹劌 （＿＿＿,＿＿＿） 2. 轍 （＿＿＿） 3. 玉帛 （＿＿＿）

4. 犧牲 （＿＿＿,＿＿＿） 5. 軾 （＿＿＿） 6. 長勺 （＿＿＿）

二 在括號中給句中加點的字注音，並選出正確的釋義 Give the pinyin romanization for each dotted word; then select the correct definition from the following list, and write it in the blank.

於(于)是　耗盡(尽)　訴訟(诉讼)案　倒下　衰落　**信服**　攻打　類(类)

1. 小信未孚 （**fú**） ＿**信服**＿ 2. 小大之獄 （　） ＿＿＿＿＿ 3. 齊師伐我 （　） ＿＿＿＿＿

4. 三而竭 （　） ＿＿＿＿＿ 5. 忠之屬也 （　） ＿＿＿＿＿ 6. 望其旗靡 （　） ＿＿＿＿＿

7. 再而衰 （　） ＿＿＿＿＿ 8. 遂逐齊師 （　） ＿＿＿＿＿

三 選擇釋義並填空 Match each word in the left column with its correct definition in the middle column. Fill in each blank in the right column with an appropriate word from the left column (some words may be used more than once).

謀謀劃(谋划)　夸大

師＿＿＿＿＿　充沛

間＿＿＿＿＿　推測(测)

鄙＿＿＿＿＿　**謀劃(谋划)**

信＿＿＿＿＿　埋伏

加＿＿＿＿＿　軍隊(军队)

盈＿＿＿＿＿　恩惠

測＿＿＿＿＿　目光短淺(浅)

懼＿＿＿＿＿　參與(参与)

伏＿＿＿＿＿　信用

克＿＿＿＿＿　振作

惠＿＿＿＿＿　戰勝(战胜)

逐＿＿＿＿＿　害怕

作＿＿＿＿＿　追逐

十年春，齊＿＿＿伐我。

其鄉人曰：“肉食者＿＿＿之，又何＿＿＿焉？”劌曰：“肉食者＿＿＿，不可遠＿＿＿。”

小＿＿＿未徧，民弗從也。

公曰：“犧牲、玉帛，弗敢＿＿＿也，必以＿＿＿。”對曰：“小＿＿＿未孚，神弗福也。”

一鼓＿＿＿氣，再而衰，三而竭。彼竭我＿＿＿，故＿＿＿之。

夫大國，難＿＿＿也，＿＿＿有＿＿＿焉。吾視其轍亂，望其旗靡，故＿＿＿之。

四 請用給出的字填空 Fill in each blank with an appropriate word from the following list (some words may be used more than once).

焉　以　夫　之　何　既　弗　其　所

1. 其鄉人曰：“肉食者謀＿＿＿，又＿＿＿間＿＿＿？”

2. ＿＿＿克。公問＿＿＿故。對曰：“＿＿＿戰，勇氣也。”

3. 公曰："衣食＿＿＿安，＿＿＿敢專也，必＿＿＿分人。

4. 公與＿＿＿乘，戰於長勺。公將鼓＿＿＿，劌曰："未可。"

五 爲加點字選擇正確釋義，並根據釋義翻譯句子 Match each dotted word with its correct modern Chinese equivalent by circling the latter. Then translate each sentence into modern Chinese.

1. 又何間焉？　　　　　　　　　　　　ⓐ爲什麼（为什么）b. 憑什麼（凭什么）c. 多少

现代文翻译：你又为什么要参与到这件事情里面？

_____

2. 乃入見，問何以戰？　　　　　　　　a. 爲什麼（为什么）b. 憑什麼（凭什么）c. 多少

现代文翻译：_____

3. 公曰："小大之獄，雖不能察，必以情。"　　a. 即使 b. 雖然（虽然）c. 而且

现代文翻译：_____

4. 夫大國，難測也。懼有伏焉。　　　　a. 嗎（吗）b. 在那裏（在那里）c. 爲什麼（为什么）

现代文翻译：_____

5. 下，視其轍，登，軾而望之。曰："可矣！"遂逐其師。　　a. 并且 b. 即使 c. 於（于）是

现代文翻译：_____

6. 夫戰，勇氣也。一鼓作氣，再而衰，三而竭。彼竭我盈，故克之。

　　　　　　　　　　　　　　　　　　　　　　a. 原因 b. 所以 c. 由於（于）

现代文翻译：_____

7. 小信未孚，神弗福也。　　　　　　　a. 保佑 b. 福氣（气）c. 有福

现代文翻译：_____

第二課

《左傳》：燭之武退秦師

"Zhu Zhiwu Convinced the Qin Army to Retreat," from *Zuo Tradition*

Introduction

This excerpt from *Zuo Tradition* recounts a famous instance of high-stakes geopolitics in ancient China. Besieged by the allied troops of the powerful Qin and Jin states in the late seventh century BCE, the lord of the small Zheng state sends his official, Zhu Zhiwu, to the Qin as a special envoy. Through a deft combination of self-effacing rhetoric and blunt warnings, this envoy gets the ear of the Duke and convinces him of the folly of military alliance against the Zheng. Heeding the envoy's warning that the fall of Zheng would only make the Jin state, the real rival of Qin, stronger and more threatening, the Duke decides to break the alliance and withdraw his troops. Fearful of being outflanked by the Qin, the Jin then decide against attacking the Zheng alone. The envoy's diplomatic persuasion accomplishes a near miracle for the Zheng: averting its annexation by two powerful neighboring states.

正文與簡體譯文 Text and Modern Chinese Translation

九月甲午，　晉侯、　秦伯圍鄭，　以其無
jiǔ yuè jiǎ wǔ　jìn hóu　qín bó wéi zhèng　yǐ qí wú

禮於晉，　且貳於楚也。[1] 晉軍函陵，　秦軍氾
lǐ yú jìn　qiě èr yú chǔ yě　jìn jūn hán líng　qín jūn fán

南。[2]
nán

九月初十，晋文公和秦穆公(率领军队)围攻郑国，因为郑文公曾对晋文公无礼，而且私下援助楚国(攻击晋国)。[1] 晋国军队驻扎在函陵，秦国军队驻扎在氾水的南边。[2]

1. 九月甲午 the tenth day of the ninth month in 630 BCE. See Cultural Note 1.
   晉(晋)侯 or 晉文公 (ancestral name 姓, Jī 姬; given name 名, Chóng ěr 重耳; r. 636–628 BCE). Lord Wen of Jin, the twenty-second king of the Jin state, is known as one of the Five Hegemons in the Spring and Autumn period of Chinese history 春秋五霸 (*Chūn qiū wǔ bà*). In his early life, he lived in exile for nineteen years in order to avoid getting framed by Li Ji 驪姬, a concubine of his father, Lord Xian of Jin 晉獻公 (r. ?–651 BCE). Thanks to Lord Mu of Qin 秦穆公, Prince Chong'er was eventually able to return to the Jin state and restore his power. See Culture Note 2.
   秦伯 or 秦穆公 (ancestral name 姓, Yíng 嬴; given name 名, Rénhǎo 任好; r. 659–621 BCE.) Lord Mu of Qin is known as one of the Five Hegemons in the Spring and Autumn period.
   圍 (围) *v.* to besiege. MdnC: 圍攻 (*wéi gōng* 围攻).
   鄭 (郑) or 鄭國 (郑国) a vassal state of the Zhou dynasty (1046–221 BCE), located in the southeastern part of the Jin state.

以 *prep.* because of. MdnC: 因爲 (*yīn wèi* 因为). See Grammar Note 1 ①.

其 *personal pron.* him. Here it refers to Lord Wen of Zheng 鄭文公. See Grammar Note 5 ①.

禮 (礼) *n.* courtesy.

無禮於晉 (无礼于晋) According to the records from the twenty-third year of Lord Xi of Lu 魯熹公 (637 BCE) in *Zuo Tradition*, Lord Wen of Zheng did not treat Chong'er with courtesy when he was exiled from the Jin state.

且 *conj.* and. MdnC: 而且 (*ér qiě*). See L13 Grammar Note 2 ①.

貳 (贰) *adj.* disloyal to. MdnC: 有貳心 (*yǒu èr xīn* 有贰心).

貳於楚 refers to the fact that the Zheng state secretly assisted the Chu state. According to "The Biography of the Zheng Family" 鄭世家 ("Zhèng shìjiā" 郑世家) in *Grand Scribe's Records* 史記 (*Shǐ jì* 史记), the Jin state and the Chu state had their first battle at Chengpu 城濮 in the Wei state in the twenty-eighth year of Lord Xi of Lu 魯熹公 (632 BCE). Lord Wen of Zheng secretly helped the Chu state to attack the Jin state because he was afraid Chong'er would take revenge on him.

2. 函陵 north of present-day Xinzheng County 新鄭, Henan Province.

氾 (fán) 南 south of the eastern Fan River 氾水. The river, which dried up long ago, is in the southern part of present-day Mou County 牟縣, Henan Province.

佚之狐言於鄭伯曰:「國危矣!若使
yì zhī hú yán yú zhèng bó yuē　　guó wēi yǐ　ruò shǐ

燭之武見秦君,師必退。」³公從之。辭
zhú zhī wǔ jiàn qín jūn　shī bì tuì　　gōng cóng zhī　cí

曰:「臣之ᵇ壯也,猶不如人;今老矣,無
yuē　chén zhī zhuàng yě　yóu bù rú rén　jīn lǎo yǐ　wú

能爲也已。」⁴公曰:「吾不能早用子,今
néng wéi yě yǐ　　gōng yuē　wú bù néng zǎo yòng zǐ　jīn

急而求子,是寡人之過也。然鄭亡,子亦
jí ér qiú zǐ　shì guǎ rén zhī guò yě　rán zhèng wáng　zǐ yì

有不利焉。」⁵許之,夜縋而出。⁶
yǒu bú lì yān　　xǔ zhī　yè zhuì ér chū

佚之狐对郑文公说:"国家情势危急了!如果派遣烛之武去面见秦君,秦军一定会撤退。"³郑文公听从他(的建议找来烛之武)。烛之武推辞说:"臣壮年的时候,尚且不如别人;现在我老了,没有什么能做的事。"⁴郑文公说:"我早先没能重用您,现在形势危急了来求您,这是我的过错。不过如果郑国灭亡了,您也有不利啊。"⁵烛之武答应了郑文公,晚上系了绳索吊出城外。⁶

3. 佚之狐 (fl. 627 BCE) a senior official in the Zheng state.

言 *v.* to speak, say.

鄭(郑)伯 or 鄭文公 (ancestral name 姓, Jī 姬; given name 名, Jié 捷; r. 673–628 BCE). Lord Wen of Zheng is the tenth king of the Zheng state.

危 *adj.* danger, critical. MdnC: 危急 (*wēi jí*).

若 *conj.* if. MdnC: 如果 (*rú guǒ*). See L4 Grammar Note 4 ②.

燭(烛)之武 (fl. 627 BCE), a person named Wu from a place named Zhu. 燭 is a place name. 武 is a person's name. 之 functions as a possessive marker. See L1 Grammar Note 2 ②.

師 (师) *n.* troops. Here it refers to the Qin army.

退 *v.* to move back, retreat. MdnC: 撤退 (*chè tuì*).

4. 從 (从) *v.* to follow. MdnC: 聽從 (*tīng cóng* 听从).

之 ₐ *personal pron.* him. See L1 Grammar Note 2 ③.

辭 (辞) *v.* to take leave, decline. MdnC: 推辭 (*tuī cí* 推辞).

之 ♭ *particle.* a nominative marker. See Grammar Note 2 ⑤.

壯 (壮) *adj.* strong. Here it refers to the prime of life 壯年 (*zhuàng nián* 壮年).

猶 (犹) *adv.* still. MdnC: 尚且 (*shàng qiě*). See L3 Grammar Note 3 ①.

如 *v.* to be comparable (with/to). MdnC: 比得上 (*bǐ dé shàng*). See L3 Grammar Note 5 ①.

爲 (为 *wéi*) *v.* to do. MdnC: 做 (*zuò*). See Grammar Note 6 ①.

也已 *ending particle.* to express an affirmative tone. See L6 Grammar Note 7 ①.

5. 是 *demonstrative pron.* this, referring to the previous situation that Lord Wen of Zheng mentioned. MdnC: 這 (*zhè* 这). See L3 Grammar Note 1 ①.

是……也 a structure of an affirmative sentence, meaning "this is…." MdnC: 這是 (*zhè shì* 这是) ……. See L3 Grammar Note 1 ②.

寡人, 寡德之人 I, the sovereign.

過 (过) *n.* fault, mistake. MdnC: 過錯 (*guò cuò* 过错).

然 *conj.* however, but. MdnC: 不過 (*bú guò* 不过). See L5 Grammar Note 2 ①.

焉 *ending particle.* MdnC: 啊 (*a*). See Grammar Note 3 ②.

6. 許 (许) *v.* to agree. MdnC: 答應 (*dā yìng* 答应).

縋 (缒) *v.* to climb down with a rope.

見秦伯, 曰:「秦、晉圍鄭, 鄭既知
jiàn qín bó　yuē　qín　jìn wéi zhèng　zhèng jì zhī

亡 ₐ 矣。若亡 ♭ 鄭而有益於君, 敢以煩執
wáng yǐ　ruò wáng zhèng ér yǒu yì yú jūn　gǎn yǐ fán zhí

事。⁷越國以鄙遠, 君知其難也。⁸焉用
shì　yuè guó yǐ bǐ yuǎn　jūn zhī qí nán yě　yān yòng

亡 ♭ 鄭以陪鄰?⁹鄰之厚, 君之薄也。¹⁰若
wáng zhèng yǐ bèi lín　lín zhī hòu　jūn zhī bó yě　ruò

舍鄭以爲東道主, 行李之往來, 共其乏
shě zhèng yǐ wéi dōng dào zhǔ　xíng lǐ zhī wǎng lái　gōng qí fá

困, 君亦無所害。¹¹
kùn　jūn yì wú suǒ hài

燭之武面见秦穆公，说："秦、晋两国围攻郑国，郑国已经知道将会灭亡。如果让郑国灭亡对您有好处，那就冒昧地拿(这件事)来劳烦您的随从。⁷越过其他的国家来把远方当作自己的边疆，您知道其中的难处。⁸为什么用灭亡郑国来增广邻国的土地呢?⁹邻国壮大了，您的力量就削弱了。¹⁰如果您放过郑国，把郑国当作东行道路的主人，秦国使臣经过往来时，(郑国)可以供给他们所需的食物和住处，对秦国也没什么害处。¹¹

7. 亡 ₐ *v.* to die, perish. MdnC: 滅亡 (*miè wáng* 灭亡).

亡 ♭ *v.* used as a causative verb here, 使……亡, meaning "to destroy." See L7 Grammar Note 1 ①.

益 *n.* benefit, profit. MdnC: 好處 (*hǎo chù* 好处).

敢 *v.* to dare. Here it means "to be bold" 冒昧 (*mào mèi*).

以 *coverb.* to use. MdnC: 拿 (*ná*). See Grammar Note 1 ②.

煩 (烦) *v.* to trouble. MdnC: 勞煩 (*láo fán* 劳烦).

執 (执) 事 *n.* retinue. MdnC: 隨從 (*suí cóng* 随从). Here Zhu Zhiwu showed his respect for Lord Mu of Qin by saying that he would bother the retinue instead of the lord.

8. 越 *v.* to cross, bypass. MdnC: 越過 (*yuè guò* 越过).

越國 (国) refers to the situation in which the Qin state had to bypass another state—namely, the Jin state—to take the lands of the Zheng state, since Qin and Zheng did not share a border.

以 *conj.* in order to. MdnC: 來 (*lái* 来). See Grammar Note 1 ③.

鄙 *n.* remote areas or areas near a border. MdnC: 邊疆 (*biān jiāng* 边疆). Here it is used as a putative verb, 以……爲 (为 *wéi*) 鄙, meaning "to regard … as remote areas." MdnC: 把 (*bǎ*) ……當作邊疆 (*dāng zuò biān jiāng* 当作边疆). See L14 Grammar Note 1 ②.

遠 (远) *adj.* far away, in the distance. MdnC: 遠方 (*yuǎn fāng* 远方).

其 *possessive pron.* its. MdnC: 其中的 (*qí zhōng de*). See Grammar Note 5 ②.

9. 焉 *interrogative particle.* why? MdnC: 爲什麼 (*wèi shén me* 为什么). See Grammar Note 3 ③.

陪 *v.* used in the sense of 倍 (*bèi*), meaning "to increase, expand" 增廣 (*zēng guǎng* 增广).

鄰 (邻) *n.* neighbor. Here it refers to the neighboring country 鄰國 (*lín guó* 邻国).

10. 之 *particle.* a nominative marker. See Grammar Note 2 ⑤.

厚 *adj.* thick. Here it means "strong" 壯大 (*zhuàng dà* 壮大).

薄 *adj.* thin. Here it means "weak" 削弱 (*xuē ruò*).

11. 舍 *v.* to abandon, to give up. Here it refers to giving up the planned attack on the Zheng state. MdnC: 放過 (*fàng guò* 放过).

以爲 (为 *wéi*) or 以 (鄭國) 爲…… to consider … to be. MdnC: 把 (*bǎ*) ……當作 (*dāng zuò* 当作). See Grammar Note 1 ④.

東 (东) 道主 the host. The Qin state was located in the northwestern corner of China proper in that period. When the Qin wanted to conquer other states, they had to go eastward. The Zheng state was on the way to the east. Therefore, Zhu Zhiwu made an offer that the Zheng state would take responsibility for hosting the Qin when they passed through.

行李 or 行理 officials who were in charge of the diplomatic mission, visit, and receptions for the guests. MdnC: 使臣 (*shǐ chén*).

之 *particle.* a nominative marker. See Grammar Note 2 ⑤.

共 *v.* used here in the sense of 供 (*gōng*), meaning "to supply" 供給 (*gōng jǐ* 供给).

乏困 *n.* tiredness. Here Zhu Zhiwu promised to offer food and lodging for the Qin officials while they were passing through the Zheng state.

「且君嘗爲晉君賜矣，許君焦、瑕，
qiě jūn cháng wéi jìn jūn cì yǐ　　xǔ jūn jiāo　　xiá

朝濟而夕設版焉，君之所知也。¹² 夫晉，
zhāo jì ér xī shè bǎn yān　　jūn zhī suǒ zhī yě　　fú jìn

何厭之有？¹³ 既東封鄭，又欲肆其西封。¹⁴
hé yàn zhī yǒu　　jì dōng fēng zhèng yòu yù sì qí xī fēng

"而且您曾对晋君有过恩惠，晋君许诺给您晋国的焦、瑕两地(作为回报)，但是早晨晋君渡河归国，晚上就在那儿设置墙板，这是您所知道的。¹² 晋国，有什么能

不闕秦， 焉取之？ ¹⁵闕秦以利<u>晉</u>， 唯君圖
bù quē qín　yān qǔ zhī　quē qín yǐ lì jìn　wéi jūn tú

之。¹⁶」
zhī

满足它的呢？¹³已经在东边把郑国作为<u>疆界</u>，又想要<u>延伸</u>其西边的领土。¹⁴（如果）不损害秦国（的利益），怎么获取土地呢？¹⁵损害秦国来让晋国得到好处，还请您考虑这件事。¹⁶"

12. 嘗 (尝) *adv.* once. MdnC: 曾經 (*céng jīng* 曾经). See L23 Grammar Note 1 ①.

　賜 (赐) *n.* favor. MdnC: 恩惠 (*ēn huì*). Here it alludes to Lord Mu of Qin helping Chong'er to get back to the Jin state and assume power as the sovereign.

　許 (许) *v.* to promise, agree. MdnC: 許諾 (*xǔ nuò* 许诺).

　焦 the Jiao state, a vassal state of the Zhou dynasty (1046–221 BCE), which was later annexed by the Jin state. It was in the southern part of present-day Shan County 陝縣, Henan Province.

　瑕 the Xia state, a vassal state of the Zhou dynasty, which was later occupied by the Jin state. It was located around the present-day city of Jiaozuo 焦作, Henan Province.

　朝 (zhāo) *n.* morning. MdnC: 早晨 (*zǎo chén*).

　濟 (济) *v.* to cross a river. MdnC: 渡河 (*dù hé*).

　朝濟 refers to the event of Chong'er crossing the river and returning to the Jin state in the morning.

　夕 *n.* evening.

　設 (设) *v.* to set up, build. MdnC: 設置 (*shè zhì* 设置).

　版 *n.* board used to build a wall. MdnC: 墙板 (*qiáng bǎn* 墙板).

　夕設 (设) 版 refers to Chong'er asking his people to set up walls between the Jin and the Qin in the evening. This is an exaggerated statement intended to show how fast Chong'er betrayed Lord Mu of Qin.

　焉 *pron.* there. See L1 Grammar Note 4 ①.

　之 *particle.* a nominative marker. See Grammar Note 2 ⑤.

13. 夫 (fú) *initial particle.* no meaning. See Grammar Note 4 ①.

　何 *interrogative pron.* what? MdnC: 什麼 (*shén me* 什么). See L1 Grammar Note 3 ①.

　厭 (厌) *v.* to dislike. Here it is used in the sense of 饜 (*yàn*), meaning "to satisfy" 满足 (*mǎn zú* 满足).

　之 *particle.* marks the inversion of objects, no meaning. See Grammar Note 2 ⑥.

14. 既 *adv.* already. MdnC: 已經 (*yǐ jīng* 已经). See L1 Grammar Note 5.

　封 *n.* boundary. MdnC: 疆界 (*jiāng jiè*). Here 封 is used as a putative verb, 以……爲 (为 *wéi*) 鄙, meaning "to regard … as their boundary." See L14 Grammar Note 1 ②.

　肆 *v.* to extend. MdnC: 延伸 (*yán shēn*). 肆其西封 means that the Jin state would eventually extend its land to the west, reaching the border with the Qin state.

15. 闕 (阙) *v.* to harm. MdnC: 損害 (*sǔn hài* 损害).

　焉 *interrogative particle.* how? MdnC: 怎麼 (*zěn me* 怎么). See Grammar Note 3 ③.

16. 唯 *particle.* used to introduce a subject. See Grammar Note 7 ①.

　圖 (图) *v.* to think about, to consider. MdnC: 考慮 (*kǎo lǜ* 考虑).

　之 *demonstrative pron.* this. See L1 Grammar Note 2 ①.

秦伯説，　與鄭人盟，　使杞子、逢孫、
qín bó yuè　　yǔ zhèng rén méng　　shǐ qǐ zǐ　　páng sūn

楊孫戍之，乃還。 ¹⁷
yáng sūn shù zhī　　nǎi huán

秦穆公很高兴，于是和郑人结盟，让杞子、逢孙、杨孙留下戍守，自己回秦国了。¹⁷

17. 説 (说) used here in the sense of 悦 (yuè), meaning "to be pleased" 高興 (gāo xìng 高兴).

   盟 v. to make an alliance. MdnC: 結盟 (jié méng 结盟).

   杞子、逢 (páng) 孫 (孙)、楊孫 (杨孙) three Qin officials.

   戍 v. to guard frontiers. MdnC: 戍守 (shù shǒu).

子犯請擊之。 ¹⁸ 公曰：「不可。微夫人
zǐ fàn qǐng jī zhī　　gōng yuē　　bù kě　　wēi fú rén

之力不及此。 ¹⁹ 因人之力而敝之，不仁；失
zhī lì bù jí cǐ　　yīn rén zhī lì ér bì zhī　　bù rén　shī

其所與，不知；以亂易整，不武。 ²⁰ 吾其還
qí suǒ yǔ　　bù zhī　　yǐ luàn yì zhěng　　bù wǔ　　wú qí huán

也。 ²¹ 」亦去之。 ²²
yě　　　　yì qù zhī

子犯请求攻击秦军。¹⁸ 晋文公说："不可以。没有秦人的助力，我们到不了今天的地步。¹⁹ 依靠他人的助力又去败坏他，不仁德；失掉我们的同盟之国，不明智；用攻击战乱代替和谐一致，不威武。²⁰ 我还是回去吧。²¹" 于是晋军也撤离郑国。²²

《春秋左傳正義》（《十三經注疏》），北京：中華書局 (2009), 3973–3974.

18. 子犯 or 狐偃 (ancestral name 姓, Jī 姬; family name 氏, Hú 狐; given name 名, Yàn 偃; style 字, Zǐfàn 子犯; 715?–629 BCE) a minister in the Jin state. Hu Yan's sister Hu Ji 狐姬 gave birth to Prince Chong'er. Hu Yan kept assisting Chong'er when he was in exile and after he regained power. See Culture Note 2.

19. 微 adv. no. MdnC: 没有 (méi yǒu).

   夫 (fú) demonstrative pron. that. 夫人, that person, refers to Lord Mu of Qin. See Grammar Note 4 ②.

   力 n. force, power. Here it refers to the Qin's help 助力 (zhù lì).

   及 v. to get to, reach. MdnC: 到 (dào).

20. 因 prep. by means of. MdnC: 依靠 (yī kào).

   敝 v. to corrupt, used in the sense of 弊 (bì). MdnC: 敗壞 (bài huài 败坏).

   仁 adj. benevolent. MdnC: 仁德 (rén dé).

   與 (与 yǔ) v. to be friendly with. 所與 refers to the Jin's ally—namely, the Qin.

   知 v. to know. It is used in the sense of 智 (zhì), meaning "wise" 明智 (míng zhì).

   易 v. to replace. MdnC: 代替 (dài tì).

   整 adj. orderly.

   武 adj. mighty. MdnC: 威武 (wēi wǔ).

21. 其 adv. 其 is used here to indicate speculation. MdnC: 還是 (hái shì 还是). See Grammar Note 5 ③.

22. 去 v. to leave. MdnC: 離開 (lí kāi 离开).

文化常識 Culture Notes

1. 天干地支 The traditional Chinese calendrical system is composed of Stems (*gān* 干) and Branches (*zhī* 支). Stems include ten Heavenly Stems (*tiān gān* 天干, see the first table), to which 甲 belongs. Branches include twelve Earthly Branches (*dì zhī* 地支, see the second table), to which 午 belongs. Stems and Branches form a cyclic numeral system of sixty combinations of the preceding two cycles (see the third table). According to the *Spring and Autumn Annals*, it is September 10 in the thirtieth year of the reign of Lord Xi of Lu (魯僖公 r. 659–627 BCE).

天　干

甲	乙	丙	丁	戊	己	庚	辛	壬	癸

地　支

子	丑	寅	卯	辰	巳	午	未	申	酉	戌	亥

天　干　地　支　表

甲子	乙丑	丙寅	丁卯	戊辰	己巳	庚午	辛未	壬申	癸酉
甲戌	乙亥	丙子	丁丑	戊寅	己卯	庚辰	辛巳	壬午	癸未
甲申	乙酉	丙戌	丁亥	戊子	己丑	庚寅	辛卯	壬辰	癸巳
甲午	乙未	丙申	丁酉	戊戌	己亥	庚子	辛丑	壬寅	癸卯
甲辰	乙巳	丙午	丁未	戊申	己酉	庚戌	辛亥	壬子	癸丑
甲寅	乙卯	丙辰	丁巳	戊午	己未	庚申	辛酉	壬戌	癸亥

2. 姓氏 There was a difference between *xìng* (姓) and *shì* (氏) in ancient China. Before the Warring States period, *xing* was a surname held by the noble clans. *Shi* appeared later. As descendants of the same ancestor multiplied, noble clans were often divided and subdivided. *Shi* appeared as the surname of one branch of the noble clan. In this way, a nobleman would hold a *xing* and a *shi*. For example, Zifan 子犯 in the text had both a *xing* (Jī 姬) and a *shi* (Hú 狐). However, *xing* and *shi* functioned differently in this period. Normally, *shi* functioned as a surname for a nobleman, while *xing* was mentioned only in relation to marriage. In other words, a man and a woman who shared the same *xing* could not get married. After the Warring States period, people often used their *shi* as their *xing*. Thus, *xing* and *shi* gradually became one—namely, *xing*. Common people also began to adopt their own surnames from then on.

語法注釋 Grammar Notes

1. 以　① *prep.* 以 is used to show the reason for an action, meaning "because" and "for the reason of." MdnC: 因爲 (*yīn wèi* 因为), 由於 (*yóu yú* 由于).

　　　晉侯、秦伯圍鄭，以其無禮於晉，且貳於楚。

　　　[晋文公、秦穆公围攻郑国，因为郑文公曾对晋文公无礼，而且私下援助楚国攻晋。]

　　② *coverb.* 以 is used in a verb phrase and often displays the features of both verb and preposition, meaning "to use," "by means of," or "with." MdnC: 用 (*yòng*), 拿 (*ná*), 憑藉 (*píng jiè* 凭借).

若亡鄭而有益於君，敢以（此）煩執事。

> ［若灭亡郑国而有利于秦国，那就冒昧地拿（灭郑国这事）劳烦您的随从。］

以亂易整，不武。

> ［用攻击战乱代替和谐一致，这是不威武（的做法）。］

③ *conj.* 以 is used to indicate a purpose, meaning "in order to." MdnC: 來 (*lái* 来), 去 (*qù*), 而 (*ér*).

越國以鄙遠，君知其難也。

> ［越过他国来把远方当作边疆，您知道其中的难处。］

焉用亡鄭以陪鄰？

> ［为什么要用灭亡郑国来增广邻国的土地？］

闕秦以利晉，唯君圖之。

> ［损害秦国而有利于晋国，还请您考虑。］

④ *v.* 以（⋯⋯）爲⋯⋯. to regard ... as.... MdnC: 把 (*bǎ*) ⋯⋯當作 (*dāng zuò* 当作) ⋯⋯.

若舍鄭以（鄭）爲東道主，⋯⋯

> ［如果您放过郑国，把（郑国）当作东行道路的主人⋯⋯］

See 以⑤ in L10 Grammar Note 2 and 以⑥ in L18 Grammar Note 4.

2. 之   Seven uses of 之 are explained in this book. In addition to the uses below, see 之①②③④ in L1 Grammar Note 2 and 之⑦ in L7 Grammar Note 2.

⑤ *particle.* a nominative marker. 之 has no meaning and is used between the subject and the predicate, converting a verb phrase or sentence into a noun or noun phrase.

臣之壯也，猶不如人。

> ［臣壮年的时候，尚且不如别人。］

行李之往來，共乏其困⋯⋯

> ［秦国使臣经行往来，（郑国）可以供给（他们的）所需⋯⋯］

⑥ *particle.* 之 marks the inversion of objects and has no meaning. In an interrogative sentence, the object is taken out of its normal position and placed in front of the verb, like the structure "object + *zhi* 之 + verb."

夫晉，何厭之有？ (L2)

> ［晋国，有什么能满足（他们的）啊！］

3. 焉   Seven uses of 焉 are explained in this book. In addition to the uses below, see 焉① in L1 Grammar Note 4, 焉④ in L5 Grammar Note 4, 焉⑤ in L6 Grammar Note 5, 焉⑥ in L12 Grammar Note 1, and 焉⑦ in L30 Grammar Note 3.

② *ending particle.* no meaning. MdnC: 啊 (*a*).

然鄭亡，子亦有不利焉。

> ［但是郑国灭亡，您也有不利啊！］

③ *interrogative particle*. what? how? why? where? MdnC: 什麼 (*shén me* 什么), 怎麼 (*zěn me* 怎么), 爲什麼 (*wèi shén me* 为什么), 哪裏 (*nǎ lǐ* 哪里).

> 焉用亡鄭以陪鄰？
>
> [为什么用灭亡郑国来增广邻国的土地？]
>
> 不闕秦，焉取之？
>
> [不侵削秦国，怎么获取土地？]

4. 夫　① *initial particle*. 夫 normally appears at the beginning of a sentence and introduces a
(fú)　　statement; it has no meaning.

> 夫晉，何厭之有？
>
> [晋国，有什么能满足（他们的）啊！]
>
> 夫大國，難測也。 (L1)
>
> [强大的国家是很难预测的！]

② *demonstrative pron*. that, those. MdnC: 那 (*nà*), 那些 (*nà xiē*).

> 微夫人之力不及此。
>
> [没有那人的助力，我们到不了今天的地步。]

See 夫③ in L8 Grammar Note 2.

5. 其　① *personal pron*. 其 is a third-person pronoun used to refer to person(s) mentioned earlier.
　　　MdnC: 他 (*tā*), 他們 (*tā mén* 他们).

> 晉侯、秦伯圍鄭，以其無禮於晉，且貳於楚。
>
> [曹刿于是拜见鲁庄公，问鲁庄公凭什么作战？]
>
> 失其所與，不知。
>
> [失去秦穆公给予的帮助，是不明智的做法。]

② *possessive pron*. 其 is equivalent to the structure of noun + 之. MdnC: ……的 (*de*).

> 越國以鄙遠，君知其難也。
>
> [越过他国来领有远方的飞地，您是知道其中的困难的。]
>
> 其鄉人曰…… (L1)
>
> [曹刿的同乡说……]

③ *adv*. 其 is used to suggest a change of tone, either meaning "probably" or "maybe" or
　　having no meaning. MdnC: 還是 (*hái shì* 还是), 大概 (*dà gài*), 應該 (*yīng gāi* 应该).

> 吾其還也。
>
> [我还是回去吧！]

See 其④ in L6 Grammar Note 6.

6. 爲　① *wéi v*. to do, make, control, manage. MdnC: 做 (*zuò*), 治理 (*zhì lǐ*).
(为)

> 今老矣，無能爲也已。
>
> [现在我老了，没有什么能做的。]

See 爲②in L7 Grammar Note 5, 爲③in L9 Grammar Note 1, 爲④in L11
Grammar Note 4, and 爲⑤in L21 Grammar Note 3.

7. 唯　①　*particle.* 唯/惟 is used to introduce the subject.

闕秦以利晉，惟君圖之。

[损害秦国而有利于晋国，还请您斟酌思量。]

See 惟/唯②in L22 Grammar Note 2.

Literary Analysis

As in the preceding passage, we find a political actor initially reluctant to undertake his mission. Why is this a recurrent trope? A person whose talent has not been recognized is given a chance to shine. What might have been the background of the storytellers who elaborate and transmit such stories? Zhu Zhiwu's masterful rhetoric saves the day for the Zheng. As a small state situated between larger and more powerful states, Zheng is constantly struggling for survival. Here it confronts Qin and Jin; elsewhere in the text, it is often caught between Jin and Chu. Perhaps as a result of the political perils it continually faced, Zheng is famous for its masters of rhetoric—the potency of which is clearly revealed as it restores the balance of power. Here a Zheng master manipulates the rivalry between Qin and Jin, and we see how political persuasion is really psychological warfare: Zhu Zhiwu, master persuader, achieves his goals by getting into the head of the Qin ruler.

☞ *HTRCProse*, chapter 1, "An Anatomy of the Chinese Prose Form: An Overview," C1.1; *HTRCProse*, chapter 2, "Pre-Qin Historical Prose: *Zuo Tradition (Zuozhuan)*," C2.6.

—WL

課後練習　Exercises

一　給加點字注音　Give the pinyin romanization for each dotted word.

1. 杞子（＿＿＿） 2. 逢孫（＿＿＿） 3. 焦（＿＿＿） 4. 瑕（＿＿＿） 5. 佚（＿＿＿）
6. 氾南（＿＿＿） 7. 函陵（＿＿＿） 8. 縋（＿＿＿） 9. 晉（＿＿＿） 10. 鄭（＿＿＿）

二　在括號中給句中加點的字注音，並選出正確的釋義　Give the pinyin romanization for each dotted word; then select the correct definition from the following list, and write it in the blank.

供給(给)　　增廣(广)　　損(损)害　　明智　　高興(兴)　　有貳(二)心　　邊(边)疆　　信服

1. 小信未孚（**fú**）　<u>信服</u>　2. 秦王說（　）＿＿＿＿＿　3. 越國以鄙遠　（　）＿＿＿＿＿

4. 共乏其困（　）＿＿＿＿＿　5. 不闕秦（　）＿＿＿＿　6. 且貳於楚　（　）＿＿＿＿＿

7. 失其所與，不知　（　）＿＿＿＿　　8. 焉用亡鄭以陪鄰（　）＿＿＿＿＿

三 選擇釋義並填空 Match each word in the left column with its correct definition in the middle column. Fill in each blank in the right column with an appropriate word from the left column (some words may be used more than once).

謀謀劃 (谋划)	敗壞 (败坏)	因人之力而＿＿之，不仁；失其所與，不知；以亂
危＿＿＿＿	放過 (过)	＿＿整，不＿＿。
師＿＿＿＿	過 (过)	闕秦以利晉，唯君＿＿之。
煩＿＿＿＿	危急	佚之狐言於鄭伯曰："國＿＿矣！ 若使燭之武見
舍＿＿＿＿	代替	秦軍，＿＿必退。
盟＿＿＿＿	軍隊 (军队)	且君嘗爲晉軍＿＿矣，許君焦、瑕，朝＿＿而夕設
濟＿＿＿＿	**謀劃 (谋划)**	版焉，君之所知也。
封＿＿＿＿	恩惠	既東＿＿鄭，又欲＿＿其西＿＿。
肆＿＿＿＿	勞煩 (劳烦)	秦伯說，與鄭人＿＿，使杞子、逢孫、楊孫＿＿
戍＿＿＿＿	考慮 (虑)	之，乃還。
敝＿＿＿＿	結 (结) 盟	若＿＿鄭以爲東道主，行李之往來，共其乏困，君
易＿＿＿＿	威武	亦無所害。
賜＿＿＿＿	延伸	
圖＿＿＿＿	封疆	
武＿＿＿＿	戍守	

四 請用給出的字填空 Fill in each blank with an appropriate word from the following list (some words may be used more than once).

焉　以　夫　之　何　其

1. 辭曰："臣＿＿壯也，猶不如人；今老矣，無能爲也已。"
2. 越國＿＿鄙遠，君知＿＿難也。＿＿用亡鄭＿＿陪鄰？鄰＿＿厚，君＿＿薄也。
3. ＿＿晉，＿＿厭＿＿有？既東封鄭，又欲肆其西封。不闕秦，將＿＿取＿＿？

五 爲加點字選擇正確釋義，並根據釋義來翻譯句子 Match each dotted word with its correct modern Chinese equivalent by circling the latter. Then translate each sentence into modern Chinese.

1. 又何間焉?　　　　　　　　　ⓐ爲什麼 (为什么) b. 憑什麼 (凭什么) c. 多少

現代文翻譯：你又为什么要参与到这件事情里面？
_____

2. 晉侯、秦伯圍鄭，以其無禮於晉，且貳於楚。　　a. 因爲 (为) b. 用 c. 來 (来)

現代文翻譯：_____

3. 若舍鄭以爲東道主，行李之往來，共其乏困，君亦無所害。　　a. 拿　b. 而　c. 把……當(当)作

現代文翻译：_____

4. 夫晉，何厭之有？　　　　　　　　　　　　a. 那　b. 先生　c. 發語詞(发语词)，沒有意思

現代文翻译：_____

5. 朝濟河而夕設版焉，君之所知也。　　　　　　　a. 啊　b. 在那裏(里)　c. 哪裏(里)

現代文翻译：_____

6. 越國以鄙遠，君知其難也。　　　　　　　　　　a. 拿　b. 來(来)　c. 由於(于)

現代文翻译：_____

7. 微夫人之力不及此。　　　　　　　　　a. 那　b. 先生　c. 發語詞(发语词)，沒有意思

現代文翻译：_____

8. 焉用亡鄭以陪鄰？　　　　　　　　a. 於(于)此　b. 爲什麽(为什么)　c. 啊

現代文翻译：_____

9. 吾其還也。　　　　　　　　　　　a. 還是(还是)　b. 他　c. 其中的

現代文翻译：_____

《國語》：邵公諫厲王弭謗

"Duke Shao Admonished the King Li of Zhou Not to Thwart Criticism,"
from *Discourses of the States*

Introduction

Discourses of the States 國語 (*Guóyǔ* 国语) is a compendium of histories of the Zhou court and seven vassal states (Lu 魯, Qi 齊, Jin 晉, Zheng 鄭, Chu 楚, Wu 吳, and Yue 越), spanning the period from 947 BCE to 453 BCE. Authorship of this text is a matter of heated debate: the Han grand historian Sima Qian 司马遷 (ca. 145–ca. 86 BCE) attributes it to Zuo Qiuming (compiler of *Zuo Tradition*), but many later scholars dispute this attribution.

As its title suggests, the text is particularly important for its extensive collection of speeches. The current excerpt, from "The Discourses of Zhou" 周語 ("Zhouyǔ" 周语), records a conversation between Duke Shao 邵公 and King Li 厲王, the latter a notorious tyrant of the late Western Zhou. Duke Shao subtly ridicules King Li's futile attempt to suppress criticism. His "Blocking people's mouths is more difficult than damming floods" has become proverbial and is frequently used to encourage rulers to welcome criticism from their people.

正文與簡體譯文 Text and Modern Chinese Translation

厲王虐，國人謗王。[1] 邵公告曰：「民
lì wáng nüè　guó rén bàng wáng　shào gōng gào yuē　mín

不堪命矣！」[2] 王怒。得衛巫，使監謗者。[3]
bù kān mìng yǐ　wáng nù　dé wèi wū　shǐ jiān bàng zhě

以告，則殺之。[4] 國人莫敢言，道路以目。[5]
yǐ gào　zé shā zhī　guó rén mò gǎn yán　dào lù yǐ mù

周厉王暴虐无道，老百姓都指责他。[1] 邵穆公告诉厉王说："老百姓不能忍受您的命令了！"[2] 厉王大怒，找来一个卫国的巫师，派他监视指责自己的人。[3] 厉王依据巫师的告密，杀害批评他的人。[4] 老百姓没有人敢再说话了，在路上见到，用眼睛来示意。[5]

1. 厲 (厉) 王 or 周厲王 (ancestral name 姓, Jī 姬; given name 名, Hú 胡; r. 877?–841? BCE). King Li of Zhou, the tenth king of the Western Zhou dynasty, is a notorious tyrant in Chinese history. His evil deeds include appointing crafty ministers, levying heavy taxes, and forbidding people to criticize his tyranny. As a result, peasants and soldiers were forced to revolt in 842 BCE, in a struggle known as the National Riot 國人暴動 (*guó rén bào dòng* 国人暴动). Afterward, King Li was exiled in Zhi 彘

and died in 828 BCE.

虐 *adj.* brutal, tyrannous. MdnC: 暴虐 (*bào nüè*).

謗 (谤) *v.* to defame, blame. MdnC: 指責 (*zhǐ zé* 指责).

2. 邵公 or 召穆公 (ancestral name 姓, Jī 姬; family name 氏, Shào 邵; given name 名, Hǔ 虎; posthumous name 謚, Mù 穆; fl. 845 BCE) Duke Shao, in the court of King Li of the Western Zhou.

堪 *v.* to bear, endure. MdnC: 忍受 (*rěn shòu*).

命 *n.* order. MdnC: 命令 (*mìng lìng*).

3. 巫 *n.* shaman. 衛 (卫) 巫 refers to a shaman from the Wei state.

監 (监) *v.* to watch, inspect. MdnC: 監視 (*jiān shì* 监视).

者 *auxiliary pron.* the one who. MdnC: ……的人 (*de rén*). See L1 Grammar Note 1 ①.

4. 以 *coverb.* according to. MdnC: 依據 (*yī jù*). See L2 Grammar Note 1 ②.

告 *v.* to tell on, inform against. MdnC: 告密 (*gào mì*).

5. 莫 *indefinite pron.* no one. MdnC: 没有人 (*méi yǒu rén*). See Grammar Note 2 ①.

以目 refers to using eyes to give a hint 示意 (*shì yì*). See L2 Grammar Note 1 ②.

王喜。告邵公曰：「吾能弭謗矣，乃不
wáng xǐ　gào shào gōng yuē　wú néng mǐ bàng yǐ　nǎi bù

敢言。」⁶邵公曰：「是障之也。⁷防民之口，
gǎn yán　　shào gōng yuē　shì zhàng zhī yě　fáng mín zhī kǒu

甚於防川。⁸川壅而潰，傷人必多，民亦如
shèn yú fáng chuān chuān yōng ér kuì　shāng rén bì duō　mín yì rú

之。⁹是故爲川者決之使導，爲民者宣之使
zhī　　shì gù wéi chuān zhě jué zhī shǐ dǎo　wéi mín zhě xuān zhī shǐ

言。¹⁰
yán

周厉王很高兴，告诉邵公说："我能消除指责我的言论，老百姓就不敢再说了。"⁶邵公说："这是堵塞他们的嘴啊！⁷堵住老百姓的嘴，其后果之严重超过堵住河流。⁸河流堵塞了，就会决堤，一定会伤到很多人。老百姓也是一样的。⁹因此治理河流的人排除阻塞，疏导河流，治理百姓的人开导他们，让他们畅所欲言。¹⁰

6. 弭 *v.* to stop, end. MdnC: 消除 (*xiāo chú*).

乃 *adv.* then. MdnC: 就 (*jiù*).

7. 是……也 a structure of an affirmative sentence, meaning "this is…." MdnC: 這是 (*zhè shì* 这是)……. See Grammar Note 1 ②.

障 *v.* to hinder, block. MdnC: 堵塞 (*dǔ sè*).

8. 防 *v.* to guard against. Here it means "to block" (*dǔ sè* 堵住).

甚 *v.* to be more than. MdnC: 超過 (*chāo guò* 超过).

川 *n.* river. MdnC: 河流 (*hé liú*).

9. 壅 *v.* to block, jam. MdnC: 堵塞 (*dǔ sè*).

潰 (溃) *v.* to burst (as a dam). MdnC: 決堤 (*jué dī* 决堤).

如 *v.* to be like. MdnC: 一樣 (*yí yàng* 一样). See Grammar Note 5 ①.

10. 是故 for this reason. MdnC: 因此 (*yīn cǐ*). See Grammar Note 1 ③.

爲 (为 *wéi*) *v.* to do, control, govern. MdnC: 治理 (*zhì lǐ*). See L2 Grammar Note 6 ①.

決 (决) *v.* to eliminate (an obstruction in the river). MdnC: 排除 (*pái chú*).

導 (导) *v.* to dredge. MdnC: 疏導 (*shū dǎo* 疏导).

宣 *v.* to free, unblock. MdnC: 開導 (*kāi dǎo* 开导).

言 *v.* to say. Here it means "to speak freely" 暢所欲言 (*chàng suǒ yù yán* 畅所欲言).

「故天子聽政，使公卿至於列士獻詩，
gù tiān zǐ tīng zhèng　shǐ gōng qīng zhì yú liè shì xiàn shī

瞽獻曲，史獻書，¹¹師箴，瞍賦，矇誦，百
gǔ xiàn qǔ　shǐ xiàn shū　shī zhēn　sǒu fù　méng sòng　bǎi

工諫，¹²庶人傳語，近臣盡規，親戚補察，
gōng jiàn　shù rén chuán yǔ　jìn chén jìn guī　qīn qī bǔ chá

瞽、史教誨，耆、艾修之，¹³而後王斟酌
gǔ　shǐ jiào huì　qí、ài xiū zhī　ér hòu wáng zhēn zhuó

焉，是以事行而不悖¹⁴。
yān　shì yǐ shì xíng ér bú bèi

"因而君王处理政务时，让三公九卿以及大小官员进献诗歌，让乐师进献乐曲，史官进献书籍，¹¹少师献箴言，没有眸子的盲人吟咏，有眸子的盲人朗诵。百官纷纷进谏，¹²老百姓传话给国君。近侍之臣尽规劝之责，国君的亲属补救过失，明察是非。乐师、史官用诗篇和史书来教导，元老们再修改整理。¹³然后国君对此斟酌取舍。于是国家的政事顺利进行，而不会互相冲突。¹⁴

11. 聽 (听) 政 *v.* to administer official affairs or to reign. MdnC: 處理政務 (*chù lǐ zhèng wù* 处理政务).
    公卿 or 三公九卿 three lords and nine ministers.
    至於 (于) *conj.* as well as. MdnC: 以及 (*yǐ jí*).
    列士 a collective name for senior officials 上士 (*shàng shì*), ordinary officials 中士 (*zhōng shì*), and junior officials 下士 (*xià shì*) in the Zhou dynasty.
    獻 (献) *v.* to present. MdnC: 進獻 (*jìn xiàn* 进献).
    瞽 *n.* blind musician. MdnC: 樂師 (*yuè shī* 乐师).
    史 *n.* historian. MdnC: 史官 (*shǐ guān*).

12. 師 (师) *n.* music official. MdnC: 少師 (*shào shī* 少师).
    箴 *n.* a literary genre for admonition.
    瞍 *n.* a blind man 盲人 (*máng rén*) who has no eyeballs (*móu zǐ* 眸子).
    賦 (赋) *v.* to recite (a poem). MdnC: 吟詠 (*yín yǒng* 吟咏).
    矇 *n.* a blind man who has dysfunctional eyeballs.
    誦 (诵) *v.* to recite. MdnC: 朗誦 (*lǎng sòng* 朗诵).
    工 *n.* officials. MdnC: 官 (*guān*).
    諫 (谏) *v.* to admonish, remonstrate. MdnC: 進諫 (*jìn jiàn* 进谏).

13. 庶人 *n.* common people. MdnC: 老百姓 (*lǎo bǎi xìng*).
    傳 (传 chuán) *v.* to transfer, deliver.
    近臣 *n.* personal attendant (*jìn shì* 近侍) of a king or an emperor.
    盡 (尽 jìn) *v.* to use up.
    規 (规) *v.* to advise. MdnC: 規勸 (*guī quàn* 规劝).

親 (亲) 戚 *n.* relatives. Here it refers to the members of the royal family.

補 (补) *v.* to repair, fix up. MdnC: 補救 (*bǔ jiù* 补救).

察 *v.* to investigate.

誨 (诲) *v.* to teach, instruct. MdnC: 教導 (*jiào dǎo* 教导).

耆艾 *n.* old people. Here it refers to seniors or veterans. MdnC: 元老 (*yuán lǎo*).

14. 斟酌 *v.* to consider.

焉 *pron.* about this. See L1 Grammar Note 4 ①.

是以 *conj.* because of this. See Grammar Note 1 ③.

悖 *v.* to go against, to be contradictory to. MdnC: 互相衝突 (*hù xiāng chōng tū* 互相冲突).

「民之有口，猶土之有山川也，財用於
mín zhī yǒu kǒu　　yóu tǔ zhī yǒu shān chuān yě　cái yòng yú

是乎出；猶其原隰之有衍沃也，衣食於是乎
shì hū chū　　yóu qí yuán xí zhī yǒu yǎn wò yě　　yī shí yú shì hū

生。¹⁵口之宣言也，善敗於是乎興。¹⁶行善而
shēng　　kǒu zhī xuān yán yě　　shàn bài yú shì hū xīng　　xíng shàn ér

備敗，其所以阜財用衣食者也。¹⁷夫民慮之
bèi bài　　qí suǒ yǐ fù cái yòng yī shí zhě yě　　　　fú mín lǜ zhī

於心而宣之於口，成而行之，胡可壅也？¹⁸
yú xīn ér xuān zhī yú kǒu　　chéng ér xíng zhī　　hú kě yōng yě

若壅其ₐ口，其ᵦ與能幾何？¹⁹」
ruò yōng qí kǒu　　qí　　yǔ néng jǐ hé

"老百姓有口，就像大地有高山河流一样，财富用度都从这里产出，就像平原和低地都有平坦肥沃的土地，衣食物品都从这里产生。¹⁵嘴能说话议论，政事好坏就从这里显露出来。¹⁶好的事情就去执行，不好的事情就多加防备，这才是增加衣食财富的方法啊！¹⁷老百姓心里担忧，然后用嘴说出来，这是想法成熟后的自然表现，怎么可以堵住呢？¹⁸如果堵住他们的嘴，那么跟随您的人还能有多少啊！¹⁹"

15. 之 *particle.* a nominative marker. See L2 Grammar Note 2 ⑤.

猶 (犹) *v.* to be like. MdnC: 就好像 (*jiù hǎo xiàng*). See Grammar Note 3 ②.

是 *demonstrative pron.* this. MdnC: 這 (*zhè* 这). See Grammar Note 1 ①.

乎 *particle.* an added syllable with no meaning. See Grammar Note 4 ①.

原隰 *n.* flatlands and marsh.

衍沃 *adj.* flat and fertile. MdnC: 平坦肥沃 (*píng tǎn féi wò*). Here it refers to a land that is flat and fertile.

16. 宣 *v.* to announce, speak in public.

善敗 (败) *n.* success and failure.

興 (兴 xīng) *v.* to rise. Here it means "to expose" 顯露 (*xiǎn lù*).

17. 行 (xíng) *v.* to do, act, conduct.

備 (备) *v.* to prepare, guard against. MdnC: 防備 (*fáng bèi* 防备).

阜 *adj.* abundant. Here it is used as a verb and means "to increase" 增加 (*zēng jiā*).

者也 used together to intensify the affirmative tone, no meaning. See L4 Grammar Note 3 ②.

18. 夫 (fú) *initial particle.* See L2 Grammar Note 4 ①.

慮 (慮) *v.* to worry. MdnC: 担忧 (*dān yōu*).

成 *v.* to complete, finish.

胡 *initial interrogative particle.* why? how come? MdnC: 怎麼 (*zěn me* 怎么). See Grammar Note 6.

19. 其 a *possessive pron.* their. MdnC: 他們的 (*tā mén de* 他们的). See L2 Grammar Note 5 ②.

其 b *adv.* used to express a change of tone, no meaning. See L2 Grammar Note 5 ③.

與 (与 *yǔ*) *v.* to get along with, follow. MdnC: 跟隨 (*gēn suí* 跟随).

幾 (几 *jǐ*) 何 how much? how many? MdnC: 多少 (*duō shǎo*). See Grammar Note 7.

王不聽。於是國人莫敢出言。三年，乃
wáng bù tīng   yú shì guó rén mò gǎn chū yán   sān nián   nǎi

流王於彘。[20]
liú wáng yú zhì

周厲王不听。于是老百姓没有人敢再公开发表言论。三年之后，人们把周厉王流放到彘这个地方去了。[20]

《國語》上海：上海古籍出版社 (1978), 9–10.

20. 莫 *indefinite pron.* none, no one. MdnC: 没有人 (*méi yǒu rén*). See Grammar Note 2 ①.

流 *v.* to send into exile. MdnC: 流放 (*liú fàng*).

彘 place name in present-day Huozhou 霍州, Shanxi Province.

語法注釋 Grammar Notes

1. 是 ① *demonstrative pron.* this, those. MdnC: 這 (*zhè* 这), 這裏 (*zhè lǐ* 这里).

財用於是乎生。

[財富用度从这里产出。]

② 是……也 a structure of an affirmative sentence, meaning "this is…." MdnC: 這是 (*zhè shì* 这是)…….

是障之也。

[这是堵塞他们的嘴啊！]

③ 是故/是以 for this reason, therefore. MdnC: 因此 (*yīn cǐ*), 由此 (*yóu cǐ*).

是故爲川者決之使導。

[因此治理河流的人排除阻塞，疏通河道。]

是以事行而不悖。

[由此政事得以顺利进行，而不会互相冲突，违背道理。]

See 是 ④ in L14 Grammar Note 4 and 是 ⑤ in L30 Grammar Note 2.

2. 莫 ① *indefinite pron.* no one, none, nothing. MdnC: 没有人 (*méi yǒu rén*), 没有什麼 (*méi yǒu shén me* 没有什么).

國人莫敢言，道路以目。

[老百姓没有人敢再说话，在路上见到，用眼睛来示意。]

See 莫② in L37 Grammar Note 1.

3. 猶　① *adv.* still, yet. MdnC: 尚且 (*shàng qiě*), 還 (*hái* 还).
(犹)

臣之壯也，猶不如人。(L2)

[臣下壮年的时候，尚且不如别人。]

② *v.* to be like. MdnC: 就好像 (*jiù hǎo xiàng*).

民之有口，猶土之有山川也，財用於是乎生。

[老百姓有口 ，就像大地有高山河流一样，（社会的）财富用度都从这里产出。]

4. 乎　① *particle.* an added syllable with no meaning.

財用於是乎生。

[财富用度从这里产出。]

See 乎②③④ in L6 Grammar Note 2.

5. 如　① *v.* to be like, be comparable (with/to). MdnC: 像 (*xiàng*) ⋯⋯一樣 (*yí yàng* 一样)，比得上 (*bǐ dé shàng*).

川壅而潰，傷人必多，民亦如之。

[河流堵塞了，就会决堤，一定会伤到很多人。老百姓也是一样的。]

臣之壯也，猶不如人。(L2)

[臣壮年的时候，尚且比不上别人。]

See 如②③④ in L6 Grammar Note 3 and 如⑤ in L15 Grammar Note 2.

6. 胡　*initial interrogative particle.* how? why? MdnC: 怎麼 (*zěn me* 怎么)，爲什麼 (*wèi shén me* 为什么).

夫民慮之於心而宣之於口，成而行之，胡可壅也？

[老百姓心里担忧，然后用嘴说出来，这是想法成熟后的自然表现，怎么可以堵住呢？]

7. 幾何　how much? how many? MdnC: 多少 (*duō shǎo*).
(几)

若壅其口，其與能幾何？

[如果堵住他们的嘴，那么跟随您的人还能有多少啊？]

Literary Analysis

Analogy is perhaps the most common method for advancing an argument in pre-Qin prose. Here, through an analogy linking criticism management and flood control, Shao Gong attempts to bring King Li to see the foolishness of his attempt to stamp out criticism of his despotic rule. Elaborating on this analogy, Shao presents both the worst- and the best-case scenarios, hoping to persuade the king to make the correct choice. According to Shao, which actions would lead to the worst-case scenarios in criticism management and flood control? Which would promote the best?

Would you call the wise actions of ancient kings praised by Shao an ancient form of the public opinion poll? What kinds of people were in charge of collecting public opinion? How were the sentiments of the humblest commoners expressed? How were these sentiments observed and reported to the rulers?

Compared to Shao's extended speech, the narrative frame is lopsidedly brief. But is this narrative brevity desirable or not? Does the narrative diminish or amplify Shao's cause-and-effect reasoning?

—ZC

課後練習 Exercises

一 給加點字注音 Give the pinyin romanization for each dotted word.

1. 衛巫 (____, ____)　2. 瞍賦 (____, ____)　3. 師箴 (____)　4. 瞽 (____)

5. 矇誦 (____, ____)　6. 耆艾 (____, ____)　7. 原隰 (____)　8. 彘 (____)

二 在括號中給句中加點的字注音，並選出正確的釋義 Give the pinyin romanization for each dotted word; then select the correct definition from the following list, and write it in the blank.

決(决)堤　　互相衝(冲)突　　增加　　消除　　**信服**　　進諫(进谏)　　指責(责)　　堵塞

1. 小信未孚 (fú) 信服　　2. 若壅其口 (　)　_____　　3. 吾能弭謗矣 (　)　_____

4. 國人謗王 (　)　_____　　5. 川壅而潰 (　)　_____　　6. 阜財用衣食者 (　)　_____

7. 百官諫 (　)　_____　　8. 事行而不悖 (　)　_____

三 選擇釋義並填空 Match each word in the left column with its correct definition in the middle column. Fill in each blank in the right column with an appropriate word from the left column.

謀謀劃(谋划)	疏導(导)	厲王____，國人謗王。邵公告曰："民不____命
障_____	防備(备)	矣！"王怒，得衛巫，使____謗者。
虐_____	監視(监视)	邵公曰："是____之也。防民之口，甚於防川。"
導_____	顯(显)露	是故爲川者____之使____，爲民者宣之使言。
備_____	**謀劃(谋划)**	庶人傳語，近臣盡____。
監_____	規勸(规劝)	口之宣言也，善敗於是乎____。行善而____敗，其所
興_____	堵塞	以阜財用衣食者也。
規_____	排除	
決_____	忍受	
堪_____	暴虐	

四 請用給出的字填空 Fill in each blank with an appropriate word from the following list (some words may be used more than once).

是　莫　以　之　何　其　焉

1. 王不聽，於是國人____敢出言。　2. 邵公曰："____障____也。防民____口，甚於防川。"

3. 若壅____口，____與能幾____？　4. 而後王斟酌____，____ ____事行而不悖。

五　爲加點字選擇正確釋義，並根據釋義來翻譯句子 Match each dotted word with its correct modern Chinese equivalent by circling the latter. Then translate each sentence into modern Chinese.

1. 又何間焉？　　　　　　　　　　　　　　　ⓐ 爲什麽（为什么）　b. 憑什麽（凭什么）　c. 多少

現代文翻译：你又为什么要参与到这件事情里面？

_____

2. 國人莫敢言，道路以目。　　　　　　　　　a. 因爲（为）　b. 用　c. 來（来）

現代文翻译：_____

3. 以告，則殺之。　　　　　　　　　　　　　a. 依據（据）　b. 而　c. 把……當（当）作

現代文翻译：_____

4. 是故爲民者決之使導，爲民者宣之使言。　a. 因此　b. 而且　c. 可是

現代文翻译：_____

5. 若壅其口，其與能幾何？　　　　　　　　　a. 那麽（么）　b. 的　c. 他

現代文翻译：_____

6. 而後王斟酌焉，是以事行而不悖。　　　　　a. 用　b. 因而　c. 這（这）是

現代文翻译：_____

7. 王不聽。於是國人莫敢出言。　　　　　　　a. 不要　b. 没有人　c. 暮

現代文翻译：_____

第四課

《戰國策》：鄒忌諷齊王納諫

"Zou Ji Admonished the Lord of Qi to Accept Criticism,"
from *The Strategies of the Warring States*

Introduction

The Strategies of the Warring States 戰國策 (*Zhànguó Cè* 战国策) is a historical text compiled by Liu Xiang 劉向 (77–6 BCE), historian of the late Western Han and member of the royal Han family. It is a compendium of the histories of twelve individual states (Eastern Zhou 東周, Western Zhou 西周, Qin 秦, Qi 齊, Chu 楚, Zhao 趙, Wei 魏, Han 韓, Yan 燕, Song 宋, Wei 衛, and Zhongshan 中山), modeled on the earlier *Discourses of the States* (see lesson 3). Covering important historical events between 455 and 221 BCE, it foregrounds eloquent, effective speeches, full of anecdotes, analogies, and other rhetorical devices.

This excerpt shows how the official Zou Ji persuaded King Wei of Qi to reform his governance by encouraging free speech and open criticism.

正文與簡體譯文 Text and Modern Chinese Translation

鄒忌脩八尺有餘，身體昳麗。朝服衣冠
zōu jì xiū bā chǐ yǒu yú　shēn tǐ yì lì　zhāo fú yī guān

窺鏡，謂其妻曰：「我孰與城北徐公美？」[1] 其
kuī jìng　wèi qí qī yuē　wǒ shú yǔ chéng běi xú gōng měi　qí

妻曰：「君美甚，徐公何能及公也！」城北徐
qī yuē　jūn měi shèn　xú gōng hé néng jí gōng yě　chéng běi xú

公，齊國之美麗者也。[2] 忌不自信，而復問其
gōng　qí guó zhī měi lì zhě yě　jì bú zì xìn　ér fù wèn qí

妾曰：「吾孰與徐公美？」妾曰：「徐公何能
qiè yuē　wú shú yǔ xú gōng měi　qiè yuē　xú gōng hé néng

及君也！」[3] 旦日，客從外來，與坐談。問之
jí jūn yě　dàn rì　kè cóng wài lái　yǔ zuò tán　wèn zhī

客曰：「吾與徐公孰美？」客曰：「徐公不若
kè yuē　wú yǔ xú gōng shú měi　kè yuē　xú gōng bù ruò

邹忌身高八尺多，而且长得很漂亮。早晨，邹忌穿戴好衣帽，偷偷照了下鏡子，对妻子说："我和城北的徐公谁更美？"[1] 他的妻子说："您很美，徐公怎么能比得上您呢！"城北徐公，是齐国有名的美男子。[2] 邹忌不太自信，然后又问他的妾："我和徐公谁更美？"妾说："徐公怎么比得上您呢！"[3] 第二天，有客人从外面来拜访。邹忌和他坐着谈话。邹忌问客

君之美也！」[4]
jūn zhī měi yě

人："我和徐公谁
美？客人说："徐公
不如您美啊！"[4]

1. 鄒 (邹) 忌 (?–?) a Qi minister in the Warring States period. He first became prime minister in the reign of King Wei of Qi 齊威王 (356–320 BCE) and later served King Xuan of Qi 齊宣王 (350?–301 BCE).

   脩 (修) *adj.* long, tall. Here it means "height" 身高 (*shēn gāo*).

   尺 *measure word.* a Chinese foot.

   餘 (余) *adj.* more than enough.

   昳麗 (丽) *adj.* beautiful, handsome. MdnC: 漂亮 (*piào liàng*).

   朝 (zhāo) *n.* morning. MdnC: 早晨 (*zǎo chén*).

   服 *v.* to wear. MdnC: 穿戴 (*chuān dài*).

   冠 (guān) *n.* hat. MdnC: 帽 (*mào*).

   窺 (窥) *v.* to spy, watch, look at. MdnC: 偷偷看 (*tōu tōu kàn*).

   謂 (谓) *v.* to talk to. MdnC: 對 (*duì* 对) ……說 (*shuō* 说).

   孰 *interrogative pron.* who? which one? MdnC: 誰 (*shuí* 谁). See Grammar Note 1 ①.

2. 甚 *adv.* very, extremely. MdnC: 很 (*hěn*).

   何 *interrogative particle.* how come? MdnC: 怎麼 (*zěn me* 怎么). See Grammar Note 2 ④.

   及 *v.* to compare with, reach. MdnC: 比得上 (*bǐ de shàng*).

   者也 *ending particle.* no meaning. See Grammar Note 3 ②.

3. 復 (复) *adv.* again. MdnC: 又 (*yòu*).

   妾 *n.* concubine.

4. 旦 *n.* dawn, day. 旦日 means "the next day" 第二天 (*dì èr tiān*).

   若 *v.* to be comparable (with/to). MdnC: 如 (*rú*). See Grammar Note 4 ①.

明日， 徐公來， 孰視之， 自以爲不如。
míng rì   xú gōng lái   shú shì zhī   zì yǐ wéi bù rú

窺鏡而自視， 又弗如遠甚。[5] 暮寢而思之。
kuī jìng ér zì shì   yòu fú rú yuǎn shèn   mù qǐn ér sī zhī

曰：「吾妻之ᵇ美我者， 私我也； 妾之ᵇ美我
yuē   wú qī zhī   měi wǒ zhě   sī wǒ yě   qiè zhī   měi wǒ

者， 畏我也； 客之ᵇ美我者， 欲有求於我
zhě   wèi wǒ yě   kè zhī   měi wǒ zhě   yù yǒu qiú yú wǒ

也。」[6]
yě

又一天，徐公来拜访，邹忌仔细看看他，觉得自己不如徐公美。照了下镜子看看自己，更觉得远远不如徐公。[5] 晚上躺在床上，想这件事情，说："我的妻子觉得我美，是她偏爱我；妾觉得我美，是她害怕我。客人觉得我美，是想有求于我。"[6]

5. 孰 *adv.* used in the sense of 熟 (*shú*), meaning "thoroughly, carefully" 仔細 (*zǐ xì* 仔细).

   之 *personal pron.* him, referring here to Xu Gong 徐公. See L1 Grammar Note 2 ③.

弗 *adv.* no, not. MdnC: 不 (*bù*). See Grammar Note 5.

如 *v.* to be comparable (with/to). See L3 Grammar Note 5 ①.

6. 暮 *n.* evening.　MdnC: 晚上 (*wǎn shàng*).

寢 *v.* to go to bed.

之ₐ *pron.* this situation. See L1 Grammar Note 2 ①.

之_b *particle.* a nominative marker. See L2 Grammar Note 2 ⑤.

美 *adj.* beautiful. Here it is used as a putative verb, 以……爲美, meaning "to think … as (a) beautiful (person)." See L14 Grammar Note 1 ①.

者……也 an equivalent of the verb *to be* in English construction. See Grammar Note 3 ③.

私 *adj.* private. Here it is used as a verb, meaning "to be partial to" 偏愛 (*piān ài* 偏爱).

畏 *v.* to be afraid. MdnC: 害怕 (*hài pà*).

於是入朝見威王曰：「臣誠知不如徐公
yú shì rù cháo jiàn wēi wáng yuē chén chéng zhī bù rú xú gōng

美。臣之妻私臣，臣之妾畏臣，臣之客欲有求
měi　chén zhī qī sī chén　chén zhī qiè wèi chén　chén zhī kè yù yǒu qiú

於臣，皆以美於徐公。⁷今齊地方千里，百二
yú chén　jiē yǐ měi yú xú gōng　jīn qí dì fāng qiān lǐ　bǎi èr

十城。宮婦左右，莫不私王；朝廷之臣，莫
shí chéng　gōng fù zuǒ yòu　mò bù sī wáng　cháo tíng zhī chén　mò

不畏王；四境之內，莫不有求於王。由此觀
bù wèi wáng　sì jìng zhī nèi　mò bù yǒu qiú yú wáng　yóu cǐ guān

之，王之蔽甚矣！⁸」
zhī　wáng zhī bì shèn yǐ

于是邹忌上朝拜见齐威王，说，"我确实知道自己不如徐公美。我的妻子偏爱我，我的妾害怕我，我的客人想要有求于我，所以都认为我比徐公美。⁷现在齐国土地方圆千里，有一百二十座城，宫中妇人和近侍，没有人不偏爱君王您的；朝廷的大臣，没有不害怕您的；齐国之内，没有不有求于您的。这样看来，君王您受到的蒙蔽一定很厉害！⁸"

7. 朝 (*cháo*) *n.* imperial court. MdnC: 朝廷 (*cháo tíng*).

威王 or 齊 (齐) 威王 (ancestral name 姓, Guǐ 媯; family name 氏, Tián 田; given name 名, Yīnqí 因其; posthumous name 謚, Wēiwáng 威王; fl. 356–320 BCE) King Wei ruled the Qi state during the Warring States period.

誠 (诚) *adv.* truly, really. MdnC: 確實 (*què shí* 确实).

8. 方 *n.* circumference. MdnC: 方圓 (*fāng yuán* 方圆).

宮婦 (妇) refers to King Wei's concubines.

左右 *n.* left and right. It refers to King Wei's attendants (*jìn shì* 近侍).

莫 *indefinite pron.* none. MdnC: 沒有人 (*méi yǒu rén*). See L3 Grammar Note 2 ①.

境 *n.* border. 四境 means "borders of a country."

蔽 *v.* to cover, deceive. MdnC: 矇蔽 (*méng bì* 蒙蔽).

甚 *adj.* much, very. MdnC: 厲害 (*lì hài* 厉害).

王曰：「善。」乃下令：「群臣吏民，能
wáng yuē shàn   nǎi xià lìng   qún chén lì mín   néng

面刺寡人之過者，受上賞。上書諫寡人者，
miàn cì guǎ rén zhī guò zhě shòu shàng shǎng shàng shū jiàn guǎ rén zhě

受中賞。能謗議於市朝，聞寡人之耳者，受
shòu zhōng shǎng néng bàng yì yú shì cháo wén guǎ rén zhī ěr zhě   shòu

下賞。」⁹
xià shǎng

齐威王说："好！"
于是下令，"各级大
小官员和老百姓，能
当面指责我过错的
人，可受到上等的赏
赐。能够上书给我进
谏的人，可受到中等
的赏赐。能够在公共
场合批评议论的人，
传到我的耳朵里的，
可以受到下等的赏
赐。"⁹

9. 善 *adj.* good, great. MdnC: 好 (*hǎo*).
   吏 *n.* low-level officials. MdnC: 官員 (*guān yuán* 官员).
   面 *n.* face. Here it is used as an adverb, meaning "face to face" 當面 (*dāng miàn* 当面).
   刺 *v.* to prick, criticize. MdnC: 指責 (*zhǐ zé* 指责).
   過 (过) *n.* mistakes. MdnC: 過錯 (*guò cuò* 过错).
   者 *auxiliary pron.* the one who. MdnC: ……的人 (*de rén*). See L1 Grammar Note 1 ①.
   受 *v.* to be awarded.
   賞 (赏) *n.* reward, award. MdnC: 賞賜 (*shǎng cì* 赏赐).
   上書 (书) *v.* to write an official letter to a higher authority.
   諫 (谏) *v.* to expostulate with. MdnC: 進諫 (*jìn jiàn* 进谏).
   謗議 (谤议) *v.* to vilify, criticize.
   市 *n.* market. MdnC: 集市 (*jí shì*). 市朝 means "public places" 公共場合 (*gōng gòng chǎng hé* 公共场合).
   聞 (闻) *v.* to hear, make known.

令初下，群臣進諫，門庭若市。數月之
lìng chū xià qún chén jìn jiàn mén tíng ruò shì   shù yuè zhī

後，時時而間進。期年之後，雖欲言，無可
hòu   shí shí ér jiàn jìn   jī nián zhī hòu   suī yù yán   wú kě

進者。燕、趙、韓、魏聞之，皆朝於齊。此
jìn zhě   yān   zhào   hán   wèi wén zhī   jiē cháo yú qí   cǐ

所謂戰勝於朝廷。¹⁰
suǒ wèi zhàn shèng yú cháo tíng

命令刚下达时，大臣
们都来进谏，宫门和
庭院像集市一样热
闹。几个月之后，有
时偶尔还有人进谏。
一年之后，即使有人
想要进谏，也没有什
么可以说的。燕国、
赵国、韩国和魏国听
说了这件事情，都来
朝拜齐国。这就是人
们所说的在朝廷上战
胜（别的国家）。¹⁰

《戰國策》，上海：上海古籍出版社 (1985), 324–326.

10. 令 *n.* order. MdnC: 命令 (*mìng lìng*).
    庭 *n.* courtyard. MdnC: 庭院 (*tíng yuàn*).
    若 *v.* to be like. MdnC: 像 (*xiàng*). See Grammar Note 4 ①.
    間 (*jiàn*) *adv.* intermittently. MdnC: 偶爾 (*ǒu ěr* 偶尔).

期 (jī) 年 *n.* one year. MdnC: 一年 (*yì nián*).

雖 (虽) *conj.* even if. MdnC: 即使 (*jí shǐ*). See Grammar Note 6.

朝 (cháo) *v.* to pay respects to a sovereign, worship. MdnC: 朝拜 (*cháo bài*).

語法注釋 Grammar Notes

1. **孰**　*interrogative pron.* who? which (of two or more people)? MdnC: 誰 (*shuí* 谁).

   ① A + 孰與 + B + adjective?

   　　我孰與城北徐公美？

   　　　[我和城北徐公谁美？]

   ② A + (與) + B 孰 + adjective?

   　　吾與徐公孰美？

   　　　[我和徐公谁美？]

2. **何**　Four uses of 何 are explained in this book. In addition to the use below, see 何①②③ in L1 Grammar Note 3 and 何如 in L6 Grammar Note 3 ④.

   ④ *interrogative particle.* how come? MdnC: 怎麼 (*zěn me* 怎么).

   　　君美甚，徐公何能及公也！

   　　　[您很美，徐公怎么能比得上您呢！]

3. **者**　Six uses of 者 are explained in this book. In addition to the uses below, see 者① in L1 Grammar Note 1, 者④ in L6 Grammar Note 8, 者⑤ in L7 Grammar Note 3, and 者⑥ in L8 Grammar Note 1.

   ② 者也, where 者 is used together with the ending particle 也 to strengthen the affirmative tone, no meaning.

   　　城北徐公，齊國之美麗者也。

   　　　[城北徐公，是齐国的美男子。]

   　　行善而備敗，其所以阜財用衣食者也。(L3)

   　　　[好的事情就去执行，不好的事情就多加防备，这才是增加衣食财富的途径啊！]

   ③ ……者，……也。　an equivalent of the verb *to be* in English construction. MdnC: ……是 (*shì*)…….

   　　吾妻之美我者，私我也。

   　　　[我的妻子觉得我美的原因是她偏爱我。]

4. **若**　① *v.* to be like, to be comparable (with/to). MdnC: 像 (*xiàng*)……一樣 (*yí yàng* 一样), 如 (*rú*).

   　　徐公不若君之美也。

   　　　[徐公不如您美。]

   　　令初下，群臣進諫，門庭若市

   　　　[命令刚下达时，大臣们都来进谏，宫门和庭院像集市一样热闹。]

② *conj.* if. MdnC: 如果 (*rú guǒ*).

若使燭之武見秦君，師必退。(L2)

[如果派遣烛之武去面见秦君，秦军一定会撤退。]

若壅其口，其與能幾何？(L3)

[如果堵住老百姓的嘴，那么跟随您的人还能有多少啊？]

See 若③ in L14 Grammar Note 3 and 若④ in L32 Grammar Note 3.

5. 弗　　*adv.* no, not. MdnC: 不 (*bù*).

窺鏡而自視，又弗如遠甚。

[照照镜子看了看自己，更觉得自己不如徐公美。]

衣食所安，弗敢專也，必以分人。(L1)

[衣服和食物这些养生的东西，不敢自己独自享用，必定把它们分给别人。]

6. 雖
(虽)　　*conj.* although, even though. MdnC: 即使 (*jí shǐ*).

期年之後，雖欲言，無可進者。

[一年后，（有人）即使想要进言，也没有什么可以说的。]

小大之獄，雖不能察，必以情。(L1)

[各种诉讼案，即使不能一一考察，一定会根据实情（来判断）。]

Literary Analysis

This text presents another well-known pre-Qin example of persuasive argument using analogy, here drawn between family and court relationships. The first half of this text tells how Zou Ji, a court minister, has been fooled by a flattering wife, concubine, and servants into believing he is handsomer than Mr. Xu, the famed best-looking man of Qi, until one day he meets Xu and discovers the truth. He realizes his flatterers have lied to him purely out of self-interest—his wife's compromised love, his concubine's fear, and others' hope for favors from him.

The next day, in an audience with King Wei of Qi, Zou alerts him to the analogous, more perilous situation facing him. He warns the king that his palace ladies are just as unreliable, his court ministers just as fearful, and his subjects just as desirous of favors. Given their obvious self-interest, all these people are bound to keep the king from knowing the truth about his governance. Unlike the despotic King Li of Zhou (see lesson 3), King Wei is convinced by his minister's admonition and takes bold action to encourage public criticism by court officials and commoners alike. If King Li's rejection of Shao Gong's analogous advice precipitates his exile and death, King Wei's acceptance of Zou's similar counsel makes possible the Qi's meteoric rise and submission of awed neighbor states.

The analogical argument in this lesson is constructed with the aid of repetitive patterning, marked by recurring repetition of diverse textual elements ranging from phrases to sentences, sentence clusters, and paragraphs. What types of repetitive patterning are employed in the first, second, and third passages? What rhetorical and/or structural functions do they perform? Comment on their effectiveness.

👉 *HTRCProse*, chapter 1, "An Anatomy of the Chinese Prose Form: An Overview," C1.4, for further comments on repetitive patterning.

—ZC

課後練習　Exercises

一 給加點字注音　Give the pinyin romanization for each dotted word.

1. 鄒忌 （＿＿, ＿＿） 2. 妾 （＿＿） 3. 燕 （＿＿） 4. 韓 （＿＿） 5. 魏 （＿＿）

二 在括號中給句中加點的字注音，並選出正確的釋義　Give the pinyin romanization for each dotted word; then select the correct definition from the following list, and write it in the blank.

偶爾(尔)　早晨　偷看　晚上　一年　身高　信服　朝拜　美麗(丽)　矇(蒙)蔽

1. 小信未孚　（fú）　信服　　2. 身體昳麗　（　）＿＿＿＿＿　　3. 朝服衣冠　（　）＿＿＿＿＿

4. 窺鏡而自視（　）＿＿＿＿＿　　5. 暮寢而思之（　）＿＿＿＿＿　　6. 王之蔽甚矣（　）＿＿＿＿＿

7. 期年之後　（　）＿＿＿＿＿　　8. 時時而間進（　）＿＿＿＿＿　　9. 皆朝於齊　（　）＿＿＿＿＿

10. 鄒忌脩八尺有餘（　）＿＿＿＿＿＿

三 選擇釋義並填空　Match each word in the left column with its correct definition in the middle column. Fill in each blank in the right column with an appropriate word from the left column (some words may be used more than once).

謀謀劃(谋划)	當(当)面
私＿＿＿＿	進諫(进谏)
畏＿＿＿＿	指責(责)
孰＿＿＿＿	穿戴
甚＿＿＿＿	**謀劃(谋划)**
面＿＿＿＿	厲(厉)害
服＿＿＿＿	仔細(细)
誠＿＿＿＿	庭院
市＿＿＿＿	害怕
諫＿＿＿＿	確實(确实)
庭＿＿＿＿	偏愛(爱)
刺＿＿＿＿	集市

鄒忌脩八尺有餘，身體昳麗，朝＿＿＿衣冠窺鏡。

明日，徐公來，＿＿＿視之，自以爲不如。

臣＿＿＿知不如徐公美，臣之妻＿＿＿臣，臣之妾＿＿＿臣，臣之客欲有求於臣。

由此觀之，王之蔽＿＿＿矣。

群臣吏民，能＿＿＿＿＿寡人之過者，受上賞。上書＿＿＿寡人者，受中賞。能謗議於＿＿＿朝，聞寡人之耳者，受下賞。

令初下，群臣進＿＿＿，門＿＿＿若＿＿＿。

四 請用給出的字填空　Fill in each blank with an appropriate word from the following list (some words may be used more than once).

孰　之　莫　其　何　弗　以

1. 謂＿＿妻曰："我＿＿與徐公美？"＿＿妻曰："君美甚，徐公＿＿能及公也！"

2. 明日，徐公來，孰視＿＿，自＿＿爲不如。窺鏡而自視，又＿＿如遠甚。

3. 宮婦左右，＿＿不私王；朝廷＿＿臣，＿＿不畏王。四境＿＿內，＿＿不有求於王。

五 爲加點字選擇正確釋義，並根據釋義來翻譯句子 Match each dotted word with its correct modern Chinese equivalent by circling the latter. Then translate each sentence into modern Chinese.

1. 又何間焉？　　　　　　　　　　　ⓐ 爲什麼（为什么） **b.** 憑什麼（凭什么） **c.** 多少

現代文翻譯：你又为什么要参与到这件事情里面？

＿＿＿＿＿＿＿＿＿＿＿＿＿＿＿＿＿＿＿＿＿＿＿＿

2. 吾孰與徐公美？　　　　　　　　　　**a.** 誰（谁） **b.** 仔細（细） **c.** 熟悉

現代文翻譯：＿＿＿＿＿＿＿＿＿＿＿＿＿＿＿＿＿＿＿＿＿

3. 君美甚，徐公何能及君也！　　　　**a.** 爲什麼（为什么） **b.** 怎麼（怎么） **c.** 多少

現代文翻譯：＿＿＿＿＿＿＿＿＿＿＿＿＿＿＿＿＿＿＿＿＿

4. 窺鏡而自視，又弗如遠甚。　　　　　　**a.** 不 **b.** 沒有人 **c.** 但是

現代文翻譯：＿＿＿＿＿＿＿＿＿＿＿＿＿＿＿＿＿＿＿＿＿

5. 吾妻之美我者，私我也。　　　　**a.** 的 **b.** 這（这） **c.** 語助詞（语助词）

現代文翻譯：＿＿＿＿＿＿＿＿＿＿＿＿＿＿＿＿＿＿＿＿＿

6. 令初下，群臣進諫，門庭若市。　　**a.** 像⋯⋯一樣（样） **b.** 如果 **c.** 比得上

現代文翻譯：＿＿＿＿＿＿＿＿＿＿＿＿＿＿＿＿＿＿＿＿＿

7. 期年之後，雖欲言，無可進者。　　　**a.** 可是 **b.** 即使 **c.** 所以

現代文翻譯：＿＿＿＿＿＿＿＿＿＿＿＿＿＿＿＿＿＿＿＿＿

單元練習

Unit Exercises

一、辨析加點字在不同句中注音和釋義的異同 Give the pinyin romanization for each dotted word, and then write in its correct definition.

1. 鄙　肉食者鄙，未能遠謀。　　　　　（ **bǐ** ）<u>目光短淺</u>
　　　越國以鄙遠，君知其難也。　　　　（　）＿＿＿＿＿

2. 甚　防民之口，甚於防川。　　　　　　（　）＿＿＿＿＿
　　　王之蔽甚矣。　　　　　　　　　　　（　）＿＿＿＿＿

3. 朝　朝濟而夕設版焉。　　　　　　　　　（　）＿＿＿＿＿
　　　燕、趙、韓、魏聞之，皆朝於齊。　（　）＿＿＿＿＿

4. 與　失其所與，不知。　　　　　　　　　（　）＿＿＿＿＿
　　　若壅其口，其與能幾何？　　　　　　（　）＿＿＿＿＿
　　　吾與徐公孰美？　　　　　　　　　　（　）＿＿＿＿＿

5. 師　十年春，齊師伐我。　　　　　　　　（　）＿＿＿＿＿
　　　師箴，瞍賦　　　　　　　　　　　　（　）＿＿＿＿＿

6. 間　肉食者謀之，又何間焉？　　　　　　（　）＿＿＿＿＿
　　　時時而間進　　　　　　　　　　　　（　）＿＿＿＿＿

二、用給出的字填空，並選擇正確的釋義 Fill in the blanks with words from list A, and then write in their modern Chinese equivalents from list B.

A. Words for Filling the Blanks　　　　　B. Modern Chinese Equivalents

窺　阜　私　悖　市　　　　　　代替　堵塞　忍受　損（损）害　　集市
壅　偏　孚　賜　靡　　　　　　增加　信服　恩惠　互相衝（冲）突　偏愛（爱）
易　闕　堪　鄙　　　　　　　　偷看　遍及　倒下　目光短淺（浅）

1. 肉食者 ＿＿鄙，未能遠謀。　**[目光短淺]**　　2. 小惠未＿＿＿，民弗從也。　　[　　]
3. 小信未＿＿＿，神弗福也。　[　　]　　4. 望其旗＿＿＿，故逐之。　　[　　]
5. 君嘗爲晉君＿＿＿矣。　[　　]　　6. 不＿＿＿秦，焉取之？　[　　]
7. 以亂＿＿＿整，不武。　[　　]　　8. 民不＿＿＿命矣！　[　　]
9. 其所以＿＿＿財用衣食者也。[　　]　　10. 是以事行而不＿＿＿。　[　　]
11. 川＿＿＿而潰，傷人必多。　[　　]　　12. ＿＿＿鏡而自視。　[　　]

13. 吾之妻美我者，＿＿＿＿我也。[　　　]　　14. 門庭若＿＿＿＿。　　　　　　　[　　　　]

三、給加點字選擇正確的釋義，並選出與加點字用法相同的句子 Circle the letter of the correct definition (a, b, c, or d) for the dotted word in each boldfaced sentence. Then circle the letter of the sentence (A, B, C, or D) that employs the dotted word in the same way as the boldfaced sentence.

1. 臣之妻私臣。　　　　　　　a. 這(这)件事情 b. 他 ⓒ 的 d. 他們(们)

　　A. 夫晉，何厭之有？　　　　　　B. 不闕秦，焉取之？

　　C. 肉食者謀之，又何間焉？　　　Ⓓ 能面刺寡人之過者，受上賞。

2. 乃入見，問何以戰。　　　a. 什麼(么) b. 多少 c. 怎麼(么) d. 為什麼(为什么)

　　A. 徐公何能及君也？　　　　　　B. 夫晉，何厭之有？

　　C. 其與能幾何？　　　　　　　　D. 肉食者謀之，又何間焉？

3. 國人莫敢言，道路以目。　a. 來(来) b. 由於(于) c. 用 d. 而

　　A. 晉侯、秦伯圍鄭，以其無禮於晉。　B. 以亂易整，不武。

　　C. 焉用亡鄭以陪鄰？　　　　　　D. 越國以鄙遠，君知其難也。

4. 焉用亡鄭以陪鄰？　　　a. 啊 b. 什麼(么) c. 怎麼(么) d. 在那裏(里)

　　A. 然鄭亡，子亦有不利焉？　　　B. 朝濟而夕設版焉。

　　C. 不闕秦，焉取之？　　　　　　D. 肉食者謀之，又何間焉？

5. 公問其故。　　　a. 他(秦穆公) b. 其中的 c. 他們(们) d. 那麼(么)

　　A. 以其無禮於晉，且貳於楚。　　B. 吾其還也。

　　C. 若壅其口，其與能幾何？　　　D. 越國以鄙遠，君知其難也。

6. 暮寢而思之⋯⋯⋯　　　a. 這(这)件事情 b. 他 c. 的 d. 他們(们)

　　A. 許之，夜縋而出。　　　　　　B. 夫晉，何厭之有？

　　C. 以告，則殺之。　　　　　　　D. 肉食者謀之，又何間焉？

7. 臣之壯也，猶不如人。　a. 如果 b. 至於(于) c. 比得上 d. 像⋯⋯一樣(样)

　　A. 若壅其口，其與能幾何？　　　B. 窺鏡而自視，又弗如遠甚。

　　C. 川壅而潰，傷人必多，民亦如之。　D. 令初下，群臣進諫，門庭若市。

四、閱讀下面的段落，選擇正確的釋義 Read the following passage and select the correct definition for each dotted word in the following list.

秦王使人謂安陵君曰:「寡人欲以五百里之地易安陵, 安陵君其許寡人? 」安陵君曰:「大王加惠, 以大易小, 甚善。雖然, 受地於先王, 願終守之, 弗敢易! 」秦王不說。安陵君因使唐且使於秦。

《戰國策 • 魏策四》上海: 上海古籍出版社 (1985), 922–923.

安陵 a vassal state of the Wei state in the Warring States period.
唐且 or 唐雎 a strategist of the Lord of Anling.

1. 寡人欲以五百里之地易安陵。　a. 因爲(为)　　b. 用　　　　c. 認爲(认为)
2. 安陵君其許寡人?　　　　　　a. 得　　　　b. 那麽(么)　c. 他
3. 以大易小, 甚善。　　　　　　a. 厲(厉)害　b. 很　　　　c. 超過(过)
4. 雖然, 受地於先王。　　　　　a. 但是　　　b. 而且　　　c. 即使
5. 弗敢易!　　　　　　　　　　a. 交換　　　b. 容易　　　c. 代替
6. 秦王不說。　　　　　　　　　a. 說話(说话)　b. 高興(兴)　c. 問題(问题)
7. 大王加惠。　　　　　　　　　a. 恩惠　　　b. 賢(贤)惠　c. 优惠
8. 弗敢易。　　　　　　　　　　a. 没有人　　b. 没(没)有　c. 不
9. 安陵君其許寡人?　　　　　　a. 這樣(这样)　b. 答應(应)　c. 贊(赞)美

五、將下列句子翻譯成現代漢語 Translate the following sentences into modern Chinese.

1. 衣食所安, 弗敢專也, 必以分人。

現代文翻译 : _____

2. 一鼓作氣, 再而衰, 三而竭。彼竭我盈, 故克之。

現代文翻译 : _____

3. 若亡鄭而有益於君, 敢以煩執事。

現代文翻译 : _____

4. 因人之力而敝之, 不仁; 失其所與, 不知; 以亂易整, 不武。

現代文翻译 : _____

5. 防民之口, 甚於防川。川壅而潰, 傷人必多, 民亦如之。

現代文翻译 : _____

6. 夫民慮之於心而宣之於口，成而行之，胡可壅也？

现代文翻译：_____

7. 吾妻之美我者，私我也；妾之美我者，畏我也；客之美我者，欲有求於我也。

现代文翻译：_____

8. 能謗議於市朝，聞寡人之耳者，受下賞。

现代文翻译：_____

第五課

《論語》選讀（上）

Selected Readings from the *Analects of Confucius* (I)

Introduction

The *Analects of Confucius* 論語 (*Lúnyǔ* 论语) is a collection of dialogues between Confucius and his disciples. Confucius, latinized name of Kong Qiu 孔丘 (courtesy name Zhongni 仲尼; 551–479 BCE), is arguably the most revered of all Chinese philosophers. Confucianism, an all-encompassing system of moral and sociopolitical ideas, beliefs, and practices based on his teachings, undergirds the development of Chinese, Japanese, Korean, and Vietnamese cultures in the premodern era. Even where it is no longer officially sanctioned, its normative influence is still felt in the daily life of these countries, as people continue to abide by many Confucian tenets concerning individual conduct, family relationships, and society at large.

The *Analects* consists of twenty short chapters, made up mostly of short passages that record political and moral views and educational principles advanced by Confucius. During the Song dynasty, it was canonized as one of the Four Books 四書 (*Sìshū* 四书), along with the *Great Learning* 大學 (*Dàxué* 大学), the *Doctrine of the Mean* 中庸 (*Zhōngyōng*), and the *Mencius* 孟子 (*Mèngzǐ*).

The three excerpts in this lesson present Confucius's ideas on learning, morality, and politics from different perspectives. Profound in thought and elegant and concise in style, they are easy for the reader to understand. A translation of the third excerpt is given in *HTRCProse*, chapter 3, "Pre-Qin Philosophical Prose: Recorded Conversations and Argumentative Essays," C3.7.

正文與簡體譯文 Text and Modern Chinese Translation

學而第一篇第一章
xué ér dì yī piān dì yī zhāng

子曰：「學而時習之，不亦説乎？[1] 有朋
zǐ yuē　　xué ér shí xí zhī　　bú yì yuè hū　　yǒu péng

自遠方來，不亦樂乎？人不知而不愠，不
zì yuǎn fāng lái　　bú yì lè hū　　rén bù zhī ér bú yùn　　bú

亦君子乎？[2]」
yì jūn zǐ hū

孔子说："学习而且时常温习知识，不是很高兴吗？[1] 有朋友从远方来，不是很快乐吗？别人不了解(我)，我也不生气，不也是一个有德行的君子吗？[2]"

《論語正義》，北京：中華書局 (1990), 2–4.

1. 子 *n.* an honorific title for a revered teacher or a person of great morality and knowledge in ancient China.
   In the *Analects*, 子 in 子曰 refers only to Confucius 孔子, which means "master" 夫子 (*fū zǐ*).
   時 (时) *adv.* often. MdnC: 時常 (*shí cháng* 时常).
   習 (习) *v.* to practice, review. MdnC: 溫習 (*wēng xí* 温习).
   之 *pron.* it. Here 之 refers to the knowledge that a student has learned. See L1 Grammar Note 2 ③.
   不亦……乎, a structure of a rhetorical question. See Grammar Note 1 ②.
   说 (说) *adj.* used in the sense of 悦 (*yuè*). MdnC: 高興 (*gāo xìng* 高兴).
2. 朋 *n.* friend. MdnC: 朋友 (*péng you*).
   自 *prep.* from. MdnC: 從 (*cóng* 从). See L31 Grammar Note 1 ①.
   樂 (乐 lè) *adj.* happy. MdnC: 快樂 (*kuài lè* 快乐).
   知 *v.* to understand. MdnC: 了解 (*liǎo jiě*).
   愠 *v.* to become angry. MdnC: 生氣 (*shēng qì* 生气).
   君子 *n.* a man of virtue.

子罕第九篇第十一章
zǐ hǎn dì jiǔ piān dì shí yī zhāng

顔淵喟然歎曰：「仰之彌高，鑽之彌堅。
yán yuān kuì rán tàn yuē　yǎng zhī mí gāo　zuān zhī mí jiān

瞻之在前，忽焉在後。³夫子循循然善誘人，
zhān zhī zài qián　hū yān zài hòu　fū zǐ xún xún rán shàn yòu rén

博我以文，約我以禮，欲罷不能。⁴既竭吾
bó wǒ yǐ wén　yuē wǒ yǐ lǐ　yù bà bù néng　jì jié wú

才，如有所立卓爾。雖欲從之，末由也
cái　rú yǒu suǒ lì zhuó ěr　suī yù cóng zhī　mò yóu yě

已。⁵」
yǐ

《論語正義》，北京：中華書局 (1990), 338–341.

顔淵感叹道："夫子的学问和德行，越仰望越觉得高远(不可及)，越钻研越觉得坚实(不可入)。看着它，好像在前面，忽然又像是在后面。³夫子善于一步步地诱导学生，用文献典籍丰富我的知识，用礼来约束我的行为，使我想停止学习都不可能。⁴我已经竭尽了我的才能去学习，(老师的学问和德行)像是高高的竖立在我的眼前。可即使我想追随上去，却没有途径了。⁵"

3. 顔淵 (颜渊) or 顔回 (family name 姓, Yán 颜; given name 名, Huí 回; style 字, Zǐyuān 子淵; 521–481 BCE), arguably the most famous of Confucius's seventy-two disciples, revered as Master Yan 顔子 (Yánzǐ 颜子) in later times.
   喟 *v.* to sigh. MdnC: 嘆息 (*tàn xī* 叹息).
   然 *particle.* functioning as an emotive particle. See Grammar Note 2 ②.
   仰 *v.* to look up at. MdnC: 仰望 (*yǎng wàng*).
   之 *personal pron.* it. Here 之 refers to Confucian learning. See L1 Grammar Note 2 ③.
   彌 (弥) *adv.* more. MdnC: 更加 (*gèng jiā*).

鑽 (钻 *zuān*) *v.* to dig into, study intensively. MdnC: 鑽研 (*zuān yán* 钻研).

堅 (坚) *adj.* solid, sturdy. MdnC: 堅實 (*jiān shí* 坚实).

瞻 *v.* to look up to, respect. MdnC: 看 (*kàn*).

忽 *adv.* all of a sudden, suddenly. MdnC: 忽然 (*hū rán*).

焉 *particle.* used as an emotive particle. See Grammar Note 4 ④.

4. 循 *v.* to follow, abide by. 循循然 means "step by step."

善 *v.* to be good at, be expert in. MdnC: 善於 (*shàn yú* 善于).

誘 (诱) *v.* to guide, lead. MdnC: 誘導 (*yòu dǎo* 诱导).

博 *adj.* rich, abundant. Here it is used as a verb, "使……博," meaning "to enrich" 豐富 (*fēng fù* 丰富). See L7 Grammar Note 1 ②.

文 *n.* essay. Here it refers to ancient books and records, classics. MdnC: 典籍 (*diǎn jí*).

約 (约) *v.* to restrain. MdnC: 約束 (*yuē shù* 约束).

禮 (礼) *n.* rules of propriety.

罷 (罢) *v.* to stop, cease. MdnC: 停止 (*tíng zhǐ*).

5. 既 *adv.* already. See L1 Grammar Note 5.

竭 *v.* to exhaust. MdnC: 竭盡 (*jié jìn* 竭尽).

卓 *adj.* tall. MdnC: 高 (*gāo*).

爾 (尔) *particle.* used as an emotive particle. See L6 Grammar Note 1 ②.

從 (从) *v.* to follow. MdnC: 追隨 (*zhuī suí* 追随).

末 *adv.* have not. MdnC: 沒有 (*méi yǒu*).

由 *n.* way. MdnC: 途徑 (*tú jìng* 途径).

也已 *ending particle.* to express an exclamation. See L6 Grammar Note 7 ①.

堯曰第二十篇第二章
yáo yuē dì èr shí piān dì èr zhāng

子張問於孔子曰：「何如斯可以從政
zǐ zhāng wèn yú kǒng zǐ yuē　hé rú sī kě yǐ cóng zhèng

矣？」子曰：「尊五美，屏四惡，斯可以從政
yǐ　zǐ yuē　zūn wǔ měi　bǐng sì è　sī kě yǐ cóng zhèng

矣。」[6] 子張曰：「何謂五美？」子曰：「君子
yǐ　zǐ zhāng yuē　hé wèi wǔ měi　zǐ yuē　jūn zǐ

惠而不費，勞而不怨，欲而不貪，泰而不
huì ér bú fèi　láo ér bú yuàn　yù ér bù tān　tài ér bù

驕，威而不猛。」[7]
jiāo　wēi ér bù měng

子张问孔子说："怎么样才能够从政呢？"孔子回答说："尊崇五种美德，摒弃四种恶政，就可以从政。"[6] 子张问："什么叫做五种美德？"孔子说："君子给他人恩惠，但自己却不浪费；君子使他人劳作却不会让他们心里产生怨恨；君子渴望追求仁德，却不贪图财物；君子庄重而不傲慢，威严而不凶猛。"[7]

6. 子張 (张) (family name 姓, Zhuānsūn 顓孫; given name 名, Shī 師; style 字, Zǐzhāng 子張; 503–447

BCE), one of seventy-two disciples of Confucius.

何如 *how*? MdnC: 怎麼樣 (*zěn me yàng* 怎么样). See L6 Grammar Note 3 ④.

斯 *conj.* then. MdnC: 則 (*zé* 则). See Grammar Note 3 ②.

從 (从) *v.* to join, be engaged in. MdnC: 從事 (*cóng shì* 从事).

政 *n.* government affairs. MdnC: 政務 (*zhèng wù* 政务).

尊 *v.* to value, esteem, honor. MdnC: 尊崇 (*zūn chóng*).

美 *adj.* beautiful. Here it is a noun, meaning "virtue" (*měi dé* 美德).

屏 (*bǐng*) *v.* to get rid of, abandon. MdnC: 摒棄 (*bǐng qì* 摒弃).

惡 (恶 *è*) *adj.* bad, evil, deplorable. Here it refers to iniquitous governance 惡政 (*è zhèng* 恶政).

7. 何 *interrogative particle.* what? MdnC: 什麼 (*shén me* 什么). See L1 Grammar Note 3 ①.

謂 (谓) *v.* to be called, be known as. MdnC: 叫做 (*jiào zuò*).

惠 *n.* favor. Here it is used as a verb, meaning "to bestow favor."

費 (费) *v.* to waste. MdnC: 浪費 (*làng fèi* 浪费).

勞 (劳) *v.* to work. Here it is used as a transitive verb, meaning "to make (people) work."

怨 *v.* to resent. MdnC: 怨恨 (*yuàn hèn*).

欲 *v.* to desire. MdnC: 渴望 (*kě wàng*).

貪 (贪) *v.* to be greedy for. MdnC: 貪圖 (*tān tú* 贪图).

泰 *adj.* great, peaceful. MdnC: 莊重 (*zhuāng zhòng* 庄重).

驕 (骄) *adj.* arrogant. MdnC: 傲慢 (*ào màn*).

威 *adj.* awe-inspiring. MdnC: 威嚴 (*wēi yán* 威严).

猛 *adj.* vicious, violent, ferocious. MdnC: 凶猛 (*xiōng měng*).

子張曰：「何謂惠而不費？」子曰：「因
zǐ zhāng yuē　　　hé wèi huì ér bú fèi　　　zǐ yuē　　　yīn

民之所利而利之，斯不亦惠而不費乎？⁸擇可
mín zhī suǒ lì ér lì zhī　　sī bú yì huì ér bú fèi hū　　zé kě

勞而勞之，又誰怨？欲仁而得仁，又焉貪？⁹
láo ér láo zhī　　yòu shuí yuàn　　yù rén ér dé rén　　yòu yān tān

君子無眾寡，無小大，無敢慢，斯不亦泰而
jūn zǐ wú zhòng guǎ　wú xiǎo dà　wú gǎn màn　sī bú yì tài ér

不驕乎？¹⁰君子正其衣冠，尊其瞻視，儼然人
bù jiāo hū　　jūn zǐ zhèng qí yī guān　zūn qí zhān shì　yǎn rán rén

望而畏之，斯不亦威而不猛乎？¹¹」
wàng ér wèi zhī　　sī bú yì wēi ér bù měng hū

子张问："什么是惠而不费？"孔子说："根据对老百姓有利的事，让他们得到利益，这不就是给人恩惠而不浪费吗？⁸选择老百姓可以劳作的事让他们劳作，还有谁会怨恨呢？想要仁德而得到仁德，还有什么要贪图的？⁹君子对人，无论是多还是少，无论势力小还是大，都不敢怠慢，这不就是庄重而不傲慢吗？¹⁰君子衣冠整齐，目光端正，严肃的样子，别人看到后敬畏他，这不就是威严而不凶猛吗？¹¹"

8. 因 *prep.* according to, on the basis of. MdnC: 根據 (*gēn jù* 根据).

利 *n.* benefit, profit. MdnC: 利益 (*lì yì*). 利 is used as a verb twice in this sentence. 所利 refers to things from which people gain benefits. Here 利之 should be 使之利, meaning "to let people reap benefits." See L7 Grammar Note 1 ③.

斯 *demonstrative pron.* this. MdnC: 這 (*zhè* 这). See Grammar Note 3 ①.

不亦……乎? a sentence structure of a rhetorical question. See Grammar Note 1 ②.

9. 擇 (择) *v.* to choose, select. MdnC: 選擇 (*xuǎn zé* 选择).

勞 (劳) *v.* to work. Here it is used as a causative verb, 使……勞 (劳), meaning "to let (people) work." See L7 Grammar Note 1 ①.

仁 *n.* benevolence, virtue, morality. MdnC: 仁德 (*rén dé*).

焉 *interrogative particle.* what? MdnC: 什麼 (*shén me* 什么). See L2 Grammar Note 3 ③.

10. 衆 (众) *adj.* many. MdnC: 人多 (*rén duō*).

寡 *adj.* few. MdnC: 人少 (*rén shǎo*).

慢 *v.* to slight. MdnC: 怠慢 (*dài màn*).

11. 正 *adj.* correct, proper. Here it is used as a verb, 使……正, meaning "to make … proper." See L7 Grammar Note 1 ②.

瞻視 (视) *v.* to look at, observe.

儼 (俨) *adj.* solemn. MdnC: 嚴肅 (*yán sù* 严肃).

然 *particle.* functioning as an emotive particle. See Grammar Note 2 ②.

畏 *v.* to fear, feel awe, respect. MdnC: 敬畏 (*jìng wèi*).

子張曰：「何謂四惡？」子曰：「不教而
zǐ zhāng yuē　　hé wèi sì è　　zǐ yuē　　bú jiào ér

殺謂之虐，不戒視成謂之暴，¹² 慢令致期謂
shā wèi zhī nüè　bú jiè shì chéng wèi zhī bào　màn lìng zhì qī wèi

之賊，¹³ 猶之與人也，出納之吝，謂之有
zhī zéi　　yóu zhī yǔ rén yě　　chū nà zhī lìn　　wèi zhī yǒu

司。¹⁴」
sī

子張问："什么是四恶？"孔子说："不教育老百姓（而他们犯错时就直接）杀戮，就是虐政。不提前告诫老百姓，却要他们直接成功完成任务就是暴政。¹²下令缓慢却要按期限完成，就是贼政。¹³同样的，给与别人时，出手很吝啬，这就叫有司。¹⁴"

《論語正義》，北京：中華書局 (1990), 766–767.

12. 教 *v.* to teach, instruct. MdnC: 教育 (*jiào yù*).

殺 (杀) *v.* to kill. MdnC: 殺戮 (*shā lù* 杀戮).

虐 *adj.* brutal, tyrannical.

戒 *v.* to warn, admonish. MdnC: 告誡 (*gào jiè* 告诫).

成 *v.* to complete, succeed. MdnC: 成功 (*chéng gōng*).

暴 *adj.* cruel, violent, tyrannical.

13. 慢 *adj.* slow. MdnC: 緩慢 (*huǎn màn* 缓慢).

令 *v.* to command, order. MdnC: 下令 (*xià lìng*).

致 *v.* to reach, cause.

期 *n.* date. MdnC: 期限 (*qī xiàn*).

賊 (贼) *adj.* evil, villainous.

14. 猶 (犹) *v.* to be like. See L3 Grammar Note 3 ②. 猶 (犹) 之 means "just the same as it" 同樣的 (*tóng yàng de* 同样的).

與 (与 *yǔ*) *v.* to give. MdnC: 給與 (*jǐ yǔ* 给予).

出 *v.* to pay (money). MdnC: 支出 (*zhī chū*).

納 (纳) *v.* to receive, accept, take in. MdnC: 納入 (*nà rù* 纳入).

吝 *adj.* stingy, mean, niggardly. MdnC: 吝嗇 (*lìn sè* 吝啬).

有司 official name in ancient time. Here it means "stingy."

語法注釋 Grammar Notes

1. 亦   ① *adv.* also. MdnC: 也 (*yě*).

然鄭亡，子亦有不利焉。(L2)

[不过郑国灭亡了，您也有不利啊！]

川壅而潰，傷人必多，民亦如之。(L3)

[河流堵塞了会决堤，伤人一定会多，老百姓也是这样的。]

② 不亦……乎? a sentence structure of a rhetorical question. MdnC: 不是 (*bú shì*) …… 嗎 (*ma* 吗)?

有朋自遠方來，不亦樂乎?

[有朋友从远方来了，不是很快乐吗?]

因民之所利而利之，斯不亦惠而不費乎?

[根据对老百姓有利的事，让他们得到利益，这不就是给人恩惠而不浪费吗?]

2. 然   ① *conj.* however, but. MdnC: 但是 (*dàn shì*), 不過 (*bú guò* 不过).

然鄭亡，子亦有不利焉。(L2)

[不过郑国灭亡了，您也有不利啊！]

② *particle.* functioning as an emotive particle. MdnC: ……的樣子 (*de yàng zi* 的样子).

顏淵喟然嘆曰：……

[颜渊（做）叹气的样子叹息说……]

夫子循循然善誘人，……

[夫子善于一步步地诱导学生，……]

See 然③ in L8 Grammar Note 5 and 然④ in L10 Grammar Note 3.

3. 斯   ① *demonstrative pron.* this. MdnC: 這 (*zhè* 这).

因民之所利而利之，斯不亦惠而不費乎?

[根据对老百姓有利的事，让他们得到利益，这不就是给人恩惠而不浪费吗?]

② *conj.* then. 斯 is used as an alternative to 則 (*zé* 则, see L11 Grammar Note 1 ①), to introduce the secondary or main clause. MdnC: 則 (*zé* 则), 才 (*cái*), 那麼 (*nà me* 那么), 就 (*jiù*).

何如斯可以从政矣?

[怎么样做，才可以从政呢？]

4. 焉   Seven uses of 焉 are explained in this book. In addition to the use below, see 焉①in L1 Grammar Note 4, 焉②③in L2 Grammar Note 3, 焉⑤in L6 Grammar Note 5, 焉⑥in L12 Grammar Note 1, and 焉⑦in L30 Grammar Note 3.

④ *particle.* a variant of 然, functioning as an emotive particle.

瞻之在前，忽焉在後。

[看看它好像在前面，忽然又像是在后面。]

Literary Analysis

For followers of Confucius, securing proper appreciation of one's talents became a theme of great importance. And yet it is precisely how one deals with the eventuality of talents passed over and professional failure that Confucius saw as revealing the difference between a true "noble man" and a person of lesser character.

The opening passage of the *Analects* reflects just this theme. While the study and practice of true nobility naturally result in a course of self-improvement that yields its own "delight," such delight in solitude is ultimately bereft of significance. True "happiness" is found only when the source of this delight is shared with others able to appreciate it, as, for instance, when friends visit from afar. Lacking any such acknowledgment undeniably proves a challenge. But for Confucius, the person who in spite of this avoids resentment and bitterness and remains focused on self-improvement achieves true nobility and the highest form of happiness—a proper, enduring contentment. Recognition may ultimately come, but it is far more important that one remain worthy of it.

Confucius himself struggled to secure employment with a lord who would appreciate and implement his advice, and this in part explains how so much of his life was devoted to teaching. Because his disciples too sought meaningful careers in government service, he tried to instill in them such virtues as moderation, deference, and humility. How, then, do we reconcile this attitude with the somewhat hyperbolic praise from Yan Hui—his favorite disciple—in the second passage? And how is this related to the broader theme of recognition? What does the question that opens the third passage tell you about what Zizhang hoped to derive from his tutelage under Confucius? What do Confucius's answers suggest about the sorts of virtues he thought his disciples needed to cultivate in order to meaningfully fulfill such ends?

☞ *HTRCProse*, chapter 3, "Pre-Qin Philosophical Prose: Recorded Conversations and Argumentative Essays" for further comments on the *Analects of Confucius*, including a discussion of happiness and a full translation of the third passage in this lesson.

—SC

課後練習 Exercises

一 給加點字注音 Give the pinyin romanization for each dotted word.

1. 顏淵 （＿＿＿,＿＿＿） 2. 虐 （＿＿＿） 3. 禮 （＿＿＿） 4. 不亦樂乎 （＿＿＿）

5. 循循 （＿＿＿,＿＿＿） 6. 帛 （＿＿＿） 7. 爾 （＿＿＿） 8. 喟然 （＿＿＿）

二 在括號中給句中加點的字注音，並選出正確的釋義 Give the pinyin romanization for each dotted word; then select the correct definition from the following list, and write it in the blank.

更加　　竭盡(尽)　　吝嗇(啬)　　高興(兴)　　摒棄(摒弃)

看　　鑽(钻)研　　**信服**　　生氣(气)　　嚴肅(严肃)

1. 小信未孚（ **fú** ）　　**信服**　　2. 不亦說乎（ ） ＿＿＿＿＿ 3. 既竭吾才 （ ） ＿＿＿＿＿

4. 鑽之彌堅（ ） ＿＿＿＿＿ 5. 瞻之在前（ ） ＿＿＿＿＿ 6. 仰之彌高 （ ） ＿＿＿＿＿

7. 出納之吝（ ） ＿＿＿＿＿ 8. 屏四惡 （ ） ＿＿＿＿＿ 9. 不知而不慍（ ） ＿＿＿＿＿

10. 儼然人望而畏之（ ） ＿＿＿＿＿

三 選擇釋義並填空 Match each word in the left column with its correct definition in the middle column. Fill in each blank in the right column with an appropriate word from the left column.

左	中
謀謀劃(谋划)	誘導(诱导)
時＿＿＿＿	停止
費＿＿＿＿	緩(缓)慢
仰＿＿＿＿	**謀劃(谋划)**
堅＿＿＿＿	約(约)束
善＿＿＿＿	溫習(温习)
驕＿＿＿＿	威嚴(严)
博＿＿＿＿	告誡(诫)
約＿＿＿＿	傳達(传达)
罷＿＿＿＿	豐(丰)富
卓＿＿＿＿	追隨(随)
由＿＿＿＿	傲慢
從＿＿＿＿	仰望
威＿＿＿＿	高
戒＿＿＿＿	浪費(费)
致＿＿＿＿	善於(于)
誘＿＿＿＿	時(时)常
慢＿＿＿＿	不可窮盡(穷尽)
習＿＿＿＿	途徑(径)

學而＿＿＿ ＿＿＿之，不亦說乎？

＿＿＿之彌高，鑽之彌＿＿＿。

夫子循循然＿＿＿ ＿＿＿人，＿＿＿我以文，＿＿＿我以禮，欲＿＿＿不能。

既竭吾才，如有所立＿＿＿爾。

雖欲＿＿＿之，末＿＿＿也已。

子曰："君子惠而不＿＿＿，勞而不怨，欲而不貪，泰而不＿＿＿，＿＿＿而不猛。"

子曰："不教而殺謂之虐，不＿＿＿視成謂之暴，＿＿＿令＿＿＿期謂之賊，猶之與人也，出納之吝，謂之有司。"

四 請用給出的字填空 Fill in each blank with an appropriate word from the following list (some words may be used more than once).

焉　以　然　之　亦　既　乎　爾(尔)　斯

1. 子曰："學而時習＿＿＿，不＿＿＿說＿＿＿？"
2. 瞻＿＿＿在前，忽＿＿＿在後。夫子循循＿＿＿善誘人，博我＿＿＿文，約我＿＿＿禮，欲罷不能。
3. ＿＿＿竭吾才，如有所立卓＿＿＿。
4. 子張問孔子曰："何如 ＿＿＿可以從政矣？"

五 爲加點字選擇正確釋義，並根據釋義來翻譯句子 Match each dotted word with its correct modern Chinese equivalent by circling the latter. Then translate each sentence into modern Chinese.

1. 又何間焉？　　　　　　　　　　　　　ⓐ 爲什麼(为什么) b. 憑什麼(凭什么) c. 多少

現代文翻譯：你又为什么要参与到这件事情里面？
＿＿＿＿＿＿＿＿＿＿＿＿＿＿＿＿＿＿＿＿＿＿＿＿＿＿＿

2. 人不知而不愠，不亦君子乎？　　　　　　a. 也 b. 不是……嗎(吗) c. 不對(对)

現代文翻譯：＿＿＿＿＿＿＿＿＿＿＿＿＿＿＿＿＿＿＿＿＿＿＿

3. 瞻之在前，忽焉在後。　　　　　　　　a. 然 b. 在那裏(里) c. 爲什麼(为什么)

現代文翻譯：＿＿＿＿＿＿＿＿＿＿＿＿＿＿＿＿＿＿＿＿＿＿＿

4. 夫子循循然善誘人，博我以文，約我以禮，欲罷不能。　　a. 因爲(为) b. 用 c. 來(来)

現代文翻譯：＿＿＿＿＿＿＿＿＿＿＿＿＿＿＿＿＿＿＿＿＿＿＿

5. 雖欲從之，末由也已。　　　　　　　　a. 即使 b. 雖(虽)然 c. 而且

現代文翻譯：＿＿＿＿＿＿＿＿＿＿＿＿＿＿＿＿＿＿＿＿＿＿＿

6. 因民之所利而利之，斯不亦惠而不費乎？　　a. 他 b. 則(则) c. 這(这)

現代文翻譯：＿＿＿＿＿＿＿＿＿＿＿＿＿＿＿＿＿＿＿＿＿＿＿

7. 欲仁而得仁，又焉貪？　　　　　　　　a. 於(于)此 b. 什麼(什么) c. 啊

現代文翻譯：＿＿＿＿＿＿＿＿＿＿＿＿＿＿＿＿＿＿＿＿＿＿＿

8. 君子正其衣冠，尊其瞻視，儼然人望而畏之，斯不亦威而不猛乎？

　　　　　　　　　　　　　a.……的樣（样）子　b.但是　c.對（对）

現代文翻译：_____

第六課

《論語》選讀（下）

Selected Readings from the *Analects of Confucius* (II)

Introduction

This lesson contains an excerpt from the "Xianjin" 先進 ("Xiān jìn" 先进) chapter in the *Analects*, in which Confucius invites his four disciples to discuss their aspirations. Unlike lesson 5 with its brief dialogues, this lesson presents longer narrative passages, delighting us with memorable character sketches. Zilu's rashness and impatience, Ran You's modesty and humility, Gongxi Hua's tact and mildness, and Zeng Xi's grace and refinement all leave indelible impressions.

☞ *HTRCProse*, chapter 3, "Pre-Qin Philosophical Prose: Recorded Conversations and Argumentative Essays."

正文與簡體譯文 Text and Modern Chinese Translation

先進第十一篇第二十六章
xiān jìn dì shí yī piān dì èr shí liù zhāng

子路、曾晳、冉有、公西華侍坐。[1] 子
zǐ lù zēng xī rǎn yǒu gōng xī huá shì zuò zǐ

曰：「以ₐ吾一日長乎爾，毋吾以ᵦ也。居則
yuē yǐ wú yí rì zhǎng hū ěr wú wú yǐ yě jū zé

曰：『不吾知也！』如或知爾，則何以哉？」[2]
yuē bù wú zhī yě rú huò zhī ěr zé hé yǐ zāi

子路率爾而對曰：「千乘之ₐ國，攝乎大國之ₐ
zǐ lù shuài ěr ér duì yuē qiān shèng zhī guó shè hū dà guó zhī

間，加之ᵦ以師旅，因之ᵦ以饑饉。[3] 由也爲
jiān jiā zhī yǐ shī lǚ yīn zhī yǐ jī jǐn yóu yě wéi

之，比及三年，可使有勇，且知方也。[4]」夫
zhī bǐ jí sān nián kě shǐ yǒu yǒng qiě zhī fāng yě fū

子哂之。[5]
zǐ shěn zhī

子路、曾晳、冉有和公西华陪孔子坐着。[1] 孔子说："因为我比你们年长一些，不任用我了。你们平时说：'都不了解我啊！'如果有人了解你们，你们会怎么做？"[2] 子路不加考虑地回答说："有一千辆兵车的国家，夹在大国之间，给它加上（入侵的）军队，继续给它加上饥荒。[3] 我来治理这个国家的话，等到三年之后，就可以使这个国家的人民变得勇敢，而且知道方向。[4]"夫子对他微微一笑。[5]

1. 子路 or 仲由 (family name 姓, Zhòng 仲; given name 名, Yóu 由; style 字, Zǐlù 子路 or Jìlù 季路; 524–480 BCE), one of the most famous disciples of Confucius. In this passage, 由 is 子路.

   曾皙 ((family name 姓, Zēng 曾; given name 名, Xī 皙; style 字, Diǎn 點; 546?–? BCE), one of seventy-two disciples of Confucius. In this passage, 點 (点) is 曾皙.

   冉有 (family name 姓, Rǎn 冉; given name 名, Qiú 求; style 字, Zǐyǒu 子有; 522–? BCE), one of seventy-two disciples of Confucius. In this passage, 求 is 冉有.

   公西華 (华) (family name 姓, Gōngxī 公西; given name 名, Chì 赤; style 字, Zǐhuá 子華; 509?–? BCE), one of seventy-two disciples of Confucius. In this passage, 赤 is 公西華.

   侍 v. to serve, wait upon. MdnC: 陪 (péi).

2. 以 ₐ prep. for the reason of. MdnC: 因爲 (yīn wèi 因为). See L2 Grammar Note 1 ①.

   長 (zhǎng 长) adj. older, elder, senior. MdnC: 年長 (nián zhǎng 年长).

   乎 prep. a variant of 於 (yú 于) here, meaning "than." MdnC: 比 (bǐ). See Grammar Note 2 ④.

   爾 (尔) pron. second-person pronoun: you. MdnC: 你們 (nǐ mén 你们). See Grammar Note 1 ①.

   毋 adv. no, not. MdnC: 不 (bù).

   以 ᵦ coverb. to employ, use. MdnC: 任用 (rèn yòng). See L2 Grammar Note 1 ②. Here the object 吾 is positioned in front of the verb 以. So is the 吾 in the next sentence 不吾知也.

   居 v. to live, stay. Here it means "usually" 平時 (píng shí 平时).

   或 indefinite pron. someone. MdnC: 有人 (yǒu rén). See Grammar Note 4 ①.

   何以 by what? how? MdnC: 怎麼做 (zěn me zuò 怎么做). See L1 Grammar Note 3 ③.

3. 率爾 (尔) adv. rashly. MdnC: 不加考慮地 (bù jiā kǎo lǜ de 不加考虑地).

   爾 (尔) particle. used as an emotive particle. See Grammar Note 1 ②.

   對 (对) v. to answer, reply. MdnC: 回答 (huí dá).

   乘 (shèng) n. a vehicle pulled by four horses, chariot. MdnC: 兵車 (bīng chē 兵车).

   之 ₐ particle. a possessive marker. MdnC: 的 (de). See L1 Grammar Note 2 ②.

   攝 (摄) v. to place in between. MdnC: 夾 (jiā 夹).

   乎 prep. as a variant of 於, meaning "between." MdnC: 在 (zài). See Grammar Note 2 ③.

   之 ᵦ demonstrative pron. this, referring to the state. See L1 Grammar Note 2 ①.

   以 coverb. to use. MdnC: 用 (yòng). See L2 Grammar Note 1 ②.

   旅 n. troops. 師 (师) 旅 refers to the army. MdnC: 軍隊 (jūn duì 军队).

   因 v. to continue, be followed. MdnC: 繼續 (jì xù 继续).

   饉 (馑) n. time of famine. MdnC: 荒年 (huāng nián).

   飢饉 (饥馑) means "famine or crop failure" 饑荒 (jī huāng 饥荒).

4. 爲 (为 wéi) v. to govern. MdnC: 治理 (zhì lǐ). See L2 Grammar Note 6 ①.

   比及 adv. by the time when, until. MdnC: 等到 (děng dào).

   方 n. direction. MdnC: 方向 (fāng xiàng).

5. 哂 v. to smile at, sneer at. MdnC: 微笑 (wēi xiào).

   之 personal pron. him. See L1 Grammar Note 2 ③.

「求！爾何如 ₐ？」對曰：「方六七十，
qiú　ěr hé rú　　　　duì yuē　　fāng liù qī shí

如 ᵦ五六十，求也爲之，比及三年，可使足
rú　wǔ liù shí　　qiú yě wéi zhī　　bǐ jí sān nián　kě shǐ zú

（孔子问:）"冉有，你怎么样？"（冉有）回答说:"一个方圆六七十里，或者五六十里的国家，我也可以去治理

民。如ᵪ其禮樂，以俟君子。」⁶「赤！爾何
mín　rú　qí lǐ yuè　yǐ sì jūn zǐ　　　chì ěr hé

如？」對曰：「非曰能之，願學焉ₐ。宗廟之
rú　　　duì yuē　　fēi yuē néng zhī　yuàn xué yān　zōng miào zhī

事，如ᵦ會同，端章甫，願爲小相焉ᵦ。」⁷
shì　rú　huì tóng　duān zhāng fǔ　yuàn wéi xiǎo xiàng yān

它。等到三年过后，可以使老百姓满足。至于那些礼乐教化，就等待有德行的君子来做吧！」⁶孔子问："公西华，你怎么样？"公西华回答说："不敢说我有能力做什么，我愿意学习做这些事情。宗庙祭祀的事情，或者诸侯会盟与朝见天子，我穿着礼服，戴着礼帽，愿意做一个司仪啊。"⁷

6. 爾 (尔) *pron.* second-person pronoun: you. MdnC: 你 (*nǐ*). See Grammar Note 1 ①.

何如ₐ or 如何 how is … like, how? MdnC: 怎麼樣 (*zěn me yàng* 怎么样). See Grammar Note 3 ④.

方 *n.* circumference. MdnC: 方圓 (*fāng yuan* 方圆).

如ᵦ *conj.* or. MdnC: 或者 (*huò zhě*). See Grammar Note 3 ②.

足 *v.* to satisfy. MdnC: 滿足 (*mǎn zú* 满足).

如ᵪ *particle.* as to, about. MdnC: 至於 (*zhì yú* 至于). See Grammar Note 3 ③.

其 *demonstrative pron.* those. MdnC: 那些 (*nà xiē*). See Grammar Note 6 ④.

禮 (礼) *n.* rules of propriety.

樂 (乐) *n.* music.

以 *coverb.* 以 (之) here, meaning "to use (them)." MdnC: 用 (*yòng*). See L2 Grammar Note 1 ②. Here 之 refers to 禮樂.

俟 *v.* to wait for. MdnC: 等待 (*děng dài*).

7. 焉ₐ *demonstrative pron.* an equivalent of 之 here, referring to how to govern a state. See Grammar Note 5 ⑤.

宗廟 *n.* ancestral temple of a ruling house.

會 (会) *n.* the territorial lords' visit to an emperor at an unscheduled time.

同 *n.* the territorial lords' visit to an emperor at a scheduled time.

端 *n.* a type of ancient dress. Here it is used as a verb, meaning "to dress in the robe."

章甫 *n.* black hat. Here it is used as a verb, meaning "to wear the black hat."

小相 *n.* a host of court ceremonies. MdnC: 司儀 (*sī yí* 司仪).

焉ᵦ *ending particle.* MdnC: 啊 (*a*). See L2 Grammar Note 3 ②.

「點！爾何如？」鼓瑟希，鏗爾，舍瑟
diǎn ěr hé rú　　gǔ sè xī　kēng ěr　shě sè

而作，對曰：「異乎三子者之撰。」⁸子曰：
ér zuò　　duì yuē　　yì hū sān zǐ zhě zhī zhuàn　　zǐ yuē

孔子问："曾皙，你怎么样？"曾皙弹瑟的声音逐渐稀疏下来，铿的一声，放下瑟站立起来，回答说："我和其

「何傷乎？亦各言其志也。」⁹曰：「莫春
hé shāng hū　　yì gè yán qí zhì yě　　　yuē　　mù chūn

者，春服既成，冠者五六人，童子六七人，
zhě　　chūn fú jì chéng　guàn zhě wǔ liù rén　　tóng zǐ liù qī rén

浴乎沂，風乎舞雩，詠而歸。」¹⁰夫子喟然
yù hū yí　　fēng hū wǔ yú　　yǒng ér guī　　　　fū zǐ kuì rán

歎曰：「吾與點也！」¹¹
tàn yuē　　wú yǔ diǎn yě

他三个人的才能不同。"⁸孔子说："有什么关系呢？也就是各自说一下自己的志向。"⁹曾皙说："暮春的时候，春天的衣服已经穿上了。（我和）五六个成年人，六七个孩子，沐浴在沂水里，然后在舞雩台吹吹风，再唱着歌回家。"¹⁰夫子长叹了一声，说："我赞同曾皙啊！"¹¹

8. 鼓 *v.* to play. MdnC: 彈 (*tán* 弹).

　瑟 *n.* stringed musical instrument.

　希 *adj.* rare. MdnC: 稀疏 (*xī shū*).

　鏗爾 (铿尔) onomatopoeic word used to describe the sound of putting down the instrument.

　爾 (尔) *particle.* used as a suffix. See Grammar Note 1 ②.

　舍 *v.* to abandon, give up. Here it means "to put down" 放下 (*fàng xià*).

　作 *v.* to stand up. MdnC: 立起來 (*lì qǐ lái* 立起来).

　異 (异) *adj.* different. MdnC: 不同 (*bù tóng*).

　乎 *particle.* a variant of 於, meaning "in comparison with." See Grammar Note 2 ④.

　撰 *n.* ability, talent. MdnC: 才能 (*cái néng*).

9. 傷 (伤) *v.* to harm, hurt, damage. MdnC: 傷害 (*shāng hài* 伤害).

　乎 *ending particle.* MdnC: 呢 (*ne*). See Grammar Note 2 ②.

　志 *n.* ambition, aspiration. MdnC: 志向 (*zhì xiàng*).

10. 莫 (暮) 春 *n.* late spring. MdnC: 暮春 (*mù chūn*).

　者 *pron.* the time when…. See Grammar Note 8 ④.

　服 *n.* clothes. MdnC: 衣服 (*yī fú*).

　冠 (guàn) 者 an adult man twenty and older. See Culture Note 1.

　童子 *n.* child.

　浴 *v.* to bathe, wash. MdnC: 沐浴 (*mù yù*).

　沂 Yi River, which originates in present-day Zou County 鄒縣 in Shandong Province, flows westward through Qufu 曲阜, and joins the Si River 泗水.

　風 (风) *n.* wind. Here it is used as a verb, meaning "to enjoy the breeze" 吹吹風 (*chuī chuī fēng* 吹吹风).

　舞雩 Wuyu altar, located in the southeastern part of present-day Qufu 曲阜. See Culture Note 2.

　詠 (咏) *v.* to sing a song or a poem, chant. MdnC: 唱 (*chàng*).

11. 喟然 *adv.* sighing.

　與 (与 *yǔ*) *v.* to agree, approve. MdnC: 贊同 (*zàn tóng* 赞同).

三子者出，曾皙後。曾皙曰：「夫三子
sān zǐ zhě chū　zēng xī hòu　zēng xī yuē　　fú sān zǐ

三个人出来，曾皙走在后面。曾皙问："那三

者之言何如？」子曰：「亦各言其志也已
zhě zhī yán hé rú   zǐ yuē   yì gè yán qí zhì yě yǐ

矣。」[12]曰：「夫子何哂由也？」曰：「為國
yǐ   yuē   fū zǐ hé shěn yóu yě   yuē   wéi guó

以禮，其言不讓，是故哂之。」[13]「唯求則
yǐ lǐ   qí yán bú ràng   shì gù shěn zhī   wéi qiú zé

非邦也與？」「安見方六七十如五六十而非
fēi bāng yě yú   ān jiàn fāng liù qī shí rú wǔ liù shí ér fēi

邦也者？」[14]「唯赤則非邦也與？」「宗廟
bāng yě zhě   wéi chì zé fēi bāng yě yú   zōng miào

會同，非諸侯而何？赤也為之小，孰能為
huì tóng   fēi zhū hóu ér hé   chì yě wéi zhī xiǎo   shú néng wéi

之大？」[15]
zhī dà

《論語正義》，北京：中華書局 (1990)，466–482.

个人的话怎么样？"孔子说："只是各自说一下自己的志向罢了！"[12]曾皙问："夫子为什么笑子路呢？"孔子回答说："治理国家要用礼义，他的话一点都不谦让，所以笑他。"[13]曾皙问："难道冉有说的不是治理国家吗？"孔子回答说："怎么见得方圆六七十或者五六十里不是国家呢？"[14]曾皙又问："难道公西华说的不是国家吗？"孔子回答说："宗庙祭祀，诸侯会盟和朝见天子这些事情，不是诸侯国的大事是什么？公西华如果做小相，谁又能做大相呢？"[15]

12. 後 (后) *v.* to walk behind.

夫 (fú) *demonstrative pron.* those. MdnC: 那 (*nà*). See L2 Grammar Note 4 ②.

也已矣 *ending particle.* nothing more. MdnC: 罷了 (*bà le* 罢了). See Grammar Note 7 ①.

13. 何 *interrogative particle.* why? MdnC: 為什麼 (*wèi shén me* 为什么). See L1 Grammar Note 3 ②.

讓 (让) *adj.* humble, modest. MdnC: 謙讓 (*qiān ràng* 谦让).

是故 for this reason, therefore. MdnC: 因此 (*yīn cǐ*). See L3 Grammar Note 1 ③.

14. 唯 *particle.* used here to introduce a subject; it has no meaning in itself. See L2 Grammar Note 7 ①.

邦 *n.* state. MdnC: 國家 (*guó jiā* 国家).

也與 (与 yú) *ending interrogative particle.* MdnC: 嗎 (*ma* 吗). See Grammar Note 7 ③.

安 *interrogative particle.* how? why? where? MdnC: 怎麼 (*zěn me* 怎么). See Grammar Note 9.

也者 *ending particle.* a variant of 也與 here. MdnC: 嗎 (*ma* 吗). See Grammar Note 7 ②.

15. 諸 (诸) 侯 *n.* territorial lords.

為 (为 wéi) *v.* to do, hold the post of. MdnC: 做 (*zuò*). See L2 Grammar Note 6 ①.

之 *personal pron.* referring to those vassal states. See L1 Grammar Note 2 ③.

小 and 大 here refer to 小相 and 大相.

孰 *interrogative pron.* who? MdnC: 誰 (*shuí* 谁). See L4 Grammar Note 1.

文化常識 Culture Notes

1. 冠禮 is a traditional Chinese coming-of-age ceremony for an educated man. According to the chapter titled "Pattern of the Family" 內則 ("Nèizé" 内则) in the *Book of Rites* 禮記 (*Lǐjì* 礼记), an educated

man would have the Guan ceremony on his twentieth birthday. After it, he would begin to learn rites.

2. 舞雩 is an altar for rain built in the Lu state during the Zhou dynasty. It is in the eastern part of present-day Qufu (Confucius's hometown), Shandong Province. 雩 is a sacrifice for rain made in the ancient time. During such sacrifices, witches would dance on the altar. Therefore, it is also called 舞雩.

語法注釋 Grammar Notes

1. 爾
(尔)

① *pron.* second-person pronoun: you. MdnC: 你 (*nǐ*), 你們 (*nǐ mén* 你们).

如或知爾, 則何以哉?

[如果有人了解你们, 那么你们怎么做呢?]

"求, 爾何如?"

[冉有, 你怎么样?]

② *particle.* functioning as an emotive particle.

子路率爾對曰……

[子路不加考虑地回答说……]

See 爾 ③ in L28 Grammar Note 1.

2. 乎
Four uses of 乎 are explained in this book. In addition to the uses below, see 乎 ① in L3 Grammar Note 4.

② *ending particle.* ends a question. MdnC: 嗎 (*ma* 吗), 呢 (*ne*).

子曰: "何傷乎? 亦各言其志也。"

[孔子说: "有什么关系呢? 也就是各自说一下自己的志向]

③ *prep.* a variant of 於 (*yú* 于), introducing a time, place, or person and meaning "at or in." MdnC: 在 (*zài*).

千乘之國, 攝乎大國之間……

[有一千辆兵车的国家, 夹在大国之间……]

冠者五六人, 童子六七人, 浴乎沂, 風乎舞雩, 詠而歸。

[(我和) 五六个成年人, 六七个孩子, 沐浴在沂水里, 在舞雩台吹吹风, 唱着歌回家。]

④ *prep.* a variant of *yú* 於 or 于, meaning "in comparison with." MdnC: 比 (*bǐ*).

子曰: "以吾一日長乎爾, 毋吾以也。"

[孔子说: "因我比你们年长一些, 不任用我了。"]

對曰: "異乎三子者之撰。"

[曾皙回答说: "不同于另外三个人的才能。"]

3. 如
Five uses of 如 are explained in this book. In addition to the uses below, see 如 ① in L3 Grammar Note 5 and 如 ⑤ in L15 Grammar Note 2.

② *conj.* or. MdnC: 或者 (*huò zhě*).

方六七十，如五六十，求也爲之。

[方圓六七十里，或者五六十里的国家，我也可以治理它。]

宗廟之事，如會同，端章甫，願爲小相焉。

[宗庙祭祀的事情，或者诸侯会盟与朝见天子，我穿着礼服，戴着礼帽，愿意做一个司仪。]

③ *particle.* as, for, about. MdnC: 至於 (*zhì yú* 至于).

如其禮樂，以俟君子。

[至于那些礼乐教化的事情，就等待有德行的君子来做吧]

④ 何如 or 如何 how is … like? how? MdnC: 怎麼樣 (*zěn me yàng* 怎么样).

"求，爾何如？"

["冉有，你怎么样？"]

何如斯可以從政矣？　(L5)

[怎么样做，可以从政呢？]

4. 或　① *indefinite pron.* some, someone, something. MdnC: 有些 (*yǒu xiē*), 有些人 (*yǒu xiē rén*).

如或知爾，則何以哉？

[如果有人了解你们，（你们）怎么做？]

See 或② in L15 Grammar Note 4, and 或③ in L32 Grammar Note 1, and 或④ in L36 Grammar Note 2.

5. 焉　Seven uses of 焉 are explained in this book. In addition to the use below, see 焉① in L1 Grammar Note 4, 焉②③ in L2 Grammar Note 3, 焉④ in L5 Grammar Note 4, 焉⑥ in L12 Grammar Note 1, and 焉⑦ in L30 Grammar Note 3.

⑤ *demonstrative pron.* an equivalent of 之. See 之① in L1 Grammar Note 2.

非曰能之，願學焉。

[（我）不敢说有能力做到什么，但是愿意学习做些东西。]

6. 其　Four uses of 其 are explained in this book. In addition to the use below, see 其①②③ in L2 Grammar Note 5.

④ *demonstrative pron.* MdnC: 那 (*nà*), 那些 (*nà xiē*).

如其禮樂，以俟君子。

[至于那些礼乐教化的事情，就等待有德行的君子来做吧。]

7. 也　*particle.* 也 is an ending particle that can be used in a statement or a question. It can also be used together with other ending particles and expresses different tones.

① 也已/也已矣 *ending particle.* used to express an affirmative or exclamatory tone.

子曰："亦各言其志也已矣。"

[孔子说："只是各自说一下自己的志向罢了。"]

臣之壯也，猶不如人；今老矣，無能爲也已。(L2)

　　[臣下年壯的时候，尚且不如别人；现今年老了，（更是）无能为力了。]

雖欲從之，末由也已。(L5)

　　[可即使我想追随上去，却没有途径了啊！]

② 也者 *ending particle.* used to express an affirmative or interrogative tone. MdnC: 呢 (*ne*).

安見方六七十如五六十而非邦也者？

　　[怎么见得方圆六七十或者五六十里（的小国）不是国家呢？]

③ 也與 (与 yú) *ending interrogative particle.* 與 (與 yú) is used in the sense of 歟 (*yú* 欤, see L15 Grammar Note 3). MdnC: 嗎 (*ma* 吗).

唯赤則非邦也與？

　　[难道公西华（说的）不是国家吗？]

8. 者 Six uses of 者 are explained in this book. In addition to the use below, see 者 ① in L1 Grammar Note 1, 者 ② ③ in L4 Grammar Note 3, 者 ⑤ in L7 Grammar Note 3, and 者 ⑥ in L8 Grammar Note 1.

④ *auxiliary pron.* time + 者 Here 者 means "the time when…." MdnC: ……的時候 (*de shí hou* 的时候).

曰：“莫春者，冠者五六人，童子六七人……”

　　[曾皙说：“暮春的时候，五六个成年人，六七个孩子……”]

9. 安 *interrogative particle.* how? why? where? MdnC: 怎麼 (*zěn me* 怎么)，哪裏 (*nǎ lǐ* 哪里).

安見方六七十如五六十而非邦也者？

　　[怎么见得（治理）方圆六七十或者五六十里（的小国）不是（治理）国家呢？]

Literary Analysis

This unusual passage revisits, in its own way, a now familiar theme: recognition of one's talents and employment in state service. When Confucius asks his disciples what they would do if their talents met with an appreciative lord, each gives an answer that reveals something of his own unique character and proclivities, a phenomenon we find throughout the *Analects*. The ever-brash Zilu, for instance, is often seen in contrast to the decidedly more timid Ran You, and these personalities are vividly reflected in this passage. Hearing Confucius's expression of disdain following Zilu's ambitious response, the other disciples offer answers that seem ever more modest, culminating in an unexpected response by Zeng Xi that has nothing whatsoever to do with service.

Why does Confucius single out Zilu for correction while perhaps tacitly approving the relatively underwhelming ambitions of Ran You and Gongxi Hua? And why, finally, is Zeng Xi's response alone singled out for approval? Might this relate in some way to the notions of happiness and self-contentment in the *Analects* discussed in the chapter on "Recorded Conversations" in *HTRCProse*?

This passage is also relatively unique in the *Analects* insofar as it provides a narrative frame, albeit a relatively skeletal one. What purposes might this narrative frame serve? In particular, what effect might be intended by having Zeng Xi strum his *se* (a type of zither) throughout the course of the conversation, ceasing his playing and putting it aside only when called on to give his own final answer to Confucius's query?

👉 *HTRCProse*, chapter 3, "Pre-Qin Philosophical Prose: Recorded Conversations and Argumentative Essays" for further comments on the *Analects of Confucius*.

—SC

課後練習　Exercises

一　給加點字注音　Give the pinyin romanization for each dotted word.

1. 鏗爾（＿＿＿）2. 瑟（＿＿＿）3. 沂（＿＿＿）4. 莫春（＿＿＿）5. 舞雩（＿＿＿）
6. 小相（＿＿＿）7. 甫（＿＿＿）8. 冉（＿＿＿）9. 冠者（＿＿＿）10. 曾皙（＿＿＿,＿＿＿）

二　在括號中給句中加點的字注音，並選出正確的釋義　Give the pinyin romanization for each dotted word; then select the correct definition from the following list, and write it in the blank.

才能　不加考慮(虑)　兵車(车)　贊(赞)同　荒年　**信服**　等待　夾(夹)　微笑　不

1. 小信未孚（fú）　信服　2. 毋吾以也（　）＿＿＿＿＿　3. 以俟君子（　）＿＿＿＿＿
4. 率爾而對（　）＿＿＿＿＿　5. 夫子哂之（　）＿＿＿＿＿　6. 攝乎大國之間（　）＿＿＿＿
7. 千乘之國（　）＿＿＿＿＿　8. 吾與點也（　）＿＿＿＿＿　9. 因之以飢饉（　）＿＿＿＿
10. 異乎三子者之撰（　）＿＿＿＿＿

三　選擇釋義並填空　Match each word in the left column with its correct definition in the middle column. Fill in each blank in the right column with an appropriate word from the left column.

謀謀劃(谋划)	稀疏
長＿＿＿＿	放下
居＿＿＿＿	沐浴
鼓＿＿＿＿	唱歌
希＿＿＿＿	**謀劃(谋划)**
舍＿＿＿＿	謙讓(谦让)
浴＿＿＿＿	贊(赞)同
風＿＿＿＿	平時(时)
詠＿＿＿＿	年長(长)
讓＿＿＿＿	彈(弹)
與＿＿＿＿	吹風(风)

子曰："以吾一日＿＿＿乎爾，毋吾以也。＿＿＿則曰：'不吾知也！'如或知爾，則何以哉？"

＿＿＿瑟＿＿＿，鏗爾，＿＿＿瑟而作。

曰："莫春者，春服既成。冠者五六人，童子六七人，＿＿＿乎沂，＿＿＿乎舞雩，＿＿＿而歸。"夫子喟然嘆曰"吾＿＿＿點也！"

曰："爲國以禮，其言不＿＿＿，是故哂之。"

四 請用給出的字填空 Fill in each blank with an appropriate word from the following list (some words may be used more than once).

乎　安　以　爾(尔)　之　如　也　唯

1. 子曰: "＿＿吾一日長＿＿爾, 毋吾＿＿也。居則曰: '不吾知也!' ＿＿或知＿＿, 則何以哉? "

2. 方六七十, ＿＿五六十, 求也為＿＿, 比及三年, 可使足民。

3. "＿＿求則非邦＿＿與? " "＿＿見六七十＿＿五六十而非邦＿＿者? "

五 爲加點字選擇正確釋義，並根據釋義來翻譯句子 Match each dotted word with its correct modern Chinese equivalent by circling the latter. Then translate each sentence into modern Chinese.

1. 又何間焉?　　　　　　　　　　ⓐ.爲什麼(为什么) b.憑什麼(凭什么) c.多少

现代文翻译：你又为什么要参与到这件事情里面?

＿＿＿＿＿＿＿＿＿＿＿＿＿＿＿＿＿＿＿＿

2. 以吾一日長乎爾, 毋吾以也。　　　　a.因爲(为) b.用 c.來(来)

现代文翻译：＿＿＿＿＿＿＿＿＿＿＿＿＿＿＿

3. 方六七十, 如五六十, 求也为之。　　a.如果 b.或者 c.至於(至于)

现代文翻译：＿＿＿＿＿＿＿＿＿＿＿＿＿＿＿

4. 如或知爾, 則何以哉?　　　　　　　a.而且 b.你們(们) c.樣(样)子

现代文翻译：＿＿＿＿＿＿＿＿＿＿＿＿＿＿＿

5. 如其禮樂, 以俟君子。　　　　　　　a.如果 b.或者 c.至於(至于)

现代文翻译：＿＿＿＿＿＿＿＿＿＿＿＿＿＿＿

6. 夫子何哂由也?　　　　　　　a.憑什麼(凭什么) b.爲什麼(为什么) c.多少

现代文翻译：＿＿＿＿＿＿＿＿＿＿＿＿＿＿＿

7. 宗廟會同, 非諸侯而何? 赤也爲之小, 孰能爲之大?　　a.熟悉 b.熟練(练) c.誰(谁)

现代文翻译：＿＿＿＿＿＿＿＿＿＿＿＿＿＿＿

第七課

《孟子》選讀（上）

Selected Readings from the *Mencius* (I)

Introduction

The *Mencius* is a collection of conversations that Mencius (Mengzi 孟子; ca. 385–305 BCE) had with kings, thinkers, and other contemporaries. In these conversations, Mencius expounds his ideas on a broad range of moral and sociopolitical issues, including human nature, principles of government, and obligations to the people.

Mencius's proposition that "human nature is good" is a further development of Confucius's core belief in *ren* 仁 (benevolence, humaneness, humanity). Mencius has also gone beyond Confucius's notion of a harmonious hieratical society, as he stresses a ruler's paramount obligations to the common people. He considers the common people the very foundation of government, even placing them above sovereigns and spirits. This people-oriented political thought has profoundly influenced successive generations (see lesson 32, " 'On the Origin of Rulership' [Huang Zongxi]").

The *Mencius* is well known for its concise and dexterously patterned prose and for the rigor of its argumentation.

正文與簡體譯文 Text and Modern Chinese Translation

得道多助，失道寡助
dé dào duō zhù　　shī dào guǎ zhù

孟子曰：「天時不如地利，地利不如人
mèng zǐ yuē　　tiān shí bù rú dì lì　　dì lì bù rú rén

和。[1]三里之城，七里之郭，環而攻之而不
hé　　sān lǐ zhī chéng　　qī lǐ zhī guō　　huán ér gōng zhī ér bú

勝。夫環而攻之，必有得天時者矣。然而不
shèng　　fú huán ér gōng zhī　　bì yǒu dé tiān shí zhě yǐ　　rán ér bú

勝者，是天時不如地利也。[2]城非不高也，
shèng zhě　　shì tiān shí bù rú dì lì yě　　chéng fēi bù gāo yě

池非不深也，兵革非不堅利也，米粟非不多
chí fēi bù shēn yě　　bīng gé fēi bù jiān lì yě　　mǐ sù fēi bù duō

孟子说："有利于作战的天气条件比不上有利的地理环境，地理优势比不上人心的统一。[1]方圆三里的内城，方圆七里的外城，包围它，攻打它，却无法取胜。包围并攻打它的，一定是得到了有利的作战天气条件。但是不能取胜，这是因为天气条件比不上有利的地理环境。[2]城墙不是不高，护城河不是

也。委而去之，是地利不如人和也。[3]
yě　　wěi ér qù zhī　　shì dì lì bù rú rén hé yě

不深，兵器和甲冑不是不锋利坚固，粮食不是不多。（守城的人）却舍弃了城池离开，这是因为有利的地理条件比不上人心所向。[3]

1. 天時 (时) *n.* opportune time.
   如 *v.* to be comparable (with/to). MdnC: 比得上 (*bǐ dé shàng*). See L3 Grammar Note 5 ①.
   地利 *n.* geographical advantages.
   人和 *n.* support of people.
2. 城 *n.* city. Here it means "inner city" 內城 (*nèi chéng*).
   郭 *n.* a wall built outside of the city. Here it refers to "outer city" 外城 (*wài chéng*).
   環 (环) *v.* to encircle, surround. MdnC: 包圍 (*bāo wéi* 包围).
   夫 *initial particle.* no meaning. See L2 Grammar Note 4 ①.
   是……也 an affirmative syntactic construction, meaning "this is…." See L3 Grammar Note 1 ②.
3. 城 *n.* wall. MdnC: 城墙 (*chéng qiáng* 城墙).
   池 *n.* moat. MdnC: 護城河 (*hù chéng hé* 护城河).
   兵 *n.* weapon. MdnC: 兵器 (*bīng qì*).
   革 *n.* leather. Here it refers to armor (*jiǎ zhòu* 甲冑).
   堅 (坚) *adj.* firm, sturdy. MdnC: 堅固 (*jiān gù* 坚固).
   利 *adj.* sharp. MdnC: 鋒利 (*fēng lì* 锋利).
   粟 *n.* millet. 米粟 refers to food.
   委 *v.* to abandon. MdnC: 捨棄 (*shě qì* 舍弃).
   去 *v.* to leave. MdnC: 離開 (*lí kāi* 离开).

「故曰：域民不以封疆之ₐ界，固國不以
gù yuē　　yù mín bù yǐ fēng jiāng zhī jiè　　gù guó bù yǐ

山谿之險，威天下不以兵革之利。[4]得道者多
shān xī zhī xiǎn　　wēi tiān xià bù yǐ bīng gé zhī lì　　dé dào zhě duō

助，失道者寡助。寡助之ᵦ至，親戚畔之ᵪ。
zhù　　shī dào zhě guǎ zhù　　guǎ zhù zhī zhì　　qīn qī pàn zhī

多助之至，天下順之。以天下之ᵈ所順，攻
duō zhù zhī zhì　　tiān xià shùn zhī　　yǐ tiān xià zhī suǒ shùn　　gōng

親戚之所畔，故君子有不戰，戰必勝矣。[5]」
qīn qī zhī suǒ pàn　　gù jūn zǐ yǒu bù zhàn　　zhàn bì shèng yǐ

《孟子注疏》(《十三經注疏》)，北京：中華書局 (2009)，5858.

"所以说，使老百姓居住下来，不是凭借划定国家的疆界。稳固国防，不是依靠山河的险要。威慑天下，不是凭借兵器甲冑坚固锋利。[4]得道的人会有很多人帮助，失去道义就少有人帮助。帮助的人少到极点，他的亲戚也会背叛他。帮助他的人多到了极点，天下的人都会归顺他。用天下人都归顺（的力量），去攻击亲戚都背叛的人。所以君子不战则已，一旦与人交战就一定会胜利。[5]"

4. 域 *n.* territory, region. Here it is used as a causative verb, 使……域, meaning "to let people live in this region." See Grammar Note 1 ③.

以 *coverb.* to depend on, rely on. MdnC: 憑藉 (*píng jiè* 凭借). See L2 Grammar Note 1 ②.

封疆 *n.* boundary.

之 ₐ *particle.* a possessive marker. MdnC: 的 (*de*). See L1 Grammar Note 2 ②.

界 *n.* boundary. MdnC: 界限 (*jiè xiàn*).

固 *adj.* firm, sturdy. Here it is used as a causative verb, 使……固, meaning "to solidify or strengthen" 穩固 (*wěn gù* 稳固). See Grammar Note 1 ②.

國 (国) *n.* state, country. Here it refers to national defense 國防 (*guó yuán* 国防).

谿 (溪) *n.* brook, creek, mountain stream.

險 (险) *adj.* strategically located and difficult to access. MdnC: 險要 (*xiǎn yào* 险要)

威 *n.* awe-inspiring strength. Here it is used as a causative verb, 使……威, meaning "to deter or frighten with power" 威懾 (*wēi shè* 威慑). See Grammar Note 1 ③.

5. 道 *n.* way, truth.

寡 *adj.* few.

之 ᵦ *v.* to reach, get to. MdnC: 到 (*dào*). See Grammar Note 2 ⑦.

至 *adv.* extremely. Here it is used as a noun, meaning "the extreme" 極點 (*jí diǎn* 极点).

畔 *n.* used here in the sense of 叛 (*pàn*), meaning "to betray" (*bèi pàn* 背叛).

之 ₒ *personal pron.* him. See L1 Grammar Note 2 ③.

順 (顺) *v.* to surrender, pledge allegiance to. MdnC: 歸順 (*guī shun* 归顺).

之 ₔ *particle.* a nominative marker. See L2 Grammar Note 2 ⑤.

魚，我所欲也
yú wǒ suǒ yù yě

孟子曰：「魚，我所欲也；熊掌，亦我所欲也。二者ₐ不可得兼，舍魚而取熊掌者ᵦ也。⁶生，亦我所欲也；義，亦我所欲也。二者不可得兼，舍生而取義者也。⁷生亦我所欲，所欲有甚於生者ₒ，故不爲苟得也。死亦我所惡，所惡有甚於死者，故患有所不辟也。⁸

孟子说："鱼，是我喜欢的东西；熊掌，也是我喜欢的东西。这两样我不能同时得到，我舍弃鱼，选取熊掌。⁶生命是我喜欢的；正义也是我喜欢的。这两样我不能同时得到，我舍弃生命，选择正义。⁷生命是我想要的，但我想要的东西有超过生命的，所以不能苟且活着。死亡是我所厌恶的，但是我厌恶的东西有超过死亡的，所以有些祸患是不去躲避的。⁸

6. 掌 *n.* palm. 熊掌 means "bear's paw."

　者 a *auxiliary pron.* used with numbers to show the category of the things mentioned earlier. See Grammar Note 3 ⑤.

　兼 *adv.* concurrently.

　舍 *v.* to abandon, give up. MdnC: 捨棄 (*shě qì* 舍弃).

　者 b 也 *ending particle.* no meaning. See L4 Grammar Note 3 ②.

7. 生 *n.* life. MdnC: 生命 (*shēng mìng*).

　義 (义) *n.* truth, justice. MdnC: 正義 (*zhèng yì* 正义).

8. 甚 *adv.* more than. MdnC: 超過 (*chāo guò* 超过).

　者 c *auxiliary pron.* the one which. MdnC: ……的東西 (*de dōng xī* 的东西). See L1 Grammar Note 1 ①.

　苟 *adv.* unscrupulously. MdnC: 苟且 (*gǒu qiě*). See L19 Grammar Note 1 ②.

　惡 (恶 wù) *v.* to dislike, hate. MdnC: 厭惡 (*yàn wù* 厌恶).

　患 *n.* trouble, suffering, disaster. MdnC: 禍患 (*huò huàn* 祸患).

　辟 *v.* used in the sense of 避 (*bì*), meaning "to avoid" 躲避 (*duǒ bì*).

「如使人之所欲莫甚於生，則凡可以得
rú shǐ rén zhī suǒ yù mò shèn yú shēng　zé fán kě yǐ dé

生者，何不用也？使人之所惡莫甚於死者，
shēng zhě　hé bú yòng yě　　shǐ rén zhī suǒ wù mò shén yú sǐ zhě

則凡可以辟患者，何不爲也？由是則生而有
zé fán kě yǐ bì huàn zhě　　hé bù wéi yě　　yóu shì zé shēng ér yǒu

不用也，由是則可以辟患而有不爲也。9是故
bù yòng yě　　yóu shì zé kě yǐ bì huàn ér yǒu bù wéi yě　　shì gù

所欲有甚於生者，所惡有甚於死者，非獨賢
suǒ yù yǒu shèn yú shēng zhě suǒ wù yǒu shén yú sǐ zhě　　fēi dú xián

者有是心也，人皆有之，賢者能勿喪耳。10
zhě yǒu shì xīn yě　　rén jiē yǒu zhī　　xián zhě néng wù sàng ěr

"如果使人想要的东西不超过生命，那么凡是可以用来获得生命的方法，有什么不可用的呢？使人所厌恶的东西不超过死亡，那么凡是可以避免祸患的方法，有什么不可做的呢？根据这样的方法可以获得生命，有人却不使用；通过这样的方法可以避免祸患，有人却不去做。9因此人们想要的东西有时会超过生命，所厌恶的东西有时会超过死亡。不是只有道德高尚的人才有这样的想法，每个人都有，只是道德高尚的人不会丧失（这种想法）罢了。10

9. 凡 *adv.* in general, whatever. MdnC: 凡是 (*fán shì*). See L10 Grammar Note 4.

　以 *coverb.* to use. MdnC: 用 (*yòng*). See L2 Grammar Note 1 ②.

　何 *interrogative pron.* MdnC: 什麼 (*shén me* 什么). See L1 Grammar Note 3 ①.

　由 *prep.* according to. MdnC: 根據 (*gēn jù* 根据).

　是 *demonstrative pron.* this, referring to the method or the situation. See L3 Grammar Note 1 ①.

10. 獨 (独) *adv.* only. MdnC: 只有 (*zhǐ yǒu*).

賢 (贤) *adj.* virtuous.

是 *demonstrative pron.* such, this. MdnC: 這樣 (*zhè yàng*). See L3 Grammar Note 1 ①.

心 *n.* heart, innate disposition. MdnC: 想法 (*xiǎng fǎ*).

勿 *adv.* do not. MdnC: 不 (*bù*).

喪 (丧) *v.* to lose. MdnC: 喪失 (*sàng shī* 丧失).

耳 *ending particle.* nothing more. MdnC: 罷了 (*bà le* 罢了). See Grammar Note 4.

「一簞食，一豆羹，得之則生，弗得則
　yì dān shí　　yí dòu gēng　　dé zhī zé shēng　　fú dé zé

死。嘑爾而與之，行道之人弗受；蹴爾而與
sǐ　　hū ěr ér yǔ zhī　　xíng dào zhī rén fú shòu　　cù ěr ér yǔ

之，乞人不屑也。¹¹萬鍾則不辯禮義而受之ₐ，
zhī　　qǐ rén bú xiè yě　　wàn zhōng zé bú biàn lǐ yì ér shòu zhī

萬鍾於我何加焉？¹²爲宮室之ᵦ美、妻妾之ᵦ
wàn zhōng yú wǒ hé jiā yān　　wèi gōng shì zhī měi　　qī qiè zhī

奉、所識窮乏者得我與？¹³鄉爲ₐ身死而不
fèng　　suǒ shí qióng fá zhě dé wǒ yú　　xiàng wèi shēn sǐ ér bú

受，今爲ₐ宮室之美爲ᵦ之；鄉爲身死而不
shòu　　jīn wèi gōng shì zhī měi wéi zhī　　xiàng wèi shēn sǐ ér bú

受，今爲妻妾之奉爲之；鄉爲身死而不受，
shòu　　jīn wèi qī qiè zhī fèng wéi zhī　　xiàng wèi shēn sǐ ér bú shòu

今爲所識窮乏者得我而爲之。¹⁴是亦不可以
jīn wèi suǒ shí qióng fá zhě dé wǒ ér wéi zhī　　shì yì bù kě yǐ

已乎？此之謂失其本心。¹⁵」
yǐ hū　　cǐ zhī wèi shī qí běn xīn

《孟子注疏》(《十三經注疏》)，北京：中華書局 (2009)，5987–5988.

"一篮子饭食，一碗汤，吃了这些食物就可以活下来，吃不到就会死掉。呼喝着给别人，过路的人不会接受；用脚踢给别人，要饭的人也看不上这些食物。¹¹优厚的俸禄，不分辨(是否合乎)礼义就接受了，这优厚的俸禄给我增加了什么好处呢？¹²为了住宅华美，妻妾侍奉，所认识的穷人感激我吗？¹³从前(有人)为了(礼义)，宁可死也不接受(施舍)，现在却有人为了住宅华美而接受；从前有人为了礼义，宁死也不接受施舍，现在有人却为了妻妾侍奉而接受；从前有人为了礼义，宁死不接受施舍，现在却为了所认识的穷人感激他而接受。¹⁴这样的行为难道不可以停止吗？这就是所说的失去了本来的善心。¹⁵

11. 簞 *n.* a small bamboo basket for holding food. MdnC: 籃子 (*lán zi* 篮子).

豆 *n.* ancient container of meat or food.

羹 *n.* soup, broth. MdnC: 湯 (*tāng* 汤).

弗 *adv.* no. MdnC: 不 (*bù*). See L4 Grammar Note 5.

嘑 (呼) *v.* to bawl, shout. MdnC: 嘑喝 (*hū hè* 呼喝).

爾 (尔) *particle.* functioning as an emotive particle. See L6 Grammar Note 1 ②.

與 (与 *yǔ*) *v.* to give. MdnC: 給 (*gěi*).

行 (*xíng*) 道 *v.* to walk on the road. MdnC: 走路 (*zǒu lù*).

受 *v.* to receive, accept. MdnC: 接受 (*jiē shòu*).

蹴 *v.* to kick. MdnC: 踢 (*tī*).

乞 *v.* to beg, request. Here it refers to begging for food 要飯 (*yào fàn* 要饭). 乞人 means "beggar."

屑 *n.* bits, crumbs. 不屑 means "to look down upon or belittle" 看不上 (*kàn bù shàng*).

12. 鍾 (钟) *measure word.* an ancient unit of capacity.

萬鍾 (万钟) ten thousand *zhong*. Here it refers to high (*yōu hòu* 优厚) emolument (*fèng lù* 俸禄).

辯 (辩) *v.* used in the sense of 辨 (*biàn*), meaning "to distinguish or discriminate" 分辨 (*fēn biàn*).

禮義 (礼义) *n.* rules of propriety and righteousness.

加 *v.* to add, increase. MdnC: 增加 (*zēng jiā*).

焉 *ending particle.* MdnC: 啊 (*a*). See L2 Grammar Note 3 ②.

13. 爲 (为 *wèi*) *prep.* for. MdnC: 爲了 (*wèi le* 为了). See Grammar Note 5 ②.

宮室 *n.* building, house. Here it refers to a residence 住宅 (*zhù zhái*).

之 ₆ *particle.* a nominative marker. See L2 Grammar Note 2 ⑤.

奉 *v.* to serve, respect. MdnC: 侍奉 (*shì fèng*).

識 (识) *v.* to know. MdnC: 認識 (*rèn shi* 认识).

乏 *adj.* lacking, poor. 窮 (穷) 乏者 means "poor people" 窮人 (*qióng rén* 穷人).

得 *v.* to get. Here it is used in the sense of 德 (*dé*), meaning "to appreciate" 感激 (*gǎn jī*).

與 (与 *yú*) *ending particle.* See Grammar Note 6.

14. 鄉 (乡) used in the sense of 向 (*xiàng*), meaning "in the past" 從前 (*cóng qián* 从前).

15. 是 *demonstrative pron.* this, referring to the behavior discussed. See L3 Grammar Note 1 ①.

已 *v.* to stop. MdnC: 停止 (*tíng zhǐ*). See L21 Grammar Note 1 ②.

本 *adj.* original, natural. MdnC: 本來 (*běn lái* 本来).

心 *n.* heart, consciousness.

語法注釋 Grammar Notes

1. 使動用法 A causative verb is a verb that causes something to happen. There are causative verbs in both English and Chinese. In English, there are only a few causative verbs, such as *let*, *make*, *have*, *get*, and *help*. A sentence made with a causative verb normally has four components:

Subject + **causative verb** + object + base verb (object)

Examples: He **made** his girlfriend cry. My mom **let** me use her car.

As shown by these examples, a causative structure always contains two verbs: the first is the causative verb, and the second is the base verb. The noun in between is at once the object of the first verb and the subject of the second verb. In the sentence "He made me do an errand," *made* is a causative verb, *me* is the object, and *do* is a base verb. The object *me* of the causative verb *made* is functioning as the logical subject of the base verb *do* in this structure.

Modern Chinese has an almost identical causative structure, and its four components appear in the same order: 讓/令

Examples: 老師讓我練習寫字。他的話令我難過。

In classical Chinese, however, causative structure is often truncated, with the initial causative verb (e.g., 使/令) being omitted and the base verb performing the causative function. Here one may ask how the base verb performs a causative function. The answer is simple and straightforward: by its inversion—that is, by its being placed before its logical subject object, as shown here:

　　焉用亡鄭以陪鄰？　　(L2)

　　亡：intransitive verb; 鄭：object

　　亡鄭 => 使鄭亡　　(causative verb 使 is added here)

　　使：causative verb; 鄭：object; 亡：base verb/infinite verb

　　[为什么用使郑国灭亡（这个办法）来增广邻国的土地？]

Here, by means of inversion, the intransitive verb 亡 before the object 鄭 performs the dual functions of the causative verb 使 and the base verb 灭亡. When it is translated into modern Chinese, a causative verb 使 should be added before the object 鄭, thus making the noun 鄭 function as both the object of 使 and the subject of 灭亡: [使郑国灭亡]. As a rule, the word performing the causative function is (1) an intransitive verb, (2) an adjective functioning as a verb, or (3) a noun functioning as a verb, as shown by the following three examples:

① Intransitive verb + object ➡ 使 (causative verb) + object + intransitive verb

　　擇可勞而勞之，又誰怨？　　　勞之 => 使之勞 (MdnC: 勞動)　(L5)

　　　[选择老百姓可以劳动的事情使他们劳动，那么还有谁会怨恨呢？]

② Adjective + object ➡ 使 (causative verb) + object + adjective

　　固國不以山谿之險。　　　固國 => 使國固 (MdnC: 穩固)

　　　[使国家稳固不是依靠山河的险要（来实现的）。]

③ Noun + object ➡ 使 (causative verb) + object + (base/infinite verb) + noun

　　域民不以封疆之界。　　　域民 => 使民(居於)域 (MdnC: 疆界)

　　　[使老百姓居住在疆界之内，不是依靠划定国家的疆界（来实现的）。]

Causative structures like these can easily be mistaken, by modern native and nonnative readers alike, for a transitive structure (i.e., transitive verb + object). Often such a transitive misreading makes sense as well, even though not as much sense as a causative reading. A judicious choice of causative reading often attests to one's mastery of classical Chinese and shows how well one contextualizes their interpretation.

2. 之　Seven uses of 之 are explained in this book. In addition to the use below, see 之 ①②③④ in L1 Grammar Note 2 and 之⑤⑥ in L2 Grammar Note 2.

　　⑦　v. to reach, go. MdnC: 到 (dào), 去 (qù).

　　　寡助之至，親戚畔之。

　　　[帮助他的人少到了极点，他的亲戚都会背叛他。]

3. 者　Six uses of 者 are explained in this book. In addition to the use below, see 者① in L1 Grammar Note 1, 者②③ in L4 Grammar Note 3, 者④ in L6 Grammar Note 8, and 者⑥ in L8 Grammar Note 1.

⑤ *auxiliary pron.* number + 者 Normally 者 is used to show the range or category of the things mentioned earlier.

魚，我所欲也；熊掌，亦我所欲也。二者不可得兼，舍魚而取熊掌者也。

[鱼是我想要的，熊掌是我想要的，这两样不能够同时得到，我舍弃鱼选择熊掌。]

4. 耳 *ending particle.* contraction of the final phrasal particle 而已 (*ér yǐ*, see L21 Grammar Note 1 ③), meaning "nothing more." MdnC: 罷了 (*bà le* 罢了).

非獨賢者有是心，人皆有之，賢者能勿喪耳。

[不是只有道德高尚的人才有这样的思想，每个人都有，只不过高尚的人能不丧失罢了。]

5. 爲 Five uses of 爲 are explained in this book. In addition to the use below, see 爲① in L2 **(为)** Grammar Note 6, 爲③ in L9 Grammar Note 1, 爲④ in L11 Grammar Note 4, and 爲⑤ in L21 Grammar Note 3.

② **wèi** *prep.* because of, for, MdnC: 爲了 (*wèi le* 为了).

爲宮室之美、妻妾之奉、所識窮乏者得我與？

[为了住宅华美，妻妾的侍奉，所认识的穷人感激我吗？]

6. 與 **yú** *ending particle.* used in the sense of 歟 (*yú* 欤, see L15 Grammar Note 3). 與/歟 is **(与)** equivalent to 嗎 (*ma* 吗) in modern Chinese and 乎 (see L6 Grammar Note 2 ②) in classical Chinese.

爲宮室之美、妻妾之奉、所識窮乏者得我與？

[为了住宅华美，妻妾的侍奉，所认识的穷人感激我吗？]

唯求則非邦也與？ (L6)

[难道冉有（说的）不是（治理）国家吗？]

Literary Analysis

In the cutthroat geopolitical world of Warring States China, rulers and ministers incessantly sought various forms of "profit" 利 (*lì*) and were generally disinclined to listen to the moralizing advice of Confucian scholars who spoke of little other than benevolence and righteousness. Mencius, however, found clever ways to emphasize the latter even while directly addressing the former. In the passage that opens the *Mencius*, King Hui of Liang 梁惠王 begins by asking Mencius what he brings to "profit" his state, to which Mencius replies: "Why must your highness speak of profit? There is only benevolence and righteousness, nothing more" 王何必曰利？亦有仁義而已矣. Nonetheless, his dialogues with King Hui demonstrate that it is precisely by focusing on these virtues that the king will ultimately fulfill all his greatest ambitions: a strong, populous, and prosperous state and indeed true kingship. How does a similar dynamic play out in the first of the two passages in this lesson?

Mencius makes great use of analogies and other forms of comparison throughout his dialogues. In the second example, a starving beggar's refusal of food that has been trampled on is particularly vivid: we all instantly relate to his indignation and appreciate that he would choose his pride over his life in the face of such contempt. And yet we easily swallow our pride and stoop to the dirtiest of deeds when it comes to the blind pursuit of wealth and status. This story functions like Mencius's example of the universal impulse to rescue a child about to fall into a well in the famous passage of *Mencius* 2A.6: we all possess this "basic heart" 本心 (*běnxīn*) or "sprout" of benevolence from birth, but we lose it all too easily when we fail to cultivate it and succumb to making viscerally moving instead of thoughtful moral decisions.

The beggar analogy was a favorite of Mencius, and we will see it employed again, to similar effect, in lesson 8.

☞ *HTRCProse*, chapter 3, "Pre-Qin Philosophical Prose: Recorded Conversations and Argumentative Essays" for further comments on the *Mencius*.

—SC

課後練習 Exercises

一 給加點字注音 Give the pinyin romanization for each dotted word.

1. 粟 （＿＿＿） 2. 羹 （＿＿＿） 3. 簞 （＿＿＿） 4. 賢 （＿＿＿） 5. 羹 （＿＿＿）

二 在括號中給句中加點的字注音，並選出正確的釋義 Give the pinyin romanization for each dotted word; then select the correct definition from the following list, and write it in the blank.

背叛　苟且　踢　躲避　嘑(呼)喝　**信服**　禍患(患)　甲胄　喪(丧)失

1. 小信未孚 （**fú**） <u>信服</u>　2. 有所不辟 （　）＿＿＿＿＿　3. 親戚畔之 （　）＿＿＿＿＿

4. 嘑爾而與之 （　）＿＿＿＿＿　5. 兵革 （　）＿＿＿＿＿　6. 勿喪耳 （　）＿＿＿＿＿

7. 蹴爾而與之 （　）＿＿＿＿＿　8. 辟患者 （　）＿＿＿＿＿　9. 苟得 （　）＿＿＿＿＿

三 選擇釋義並填空 Match each word in the left column with its correct definition in the middle column. Fill in each blank in the right column with an appropriate word from the left column (some words may be used more than once).

<u>謀謀劃 (谋划)</u>	護(护)城河
利＿＿＿＿＿	離開(离开)
池＿＿＿＿＿	增加
威＿＿＿＿＿	險(险)要
去＿＿＿＿＿	鋒(锋)利
委＿＿＿＿＿	捨棄(舍弃)
加＿＿＿＿＿	**謀劃 (谋划)**
界＿＿＿＿＿	威懾(慑)
險＿＿＿＿＿	分辨
辯＿＿＿＿＿	界限

城非不高也，＿＿＿非不深也，兵革非不堅＿＿＿也，米粟非不多也。＿＿＿而＿＿＿之，是地利不如人和也。

故曰：域民不以封疆之＿＿＿，固國不以山谿之＿＿＿，＿＿＿天下不以兵革之＿＿＿。得道者多助，失道者寡助。

萬鍾則不＿＿＿禮義而受之，萬鍾於我何＿＿＿焉？

四 請用給出的字填空 Fill in each blank with an appropriate word from the following list (some words may be used more than once).

如　者　以　之　何　爲(为)　與(与)

1. 寡助＿＿＿至，親戚畔＿＿＿。多助＿＿＿至，天下順＿＿＿。
2. ＿＿＿使人之所欲莫甚於生，則凡可＿＿＿得生＿＿＿，＿＿＿不用也？
3. ＿＿＿宮室＿＿＿美，妻妾＿＿＿奉，所識窮乏＿＿＿得我＿＿＿？

五 爲加點字選擇正確釋義，並根據釋義來翻譯句子 Match each dotted word with its correct modern Chinese equivalent by circling the latter. Then translate each sentence into modern Chinese.

1. 又何間爲?　　　　　　　　　　ⓐ 爲什麼(为什么)　b. 憑什麼(凭什么)　c. 多少

現代文翻译：你又为什么要参与到这件事情里面？

＿＿＿＿＿＿＿＿＿＿＿＿＿＿＿＿＿＿＿＿＿＿＿＿＿＿＿＿

2. 域民不以封疆之界。　　　　　　　a. 因爲(为)　b. 用　c. 來(来)

現代文翻译：＿＿＿＿＿＿＿＿＿＿＿＿＿＿＿＿＿＿＿＿＿＿＿

3. 固國不以山谿之險。　　　　　　　a. 堅(坚)固　b. 使……穩(稳)固　c. 久

現代文翻译：＿＿＿＿＿＿＿＿＿＿＿＿＿＿＿＿＿＿＿＿＿＿＿

4. 天時不如地利，地利不如人和。　　　a. 如果　b. 或者　c. 比

現代文翻译：＿＿＿＿＿＿＿＿＿＿＿＿＿＿＿＿＿＿＿＿＿＿＿

5. 非獨賢者有是心。　　　　　　　　a. 但是　b. 所以　c. 這(这)

現代文翻译：＿＿＿＿＿＿＿＿＿＿＿＿＿＿＿＿＿＿＿＿＿＿＿

6. 多助之至，天下順之。　　　　　　a. 到　b. 的　c. 他

現代文翻译：＿＿＿＿＿＿＿＿＿＿＿＿＿＿＿＿＿＿＿＿＿＿＿

7. 鄉爲身死而不受，今爲妻妾之奉而爲之。　　a. 做　b. 治理　c. 爲(为)了

現代文翻译：＿＿＿＿＿＿＿＿＿＿＿＿＿＿＿＿＿＿＿＿＿＿＿

《孟子》選讀（下）

Selected Readings from the *Mencius* (II)

Introduction

The first excerpt in this lesson is an allegorical tale in which Mencius castigates those in high position who unscrupulously pursue wealth and distinction. In the second, he discusses human nature with his intellectual opponent Gao Zi. Through a metaphor of water, Gao argues that human nature is neither good nor bad. Employing the same metaphor differently, Mencius refutes Gao's position and argues that human nature is good. Mencius's view of human nature stands in sharp contrast to that of Xunzi 荀子 (313–238 BCE), who saw human nature as inherently evil (see lesson 10, " 'Human Nature Is Deplorable,' Excerpt from the *Xunzi*").

正文與簡體譯文 Text and Modern Chinese Translation

齊人有一妻一妾
qí rén yǒu yì qī yí qiè

齊人有一妻一妾而處室者，其良人出，則
qí rén yǒu yì qī yí qiè ér chǔ shì zhě　qí liáng rén chū　zé

必饜酒肉而後反。[1] 其妻問所與飲食者，則盡
bì yàn jiǔ ròu ér hòu fǎn　qí qī wèn suǒ yǔ yǐn shí zhě　zé jìn

富貴也。[2] 其妻告其妾曰：「良人出，則必饜酒
fù guì yě　qí qī gào qí qiè yuē　liáng rén chū　zé bì yàn jiǔ

肉而後反。問其與飲食者，盡富貴也，而未
ròu ér hòu fǎn　wèn qí yǔ yǐn shí zhě　jìn fù guì yě　ér wèi

嘗有顯者來。吾將瞷良人之 ₐ所之 ᵦ也。」[3]
cháng yǒu xiǎn zhě lái　wú jiāng jiàn liáng rén zhī suǒ zhī　yě

齐国有个人和一妻一妾住在一起。那丈夫（每次）出门，一定会饱食酒肉，然后才回家。[1] 他的妻子问，同他一起吃吃喝喝的都是什么人，（他说）都是些有钱有地位（的人）。[2] 他的妻子告诉他的小妾说："夫君每次出门，一定会饱食酒肉后才回家。问他和谁一起饮酒吃肉，他说都是些富贵的人。但却不曾看到有显贵的人来（我们家）。我要偷偷去看看夫君去的地方。"[3]

---

1. 處（处 chǔ）*v.* to live, stay. MdnC: 居住 (*jū zhù*).

室 *n.* room, home, house.

有……者 See Grammar Note 1 ⑥.

其 *demonstrative pron.* that. MdnC: 那 (*nà*). See L6 Grammar Note 6 ④.

良人 *n.* husband. MdnC: 丈夫 (*zhàng fū*), 夫君 (*fū jūn*).

饜 (餍) *v.* to satiate, eat one's fill, be satisfied. MdnC: 飽食 (*bǎo shí* 饱食).

反 *n.* opposite. Here it is used in the sense of 返 (*fǎn*), meaning "to return home" 回家 (*huí jiā*).

2. 飲 (饮) *v.* to drink. MdnC: 喝酒 (*hē jiǔ*).

食 *v.* to eat. MdnC: 吃 (*chī*).

盡 (尽 *jìn*) *adv.* all. MdnC: 都 (*dōu*).

貴 *adj.* expensive, noble, honorable. 富貴 means "wealthy and honorable."

3. 未 *adv.* not yet, never. MdnC: 不 (*bù*).

嘗 (尝) *adv.* once, ever. MdnC: 曾經 (*céng jīng* 曾经). See L23 Grammar Note 1 ①.

顯 (显) *adj.* illustrative, celebrated. MdnC: 顯貴 (*xiǎn guì* 显贵).

瞷 *v.* to peek at. MdnC: 偷偷看 (*tōu tōu kàn*).

之 a *particle.* a nominative marker. See L2 Grammar Note 2 ⑤.

之 b *v.* to go, get to. MdnC: 去 (*qù*). See L7 Grammar Note 2 ⑦.

蚤起，施從良人之所之。⁴徧國中無與立
zǎo qǐ　　yí cóng liáng rén zhī suǒ zhī　　biàn guó zhōng wú yǔ lì

談者。⁵卒之東郭墦間，之祭者，乞其餘。⁶
tán zhě　　zú zhī dōng guō fán jiān　　zhī jì zhě　　qǐ qí yú

不足，又顧而之他，此其爲饜足之道也。⁷其
bù zú　　yòu gù ér zhī tā　　cǐ qí wéi yàn zú zhī dào yě　　qí

妻歸告其妾曰：「良人者，所仰望而終身也。
qī guī gào qí qiè yuē　　liáng rén zhě　suǒ yǎng wàng ér zhōng shēn yě

今若此。」⁸與其妾訕其良人，而相泣於中
jīn ruò cǐ　　yǔ qí qiè shàn qí liáng rén　　ér xiāng qì yú zhōng

庭。⁹而良人未之知也，施施從外來，驕其妻
tíng　　ér liáng rén wèi zhī zhī yě　　yí yí cóng wài lái　　jiāo qí qī

妾。¹⁰
qiè

（第二天）早晨起来，（妻子）偷偷地跟踪丈夫到他去的地方。⁴（走）遍国都，也没见有人站住和他交谈。⁵最后到了东城外的坟墓间，丈夫走到祭拜的人前，乞讨他们剩下的食物。⁶（食物）不够，丈夫又四下看看，到别的墓前（要），这就是他吃饱喝足的方法。⁷他的妻子回家告诉小妾说："夫君是我们要依靠终身的人，现在却像这样的。"⁸妻子和小妾在院子里骂着丈夫，一起哭了起来。⁹可是（她们的）丈夫还不知道这件事，得意洋洋地从外面回来，骄傲地（面对）他的妻妾。¹⁰

4. 蚤 *n.* used here in the sense of 早 (*zǎo*), meaning "morning" (*zǎo chén* 早晨).

施 *v.* to give, act. Here it is used in the sense of 迤 (*yí*), which means "meandering" (*wēi yí* 逶迤). In this context, it means "secretly (following)." MdnC: 偷偷地 (*tōu tōu de*).

從 (从) *v.* to follow. MdnC: 跟蹤 (*gēn zōng* 跟踪).

5. 徧 (遍) *adv.* all over, everywhere.

國 (国) *n.* state, country. Here it refers to the capital 國都 (*guó dū* 国都).

6. 卒 *adv.* at last, finally. MdnC: 最後 (*zuì hòu* 最后).

之 *v.* to go, get to. MdnC: 去 (*qù*). See L7 Grammar Note 2 ⑦.

郭 *n.* a wall built outside of the city. 東 (东) 郭 refers to the east side of the outer city.

墦 *n.* grave, tomb. MdnC: 坟墓 (*fén mù*).

祭 *v.* to sacrifice. MdnC: 祭祀 (*jì sì*).

乞 *v.* to beg, request. MdnC: 乞討 (*qǐ tǎo* 乞讨).

餘 (余) *n.* leftover.

7. 顧 (顾) *v.* to look, look back. MdnC: 看 (*kàn*).

道 *n.* way, method. MdnC: 辦法 (*bàn fǎ* 办法).

8. 仰望 *v.* to look up at, look up to. Here it means "to rely on or depend on" 依靠 (*yī kào*).

若 *v.* to be like. MdnC: 像 (*xiàng*). See L4 Grammar Note 4 ①.

終 (终) 身 *adv.* lifelong, all one's life. Here it means "to live together all one's life."

9. 訕 (讪) *v.* to ridicule. MdnC: 譏諷 (*jī fěn* 讥讽).

泣 *v.* to cry. MdnC: 哭 (*kū*).

庭 *n.* courtyard. MdnC: 庭院 (*tíng yuàn*).

10. 未之知 the normal order should be 未知之. 之, the object, is taken out of its normal position and placed before the verb 知.

施施 (*yí yí*) *adv.* immensely proud. MdnC: 得意洋洋 (*dé yì yáng yáng*).

驕 (骄) *adj.* arrogant. MdnC: 驕傲地 (*jiāo ào de* 骄傲地).

由君子觀之，　則人之所以求富貴利達者，
yóu jūn zǐ guān zhī　　zé rén zhī suǒ yǐ qiú fù guì lì dá zhě

其妻妾不羞也，　而不相泣者，　幾希矣。[11]
qí qī qiè bù xiū yě　　ér bù xiāng qì zhě　　jī xī yǐ

在君子看来，人们用来追求富贵利益和显达的社会地位的方法，让他们的妻子和小妾不感到羞愧，不在院子中哭泣的，几乎太少见了！[11]

《孟子注疏》(《十三經注疏》)，北京：中華書局 (2009), 5972.

11. 之所以……者 the way of…. MdnC: ……的方法 (*de fāng fǎ*). See L9 Grammar Note 2.

利 *n.* profit, benefit. MdnC: 利益 (*lì yì*).

達 (达) *v.* to be smooth and successful in one's political career. MdnC: 顯達 (*xiǎn dá* 显达).

羞 *v.* to feel ashamed. MdnC: 羞愧 (*xiū kuì*).

幾 (几 *jī*) *adv.* almost. MdnC: 幾乎 (*jī hū* 几乎).

希 *n.* hope. Here it is used in the sense of 稀 (*xī*), meaning "few" 少 (*shǎo*).

性猶湍水也
xìng yóu tuān shuǐ yě

告子曰：「性，　猶杞柳也。義，　猶桮棬
gào zǐ yuē　　xìng　yóu qǐ liǔ yě　　yì　yóu bēi quān

告子说："人性就像杞柳一样，仁义就像杯

也。以人性爲仁義，猶以杞柳爲桮棬。」 12
yě　yǐ rén xìng wéi rén yì　yóu yǐ qǐ liǔ wéi bēi quān

孟子曰：「子能順杞柳之性，而以爲桮棬
mèng zǐ yuē　zǐ néng shùn qǐ liǔ zhī xìng　ér yǐ wéi bēi quān

乎？將戕賊杞柳，而後以爲桮棬也？如將戕賊
hū　jiāng qiāng zéi qǐ liǔ　ér hòu yǐ wéi bēi quān yě　rú jiāng qiāng zéi

杞柳而以爲桮棬，則亦將戕賊人以爲仁義與？
qǐ liǔ ér yǐ wéi bēi quān　zé yì jiāng qiāng zéi rén yǐ wéi rén yì　yú

率天下之人而禍仁義者，必子之言夫！」 13
shuài tiān xià zhī rén ér huò rén yì zhě　bì zǐ zhī yán fú

子一样。把人性说成是仁义的，就像把杞柳直接当成杯子一样。" 12

孟子说："您能够顺着杞柳的本性，然后把它做成杯子吗？还是要砍断杞柳，然后把它制成杯子呢！如果要砍断杞柳，然后把它做成杯子，那么也要残害人的本性，然后把这说成是仁义吗？率领天下的人来祸害仁义的人，一定是您的言论啊！" 13

12. 告子 a contemporary of Mencius.
性 *n.* human nature. MdnC: 人性 (*rén xìng*).
猶 (犹) *v.* to be like, just as. MdnC: 像 (*xiàng*). See L3 Grammar Note 3 ②.
杞柳 *n.* a type of willow tree.
義 (义) *n.* righteousness. MdnC: 仁義 (*rén yì* 仁义).
桮 (杯) *n.* cup, glass. MdnC: 杯子 (*bēi zi*).
棬 *n.* drinking vessel made of wood.

13. 順 (顺) *v.* to go in the same direction, go along with.
以爲 (为 wéi) or 以 (杞柳) 爲…… See L2 Grammar Note 1 ④.
將 (将 jiāng) *adv.* will, going to.
戕賊 (贼) *v.* to kill, hurt, injure. Here it means "to cut (the willow)" 砍斷 (*kǎn duàn* 砍断) or "to destroy (people)" 殘害 (*cán hài* 残害).
與 (与 yú) *ending particle.* See L7 Grammar Note 6.
率 *v.* to lead. MdnC: 率領 (*shuài lǐng* 率领).
禍 (祸) *n.* disaster. Here it is a verb, meaning "to ruin" 禍害 (*huò hài* 祸害).
夫 (fú) *ending particle.* See Grammar Note 2 ③.

告子曰：「性猶湍水也，決諸東方則東
gào zǐ yuē　xìng yóu tuān shuǐ yě　jué zhū dōng fāng zé dōng

流，決諸西方則西流。人性之無分於善不善
liú　jué zhū xī fāng zé xī liú　rén xìng zhī wú fēn yú shàn bù shàn

也，猶水之無分於東西也。」 14
yě　yóu shuǐ zhī wú fēn yú dōng xī yě

孟子曰：「水信無分於東西，無分於上下
mèng zǐ yuē　shuǐ xìn wú fēn yú dōng xī　wú fēn yú shàng xià

告子说："人性就像湍急的流水，在东边决口，就向东边流，在西边决口，就向西边流。人的本性没有善和不善的分别，就像水没有向东流还是向西流的分别一样。" 14

孟子说："水确实没有向东流还是向西流的

乎？ 人性之善也， 猶水之就下也。 人無有不
hū　　rén xìng zhī shàn yě　　yóu shuǐ zhī jiù xià yě　　rén wú yǒu bù

善， 水無有不下。 ¹⁵今夫水， 搏而躍之， 可
shàn　　shuǐ wú yǒu bù xià　　jīn fú shuǐ　　bó ér yuè zhī　　kě

使過顙； 激而行之， 可使在山。 ¹⁶是豈水之
shǐ guò sǎng　　jī ér xíng zhī　　kě shǐ zài shān　　shì qǐ shuǐ zhī

性哉？ 其勢則然也。 人之可使爲不善， 其性
xìng zāi　　qí shì zé rán yě　　rén zhī kě shǐ wéi bù shàn　　qí xìng

亦猶是也。 ¹⁷」
yì yóu shì yě

《孟子注疏》（《十三經注疏》）, 北京：中華書局 (2009), 5978.

分别，但也没有向上流还是向下流的分别吗？人的本性善良，就像水会向下流一样。人（的本性）没有不善良的，水也没有不向下流的。¹⁵现在，这水流，拍打它使它溅起来，可以使它高过额头；阻遏它，使它（往回）流，可以迫使它流上山。¹⁶这难道是水的本性吗？地势迫使它这样。人可以（被态势）迫使做不善良的事情，他的本性也像这样的。¹⁷"

14. 湍 *adj.* rapid (water), running (water). MdnC: 湍急 (*tuān jí*).

决 (决) *v.* to burst (the dike). MdnC: 決口 (*jué kǒu* 决口).

諸 (诸) *particle.* contraction of 之於 (*zhī yú*). See Grammar Note 3.

之 *particle.* a nominative marker. See L2 Grammar Note 2 ⑤.

15. 信 *adv.* indeed. MdnC: 確實 (*què shí* 确实).

就 *v.* to move toward, go to.

16. 夫 (fú) *demonstrative pron.* this. MdnC: 這 (*zhè* 这). See L2 Grammar Note 4 ②.

搏 *v.* to beat, fight. MdnC: 拍打 (*pāi dǎ*).

躍 (跃) *v.* to jump, skip. MdnC: 跳 (*tiào*). Here it is used as a causative verb, meaning "to make (water) splash" 使 (*shǐ*) ……溅起來 (*jiàn qǐ lái* 溅起来). See L7 Grammar Note 1 ①.

顙 (颡) *n.* forehead. MdnC: 額頭 (*é tóu* 额头).

激 *v.* to dam. MdnC: 阻遏 (*zǔ è*).

使 *v.* to make, force. MdnC: 迫使 (*pò shǐ*).

17. 是 *demonstrative pron.* this, referring to the situation. MdnC: 這 (*zhè* 这). See L3 Grammar Note 1 ①.

豈 (岂) *particle.* rhetorical question marker. MdnC: 難道 (*nán dào* 难道). See Grammar Note 4.

勢 (势) *n.* terrace. MdnC: 地勢 (*dì shì* 地势).

然 *pron.* like this. MdnC: 這樣 (*zhè yàng* 这样). See Grammar Note 5 ③.

語法注釋 Grammar Notes

1. 者　　Six uses of 者 are explained in this book. In addition to the use below, see 者① in L1 Grammar Note 1, 者②③ in L4 Grammar Note 3, 者④ in L6 Grammar Note 8, and 者⑤ in L7 Grammar Note 3.

⑥ 有……者 means "there is the one who/which…." MdnC: 有 (*yǒu*) ……的人 (*de rén*), 有 (*yǒu*) ……的東西 (*de dōng xi* 的东西), 有 (*yǒu*) ……的情況 (*de qíng kuàng*).

齊人有一妻一妾而處室者……

[齐国有个和一个妻子一个小妾共同居住的人……]

是故所欲有甚於生者，所惡有甚於死者。(L7)

[所以人们想要的东西里有超越生命的，厌恶的东西里有超过死亡的。]

2. 夫   Three uses of 夫 are explained in this book. In addition to the use below, see 夫①② in
(fú)   L2 Grammar Note 4.

③ *ending particle.* used at the end of a sentence to sigh. MdnC: 啊 (*a*).

率天下之人而禍仁義者，必子之言夫！

[率领天下的人来祸害仁义的人，一定是您的言论啊！]

3. 諸   *particle.* contraction of 之乎 (or 之於): 之 is a pronoun, and 乎 (or 於) is a preposition
(诸)   here.

性猶湍水也，決諸東方則東流，決諸西方則西流。

[人性就像湍急的流水，在东边决口了，就向东流，在西边决口了，就向西流。]

4. 豈   *particle.* rhetorical question marker: why? how? MdnC: 難道 (*nán dào* 难道)，怎麼 (*zěn me* 怎
(岂)   么).

是豈水之性哉？

[这难道是水的本性吗？]

5. 然   Four uses of 然 are explained in this book. In addition to the use below, see 然①② in L5
Grammar Note 2 and 然④ in L10 Grammar Note 3.

③ *pron.* like this/that. MdnC: 這樣 (*zhè yàng* 这样)，那樣 (*nà yàng* 那样)，一樣 (*yí yàng* 一
样).

其勢則然也。

[它的形势迫使它这样的。]

Literary Analysis

The parable of the man who puts on airs before his wife and concubine while guilty of shameful acts out of their sight powerfully drives home the hypocrisy of wealth and status obtained by corrupt means. How might you relate this to the analogies employed in the passage describing the choice between fish and bear paws you read in lesson 7?

The structural analogies to wood and water seen in the final pair of passages constitute some of Mencius's most enduring statements on the intrinsic goodness of human nature. Designed to give Mencius the final word, it seems Gao Zi was simply at a loss for any rebuttal. Can you think of any ways that Gao Zi, given the chance, might have turned Mencius's cups-and-bowls analogy against him? If so, you might anticipate some of Xunzi's later analogies suggesting the basically deplorable state of unrefined human nature.

👉 *HTRCProse*, chapter 3, "Pre-Qin Philosophical Prose: Recorded Conversations and Argumentative Essays" for further comments on the *Mencius*, including a translation of the last of the preceding passages as well as 2A.2, in which Gao Zi also figures prominently; see also the comments on the *Xunzi* in the same chapter, where Xunzi's own use of analogies related to human nature is discussed.

—SC

課後練習 Exercises

一　給加點字注音　Give the pinyin romanization for each dotted word.

1. 杞柳 （____, ____）　2. 墦 （____）　3. 徧 （____）　4. 施從 （____）

5. 桮棬 （____, ____）　6. 祭 （____）　7. 顙 （____）　8. 戕賊 （____）

二　在括號中給句中加點的字注音，並選出正確的釋義　Give the pinyin romanization for each dotted word; then select the correct definition from the following list and write it in the blank.

饱(饱)食　偷偷看　幾(几)乎　湍急　決(决)口　**信服**　譏諷(讥讽)

使……濺起 (溅起)

1. 小信未孚 （ **fú** ）　**信服**　2. 饜足之道（　）_____　3. 訕其良人（　）_____

4. 搏而躍之 （　）_____　5. 幾希矣 （　）_____　6. 決諸東方（　）_____

7. 性猶湍水也（　）_____　8. 吾將瞷良人之所之（　）_____

三　選擇釋義並填空　Match each word in the left column with its correct definition in the middle column. Fill in each blank in the right column with an appropriate word from the left column.

謀謀劃（谋划）	回家	齊人有一妻一妾而____室者，其良人出，則必饜酒肉
處_____	看	而後____。
顯_____	稀少	問其與飲食者，盡富貴也，而未嘗有____者來。吾將
反_____	**謀劃（谋划）**	瞷良人之所之。
乞_____	顯貴（显贵）	卒之东郭墦间，之祭者，____其餘。不足，又____
顧_____	羞愧	而之他，此其爲饜足之道也。
達_____	率領（领）	由君子觀之，則人之所以求富貴利____者，其妻妾不
希_____	居住	____也，而不相泣者，幾____矣。
羞_____	禍(祸)害	___天下之人而____仁義者，必子之言夫！
率_____	乞討(讨)	
禍_____	顯達（显达）	

四　請用給出的字填空　Fill in each blank with an appropriate word from the following list (some words may be used more than once).

者　　之　　豈(岂)　以　　爲(为)　　如

1. 問其與飲食____，盡富貴也，而未嘗有顯____來。吾將瞷良人____ 所 ____。
2. 卒____东郭墦间，____祭____，乞其餘。不足，又顧而____他，此其____饜足之道也。
3. 由君子觀____，則人____所____求富貴利達____，其妻妾不羞也，而不相泣____，幾希矣。
4. ____將戕賊杞柳而____ ____桮棬，則將戕賊人____ ____仁義與？

五　爲加點字選擇正確釋義，並根據釋義來翻譯句子 Match each dotted word with its correct modern Chinese equivalent by circling the latter. Then translate each sentence into modern Chinese.

1. 又何間焉？　　　　　　　　　　ⓐ 爲什麼(为什么)　b. 憑什麼(凭什么)　c. 多少

現代文翻译：你又为什么要参与到这件事情里面？

_____

2. 其妻問所與飲食者，則盡富貴也。　　A. ……的人 b. ……的原因 c. ……的東西(东西)

現代文翻译：_____

3. 卒之东郭墦间，之祭者，乞其餘。　　　　　a. 的 b. 這(这) c. 到

現代文翻译：_____

4. 良人者，所仰望而終身也。　　　　a. 的 b. ……的人 c. ……是……

現代文翻译：_____

5. 是豈水之性哉？其勢則然也。　　　a. 可是 b. 難(难)道 c. 那麼(么)

現代文翻译：_____

6. 性猶湍水也，決諸東方則東流，決諸西方則西流。　　a. 之於(于) b. 即使 c. 如果

現代文翻译：_____

7. 率天下之人而禍仁義者，必子之言夫！　　a. 這(这) b. 發語詞(发语词) c. 啊

現代文翻译：_____

8. 人之可使爲不善，其性亦猶是也。　　　a. 爲(为)了 b. 做 c. 因爲(为)

現代文翻译：_____

單元練習

Unit Exercises

一、辨析加點字在不同句中注音和釋義的異同 Give the pinyin romanization for each dotted word, and then write in its correct definition.

1. 鄙　　肉食者鄙，未能遠謀。　　　　　　（ **bǐ** ）目光短浅
　　　越國以鄙遠，君知其難也。　　　　　（　　）＿＿＿＿＿

2. 樂　　有朋自遠方來，不亦樂乎？　　　　　（　　）＿＿＿＿＿
　　　如其禮樂，以俟君子。　　　　　　　（　　）＿＿＿＿＿

3. 威　　威天下不以兵革之利。　　　　　　　（　　）＿＿＿＿＿
　　　泰而不驕，威而不猛。　　　　　　　（　　）＿＿＿＿＿

4. 與　　蹴爾而與之，乞人不屑也。　　　　　（　　）＿＿＿＿＿
　　　夫子喟然嘆曰："吾與點也！"　　　　（　　）＿＿＿＿＿

5. 方　　方六七十，如五六十，求也爲之。　　（　　）＿＿＿＿＿
　　　比及三年，可使有勇，且知方也。　　（　　）＿＿＿＿＿

6. 惡　　尊五美，屏四惡。　　　　　　　　　（　　）＿＿＿＿＿
　　　所惡有甚於死者。　　　　　　　　　（　　）＿＿＿＿＿

7. 慢　　慢令致期謂之賊。　　　　　　　　　（　　）＿＿＿＿＿
　　　君子無眾寡、無小大、無敢慢。　　　（　　）＿＿＿＿＿

8. 乘　　千乘之國，攝乎大國之間。　　　　　（　　）＿＿＿＿＿
　　　公與之乘。　　　　　　　　　　　　（　　）＿＿＿＿＿

二、用給出的字填空，並選擇正確的釋義 Fill in the blanks with words from list A, and then write in their modern Chinese equivalents from list B.

A. Words for Filling the Blanks

慍	約	竭	屏	咎
攝	徧	哂	俟	撰
畔	處	卒	**鄙**	信

B. Modern Chinese Equivalents

微笑	背叛	最後(后)	生氣(气)	摒棄(弃)
等待	居住	確實(确实)	竭盡(尽)	夾(夹)
才能	走遍	咎醬(啬)	**目光短浅**	約(约)束

1. 肉食者 ＿＿鄙，未能遠謀。　　**[目光短浅]**　　2. ＿＿＿國中無與立談者。　　　　　[　　　　　]

3. 出納之＿＿＿＿，謂之有司。　[　　　] 　　4. 博我以文，＿＿＿＿我以禮。　[　　　]

5. 如其禮樂，以＿＿＿＿君子。　[　　　] 　　6. 齊人有一妻一妾而＿＿＿＿室者。　[　　　]

7. 寡助之至，親戚＿＿＿＿之。　[　　　] 　　8. 水＿＿＿＿無分於東西。　[　　　]

9. 異乎三子者之＿＿＿＿。　[　　　] 　　10. 既＿＿＿＿吾才，如有所立卓爾。　[　　　]

11. 夫子＿＿＿＿之。　[　　　] 　　12. 人不知而不＿＿＿＿，不亦君子乎。[　　　]

13. 尊五美，＿＿＿＿四惡。　[　　　] 　　14. 千乘之國，＿＿＿＿乎大國之間。　[　　　]

15. ＿＿＿＿之東郭墦間。　[　　　]

三、給加點字選擇正確的釋義，並選出與加點字用法相同的句子 Circle the letter of the correct definition (a, b, c, or d) for the dotted word in each boldfaced sentence. Then circle the letter of the sentence (A, B, C, or D) that employs the dotted word in the same way as the boldfaced sentence.

1. **臣之妻私臣。**　　　　　　a. 這(这)件事情　b. 他　ⓒ 的　d. 他們

    A. 夫晉，何厭之有？　　　　　　**B. 不闕秦，將焉取之？**

    C. 肉食者謀之，又何間焉？　　Ⓓ 能面刺寡人之過者，受上賞。

2. **子路率爾而對曰：……**　　a. 樣(样)子　b. 你　c. 而且　d. 你們(们)

    A. 以吾一日長乎爾，毋吾以也。　　B. 求，爾何如？

    C. 嘑爾而與之，行道之人弗受。　　D. 如或知爾，則何以哉？

3. **千乘之國，攝乎大國之間。**　a. 嗎(吗)　b. 比　c. 在　d. 呢

    A. 浴乎沂，風乎舞雩。　　　　　B. 以吾一日長乎爾，毋吾以也。

    C. 何傷乎？　　　　　　　　　　D. 有朋自遠方來，不亦樂乎？

4. **夫子循循然善誘人。**　　　a. 而且　b. 但是　c. 這樣(这样)　d. 樣(样)子

    A. 然鄭亡，子亦有不利焉？　　　B. 顏淵喟然嘆曰……

    C. 其勢則然也。　　　　　　　　D. 雖然，受地於先王，願終守之，弗敢易。

5. **天時不如地利。**　　　　　a. 至於(于)　b. 比　c. 如果　d. 或者

    A. 如使人之所欲莫甚於生……　　B. 方六七十，如五六十，求也為之。

    C. 如其禮樂，以俟君子。　　　　D. 臣之壯也，猶不如人。

6. **赤也為之小，孰能為之大？**　a. 為(为)了　b. 做　c. 因此　d. 治理

    A. 鄉為身死而不受……　　　　　B. 今為妻妾之奉為之。

    C. 是故為川者決之使導……　　　D. 為民者宣之使言。

7. **與其妾訕其良人。**　　　　a. 給(给)　b. 贊(赞)同　c. 跟　d. 嗎(吗)

    A. 失其所與，不知。　　　　　　B. 秦伯說，與鄭人盟。

C. 蹴爾而與之，乞人不屑也。　　　　D. 唯求則非邦也與？

8. **而未嘗有顯者來。**　　　a. ……是…… b. ……的人

　　　　　　　　　　　c. ……的原因 d. ……的東(东)西

A. 良人者，所仰望而終身也。　　　B. 二者不可得兼，舍魚而取熊掌者也。

C. 吾妻之美我者，私我也。　　　　D. 卒之東郭墦間，之祭者，乞其餘。

四、閱讀下面的段落，選擇正確的釋義 Read the following passage, and select the correct definition for each dotted word in the following list.

　　　　梁惠王曰：「寡人之於國也，盡心焉耳矣。河內凶，則移其民於河東，移其粟於河內。河東凶亦然。察鄰國之政，無如寡人之用心者。鄰國之民不加少，寡人之民不加多，何也？」孟子對曰：「王好戰，請以戰喻。填然鼓之，兵刃既接，棄甲曳兵而走。或百步而後止。或五十步而後止。以五十步笑百步，則何如？」曰：「不可！直不百步耳，是亦走也！」曰：「王如知此，則無望民之多於鄰國也。」

《孟子・梁惠王上》北京：中華書局 (2009), 5798.

梁惠王 King Hui of Liang (r. 369–319 BCE).

河 or 黃河 Yellow River. 　凶 *adj.* famine. 　加 *adv.* more.

好 (hào) *v.* to like, be fond of. 　喻 *v.* to make an analogy. 　填 onomatopoeia.

刃 *n.* blade. 　棄 (弃) *v.* to abandon. 　甲 n. shell, armor.

走 *v.* to run, escape. 　直 *adj.* a loanword of 只 (zhǐ), here meaning "only."

1. 河東凶亦然。　　　　a. 這樣(这样)　b. 但是　　c. 樣(样)子
2. 察鄰國之政。　　　　a. 找　　　　b. 望　　　c. 考察
3. 無如寡人之用心者。　a. 比　　　　b. 如果　　c. 或者
4. 無如寡人之用心者。　a. 的東(东)西　b. 的人　　c. 的時(时)候
5. 何也？　　　　　　　a. 怎麼(么)　　b. 多少　　c. 爲什麼(为什么)
6. 填然鼓之。　　　　　a. 這樣(这样)　b. 但是　　c. 樣(样)子
7. 兵刃既接。　　　　　a. 從(从)　　b. 已经　　c. 即使
8. 以五十步笑百步。　　a. 憑藉(凭借)　b. 而且　　c. 来
9. 是亦走也。　　　　　a. 這(这)　　b. 所以　　c. 是的
10. 王如知此。　　　　　a. 至於(于)　　b. 如果　　c. 或者

五、將下列句子翻譯成現代漢語 Translate the following sentences into modern Chinese.

1. 人不知而不慍，不亦君子乎？

現代文翻译：＿＿＿＿＿＿＿＿＿＿＿＿＿＿＿＿＿＿＿＿＿＿＿＿＿＿＿

2. 夫子循循然善誘人，博我以文，約我以禮，欲罷不能。

現代文翻译：＿＿＿＿＿＿＿＿＿＿＿＿＿＿＿＿＿＿＿＿＿＿＿＿＿＿＿

3. 因民之所利而利之，斯不亦惠而不費乎？擇可勞而勞之，又誰怨？欲仁而得仁，又焉貪？

現代文翻译：＿＿＿＿＿＿＿＿＿＿＿＿＿＿＿＿＿＿＿＿＿＿＿＿＿＿＿

4. 千乘之國，攝乎大國之間，加之以師旅，因之以飢饉。由也爲之，比及三年，可使有勇，且知方也。

現代文翻译：＿＿＿＿＿＿＿＿＿＿＿＿＿＿＿＿＿＿＿＿＿＿＿＿＿＿＿

5. 域民不以封疆之界，固國不以山谿之險，威天下不以兵革之利。得道者多助，失道者寡助。

現代文翻译：＿＿＿＿＿＿＿＿＿＿＿＿＿＿＿＿＿＿＿＿＿＿＿＿＿＿＿

6. 萬鍾則不辯禮義而受之，萬鍾於我何加焉？

現代文翻译：＿＿＿＿＿＿＿＿＿＿＿＿＿＿＿＿＿＿＿＿＿＿＿＿＿＿＿

7. 卒之東郭墦間，之祭者，乞其餘。不足，又顧而之他，此其爲饜足之道也。

現代文翻译：＿＿＿＿＿＿＿＿＿＿＿＿＿＿＿＿＿＿＿＿＿＿＿＿＿＿＿

8. 今夫水，搏而躍之，可使過顙；激而行之，可使在山。是豈水之性哉？其勢則然也。

現代文翻译：＿＿＿＿＿＿＿＿＿＿＿＿＿＿＿＿＿＿＿＿＿＿＿＿＿＿＿

第九課

《孫子・謀攻》

"Attacking Strategically," from the *Sunzi*

Introduction

The *Sunzi*, commonly translated as *The Art of War*, is the earliest extant Chinese treatise on war. Its authorship and dating are shrouded in uncertainty even now, attributed alternatively to the great general Sun Wu 孫武 (545–470 BCE) and the great military strategist Sun Bing 孫臏 (382–316 BCE). Recent archaeological discoveries at Yinqueshan 銀雀山 confirm the existence of two distinct texts, probably by different authors, that share an overlapping core on the fundamental principles of warfare: awareness of the psychological aspects of war, familiarity with different terrains, the ultimate goal of conquering an enemy without the use of force, and so on.

The *Sunzi* is celebrated for its terse, powerful statements, neatly wrought in parallel sentences. The following excerpt, "Attacking Strategically" 謀攻 ("Móugōng" 谋攻), compares various strategies of military offense and concludes that "one who is adept at using troops subdues the enemy's troops, but not through battle."

正文與簡體譯文 Text and Modern Chinese Translation

孫子曰：凡用兵之法，全國爲上，破國
sūn zǐ yuē　　fán yòng bīng zhī fǎ　quán guó wéi shàng　pò guó

次之；全軍爲上，破軍次之；全旅爲上，
cì　zhī　　quán jūn wéi shàng　pò jūn cì　zhī　　quán lǚ wéi shàng

破旅次之；全卒爲上，破卒次之；全伍爲
pò lǚ cì zhī　　quán zú wéi shàng　pò zú cì zhī　　quán wǔ wéi

上，破伍次之。[1] 是故百戰百勝，非善之善
shàng　pò wǔ cì zhī　　shì gù bǎi zhàn bǎi shèng　fēi shàn zhī shàn

者也；不戰而屈人之兵，善之善者也。[2]
zhě yě　　bú zhàn ér qū rén zhī bīng　　shàn zhī shàn zhě yě

孙子说："凡是战争(胜利)的原则是，使敌国全部投降(自己没有受到任何损伤)是上策；(用武力攻破)使敌国受到损害，就差一等。使敌人一个军的士兵全部投降是上策，用武力击破敌军就差一等。使敌人一个旅全部投降是上策，用武力击破敌人就差一等。使敌人一个卒全部投降是上策，用武力击破敌人就差一等。使敌人一个伍全部投降是上策，用武力击破敌人就差一等。[1]因此，百战百胜，不一定是高明的(军

事家中)最高明的人。不
交战就能使敌人的军队投
降，才是最高明的。[2]

1. 凡 *adv.* in general, overall. MdnC: 凡是 (*fán shì*). See L10 Grammar Note 4.

   兵 *n.* army, troops. MdnC: 軍隊 (*jūn duì* 军队). Here 用兵 means "war" 戰爭 (*zhàn zhēng* 战争).

   全 *adj.* complete. Here it is used as a causative verb, 使……全, meaning "to capture … intact." See L7 Grammar Note 1 ②.

   國 (国) *n.* state, country. Here it refers to the enemy's state 敵國 (*dí guó* 敌国).

   爲 (为 wéi) *v.* to be. MdnC: 是 (*shì*). See Grammar Note 1 ③.

   上 *adv.* above, up. Here it is a noun, meaning "the best plan" 上策 (*shàng cè*).

   破 *adj.* broken, damaged. Here it is used as a causative verb, 使……破, meaning "to make … broken." See L7 Grammar Note 1 ②.

   次 *n.* sequence, next. Here it is a verb, meaning "to be inferior or be second-rate" 差一等 (*chà yì děng*).

   軍 (军) *n.* an army in ancient China that consists of 12,500 soldiers.

   旅 *n.* a battalion that consists of five hundred soldiers.

   卒 *n.* a company that consists of one hundred soldiers.

   伍 *n.* a group that consists of five soldiers.

2. 是故 therefore, so. MdnC: 因此 (*yīn cǐ*). See L3 Grammar Note 1 ③.

   勝 (胜 shèng) *n.* victory. MdnC: 勝利 (*shèng lì* 胜利).

   善 *adj.* good, brilliant. MdnC: 高明 (*gāo míng*).

   之 *particle.* a possessive marker. MdnC: 的 (*de*). See L1 Grammar Note 2 ②.

   善者 *n.* the most brilliant general, the wisest general. See L1 Grammar Note 1 ① for 者.

   屈 *v.* to surrender. MdnC: 屈服 (*qū fú*). Here it means "to make … surrender" 使 (*shǐ*) ……屈服 (*qū fú*). See L7 Grammar Note 1 ①.

故上兵 a 伐謀，其次伐交，其次伐兵 b，
gù shàng bīng   fá móu   qí cì fá jiāo   qí cì fá bīng

其下攻城。[3] 攻城之法，爲不得已；修櫓轒
qí xià gōng chéng   gōng chéng zhī fǎ   wéi bù dé yǐ   xiū lǔ fén

輼，具器械，三月而後成；距闉，又三月而
wēn   jù qì xiè   sān yuè ér hòu chéng   jù yīn   yòu sān yuè ér

後已。[4] 將不勝其忿而蟻附之，殺士三分之
hòu yǐ   jiāng bù shēng qí fèn ér yǐ fù zhī   shā shì sān fēn zhī

一，而城不拔者，此攻之災也。[5]
yī   ér chéng bù bá zhě   cǐ gōng zhī zāi yě

所以最好的兵法是破坏
(敌人的)计谋，差一等
是破坏敌人(与别国)联
合，再差一等是攻打敌
人的军队，最下一等是
攻打敌人的城池。[3] 攻城
这一办法，是不得已
(才用的)。制造大盾牌
和战车，准备战争的装
备，要三个月之后才能
完成。堆积攻城用的土
山，又要三个月之后才
能完。[4] (如果)军队的将
领承受不了自己的愤怒
心情，(命令士兵)像蚂
蚁一样去爬上敌人的城
墙，三分之一的士兵因

此被杀，但是敌人的城池还没有被<u>占领</u>，这是攻城的<u>灾难</u>啊！[5]

3. 上 *adj.* best. MdnC: 最好的 (*zuì hǎo de*).

兵 ₐ *n.* strategy. MdnC: 兵法 (*bīng fǎ*).

伐 *v.* to attack, break. MdnC: 破壞 (*pò huài* 破坏), 攻打 (*gōng dǎ*).

謀 (谋) *n.* strategy, plan. MdnC: 計謀 (*jì móu* 计谋).

交 *v.* to befriend, join with. MdnC: 聯合 (*lián hé* 联合). Here it means "alliance."

兵 ᵦ *n.* army, troops. MdnC: 軍隊 (*jūn duì* 军队).

4. 爲 (为 *wéi*) *v.* to be. MdnC: 是 (*shì*). See Grammar Note 1 ③.

不得已 have no alternative but to, have to.

修 *v.* to make, produce. MdnC: 製造 (*zhì zào* 制造).

櫓 (橹) *n.* a large shield made of rattan. MdnC: 大盾牌 (*dà dùn pái*).

轒轀 *n.* an ancient chariot used to cover soldiers when attacking the enemy's city. MdnC: 戰車 (*zhàn chē* 战车).

具 *v.* to prepare. MdnC: 準備 (*zhǔn bèi* 准备).

器械 *n.* equipment. Here it refers to siege equipment or weapons.

闉 *n.* used in the sense of 堙 (*yīn*), meaning "mound."

距闉 *n.* earthworks.

已 *v.* to stop. MdnC: 停止 (*tíng zhǐ*). See L21 Grammar Note 1 ②.

5. 將 (将 *jiàng*) *n.* commander, general. MdnC: 將領 (*jiàng lǐng* 将领).

勝 (胜 *shēng*) *v.* to be able to bear, endure. MdnC: 承受 (*chéng shòu*).

忿 *n.* fury. MdnC: 憤怒 (*fèn nù* 愤怒).

蟻 (蚁) *n.* ants. MdnC: 螞蟻 (*mǎ yǐ* 蚂蚁). Here it means "like ants."

附 *v.* to attach. Here it means "to climb" 爬 (*pá*).

之 *demonstrative pron.* 之 refers to the wall of the enemy's city. MdnC: 城墙 (*chéng qiáng* 城墙). See L1 Grammar Note 2 ①.

士 *n.* soldiers. MdnC: 士兵 (*shì bīng*).

拔 *v.* to capture, seize. MdnC: 占領 (*zhàn lǐng* 占领).

災 (灾) *n.* disaster. MdnC: 災難 (*zāi nàn* 灾难).

故善用兵者，屈人之兵而非戰也，拔人
gù shàn yòng bīng zhě　qū rén zhī bīng ér fēi zhàn yě　　bá rén

之城而非攻也，毀人之國而非久也。[6]必以
zhī chéng ér fēi gōng yě　　huǐ rén zhī guó ér fēi jiǔ yě　　　bì yǐ

全爭於天下，故兵不頓而利可全，此謀攻之
quán zhēng yú tiān xià　gù bīng bú dùn ér lì kě quán　　cǐ móu gōng zhī

法也。[7]
fǎ yě

所以<u>擅长</u>用兵的人，使敌人的军队屈服投降，不是通过与敌人作战（来实现的）。占领敌人的城池，不是通过进攻敌人的城池来实现的。毁掉敌人的国家，不是通过<u>长时间</u>与敌国作战来实现的。[6]一定是用"全胜"的谋略来争胜于天下。这样兵力不会受到<u>挫伤</u>，而且<u>利益</u>可以保

全，这就是谋攻的方法。[7]

6. 毀 *v.* to destroy.

久 *adj.* long time. MdnC: 長時間 (*cháng shí jiān* 长时间).

7. 全 *adj.* complete. Here it refers to the best strategy—for example, 全國爲上.

爭 (争) *v.* to contend with. MdnC: 爭勝 (*zhēng sheng* 争胜).

兵 *n.* troops. MdnC: 兵力 (*bīng lì*).

頓 (顿) *v.* thwart. MdnC: 挫傷 (*cuò shāng* 挫伤).

利 *n.* gain. MdnC: 利益 (*lì yì*).

故用兵之法： 十則圍之， 五則攻之， 倍
gù yòng bīng zhī fǎ　　shí zé wéi zhī　　wǔ zé gōng zhī　　bèi

則分之， 敵則能戰之， 少則能逃之， 不若則
zé fēn zhī　　dí zé néng zhàn zhī　　shǎo zé néng táo zhī　　bú ruò zé

能避之。[8] 故小敵之堅， 大敵之擒也。[9]
néng bì zhī　　gù xiǎo dí zhī jiān　　dà dí zhī qín yě

所以用兵的方法是，（如果有敵人）十倍的兵力，就圍攻敵軍。有敵人五倍的兵力，就进攻敵軍。有敵人两倍的兵力，就分割敵軍（然后各个击破）。兵力与敵軍相匹敌，就与敵軍一战。兵力略少于敵軍，就逃离敌人。兵力不如敵軍，就要能避开敵軍。[8] 因此（敌对的双方），弱小的一方（如果）坚守（不躲避），（最后必会被）强大的一方捉住。[9]

8. 十 *number.* ten. Here it means "ten times" 十倍 (*shí bèi*).

圍 (围) *v.* to besiege. MdnC: 圍攻 (*wéi gōng* 围攻).

之 *personal pron.* 之 refers to the enemy. See L1 Grammar Note 2 ③.

五 *number.* five. Here it means "five times."

倍 *adj.* double. MdnC: 兩倍 (*liǎng bèi* 两倍).

分 (fēn) *v.* to break up. MdnC: 分割 (*fēn gē*).

敵 (敌) *adj.* equal to, a match for. MdnC: 匹敵 (*pǐ dí* 匹敌).

逃 *v.* to escape.

若 *v.* to be comparable (with/to). MdnC: 如 (*rú*). See L4 Grammar Note 4 ①.

避 *v.* to avoid. MdnC: 避開 (*bì kāi* 避开).

9. 敵 (敌) *n.* match, opponent, rivalry. MdnC: 敵手 (*dí shǒu* 敌手).

小敵 refers to the weak side of a rivalry.

大敵 refers to the strong side of a rivalry.

之 *particle.* a nominative marker. See L2 Grammar Note 2 ⑤.

堅 (坚) *adj.* resistant, durable. Here it refers to the situation in which the small force holds fast to its ground. MdnC: 堅守 (*jiān shǒu* 坚守).

擒 *v.* to capture, seize. MdnC: 捉住 (*zhuō zhù*).

夫將者，　國之輔也，　輔周則國必強，　輔
fú jiàng zhě　guó zhī fǔ yě　fǔ zhōu zé guó bì qiáng　fǔ

隙則國必弱。[10]
xì zé guó bì ruò

将帅是国家的<u>辅助</u>，　辅助得周密，则国家必然强大，辅助有<u>缺陷</u>，则国家必然变弱。[10]

10. 夫 (fú) *initial particle.* See L2 Grammar Note 4 ①.
　　將 (将 jiàng) *n.* general. MdnC: 將帥 (*jiàng shuài* 将帅).
　　……者……也 a construction of a declarative statement. MdnC: ……是…… (*shì*). See L4 Grammar Note 3 ③.
　　輔 (辅) *v.* to assist a ruler in governing a country. MdnC: 輔助 (*fǔ zhù* 辅助). Here it is a noun, referring to the person who assists a ruler.
　　周 *adj.* careful, thorough. MdnC: 周密 (*zhōu mì*).
　　隙 *n.* crack in a wall. Here it means "defect or flaw" 缺陷 (*quē xiàn*).

故君之ₐ所以患於軍者三：不知軍之ᵦ不
gù jūn zhī　suǒ yǐ huàn yú jūn zhě sān　bù zhī jūn zhī bù

可以進，而謂ₐ之꜀進；不知軍之不可以退，
kě yǐ jìn　ér wèi zhī jìn　bù zhī jūn zhī bù kě yǐ tuì

而謂之退，是謂ᵦ縻軍。[11] 不知三軍之事，而
ér wèi zhī tuì　shì wèi mí jūn　bù zhī sān jūn zhī shì　ér

同三軍之政者，則軍士惑矣。不知三軍之
tóng sān jūn zhī zhèng zhě zé jūn shì huò yǐ　bù zhī sān jūn zhī

權，而同三軍之任，則軍士疑矣。[12] 三軍既惑
quán　ér tóng sān jūn zhī rèn　zé jūn shì yí yǐ　sān jūn jì huò

且疑，則諸侯之難至矣，是謂亂軍引勝。[13]
qiě yí　zé zhū hóu zhī nàn zhì yǐ　shì wèi luàn jūn yǐn shèng

所以君王<u>危害</u>军队的情况有三种：不知道军队<u>不可以前进</u>时，命令军队前进；不知道军队不可以后退时，命令军队后退，这叫做<u>牵制</u>军队。[11] 不知道军队的事务，却要干涉军队的政务，那么军队的将士就会感到困惑。不知道军队的权变，却要干涉军队的指挥，那么军队的将士会有疑虑。[12] 军队既困惑又有疑虑，那么诸侯的进攻就会<u>降临</u>，这就是扰乱军队<u>夺走</u>胜利。[13]

11. 之ₐ所以……者 the situation of…. MdnC: ……的情况 (*de qíng kuàng*). See Grammar Note 2.
　　患 *n.* trouble, disaster. Here it is a verb, meaning "to make trouble" 危害 (*wēi hài*).
　　軍 (军) *n.* army, troops. MdnC: 軍隊 (*jūn duì* 军队).
　　之ᵦ *particle.* a nominative marker. See L2 Grammar Note 2 ⑤.
　　進 (进) *v.* to move forward, advance. MdnC: 前進 (*qián jìn* 前进).
　　謂ₐ (谓) *v.* to tell. Here it means "to command" 命令 (*mìng lìng*).
　　之꜀ *personal pron.* Here 之 refers to the army. See L1 Grammar Note 2 ③.
　　退 *v.* to move back, retreat. MdnC: 撤退 (*chè tuì*).
　　謂ᵦ (谓) *v.* to call. MdnC: 叫做 (*jiào zuò*).
　　縻 *v.* to tie up, pin down an enemy. MdnC: 牽制 (*qiān zhì*).

12. 三軍 (军) *n.* the army. MdnC: 軍隊 (*jūn duì* 军队).

　　同 *v.* to participate, intervene. MdnC: 干涉 (*gān shè*).

　　政 *n.* political affairs. MdnC: 政務 (*zhèng wù* 政务).

　　惑 *v.* to be confused. MdnC: 困惑 (*kùn huò*).

　　權 (权) *n.* power, authority. Here it refers to flexibility in tactics 權變 (*quán biàn* 权变).

　　任 *n.* duty, responsibility. Here it refers to command 指揮 (*zhǐ huī* 指挥).

　　疑 *v.* to have doubts, be uncertain about. MdnC: 有疑慮 (*yǒu yí lù* 有疑虑).

13. 既……且…… both … and…. MdnC: 既 (*jì*) ……又 (*yòu*) ……. See Grammar Note 3.

　　諸 (诸) 侯 *n.* territorial lords.

　　難 (难 *nàn*) *n.* trouble, disaster. Here it refers to the duke's attacks or invasion 進攻 (*jìn gōng* 进攻).

　　至 *v.* to arrive. MdnC: 降臨 (*jiàng lín* 降临).

　　亂 (乱) *v.* to throw into chaos. MdnC: 擾亂 (*rǎo luàn* 扰乱).

　　引 *v.* to retreat, draw back. Here it refers to taking (victory) away 奪走 (*duó zǒu* 夺走).

　　勝 (胜 *shèng*) *n.* victory, win. MdnC: 勝利 (*shèng lì* 胜利).

故知勝有五： 知可以戰與不可以戰者勝，
gù zhī shèng yǒu wǔ　 zhī kě yǐ zhàn yǔ　bù kě yǐ zhàn zhě shèng

識眾寡之用者勝，　上下同欲者勝，以虞待不
shí zhòng guǎ zhī yòng zhě shèng shàng xià tóng yù zhě shèng yǐ yú dài bù

虞者勝，將能而君不御者勝。¹⁴ 此五者，知勝
yú zhě shèng　jiàng néng ér jūn bú yù zhě shèng　　cǐ wǔ zhě　 zhī shèng

之道也。
zhī dào yě

所以知道胜利有五种情况：知道什么时候可以作战，什么时候不可以作战，就能取胜。懂得军队多或者军队少的不同用法，就能取胜。全国上下，全军上下心意相同，就能取胜。用有准备的军队对待没有准备的，就能取胜。将帅有指挥才能，而君主不干涉，能够取胜。¹⁴ 这五点，就是预知胜利的办法。

14. 者 *auxiliary pron.* the one who. See L1 Grammar Note 1 ①.

　　勝 (胜 *shèng*) *v.* to win. MdnC: 取勝 (*qǔ shèng* 取胜).

　　識 (识) *v.* to know, understand. MdnC: 懂得 (*dǒng dé*).

　　眾 (众) *adj.* numerous. MdnC: 多 (*duō*).

　　寡 *adj.* few, scant. MdnC: 少 (*shǎo*).

　　欲 *n.* desire. MdnC: 心愿 (*xīn yuàn*).

　　以 *coverb.* to use. MdnC: 用 (*yòng*). See L2 Grammar Note 1 ②.

　　虞 *v.* to expect. Here it means "to be well prepared." MdnC: 有準備的 (*yǒu zhǔn bèi de* 有准备的).

　　待 *v.* to treat. MdnC: 對待 (*duì dài* 对待).

　　將 (将 *jiàng*) *n.* general. MdnC: 將帥 (*jiàng shuài* 将帅).

　　御 *v.* to manage, govern. Here it means "to intervene" 干涉 (*gān shè*).

故曰：知彼知己者，百戰不殆；不知彼
gù yuē　zhī bǐ zhī jǐ zhě　bǎi zhàn bù dài　bù zhī bǐ

而知己，一勝一負；不知彼，不知己，每戰
ér zhī jǐ　yí shèng yí fù　bù zhī bǐ　bù zhī jǐ　měi zhàn

必殆。¹⁵
bì dài

所以说，了解对手了解自己，百战都没有危险；不了解对手，但了解自己，可能一场胜利，一场失败；不了解对手，不了解自己，每场战斗都会很危险。¹⁵

《十一家注孫子校理》，北京：中華書局 (1999), 44–63.

15. 彼 *demonstrative pron.* those, indicating opponents or enemies. MdnC: 對手 (*duì shǒu* 对手). See L14 Grammar Note 2 ①.

己 *n.* self. MdnC: 自己 (*zì jǐ*).

殆 *n.* danger. MdnC: 危險 (*wēi xiǎn* 危险).

負 (负) *v.* to lose. MdnC: 失敗 (*shī bài* 失败).

語法注釋 Grammar Notes

1. 爲 (为)　Five uses of 爲 are explained in this book. In addition to the use below, see 爲① in L2 Grammar Note 6, 爲② in L7 Grammar Note 5, 爲④ in L11 Grammar Note 4, and 爲⑤ in L21 Grammar Note 3.

　③ **wéi** *v.* to be. MdnC: 是 (*shì*).

　　攻城之法，爲不得已。

　　　[攻打敌人的城池，是不得已（才去做的）。]

2. 之所以……者　the way of…, the situation of…, the reason of…. MdnC: ……的方法 (*de fāng fǎ*), ……的情况 (*de qíng kuàng*), ……的原因 (*de yuán yīn*).

　　故君之所以患於軍者三……

　　　[所以君王危害军队的情况有三种……]

　　人之所以求富貴利達者，其妻妾不羞也，而不相泣者，幾希矣。(L8)

　　　[人们用来追求富贵利益和显达的社会地位的方法，能让他们的妻子小妾不感到羞愧，不在院子中哭泣，是很少见的。]

3. 既……且……　both … and…. Used to join two adjectives or descriptive phrases. MdnC: 既 (*jì*) ……又 (*yòu*) …….

　　三軍既惑且疑，則諸侯之難至矣，……

　　　[军队既困惑又有疑虑，那么诸侯的进攻就会降临，……]

Literary Analysis

1. What does knowledge (*zhī* 知, *shí* 識, etc.) have to do with battle? What are the most important characteristics of a commander, and why do they have nothing to do with physical talent or training?

2. How do the ideals of this passage compare with conceptions of martial skill in other traditions (both in China and beyond)? Why is 百戰百勝，非善之善者也 not an expression of pacifism? And what is wrong with besieging cities?

3. How does the literary style of this text, with its tight parallel phrases and bold, arresting declarations, suit the argument? Does it suggest real combat experience on the part of the author? Why or why not?

—PRG

課後練習 Exercises

一 給加點字注音 Give the pinyin romanization for each dotted word.

1. 旅 (＿＿＿)　2. 伍 (＿＿＿)　3. 轒輼 (＿＿＿, ＿＿＿)　4. 器械 (＿＿＿, ＿＿＿)
5. 卒 (＿＿＿)　6. 櫓 (＿＿＿)　7. 距闉 (＿＿＿, ＿＿＿)　8. 蟻附 (＿＿＿, ＿＿＿)

二 在括號中給句中加點的字注音，並選出正確的釋義 Give the pinyin romanization for each dotted word; then select the correct definition from the following list, and write it in the blank.

缺陷　承受　捉住　有准備(備)　助手　牽(牽)制
信服　破壞(坏)　危險(險)　堅(堅)守

1. **小信未孚**（ fú ）　　**信服**　　2. 百戰不殆（ ）＿＿＿＿＿＿　3. 上兵伐謀（ ）＿＿＿＿＿＿
4. 小敵之堅（ ）＿＿＿＿＿＿　　5. 大敵之擒（ ）＿＿＿＿＿＿　6. 是謂縻軍（ ）＿＿＿＿＿＿
7. 將不勝其忿而蟻附之（ ）＿＿＿＿＿＿　　8. 輔隙則國必弱　（ ）＿＿＿＿＿＿
9. 國之輔也　　　　　　　（ ）＿＿＿＿＿＿　10. 以虞待不虞者勝（ ）＿＿＿＿＿＿

三 選擇釋義並填空 Match each word in the left column with its correct definition in the middle column. Fill in each blank in the right column with an appropriate word from the left column (some words may be used more than once).

謀謀劃（谋划）	挫傷(挫伤)
交＿＿＿＿	製造(制造)
修＿＿＿＿	危害
具＿＿＿＿	疑慮(虑)
拔＿＿＿＿	困惑
頓＿＿＿＿	屈服
患＿＿＿＿	**謀劃（谋划）**
惑＿＿＿＿	奪(夺)走
久＿＿＿＿	周密
引＿＿＿＿	聯合(联合)
屈＿＿＿＿	準備(准备)

故上兵伐謀，其次伐＿＿＿＿，其次伐兵，其下攻城。攻城之法，爲不得已；＿＿＿＿櫓轒，＿＿＿＿器械，三月而後成。

故善用兵者，＿＿＿＿人之兵而非戰也，＿＿＿＿人之城而非攻也，毀人之國而非＿＿＿＿也。必以全＿＿＿＿於天下，故兵不＿＿＿＿而利可全，此＿＿＿＿攻之法也。

故君之所以＿＿＿＿於軍者三。

不知三軍之事，而同三軍之政者，則軍士＿＿＿＿矣。不知三軍之權，而同三軍之＿＿＿＿，則軍士＿＿＿＿矣。三軍

爭_____	攻下
周_____	指揮
任_____	爭勝(争胜)
疑_____	長時間(长时间)

既____且____，則諸侯之難至矣，是謂亂軍____勝。

夫將者，國之輔也，輔____則國必強，輔隙則國必弱。

四 請用給出的字填空 Fill in each blank with an appropriate word from the following list (some words may be used more than once).

凡　是　者　之　以　為(为)　則(则)　與(与)

1. ____用兵之法，全國____上，破國次____。

2. ____故，百戰百勝，非善____善____也；不戰而屈人____兵，善____善____也。

3. 十____圍____，五____攻____，倍____分____，敵____能戰____，少____能逃____，五不若____能避____。

4. 知可____戰____不可____戰____勝，識眾寡____用____勝，上下同欲____勝，____虞待不虞____勝，將能而君不御____勝。

五 為加點字選擇正確釋義，並根據釋義來翻譯句子 Match each dotted word with its correct modern Chinese equivalent by circling the latter. Then translate each sentence into modern Chinese.

1. 又何間焉?　　　　　　　　　ⓐ.為什麼(为什么) b.憑什麼(凭什么) c.多少

现代文翻译：你又为什么要参与到这件事情里面？

_____

2. 凡用兵之法：全國為上，破國次之。　　　a.平凡 b.都 c.凡是

现代文翻译：_____

3. 不戰而屈人之兵，善之善者也。　　　a.使……屈服 b.委屈 c.彎(弯)曲

现代文翻译：_____

4. 是故百戰百勝，非善之善者也。　　　a.因此 b.因為(为) c.可是

现代文翻译：_____

5. 不知三軍之權，而同三軍之任，則軍士疑矣。　　　a.雖(虽)然 b.那麼(么) c.但是

现代文翻译：_____

6. 三軍既惑且疑，則諸侯之難至矣，是謂亂軍引勝。　　　a. 已經（经）　b. 既然　c. 既……又……

现代文翻译：_____

7. 知己知彼者，百戰不殆。　　　　　　　　　　　　　　　a. ……人　b. ……事　c. …… 的情況

现代文翻译：_____

第十課

《荀子・性惡篇》節選

"Human Nature Is Deplorable," Excerpt from the *Xunzi*

Introduction

The *Xunzi* is a collection of argumentative essays attributed to Xun Kuang (ca. 316–ca. 237 BCE), a Confucian philosopher of the late Warring States period, also known as Xunzi. Though a contemporary of Mencius, Xunzi develops Confucian thought along a considerably different path from Mencius. Their views of human nature are diametrically opposed, as Xunzi claims that human beings are born evil and become good only through rituals and education. His view of the past is also different: he valorizes later kings (such as King Wen, King Wu, and Duke Zhou of the Zhou dynasty) rather than reserving his praise only for the legendary ancient kings, as Mencius does. Another distinctive feature of Xunzi's political thought is his endorsement of strict laws of reward and punishment primarily intended to secure the ruler's absolute authority. His position is generally thought to have influenced Qin Legalist thinking, and this affinity with Legalism is probably why the *Xunzi* was excluded from the Confucian canon and even from mainstream Confucianism until the Qing dynasty.

In this excerpt, Xunzi refutes, point by point, Mencius's view of inborn human goodness until he reaches the conclusion that all human goodness, instead of being innate, is acquired through moral education and ritual discipline. Xunzi's prose is renowned for its masterful deployment of textual patterning to facilitate analytical reasoning.

正文與簡體譯文 Text and Modern Chinese Translation

人之性惡，其善者偽也。[1] 今人之性，生
rén zhī xìng è　　 qí shàn zhě wěi yě　　 jīn rén zhī xìng　shēng

而有好利焉，順是，故爭奪生而辭讓亡焉；[2]
ér yǒu hào lì yān　 shùn shì　 gù zhēng duó shēng ér cí ràng wáng yān

生而有疾惡焉，順是，故殘賊生而忠信亡
shēng ér yǒu jí wù yān　　 shùn shì　 gù cán zéi shēng ér zhōng xìn wáng

焉；[3] 生而有耳目之欲，有好聲色焉，順是，
yān　　 shēng ér yǒu ěr mù zhī yù　　 yǒu hào shēng sè yān　 shùn shì

故淫亂生而禮義文理亡焉。[4]
gù yín luàn shēng ér lǐ yì wén lǐ wáng yān

人的本性是不好的，它好的一面是人为做出来的。[1] 现在人的本性，一出生就喜欢利益啊！顺着这个本性，争抢和掠夺就产生了，而推辞和谦让就消失了；[2] 人一出生就会嫉恨和厌恶别人啊！顺着这个本性，于是残害（别人的事）就产生了，而忠诚和信任就消失了；[3] 人一出生就有耳朵和眼睛的本能欲望，喜欢（美

妙的）声音和颜色啊！顺着这个本性，于是淫荡、混乱就产生了，而礼义条理就消失了！[4]

1. 性 *n.* human nature. MdnC: 本性 (*běn xìng*).

  惡 (恶 *è*) *adj.* bad, evil, deplorable. MdnC: 不好 (*bù hǎo*).

  善 *adj.* good.

  僞 *adj.* man-made, contrived. MdnC: 人爲 (*rén wéi* 人为).

2. 生 ₐ *v.* to be born. MdnC: 出生 (*chū shēng*).

  好 (hào) *v.* to like, be fond of, desire. MdnC: 喜歡 (*xǐ huāng* 喜欢).

  利 *n.* benefit, profit. MdnC: 利益 (*lì yì*).

  爲 *ending particle.* MdnC: 啊 (*a*). See L2 Grammar Note 3 ②.

  順 (顺) *v.* to go along with, accept. MdnC: 順著 (*shùn zhe* 顺着).

  是 *demonstrative pron.* this, referring to one's human nature. See L3 Grammar Note 1 ①.

  爭 *v.* to contend for, fight for. MdnC: 爭搶 (*zhēng qiǎng* 争抢).

  奪 (夺) *v.* to take by force. MdnC: 掠奪 (*lüè duó* 掠夺).

  生 ᵦ *v.* to come into being. MdnC: 產生 (*chǎn shēng* 产生).

  辭 (辞) *v.* to decline. MdnC: 推辭 (*tuī cí* 推辞).

  讓 (让) *v.* to yield, modestly decline. MdnC: 謙讓 (*qiān ràng* 谦让).

  亡 *v.* to lose, be absent. MdnC: 消失 (*xiāo shī*).

3. 疾 *n.* illness. Here it is used in the sense of 嫉 (*jí*), meaning "to envy and hate" 嫉恨 (*jí hèn*).

  惡 (恶 *wù*) *v.* to dislike, hate. MdnC: 厭惡 (*yàn wù* 厌恶).

  殘賊 (残贼) *v.* to injure, kill, harm. MdnC: 殘害 (*cán hài* 残害).

  忠 *adj.* loyal. MdnC: 忠誠 (*zhōng chéng* 忠诚).

  信 *v.* to trust. MdnC: 信任 (*xìn rèn*).

4. 聲 *n.* sound. MdnC: 聲音 (*shēng yīn* 声音).

  色 *n.* color, beauty. MdnC: 顏色 (*yán sè* 颜色).

  淫 *adj.* licentious. MdnC: 淫蕩 (*yín dàng* 淫荡).

  亂 (乱) *adj.* chaotic, disorderly. MdnC: 混亂 (*hùn luàn* 混乱).

  文 *n.* pattern. Here it means "ritual" 禮義 (*lǐ yì* 礼义).

  理 *n.* order, principle, reason. MdnC: 條理 (*tiáo lǐ* 条理).

然則從人之性，順人之情，必出於爭
rán zé zòng rén zhī xìng　shùn rén zhī qíng　　bì chū yú zhēng

奪，合於犯分亂理而歸於暴。[5] 故必將有師法
duó　　hé yú fàn fèn luàn lǐ ér　guī yú bào　　　gù bì jiāng yǒu shī fǎ

之化，禮義之道，然後出於辭讓，合於文
zhī huà　　lǐ yì zhī dǎo　　rán hòu chū yú cí ràng　　hé yú wén

理，而歸於治。[6] 用此觀之，然則人之性惡明
lǐ　　ér　guī yú zhì　　　yòng cǐ guān zhī　　rán zé rén zhī xìng è míng

既然如此，那么放纵人的本性，顺着人的喜好，必然会生出争抢和掠夺，（会有与）违犯名分等级、扰乱条理相符合（的行为），从而（使社会）趋向于暴乱。[5] 所以一定要有老师和法度（对人的）教化，礼义的引导，然后产生出推辞

矣，其善者偽也。[7]

yǐ　　qí shàn zhě wěi yě

和谦让，符合礼义和条理，从而使社会趋向于安定。[6]由此看来，人的本性不好是很清楚的，人的善良是人为出来的。[7]

5. 然則 (则) *conj.* if it is so, then…. MdnC: 既然如此，那麼 (*jì rán rú cǐ nà me* 那么). See Grammar Note 1.

從 (从) *v.* to follow. Here it is used in the sense of 縱 (*zòng* 纵), meaning "to indulge or give free rein to" 放縱 (*fàng zòng* 放纵).

情 *n.* affection, feeling. MdnC: 喜好 (*xǐ hào*).

合 *v.* to coincide with. MdnC: 符合 (*fú hé*).

犯 *v.* to violate. MdnC: 違犯 (*wéi fàn* 违犯).

分 (fèn) *n.* allocated duty, assignment. MdnC: 名分 (*míng fèn*).

歸 (归) *v.* to tend to, incline to. MdnC: 趨向 (*qū xiàng* 趋向).

暴 (暴) *n.* violence. MdnC: 暴亂 (*bào luàn* 暴乱).

6. 師 *n.* teacher. MdnC: 老師 (*lǎo shī* 老师).

法 *n.* law, standard, regulation. MdnC: 法度 (*fǎ dù*).

化 *v.* to transform. MdnC: 教化 (*jiào huà*).

道 *n.* way. Here it is used in the sense of 導 (*dǎo*), meaning "to guide" 引導 (*yǐn dǎo* 引导).

治 *n.* order. MdnC: 安定 (*ān dìng*).

7. 明 *adj.* clear, obvious. MdnC: 清楚 (*qīng chǔ*).

故枸木必將待檃栝、烝、矯然後直；鈍

gù gōu mù bì jiāng dài yǐn guā　zhēng　jiǎo rán hòu zhí　dùn

金必將待礱、厲然後利。[8]今人之性惡，必將

jīn bì jiāng dài lóng　lì rán hòu lì　jīn rén zhī xìng è　bì jiāng

待師法然後正，得禮義然後治。今人無師法

dài shī fǎ rán hòu zhèng　dé lǐ yì rán hòu zhì　jīn rén wú shī fǎ

則偏險而不正，無禮義則悖亂而不治。[9]古者

zé piān xiǎn ér bú zhèng　wú lǐ yì zé bèi luàn ér bú zhì　gǔ zhě

聖王以ₐ人之性惡，以爲偏險而不正，悖亂而

shèng wáng yǐ rén zhī xìng è　yǐ wéi piān xiǎn ér bú zhèng　bèi luàn ér

不治，是以爲之起禮義，制法度，以ᵦ矯飾

bú zhì　shì yǐ wèi zhī qǐ lǐ yì　zhì fǎ dù　yǐ jiǎo shì

人之情性而正之，以擾化人之情性而導之

rén zhī qíng xìng ér zhèng zhī　yǐ rǎo huà rén zhī qíng xìng ér dǎo zhī

所以弯曲的木头必定要等到用火烤，用工具矫正，然后才变成直的；不锋利的金属一定要等到磨过，然后才变得锋利。[8]现在人的本性不好，一定要等到老师法度教化，然后才能端正，得到礼义的引导，然后社会才能安定。现在没有老师和法度，人心偏颇险恶而不端正，没有礼义引导，人们互相冲突，社会混乱而不安定。[9]古时候圣明的君王认为人的本性不好，认为人性偏颇险恶而不端正，人们互相冲突混乱，社会不安定。因此

也。[10] 始皆出於治，合於道者也。今之人，化
yě　　　shǐ jiē chū yú zhì　　hé yú dào zhě yě　　jīn zhī rén　　huà

師法，積文學，道禮義者爲君子；縱性情，
shī fǎ　　jī wén xué　　dào lǐ yì zhě wéi jūn zǐ　　zòng xìng qíng

安恣睢，而違禮義者爲小人。[11] 用此觀之，
ān zì suī　　ér wéi lǐ yì zhě wéi xiǎo rén　　yòng cǐ guān zhī

然則人之性惡明矣，其善者僞也。
rán zé rén zhī xìng è míng yǐ　　qí shàn zhě wěi yě

（圣王）为人们建立礼义，制定法度，来矫正整饬人的喜好本性，使其变得端正，来驯服教化人的情性，从而引导他们。[10]（使他们能）开始从社会安定（的角度）出发，符合（正确）的道理。现在的人，接受老师和法度的教化，积累文献经典（的知识），遵行礼义的人成为君子；放纵本性喜好，习惯恣意狂妄，而且违反礼义的人成为小人。[11] 由此来看，人本性是邪恶的是很清楚的，他善良的（一面）是人为的。

8. 枸 (gōu) *adj.* curved, crooked. MdnC: 彎曲 (*wān qū* 弯曲).

   待 *v.* to wait, rely on. MdnC: 等 (*děng*).

   檃栝 *n.* a machine used to straighten curved wood.

   烝 *v.* to heat wood with fire in order to soften it. MdnC: 用火烤 (*yòng huǒ kǎo*).

   矯 (矫) *v.* to bend, mold. MdnC: 矯正 (*jiǎo zhèng* 矫正).

   鈍 (钝) *adj.* dull. MdnC: 不鋒利 (*bù fēng lì* 不锋利).

   礱 (砻) *v.* to grind, sharpen. MdnC: 磨 (*mó*).

   厲 (厉) *v.* to sharpen. MdnC: 磨 (*mó*).

   利 *adj.* sharp. MdnC: 鋒利 (*fēng lì* 锋利).

9. 正 *adj.* right, proper, correct. MdnC: 端正 (*duān zhèng*).

   偏 *adj.* inclined to one side, partial, prejudiced. MdnC: 偏頗 (*piān pō* 偏颇).

   險 (险) *adj.* sinister, vicious, venomous. MdnC: 險惡 (*xiǎn è* 险恶).

   悖 *v.* to be contradictory to, go against. MdnC: 互相衝突 (*hù xiāng chōng tū* 互相冲突).

10. 者 *auxiliary pron.* the time when…. MdnC: ……的時候 (*de shí hou* 的时候). See L6 Grammar Note 8 ④.

   聖 (圣) *adj.* holy, sage.

   以 ₐ *v.* to think, regard. MdnC: 認爲 (*rèn wéi* 认为). See Grammar Note 2 ⑤.

   是以 for this reason, therefore. MdnC: 因此 (*yīn cǐ*). See L3 Grammar Note 1 ③.

   爲 (为 wèi) *prep.* because of, for. MdnC: 爲了 (*wèi le* 为了). See L7 Grammar Note 5 ②.

   起 *v.* to build, produce. MdnC: 建立 (*jiàn lì*).

   制 *v.* to formulate, draw up. MdnC: 制定 (*zhì dìng*).

   以 ᵦ *conj.* in order to. MdnC: 來 (*lái* 来). See L2 Grammar Note 1 ③.

   矯 (矫) *v.* to rectify, set right, straighten out. MdnC: 矯正 (*jiǎo zhèng*).

   飾 (饰) *v.* to decorate. Here it is used in the sense of 飭 (*chì* 饬), meaning "to straighten up or put in order" 整飭 (*zhěng chì* 整饬).

擾 (扰) *v.* to tame, to make docile or tractable. MdnC: 馴服 (*xùn fú* 驯服).

11. 始 *v.* to begin, start. MdnC: 開始 (*kāi shǐ* 开始).

積 (积) *v.* to accumulate, collect. MdnC: 積纍 (*jī lěi* 积累).

文學 (学) *n.* literature and classics. MdnC: 文獻經典 (*wén xiàn jīng diǎn* 文献经典).

道 *n.* path, way. Here it is used as a verb, meaning "taking the path of" 遵行 (*zūn xíng*).

縱 (纵) *v.* to give free rein to, indulge in. MdnC: 放縱 (*fàng zòng* 放纵).

安 *v.* to satisfy. Here it means "to be used to" 習慣 (*xí guàn* 习惯).

恣睢 *adj.* uncontrolled. MdnC: 狂妄 (*kuáng wàng*).

孟子曰：「人之學者，其性善。」[12]
mèng zǐ yuē　　rén zhī xuézhě　　qí xìng shàn

曰：是不然。是不及知人之性，而不察
yuē　　shì bù rán　　shì bù jí zhī rén zhī xìng　　ér bù chá

乎人之性、偽之分者也。[13] 凡性者，天之就
hū rén zhī xìng　　wěi zhī fēn zhě yě　　fán xìng zhě　　tiān zhī jiù

也，不可學，不可事。[14] 禮義者，聖人之所
yě　　bù kě xué　　bù kě shì　　lǐ yì zhě　　shèng rén zhī suǒ

生也，人之所學而能，所事而成者也。不可
shēng yě　　rén zhī suǒ xué ér néng　　suǒ shì ér chéng zhě yě　　bù kě

學、不可事而在人者謂之性，可學而能、可
xué　　bù kě shì　　ér zài rén zhě　　wèi zhī xìng　　kě xué ér néng　　kě

事而成之在人者謂之偽。是性、偽之分也。
shì ér chéng zhī zài rén zhě wèi zhī wěi　　shì xìng　　wěi zhī fēn　yě

今人之性，目可以見，耳可以聽。夫可以見
jīn rén zhī xìng　　mù kě yǐ jiàn　　ěr kě yǐ tīng　　fú kě yǐ jiàn

之明不離目，可以聽之聰不離耳，目明而耳
zhī míng bù lí mù　　kě yǐ tīng zhī cōng bù lí ěr　　mù míng ér ěr

聰，不可學明矣。[15]
cōng　　bù kě xué míng yǐ

孟子说："人们学习的，是人本性的善良。"[12]

（我）说："这是不对的。这是不够了解人的本性，而且没有考察人的天性和后天人为的不同。"[13] 凡是人的本性，都是天生造就的，不可以学到，不可以（通过人为）做到的。[14] 礼义是圣人制造出来的，人学习了才能会，做了才可以完成的。在人身上，不可以学到，不可以做成的，是本性；人可以学会，可以做成的，就是人为。这是本性和人为的不同。现在人的本性，眼睛可以看到，耳朵可以听到。那么可以看见东西的视力离不开眼睛，可以听到的听力离不开耳朵。眼睛的视力和耳朵的听力，不可通过学习而达到，是很清楚的。[15]

《荀子集解》，北京：中華書局 (1988), 434–436.

12. 之 *particle.* a nominative marker. See L2 Grammar Note 2 ⑤.

者 *auxiliary pron.* the one which. See L1 Grammar Note 1 ①.

13. 是 *pron.* this point. MdnC: 這 (*zhè* 这). See L3 Grammar Note 1 ①.

然 *adj.* it is so. MdnC: 對 (*duì* 对). See Grammar Note 3 ④.

及 *v.* to reach, get to. MdnC: 達到 (*dá dào* 达到).

察 *v.* to investigate, examine. MdnC: 考察 (*kǎo chá*).

分 (fēn) *n.* difference. MdnC: 不同 (*bù tóng*).

14. 就 *v.* to accomplish. MdnC: 造就 (*zào jiù*).

事 *v.* to do, work at. MdnC: 做 (*zuò*).

15. 明 *n.* vision, sight. MdnC: 視力 (*shì lì* 视力).

離 (离) *v.* to leave. MdnC: 離開 (*lí kāi* 离开).

聰 (聪) *n.* hearing. MdnC: 聽力 (*tīng lì* 听力).

語法注釋 Grammar Notes

1. 然則 *conj.* if it is so, then…. MdnC: 既然如此，那麼 (*jì rán rú cǐ nà me* 那么).

然則從人之性，順人之情，必出於争奪……

[既然如此，那么放纵人的本性，顺着人的喜好，必然会生出争抢和掠夺……

用此觀之，然則人之性惡明矣。

[由此看来，既然如此，那么人的本性是邪恶的是很清楚的。]

2. 以 Six uses of 以 are explained in this book. In addition to the use below, see 以①②③④ in L2 Grammar Note 1 and 以⑥ in L18 Grammar Note 4.

⑤ *v.* to think, regard. MdnC: 認爲 (*rèn wéi* 认为), 以爲 (*yǐ wéi* 以为).

古者聖王以人性惡……

[古时候圣明的君王认为人性是邪恶的……]

3. 然 Four uses of 然 are explained in this book. In addition to the use below, see 然①② in L5 Grammar Note 2 and 然③ in L8 Grammar Note 5.

④ *adj.* it is so, all right. MdnC: 是的 (*shì de*), 對 (*duì* 对).

曰：是不然，……

[（荀子）说：这不对，……]

4. 凡 *adv.* all, overall, in general. MdnC: 凡是 (*fán shì*).

凡性者，天之就也，不可學，不可事。

[凡是人的本性，都是天生造就的，不可以学到，不可以（通过人为）做到的。]

Literary Analysis

Mencius and Xunzi clearly held diametrically different views of human nature, but what does this entail in practice? Xunzi finds study of the canonical works and practices of the ancient sages indispensable for the proper refinement of human nature—but does Mencius have no use for such things? If, for Mencius, people are basically good at birth, does this mean we have no need for study? What exactly is at stake in this debate?

In what ways does Xunzi employ analogies to make his arguments about human nature? How might these relate to analogies employed, to opposite ends, by Mencius before him? What does Xunzi gain, and what does he lose, by laying this out in the form of an essay rather than a staged dialogue with a philosophical rival? (See also the *Mencius* examples in lessons 7 and 8.)

☞ *HTRCProse*, chapter 3, "Pre-Qin Philosophical Prose: Recorded Conversations and Argumentative Essays" for further comments on the *Xunzi* (along with the *Mencius*) as it relates to some of these issues as well as a complete translation of the excerpt here.

—SC

課後練習 Exercises

一　給加點字注音　Give the pinyin romanization for each dotted word.

1. 歸於暴　（＿＿）　2. 檃栝　（＿＿, ＿＿）　3. 烝　（＿＿）　4. 礱　（＿＿）　5. 恣睢　（＿＿, ＿＿）

二　在括號中給句中加點的字注音，並選出正確的釋義　Give the pinyin romanization for each dotted word; then select the correct definition from the following list, and write it in the blank.

彎(弯)曲　　人爲(为)　　整飭(饬)　　不鋒(锋)利　　**信服**　　放縱(纵)　　矯(矫)正　　嫉妒

1. **小信未孚　（fú）　　信服**　　2. 鈍金　（　）　　　　　　3. 其善偽也　（　）　　　　
4. 枸木　　（　）　　　　　5. 矯飾　（　）　　　　　　6. 矯飾　　（　）　　　　
7. 從人之性　（　）　　　　　8. 生而有疾惡焉　（　）　　　　

三　選擇釋義並填空　Match each word in the left column with its correct definition in the middle column. Fill in each blank in the right column with an appropriate word from the left column (some words may be used more than once).

謀謀劃(谋划)	殘(残)害	今人之性，生而有好利焉，順是，故爭奪生而＿＿＿亡焉。生而有疾惡焉，順是，故殘＿＿＿生而忠信亡焉。
辭＿＿＿＿＿	符合	
讓＿＿＿＿＿	馴(驯)服	然則從人之性，順人之情，必出於爭奪，＿＿＿於分亂理而歸於暴。故必將有師法之化，禮義之道，然後出於＿＿＿＿，＿＿＿於文理，而歸於＿＿＿。
賊＿＿＿＿＿	端正	
合＿＿＿＿＿	**謀劃(谋划)**	
犯＿＿＿＿＿	造就	是以爲之＿＿＿禮義，制法度，以矯飾人之情性而＿＿＿之，以＿＿＿化人之情性而導之也。始皆出於＿＿＿，＿＿＿於道者也。
治＿＿＿＿＿	推辭(辞)	
正＿＿＿＿＿	違(违)犯	
起＿＿＿＿＿	聽(听)力	凡性者，天之＿＿＿也，不可學，不可事。
擾＿＿＿＿＿	視(视)力	
就＿＿＿＿＿	制定	夫可以見之＿＿＿不離目，可以聽之＿＿＿不離耳。
明＿＿＿＿＿	謙讓(谦让)	
聰＿＿＿＿＿	安定	

四 請用給出的字填空 Fill in each blank with an appropriate word from the following list (some words may be used more than once).

焉　者　是　之　其　凡　然　則(则)

1. 今人____性，生而有好利____，順____，故爭奪生而辭讓亡____。

2. 用此觀____，____ ____人____性惡明矣，____善____偽也。

3. ____性____，天____就也，不可學，不可事。

五 爲加點字選擇正確釋義，並根據釋義來翻譯句子 Match each dotted word with its correct modern Chinese equivalent by circling the latter. Then translate each sentence into modern Chinese.

1. 又何間焉?　　　　　　　　　　　ⓐ 爲什麼(为什么) b. 憑什麼(凭什么) c. 多少

現代文翻译：你又为什么要参与到这件事情里面？

_____

2. 今人之性，生而有好利焉。　　　　a. 嗎(吗) b. 在那裏(在那里) c. 爲什麼(为什么)

現代文翻译：_____

3. 順是，故爭奪生而辭讓亡焉。　　　　　　　a. 但是 b. 所以 c. 這(这)

現代文翻译：_____

4. 然則從人之性，順人之情，必出於爭奪。　　a. 雖(虽)然 b. 那麼(么) c. 但是

現代文翻译：_____

5. 古者聖王以人性惡，以爲偏險而不正，悖亂而不治。　　a. 認爲(认为) b. 來(来) c. 由於(于)

現代文翻译：_____

6. 縱性情，安恣睢，而違禮義者爲小人。　　　a. 成爲(为) b. 治理 c. 爲(为)了

現代文翻译：_____

7. 凡性者，天之就也，不可學，不可事。　　　　a. 平凡 b. 都 c. 凡是

現代文翻译：_____

第十一課

《莊子》選讀

Selected Readings from the *Zhuangzi*

Introduction

The *Zhuangzi* is attributed to the historical Zhuangzi of the mid–Warring States period, the second-most important figure of Daoism (after Laozi). This text is traditionally divided into three parts: the first seven chapters make up the "inner chapters" 內篇 (*nèipiān*) and are considered authentic work of Zhuangzi; the remaining "outer chapters" 外篇 (*wàipiān*) and "miscellaneous chapters" 雜篇 (*zápiān* 杂篇) include remarkable ideas of his followers, fellow Daoist scholars. The *Zhuangzi* is acknowledged as one of the two most important works (with the *Laozi*) of Daoism.

Employing parables, anecdotes, astonishing images, and imaginary tales, Zhuangzi creates a fictional world of great depth. His masterful use of hyperbole, sarcasm, and sharp-witted sophistry demonstrates the exuberant power and beauty of classical Chinese language. Both the content and the style of his writing have exerted an enduring influence on generations of literary creations.

In the first excerpt, "Zhuang Zhou Dreams of Being a Butterfly," probably the best loved of all Zhuangzi's tales, the author loses himself in the ambiguous space between dream and reality: "He didn't know if he was Zhuang Zhou who had dreamt he was a butterfly, or a butterfly dreaming that he was Zhuang Zhou" (Burton Watson's translation). Such marvelous imagination, propelled by elegant writing and witty insight, exhibits a profound understanding of the transformation of things.

The second excerpt, "Free and Easy Wandering" 逍遙遊 ("Xiāoyáo You" 逍遥游), expresses the philosophical aspiration to unfetter oneself from all forms of dependence. Zhuangzi begins by illustrating the distinction between large and small through the sharp contrast between the gigantic bird Peng and little creatures like the cicada and dove. He further points out that whatever their disparities in body and ability, they all must borrow wind to fly up. The tale is meant to illustrate the relative distinctions of large and small, freedom and limitation. All things physical are subject to external conditions. A translation of this excerpt is given in *HTRCProse*, chapter 4, "The Pre-Qin Philosophical Prose: The Inner Chapters of the *Zhuangzi*," C4.3.

正文與簡體譯文 Text and Modern Chinese Translation

《齊物論》選段
qí wù lùn   xuǎn duàn

昔者莊周夢爲胡蝶，栩栩然胡蝶也，自
xī zhě zhuāng zhōu mèng wéi hú dié xǔ xǔ rán hú dié yě　zì

从前庄周做梦变成了蝴蝶，很生动的蝴蝶，自

喻適志與！不知<u>周</u>也。[1] 俄然覺，則蘧蘧然周
yù shì zhì yú　　bù zhī zhōu yě　　é rán jué　　zé qú qú rán zhōu

也。[2] 不知<u>周</u>之夢爲胡蝶與，胡蝶之夢爲<u>周</u>
yě　　bù zhī zhōu zhī mèng wéi hú dié yú　　hú dié zhī mèng wéi zhōu

與？<u>周</u>與胡蝶，則必有<u>分</u>矣。此之謂物化。[3]
yú　　zhōu yǔ hú dié　　zé bì yǒu fēn yǐ　　cǐ zhī wèi wù huà

《莊子集解》，北京：中華書局 (1987), 26–27.

己<u>明白</u>(变成蝴蝶)<u>适应</u>了心意啊！(都)不知道自己是庄周了！[1] 突然<u>醒</u>了，<u>惊讶地</u>(发现自己)是庄周(不是蝴蝶)。[2] 不知道是庄周做梦变成了蝴蝶呢？还是蝴蝶做梦变成了庄周呢？庄周和蝴蝶，一定是有<u>不同</u>的！这就叫做物化。[3]

1. 昔 *n.* former times, the past. MdnC: 從前 (*cóng qián* 从前).
   者 *auxiliary pron.* the time when.... See L6 Grammar Note 8 ④.
   爲 (为 *wéi*) *v.* to change into. MdnC: 變成 (*biàn chéng* 变成).
   胡蝶 or 蝴蝶 *n.* butterfly.
   栩栩 used to describe the vivid image of a butterfly. MdnC: 生動的 (*shēng dòng de* 生动的).
   然 *particle.* functioning here as an emotive particle. See L5 Grammar Note 2 ②.
   喻 *v.* to understand. MdnC: 明白 (*míng bái*).
   適 (适) *v.* to fit, be suitable, satisfy. MdnC: 適應 (*shì yìng* 适应).
   志 *n.* feelings, purpose. MdnC: 心意 (*xīn yì*).
   與 (与 *yú*) *ending particle.* See L7 Grammar Note 6.
2. 俄然 *adv.* in a very short time, suddenly. MdnC: 突然 (*tū rán*).
   覺 (觉 *jué*) *v.* to awake. MdnC: 醒 (*xǐng*).
   蘧蘧然 *adv.* all of a sudden, startled. MdnC: 驚訝地 (*jīng yà de* 惊讶地).
3. 之 *particle.* a nominative marker. See L2 Grammar Note 2 ⑤.
   分 (*fēn*) *n.* difference. MdnC: 不同 (*bù tóng*).
   化 *n.* transformation.

《逍遙遊》節選
xiāo yáo yóu　　jié xuǎn

北冥有魚，其名爲鯤。鯤之大，不知其
běi míng yǒu yú　　qí míng wéi kūn　　kūn zhī dà　　bù zhī qí

幾千里也。化而爲鳥，其名爲鵬。[4] 鵬之背，
jǐ qiān lǐ yě　　huà ér wéi niǎo　　qí míng wéi péng　　péng zhī bèi

不知其幾千里也；怒而飛，其翼若垂天之
bù zhī qí jǐ qiān lǐ yě　　nù ér fēi　　qí yì ruò chuí tiān zhī

雲。[5] 是鳥也，海運則將徙於南冥。南冥者，
yún　　shì niǎo yě　　hǎi yùn zé jiāng xǐ yú nán míng　　nán míng zhě

天池也。[6]
tiān chí yě

北方的大海里有条鱼，它的名字叫做鯤，鯤很大，不知道它有几千里啊！<u>化身成为鸟</u>，它的名字叫做鵬。[4] 鵬的后背，不知道它有几千里啊！<u>奋起而飞</u>，它的翅膀就像垂挂在天上的云彩。[5] 这只鸟，大海动起来(时)就会<u>迁徙</u>到南海去。南海，是天上的湖。[6]

4. 冥 *adj.* dark. Here it is used in the sense of 溟 (*míng*), meaning "sea" 海 (*hǎi*).

  之 *particle.* a nominative marker. See L2 Grammar Note 2 ⑤.

  化 *v.* to transform, change. MdnC: 化身 (*huà shēn*).

5. 之 *particle.* a possessive marker. MdnC: 的 (*de*). See L1 Grammar Note 2 ②.

  怒 *v.* to take flight vigorously. MdnC: 奮起 (*fèn qǐ* 奋起).

  翼 *n.* wing. MdnC: 翅膀 (*chì bǎng*).

  若 *v.* to be like. MdnC: 像 (*xiàng*). See L4 Grammar Note 4 ①.

  垂 *v.* to droop, hang down. MdnC: 垂挂 (*chuí guà*).

6. 是 *demonstrative pron.* this. MdnC: 這 (*zhè* 这). See L3 Grammar Note 1 ①.

  運 (运) *v.* to move. MdnC: 動 (*dòng* 动).

  徙 *v.* to move, migrate. MdnC: 遷徙 (*qiān xǐ* 迁徙).

  池 *n.* pond, lake.

《齊諧》者，志怪者也。[7]《諧》之言
qí xié zhě　zhì guài zhě yě　　　xié zhī yán

曰：「鵬之徙於南冥也，水擊三千里，摶扶搖
yuē　péng zhī xǐ yú nán míng yě　shuǐ jī sān qiān lǐ　tuán fú yáo

而上者九萬里，去以六月息者也。」[8]野馬也，
ér shàng zhě jiǔ wàn lǐ　qù yǐ liù yuè xī zhě yě　　　yě mǎ yě

塵埃也，生物之以息相吹也。[9]天之蒼蒼，其
chén āi yě　shēng wù zhī yǐ xī xiāng chuī yě　tiān zhī cāng cāng　qí

正色邪？其遠而無所至極邪？[10]其視下也亦若
zhèng sè yé　qí yuǎn ér wú suǒ zhì jí yé　　　qí shì xià yě yì ruò

是，則已矣。[11]
shì　zé yǐ yǐ

《齐谐》是一本记述怪异事物的书。[7]《谐》里有话说："大鹏鸟迁徙去南海，（翅膀）拍打水面，（水浪达）三千里之高，盘旋着依着旋风向上飞到九万里的高空；离开时用六个月（的时间飞到南海才）休息。"[8]像野马飞腾一样的雾气，（飘扬的）尘埃，都是生物的气息互相吹动的结果。[9]天的深蓝色，是它真正的颜色吗？还是太远了，没有达到尽头的地方呢？[10]大鹏鸟（从高空）看下面，也像这样罢了！[11]

7. 《齊諧》(齐谐) book title. 《諧》is the short title for it.

  志 *v.* to record, note down. MdnC: 記述 (*jì shù* 记述).

  怪 *adj.* uncommon, peculiar, bizarre. MdnC: 怪異 (*guài yì* 怪异). Here it refers to fantastic or bizarre things.

8. 擊 (击) *v.* to attack. MdnC: 拍打 (*pāi dǎ*).

  摶 (抟) *v.* to wheel, fly around in a circle. MdnC: 盤旋 (*pán xuán* 盘旋).

  扶搖 *n.* whirlwind. MdnC: 旋風 (*xuàn fēng* 旋风).

  去 *v.* to leave, go away. MdnC: 離開 (*lí kāi* 离开).

  以 *coverb.* to use. MdnC: 用 (*yòng*). See L2 Grammar Note 1 ②.

  息 *v.* to rest, take a break. MdnC: 休息 (*xiū xi*).

9. 野馬 (马) *n.* wild horse. Here it refers to the smoky haze hanging over the hills or swamps in the spring, appearing like wild horses galloping. MdnC: 霧氣 (*wù qì* 雾气).

塵 (尘) 埃 *n.* dust.

之 *particle.* a nominative marker. See L2 Grammar Note 2 ⑤.

息 *n.* breath. MdnC: 氣息 (*qì xī* 气息).

10. 蒼蒼 (苍) *adj.* blue, dark blue. MdnC: 深藍色 (*shēn lán sè* 深蓝色).

    邪 (yé) *ending interrogative particle.* MdnC: 嗎 (*ma* 吗). See Grammar Note 2.

    其 *adv.* used to suggest a tentative thought. See L2 Grammar Note 5 ③.

    至 *v.* to get to, reach. MdnC: 達到 (*dá dào* 达到).

    極 (极) *n.* the furthest edge. MdnC: 盡頭 (*jìn tóu* 尽头).

11. 其 *personal pron.* 其 refers to 大鵬 here. See L2 Grammar Note 5 ①.

    是 *demonstrative pron.* this. MdnC: 這樣 (*zhè yàng* 这样). See L3 Grammar Note 1 ①.

    則 (则) 已 *ending particle.* nothing more. MdnC: 罷了 (*bà le* 罢了). See Grammar Note 1 ②.

且夫水之積也不厚，　則其負大舟也無力。
qiě fú shuǐ zhī jī yě bú hòu　zé qí fù dà zhōu yě wú lì

覆杯水於坳堂之上，　則芥爲之舟，　置杯焉則
fù bēi shuǐ yú ào táng zhī shàng　zé jiè wéi zhī zhōu　zhì bēi yān zé

膠，水淺而舟大也。風之積也不厚，　則其負
jiāo　shuǐ qiǎn ér zhōu dà yě　fēng zhī jī yě bù hòu　zé qí fù

大翼也無力。[12] 故九萬里則風斯在下矣，而後
dà yì yě wú lì　gù jiǔ wàn lǐ zé fēng sī zài xià yǐ　ér hòu

乃今培風；背負青天而莫之夭閼者，而後乃
nǎi jīn péi fēng　bēi fù qīng tiān ér mò zhī yāo è zhě　ér hòu nǎi

今將圖南。[13]
jīn jiāng tú nán

況且水積累得不深，那么要它負載大船也沒有力量。在堂前洼地上倒杯水，那么小草就可以給它當船；放個杯子在那里就粘住不動了，(因為)水太浅而船太大了。風積累得不夠，那么它也沒有力量負載大鵬鳥的翅膀。[12] 所以(大鵬鳥飛到)九万里的高空，風就在下面了，然後才凭借着風力，背負着青天，沒有什么東西阻隔(它)，然後才計划着向南飞。[13]

12. 且夫 (fú) *conj.* besides, furthermore. MdnC: 況且 (*kuàng qiě* 况且). See L13 Grammar Note 2 ②.

    積 (积) *v.* to accumulate, collect. MdnC: 積累 (*jī lěi* 积累).

    厚 *adj.* deep. MdnC: 深 (*shēn*).

    負 (负) *v.* to bear up, carry. MdnC: 負載 (*fù zài* 负载).

    舟 *n.* boat. MdnC: 船 (*chuán*).

    覆 *v.* to turn over. MdnC: 倒 (*dào*).

    坳 (ào) *n.* low-lying land. MdnC: 窪地 (*wā dì* 洼地).

    芥 *n.* grass. MdnC: 小草 (*xiǎo cǎo*).

    爲 (为 wéi) 之舟 Here 之 and 舟 are double objects of the verb 爲. 之 refers to water in this phrase.

    置 *v.* to set, place, put. MdnC: 放 (*fàng*).

    焉 *pron.* there. MdnC: 在那裏 (*zài nà lǐ* 在那里). See L1 Grammar Note 4 ①.

    膠 (胶) *v.* to stick. MdnC: 粘住 (*zhān zhù*).

13. 斯 *conj.* then. MdnC: 就 (*jiù*). See L5 Grammar Note 3 ②.

    培 *v.* to cultivate. Here it means "with (wind)" 憑藉 (*píng jiè* 凭借).

莫 *indefinite pron.* none. MdnC: 沒有什麼 (*méi yǒu shén me* 没有什么). See L3 Grammar Note 2 ①.

夭閼 (阏 è) *v.* to hinder, block. MdnC: 阻隔 (*zǔ gé*).

圖 (图) *v.* to plan. MdnC: 計劃 (*jì huà* 计划).

蜩與學鳩笑之ₐ曰：「我決起而飛，槍
tiáo yǔ xué jiū xiào zhī　yuē　　　wǒ xuè qǐ ér fēi　qiāng

榆、枋，時則不至而控於地而已矣，奚以之ᵦ
yú　fāng　shí zé bú zhì ér kòng yú dì ér yǐ yǐ　xī yǐ zhī

九萬里而南爲？」¹⁴適莽蒼者三飡而反，腹猶
jiǔ wàn lǐ ér nán wéi　　　shì mǎng cāng zhě sān cān ér fǎn　fù yóu

果然；適百里者宿舂糧；適千里者三月聚糧。
guǒ rán　shì bǎi lǐ zhě sù chōng liáng　shì qiān lǐ zhě sān yuè jù liáng

之二蟲又何知！¹⁵
zhī èr chóng yòu hé zhī

蟬跟斑鳩笑话大鵬鳥说："我迅速地起飞，碰到榆树、檀树，有时到不了(树上)就落到地上罢了，哪里用得着飞到九万里还要往南飞呢？"¹⁴去郊野的人三顿饭之后就回来，肚子还是饱的；去百里之外的人要隔夜准备粮食；去千里之外的人要用三个月积累(路上的)粮食。这两只虫鸟又知道什么！¹⁵

14. 蜩 *n.* cicada. MdnC: 蟬 (*chán* 蝉).

學鳩 (学鸠) *n.* dove. MdnC: 斑鳩 (*bān jiū* 斑鸠).

之ₐ *pron.* Here 之 refers to 大鵬鳥. See L1 Grammar Note 2 ③.

決 (xuè) *adv.* swiftly, rapidly. MdnC: 迅速地 (*xùn sù de*).

槍 (枪) used here in the sense of 搶 (*qiāng* 抢), meaning "to bump against" 碰到 (*pèng dào*).

榆 *n.* elm tree. MdnC: 榆樹 (*yú shù* 榆树).

枋 *n.* sandalwood. MdnC: 檀樹 (*tán shù* 檀树).

控 *v.* to throw, throw down. MdnC: 落 (*luò*).

而已矣 *ending particle.* nothing more. MdnC: 罷了 (*bà le* 罢了). See L21 Grammar Note 1 ③.

奚 *interrogative particle.* how come? MdnC: 哪裏 (*nǎ lǐ* 哪里). See Grammar Note 3.

以 *coverb.* use. MdnC: 用 (*yòng*). See L2 Grammar Note 1 ②.

之ᵦ *v.* to go. MdnC: 去 (*qù*). See L7 Grammar Note 2 ⑦.

爲 (为 wéi) *ending particle.* MdnC: 呢 (*ne*). See Grammar Note 4 ④.

15. 適 (适) *v.* to go to, get to. MdnC: 去 (*qù*).

莽 *n.* grass. Here 莽蒼 (苍) refers to green woods nearby 郊野 (*jiāo yě*).

飡 (餐) *n.* meal. MdnC: 飯 (*fàn* 饭).

反 *adj.* opposite. Here it is used in the sense of 返 (*fǎn*), meaning "to return" 回來 (*huí lái* 回来).

腹 *n.* belly. MdnC: 肚子 (*dù zi*).

猶 (犹) *adv.* still. MdnC: 還 (*hái* 还). See L3 Grammar Note 3 ①.

果然 *adj.* full. MdnC: 飽 (*bǎo* 饱). 然 functions as an emotive particle. See L5 Grammar Note 2 ②.

宿 (sù) *adj.* of the previous night. MdnC: 隔夜 (*gé yè*).

舂 *v.* to grind. 宿舂糧 means "to grind the grain the whole night before leaving."

聚 *v.* to accumulate, gather. MdnC: 積累 (*jī lěi* 积累).

之 *demonstrative pron.* this. MdnC: 這 (*zhè* 这). See L1 Grammar Note 2 ①.

小知 ᵃ 不及大知， 小年不及大年。 奚以知 ᵇ
xiǎo zhì   bù jí dà zhì   xiǎo nián bù jí dà nián   xī yǐ zhī

其然也？ ¹⁶朝菌不知晦朔， 惠蛄不知春秋， 此
qí rán yě   zhāo jūn bù zhī huì shuò   huì gū bù zhī chūn qiū   cǐ

小年也。 ¹⁷楚之南有冥靈者， 以五百歲爲春，
xiǎo nián yě   chǔ zhī nán yǒu míng líng zhě   yǐ wǔ bǎi suì wéi chūn

五百歲爲秋； 上古有大椿者， 以八千歲爲春，
wǔ bǎi suì wéi qiū   shàng gǔ yǒu dà chūn zhě   yǐ bā qiān suì wéi chūn

八千歲爲秋。 ¹⁸而彭祖乃今以久特聞， 衆人匹
bā qiān suì wéi qiū   ér péng zǔ nǎi jīn yǐ jiǔ tè wén   zhòng rén pǐ

之，不亦悲乎！ ¹⁹
zhī   bú yì bēi hū

小智慧不及大智慧，短命不及长寿。根据什么知道这些情况是这样的呢？¹⁶朝菌不知道每个月的最后一天和第一天，蟪蛄不知道春天和秋天，这是短命。¹⁷楚南有种叫冥灵的树，把五百年当作春天，把五百年当作秋天；上古有种树叫大椿，把八千年当作春天，八千年当作秋天。¹⁸而彭祖现在因为长寿特别闻名。普通人和他比，不是很悲哀吗！¹⁹

《莊子集解》，北京：中華書局 (1987), 1–3.

16. 知 ᵃ (zhì) *n.* used in the sense of 智 (zhì), meaning "wisdom" 智慧 (zhì huì).

年 *n.* age. MdnC: 年歲 (nián suì 年岁). 小年 means "short-lived" 短命 (duǎn mìng), and 大年 means "long-lived" 長壽 (cháng shòu 长寿).

奚 *interrogative particle.* what? MdnC: 什麼 (shén me 什么). See Grammar Note 3.

以 *coverb.* by means of. MdnC: 根據 (gēn jù 根据). See L2 Grammar Note 1 ②.

知 ᵇ (zhī) *v.* to know. MdnC: 知道 (zhī dào).

其 *demonstrative pron.* these. MdnC: 這些 (zhè xiē 这些). See L6 Grammar Note 6 ④.

然 *pron.* like this. MdnC: 這樣 (zhè yàng 这样). See L8 Grammar Note 5 ③.

17. 朝 (zhāo) 菌 *n.* morning mushroom, which appears in the morning and dies in the evening.

晦 *n.* the last day of the lunar month.

朔 *n.* the first day of the lunar month.

惠蛄 or 蟪蛄 *n.* a kind of cicada born in the spring and dead in the fall.

春秋 *n.* spring and autumn—namely, a year.

18. 楚 the Chu state.

冥靈 (灵) *n.* tree name.

歲 (岁) *n.* a year. MdnC: 年 (nián).

上古 *n.* antiquity.

大椿 *n.* tree name.

19. 彭祖 a legendary man of longevity, living for eight hundred years.

乃今 now. MdnC: 現在 (xiàn zài 现在).

以 *prep.* for the reason of. MdnC: 因爲 (yīn wèi 因为). See L2 Grammar Note 1 ①.

久 *n.* longevity. MdnC: 長壽 (cháng shòu 长寿).

特 *adj.* special, unique. MdnC: 特別 (tè bié).

聞 *v.* to be known. MdnC: 聞名 (wén míng 闻名).

匹 *v.* to compare. MdnC: 比 (bǐ).

不亦⋯⋯乎 a sentence structure of a rhetorical question. MdnC: 不是 (*bú shì*) ⋯⋯嗎 (*ma* 吗). See L5 Grammar Note 1 ②.

語法注釋 Grammar Notes

1. 則
(则)

① *conj.* then. MdnC: 那麼 (*nà me* 那么), 就 (*jiù*).

俄然覺，則蘧蘧然周也。

[突然（庄周）醒了，就很惊讶地发现自己还是庄周（不是蝴蝶）。]

且夫水之積也不厚，則其負大舟也無力。

[如果水积累得不深，那么它也没有力量负载大船。]

② 則 (则) 已 *ending particle.* nothing more. 則已 is used as a variant of 而已 (*ér yǐ*, see L21 Grammar Note 1 ③). MdnC: 罷了 (*bà le* 罢了).

其視下也亦若是，則已矣。

[大鹏鸟（从高空中）看下面，也不过像这样罢了。]

2. 邪
(yé)

ending interrogative particle. MdnC: 嗎 (*ma* 吗), 呢 (*ne*).

天之蒼蒼，其正色邪？

[天的深蓝色，是它真正的颜色吗？]

其遠而無所至極邪？

[还是太远了而没有达到尽头的地方（所以看不清楚而造成的）呢？]

3. 奚

initial interrogative particle. used as an alternative to 何 (*hé*, see L1 Grammar Note 3 ①), meaning "what? or how? or how come?" MdnC: 什麼 (*shén me* 什么), 哪裏 (*nǎ lǐ* 哪里).

奚以之九萬里而南爲？

[哪里用得着飞到九万里之后还要向南飞啊！]

奚以知其然也？

[根据什么知道这些情况是这样的呢？]

4. 爲
(为)

Five uses of 爲 are explained in this book. In addition to the use below, see 爲① in L2 Grammar Note 6, 爲② in L7 Grammar Note 5, 爲③ in L9 Grammar Note 1, and 爲 ⑤ in L21 Grammar Note 3.

④ **wéi** *ending particle.* usually appears in general questions and rhetorical questions. MdnC: 啊 (*a*), 呢 (*ne*).

奚以之九萬里而南爲？

[哪里用得着飞到九万里之后还要向南飞啊！]

Literary Analysis

A good grasp of the three modes of discourse is key to appreciating the prose art of the inner chapters. Early Qing scholar Xuan Ying 宣穎 (fl. early eighteenth c.) may have offered the best literal definition of *yuyan* 寓言 (*yù yán*) when he calls it "speech that contains an implied meaning" (*jì yù zhī yán* 寄寓之言). The term fundamentally means something like "metaphorical language" in English. As used by the authors of chapters 27 and 33 of the *Zhuangzi*, *yuyan* also refers to anecdotes and stories in addition to individual words and phrases. The metaphorical language that contains a narrative element can be further divided into two types: fables involving animal characters and parables with human characters. Fables and parables are actually extended metaphors—that is, metaphors that are expanded into anecdotes and stories. Finally, *yuyan* can also be understood as "putting one's words in the mouths of other people" 寄之他人之言 (*jì zhī tārén zhī yán*), which brings to mind the idea of the literary mask in modern Western criticism.

Although *zhongyan* 重言 can also be pronounced *chóngyán* (lit. "repeating others' words"), reading it as *zhòngyán* so that it means "employing words of those whom people respect" is most likely what the authors of the *Zhuangzi* intended. In the inner chapters, "those whom people respect" include legendary heroes, ancient emperors, sages, and people from all walks of life who have achieved a high level of spirituality—all used as the author's masks so that his own words, thus disguised, might carry more authority and "ring true."

The last discursive mode here is *zhīyán* 卮言, from *zhi* (lit. "goblet" or "wine vessel"). In the context of the *Zhuangzi*, *zhi* refers not to any ordinary drinking vessel but to the "tilting vessel" 攲器 (*qīqì* 攲器) in ancient China, an unusual vessel designed to remain upright when empty and tip over when full, thus illustrating the concept of emptiness, a core Daoist value. The authors of chapters 27 and 33 seem to have chosen this goblet as a metaphor for the ideal use of the heart in relation to speech: the heart should remain empty of preconceived ideas and values until the occasion for speech arises and it can pour out ideas and values taken in from outside. The term *goblet words* refers to speech that is natural, unpremeditated, and responsive to changes in the flow of discourse and that always returns the heart to its pristine emptiness on completion. Applied to the writing of the inner chapters, apart from denoting the overall mode of responding to changes in the natural flow of discourse, goblet words also refer to the ad hoc comments that emerge from the author's heart in the course of writing an essay or presenting a fable or parable. In the prose of the inner chapters, we find that metaphorical words, "words of those whom people respect," and goblet words do not appear as three sharply distinct modes of discourse but overlap and intertwine throughout. They include the author's figurative language, quoted words from other texts, stories he has made up himself, statements from previous passages and chapters, and anecdotes borrowed from common knowledge, myths, and folktales. It should be particularly noted that Zhuangzi, in contrast to the Confucian tradition, seldom, if ever, just "quotes" existing stories and texts to express his authorial intent. Instead, he changes them and uses them as metaphors to articulate his own philosophical thinking. When we read the inner chapters, it is critical to keep this in mind.

☞ *HTRCProse*, chapter 4, "The Pre-Qin Philosophical Prose: The Inner Chapters of the *Zhuangzi*" for further comments on the *Zhuangzi*.

—SL

課後練習 **Exercises**

一 給加點字注音 Give the pinyin romanization for each dotted word.

1. 栩栩然 （＿＿＿,＿＿＿） 2. 鯤 （＿＿＿） 3. 學鳩 （＿＿＿） 4. 舂糧 （＿＿＿） 5. 朝菌 （＿＿＿）

6. 蓬蓬然 (____,____) 7. 蜩 (____) 8. 坳堂 (____) 9. 惠蛄 (____) 10. 大椿 (____)

二 在括號中給句中加點的字注音，並選出正確的釋義 Give the pinyin romanization for each dotted word; then select the correct definition from the following list, and write it in the blank.

醒了　　小草　　遷(迁)徙　　粘住　　迅速地　　明白　　飯(饭)　　**信服**　　智慧　　盘旋

1. 小信未孚 （**fú**） 信服　　2. 自喻適志 （　） _____　　3. 俄然覺 （　） _____

4. 搏扶搖而上 （　） _____　　5. 芥爲之舟 （　） _____　　6. 三湌 （　） _____

7. 海運則將徙於南冥（　） _____　　8. 置杯焉則膠 （　） _____

9. 我決起而飛 （　） _____　　10. 小知不如大知 （　） _____

三 選擇釋義並填空 Match each word in the left column with its correct definition in the middle column. Fill in each blank in the right column with an appropriate word from the left column.

謀謀劃(谋划)	奮(奋)起	____然覺，則蓬蓬然周也。
俄_____	倒	周與胡蝶，則必有____矣。
分_____	計劃(计划)	鵬之背，不知其幾千里也，____而飛，其____若____天之雲。
怒_____	**謀劃(谋划)**	
翼_____	落	
垂_____	憑藉(凭借)	天之蒼蒼，其正色邪？其遠而無所至____邪？
負_____	隔夜	且夫水之積也不厚，其____大舟也無力。
覆_____	聞(闻)名	____杯水於坳堂之上，則芥爲之舟。
培_____	盡頭(尽头)	
圖_____	飽(饱)	故九萬里則風斯在下矣，而後乃今____風。
槍_____	突然	背負青天而莫之夭閼者，而後乃今將____南。
控_____	翅膀	我決起而飛，____榆、枋，時則不至而____於地而已矣。
聚_____	不同	
反_____	碰到	
果_____	垂挂	適蒼莽者，三湌而____，腹猶____然；適百里者____春糧；適千里者三月____糧。
宿_____	纍積(累计)	
極_____	負載(负载)	
聞_____	比	而彭祖乃今以久特____，衆人____之，不亦悲乎！
匹_____	回來(来)	

四 請用給出的字填空 Fill in each blank with an appropriate word from the following list (some words may be used more than once).

亦　　乎　　然　　之　　奚　　邪　　則(则)已　　者　　爲(为)　　與(与)

1. 昔____莊周夢爲胡蝶，栩栩____胡蝶也，自喻適志____！

2. 天＿＿＿蒼蒼，其正色＿＿＿？其遠而無所至極＿＿＿？其視下也＿＿＿若是，＿＿＿＿＿＿矣。

3. ＿＿＿以＿＿＿九萬里而南＿＿＿？　4. 而彭祖乃今以久特聞，衆人匹＿＿＿，不＿＿＿悲＿＿＿！

五　爲加點字選擇正確釋義，並根據釋義來翻譯句子 Match each dotted word with its correct modern Chinese equivalent by circling the latter. Then translate each sentence into modern Chinese.

1. 又何間焉？　　　　　　　　　　　　　ⓐ 爲什麼（为什么）b. 憑什麼（凭什么）c. 多少

現代文翻译：你又为什么要参与到这件事情里面？

＿＿＿＿＿＿＿＿＿＿＿＿＿＿＿＿＿＿＿＿＿

2. 周與胡蝶，則必有分矣。　　　　　　　　a. 也　b. 就　c. 罷（罢）了

現代文翻译：＿＿＿＿＿＿＿＿＿＿＿＿＿＿＿

3. 是鳥也，海運則將徙於南冥。　　　　　　a. 但是　b. 所以　c. 這（这）

現代文翻译：＿＿＿＿＿＿＿＿＿＿＿＿＿＿＿

4. 置杯焉則膠，水淺而舟大也。　　　　　　a. 然　b. 在那裏（在那里）c. 爲什麼（为什么）

現代文翻译：＿＿＿＿＿＿＿＿＿＿＿＿＿＿＿

5. 天之蒼蒼，其正色邪？其遠而無所至極邪？　a. 這（这）b. 它　c. 還（还）是

現代文翻译：＿＿＿＿＿＿＿＿＿＿＿＿＿＿＿

6. 之二蟲又何知？　　　　　　　　　　　　a. 的　b. 這（这）c. 到

現代文翻译：＿＿＿＿＿＿＿＿＿＿＿＿＿＿＿

7. 小知不及大知，小年不及大年。奚以知其然也？　a. 什麼（什么）b. 在哪　c. 來（来）

現代文翻译：＿＿＿＿＿＿＿＿＿＿＿＿＿＿＿

8. 而彭祖乃今以久特聞，衆人匹之，不亦悲乎！　a. 因爲（为）b. 用　c. 來（来）

現代文翻译：＿＿＿＿＿＿＿＿＿＿＿＿＿＿＿

第十二課

《墨子》兼愛上

"Universal Love, I," from the *Mozi*

Introduction

The *Mozi*—a collection of sayings and ideas attributed to the historical figure Mozi, named Mo Di 墨翟 (ca. 479–381 BCE)—is believed to have been recorded and compiled by his disciples. The extant edition of the *Mozi* has fifty-three chapters and is a voluminous source of Mohism, one of the two most influential philosophical schools (with Confucianism) during the Warring States period. The *Mozi* is best known for its advocacy of thrift, opposition to military action, and ideal of equal, universal love in contradistinction to Confucian notions of differentiated love grounded in strict social hierarchy. This excerpt expounds the ultimate value of universal love: if each person loves everyone else in the way he loves himself, there will be lasting peace and order in the world.

The *Mozi* provides one of the earliest models of argument writing, marked by a self-conscious process of logical thinking aided by analogies and tactful repetitions.

正文與簡體譯文 Text and Modern Chinese Translation

聖人以治天下爲事者也，必知亂之所自
shèng rén yǐ zhì tiān xià wéi shì zhě yě　bì zhī luàn zhī suǒ zì

起，焉能治之；不知亂之所自起，則不能
qǐ　　yān néng zhì zhī　bù zhī luàn zhī suǒ zì qǐ　　zé bù néng

治。[1] 譬之如醫之攻人之疾者然：必知疾之所
zhì　　pì zhī rú yī zhī gōng rén zhī jí zhě rán　　bì zhī jí zhī suǒ

自起，焉能攻之；不知疾之所自起，則弗能
zì qǐ　　yān néng gōng zhī bù zhī jí zhī suǒ zì qǐ　　zé fú néng

攻。[2] 治亂者何獨不然？必知亂之所自起，焉
gōng　　zhì luàn zhě hé dú bù rán　　bì zhī luàn zhī suǒ zì qǐ　　yān

能治之；不知亂之所自起，則弗能治。[3]
néng zhì zhī　bù zhī luàn zhī suǒ zì　qǐ　　zé fú néng zhì

圣人把治理天下作为自己的事业，必然知道（社会的）祸乱是从哪里产生的，于是才能治理它；不知祸乱从哪里产生，就不能治理。[1] 比如说这就像医生给病人治病一样，一定知道病从哪里来的，然后才能治病。不知病从哪里来的，就不能治。[2] 治理祸乱难道有什么不一样吗？一定知道祸乱从哪里产生的，然后才能治理它。不知道祸乱从哪里产生的，就不能治。[3]

1. 聖 (圣) 人 *n.* sage.
　　以⋯⋯爲(为)⋯⋯ to regard... as.... See L2 Grammar Note 1 ④.

治 *v.* to govern, direct. MdnC: 治理 (*zhì lǐ*).

事 *n.* deeds, task, duty. MdnC: 事業 (*shì yè* 事业).

亂 (乱) *n.* disorder, chaos. MdnC: 禍亂 (*huò luàn* 祸乱).

自 *prep.* from. MdnC: 從 (*cóng* 从). See L31 Grammar Note 1 ①.

起 *v.* to produce, give rise to, arouse. MdnC: 產生 (*chǎn shēng* 产生).

焉 *conj.* then. MdnC: 於是 (*yú shì* 于是). See Grammar Note 1 ⑥.

2. 譬 *v.* to draw an analogy, propose an example. MdnC: 比如 (*bǐ rú*).

之 *demonstrative pron.* this. MdnC: 這 (*zhè* 这). See L1 Grammar Note 2 ①.

醫 (医) *n.* doctor. MdnC: 醫生 (*yī shēng* 医生).

攻 *v.* to attack, work at. Here it means "to suppress a patient's disease" 治 (*zhì*).

疾 *n.* disease, illness. MdnC: 病 (*bìng*).

3. 何 *interrogative pron.* what? MdnC: 什麼 (*shén me* 什么). See L1 Grammar Note 3 ①.

獨 (独) *adv.* once, ever. MdnC: 難道 (*nán dào* 难道).

然 *pron.* like this, similar. MdnC: 一樣 (*yí yàng* 一样). See L8 Grammar Note 5 ③.

弗 *adv.* no, not. See L4 Grammar Note 5.

聖人以治天下爲事者也，不可不察亂之
shèng rén yǐ zhì tiān xià wéi shì zhě yě　　bù kě bù chá luàn zhī

所自起。當察亂何自起？起不相愛。臣子之
suǒ zì qǐ　　dāng chá luàn hé zì qǐ　　qǐ bù xiāng ài　　chén zǐ zhī

不孝君父，所謂亂也。⁴子自愛不愛父，故虧
bù xiào jūn fù　　suǒ wèi luàn yě　　zǐ zì ài bú ài fù　　gù kuī

父而自利；弟自愛不愛兄，故虧兄而自利；臣
fù ér zì lì　　dì zì ài bú ài xiōng　　gù kuī xiōng ér zì lì　　chén

自愛不愛君，故虧君而自利，此所謂亂也。⁵
zì ài bú ài jūn　　gù kuī jūn ér zì lì　　cǐ suǒ wèi luàn yě

雖父之不慈子，兄之不慈弟，君之不慈臣，此
suī fù zhī bù cí zǐ　　xiōng zhī bù cí dì　　jūn zhī bù cí chén　　cǐ

亦天下之所謂亂也。⁶父自愛也不愛子，故虧
yì tiān xià zhī suǒ wèi luàn yě　　fù zì ài yě bú ài zǐ　　gù kuī

子而自利；兄自愛也不愛弟，故虧弟而自利；
zǐ ér zì lì　　xiōng zì ài yě bú ài dì　　gù kuī dì ér zì lì

君自愛也不愛臣，故虧臣而自利。是何也？
jūn zì ài yě bú ài chén　　gù kuī chén ér zì lì　　shì hé yě

皆起不相愛。⁷
jiē qǐ bù xiāng ài

圣人把治理天下作为自己的事业，不可以不考察祸乱是从哪里产生的。应当考察祸乱从哪里产生的？产生于(人与人之间)不相爱。臣和子不孝敬君和父，就是所说的祸乱。⁴儿子爱自己，不爱父亲，所以使父亲亏损，使自己获利。弟弟爱自己，不爱兄长，所以使兄长亏损，使自己获利。大臣爱自己，不爱君主，所以使君主亏损，使自己获利。这就是所说的祸乱。⁵即使父亲不爱儿子，兄长不爱弟弟，君主不爱大臣，这也是天下所说的祸乱啊！⁶父亲爱自己，不爱儿子，所以使儿子亏损，使自己获利。兄长爱自己，不爱弟弟，所以使弟弟亏损，使自己

获利。君王爱自己，不爱大臣，所以使大臣亏损，使自己获利。这是为什么呢？都是不相爱造成的。[7]

4. 察 *v.* to investigate, examine. MdnC: 考察 (*kǎo chá*).

當 (当 *dāng*) *adv.* ought to, should. MdnC: 應當 (*yīng dāng* 应当).

愛 (爱) *v.* to care for, be chary of.

臣 *n.* subject, minister, servitor.

子 *n.* son.

孝 *v.* to show filial piety. MdnC: 孝敬 (*xiào jìng*).

君 *n.* lord, king.

5. 自 *pron.* self. See L31 Grammar Note 1 ②.

虧 (亏) *v.* to lose, have a deficit. MdnC: 虧損 (*kuī sǔn* 亏损). Here it is 使 (父) 虧, meaning "to make (father) have a deficit." See L7 Grammar Note 1 ①.

利 *v.* to benefit, gain a profit. MdnC: 獲利 (*huò lì* 获利). Here it is 使 (自) 利, meaning "to make (oneself) gain a profit." See L7 Grammar Note 1 ①.

6. 雖 (虽) *conj.* even though. MdnC: 即使 (*jí shǐ*). See L4 Grammar Note 6.

慈 *v.* to love, care. MdnC: 愛 (*ài* 爱).

之 *particle.* a nominative marker. See L2 Grammar Note 2 ⑤.

7. 是 *demonstrative pron.* these. MdnC: 這些 (*zhè xiē* 这些). See L3 Grammar Note 1 ①.

何 *interrogative particle.* for what reason? why? MdnC: 爲什麼 (*wèi shén me* 为什么). See L1 Grammar Note 3 ②.

雖至天下之爲盜賊[a]者亦然，盜愛其室，不
suī zhì tiān xià zhī wéi dào zéi zhě yì rán dào ài qí shì bú
愛其異室，故竊異室以利其室；賊愛其身，不
ài qí yì shì gù qiè yì shì yǐ lì qí shì zéi ài qí shēn bú
愛人，故賊[b]人以利其身。[8]此何也？皆起不相
ài rén gù zéi rén yǐ lì qí shēn cǐ hé yě jiē qǐ bù xiāng
愛。
ài

至于天下做小偷和强盗的人也是这样。小偷爱自己的家，不爱别人的家，所以偷别人的家，来使自己的家获利。强盗爱护自己的身体，不爱别人的身体，所以残害别人来使自己获利。[8]这是为什么呢？都是不相爱造成的。

8. 至 *conj.* as for, about. MdnC: 至於 (*zhì yú* 至于).

爲 (为 *wéi*) *v.* to do. MdnC: 做 (*zuò*). See L2 Grammar Note 6 ①.

盜 *n.* thief. MdnC: 小偷 (*xiǎo tōu*).

賊 [a] (贼) *n.* outlaw. MdnC: 强盗 (*qiáng dào*).

亦 *adv.* also. MdnC: 也 (*yě*). See L5 Grammar Note 1 ①.

然 *pron.* like this/that. MdnC: 這樣 (*zhè yàng* 这样). See L8 Grammar Note 5 ③.

室 *n.* room, home, house. MdnC: 家 *(jiā)*.

異 (异) *adj.* different. Here it refers to other people's 別人的 *(bié rén de)*.

竊 (窃) *v.* to steal. MdnC: 偷 *(tōu)*.

賊 b (贼) *v.* to kill, harm. MdnC: 殘害 *(cán hài* 残害*)*.

雖至大夫之相亂家、諸侯之相攻國者，亦
suī zhì dà fū zhī xiāng luàn jiā　zhū hóu zhī xiāng gōng guó zhě yì

然。大夫各愛其家，不愛異家，故亂異家以利
rán　dà fū gè ài qí jiā　bú ài yì jiā　gù luàn yì jiā yǐ lì

其家。諸侯各愛其國，不愛異國，故攻異國以
qí jiā　zhū hóu gè ài qí guó　bú ài yì guó　gù gōng yì guó yǐ

利其國，天下之亂物具此而已矣。⁹察此何自
lì qí guó　tiān xià zhī luàn wù jù cǐ ér yǐ yǐ　chá cǐ hé zì

起？皆起不相愛。
qǐ　jiē qǐ bù xiāng ài

至于大夫互相扰乱对方的家族，诸侯互相攻击对方的诸侯国都是这样的。大夫各自爱自己的家族，不爱别人的家，所以扰乱别人的家族来使自己家族获利。诸侯各自爱自己的诸侯国，不爱别人的诸侯国，所以攻击别人的诸侯国来使自己的诸侯国获利。天下的祸乱事，都在这里了！⁹考察这些祸乱从哪里产生的，都是不相爱造成的。

9. 大夫 *n.* senior official.

諸 (诸) 侯 *n.* territorial lords.

相 *(xiāng) adv.* each other. MdnC: 互相 *(hù xiāng)*.

物 *n.* thing. MdnC: 事 *(shì)*.

具 *v.* all, complete. MdnC: 完備 *(wán bèi* 完备*)*.

而已矣 *ending particle.* nothing more. MdnC: 罷了 *(bà le* 罢了*)*. See L21 Grammar Note 1 ③.

若 a使天下兼相愛，愛人若 b愛其身，猶
ruò shǐ tiān xià jiān xiāng ài　ài rén ruò ài qí shēn　yóu

有不孝者乎？視父兄與君若其身，惡施不孝？
yǒu bú xiào zhě hū　shì fù xiōng yǔ jūn ruò qí shēn　wū shī bú xiào

猶有不慈者乎？視弟子與臣若其身，惡施不
yóu yǒu bù cí zhě hū　shì dì zǐ yǔ chén ruò qí shēn　wū shī bù

慈？故不孝不慈亡有。猶有盜賊乎？¹⁰故視人
cí　gù bú xiào bù cí wú yǒu　yóu yǒu dào zéi hū　gù shì rén

之室若其室，誰竊？視人身若其身，誰賊？
zhī shì ruò qí shì　shuí qiè　shì rén shēn ruò qí shēn　shuí zéi

如果使天下人都相亲相爱，爱别人就像爱自己，还会有不孝的人吗？看待父亲、兄长和君王就像看待自己，怎么会施行不孝呢？还会有不慈爱的人吗？看待弟弟，儿子和大臣就像自己一样，怎么会做不爱护的事情呢？所以不孝不慈都没有了。还会有小偷和强盗吗？¹⁰所

故盜賊亡有。猶有大夫之相亂家、諸侯之相
gù dào zéi　wú yǒu　　yóu yǒu dà fū zhī xiāng luàn jiā　　zhū hóu zhī xiāng

攻國者乎？視人家若其家，誰亂？視人國若
gōng guó zhě hū　　shì rén jiā ruò qí jiā　　shuí luàn　　shì rén guó ruò

其國，誰攻？故大夫之相亂家、諸侯之相攻
qí guó　　shuí gōng　　gù dà fū zhī xiāng luàn jiā　　zhū hóu zhī xiāng gōng

國者亡有。若使天下兼相愛，國與國不相攻，
guó zhě wú yǒu　　ruò shǐ tiān xià jiān xiāng ài　　guó yǔ guó bù xiāng gōng

家與家不相亂，盜賊無有，君臣父子皆能孝
jiā yǔ jiā bù xiāng luàn　　dào zéi wú yǒu　　jūn chén fù zǐ jiē néng xiào

慈，若此則天下治。
cí　　　ruò cǐ zé tiān xià zhì

以看待别人的家像自己的家一样，谁还去偷呢？看待别人就像看待自己一样，谁还去害人呢？所以小偷和强盗没有了。还会有大夫互相祸乱别人的家族，诸侯互相攻击别人的诸侯国吗？看待别的家族像对自己的家族一样，谁还去扰乱？看待别的诸侯国就像自己的诸侯国一样，谁还去攻击？所以大夫互相扰乱彼此的家族，诸侯之间互相攻击彼此的情况没有了。如果使天下都互相爱护，诸侯国之间不互相攻击，家族之间不互相扰乱，小偷和强盗没有了，君主、大臣、父亲、儿子都能孝顺慈爱，如果这样，那么天下就安定了！

10. 若 a *conj.* if. MdnC: 如果 (*rú guǒ*). See L4 Grammar Note 4 ②.

兼 *adv.* impartially, indiscriminately.

若 b *v.* to be like. MdnC: 像 (*xiàng*). See L4 Grammar Note 4 ①.

猶 (犹) *adv.* still. MdnC: 還 (*hái* 还). See L3 Grammar Note 3 ①.

視 (视) *v.* to regard, view. MdnC: 看待 (*kàn dài*).

惡 (恶 *wū*) *interrogative particle*. how come? MdnC: 怎麼 (*zěn me* 怎么). See Grammar Note 2 ①.

施 *v.* to act, execute, carry out. MdnC: 施行 (*shī xíng*), 做 (*zuò*).

賊 (贼) *v.* to kill, harm. Here 戕賊 (贼) means "to cut the willow."

亡 *n.* death, loss. Here it is used in the sense of 無 (*wú* 无), meaning "have not" 没 (*méi*).

故聖人以治天下爲事者，惡 a 得不禁惡 b
gù shèng rén yǐ zhì tiān xià wéi shì zhě　　wū　　dé bú jìn wù

而勸愛？故天下兼相愛則治，交相惡則亂。
ér quàn ài　　gù tiān xià jiān xiāng ài zé zhì　　jiāo xiāng wù zé luàn

所以圣人把治理天下当作自己的事业，怎么能不禁止(大家)互相憎恨而劝导互相爱护呢？所以天下都相

故 子 _a 墨 子 _b 曰： 不 可 以 不 勸 愛 人 者， 此 也。 ¹¹

gù zǐ   mò zǐ   yuē   bù kě yǐ bú quàn ài rén zhě   cǐ yě

《墨子閒詁》，北京：中華書局 (2001), 99–101.

爱就安定了，都相互憎恨就祸乱了。因此墨子说："不可不劝导大家爱护别人。"道理就在这里！¹¹

11. 惡 _a (惡 wū) *interrogative particle.* how come? MdnC: 怎麼 (*zěn me* 怎么). See Grammar Note 2 ①.

禁 (jìn) *v.* to prohibit, ban, forbid. MdnC: 禁止 (*jìn zhǐ*).

惡 _b (惡 wù) *v.* to hate, detest. MdnC: 憎恨 (*zèng hèn*).

勸 (劝) *v.* to urge, advise, exhort. MdnC: 勸導 (*quàn dǎo* 劝导).

交 *adv.* each other. MdnC: 互相 (*hù xiāng*).

子 _a *n.* honorific designation of a teacher.

子 _b *n.* honorific designation of a gentleman.

語法注釋 Grammar Notes

1. 焉   Seven uses of 焉 are explained in this book. In addition to the use below, see 焉① in L1 Grammar Note 4, 焉②③ in L2 Grammar Note 3, 焉④ in L5 Grammar Note 4, 焉⑤ in L6 Grammar Note 5, and 焉⑦ in L30 Grammar Note 3.

⑥ *conj.* then. MdnC: 於是 (*yú shì* 于是), 乃 (*nǎi*).

聖人以治天下為事者，必知亂之所自起，焉能治之。

[圣人把治理天下作为自己的事业，必然知道混乱从哪里开始的，于是才能够治理它。]

2. 惡
(恶)   ① **wū** *interrogative particle.* how? where? how come? MdnC: 怎麼 (*zěn me* 怎么).

故聖人以治天下為事者，惡得不禁惡而勸愛？

[所以圣人把治理天下当作自己的事业，怎么能不禁止互相憎恨而劝导互相爱护呢？]

See 惡② in L33 Grammar Note 2.

Literary Analysis

1. There is considerable debate over the best translation of 愛 in this text. Does it mean "love"? Why or why not? What other word would you suggest?

2. How does the ideal of 兼愛 compare to the Confucian virtue of 恕 (reciprocity—that is, treating others as you would want them to treat you)? Why are they not the same?

👉 *HTRCProse*, chapter 5, "Pre-Qin and Han Philosophical and Historical Prose: Self-Interest, Manipulation, and the Philosophical Marketplace."

—PRG

課後練習 Exercises

一 在括號中給句中加點的字注音，並選出正確的釋義 Give the pinyin romanization for each dotted word; then select the correct definition from the following list, and write it in the blank.

禁止　小偷　病　憎恨　偷　**信服**　强盜　比如　没　使……吃虧(亏)

1. 小信未孚（**fú**）　**信服**　2. 譬之如（　）＿＿＿＿　3. 虧父而自利（　）＿＿＿＿

4. 盜愛其室（　）＿＿＿＿　5. 不禁惡（　）＿＿＿＿　6. 疾之所自起（　）＿＿＿＿

7. 賊愛其身（　）＿＿＿＿　8. 竊異室（　）＿＿＿＿　9. 交相惡則亂（　）＿＿＿＿

10. 故盜賊亡有（　）＿＿＿＿

二 選擇釋義並填空 Match each word in the left column with its correct definition in the middle column. Fill in each blank in the right column with an appropriate word from the left column (some words may be used more than once).

左	中	右
謀謀劃(谋划)	殘(残)害	聖人以＿＿天下爲事者，必知＿＿之所自＿＿，焉能＿＿之。
治＿＿＿＿	產(产)生	
亂＿＿＿＿	完備(备)	＿＿＿＿者何＿＿不然？
起＿＿＿＿	**謀劃(谋划)**	＿＿＿察＿＿何自＿＿？ ＿＿＿不相愛。
獨＿＿＿＿	勸導(劝导)	
當＿＿＿＿	看待	賊愛其身，不愛人，故＿＿人以利其身。
賊＿＿＿＿	禍亂(祸乱)	天下之＿＿物＿＿此而已矣。
具＿＿＿＿	施行	
施＿＿＿＿	禍(祸)害	＿＿＿父兄與君若其身，惡＿＿不孝？
勸＿＿＿＿	應當(应当)	故聖人以＿＿天下爲事者，惡得不禁惡而＿＿愛？
視＿＿＿＿	難(难)道	

三 請用給出的字填空 Fill in each blank with an appropriate word from the following list (some words may be used more than once).

所　者　然　焉　猶(犹)　惡(恶)　以　爲(为)　如

1. 聖人＿＿治天下＿＿事＿＿也，必知亂之＿＿自起，＿＿能治之。

2. 譬之＿＿醫之攻人之疾＿＿＿＿：必知疾之＿＿自起，＿＿能攻之。

3. 雖至天下之＿＿盜賊＿＿亦＿＿。　4. 視父兄與君若其身，＿＿施不孝？ ＿＿有不慈者乎？

四 爲加點字選擇正確釋義，並根據釋義來翻譯句子 Match each dotted word with its correct modern Chinese equivalent by circling the latter. Then translate each sentence into modern Chinese.

1. 又何間焉?　　　　　　　　　　　　　ⓐ 爲什麼(为什么) b. 憑什麼(凭什么) c. 多少

現代文翻译： 你又为什么要参与到这件事情里面？

_____

2. 必知亂之所自起，焉能治之。　　　　　a. 於(于)是 b. 什麼(么) c.啊

現代文翻译： _____

3. 當察亂何自起？起不相愛。　　　　　　a. 爲什麼(为什么) b. 多少 c. 什麼(么)地方

現代文翻译： _____

4. 是何也？皆起不相愛。　　　　　　　　a. 但是 b. 所以 c. 這(这)

現代文翻译： _____

5. 雖至大夫之相亂家、諸侯之相攻國，亦然。　a. 但是 b. 一樣(样) c. 對(对)

現代文翻译： _____

6. 視弟子與臣若其身，惡施不慈?　　　　　a. 對誰(对谁) b. 憎恨 c.惡(恶)行

現代文翻译： _____

7. 故不慈不孝亡有。猶有盜賊乎?　　　　　a. 像 b. 還(还) c. 猶(犹)豫

現代文翻译： _____

單元練習

Unit Exercises

一、辨析加點字在不同句中注音和釋義的異同 Give the pinyin romanization for each dotted word, and then write in its correct definition.

1. 鄙　　肉食者鄙，未能遠謀。　　　　　　（ bǐ ）目光短淺
　　　　越國以鄙遠，君知其難也。　　　　（　　）_____

2. 適　　栩栩然胡蝶也，自喻適志與？　　　（　　）_____
　　　　適百里者宿舂糧。　　　　　　　　（　　）_____

3. 勝　　將不勝其忿而蟻附之。　　　　　　（　　）_____
　　　　知可以戰與不可以戰者勝。　　　　（　　）_____

4. 與　　栩栩然胡蝶也，自喻適志與？　　　（　　）_____
　　　　視父兄與君若其身，惡施不孝？　　（　　）_____

5. 敵　　敵則能戰之，少則逃之，不若則避之。（　　）_____
　　　　小敵之堅，大敵之擒也。　　　　　（　　）_____

6. 惡　　生而有疾惡焉，順是，故殘賊生而忠信亡焉。（　　）_____
　　　　人之性惡明矣，其善者偽也。　　　（　　）_____

7. 亡　　故盜賊亡有。　　　　　　　　　　（　　）_____
　　　　焉用亡鄭以陪鄰？　　　　　　　　（　　）_____

8. 知　　小知不及大知，小年不及大年。　　（　　）_____
　　　　奚以知其然也？　　　　　　　　　（　　）_____

二、用給出的字填空，並選擇正確的釋義 Fill in the blanks with words from list A, and then write in their modern Chinese equivalents from list B.

A. Words for Filling the Blanks

槍　宿　果　培　從
安　矯　忿　拔　施
擒　殆　竊　鄙

B. Modern Chinese Equivalents

飽(饱)　偷　放縱(纵)　危險(险)　憤(愤)怒
隔夜　捉住　憑藉(凭借)　矯(矫)正　占領(领)
施行　碰到　習慣(习惯)　目光短淺

1. 肉食者 __鄙__，未能遠謀。 [目光短淺]　　2. _____人之城而非攻也。　　[　　]

3. 縱性情，_____忿睢。　　[　　]　　4. 我決起而飛，_____榆、枋。　　[　　]

5. 將不勝其_____而蟻附之。 [　　]　　6. _____人之性，順人之情。 [　　]

7. 適百里者_____春糧。 [　　]　　8. 故_____異室以利其室。 [　　]

9. 惡_____不孝？ [　　]　　10. 而後乃今_____風。 [　　]

11. 腹猶_____然。 [　　]　　12. 以_____飾人之情性而正之。 [　　]

13. 小敵之堅，大敵之_____。 [　　]　　14. 知彼知己者，百戰不_____。 [　　]

三、給加點字選擇正確的釋義，並選出與加點字用法相同的句子 Circle the letter of the correct definition (a, b, c, or d) for the dotted word in each boldfaced sentence. Then circle the letter of the sentence (A, B, C, or D) that employs the dotted word in the same way as the boldfaced sentence.

1. 臣之妻私臣。　　a. 這(这)件事情 b. 他 ⓒ 的 d. 他們

　　A. 夫晉，何厭之有？　　B. 不闕秦，將焉取之？

　　C. 肉食者謀之，又何間焉？　　Ⓓ 能面刺寡人之過者，受上賞。

2. 奚以知其然？　　a. 哪裏(里) b. 爲什麼(为什么) c. 而且 d. 什麼(么)

　　A. 奚以之九萬里而南爲？　　B. 乃入見，問何以戰？

　　C. 肉食者謀之，又何間焉？　　D. 徐公何能及君？

3. 之二蟲又何知？　　a. 去 b. 的 c. 這(这) d. 他們

　　A. 譬之如醫之攻人之疾者然。　　B. 風之積也不厚，則其負大翼也無力。

　　C. 楚之南有冥靈者。　　D. 卒之東郭墦間，之祭者，乞其餘。

4. 今之人性，生而有好利焉。　　a. 啊 b. 什麼(么) c. 怎麼(么) d. 在那裏(里)

　　A. 焉用亡鄭以陪鄰？　　B. 必知亂之所自起，焉能治之。

　　C. 故淫亂生而禮義文理亡焉。　　D. 置杯焉則膠，水淺而舟大也。

5. 猶有不孝者乎？　　a. 就像 b. 還(还) c. 如果 d. 一樣(样)

　　A. 民之有口，猶土之有山川也。　　B. 適莽蒼者三湌而反，腹猶果然。

　　C. 猶之與人也，出納之吝，謂之有司。　　D. 性猶湍水也。

6. 視父兄與君若其身，惡施不孝？　　a. 惡(恶)行 b. 憎恨 c. 怎麼(么) d. 邪惡(恶)

　　A. 惡得不禁惡而勸愛？　　B. 天下兼相愛則治，交相惡則亂。

　　C. 人之性惡，其善者偽也。　　D. 視弟子與臣若其身，惡施不慈？

7. 昔者莊周夢爲胡蝶，栩栩然胡蝶也。　a. 而且 b. 但是 c. 這樣(这样) d. 樣(样)子

　　A. 曰："是不然。"　　B. 然則從人之性，順人之情，必出於争奪。

C. 適莽蒼者三湌而反，腹猶果然。　　　D. 奚以知其然也？

四、閱讀下面的段落，選擇正確的釋義 Read the following passage, and select the correct definition for each dotted word in the following list.

　　楚昭王失國，屠羊說走而從於昭王。昭王反國，將賞從者，及屠羊說。

　　屠羊說曰：「大王失國，說失屠羊；大王反國，說亦反屠羊。臣之爵祿已復矣，又何賞之言？」

　　王曰：「強之。」

　　屠羊說曰：「大王失國，非臣之罪，故不敢伏其誅；大王反國，非臣之功，故不敢當其賞。」

　　王曰：「見之！」

　　屠羊說曰：「楚國之法，必有重賞大功而後得見。今臣之知不足以存國，而勇不足以死寇。吳軍入郢，說畏難而避寇，非故隨大王也。今大王欲廢法毀約而見說，此非臣之所以聞於天下也。」

　　王謂司馬子綦曰：「屠羊說居處卑賤而陳義甚高，子綦爲我延之以三旌之位。」

　　屠羊說曰：「夫三旌之位，吾知其貴於屠羊之肆也；萬鍾之祿，吾知其富於屠羊之利也。然豈可以食爵祿而使吾君有妄施之名乎！說不敢當，願復反吾屠羊之肆。」

　　遂不受也。

《莊子集解》卷八《讓王第二十八》，北京：中華書局 (1987), 254–255.

楚昭王 King Zhao of Chu (r. 516–489 BCE).
屠羊說 (yuè) a sheep-butcher whose name is Yue 說.

爵 *n.* ranks of nobility.　　祿 *n.* salary.　　強(qiǎng) *v.* to force.
伏 *v.* to acknowledge a crime.　誅 *v.* to punish.　見 *v.* to receive, meet
寇 *n.* invaders, bandits.　　郢 capital of the Chu state.　司馬 *n.* minister of war.
子綦 a name.　　　　肆 *n.* shop.　　延 *v.* to invite.
三旌之位 the high official position.

1. 屠羊說走而從於昭王　　a. 逃跑　　　b. 走路　　　c. 來(来)
2. 昭王反國　　　　　　　a. 反面　　　b. 返回　　　c. 對(对)
3. 將賞從者　　　　　　　a. 跟從(从)　b. 縱(纵)容　c. 從(从)前
4. 今臣之知(zhi)不足以存國　a. 知識(识)　b. 智慧　　　c. 知道
5. 勇不足以死寇　　　　　a. 死了　　　b. 重大的　　c. 使……死去
6. 此非臣之所以聞於天下也　a. 聽説(听说)　b. 聽(听)　　c. 聞(闻)名

7. 延之以三旌之位　　a. 憑藉（凭借）　b. 用　　　c. 來（来）

8. 吾知其富於屠羊之利　a. 有利　　b. 便利　　c. 利益

9. 然豈可以……　　　a. 但是　　b. 對（对）　c. 一樣（样）

五、將下列句子翻譯成現代漢語 Translate the following sentences into modern Chinese.

1. 鵬之徙于南冥也，水擊三千里，搏扶搖而上者九萬里，去以六月息者也。

現代文翻译：＿＿＿＿＿＿＿＿＿＿＿＿＿＿＿＿＿＿＿＿＿＿＿＿＿＿

2. 野馬也，塵埃也，生物之以息相吹也。

現代文翻译：＿＿＿＿＿＿＿＿＿＿＿＿＿＿＿＿＿＿＿＿＿＿＿＿＿＿

3. 古者聖王以人性惡，以爲偏險而不正，悖亂而不治，是以爲之起禮義，制法度，以矯飾人之情性而正之，以擾化人之情性而導之也。

現代文翻译：＿＿＿＿＿＿＿＿＿＿＿＿＿＿＿＿＿＿＿＿＿＿＿＿＿＿

4. 夫可以見之明不離目，可以聽之聰不離耳，目明而耳聰，不可學明矣。

現代文翻译：＿＿＿＿＿＿＿＿＿＿＿＿＿＿＿＿＿＿＿＿＿＿＿＿＿＿

5. 故善用兵者，屈人之兵而非戰也，拔人之城而非攻也，毀人之國而非久也。

現代文翻译：＿＿＿＿＿＿＿＿＿＿＿＿＿＿＿＿＿＿＿＿＿＿＿＿＿＿

6. 知彼知己者，百戰不殆；不知彼而知己，一勝一負；不知彼，不知己，每戰必殆。

現代文翻译：＿＿＿＿＿＿＿＿＿＿＿＿＿＿＿＿＿＿＿＿＿＿＿＿＿＿

7. 聖人以治天下爲事者也，必知亂之所自起，焉能治之；不知亂之所自起，則不能治。

現代文翻译：＿＿＿＿＿＿＿＿＿＿＿＿＿＿＿＿＿＿＿＿＿＿＿＿＿＿

8. 故天下兼相愛則治，交相惡則亂。

現代文翻译：＿＿＿＿＿＿＿＿＿＿＿＿＿＿＿＿＿＿＿＿＿＿＿＿＿＿

第十三課

《史記・伯夷列傳》（上）

"Biography of Boyi" (I), from *Grand Scribe's Records* (Sima Qian)

Introduction

The famous early Han historian Sima Qian 司馬遷 (ca. 145—90 BCE) wrote *Grand Scribe's Records*, hereafter the *Records*, the earliest comprehensive history of China. It covers roughly twenty-five hundred years from the legendary Yellow Emperor to Emperor Wu of Han.

The *Records* consists of twelve *Basic Annals* 本紀 (*Běnjì* 本纪), thirty *Hereditary Houses* 世家 (*Shìjiā* 世家), seventy *Arrayed Memoirs* 列傳 (*Lièzhuàn* 列传), ten *Chronological Tables* 表 (*Biǎo* 表), and eight *Treatises* 書 (*Shū* 书). The *Basic Annals* contain the biographies of dynastic rulers, while the *Hereditary Houses* record significant events in the history of ruling houses of both vassal states and nobles, and the *Ordered Biographies* contain biographies of important officials and non-nobles. The *Records* adopts a unique biographical style 紀傳體 (*jìzhuàn tǐ* 纪传体) as it presents a grand history through a series of individual profiles. This biographical approach became the model of history writing in dynastic China.

Sima Qian's *Records* is hailed not only as a masterpiece of historiography but also as a great work of biographical literature, lauded for its lifelike portrayal of human characters through their dialogues, speeches, and actions. Making bold use of the vernacular, *Records* profoundly influenced later Chinese prose, especially narrative writings.

"The Biography of Boyi and Shuqi," first of the ordered biographies, gives an account of two historical figures lionized by Confucius as moral paragons. For a synopsis of this biography, see the introduction to lesson 14.

正文與簡體譯文 Text and Modern Chinese Translation

夫學者載籍極博，猶考信於六藝。[1]
fú xué zhě zǎi jí jí bó　　yóu kǎo xìn yú liù yì

《詩》《書》雖缺，然虞夏之文可知也。[2]
shī　　shū　suī quē　　rán yú xià zhī wén kě zhī yě

堯將遜位，讓於虞舜，[3]舜禹之間，岳牧咸
yáo jiāng xùn wèi　ràng yú yú shùn　　shùn yǔ zhī jiān　　yuè mù xián

薦，[4]乃試之於位，典職數十年，功用既興，
jiàn　　nǎi shì zhī yú wèi　　diǎn zhí shù shí nián　gōng yòng jì xīng

学者(读的)书籍非常多，(但)还要在六经中考察真实可信的(记录)。[1]《诗经》和《尚书》虽然残缺不全，但是记录虞朝和夏朝的文字还是可以知道的。[2]尧将要退位时，把王位让给了虞舜。[3]舜和禹之间传位的时候，四岳十二

然後授政。⁵示天下重器，王者大統，傳天下
rán hòu shòu zhèng　shì tiān xià zhòng qì　wáng zhě dà tǒng chuán tiān xià

若斯之難也。⁶而說者曰堯讓天下於許由，許
ruò sī zhī nán yě　　ér shuō zhě yuē yáo ràng tiān xià yú xǔ yóu　　xǔ

由不受，恥之逃隱。⁷及夏之時，有卞隨、務
yóu bú shòu　chǐ zhī táo yǐn　　jí xià zhī shí　　yǒu biàn suí　wù

光者。此何以稱焉？⁸
guāng zhě　　cǐ hé yǐ chēng yān

牧(的诸侯和官员们)都来推荐，⁴这才用王位来考察他，让他主管职务数十年，等到他功绩已经建立了，然后才传给他政权。⁵这显示出天下最重要的宝器，王者帝位，传下去像这样的难啊！⁶但一些杂说记载尧把天下让给许由，许由不接受，以之为耻，逃走并隐居起来。⁷等到夏朝的时候，又有了卞随和务光。这凭什么称赞他们呢？⁸

1. 夫 (fú) *initial particle*. See L2 Grammar Note 4 ①.

   學 (学) 者 *n.* scholars.

   載 (载 zǎi) *v.* to record, describe. MdnC: 記錄 (*jì lù* 记录).

   籍 *n.* book. 載籍 means "books" 書籍 (*shū jí* 书籍).

   博 *adj.* rich, plentiful. MdnC: 多 (*duō*).

   猶 (犹) *adv.* still. MdnC: 還 (*hái* 还). See L3 Grammar Note 3 ①.

   考 *v.* to examine, investigate. MdnC: 考察 (*kǎo chá*).

   信 *adj.* true. MdnC: 真實 (*zhēn shí* 真实).

   六藝 (艺) six Confucian classics. See Culture Note 1.

2. 《詩》(诗) *Book of Poetry* 詩經 (*Shī jīng* 诗经).

   《書》(书) *Book of History* 尚書 (*Shàng shū* 尚书).

   缺 *adj.* incomplete. MdnC: 殘缺 (*cán quē* 残缺).

   虞 a legendary ancient dynasty ruling China before the Xia 夏 (2070?–1600? BCE), Shang 商 (1600?–1046 BCE), and Zhou 周 (1046–256 BCE) dynasties according to *Zuo Tradition* 左傳, *Discourses of the States* 國語, and some other sources. The *Book of History* also begins with "Book of Yu" 虞書 (Yú shū 虞书).

   夏 the Xia dynasty, the first dynasty recorded in Chinese history books.

3. 堯 (尧) (ancestral name 姓, Yīqí 伊祁; family name 氏, Táotáng 陶唐; given name 名, Fàngxūn 放勋; 2356?–2255? BCE), a legendary ancient ruler also known as 唐堯 (Táng Yáo).

   遜 (逊) *v.* to abdicate. MdnC: 退 (*tuì*).

   位 *n.* seat, position. Here it refers to the position of being a ruler. MdnC: 王位 (*wáng wèi*).

   讓 (让) *v.* to give away, yield. MdnC: 讓給 (*ràng gěi* 让给).

   虞舜 or 舜 (ancestral name 姓, Yáo 姚; family name 氏, Yǒuyú 有虞氏; given name 名, Chóng huá 重華), Yao's 堯 successor as ruler of China at that time. Shun's 舜 clan name 氏 is Yǒu Yú 有虞(氏), so he is also called Yu Shun 虞舜 in some historical records.

4. 禹 (ancestral name 姓, Sì 姒; given name 名, Wénmìng 文命; style 字, Gāomì 高密; r. ?–2025 BCE), a legendary ancient ruler known for successfully controlling floods and for establishing the Xia dynasty, the first in Chinese history.

岳 or 四岳 the legendary four dukes of the Shun period.

牧 or 十二牧 the legendary twelve governors of the Shun period.

咸 *adv.* all, completely. MdnC: 都 (*dōu*). See L24 Grammar Note 1 ①.

薦 (荐) *v.* to recommend. MdnC: 推薦 (*tuī jiàn* 推荐).

5. 試 (试) *v.* to test, examine, try. MdnC: 考察 (*kǎo chá*).

之 *personal pron.* him. Here 之 refers to 禹. See L1 Grammar Note 2 ③.

典 *v.* to be in charge of. MdnC: 主管 (*zhǔ guǎn*).

職 (职) *n.* duty, position, office. MdnC: 職務 (*zhí wù* 职务).

功用 *n.* merits and achievements, contributions. MdnC: 功績 (*gōng jì* 功绩).

既 *adv.* already. MdnC: 已經 (*yǐ jīng* 已经). See L1 Grammar Note 5.

興 (兴 xīng) *v.* to rise, prosper. MdnC: 建立 (*jiàn lì*).

授 *v.* to give to, transfer. MdnC: 傳給 (*chuán gěi* 传给).

政 *n.* regime. MdnC: 政權 (*zhèng quán* 政权).

6. 示 *v.* to show, demonstrate. MdnC: 顯示 (*xiǎn shì* 显示).

器 *n.* vessel, container, receptacle. Here it means "the precious vessel."

統 (统) *n.* succession. 大統 (统) means "the position of being an emperor" 帝位 (*dì wèi*).

傳 (传 chuán) *v.* to transmit, transfer, hand down.

斯 *demonstrative pron.* this. It refers to the long procedure by which Yao 堯 and Shun 舜, respectively, transferred their throne to Shun 舜 and Yu 禹. MdnC: 這樣 (*zhè yàng* 这样). See L5 Grammar Note 3 ①.

之 *particle.* a possessive marker. MdnC: 的 (*de*). See L1 Grammar Note 2 ②.

7. 說 (说) *v.* to speak, say. 說者 refers to miscellaneous records.

許 (许) 由 a legendary recluse who lived during the reign of the Yao 堯.

受 *v.* to accept. MdnC: 接受 (*jiē shòu*).

恥 (耻) *adj.* shameful. Here 恥 is used as a putative verb, 以……爲恥 (为耻), meaning "to consider something shameful." See L14 Grammar Note 1 ①.

逃 *v.* to run, escape. MdnC: 逃走 (*táo zǒu*).

隱 (隐) *v.* to live in seclusion. MdnC: 隱居 (*yǐn jū* 隐居).

8. 及 *prep.* with regard to (time). MdnC: 等到 (*děng dào*).

卞隨 (随) a renowned recluse in ancient China. According to "Rising Above the Worldly" 離俗 ("Lí sú" 离俗) in *Mr. Lü's Spring and Autumn Annals* 呂氏春秋 (*Lǚ shì chūn qiū*), King Tang 湯 of the Shang dynasty gave the throne to Bian Sui after he defeated King Jie 傑 of the Xia dynasty. However, Bian Sui refused to accept it. Then he threw himself into the river and died.

務 (务) 光 a recluse known for refusing the offer of the throne by King Tang of the Shang dynasty. Later he sank himself in the river with a stone. His story is also recorded in "Rising Above the Worldly" in *Mr. Lü's Spring and Autumn Annals*.

何以 by what? MdnC: 憑什麼 (*píng shén me* 凭什么). See L1 Grammar Note 3 ③.

稱 (称) *v.* to praise, compliment. MdnC: 稱贊 (*chēng zàn* 称赞).

焉 *ending particle.* MdnC: 呢 (*ne*). See L2 Grammar Note 3 ②.

太史公曰： 余登箕山， 其上蓋有許由冢
tài shǐ gōng yuē　　yú dēng jī shān　　qí shàng gài yǒu xǔ yóu zhǒng

太史公说：我登上箕山，据说山上可能有许

云。⁹孔子序列古之仁聖賢人，如吳太伯、伯
yún　　kǒng zǐ xù liè gǔ zhī rén shèng xián rén　rú wú tài bó　bó

夷之倫詳矣。¹⁰余以所聞由、光義至高，其文
yí　zhī lún xiáng yǐ　　　yú　yǐ suǒ wén yóu　guāng yì zhì gāo　　qí wén

辭不少概見，何哉？¹¹
cí　bù shāo gài jiàn　　hé zāi

由的墓。⁹孔子依次论述古代的仁人、圣人、贤人，像吴太伯和伯夷之类的人(记录得很)详细。¹⁰我认为我所听到的许由和务光德行极高，(但)孔子的文字中看不到略微一点概述，为什么呢？¹¹

9. 太史公 *n.* grand historian, the form of self-address used by Sima Qian 司馬遷 in *Grand Scribe's Records*.

   登 *v.* to climb, ascend.

   箕山 Ji Mountain, in present-day Dengfeng 登封, Henan Province.

   蓋 (盖) *adv.* probably. MdnC: 可能 (*kě néng*). See Grammar Note 1.

   冢 *n.* tomb. MdnC: 墓 (*mù*).

   云 *ending particle.* ends an indirect quotation or summary. See L17 Grammar Note 1.

10. 序 *n.* sequence, order. Here it is a verb, meaning "to put in order."

    列 *v.* to arrange in order, classify.

    序列 means "to expound on … in sequence 依次論述" (*yī cì lùn shù* 依次论述).

    仁 *adj.* humane, kind.

    聖 (圣) *adj.* sage.

    賢 (贤) *adj.* worthy, virtuous, good.

    如 *v.* to be like, such as. MdnC: 像 (*xiàng*). See L3 Grammar Note 5 ①.

    吳太伯 or 泰伯 (ancestral name 姓, Jī 姬; given name 名, Tàibó 泰伯), the eldest son of King Tai of Zhou 周太王. Since his father gave the throne to his youngest brother, Jili 季歷, Taibo went to the southeast and built the Wu state (in present-day Jiangsu Province).

    伯夷 (ancestral name 姓, Zǐ 子; family name 氏, Mòtāi 墨胎; given name 名, Yǔn 允), the eldest son of the eighth king of the Guzhu state 孤竹國 in the Shang dynasty.

    倫 (伦) *n.* category, group. MdnC: 類 (*lèi* 类).

    詳 *adj.* detailed, in detail, precise. MdnC: 詳細 (*xiáng xì* 详细).

11. 以 *v.* to think, regard. MdnC: 認爲 (*rèn wéi* 认为). See L10 Grammar Note 2 ⑤.

    聞 (闻) *v.* to hear. MdnC: 聽到 (*tīng dào* 听到).

    義 (义) *n.* righteousness. MdnC: 德行 (*dé xíng*).

    至 *adv.* extremely, most. MdnC: 極 (*jí* 极).

    辭 (辞) *n.* words, phrase, expression.

    少 (shāo) *adv.* used in the sense of 稍 (*shāo*), meaning "a little" 略微 (*lüè wēi*).

    概 *n.* summary. MdnC: 概述 (*gài shù*).

孔子曰：「伯夷、叔齊，不念舊惡，怨
kǒng zǐ yuē　　　bó yí　shū qí　bú niàn jiù è　yuàn

是用希。」¹²「求仁得仁，又何怨乎？」¹³余
shì yòng xī　　　qiú rén dé rén　yòu hé yuàn hū　　yú

孔子说："伯夷、叔齐不想着以前(别人的)恶行，怨恨因此也少了。"¹² "(他们)追求仁德而得到仁德，还有什

悲<u>伯夷</u>之意，睹<u>軼</u>詩可異焉。¹⁴ 其傳曰：¹⁵
bēi bó yí zhī yì　　dǔ yì shī kě yì yān　　qí zhuàn yuē

么可怨恨的呢？"¹³我同情伯夷的意志，看散失的诗篇又觉得奇怪啊！¹⁴他的传记上说：¹⁵

12. 孔子曰 a quotation of Confucius from chapter 5 公冶長 ("Gōng yě cháng" 公冶长) of the *Analects*.

　　叔齊 (齐) (ancestral name 姓, Zǐ 子; family name 氏, Mòtāi 墨胎; given name 名, Zhì 致), the third son of the eighth king of the Guzhu state 孤竹國 in the Shang dynasty.

　　念 *v.* to think of, recall. MdnC: 想 (*xiǎng*).

　　舊 (旧) *adj.* old, past, former. MdnC: 以前 (*yǐ qián*).

　　惡 (恶 è) *n.* evil, vice, wickedness. MdnC: 惡行 (*è xíng* 恶行).

　　是 *demonstrative pron.* this. Here it refers to Boyi 伯夷 and Shuqi 叔齊 not complaining about any wrong done to them. MdnC: 這樣 (*zhè yàng* 这样). See L3 Grammar Note 1 ①.

　　用 *prep.* because of. MdnC: 因 (*yīn*).

　　是用 the normal word order should be 用是 here, meaning "because of this."

　　希 *adj.* used in the sense of 稀 (*xī*), meaning "few or rare" 少 (*shǎo*).

13. 求仁得仁 a quotation of Confucius from chapter 7 述而 ("Shù ér") of the *Analects*.

　　求 *v.* to pursue, chase after. MdnC: 追求 (*zhuīqiú*).

　　仁 *n.* benevolence, virtue. MdnC: 仁德 (*rén dé*).

　　得 *v.* to get, obtain. MdnC: 得到 (*dé dào*).

14. 悲 *v.* to feel sorry for, pity. MdnC: 同情 (*tóng qíng*).

　　意 *n.* will, determination. MdnC: 意志 (*yì zhì*).

　　睹 *v.* to see. MdnC: 看 (*kàn*).

　　軼 (轶) *adj.* scattered, lost. MdnC: 散失 (*sàn shī*).

　　異 *adj.* strange, odd. MdnC: 奇怪 (*qí guài*).

　　焉 *ending particle.* MdnC: 啊 (*a*). See L2 Grammar Note 3 ②.

15. 傳 (传 zhuàn) *n.* biography. MdnC: 傳記 (*zhuàn jì* 传记).

<u>伯夷</u>、<u>叔齊</u>，<u>孤竹君</u>之二子也。父欲立
bó yí　　shū qí　　gū zhú jūn zhī èr zǐ yě　　fù yù lì

<u>叔齊</u>，及父卒，<u>叔齊</u>讓<u>伯夷</u>。¹⁶ <u>伯夷</u>曰：「父
shū qí　　jí fù zú　　shū qí ràng bó yí　　bó yí yuē　　fù

命也。」遂逃去。<u>叔齊</u>亦不肯立而逃之。國
mìng yě　　suì táo qù　　shū qí yì bù kěn lì ér táo zhī　　guó

人立其中子。¹⁷ 於是<u>伯夷</u>、<u>叔齊</u>聞<u>西伯昌</u>善養
rén lì qí zhōng zǐ　　yú shì bó yí　　shū qí wén xī bó chāng shàn yǎng

老，盍往歸焉。¹⁸ 及至，<u>西伯</u>卒，<u>武王</u>載木
lǎo　　hé wǎng guī yān　　jí zhì　　xī bó zú　　wǔ wáng zài mù

伯夷和叔齐是孤竹国君的两个儿子。父亲要立叔齐为下一任国君。等父亲死了，叔齐让位给伯夷。¹⁶伯夷说："这是父亲的命令啊！"于是逃走了。叔齐也不肯当孤竹国的国君，也逃走了。孤竹国人就立了孤竹国君的第二个儿子为新的国君。¹⁷于是伯夷和叔齐听说西伯昌善养老人，（觉得）何不去

主，號爲文王，東伐紂。[19]伯夷、叔齊叩馬而
zhǔ　　hào wéi wén wáng　dōng fá zhòu　　bó yí　　shū qí kòu mǎ ér

諫曰：「父死不葬，爰及干戈，可謂孝乎？
jiàn yuē　　fù sǐ bú zàng　yuán jí gān gē　kě wèi xiào hū

以臣弒君，可謂仁乎？」[20]左右欲兵之。太公
yǐ chén shì jūn　kě wèi rén hū　　zuǒ yòu yù bīng zhī　tài gōng

曰：「此義人也。」扶而去之。[21]
yuē　　cǐ yì rén yě　　fú ér qù zhī

归附他呢！[18]等到了那儿，西伯昌已经死了，武王载着西伯昌的牌位，尊他谥号为文王，向东讨伐商纣王。[19]伯夷和叔齐勒住马向武王进谏说："父亲去世不下葬，就开始战争，可以称作孝顺吗？凭着臣子的身份去杀死国君，可以称作仁义吗？"[20]武王的侍从要杀他们。姜太公说："这是有节义的人啊！"扶着他们让他们离开了。[21]

16. 君 *n.* king. MdnC: 國君 (*guó jūn* 国君).
    立 *v.* to determine an heir to the throne.
    卒 *v.* to die, pass away. MdnC: 死 (*sǐ*).

17. 命 *n.* order, will. MdnC: 命令 (*mìng lìng*).
    遂 *conj.* then, thus. MdnC: 於是 (*yú shì* 于是).
    之 *particle.* an added syllable with no meaning in itself. See L1 Grammar Note 2 ④.
    中子 the second son.

18. 西伯昌 or 周文王 (ancestral name 姓, Jī 姬; given name 名, Chāng 昌; posthumous name 諡 (谥), Zhōu Wén Wáng 周文王; 1152–1056 BCE). Ji Chang was given the title of Duke Xibo 西伯 after his father died. His son, King Wu of Zhou 周武王, defeated the last king of the Shang and founded the Zhou dynasty. Thus, Ji Chang was posthumously honored by his son as King Wen of Zhou.
    善 *v.* to be good at, be inclined to.
    老 *adj.* old. Here it refers to old people.
    盍 *initial interrogative particle.* why not? MdnC: 何不 (*hé bù*). See Grammar Note 3.
    往 *v.* to go. MdnC: 去 (*qù*).
    歸 (归) *v.* to take refuge with. MdnC: 歸附 (*guī fù* 归附).
    焉 *demonstrative pron.* an equivalent of 之, here referring to 西伯昌. See L6 Grammar Note 5 ⑤.

19. 武王 or 周武王 (ancestral name 姓, Jī 姬; given name 名, Fā 發; posthumous name 諡, Zhōu Wǔ Wáng 周武王; ?–1043 BCE), King Wu of Zhou, the founder of the Zhou dynasty. Ji Fa was the second son of King Wen of Zhou 周文王. He overthrew the Shang dynasty when he defeated King Zhou of Shang 商紂王 at the Battle of Muye 牧野之戰 (*Mùyě zhī zhàn*) in 1046 BCE. Ji Fa was posthumously called King Wu of Zhou.
    載 (载 *zài*) *v.* to carry.
    木主 wooden tablet of King Wen of Zhou. MdnC: 牌位 (*pái wèi*).
    號 (号 *hào*) *n.* posthumous title. MdnC: 諡號 (*shì hào* 谥号). Here it used as a verb, meaning "to bestow a posthumous title upon."
    爲 (为 *wéi*) *v.* to be. See L9 Grammar Note 1 ③.

東 (东) *n.* east. Here it is an adverb, meaning "eastward" 向東 (*xiàng dōng* 向东).

伐 *v.* to attack. MdnC: 討伐 (*tǎo fá* 讨伐).

紂 (纣) or 商紂王 (ancestral name 姓, Zǐ 子; given name 名, Shòu 受; posthumous name 諡, Zhòu 紂; 1090?–1044 BCE), a tyrannical king and the last of the Shang dynasty. Zhou 紂 is his derogatory posthumous title.

20. 叩 *v.* to bow, kowtow. Here it is used in the sense of 扣 (*kòu*), meaning "to pull/take the reins" 勒住韁繩 (*lè zhù jiāng shéng* 勒住缰绳).

諫 (谏) *v.* to admonish, remonstrate. MdnC: 進諫 (*jìn jiàn* 进谏).

葬 *v.* to bury, inter. MdnC: 下葬 (*xià zàng*).

爰 *conj.* then, therefore. MdnC: 就 (*jiù*).

干 (*gān*) *n.* shield. MdnC: 盾 (*dùn*).

戈 *n.* spear. MdnC: 矛 (*máo*).

干戈 *n.* weapons of war, war. MdnC: 戰爭 (*zhàn zhēng* 战争).

以 *coverb.* by means of. See L2 Grammar Note 1 ②.

弒 *v.* to kill. MdnC: 殺死 (*shā sǐ* 杀死).

21. 左右 *n.* left and right. It refers to the king's attendants 侍從 (*shì cóng* 侍从).

兵 *n.* weapon. Here it is used as a verb, meaning "to kill … by using a weapon."

之 *pron.* them, Boyi and Shuqi. See L1 Grammar Note 2 ③.

太公 or 姜太公 (ancestral name 姓, Jiāng 姜; family name 氏, Lǚ 吕; given name 名, Shàng 尚; style 字, Zǐyá 子牙; fl. 1128?–1015? BCE), a known strategist in the late Shang and early Zhou dynasties. Jiang Shang was first hired by King Wen of Zhou 周文王 and given an official position as master 太師 (*tài shī* 太师). After King Wen of Zhou died, Jiang continued to assist King Wu of Zhou 周武王 in building the Zhou dynasty. He is often called 太公望 (*Tàigōng Wàng*) or 太公.

義 (义) *n.* righteousness. MdnC: 節義 (*jié yì* 节义).

扶 *v.* to hold by the arm.

去 *v.* to leave. 去 is an intransitive verb, but here, with 之, 去 is used as a causative verb, 使之去, meaning "to let them leave." See L7 Grammar Note 1 ①.

武王已平殷亂，天下宗周，而伯夷、叔
wǔ wáng yǐ píng yīn luàn tiān xià zōng zhōu ér bó yí shū

齊恥之，義不食周粟，隱於首陽山，采薇而
qí chǐ zhī   yì bù shí zhōu sù   yǐn yú shǒu yáng shān   cǎi wēi ér

食之。²² 及餓且死，作歌。²³ 其辭曰：「登彼
shí zhī   jí è qiě sǐ   zuò gē   qí cí yuē   dēng bǐ

西山兮，采其薇矣。以暴易暴兮，不知其非
xī shān xī   cǎi qí wēi yǐ   yǐ bào yì bào xī   bù zhī qí fēi

矣。²⁴ 神農、虞、夏忽焉沒兮，我安適歸
yǐ   shén nóng yú   xià hū yān mò xī   wǒ ān shì guī

武王已经平定了商朝的叛乱，天下都以周为宗主，但伯夷和叔齐以此为耻，坚持节义，不吃周朝的粮食，隐居在首阳山，采野菜来吃。²² 等到饿得要死去时，做了首歌。²³ 这首歌是："登上那个西山呀！采摘它上面的野菜！用残暴（的臣子）来换残暴（的君王）啊！不知这是错误的！²⁴ 神农、虞

矣？ ²⁵ 于嗟徂兮，命之衰矣！ ²⁶」遂餓死於首
yǐ　　　xū jiē cú xī　　mìng zhī shuāi yǐ　　　suì è sǐ yú shǒu

陽山。
yáng shān

由此觀之，怨邪非邪？ ²⁷
yóu cǐ guān zhī　　yuàn yé fēi yé

舜、夏禹(这些君王)忽
然都消失了！我能归附
去哪里！²⁵哎！只有死
亡啊！命运这样不济
啊！²⁶」(伯夷和叔齐)
于是饿死在首阳山上。
从这首歌来看他们，他
们是怨恨还是不怨恨
呢？²⁷

《史記》，北京：中華書局 (1982), 2121–2123.

22. 平 *v.* to suppress. MdnC: 平定 (*píng dìng*).

　　殷 the Shang dynasty.

　　亂 (乱) *n.* chaos.

　　宗 *n.* ancestor, founding ancestor of a clan. MdnC: 宗主 (*zōng zhǔ*). Here 宗 is used as a putative verb,
　　　以……爲宗, meaning "to regard … as the ancestor." See L14 Grammar Note 1 ②.

　　恥 (耻) *adj.* shameful. Here 恥 is used as a putative verb. 恥之 means 以之爲恥 (为耻), "to consider it
　　　shameful." See L14 Grammar Note 1 ①.

　　粟 *n.* grain. Here it refers to food 糧食 (*liáng shí* 粮食).

　　首陽 (阳) 山 Mount Shouyang, in present-day Yanshi 偃師, Henan Province.

　　薇 *n.* edible wild plants. MdnC: 野菜 (*yě cài*).

23. 且 *adv.* marker of future action, about to. MdnC: 將要 (*jiāng yào* 将要). See Grammar Note 2 ③.

24. 彼 *demonstrative pron.* that. MdnC: 那 (*nà*). See L14 Grammar Note 2 ①.

　　西山 west mountain. Here it refers to Mount Shouyang.

　　兮 *particle.* rhythmic particle placed at the middle or end of lines of some verse.

　　以 *coverb.* to use. MdnC: 用 (*yòng*). See L2 Grammar Note 1 ②.

　　暴 *adj.* tyrannical. MdnC: 殘暴 (*cán bào* 残暴).

　　易 *v.* to exchange. MdnC: 換 (*huàn*).

　　非 *n.* error, wrong. MdnC: 錯誤 (*cuò wù* 错误).

25. 神農 (农) divine farmer, a legendary ruler of ancient China. He was venerated as the legendary creator
　　of Chinese agriculture and medicine.

　　忽 *adv.* all of sudden. MdnC: 忽然 (*hū rán*).

　　焉 *particle.* functioning here as an emotive particle. See L5 Grammar Note 4 ④.

　　沒 (mò) *v.* to disappear. MdnC: 消失 (*xiāo shī*).

　　安 *interrogative particle.* where? MdnC: 哪裏 (*nǎ lǐ* 哪里). See L6 Grammar Note 9.

　　適 (适) *v.* to go to, get to. MdnC: 去 (*qù*).

26. 于 (xū) 嗟 an exclamation of surprise.

　　徂 used in the sense of 殂 (*cú*), meaning "to die" 死 (*sǐ*).

　　命 *n.* fate, destination. MdnC: 命運 (*mìng yùn* 命运).

　　衰 *v.* to decline, weaken. Here it means "bad (fate)" 不濟 (*bú jì* 不济).

27. 怨 *v.* to resent. MdnC: 怨恨 (*yuàn hèn*).

　　非 *v.* to negate. MdnC: 不 (*bù*).

　　邪 *ending interrogative particle.* MdnC: 呢 (*ne*). See L11 Grammar Note 2.

文化常識 Culture Note

1. 六藝(藝、艺) Six Arts. *Six Arts* has two meanings in the pre-Qin period. The first refers to the six basic skills that Confucian scholars must master. According to the *Rites of Zhou* 周禮 (*Zhōulǐ* 周礼), the Six Arts are the six disciplines of aristocratic education before the Western Zhou dynasty: rites 禮 (*lǐ* 礼), music 樂 (*yuè* 乐), archery 射 (*shè*), charioteering 御 (*yù*), calligraphy 書 (*shū* 书), and mathematics 數 (*shù* 数).

    The second refers to the six classics allegedly edited by Confucius: *Book of Poetry* 詩經 (*Shījīng* 诗经), *Book of History* 尚書 (*Shàngshū* 尚书), *Book of Rites* 禮記 (*Lǐjì* 礼记), *Records of Music* 樂記 (*Yuèjì* 乐记), *Book of Changes* 易經 (*Yìjīng* 易经), and *Spring and Autumn Annals* 春秋 (*Chūnqiū*).

語法注釋 Grammar Notes

1. 蓋   *adv.* indicating a measure of uncertainty, probably. MdnC: 可能 (*kě néng*).
(盖)

    余登箕山，其上蓋有許由冢云。

      [我登上箕山，据说山上可能有许由的墓。]

2. 且   ① *conj.* and, moreover, in addition. MdnC: 而且 (*ér qiě*).

    晉侯、秦伯圍鄭，以其無禮於晉，且貳於楚也。(L2)

      [晋文公联合秦穆公围攻郑国，因为郑文公曾对晋文公无礼，而且私下援助楚国攻晋。]

    由也爲之，比及三年，可使有勇，且知方也。(L6)

      [我来治理这个国家，等到三年后，可使这个国家的人民变得勇敢，而且知道方向。]

    ② 且夫 (*fú*) *conj.* besides, furthermore, moreover. MdnC: 況且 (*kuàng qiě* 况且).

    且夫水之積也不厚，則其負大舟也無力之。(L11)

      [况且如果水积聚得不深，那么它也没有力量负载大船。]

    ③ *adv.* marker of future action, about to, will. MdnC: 將要 (*jiāng yào* 将要).

    及餓且死，作歌。

      [等到（他们）饿得将要死去的时候，做了首歌。]

3. 盍   *initial interrogative particle.* why not? MdnC: 何不 (*hé bù*).

    伯夷、叔齊聞西伯昌善養老，盍往歸焉。

      [伯夷和叔齐听说西伯昌善于养老人，（觉得）何不去归顺他呢！]

Literary Analysis

This first of the *lièzhuàn* 列传 (arrayed memoirs), like the first of the *shìjiā* 世家 (hereditary houses), serves as a preface to the memoirs that follow and a key to Sima Qian's thinking on what the biographical form should incorporate. It begins with a short survey of sage rulers who initially refused the throne as well as those who remained steadfast in their refusal of power. Sima Qian in his comments—which normally *end* a chapter—here begins by lamenting how tradition has overlooked the latter group. After citing Confucius's opinion that Boyi and Shuqi did not resent their fate, Sima embeds in his version a *zhuan* (probably an orally transmitted narrative) of the Boyi and Shuqi story that ends with the brothers condemning in song the founders of the Zhou dynasty, Kings Wen and Wu. Boyi and Shuqi were unwilling not only to serve the Zhou but even to eat their grain, preferring to starve on Mount Shouyang. The shifts from expository to narrative to lyric style create a layered account of the brothers' fate and show Sima Qian at his most creative. Note, however, that following this dramatic climax, Sima returns to the question of whether Boyi and Shuqi resented their fate. This becomes a theme of what follows.

☞ *HTRCProse*, chapter 6, "Han Historical Prose: Sima Qian and the *Grand Scribe's Records (Shiji)*" for further comments on Sima Qian's prose writings.

—WHN

課後練習　Exercises

一　給加點字注音　Give the pinyin romanization for each dotted word.

1. 虞舜（＿＿＿, ＿＿＿）2. 堯（＿＿＿）3. 卞隨（＿＿＿）4. 箕山（＿＿＿）5. 伯夷（＿＿＿）
6. 于嗟（＿＿＿, ＿＿＿）7. 冢（＿＿＿）8. 殷亂（＿＿＿）9. 伐紂（＿＿＿）10. 兮（＿＿＿）

二　在括號中給句中加點的字注音，並選出正確的釋義　Give the pinyin romanization for each dotted word; then select the correct definition from the following list, and write it in the blank.

建立　　散失　　消失　　推薦(荐)　　野菜　　死　　退　　殺(杀)　　**信服**　　看

1. 小信未孚（ **fú** ）　**信服**　2. 堯將遜位（　）＿＿＿＿＿　3. 睹軼詩可異焉（　）＿＿＿＿＿
4. 岳牧咸薦（　）＿＿＿＿＿　5. 功用既興（　）＿＿＿＿＿　6. 睹軼詩可異焉（　）＿＿＿＿＿
7. 以臣弒君（　）＿＿＿＿＿　8. 忽焉沒兮（　）＿＿＿＿＿　9. 采薇而食之（　）＿＿＿＿＿
10. 于嗟徂兮（　）＿＿＿＿＿

三　選擇釋義並填空　Match each word in the left column with its correct definition in the middle column. Fill in each blank in the right column with an appropriate word from the left column.

謀謀劃(谋划)	追求	夫學者載籍極＿＿＿＿，猶考＿＿＿＿於六蓺。
博＿＿＿＿＿＿	概述	堯將遜位，＿＿＿＿於虞舜，舜禹之閒，岳牧＿＿＿＿薦，
讓＿＿＿＿＿＿	進諫(进谏)	乃試之於位，＿＿＿＿職數十年，功用既興，然後授政。
咸＿＿＿＿＿＿	**謀劃(谋划)**	
信＿＿＿＿＿＿	想	
典＿＿＿＿＿＿	去	

倫＿＿＿＿＿＿ 少
概＿＿＿＿＿＿ 討(讨)伐
念＿＿＿＿＿＿ 不濟(济)
伐＿＿＿＿＿＿ 類(类)
諫＿＿＿＿＿＿ 都
適＿＿＿＿＿＿ 主管
衰＿＿＿＿＿＿ 真實(实)
求＿＿＿＿＿＿ 讓給(让给)
希＿＿＿＿＿＿ 多

孔子序列古之仁聖賢人，知吳太伯、伯夷之＿＿＿詳矣。余以所聞由、光義至高，其文辭不少＿＿＿見，何哉？

伯夷、叔齊，不＿＿＿舊惡，怨用是＿＿＿。

＿＿＿仁得仁，又何怨乎？

及至，西伯卒，武王載木主，號爲文王，東＿＿＿紂。伯夷、叔齊叩馬而＿＿＿。

神農、虞、夏忽焉没兮，我安＿＿＿歸矣？于嗟徂兮，命之＿＿＿矣！

四 請用給出的字填空 Fill in each blank with an appropriate word from the following list (some words may be used more than once).

焉 以 何 之 安 邪 且 者 蓋(盖)

1. 而說＿＿＿曰堯讓天下於許由，許由不受，恥＿＿＿逃隱。及夏＿＿＿時，有卞隨、務光＿＿＿。此＿＿＿＿＿＿稱＿＿＿？

2. 余登箕山，其上＿＿＿有許由冢云。

3. 伯夷、叔齊恥＿＿＿，義不食周粟，隱於首陽山，采薇而食＿＿＿。及餓＿＿＿死，作歌。

4. ＿＿＿暴易暴兮，不知其非矣。神農、虞、夏忽＿＿＿没兮，我＿＿＿適歸矣？

5. 由此觀＿＿＿，怨＿＿＿非＿＿＿？

五 爲加點字選擇正確釋義，並根據釋義來翻譯句子 Match each dotted word with its correct modern Chinese equivalent by circling the latter. Then translate each sentence into modern Chinese.

1. 又何間焉? 　　　　　　　　　　ⓐ爲什麽(为什么) b.憑什麽(凭什么) c.多少

現代文翻譯：你又为什么要参与到这件事情里面？
＿＿＿＿＿＿＿＿＿＿＿＿＿＿＿＿＿＿＿＿

2. 夫學者載籍極博，猶考信於六蓺。 　　　a.猶豫(犹豫) b.但是 c.還(还)

現代文翻譯：＿＿＿＿＿＿＿＿＿＿＿＿＿＿＿＿

3. 乃試之於位，典職數十年，功用既興，然後授政。 　a.已經(经) b.既然 c.即使

現代文翻譯：＿＿＿＿＿＿＿＿＿＿＿＿＿＿＿＿

4.余登箕山，其上蓋有許由冢云。　　　　　　　　　a.可能 b.建造 c.何不

现代文翻译：_____

5.伯夷、叔齊，不念舊惡，怨是用希。　　　　　　　a.是的 b.這樣(这样) c.到

现代文翻译：_____

6.於是伯夷、叔齊聞西伯昌善養老，盍往歸焉。　　　a.可能 b.建造 c.何不

现代文翻译：_____

7.神農、虞、夏忽焉没兮，我安適歸矣？　　　a.哪裏(哪里) b.安静 c.爲什麼(为什么)

现代文翻译：_____

第十四課

《史記・伯夷列傳》（下）

"Biography of Boyi" (II), from *Grand Scribe's Records* (Sima Qian)

Introduction

In recounting the lives of Boyi and Shuqi, Sima Qian focuses on their three famous deeds. First, these princes of the state of Guzhu 孤竹 try but fail to convince each other to accept the throne; both end up fleeing their homeland instead. They then risk their lives when they reprimand King Wen of Zhou for launching a military campaign against the Shang when he should have been mourning his father. Finally, after King Wen conquers the Shang and establishes the Zhou dynasty, Boyi and Shuqi refuse to eat Zhou grain, which eventually leads to their deaths. At the end of this biography, Sima Qian steps out of the narrative to express his doubts about the existence of heavenly justice, as Boyi, Shuqi, and other moral paragons end so tragically while many of the most wicked characters enjoy wealth, power, and a ripe old age. The final section reads almost like an essay.

正文與簡體譯文 Text and Modern Chinese Translation

或曰：「天道無親，常與善人。」¹ 若伯
huò yuē　　　tiān dào wú qīn　　cháng yǔ shàn rén　　　　ruò bó

夷、叔齊，可謂善人者非邪？積仁絜行如此
yí　　shū qí　　　kě wèi shàn rén zhě fēi yé　　　jī rén jié xíng rú cǐ

而餓死！² 且七十子之徒，仲尼獨薦顏淵爲好
ér è sǐ　　　qiě qī shí zǐ zhī tú　　zhòng ní dú jiàn yán yuān wéi hào

學。³ 然回也屢空，糟糠不厭，而卒蚤夭。⁴ 天
xué　　　rán huí yě lǚ kōng　　zāo kāng bú yàn　　ér zú zǎo yāo　　tiān

之報施善人，其何如哉？⁵ 盜蹠日殺不辜，肝
zhī bào shī shàn rén　　qí hé rú zāi　　　　dào zhí rì shā bù gū　　gān

人之肉，暴戾恣睢，聚黨數千人橫行天下，
rén zhī ròu　　bào lì zì suī　　jù dǎng shù qiān rén héng xíng tiān xià

竟以壽終。⁶ 是遵何德哉？此其尤大彰明較著
jìng yǐ shòu zhōng　　shì zūn hé dé zāi　　cǐ qí yóu dà zhāng míng jiào zhù

有人说："天道没有亲疏，常给与好人（好报）。"¹ 像伯夷和叔齐，可称为好人还是坏人呢？他们积累仁义，使自己的品行高洁，却饿死了！² 而且孔子的七十位门徒，他只推荐颜渊好学。³ 但颜回也很穷困，粗粮都吃不饱，最终早早夭折了。⁴（所谓）上天报答好人，又怎么样呢！⁵ 盗蹠每天杀害无辜的人，吃人心肝，残暴狂妄，聚集数千人的党徒横行天下，竟然长寿终老。⁶ 这遵循的是什么品德

者也。 [7]
zhě yě

啊！这些都是很明显的
例子啊！ [7]

1. 或 *indefinite pron.* someone. MdnC: 有人 (*yǒu rén*). See L6 Grammar Note 4 ①.
   天道 *n.* the heaven's will.
   親 (亲) *adj.* close to. Here it means "close to or distant from (somebody)" 親疏 (*qīn shū* 亲疏).
   與 (与 *yǔ*) *v.* to give. MdnC: 給與 (*jǐ yǔ* 给与).

2. 若 *v.* to be like. MdnC: 像 (*xiàng*). See L4 Grammar Note 4 ①.
   邪 (*yé*) *ending interrogative particle.* MdnC: 呢 (*ne*). See L11 Grammar Note 2.
   積 (积) *v.* to accumulate, gather. MdnC: 積纍 (*jī léi* 积累).
   絜 (*jié*) an equivalent of 潔 (*jié* 洁), meaning "clean." Here it is used as a causative verb, 使……潔, meaning "to make … clean." See L7 Grammar Note 1 ②.

3. 且 *conj.* moreover, in addition. MdnC: 而且 (*ér qiě*). See L13 Grammar Note 2 ①.
   徒 *n.* disciple, follower. MdnC: 門徒 (*mén tú* 门徒).
   仲尼 Confucius.
   獨 (独) *adv.* only. MdnC: 只 (*zhǐ*).
   薦 (荐) *v.* to recommend, endorse. MdnC: 推薦 (*tuī jiàn* 推荐).
   顏淵 (颜渊) or 顏回, also 回 in the next line. See L5 note 3 for Yan Yuan's brief biography.

4. 屢 (屡) *adv.* often. MdnC: 常 (*cháng*).
   空 (*kōng*) *adj.* empty. Here it means "poor" 窮困 (*qióng kùn* 穷困).
   糟糠 *n.* chaff. MdnC: 粗糧 (*cū liáng* 粗粮). 糟 is sediment left after fermentation of alcohol, and 糠 is the husk of grain.
   厭 (厌) an equivalent of 饜 (*yàn* 餍), meaning "to eat one's fill" 吃飽 (*chī bǎo* 吃饱).
   卒 *adv.* at last, finally. MdnC: 終於 (*zhōng yú* 终于).
   蚤 used in the sense of 早 (*zǎo*), meaning "early."
   夭 *v.* to die young. MdnC: 夭折 (*yāo zhé*).

5. 之 *particle.* a nominative marker. See L2 Grammar Note 2 ⑤.
   報 (报) 施 *v.* to repay. MdnC: 報答 (*bào dá* 报答).
   其 *adv.* used to suggest a tentative thought. See L2 Grammar Note 5 ③.
   何如 how? MdnC: 怎麼樣 (*zěn me yàng* 怎么样). See L6 Grammar Note 3 ④.

6. 盜蹠 or 盜跖 Robber Zhi, a legendary leader of thousands of robbers in the Spring and Autumn period. 蹠 (or *zhí* 跖) is his name.
   日 *n.* day. Here it is used as an adverb, meaning "every day" 每天 (*měi tiān*).
   辜 *adj.* guilt. 不辜 means "innocent or not guilty" 無辜 (*wú gū* 无辜).
   肝 *n.* liver. Here it is used as a verb, meaning "to eat" 吃 (*chī*).
   戾 *adj.* brutal, cruel, violent. MdnC: 殘暴 (*cán bào* 残暴).
   恣睢 *adj.* uncontrolled. MdnC: 狂妄 (*kuáng wàng*).
   聚 *v.* to gather. MdnC: 聚集 (*jù jí*).
   黨 (党) *n.* party, partisan. Here it means "followers or clique" 黨徒 (*dǎng tú* 党徒).
   橫行 *v.* to run amok, be on a rampage.
   竟 *adv.* at last, finally. MdnC: 竟然 (*jìng rán*).
   壽 (寿) *n.* longevity, long life. MdnC: 長壽 (*cháng shòu* 长寿).
   終 (终) *v.* to end. MdnC: 終老 (*zhōng lǎo* 终老).

7. 遵 *v.* to follow, obey. MdnC: 遵循 (*zūn xún*).

　　德 *n.* morality, virtue. MdnC: 道德 (*dào dé*).

　　尤 *adv.* especially, particularly. MdnC: 尤其 (*yóu qí*).

　　彰明較 (较) 著 *adj.* evident, clearly displayed. MdnC: 明顯 (*míng xiǎn* 明显).

　　者 *auxiliary pron.* the case that…. MdnC: ……的例子 (*de lì zi*). See L1 Grammar Note 1 ①.

若至近世， 操行不軌， 專犯忌諱， 而終
ruò zhì jìn shì　　cāo xíng bù guǐ　　zhuān fàn jì huì　　ér zhōng

身逸樂， 富厚累世不絕。⁸或擇地而蹈之， 時
shēn yì lè　　fù hòu lěi shì bù jué　　huò zé dì ér dǎo zhī　　shí

然後出言， 行不由徑， 非公正不發憤， 而遇
rán hòu chū yán　　xíng bù yóu jìng　　fēi gōng zhèng bù fā fèn　　ér yù

禍災者， 不可勝數也。⁹余甚惑焉， 儻所謂天
huò zāi zhě　　bù kě shēng shǔ yě　　yú shèn huò yān　　tǎng suǒ wèi tiān

道， 是邪非邪？¹⁰
dào　　shì yé fēi yé

到了近代，那些操守品行不轨，专门违犯忌讳(的人)，却终身安逸快乐，过着富裕丰厚的生活，世世代代都不断。⁸有人选择好地方才踩上去，选择好时机才开口说话，走路不走小路，不是公正(的事情)不会奋力去做。可这样的人遭遇祸事灾难的，数不过来。⁹我很困惑啊！倘若有所说的天道，(这是)对的呢？还是不对的呢？¹⁰

8. 若 *conj.* as for. See Grammar Note 3 ③.

　　近世 *n.* modern times. MdnC: 近代 (*jìn dài*).

　　操行 *n.* moral character and behavior. MdnC: 操守品行 (*cāo shǒu pǐn xíng*).

　　軌 (轨) *n.* rule, law. 不軌 (轨) means "against the law and moral norms."

　　專 (专) *adv.* specially, particularly. MdnC: 專門 (*zhuān mén* 专门).

　　犯 *v.* to violate, offend (against the law, rules, etc.). MdnC: 違犯 (*wéi fàn* 违犯).

　　忌諱 (讳) *n.* taboo. Here it refers to law or discipline.

　　逸 *adj.* ease, leisure. MdnC: 安逸 (*ān yì*).

　　富 *adj.* rich, wealthy. MdnC: 富裕 (*fù yù*).

　　厚 *adj.* rich and generous. MdnC: 豐厚 (*fēng hòu* 丰厚).

　　累 (*lěi*) *adj.* successive, continuous. 累世 means "successive generations" 世世代代 (*shì shì dài dài*).

　　絕 (绝) *v.* to break off, cut off, stop. MdnC: 斷 (*duàn* 断).

9. 或 *indefinite pron.* some. MdnC: 有人 (*yǒu rén*). See L6 Grammar Note 4 ①.

　　擇 (择) *v.* to select, choose. MdnC: 選擇 (*xuǎn zé* 选择).

　　蹈 *v.* to stamp, stomp. MdnC: 踩 (*cǎi*).

　　時 (时) *n.* time, moment, opportunity. MdnC: 時機 (*shí jī* 时机).

　　行 *v.* to walk. MdnC: 走 (*zǒu*).

　　由 *v.* by way of. MdnC: 經由 (*jīng yóu* 经由).

　　徑 (径) *n.* path. MdnC: 小路 (*xiǎo lù*).

　　發憤 (发愤) *v.* to make a determined effort. MdnC: 奮力 (*fèn lì* 奋力).

　　遇 *v.* to come upon, meet unexpectedly. MdnC: 遭遇 (*zāo yù*).

　　禍災 (祸灾) *n.* misfortune, disaster. MdnC: 禍事災难 (*huò shì zāi nàn* 祸事灾难).

勝 (胜 shēng) *v.* to be capable of. 不勝數 means "innumerable" 數不過來 (*shǔ bú guò lái* 数不过来).

10. 惑 *v.* to puzzle, feel confused. MdnC: 迷惑 (*mí huò*).

焉 *ending particle.* MdnC: 啊 (*a*). See L2 Grammar Note 3 ②.

儻 (傥) *conj.* an equivalent of 倘 (*tǎng*), meaning "if" 倘若 (*tǎng ruò*). See L35 Grammar Note 1.

是 *adj.* correct, right. MdnC: 對 (*duì* 对). See Grammar Note 4 ④.

子曰「道不同不相爲謀」，亦各從其志
zǐ yuē dào bù tóng bù xiāng wéi móu yì gè cóng qí zhì

也。¹¹ 故曰：「富貴如可求，雖執鞭之士，吾
yě gù yuē fù guì rú kě qiú suī zhí biān zhī shì wú

亦爲之。如不可求，從吾所好」。¹² 「歲寒，
yì wéi zhī rú bù kě qiú cóng wú suǒ hào suì hán

然後知松柏之後凋」。¹³ 舉世混濁，清士乃
rán hòu zhī sōng bǎi zhī hòu diāo jǔ shì hùn zhuó qīng shì nǎi

見。¹⁴ 豈以其重若彼，其輕若此哉？¹⁵
xiàn qǐ yǐ qí zhòng ruò bǐ qí qīng ruò cǐ zāi

孔子说，"道路不同，就不互相商量"，（就是说）各人按自己的志向（来走）。¹¹ 所以说："富贵如果可求，即使是拿鞭子的马车夫，我也会做。如求不到，就按我的喜好来吧！"¹² "寒冷（时）才知道松树和柏树最后凋谢。"¹³ 整个社会混乱污浊，品行好的人才能显现出来。¹⁴ 难道不是因为他们那么看重（道德），这样看轻（富贵）吗？¹⁵

11. 道不同不相爲謀 a quotation of Confucius from chapter 15 衛靈公 ("Wèi líng gōng" 卫灵公) of the *Analects*.

道 *n.* way.

謀 (谋) *v.* to consult. MdnC: 商量 (*shāng liáng*).

亦 *adv.* also. See L5 Grammar Note 1 ①.

從 (从) *v.* to follow. MdnC: 按照 (*àn zhào*).

志 *n.* purpose, will. MdnC: 志向 (*zhì xiàng*).

12. 富貴如可求 a quotation of Confucius from chapter 7 述而 ("Shù ér") of the *Analects*.

雖 (虽) *conj.* even though. MdnC: 即使 (*jí shǐ*). See L4 Grammar Note 6.

執 (执) *v.* to hold in hand, carry. MdnC: 拿 (*ná*).

鞭 *n.* whip.

執鞭之士 the person who holds a whip. It refers to a coachman. MdnC: 馬車夫 (*mǎ chē fū*).

好 (hào) *v.* to be fond of. MdnC: 喜好 (*xǐ hào*).

13. 歲寒 a quotation of Confucius from chapter 9 子罕 ("Zǐ hǎn") of the *Analects*.

歲 (岁) *n.* year. MdnC: 年 (*nián*).

寒 *adj.* cold. MdnC: 寒冷 (*hán lěng*).

松柏 *n.* pine and cypress.

之 *particle.* a nominative marker. See L2 Grammar Note 2 ⑤.

凋 *v.* to wither, fall. MdnC: 凋謝 (*diāo xiè* 凋谢).

14. 舉 (举) *adj.* complete, entire. MdnC: 全 (*quán*). 舉 (举) 世 means the entire world, the whole society.

混濁 (浊) *adj.* chaotic and turbid. MdnC: 混亂污濁 (*hùn luàn wū zhuó* 混乱污浊).

清士 *n.* a good, honest, upright man.

見 (见 *xiàn*) an equivalent of 現 (*xiàn* 现), meaning "to appear or show" 顯現 (*xiǎn xiàn* 显现).

15. 豈 (岂) *particle.* usually used in a rhetorical question. MdnC: 難道 (*nán dào* 难道). See L8 Grammar Note 4.

以 *prep.* because. MdnC: 因爲 (*yīn wèi* 因为). See L2 Grammar Note 1 ①.

重 *adj.* heavy, important. Here it is used as a putative verb, 以……爲重, meaning "to consider something important." MdnC: 看重 (*kàn zhòng*). See Grammar Note 1 ①.

若 *v.* to be like. MdnC: 像 (*xiàng*). See L4 Grammar Note 4 ①.

彼 *pron.* that. 彼 is used together with 此 (this) to make a contrast between two different types of personalities. See Grammar Note 2 ②.

輕 (轻) *adj.* light, trivial. Here it is used as a putative verb, 以……爲輕, meaning "to consider something unimportant." MdnC: 看輕 (*kàn qīng* 看轻). See Grammar Note 1 ①.

「君子疾沒世而名不稱焉。」[16] 賈子曰：
jūn zǐ　jí mò shì ér míng bú chēng yān　jiǎ zǐ yuē

「貪夫徇財，烈士徇名，夸者死權，衆庶馮
tān fū xùn cái　liè shì xùn míng　kuā zhě sǐ quán　zhòng shù píng

生。」[17]「同明相照，同類相求。」[18]「雲從
shēng　　tóng míng xiāng zhào, tóng lèi xiāng qiú　　yún cóng

龍，風從虎，聖人作而萬物覩。」[19] 伯夷、叔
lóng　fēng cóng hǔ　shèng rén zuò ér wàn wù dǔ　　bó yí　shū

齊雖賢，得夫子而名益彰。[20] 顏淵雖篤學，附
qí suī xián　dé fū zǐ ér míng yì zhāng　yán yuān suī dǔ xué　fù

驥尾而行益顯。[21] 巖穴之士，趣舍有時若此，
jì wěi ér xíng yì xiǎn　yán xué zhī shì　qū shě yǒu shí ruò cǐ

類名堙滅而不稱，悲夫！[22] 閭巷之人，欲砥行
lèi míng yān miè ér bù chēng　bēi fú　lú xiàng zhī rén　yù dǐ xíng

立名者，非附青雲之士，惡能施于後世哉？[23]
lì míng zhě　fēi fù qīng yún zhī shì　wū néng shī yú hòu shì zāi

《史記》，北京：中華書局 (1982), 2124–2127.

（孔子说：）"君子痛恨死后名声不被后人称道啊！"[16] 贾谊说："贪婪的人为财富而死，品行好的人为名声而死，自大的人为权势而死，老百姓（只能）依靠自己的生命。[17]（《易经》：）"同样明亮的事物互相照亮，同类的东西互相应求。"[18]（又说：）"云彩跟随飞龙，风跟随猛虎，圣人出现了，天下万物才能显现。"[19] 伯夷和叔齐即使贤良，得到孔子（的赞美）后，名声才更加显著。[20] 颜渊即使专心好学，（因为像）依附千里马的尾巴（一样追随孔子），品行才更加明显。[21] 住在洞穴的人，向前（名声显著的还是）退避（默默无闻的），大多名声被埋没而不被人称道，令人悲哀啊！[22] 老百姓想要磨砺品行确立名声，不依附德高望重的人，怎么能在后代留名呢！[23]

16. 君子疾沒世而名不稱焉 a quotation of Confucius from chapter 15 衛靈公 ("Wèi líng gōng" 卫灵公) of the *Analects*. Lesson 31, "A Superior Man Detests Dying Without Achieving Renown" 君子疾沒世而名不稱焉, is an eight-legged essay on this famous quotation.

　　疾 *v.* to hate. MdnC: 痛恨 (*tòng hèn*).

　　沒 (没 *mò*) 世 died. MdnC: 死 (*sǐ*).

　　名 *n.* reputation. MdnC: 名聲 (*míng shēng* 名声).

　　稱 (称 *chēng*) *v.* to speak highly of, praise. MdnC: 稱道 (*chēng dào* 称道).

17. 賈子曰 a quotation of Jia Yi 賈誼 (200–168 BCE) from his "On the Giant Bird" 鵬鳥賦 ("Péngniǎo fù" 鹏鸟赋). He was a renowned writer and politician in the Western Han dynasty and is well known for his prose and rhapsodies 賦 (*fù* 赋).

　　貪 (贪) *adj.* greedy. MdnC: 貪婪 (*tān lán* 贪婪).

　　夫 *n.* man. MdnC: 人 (*rén*).

　　徇 *v.* used here in the sense of 殉 (*xùn*), meaning "to follow to the death" 爲 (*wèi* 为) ……而死 (*ér sǐ*).

　　財 (财) *n.* wealth, property, possessions. MdnC: 財富 (*cái fù* 财富).

　　烈士 *n.* a person of high endeavor.

　　夸 *v.* to show off, exaggerate. MdnC: 自大 (*zì dà* 自大).

　　死 *v.* to die for.

　　權 (权) *n.* power, authority. MdnC: 權勢 (*quán shì* 权势).

　　衆 (众) 庶 *n.* common people. MdnC: 百姓 (*bǎi xìng*).

　　馮 (冯) *n.* used here in the sense of 憑 (*píng* 凭), meaning "to rely on" 依靠 (*yī kào*).

18. 同明相照 a quotation from the chapter titled "Patterned Words" 文言 ("Wén Yán") in the *Book of Changes* 易經 (*Yì Jīng* 易经).

　　明 *adj.* bright. MdnC: 明亮 (*míng liàng*).

　　照 *v.* to shine, light.

　　類 (类) *n.* category, group.

19. 作 *v.* to rise, appear. MdnC: 出現 (*chū xiàn* 出现).

　　覩 (睹) *v.* to observe, see. Here it means "to be seen."

20. 賢 (贤) *adj.* virtuous, good, worthy. MdnC: 賢良 (*xián liáng* 贤良).

　　益 *adv.* more. MdnC: 更加 (*gèng jiā*).

　　彰 *adj.* evident, clearly displayed. MdnC: 明顯 (*míng xiǎn* 明显).

21. 篤 (笃) *adj.* devoted to, dedicated. MdnC: 專心 (*zhuān xīn* 专心).

　　附 *v.* to adhere to, rely on. MdnC: 依附 (*yī fù*).

　　驥 (骥) *n.* steed. MdnC: 千里馬 (*qiān lǐ mǎ* 千里马).

　　行 *n.* behavior, conduct. MdnC: 品行 (*pǐn xíng*).

　　顯 (显) *adj.* evident, clear. MdnC: 明顯 (*míng xiǎn* 明显).

22. 巖 (岩) 穴 *n.* cave. MdnC: 洞穴 (*dòng xuè*).

　　趣舍 (qū shě) *v.* to go forward or to stop. 趣 is used here in the sense of 趨 (*qū* 趋), meaning "to walk fast." 舍 means "to give up or quit."

　　類 (类) *adv.* mostly, approximately. MdnC: 大多 (*dà duō*).

　　埋滅 (灭) *v.* to be buried, be covered. MdnC: 埋沒 (*mián mò*).

　　悲夫 *exclamatory word.* alas.

23. 閭 (闾) 巷 *n.* alley, alleyway. 閭巷之人 refers to common people.

　　砥 *n.* whetstone. Here it is a verb, meaning "to sharpen" 磨礪 (*mó lì* 磨砺).

行 *n.* behavior, conduct. MdnC: 品行 (*pǐn xíng*).

青雲 (云) 之士 a venerable and prominent person.

惡 (恶 *wū*) *interrogative particle.* how come? MdnC: 怎麼 (*zěn me* 怎么). See L12 Grammar Note 2 ①.

施 *v.* to act, execute, carry out. MdnC: 施行 (*shī xíng*).

語法注釋 Grammar Notes

1. 意動
用法　Classical Chinese has a *putative structure* 意動結構 (*yìdòng jiégòu*), which is similar in form to a causative structure but different in signification (see L7 Grammar Note 1). It is similar in form because it also entails a syntactical inversion. The normal "object + complement (adjective/noun)" is inverted as "complement (adjective/noun) + object," as shown here:

① Adjective + object ➡ 以 + object + 爲 + adjective.

吾妻之美我者，私我也。　　美我 => 以我爲美　MdnC: 認爲我美　(L4)

[我的妻子认为我美，是（因为）她偏爱我。]

而伯夷、叔齊恥之。　　恥之 => 以之爲恥　MdnC: 認爲它令人羞恥　(L13)

[但是伯夷和叔齐认为宗周令人羞耻。]

② Noun + object ➡ 以 + object + 爲 + noun.

越國以鄙遠，君知其難也。

鄙遠 => 以遠爲鄙　MdnC: 把遠方當作邊疆 (L2)

[越过其他的国家来把远方当作自己的边疆，您是知道其中难处的。]

既東封鄭，又欲肆其西封。

封鄭 => 以鄭爲封　MdnC: 把鄭國當作疆界 (L2)

[既已在东边把郑国作为疆界，势必又要延伸其西部领土。]

In explaining the putative structure, we have added the Chinese characters 以 and 爲, which give us clues to the essential differences between putative and causative structures. First, 爲 is a copula (verb *to be*), and therefore what follows it is necessarily a passive predicative complement 表語 (*biǎoyǔ*) rather than an active verb or a noun/adjective functioning as a verb, as is the case with the causative structure. Second, 以 is a word indicative of subjective judgment, equivalent to *consider*, *take*, or *regard something as* in English. The labeling of this structure as *putative* is very appropriate because its Latin root, *putare*, meaning "think, believe, suppose, or hold," exactly captures the unique semantic signification of this structure—an invariable suggestion of subjective judgment, even when the thinking subject is omitted in a sentence.

2. 彼　① *demonstrative pron.* that, those. MdnC: 那 (*nà*), 那些 (*nà xiē*), 他們 (*tā men*).

彼竭我盈，故克之。(L1)

[他们的士气耗尽了，我们的却很充沛，因此战胜他们。]

知彼知己者，百戰不殆。(L11)

[了解他们（对手）了解自己，百战都没有危险。]

登彼西山兮，采其薇矣。 (L13)

[登上那西山呀，采摘山上的野菜。]

② 彼 (that, over there) is used with 此 (this, here) to make a contrast between the two.

豈以其重若彼，其輕若此哉？

[难道不是因为他们把（道德品行）看得那样重，把（富贵）看得这样轻吗？]

3. 若　Four uses of 若 are explained in this book. In addition to the use below, see 若①② in L4 Grammar Note 4 and 若④ in L32 Grammar Note 3.

③ *conj.* as for, about. MdnC: 至於 (*zhì yú* 至于).

若至近世，操行不軌，專犯忌諱，而終身逸樂，富厚累世不絕。

[至于到了近代，操守品行不轨，专门违犯忌讳的人，却终身安逸快乐，过着富裕丰厚的生活，世世代代都不断。]

4. 是　Five uses of 是 are explained in this book. In addition to the use below, see 是①②③ in L3 Grammar Note 1 and 是⑤ in L30 Grammar Note 2.

④ *adj.* correct, right. MdnC: 對 (*duì* 对).

余甚惑焉，儻所謂天道，是邪非邪？

[我非常困惑啊！倘若有所说的天道，（这是）对的呢？还是不对的呢？]

Literary Analysis

Many scholars, misunderstanding Sima Qian's intent, focus on why the account of Boyi and Shuqi cannot be accepted as historical fact. Liang Yusheng 梁玉繩 (1745–1819), perhaps the greatest traditional *Shiji* exegete, gives ten reasons for his skepticism. But others have seen the text as it must have been intended—as a preface of sorts to the accounts of 308 men in the 68 memoirs (*lièzhuàn* 列傳) that follow. As Stephen Durrant put it in explaining why this chapter did not conclude with the usual historian's comment, "a judgment is unnecessary precisely because the entire chapter is a judgment." But a judgment of what?

"It is one of the vagaries of the Way of Heaven to sometimes reward those who do not follow the proper path, while bringing disaster and catastrophe to those who have carefully chosen where they put their feet." Sima Qian must be thinking of himself here. He followed the proper path but met with personal disaster, as he was forced to endure castration. He comprehends, even better than Confucius, the resentment he must have believed Boyi and Shuqi embodied. The chapter closes with Confucius's arguments about when to take office and when to refuse, and in citing Boyi and Shuqi, he thereby exonerates them—and perhaps himself as well. The final line can be read on two levels: by addressing Boyi and Shuqi, Confucius has preserved their names for the ages, but Sima Qian in his biographies will also establish the names of many men of the highest principles who barely survive historical record. Sima Qian, in effect, begins his *Arrayed Memoirs* section with an essay on recognition and resentment and an introduction to his accounts of other men who deserve equal recognition, and he ends it in similar fashion—with an account, in his postface, of why he composed the *Shiji*.

☞ *HTRCProse*, chapter 6, "Han Historical Prose: Sima Qian and the *Grand Scribe's Records (Shiji)*" for further comments on Sima Qian's prose writings.

—WHN

課後練習 Exercises

一 給加點字注音 Give the pinyin romanization for each dotted word.

1. 糟糠 （＿＿＿，＿＿＿） 2. 蹠 （＿＿＿） 3. 不軌 （＿＿＿） 4. 松柏 （＿＿＿） 5. 驥尾 （＿＿＿）

6. 忌諱 （＿＿＿，＿＿＿） 7. 鞭 （＿＿＿） 8. 閭巷 （＿＿＿ ＿＿＿） 9. 不可勝數 （＿＿＿）

二 在括號中給句中加點的字注音，並選出正確的釋義 Give the pinyin romanization for each dotted word; then select the correct definition from the following list, and write it in the blank.

夭折　依靠　吃飽(饱)　凋謝(谢)　爲(为)……而死　磨礪(砺)　明顯(显)　**信服**　殘(残)暴

1. 小信未孚 （**fú**） **信服** 　　2. 糟糠不厭 （　） ＿＿＿＿＿＿　　3. 彰明較著 （　） ＿＿＿＿＿＿

4. 而卒蚤夭 （　） ＿＿＿＿＿＿　　5. 衆庶馮生 （　） ＿＿＿＿＿＿　　6. 暴戾恣睢 （　） ＿＿＿＿＿＿

7. 貪夫徇財 （　） ＿＿＿＿＿＿　　8. 砥行立名 （　） ＿＿＿＿＿＿　　9. 松柏之後凋 （　） ＿＿＿＿＿＿

三 選擇釋義並填空 Match each word in the left column with its correct definition in the middle column. Fill in each blank in the right column with an appropriate word from the left column.

<u>謀謀劃(谋划)</u>	經(经)由	或曰："天道無＿＿＿，常與善人。"
親＿＿＿＿＿＿	災難(灾难)	然回也＿＿＿空，而＿＿＿蚤夭。
屢＿＿＿＿＿＿	倘若	
卒＿＿＿＿＿＿	**謀劃(谋划)**	盜蹠日殺不辜，肝人之肉，暴戾恣睢，聚＿＿＿數千
黨＿＿＿＿＿＿	斷(断)	人橫行天下，竟以＿＿＿終。是遵何德哉？此其尤大彰明
壽＿＿＿＿＿＿	踩	較著者也。
絕＿＿＿＿＿＿	出現(现)	雲從龍，風從虎，聖人＿＿＿而萬物覩。
由＿＿＿＿＿＿	親(亲)疏	
災＿＿＿＿＿＿	依附	若至近世，操行不軌，專犯忌諱，而終身逸樂，富
儻＿＿＿＿＿＿	黨(党)徒	厚累世不＿＿＿。
蹈＿＿＿＿＿＿	常	或擇地而＿＿＿之，時然後出言，行不＿＿＿徑，非公
作＿＿＿＿＿＿	專(专)心	正不發憤，而遇禍＿＿＿者，不可勝數也。
篤＿＿＿＿＿＿	終於(终于)	余甚惑焉，＿＿＿所謂天道，是邪非邪？
附＿＿＿＿＿＿	長壽(寿)	顏淵雖＿＿＿學，＿＿＿驥尾而行益顯。

四 請用給出的字填空 Fill in each blank with an appropriate word from the following list (some words may be used more than once).

彼　此　焉　以　何　之　若　邪　者

1. ＿＿伯夷、叔齊，可謂善人＿＿非＿＿？　　2. 天＿＿報施善人，其＿＿如哉？

3. 余甚惑＿＿，儻所謂天道，是＿＿非＿＿？　　4. 豈＿＿其重＿＿＿＿，其輕＿＿＿＿哉？

五 爲加點字選擇正確釋義，並根據釋義來翻譯句子 Match each dotted word with its correct modern Chinese equivalent by circling the latter. Then translate each sentence into modern Chinese.

1. 又何間焉?　　　　　　　　　　ⓐ 爲什麼(为什么)　b. 憑什麼(凭什么)　c. 多少

現代文翻譯：你又为什么要参与到这件事情里面？

＿＿＿＿＿＿＿＿＿＿＿＿＿＿＿＿＿＿＿＿＿＿＿＿＿＿＿＿＿＿

2. 積仁絜行如此而餓死。　　　　　a. 乾(干)净　b. 廉潔(洁)　c. 使⋯⋯高潔(洁)

現代文翻譯：＿＿＿＿＿＿＿＿＿＿＿＿＿＿＿＿＿＿＿＿＿＿＿＿＿

3. 若至近世，操行不軌，專犯忌諱，而終身逸樂，富厚累世不絕。　a. 至於(于)　b. 像 c. 你

現代文翻譯：＿＿＿＿＿＿＿＿＿＿＿＿＿＿＿＿＿＿＿＿＿＿＿＿＿

4. 豈以其重若彼，其輕若此哉？　　　　a. 重量　b. 以⋯⋯爲(为)重 c. 多

現代文翻譯：＿＿＿＿＿＿＿＿＿＿＿＿＿＿＿＿＿＿＿＿＿＿＿＿＿

5. 君子疾没世而名不稱焉。　　　　a. 爲什麼(为什么) b. 這樣(这样)　c. 啊

現代文翻譯：＿＿＿＿＿＿＿＿＿＿＿＿＿＿＿＿＿＿＿＿＿＿＿＿＿

6. 顏淵雖篤學，附驥尾而行益顯。　　　　a. 即使　b. 而且　c. 但是

現代文翻譯：＿＿＿＿＿＿＿＿＿＿＿＿＿＿＿＿＿＿＿＿＿＿＿＿＿

7. 閭巷之人，欲砥行立名者，非附青雲之士，惡能施於後世哉？

　　　　　　　　　　　　　　a. 怎麼(怎么)　b. 坏 c. 爲什麼(为什么)

現代文翻譯：＿＿＿＿＿＿＿＿＿＿＿＿＿＿＿＿＿＿＿＿＿＿＿＿＿

第十五課

陶淵明《五柳先生傳》

"Biography of Mr. Five Willows" (Tao Yuanming)

Introduction

Widely considered a brief *spiritual* autobiography of Tao Yuanming (ca. 365–427), one of China's greatest poets and cultural icons, this work is spiritual in that it projects an ideal rather a factual image of the self. In other words, Mr. Five Willows is more what Tao wishes to be rather than what even he believes he has become. Nonetheless, thanks to the transformative power of his poetic and prose writings about his life as a hermit-farmer, Tao's readers have gradually come to identify the historical poet with his creation, Mr. Five Willows. This merging of ideal and historical has elevated Tao Yuanming to the status of an enduring cultural icon.

Throughout the Six Dynasties, the literary reception of Tao's work was lukewarm, as he was primarily known, in the words of Zhong Rong 鍾嶸 (ca. 468–518), as "the patriarch of poets of reclusion, past and present." But by the Tang, the hermit-poet and his works had become objects of praise, imitation, and even adulation by eminent literati, including Li Bai 李白 (701–762), Wang Wei 王維 (699–761), Meng Haoran 孟浩然 (689–740), Bai Juyi 白居易 (772–846), and others. During the Song, writing "Tao-matching poems"—namely, poems that matched Tao's in both theme and rhyme—was all the rage. The most famous, of course, is Su Shi's 蘇軾 (1037–1101) matching of Tao's entire corpus.

Apart from his literary prowess, what endears Tao to great literati and common readers alike is the combination of qualities exemplified in "Biography of Mr. Five Willows": his dislike of obsequious officialdom, appreciation of the simple rustic life, disinterested love of reading, fondness for wine as relief from mundane cares, and attunement with the Dao and nature's eternal rhythms.

正文與簡體譯文 Text and Modern Chinese Translation

先生不知何許人也，亦不詳其姓字。[1] 宅
xiān shēng bù zhī hé xǔ rén yě　yì bù xiáng qí xìng zì　zhái

邊有五柳樹，因以爲號焉。[2]
biān yǒu wǔ liǔ shù　yīn yǐ wéi hào yān

不知道先生是什么地方的人，也不知道他的姓名和字。[1] 住处边有五棵柳树，因此把五柳作为他的号！[2]

1. 許 (许) *n.* place. MdnC: 地方 (*dì fāng*).
   詳 (详) *v.* to know something in detail. MdnC: 知道 (*zhī dào*).
   姓字 *n.* name and style.
2. 宅 *n.* residence, house. MdnC: 住處 (*zhù chù* 住处).
   柳 *n.* willow tree.

以爲 or 以 (五柳) 爲…… regard (five willow) as…. See L2 Grammar Note 1 ④.

號 (号) *n.* a special name or title given by oneself or someone else.

焉 *ending particle.* See L2 Grammar Note 3 ②.

閑静少言， 不慕榮利。³好讀書， 不求甚
xián jìng shǎo yán　bú mù róng lì　　hào dú shū　　bù qiú shèn

解， 每有會意， 便欣然忘食。⁴性嗜酒， 家貧
jiě　měi yǒu huì yì　biàn xīn rán wàng shí　xìng shì jiǔ　jiā pín

不能常得， 親舊知其如此， 或置酒而招之。⁵
bù néng cháng dé　qīn jiù zhī qí rú cǐ　huò zhì jiǔ ér zhāo zhī

造飲輒盡， 期在必醉， 既醉而退， 曾不吝情
zào yǐn zhé jìn　qī zài bì zuì　jì zuì ér tuì　zēng bú lìn qíng

去留。⁶環堵蕭然， 不蔽風日， 短褐穿結， 簞
qù liú　huán dǔ xiāo rán　bú bì fēng rì　duǎn hè chuān jié　dān

瓢屢空。⁷晏如也。 常著文章自娛， 頗示己
piáo lǚ kōng　yàn rú yě　cháng zhù wén zhāng zì yú　pō shì jǐ

志。⁸忘懷得失， 以此自終。⁹
zhì　wàng huái dé shī　yǐ cǐ zì zhōng

（五柳先生）安静不爱说话，不向往荣耀和利益。³喜好读书，不追求细致的解释。每当有领悟时，就会高兴得忘记吃饭。⁴（他）生性喜欢喝酒，（但）他很穷，不能常常买酒，亲戚朋友知道他这样，有时摆酒来招待他。⁵他去饮酒就喝得尽兴，期望一定喝醉，喝醉了就离开，甚至不会在意去留的问题。⁶（他家）墙四周空空的，不能遮蔽大风烈日；粗布短衣破了，缝满了补丁；装饭的篮子和水瓢常是空的。⁷（即使这样，他仍然）安然闲适。常写文章来娱乐自己，很能展现自己的志向。⁸（他就这样）忘记自己的得失，过完一生。⁹

3. 閑 (闲) *adj.* an early graph form of 閒 (*xián* 闲), meaning "quiet" 安静 (*ān jìng*).

　慕 *v.* to long for, admire, desire. MdnC: 向往 (*xiàng wǎng*).

　榮 (荣) *n.* glory, honor. MdnC: 榮耀 (*róng yào* 荣耀).

　利 *n.* benefit, profit. MdnC: 利益 (*lì yì*).

4. 好 (hào) *v.* to like, be fond of. MdnC: 喜好 (*xǐ hào*).

　不求甚解 not to pursue a thorough understanding. 甚 means "excessively, too much, or extremely," and 解 means "explanation" 解釋 (*jiě shì* 解释).

　每 *adv.* every time. MdnC: 每當 (*měi dāng* 每当).

　會意 *n.* understanding. MdnC: 領悟 (*lǐng wù* 领悟).

　欣然 *adv.* joyfully. MdnC: 高興地 (*gāo xìng de* 高兴地).

5. 嗜 *v.* to be addicted to, be fond of. MdnC: 喜好 (*xǐ hào*).

　貧 (贫) *adj.* poor. MdnC: 窮 (*qióng* 穷).

　親舊 (亲旧) *n.* relatives and friends. MdnC: 親戚朋友 (*qīn qī péng yǒu* 亲戚朋友).

　或 *adv.* sometimes. MdnC: 有時 (*yǒu shí* 有时). See Grammar Note 4 ②.

置 *v.* to place, arrange, set in a certain place. MdnC: 摆 (*bǎi*).

招 *v.* to receive, serve. MdnC: 招待 (*zhāo dài*).

6. 造 *v.* to go to. MdnC: 去 (*qù*).

輒 (辄) *adv.* always, every time. MdnC: 就 (*jiù*).

盡 (尽 jìn) *v.* to exhaust. Here it means "to enjoy oneself to the fullest" 盡興 (*jìn xìng* 尽兴).

期 *v.* to expect, hope. MdnC: 期望 (*qī wàng*).

醉 *adj.* drunk.

退 *v.* to move back, retreat. Here it means "to leave" 離開 (*lí kāi* 离开).

曾 (zēng) *adv.* just, even. MdnC: 甚至 (*shèn zhì*). See Grammar Note 1.

吝情 means "to care about" 在意 (*zài yì*).

去留 *v.* to leave or stay. Here it means "to leave."

7. 環 *v.* to surround, encircle. Here it means "surrounding" 四周 (*sì zhōu*).

堵 *n.* wall. MdnC: 墙 (*qiáng* 墙).

蕭 (萧) 然 *adj.* empty. MdnC: 空 (*kōng*).

蔽 *v.* to cover, hide, shelter. MdnC: 遮蔽 (*zhē bì*).

褐 *n.* coarse wool cloth. MdnC: 粗布衣服 (*cū bù yī fu*).

穿 *adj.* broken. MdnC: 破 (*pò*).

結 (结) *v.* to knot, knot up. MdnC: 縫補 (*féng bǔ* 缝补).

簞 (箪) *n.* small bamboo basket for holding things. MdnC: 籃子 (*lán zi* 篮子).

瓢 *n.* ladle made from a dried gourd. MdnC: 水瓢 (*shuǐ piáo*).

屢 *adv.* frequently, often, repeatedly. MdnC: 經常 (*jīng cháng* 经常).

8. 晏 *adj.* peaceful, quiet. MdnC: 安然 (*ān rán*).

如 *particle.* functioning as an emotive particle. See Grammar Note 2 ⑤.

著 *v.* to write. MdnC: 寫 (*xiě* 写).

娛 *v.* to entertain, amuse. MdnC: 娛樂 (*yú lè* 娱乐).

頗 (颇) *adv.* very. MdnC: 很 (*hěn*).

示 *v.* to present, display, show. MdnC: 展現 (*zhǎn xiàn* 展现).

志 *n.* intention, aspiration. MdnC: 志向 (*zhì xiàng*).

9. 忘懷 (怀) *v.* to forget (all the mundane cares), erase the memory of. MdnC: 忘記 (*wàng jì* 忘记).

終 (终) *v.* to end, finish. MdnC: 完 (*wán*).

贊曰：黔婁之妻有言：「不戚戚於貧
zàn yuē　qián lóu zhī qī yǒu yán　　　bù qī qī yú pín

賤，不汲汲於富貴。」[10] 極其言茲若人之儔
jiàn　　bù jí jí yú fù guì　　　jí qí yán zī ruò rén zhī chóu

乎？[11] 酣觴賦詩，以樂其志，無懷氏之民
hū　　　hān shāng fù shī　　yǐ lè qí zhì　　wú huái shì zhī mín

歟！葛天氏之民歟！[12]
yú　　　gě tiān shì zhī mín yú

赞语称：黔娄的妻子曾说过："不因贫穷地位低下而忧愁，不因富有和地位高贵而心情急切。"[10] 推究这句话，五柳先生(是)那类人吧？[11] 喝酒写诗，来快乐地抒发自己的志向。(他是)无怀氏时的人呢！还是葛天氏时的人呢！[12]

《陶淵明集》，北京：中華書局 (2001), 175.

10. 贊 (赞) *n.* prose genre: appraisal at the end of a chapter of a biography.

   黔婁 (娄) a famous Daoist of the Qi state in the Warring States period. Duke Gong of Lu 魯恭公 and King Wei of Qi 齊威王 both invited him to be a minister, but he refused them. He later stayed in seclusion and wrote books at the Southern Mountain of the Ji (in the present-day city of Jinan 濟南, Shandong Province). Tao Qian also wrote a poem entitled "In Praise of Poor Gentleman" 詠貧士 ("Yǒng pínshì" 咏贫士) to praise him for keeping his noble character and the purity of his belief unsullied under the poor living conditions.

   戚 *adj.* sad, worried. MdnC: 憂愁 (*yōu chou* 忧愁).

   賤 (贱) *adj.* lacking dignity, lowly. MdnC: 地位低下 (*dì wèi dī xià*).

   汲汲 *adj.* overly anxious, impatient. MdnC: 急切 (*jí qiè*).

11. 極 (极) *n.* extreme, utmost. Here it means to "think deeply" 推究 (*tuī jiù*).

   茲 *demonstrative pron.* this. Here it refers to 五柳先生. MdnC: 此 (*cǐ*). See L26 Grammar Note 1.

   若人 *n.* the kind of people mentioned by Qian Lou's wife.

   儔 (俦) *n.* kind, class. MdnC: 類 (*lèi* 类).

12. 酣 *adj.* tipsy, slightly drunk.

   觴 (觞) *n.* wine goblet. MdnC: 酒杯 (*jiǔ bēi*).

   賦 (赋) *v.* to compose (verse or poem). MdnC: 作 (*zuò*).

   以 *conj.* in order to. MdnC: 來 (*lái* 来). See L2 Grammar Note 1 ③.

   樂 (乐 *lè*) *adj.* happy. Here it means 使……樂, "to let … be happy." See L7 Grammar Note 1 ②.

   志 *n.* purpose, will. MdnC: 志向 (*zhì xiàng*).

   無懷 (无怀) 氏 a legendary tribal leader in ancient China. His tribe was located in Huaicheng 懷城 (in present-day Jiaozuo 焦作, Henan Province). Later generations regarded his reign as an ideal society.

   歟 (欤) *ending interrogative particle.* See Grammar Note 3.

   葛天氏 a legendary tribal leader in ancient China. His tribe was located in present-day Ningxian 寧縣, Henan Province. Later generations regarded his reign as an ideal society.

語法注釋 Grammar Notes

1. 曾 (zēng) *adv.* even. MdnC: 竟 (*jìng*), 甚至 (*shèn zhì*). 曾 is often used together with 不. MdnC: 連 (*lián* 连) ……都…….

> 既醉而退，曾不吝情去留。
>
> [已经喝醉了就离开，甚至不会在意去留的问题。]

2. 如 Five uses of 如 are explained in this book. In addition to the use below, see 如① in L3 Grammar Note 5 and 如②③④ in L6 Grammar Note 3.

   ⑤ *particle.* used as an emotive particle.

> 晏如也。
>
> [(即使这样，他仍然过得) 安然啊！]

3. 歟 (欤) *ending interrogative particle.* an equivalent to the ending particle 乎 (see L6 Grammar Note 2 ②). MdnC: 嗎 (*ma* 吗), 呢 (*ne*).

無懷氏之民歟！葛天氏之民歟！

[他是无怀氏时代的人吗！还是葛天氏时代的人吗！]

4. 或　Four uses of 或 are explained in this book. In addition to the use below, see 或① in L6 Grammar Note 4, 或③ in L32 Grammar Note 1, and 或④ in L36 Grammar Note 2.

　② *adv.* sometimes, occassionally. MdnC: 有時 (*yuán yīn* 有时).

　　親舊知其如此，或置酒而招之。

　　[亲戚朋友知道他这样，有时摆酒来招待他。]

Literary Analysis

1. This brief biography has been regarded by many as Tao Yuanming's de facto autobiography. If you agree with this assessment, explain on what grounds Mr. Five Willows can be identified with the author. If you disagree with this view, identify and comment on any evidence of fictionality in this biographical sketch.
2. How would you compare the lifestyle of Mr. Five Willows with that of the Peach Blossom Spring inhabitants as portrayed by Tao Yuanming (lesson 24)?
3. Discuss the philosophical concepts and beliefs undergirding the lifestyles of Mr. Five Willows and the Peach Blossom Spring inhabitants.

　　　　　　　　　　　　　　　　　　　　　　　　　　　—ZC

課後練習 Exercises

一 給加點字注音 Give the pinyin romanization for each dotted word.

1. 柳 （＿＿＿） 2. 簞瓢 （＿＿＿, ＿＿＿） 3. 曾 （＿＿＿） 4. 短褐 （＿＿＿） 5. 黔婁 （＿＿＿, ＿＿＿）

二 在括號中給句中加點的字注音，並選出正確的釋義 Give the pinyin romanization for each dotted word; then select the correct definition from the following list, and write it in the blank.

　　　　向往　　捨(舍)得　　酒杯　　住處(处)　　**信服**　　安然　　喜好　　地方

1. 小信未孚 （**fú**）<u>信服</u> 2. 宅邊 （　）＿＿＿ 3. 嗜酒 （　）＿＿＿ 4. 酣觴 （　）＿＿＿

5. 何許人也 （　）＿＿＿ 6. 晏如 （　）＿＿＿ 7. 吝情 （　）＿＿＿ 8. 不慕 （　）＿＿＿

三 選擇釋義並填空 Match each word in the left column with its correct definition in the middle column. Fill in each blank in the right column with an appropriate word from the left column (some words may be used more than once).

<u>謀謀劃 (谋划)</u>　　招待　　　　先生不知何許人也，亦不＿＿＿其姓字。

詳＿＿＿＿＿＿　　摆

榮＿＿＿＿＿＿	墙(墙)
解＿＿＿＿＿＿	去
置＿＿＿＿＿＿	**謀劃(谋划)**
招＿＿＿＿＿＿	知道
造＿＿＿＿	解釋(释)
盡＿＿＿＿＿＿	憂愁(忧愁)
堵＿＿＿＿＿＿	榮(荣)耀
結＿＿＿＿＿＿	急切
戚＿＿＿＿＿＿	盡興(尽兴)
汲＿＿＿＿＿＿	縫補(缝补)

閑静少言，不慕＿＿＿利。好讀書，不求甚＿＿＿。

親舊知其如此，或＿＿＿酒而＿＿＿之。

＿＿＿飲輒＿＿＿，期在必醉。

環＿＿＿蕭然，不蔽風日，短褐穿＿＿＿，簞瓢屢空。

黔婁之妻有言："不＿＿＿＿＿＿於貧賤，不＿＿＿＿＿＿於富貴。"

四 請用給出的字填空 Fill in each blank with an appropriate word from the following list.

以　若　其　或　然　歟(欤)　兹

1. 每有會意，便欣＿＿＿忘食。　　2. 親舊知＿＿＿如此，＿＿＿置酒而招之。

3. 極其言＿＿＿＿＿＿人之儔乎？　　4. 酣觴賦詩，＿＿＿樂其志，無懷氏之民＿＿＿？

五 為加點字選擇正確釋義，並根據釋義來翻譯句子 Match each dotted word with its correct modern Chinese equivalent by circling the latter. Then translate each sentence into modern Chinese.

1. 又何間焉?　　　　　　　　　　ⓐ爲什麼(为什么)　b.憑什麼(凭什么)　c.多少

現代文翻譯：你又为什么要参与到这件事情里面？

＿＿＿＿＿＿＿＿＿＿＿＿＿＿＿＿＿＿＿＿＿＿＿＿＿

2. 宅邊五柳樹，因以爲號焉。　　　a.把……當(当)作　b.來(来)　c.認爲(认为)

現代文翻譯：＿＿＿＿＿＿＿＿＿＿＿＿＿＿＿＿＿＿＿＿＿＿＿

3. 親舊知其如此，或置酒而招之。　　　a.或許(许)　b.可能　c.有時(时)

現代文翻譯：＿＿＿＿＿＿＿＿＿＿＿＿＿＿＿＿＿＿＿＿＿＿＿

4. 既醉而退，曾不吝情去留。　　　　a.竟　b.姓　c.曾經(经)

現代文翻譯：＿＿＿＿＿＿＿＿＿＿＿＿＿＿＿＿＿＿＿＿＿＿＿

5. 酣觴賦詩，以樂其志。　　　a.快樂(乐)　b.音樂(乐)　c.使……樂(乐)

現代文翻譯：＿＿＿＿＿＿＿＿＿＿＿＿＿＿＿＿＿＿＿＿＿＿＿

第十六課

柳宗元《李赤傳》

"An Account of Li Chi" (Liu Zongyuan)

Introduction

Liu Zongyuan 柳宗元 (courtesy name Zihou 子厚; 773–814) is one of the Eight Prose Masters of Tang and Song 唐宋八大家 (*Táng Sòng bādàjiā*, see Culture Note 1). Together with his contemporary Han Yu, he launched the Ancient Prose Movement 古文運動 (*gǔwén yùndòng* 古文运动) in the mid-Tang and sought to elevate the status of ancient prose as a means of illuminating the Confucian Dao. He denounced the rigid formalism of parallel prose and consciously employed lines of varying lengths in his prose writings. He also emphasized the importance of using one's genuine language.

In this biographical account, Liu demonstrates his flair for drawing a character sketch. Through a careful depiction of Li Chi's boastful language, stupid actions, and obsessive thoughts, Liu conveys a vivid image of the madman and reveals his own satirical intent: Li Chi is nothing but a despicable exemplum of all who madly pursue wealth and power at any cost. A translation of this text is given in *HTRCProse*, chapter 13, "Tang and Song Biographical Prose: Allegorical and Fictional," C13.4.

正文與簡體譯文 Text and Modern Chinese Translation

李赤，江湖浪人也。嘗曰：「吾善爲歌
lǐ chì jiāng hú làng rén yě cháng yuē wú shàn wéi gē

詩，詩類李白。」故自號曰李赤。[1] 遊宣州，
shī shī lèi lǐ bái gù zì hào yuē lǐ chì yóu xuān zhōu

州人館之。其友與俱遊者有姻焉，間纍日，
zhōu rén guǎn zhī qí yǒu yǔ jù yóu zhě yǒu yīn yān jiàn léi rì

乃從之館。[2] 赤方與婦人言，其友戲之。赤
nǎi cóng zhī guǎn chì fāng yǔ fù rén yán qí yǒu xì zhī chì

曰：「是ₐ媒我也，吾將娶乎是ᵦ。」[3] 友大
yuē shì méi wǒ yě wú jiāng qǔ hū shì yǒu dà

駭，曰：「足下妻固無恙，太夫人在堂，安
hài yuē zú xià qī gù wú yàng tài fū rén zài táng ān

李赤是江湖上游荡的人。他曾经说："我擅长写歌行和诗，我的诗类似李白的。"所以他自称为李赤。[1] (李赤) 到宣州游玩，宣州人安排他的客舍。他的朋友和一同游玩的人有姻亲，隔些日子，也跟着住到了客舍。[2] (遇到) 李赤正在与一女人说话，他的朋友就开他的玩笑。李赤说："这是给我做媒啊！我要娶这个女人。"[3] 朋友大惊，说："您的妻子本来就 (身体健康) 没生

得有是？豈狂易病惑耶？」⁴取絳雪餌之，<u>赤</u>
dé yǒu shì　　qǐ kuáng yì bìng huò yé　　qǔ jiàng xuě ěr zhī　　chì

不肯。有間，婦人至，又與<u>赤</u>言。即取巾經
bù kěn　　yǒu jiàn　　fù rén zhì　　yòu yǔ chì yán　　jí qǔ jīn jīng

其脰，<u>赤</u>兩手助之，舌盡出。⁵其友號而救
qí dòu　　chì liǎng shǒu zhù zhī　　shé jìn chū　　qí yǒu háo ér jiù

之，婦人解其巾走去。<u>赤</u>怒曰：「汝無道。
zhī　　fù rén jiě qí jīn zǒu qù　　chì nù yuē　　rǔ wú dào

吾將從吾妻，汝何爲者？」⁶
wú jiāng cóng wú qī　　rǔ hé wéi zhě

病，您的母亲还健在，您怎么能有这样的想法？难道是受了<u>诱惑</u>得了精神失常的病吗？"⁴（朋友）取了绛雪丹药来引诱他吃，李赤不肯。过了一会儿，女人来了，又与李赤说话。（她）取了一个头巾，<u>勒住</u>李赤的<u>脖子</u>，李赤用两只手帮助她，舌头（被勒得）全出来了。⁵朋友（见了）大声呼叫来救李赤，那个女人解开头巾逃走了。李赤生气地说："你没道理，我要跟从我的妻子，你为什么啊！"⁶

1. 江湖 *n.* rivers and lakes. It refers to the world outside of the government.

   浪人 *n.* vagabond, wanderer.

   嘗 (尝) *adv.* once. MdnC: 曾經 (*céng jīng* 曾经). See L23 Grammar Note 1 ①.

   善 *v.* to be good at. MdnC: 擅長 (*shàng cháng* 擅长).

   爲 (为 *wéi*) *v.* to do, make. MdnC: 寫 (*xiě* 写). See L2 Grammar Note 6 ①.

   歌 *n.* song. Here it refers to a subgenre of ancient-style poetry 歌行 (*gē xíng*) in the Tang dynasty.

   詩 (诗) *n.* poem.

   類 (类) *v.* to conform to, be similar to. MdnC: 類似 (*lèi sì* 类似).

   李白 (style 字, Tàibái 太白; literary name 號, Qīnglián jūshì 青蓮居士; 701–762), one of the greatest poets in Chinese history. He is known as the "immortal poet" 詩仙 (*shī xiān* 诗仙) for his quest for immortality in the Daoist vein and for his extraordinary power of imagination.

   號 (号) *n.* literary name. Here it is a verb, meaning "to name" 稱呼 (*chēng hū* 称呼).

   宣州 place name. Xuanzhou of the Tang dynasty includes parts of the present-day Anhui and Jiangsu Province. Li Bai once visited Xuanzhou and wrote some famous poems about Xuanzhou's landscape and experience, such as "Sitting Alone at the Jingting Mountain" 獨坐敬亭山 ("Dú zuò Jìngtíng shān" 独坐敬亭山).

   館 (馆) *n.* accommodation for guests. MdnC: 客舍 (*kè shè*). Here it is used as a verb, meaning "to accommodate."

2. 俱 *adv.* together. MdnC: 一同 (*yì tóng*).

   姻 *n.* relation by marriage. MdnC: 姻親 (*yīn qīn* 姻亲).

   焉 *pron.* in this place, there. MdnC: 在當地 (*zài dāng dì* 在当地). See L1 Grammar Note 4 ①.

   間 (间 *jiàn*) *prep.* after an interval of time. MdnC: 隔 (*gé*).

   纍 (累 *léi*) *adj.* continuous. MdnC: 連續 (*lián xù* 连续).

   從 (从) *v.* to follow. MdnC: 跟隨 (*gēn suí* 跟随).

3. 方 *adv.* just, just now. MdnC: 正在 (*zhèng zài*).

   戲 (戏) *v.* to joke. MdnC: 開玩笑 (*kāi wán xiào* 开玩笑).

是 ₐ……也 this is. MdnC: 這是 (*zhè shì* 这是). See L3 Grammar Note 1 ②.

媒 *n.* matchmaker. Here it is used as a verb, meaning "to make a match" 做媒 (*zuò méi*).

娶 *v.* to marry, take as wife.

乎 *prep.* a variant of 於 (*yú* 于). See L6 Grammar Note 2 ③.

是 ₆ *demonstrative pron.* this (woman). See L3 Grammar Note 1 ①.

4. 駭 (骇) *v.* to be shocked. MdnC: 驚 (*jīng* 惊).

足下 you, sir, a respectful way to address a friend.

固 *adv.* in fact, certainly. MdnC: 本來 (*běn lái* 本来).

恙 *n.* illness. MdnC: 病 (*bìng*).

太夫人 a respectful way to address Li Chi's mother.

在堂 literally means "in a hall," but here it means that Li Chi's mother is still alive. MdnC: 健在 (*jiàn zài*).

安 *interrogative particle.* how? MdnC: 怎麼 (*zěn me* 怎么). See L6 Grammar Note 9.

是 *demonstrative pron.* this (decision/behavior). See L3 Grammar Note 1 ①.

豈 (岂) *particle.* MdnC: 難道 (*nán dào* 难道). See L8 Grammar Note 4.

狂易 *n.* mental disorder. MdnC: 精神失常 (*jīng shén shī cháng*).

惑 *v.* to delude. MdnC: 誘惑 (*yòu huò* 诱惑).

耶 *ending interrogative particle.* MdnC: 呢 (*ne*). See Grammar Note 3.

5. 絳 (绛) 雪 elixir made by Daoist adepts.

餌 (饵) *n.* bait. Here it is used as a verb, meaning "to entice" 引誘 (*yǐn yòu* 引诱).

間 (间 jiàn) *n.* interval. MdnC: 一會兒 (*yí huìr* 一会儿).

即 *adv.* quickly, immediately. MdnC: 立刻 (*lì kè*).

巾 *n.* a piece of cloth.

經 *v.* to hang, strangle. MdnC: 勒住 (*lēi zhù*).

脰 *n.* neck. MdnC: 脖子 (*bó zi*).

盡 (尽 jìn) *adv.* completely, entirely. MdnC: 全 (*quán*).

6. 號 (号 háo) *v.* to shout, cry out. MdnC: 大聲呼叫 (*dà shēng hū jiào* 大声呼叫).

解 *v.* to untie, unknot. MdnC: 解開 (*jiě kāi* 解开).

走 *v.* to run away. MdnC: 逃 (*táo*).

汝 *pron.* you. MdnC: 你 (*nǐ*). See Grammar Note 1.

赤乃就牖間爲書，輾而圓封之。⁷又爲
chì nǎi jiù yǒu jiān wéi shū　zhǎn ér yuán fēng zhī　yòu wéi

書，博封之。訖，如厕。⁸久，其友從之，
shū　bó fēng zhī　qì　rú cè　jiǔ　qí yǒu cóng zhī

見赤軒厠抱甕，詭笑而側視，勢且下入。
jiàn chì xuān cè bào wèng　guǐ xiào ér cè shì　shì qiě xià rù

乃倒曳得之。⁹又大怒曰：「吾已升堂面吾
nǎi dào yè dé zhī　yòu dà nù yuē　wú yǐ shēng táng miàn wú

李赤于是靠近窗边写书信，(写完后)翻转过来完全封好。⁷之后又写了信，都封好了。做完后去了厕所。⁸(李赤进了厕所)很久(都没出来)，他的朋友就跟着进去了，看到李赤在厕所抱着瓮(一边)诡异地笑着(一边)斜着眼睛看人，

妻。吾妻之容，世固無有。¹⁰堂之飾，宏大
qī　wú qī zhī róng　shì gù wú yǒu　táng zhī shì　hóng dà

富麗，椒蘭之氣，油然而起。¹¹顧視汝之世，
fù lì　jiāo lán zhī qì　yóu rán ér qǐ　gù shì rǔ zhī shì

猶溷厠也。¹²而吾妻之居，與帝居鈞天、清
yóu hùn cè yě　ér wú qī zhī jū　yǔ dì jū jūn tiān　qīng

都無以異，若何苦余至此哉？¹³」然後其友
dōu wú yǐ yì　ruò hé kǔ yú zhì cǐ zāi　rán hòu qí yǒu

知赤之所遭，乃厠鬼也。¹⁴
zhī chì zhī suǒ zāo　nǎi cè guǐ yě

（眼看）要掉下去了。（朋友）就（把他）拉上来。⁹（李赤）又大怒，说："我已经登上大堂见到我妻子了！我妻子的容貌，世上就没有（可与之相比的）。¹⁰大堂的装饰宏大富丽，椒兰的香气自然而然地散发着。¹¹回头看你的世界，像肮脏的厕所。¹²而我妻子的住所与天帝居住的钧天、清都没有不同，为什么害我到这种地步呢！¹³"然后他的朋友知道李赤所遇到的是厕鬼。¹⁴

7. 就 *v.* to approach, draw close to. MdnC: 靠近 (*kào jìn*).
   牖 *n.* window. MdnC: 窗户 (*chuāng hù*).
   間 (间 jiān) *n.* space inside a room.
   書 (书) *n.* letter. MdnC: 書信 (*shū xìn* 书信).
   輾 (辗) *v.* to roll over. MdnC: 翻轉 (*fān zhuǎn* 翻转).
   圓 (圆) *adj.* complete. MdnC: 完全 (*wán quán*).
   封 *v.* to seal.

8. 博 *adv.* generally, widely.
   訖 (讫) *v.* to finish. MdnC: 完 (*wán*).
   如 *v.* to go. MdnC: 去 (*qù*).
   厠 (厕) *n.* lavatory. MdnC: 厠所 (*cè suǒ* 厕所).

9. 久 *adj.* long time. MdnC: 長時間 (*cháng shí jiān* 长时间).
   軒 (轩) *n.* a small room.
   甕 (瓮) *n.* earthen jar, receptacle.
   詭 (诡) *adj.* weird, peculiar, eerie. MdnC: 詭異 (*guǐ yì* 诡异).
   側 (侧) *v.* to slant, lean. MdnC: 斜 (*xié*).
   勢 (势) *n.* posture. MdnC: 姿勢 (*zī shì* 姿势).
   且 *adv.* about to. MdnC: 將要 (*jiāng yào* 将要). See L13 Grammar Note 2 ③.
   倒 (dào) *v.* to move backward. MdnC: 向後 (*xiàng hòu* 向后).
   曳 *v.* to pull, drag. MdnC: 拉 (*lā*).

10. 升 *v.* to ascend, go up. MdnC: 登上 (*dēng shàng*).
    堂 *n.* hall. MdnC: 大堂 (*dà táng*).
    面 *v.* to face, meet. MdnC: 見到 (*jiàn dào* 见到).
    容 *n.* looks, appearance. MdnC: 容貌 (*róng mào*).
    世 *n.* the human world. MdnC: 世上 (*shì shàng*).

11. 飾 (饰) *n.* decoration. MdnC: 裝飾 (*zhuāng shì* 装饰).

宏大 *adj.* grand.

富麗 (丽) *adj.* magnificent, gorgeous.

椒蘭 (兰) *n.* pepper and orchid. Here it refers to all kinds of fragrant grass.

油然 *adv.* spontaneously. MdnC: 自然而然 (*zì rán ér rán*).

12. 顧 (顾) *v.* to look back. MdnC: 回頭看 (*huí tóu kàn* 回头看).

猶 (犹) *v.* to be like. MdnC: 就像 (*jiù xiàng*). See L3 Grammar Note 3 ②.

溷 *adj.* dirty. MdnC: 骯髒 (*āng zāng* 肮脏).

13. 居 *n.* residence, house. MdnC: 住所 (*zhù suǒ*).

帝 *n.* heavenly emperor. MdnC: 天帝 (*tiān dì*).

鈞 (钧) 天 the heavenly emperor's palace in ancient Chinese legends.

清都 Capital Qing, the heavenly emperor's palace.

異 (异) *adj.* different. MdnC: 不同 (*bù tóng*).

若何 or 如何 why?

苦 *adj.* bitter, hard. Here it is used as a causative verb, 使……苦, meaning "to make … suffer." MdnC: 害苦 (*hài kǔ*). See L7 Grammar Note 1 ②.

14. 遭 *v.* to come across, encounter. MdnC: 遇到 (*yù dào*).

鬼 *n.* ghost.

聚僕謀曰：「亟去是廁。」遂行宿三十
jù pú móu yuē   jí qù shì cè   suì xíng sù sān shí

里。夜，赤又如廁久，從之，且復入矣。[15]
lǐ yè chì yòu rú cè jiǔ cóng zhī qiě fù rù yǐ

持出，洗其汙，眾環之以至旦。[16]
chí chū xǐ qí wū zhòng huán zhī yǐ zhì dàn

(朋友)聚集仆人商量说："赶快离开那个厕所。"于是走了三十里然后停下来住宿一晚。晚上，李赤又去厕所很久(不出来)，(朋友)跟着进去，(发现他)又要掉进去了。[15](朋友把李赤)拉出来，洗去他身上的脏(东西)，众人围着他一直到天亮。[16]

15. 聚 *v.* to gather. MdnC: 聚集 (*jù jí*).

僕 (仆) *n.* servants. MdnC: 僕人 (*pú rén* 仆人).

謀 (谋) *v.* to consult. MdnC: 商量 (*shāng liáng*).

亟 *adv.* urgently, immediately. MdnC: 趕快 (*gǎn kuài* 赶快).

去 *v.* to leave, get away. MdnC: 離開 (*lí kāi* 离开).

是 *demonstrative pron.* this. See L3 Grammar Note 1 ①.

遂 *adv.* then. MdnC: 於是 (*yú shì* 于是).

宿 *v.* to stop, lodge, rest. Here 行宿三十里 should be 行三十里，宿. The meaning is "to travel thirty *li* and then stop at lodging."

復 (复) *adv.* again. MdnC: 又 (*yòu*).

16. 持 *v.* to hold in one's hand, grasp. MdnC: 拉 (*lā*).

汙 (污) *adj.* dirty. MdnC: 髒 (*zāng* 脏).

眾 (众) *n.* all the people, everybody. MdnC: 眾人 (*zhòng rén* 众人).

環 (环) *v.* to encircle, surround. MdnC: 圍 (*wéi* 围).

以 *conj.* and. See L2 Grammar Note 1 ③.
旦 *n.* sunrise, dawn. MdnC: 天亮 (*tiān liàng*).

去抵他縣， 縣之吏方宴， 赤拜揖跪起無
qù dǐ tā xiàn　　xiàn zhī lì fāng yàn　　chì bài yī guì qǐ wú

異者。[17] 酒行， 友未及言， 已飲而顧赤， 則
yì zhě　　　jiǔ xíng　　yǒu wèi jí yán　　yǐ yǐn ér gù chì　　zé

已去矣。 走從之。 赤入廁， 舉其牀捍門， 門
yǐ qù yǐ　　zǒu cóng zhī　　chì rù cè　　jǔ qí chuáng hàn mén　mén

堅不可入， 其友叫且言之。[18] 眾發牆以入，
jiān bù kě rù　　qí yǒu jiào qiě yán zhī　　zhòng fā qiáng yǐ rù

赤之面陷不潔者半矣。 又出洗之。[19] 縣之吏
chì zhī miàn xiàn bù jié zhě bàn yǐ　　yòu chū xǐ zhī.　　xiàn zhī lì

更召巫師善呪術者守赤， 赤自若也。[20]
gèng zhào wū shī shàn zhòu shù zhě shǒu chì　chì zì ruò yě

(第二天他们)离开到了另一个县，县里的官员正在(举行)宴会，李赤(见到官员)下拜、作揖、跪拜、站起(这一切都和正常人)没有不同的地方。[17] 酒宴正进行着，朋友还没来得及说话，已经喝(了点酒)，回头看李赤，(发现他)已经离开了。(朋友)跑去跟上他。李赤进了厕所，举起坐具护着门。门很坚固，(外面的人)不能进入，他的朋友一边叫着，一边对李赤说话。[18] 众人打破墙进去，(发现)李赤的脸一半都陷到了不干净的东西里面。(大家)又(把他拉)出来，洗干净。[19] 县里的官员更是召来擅长咒术的巫师来守护李赤，李赤(看起来)很自然很正常。[20]

17. 去 *v.* to leave. MdnC: 離開 (*lí kāi* 离开).
　　抵 *v.* to reach, arrive. MdnC: 到 (*dào*).
　　他 *pron.* another. MdnC: 另一個 (*lìng yí gè* 另一个).
　　縣 (县) *n.* county.
　　吏 *n.* functionaries, low-level officials. MdnC: 官員 (*guān yuán* 官员).
　　方 *adv.* just. MdnC: 正在 (*zhèng zài*).
　　宴 *n.* banquet. MdnC: 宴會 (*yàn huì* 宴会).
　　拜 *v.* to bow with respect.
　　揖 *v.* to bow, salute. MdnC: 作揖 (*zuō yī*).
　　跪 *v.* to kneel. MdnC: 跪拜 (*guì bài*).
　　異 (异) *adj.* different. MdnC: 不同 (*bù tóng*).
18. 行 *v.* to be underway. MdnC: 進行 (*jìn xíng* 进行).
　　飲 (饮) *v.* to drink. MdnC: 喝 (*hē*).
　　顧 (顾) *v.* to look back. MdnC: 回頭看 (*huí tóu kàn* 回头看).
　　舉 (举) *v.* to raise up, lift up.
　　牀 *n.* couch, bench. MdnC: 坐具 (*zuò jù*).

捍 *v.* to defend, protect, guard. MdnC: 保護 (*bǎo hù* 保护).

堅 (坚) *adj.* solid, firm, resistant. MdnC: 堅固 (*jiān gù* 坚固).

19. 發 (发) *v.* to send out. Here it means "to breach or break." MdnC: 破 (*pò*).

　　以 *conj.* and thereby, in order to. MdnC: 來 (*lái* 来).

　　面 *n.* face. MdnC: 臉 (*liǎn* 脸).

　　陷 *v.* to fall into.

　　潔 (洁) *adj.* clean. MdnC: 乾净 (*gān jìng* 干净).

20. 更 (gèng) *adv.* more, furthermore.

　　召 (zhào) *v.* to summon.

　　巫師 (师) *n.* wizard.

　　善 *v.* to be good at. MdnC: 擅長 (*shàng cháng* 擅长).

　　呪 (咒) *n.* charm, spell.

　　術 (术) *n.* skills.

　　守 *v.* to guard. MdnC: 守護 (*shǒu hù* 守护).

　　自若 *adj.* ease and calm.

夜半，守者怠，皆睡。及覺，更呼而求
yè bàn　shǒu zhě dài　jiē shuì　jí jué　gèng hū ér qiú

之，見其足於廁外，赤死久矣。²¹ 獨得尸歸
zhī　jiàn qí zú yú cè wài　chì sǐ jiǔ yǐ　dú dé shī guī

其家。取其所爲書讀之，蓋與其母妻訣，其
qí jiā　qǔ qí suǒ wéi shū dú zhī　gài yǔ qí mǔ qī jué　qí

言辭猶人也。²²
yán cí yóu rén yě

半夜，守护李赤的人累了，都睡了。等到醒来，（发现李赤不见了），又呼喊着找他。只见李赤的脚在厕所外，李赤已经死了很长时间了。²¹（朋友）得到了李赤的尸体，把他送回到家。取出他所写的信来读，大致都是和母亲妻子诀别（的话），他的言辞像正常人一样。²²

21. 夜半 *n.* midnight. MdnC: 半夜 (*bàn yè*).

　　怠 *adj.* tired. MdnC: 累 (*lèi*).

　　皆 *adv.* all. MdnC: 都 (*dōu*). See L24 Grammar Note 1 ③.

　　覺 (觉 jué) *v.* to wake up. MdnC: 醒 (*xǐng*).

　　呼 *v.* to shout, cry.

22. 尸 *n.* corpse, dead body. MdnC: 尸體 (*shī tǐ*).

　　蓋 (盖) *adv.* probably. MdnC: 大致 (*dà zhì*). See L13 Grammar Note 1.

　　訣 (诀) *v.* to bid farewell. MdnC: 訣別 (*jué bié* 诀别).

　　言辭 (辞) *n.* words.

柳先生曰：李赤之傳不誣矣。是其病心
liú xiān shēng yuē　lǐ chì zhī zhuàn bù wū yǐ　shì qí bìng xīn

而爲是耶？抑固有廁鬼耶？²³ 赤之名聞江湖
ér wéi shì yé　yì gù yǒu cè guǐ yé　chì zhī míng wén jiāng hú

柳先生说：李赤的传记不是不真实的。这是（因为）他的精神生病了而做这样的事情呢？抑或本来真的有厕鬼（诱

間，其始爲士，無以異於人也。²⁴一惑於怪，
jiān　qí shǐ wéi shì　wú yǐ yì yú rén yě　　　yí huò yú guài

而所爲若是，乃反以世爲溷，溷爲帝居清
ér suǒ wéi ruò shì　nǎi fǎn yǐ shì wéi hùn　hùn wéi dì　jū qīng

都，其屬意明白。²⁵今世皆知笑赤之惑也，及
dū　　qí zhǔ yì míng bái　　jīn shì jiē zhī xiào chì zhī huò yě　　jí

至是非取與向背決不爲赤者，幾何人耶？²⁶反
zhì shì fēi qǔ yǔ xiàng bèi jué bù wéi chì zhě　　jǐ hé rén yé　　fǎn

修而身，無以欲利好惡遷其神而不返，則幸
xiū ér shēn　　wú yǐ　yù lì hào wù qiān qí shén ér　bù fǎn　　zé xìng

矣，又何暇赤之笑哉？²⁷
yǐ　　yòu hé xiá chì zhī xiào zāi

《柳宗元集校注》，北京：中華書局 (2013), 1204–1205.

惑他）呢？²³李赤在江湖間聞名，他开始作为士人，没有什么和其他人不同。²⁴一旦被怪异（的事物）迷惑，所做的事情像这样，竟反而以为人世是肮脏的，肮脏（的厕所倒）是天帝居住的清都，他的用意是很明白的。²⁵现在世人都知道笑话李赤被迷惑（这件事），有多少人能不像李赤那样来决断是非、取与、向背呢？²⁶反过来修养自身，不因为欲望、利益、喜好、厌恶来改变自己的心神，从而一去不返，才是幸运的！又怎么有空闲去笑话李赤呢！²⁷

23. 柳先生 Mr. Liu, the author 柳宗元.

　　誣 (诬) *adj.* not true, false. MdnC: 不真實 (*bù zhēn shí* 不真实).

　　心 *n.* mind. MdnC: 精神 (*jīng shén*).

　　抑 *conj.* or. MdnC: 抑或 (*yì huò*). See Grammar Note 2.

24. 聞 *v.* to be known. MdnC: 聞名 (*wén míng* 闻名).

　　始 *n.* beginning. MdnC: 開始 (*kāi shǐ* 开始).

　　士 *n.* scholar. MdnC: 士人 (*shì rén*).

25. 一 *conj.* once, now that. MdnC: 一旦 (*yí dàn*).

　　惑 *v.* to puzzle, delude. MdnC: 迷惑 (*mí huò*).

　　怪 *adj.* bizarre, fantastic, weird. MdnC: 怪異 (*guài yì* 怪异).

　　乃 *adv.* unexpectedly. MdnC: 竟 (*jìng*).

　　反 *adv.* on the contrary, instead. MdnC: 反而 (*fǎn ér*).

　　以 *v.* to think, regard. MdnC: 認爲 (*rèn wéi* 认为). See L10 Grammar Note 2 ⑤.

　　溷 *adj.* dirty. MdnC: 骯髒 (*āng zāng* 肮脏).

　　屬 (属 *zhǔ*) 意 *n.* determination, will. MdnC: 用意 (*yòng yì*).

26. 笑 *v.* to laugh at. MdnC: 笑話 (*xiào huà* 笑话).

　　是非 *n.* right or wrong.

　　取與 (与 *yǔ*) *v.* to take or give.

　　向背 *n.* to support or oppose.

　　決 (决) *v.* to determine, decide. MdnC: 決斷 (*jué duàn* 决断).

　　幾何 how many? how much? MdnC: 多少 (*duō shǎo*). See L3 Grammar Note 7.

27. 修 *v.* to cultivate. MdnC: 修養 (*xiū yǎng* 修养).

而 *pron.* used in the sense of 爾 (*ěr* 尔), meaning "your."

以 *prep.* because of, for the reason of. MdnC: 因爲 (*yīn wèi* 因为). See L2 Grammar Note 1 ①.

遷 (迁) *v.* to change, shift, move. MdnC: 改變 (*gǎi biàn* 改变).

返 *v.* to return.

幸 *adj.* lucky, fortunate. MdnC: 幸運 (*xìng yùn* 幸运).

暇 *n.* free time, spare time. MdnC: 空閑 (*kòng xián* 空闲).

文化常識 Culture Note

1. 唐宋八大家 or 唐宋八大散文家 (Eight Masters of Prose of Tang and Song) refers to Han Yu 韓愈 (768–824) and Liu Zongyuan 柳宗元 in the Tang dynasty and to Ouyang Xiu 歐陽修 (1007–1072), Su Shi 蘇軾 (1037–1101), Su Xun 蘇洵 (1009–1066), Su Zhe 蘇轍 (1039–1112), Wang Anshi 王安石 (1021–1186), and Zeng Gong 曾鞏 (1019–1083) in the Song dynasty. Han Yu and Liu Zongyuan are the leaders of the Ancient Prose Movement 古文運動 in the Tang dynasty, while Ouyang Xiu and the three Sus are the key figures of that movement in the Song dynasty.

    The title of Eight Great Masters of Prose first appeared in the *Prose Anthology of Eight Masters* 八先生文集 (*Bāxiānshēng wénjí*), edited by the Ming scholar Zhu You 朱右 (1314–1376). Then in the late Ming, Mao Kun 茅坤 (1512–1601) edited *Prose Anthology of Eight Great Masters of the Tang and Song* 唐宋八大家文鈔 (*Táng Sòng bādàjiā wénchāo*). Mao's anthology was very popular at that time, and thus this title was widely accepted by scholars and readers from then on.

語法注釋 Grammar Notes

1. **汝** *pron.* second-person pronoun: you. MdnC: 你 (*nǐ*), 你們 (*nǐ mén* 你们).

    吾將從吾妻，汝何爲者？

    [我要跟从我的妻子，你为什么这么做？]

    顧視汝之世，猶溷厠也。

    [回过头来看看你们的世界，就像肮脏的厕所。]

2. **抑** *conj.* or. MdnC: 抑或 (*yì huò*).

    抑固有厠鬼耶？

    [抑或本来真的有厕鬼（诱惑他）呢？]

3. **耶** *ending interrogative particle.* MdnC: 嗎 (*ma* 吗), 呢 (*ne*).

    豈狂易病惑耶？

    [难道是受了诱惑得了精神失常的病吗？]

    抑固有厠鬼耶？

    [抑或因为真的有厕鬼（诱惑他）呢？]

Literary Analysis

1. "An Account of Li Chi" ("Li Chi zhuan") tells the story of the protagonist's tragic death in a tight, fascinating narrative: to understand it, the reader must pay close attention to what the protagonist does and says. The message of the story, however, is clear. The purpose of such writings, according to Liu Zongyuan, is to "elucidate the Way" 明道 (*míng dào*). What is it that Liu tries to elucidate or promote in the story? Do you find his argument in the last paragraph convincing?

2. Liu focuses on Li Chi's deluded actions and their consequences but leaves the sources of his delusion unspecified. What do you think might be the sources of Li Chi's delusion, and for that matter, what are some of the possible sources of delusion for us all?

3. Liu sets the fantastic story of Li Chi in a realistic environment where everyone around him seems to act according to the logic and reason of the material world; Li Chi is the one exception. How unreasonable or fantastic are Li Chi's actions? Putting yourself in his shoes, can you see, understand, or imagine the rationale behind his actions? How would you describe the world that eventually leads to Li's demise?

4. In our modern understanding, a *zhuàn* 傳 or "biographical account" is supposed to span a subject's entire life. In "Li Chi zhuan," the reader is plunged directly into the last dramatic moments of Li Chi's life. How would you work backward from the story to Li Chi's life prior to his arrival of Xuanzhou? In other words, can you build a connection between his story as told in the main text and a prequel to the story, as suggested in the opening sentence: "Li Chi was a vagabond scholar wandering among the rivers and lakes"?

☞ *HTRCProse*, chapter 13, "Tang and Song Biographical Prose: Allegorical and Fictional" for further comments on Liu Zongyuan's prose writings.

—YW

課後練習 Exercises

一 給加點字注音 Give the pinyin romanization for each dotted word.

1. 姻 (＿＿＿)　2. 牖 (＿＿＿)　3. 絳雪 (＿＿＿, ＿＿＿)　4. 呪術 (＿＿＿, ＿＿＿)
5. 甕 (＿＿＿)　6. 胵 (＿＿＿)　7. 椒蘭 (＿＿＿, ＿＿＿)　8. 揖 (＿＿＿)

二 在括號中給句中加點的字注音，並選出正確的釋義 Give the pinyin romanization for each dotted word; then select the correct definition from the following list, and write it in the blank.

病　完　趨(赶)快　引誘(诱)　拉　驚(惊)　**信服**　翻轉(转)　骯髒(肮脏)　大聲(声)呼叫

1. 小信未孚（ fú ）　信服　2. 友大駭（　）＿＿＿＿　3. 取絳雪餌之（　）＿＿＿＿
4. 號而救之（　）＿＿＿＿　5. 無恙（　）＿＿＿＿　6. 輾而圓封之（　）＿＿＿＿

7. 訖，如厠（　）_____　　8. 溷厠　（　）_____　　9. 乃倒曳得之（　）_____

10. 亟去是厠（　）_____

三 選擇釋義並填空 Match each word in the left column with its correct definition in the middle column. Fill in each blank in the right column with an appropriate word from the left column.

謀謀劃(谋划)	累	其友與俱遊者有姻焉，間____日，乃從之館。
纍_____	回頭(头)看	赤方與婦人言，其友____之。
戲_____	不真實(实)	赤乃____牖間爲書，輾而____封之。
就_____	連續(连续)	____視汝之世，猶溷厠也。
圓_____	醒	持出，洗其____，眾____之以至旦。去____他縣，
顧_____	空閑(闲)	縣之吏方宴，赤拜揖跪起無異者。
環_____	**謀劃(谋划)**	夜半，守者____，皆睡。及____，更呼而求之，見
汙_____	訣(诀)別	其足於厠外，赤死久矣。
抵_____	靠近	取其所爲書讀之，蓋與其母妻____，其言辭猶人
悤_____	開(开)玩笑	也。
覺_____	改變(变)	柳先生曰：李赤之傳不____矣。
訣_____	完全	反修而身，無以欲利好惡____其神而不返，則幸
誣_____	到	矣，又何____赤之笑哉？
遷_____	髒(脏)	
暇_____	圍(围)	

四 請用給出的字填空 Fill in each blank with an appropriate word from the following list (some words may be used more than once).

汝　是　者　之　安　以　耶　何

1. 赤曰：“____媒我也，吾將娶乎____。”

2. 友大駭，曰：“足下妻固無恙，太夫人在堂，____得有____？豈狂易病惑____？”

3. 赤怒曰：“____無道。吾將從吾妻，____ ____爲____？”

4. 而吾妻____居，與帝居天、清都無____異，若____苦余至此哉？

五 爲加點字選擇正確釋義，並根據釋義來翻譯句子 Match each dotted word with its correct modern Chinese equivalent by circling the latter. Then translate each sentence into modern Chinese.

1. 又何間焉?　　　　　　　　　　ⓐ 爲什麽(为什么)　**b.** 憑什麽(凭什么)　**c.** 多少

現代文翻譯：你又为什么要参与到这件事情里面？

_____

2. 其友從之，見赤軒厠抱甕，詭笑而側視，勢且下入。　　　a. 而且　b. 將（将）要　c. 和

现代文翻译：＿＿＿＿＿＿＿＿＿＿＿＿＿＿＿＿＿＿＿＿＿＿

3. 而吾妻之居，與帝居鈞天、清都無以異，若何苦余至此哉？　a. 使……受苦　b. 痛苦　c. 何苦呢？

现代文翻译：＿＿＿＿＿＿＿＿＿＿＿＿＿＿＿＿＿＿＿＿＿＿

4. 眾發墻以入，赤之面陷不潔者半矣。　　　　　　　　　a. 認爲（认为）　b. 來（来）　c. 用

现代文翻译：＿＿＿＿＿＿＿＿＿＿＿＿＿＿＿＿＿＿＿＿＿＿

5. 取其所爲書讀之，蓋與其母妻訣，其言辭猶人也。　　　a. 雖（虽）然　b. 那麼（么）　c. 大致

现代文翻译：＿＿＿＿＿＿＿＿＿＿＿＿＿＿＿＿＿＿＿＿＿＿

6. 是其病心而爲是耶？抑固有厠鬼耶？　　　　　　　a. 抑或　b. 抑制　c. 因此

现代文翻译：＿＿＿＿＿＿＿＿＿＿＿＿＿＿＿＿＿＿＿＿＿＿

7. 今世皆知笑赤之惑也，及至是非取與向背決不爲赤者，幾何人也？

　　　　　　　　　　　　　　　　　a. 多少　b. 怎麼（么）　c. 爲什麼（为什么）

现代文翻译：＿＿＿＿＿＿＿＿＿＿＿＿＿＿＿＿＿＿＿＿＿＿

第十七課

方苞《左忠毅公逸事》

"An Anecdote Concerning Zuo the Loyal and Steadfast" (Fang Bao)

Introduction

Fang Bao 方苞 (courtesy names Fengjiu 鳳九 and Linggao 靈皋; pseudonym Wangxi 望溪; 1668–1749), an advocate of simple, lucid language, is generally regarded as the founder of the Tongcheng school of ancient-style prose. He models his prose on *Zuo Tradition* and *Grand Scribe's Records* and at the same time emulates Tang prose masters Han Yu and Liu Zongyuan. Fang establishes the ideal of "Righteousness and Methods" 義法 (*yìfǎ* 义法), balancing emphasis on moral content and refined form. His ancient-style prose greatly influenced the development of prose throughout the Qing dynasty.

This biographical account is a perfect example of Fang's ideal of "Righteousness and Methods." It not only illuminates the Confucian virtue of unbending loyalty but also exemplifies Fang's amazing art of narrative structuring. A translation of this text is given in *HTRCProse*, chapter 15, "Ming and Qing Occasional Prose: Letters and Funerary Inscriptions," C15.2.

正文與簡體譯文 Text and Modern Chinese Translation

先君子嘗言，鄉先輩<u>左忠毅公</u>視學京
xiān jūn zǐ cháng yán　xiāng xiān bèi zuǒ zhōng yì gōng shì xué jīng

畿。[1] 一日，風雪嚴寒，從數騎出，微行，入
jī　　yí rì　　fēng xuě yán hán　cóng shù jì chū　wēi xíng　rù

古寺。[2] 廡下一生伏案臥，文方成草。[3] 公閱
gǔ sì　　wǔ xià yì shēng fú àn wò　wén fāng chéng cǎo　gōng yuè

畢，即解貂覆生，爲掩戶，叩之寺僧，則<u>史</u>
bì　jí jiě diāo fù shēng　wèi yǎn hù　kòu zhī sì sēng　zé shǐ

<u>公可法</u>也。[4] 及試，吏呼名至<u>史公</u>，公瞿然注
gōng kě fǎ yě　　jí shì　lì hū míng zhì shǐ gōng　gōng jù rán zhù

視，呈卷，即面署第一。[5] 召入，使拜夫人，
shì　chéng juàn　jí miàn shǔ dì yī　　zhào rù　shǐ bài fū rén

曰：「吾諸兒碌碌，他日繼吾志事，惟此生
yuē　wú zhū ér lù lù　tā rì jì wú zhì shì　wéi cǐ shēng

先父曾经说过，同乡先辈左忠毅公(任)视察京城地区的学政(时)。[1] 一天，刮风下雪，天非常冷，(他带着)几个骑马的随从，微服出行，进入一座古寺。[2] 厢房里一个书生趴在桌上睡着了，(桌上的)文章刚刚写完草稿。[3] 左光斗读完，立刻解下貂裘给书生盖上，为他关上门。向寺里的僧人询问书生的事情，(知道)是史可法。[4] 等到考试时，官吏叫名字叫到史可法，左光斗惊喜地注视着他。(等他)呈上考卷，立刻

耳。」⁶
ěr

当面列为第一名。⁵(左光斗还把史可法)召到家里，使他拜见夫人，说："我的几个儿子都很平庸，将来继承我的志向事业的，只有这个书生罢了！"⁶

1. 先君子 the author's respectful way of referring to his deceased father, Fang Zhongshu 方仲舒.

   嘗 (尝) *adv.* once. MdnC: 曾經 (*céng jīng* 曾经). See L23 Grammar Note 1 ①.

   鄉 (乡) *n.* county. Here it refers to the people from the same hometown 同鄉 (*tóng xiāng* 同乡).

   先輩 (辈) *n.* elder, senior.

   左忠毅公 or 左光斗 (family name 姓, Zuǒ 左; given name 名, Guāngdǒu 光斗; style 字, Yízhí 遺直/Gǒngzhī 拱之; posthumous name 諡, Zhōngyì 忠毅; 1575–1625), one of the representatives of the Donglin Party 東林黨 (*Dōnglín dǎng* 东林党) in the late Ming.

   視 (视) *v.* to watch, inspect. MdnC: 視察 (*shì chá* 视察).

   學 (学) *v.* to study. Here it is a noun, referring to educational affairs 學政 (*xué zhèng* 学政).

   京 *n.* capital. MdnC: 京城 (*jīng chéng*).

   畿 *n.* area close to the capital.

2. 嚴 (严) 寒 *adj.* very cold, extremely cold.

   從 (从) *v.* to follow. MdnC: 跟從 (*gēn cóng* 跟从). Here it is used as a causative verb, 使……從, meaning "to make … follow." See L7 Grammar Note 1 ①.

   騎 (骑 jì) *n.* cavalry.

   微 *adv.* incognito, disguised. MdnC: 微服 (*wēi fú*).

   行 (xíng) *v.* to travel. MdnC: 出行 (*chū xíng*).

   寺 *n.* temple.

3. 廡 (庑) *n.* wing room. MdnC: 廂房 (*xiāng fáng* 厢房).

   生 *n.* scholar. MdnC: 書生 (*shū shēng* 书生).

   伏 *v.* to bend over. MdnC: 趴 (*pā*).

   案 *n.* small rectangular table. MdnC: 桌子 (*zhuō zi*).

   臥 (卧) *v.* to lie, sleep.

   方 *adv.* just, just now. MdnC: 剛剛 (*gāng gāng* 刚刚).

   成 *v.* to complete, finish.

   草 *n.* draft. MdnC: 草稿 (*cǎo gǎo*).

4. 閱 (阅) *v.* to read. MdnC: 讀 (*dú* 读).

   畢 (毕) *v.* to end, complete. MdnC: 完 (*wán*).

   即 *adv.* quickly, immediately. MdnC: 立刻 (*lì kè*).

   解 (jiě) *v.* to untie.

   貂 *n.* marten. Here it means "marten coat" 貂裘 (*diāo qiú*).

   覆 *v.* to cover. MdnC: 蓋 (*gài* 盖).

   掩 *v.* to shut, close. MdnC: 關 (*guān* 关).

   戶 *n.* door. MdnC: 門 (*mén* 门).

   叩 *v.* to ask about, make inquiries about. MdnC: 詢問 (*xún wèn* 询问).

之 *personal pron.* him. It refers to the young scholar Shi Kefa. See L1 Grammar Note 2 ③.

僧 *n.* monk.

史可法 (family name 姓, Shǐ 史; given name 名, Kěfǎ 可法; style 字, Xiànzhī 憲之/Dàolín 道鄰; posthumous names 謚, Wénzhōng 文忠/Zhōngzhèng 忠正; 1602–1645), a renowned late-Ming general and hero in fighting against the Manchu army.

5. 試 (试) *n.* examination. MdnC: 考試 (*kǎo shì* 考试).

  吏 *n.* functionaries, low-level officials. MdnC: 官員 (*guān yuan* 官员).

  瞿 (jù) 然 *adj.* surprised. MdnC: 驚訝 (*jīng yà* 惊讶).

  注視 (视) *v.* to gaze, watch.

  呈 *v.* to submit respectfully. MdnC: 呈上 (*chéng shàng*).

  卷 *n.* test sheet. MdnC: 考卷 (*kǎo juàn*).

  面 *n.* face. Here it means "face to face" 當面 (*dāng miàn* 当面).

  署 *v.* to sign, endorse. MdnC: 簽 (*qiān* 签).

6. 召 (zhào) *v.* to call over, summon.

  拜 *v.* to pay a formal visit to. MdnC: 拜見 (*bài jiàn* 拜见).

  諸 (诸) *adj.* various, all of.

  碌碌 *adj.* mediocre, ordinary, so-so. MdnC: 平庸 (*píng yōng*).

  他日 another day in the future. MdnC: 將来 (*jiāng lái* 将来).

  繼 (继) *v.* to continue, succeed, inherit. MdnC: 繼承 (*jì chéng* 继承).

  志 *n.* aspiration, goal. MdnC: 志向 (*zhì xiàng*).

  事 *n.* career. MdnC: 事業 (*shì yè* 事业).

  惟 *adv.* only. MdnC: 只有 (*zhǐ yǒu*).

  耳 *ending particle.* MdnC: 罷了 (*bà le* 罢了). See L7 Grammar Note 4.

及左公下廠獄，　史朝夕獄門外；　逆閹防伺
jí zuǒ gōng xià chǎng yù　shǐ zhāo xī yù mén wài　　nì yān fáng sì

甚嚴，雖家僕不得近。⁷久之，聞左公被炮烙，
shèn yán　suī jiā pú bù dé jìn　　jiǔ zhī　wén zuǒ gōng bèi páo luò

旦夕且死。持五十金，涕泣謀於禁卒，卒感
dàn xī qiě sǐ　chí wǔ shí jīn　tì qì móu yú jìn zú　zú gǎn

焉。⁸一日，使史更敝衣草屨，背筐，手長鑱，
yān　yí rì　shǐ shǐ gēng bì yī cǎo jù　bēi kuāng shǒu cháng chán

爲除不潔者，引入，微指左公處，⁹則席地倚
wéi chú bù jié zhě　yǐn rù　wēi zhǐ zuǒ gōng chù　zé xí dì yǐ

牆而坐，面額焦爛不可辨，左膝以下，筋骨
qiáng ér zuò　miàn é jiāo làn bù kě biàn　zuǒ xī yǐ xià　jīng gǔ

盡脫矣。¹⁰
jìn tuō yǐ.

到左光斗被关进了东厂的监狱时，史可法每天(都守)在监狱外。宦官逆党防备监视得很严，即使是(左光斗)家的仆人也不能靠近。⁷过了很久，听说左光斗被(施行了)炮烙酷刑，很快就要死了。(史可法)拿着五十两银子，流着泪与狱卒商量，狱卒被他感动了。⁸一天，(狱卒)让史可法换上破衣服和草鞋，背着筐，手(拿)长镵，(扮)做清除脏东西的人。(狱卒)领着(他)进(了监狱)，稍微指了指左光斗在的地方。⁹(史可法就看到左

光斗）靠着墙坐在地
上，脸和额头都烧焦溃
烂了，不能辨认，左膝
以下，筋骨全都脱落
了。[10]

7. 廠 (厂) or 東廠 (东厂) Eastern Bureau, a secret agency run by eunuchs during the Ming dynasty for surveillance of government officials.

獄 (狱) *n.* prison, jail. MdnC: 監獄 (*jiān yù* 监狱).

朝 (zhāo) 夕 *n.* morning and evening. MdnC: 早晚 (*zǎo wǎn*). Here it refers to every day.

逆 *adj.* refractory.

閹 (阉) *n.* eunuch. MdnC: 宦官 (*huàn guān*).

逆閹 here refers to Wei Zhongxian 魏忠賢 (1568–1627), a powerful eunuch during the reign of Emperor Tianqi (r. 1620–1627) of the Ming dynasty.

防 *v.* to guard against. MdnC: 防備 (*fáng bèi* 防备).

伺 *v.* to keep watch over. MdnC: 監視 (*jiān shì* 监视).

嚴 (严) *adj.* severe, rigorous.

雖 (虽) *conj.* even though. MdnC: 即使 (*jí shǐ*). See L4 Grammar Note 6.

僕 (仆) *n.* servant. MdnC: 僕人 (*pú rén* 仆人).

近 *v.* to come close, draw near. MdnC: 靠近 (*kào jìn*).

8. 聞 (闻) *v.* to hear. MdnC: 聽説 (*tīng shuō* 听说).

炮烙 *n.* branding with an iron, a form of torture.

旦 *n.* dawn.

旦夕 *n.* morning and night. It refers to a very short time.

且 *adv.* about to, will. MdnC: 將要 (*jiāng yào* 将要). See L13 Grammar Note 2 ③.

持 *v.* to hold in one's hand. MdnC: 拿 (*ná*).

金 *n.* money. Here it refers to silver taels. MdnC: 銀子 (*yín zi* 银子).

涕泣 *v.* to weep. MdnC: 流淚 (*liú lèi* 眼泪).

謀 (谋) *v.* to consult. MdnC: 商量 (*shāng liáng*).

禁 *v.* to forbid, prohibit. Here it is a noun, referring to prison 監獄 (*jiān yù* 监狱).

卒 *n.* soldier, guard.

感 *v.* to be moved, be touched. MdnC: 感動 (*gǎn dòng* 感动).

焉 *pron.* 焉 here is a combination of 於 and 之. See L1 Grammar Note 4 ①.

9. 更 (gēng) *v.* to change. MdnC: 換 (*huàn* 换).

敝 *adj.* tattered, ragged. MdnC: 破 (*pò*).

屨 *n.* straw sandals. MdnC: 鞋 (*xié*).

背 (bēi) *v.* to carry on one's back.

筐 *n.* bamboo basket.

長 (长 cháng) 鑱 (镵) *n.* a farming tool with a long handle.

爲 (为 wéi) *v.* to do, act. MdnC: 做 (*zuò*). See L2 Grammar Note 6 ①.

除 *v.* to remove, get rid of. MdnC: 清除 (*qīng chú*).

引 *v.* to lead. MdnC: 領 (*lǐng* 领).

微 *adv.* a little, a bit. MdnC: 稍微 (*shāo wēi*).

指 *v.* to point to.

處 (处 chù) *n.* location, place. MdnC: 地方 (*dì fāng*).

10. 席 *n.* mat, seat. Here it is used as a putative verb, 以……爲席, meaning "to use … as a seat." See L14 Grammar Note 1 ②.

倚 *v.* to lean on. MdnC: 靠 (*kào*).

面 *n.* face. MdnC: 臉 (*liǎn* 脸).

額 (额) *n.* forehead. MdnC: 額頭 (*é tóu* 额头).

焦 *adj.* burned.

爛 (烂) *adj.* ulcerated, festered. MdnC: 潰爛 (*kuì làn* 溃烂).

辨 *v.* to distinguish, tell. MdnC: 辨認 (*biàn rèn* 辨认).

膝 *n.* knee.

筋 *n.* tendon.

盡 (尽 jìn) *adv.* completely. MdnC: 全 (*quán*).

脫 *v.* to come off. MdnC: 脫落 (*tuō luò*).

史前跪，抱公膝而嗚咽。公辨其聲，而目不可開，乃奮臂以指撥眥；目光如炬。[11] 怒曰：「庸奴，此何地也，而汝來前！國家之事，糜爛至此。[12] 老夫已矣，汝復輕身而昧大義，天下事誰可支拄者！[13] 不速去，無俟姦人構陷，吾今即撲殺汝！[14]」因摸地上刑械，作投擊勢。[15] 史噤不敢發聲，趨而出。後常流涕述其事以語人曰：「吾師肺肝，皆鐵石所鑄造也！」[16]

shǐ qián guì, bào gōng xī ér wū yè. gōng biàn qí shēng, ér mù bù kě kāi, nǎi fèn bì yǐ zhǐ bō zì; mù guāng rú jù. nù yuē: yōng nú, cǐ hé dì yě, ér rǔ lái qián! guó jiā zhī shì, mí làn zhì cǐ. lǎo fū yǐ yǐ, rǔ fù qīng shēn ér mèi dà yì, tiān xià shì shuí kě zhī zhǔ zhě! bú sù qù, wú sì jiān rén gòu xiàn, wú jīn jí pū shā rǔ! yīn mō dì shàng xíng xiè, zuò tóu jī shì. shǐ jìn bù gǎn fā shēng, qū ér chū. hòu cháng liú tì shù qí shì yǐ yǔ rén yuē: wú shī fèi gān, jiē tiě shí suǒ zhù zào yě.

史可法走上前跪下，抱着左光斗的膝盖小声哭起来。左光斗辨认出他的声音，但是眼睛不能睁开，于是奋力举起手臂，用手指拨开眼角，目光像火炬(一样明亮)。[11] (左光斗)生气地说："不明事理的家伙，这是什么地方？而你来到这里！国家的事情已经糜烂到这种地步。[12] 我已经完了，你又看轻自己，不明大义，天下的事情谁还能支撑啊！[13] 你还不赶快离开，不等奸诈小人来设计陷害你，我现在就击杀了你！[14]" 说着，(左光斗)摸起地上的用刑器具，作出投击的姿势。[15] 史可法闭口不敢出声，快步走了出去。后来(史可法)常流着眼泪跟别人讲左光斗的事情，说："我老师的肺肝，都是铁石铸成的！"[16]

11. 跪 *v.* to kneel.

    嗚 (呜) 咽 *v.* to sob, whimper.

    奮 (奋) *v.* to raise. MdnC: 舉起 (*jǔ qǐ* 举起).

    臂 *n.* arm.

    撥 (拨) *v.* to spread out.

    眥 *n.* eye sockets, the corner of eyes. MdnC: 眼角 (*yǎn jiǎo*).

    炬 *n.* torch. MdnC: 火炬 (*huǒ jù*).

12. 庸 *adj.* mediocre, so-so.

    奴 *n.* slave, servant, fellow.

    汝 *pron.* you. MdnC: 你 (*nǐ*). See L16 Grammar Note 1.

    糜爛 (烂) *adj.* rotten to the core.

13. 已 *v.* to stop, end. MdnC: 完 (*wán*). See L21 Grammar Note 1 ②.

    復 (复) *adv.* again. MdnC: 又 (*yòu*).

    輕 (轻) *adj.* unimportant. Here it is used as a putative verb, 以⋯⋯爲輕, meaning "to treat ... as unimportant." MdnC: 看輕 (*kàn qīng* 看轻). See L14 Grammar Note 1 ①.

    昧 *v.* to be ignorant of. MdnC: 不明 (*bù míng*).

    大義 (义) *n.* cardinal principle of righteousness.

    拄 *v.* to support. MdnC: 支撐 (*zhī chēng* 支撑).

14. 速 *adv.* fast, quickly. MdnC: 趕快 (*gǎn kuài* 赶快).

    去 *v.* to leave. MdnC: 離開 (*lí kāi* 离开).

    俟 *v.* to wait for, wait until. MdnC: 等 (*děng*).

    奸 *adj.* evil, treacherous. MdnC: 奸詐 (*jiān zhà* 奸诈).

    構 (构) 陷 *v.* to frame somebody. MdnC: 設計陷害 (*shè jì xiàn hài* 设计陷害).

    撲殺 (扑杀) *v.* to attack and kill. MdnC: 擊殺 (*jī shā* 击杀).

15. 刑 *n.* torture and mutilation. MdnC: 用刑 (*yòng xíng*).

    械 *n.* instrument. MdnC: 器具 (*qì jù*).

    投 *v.* to throw.

    擊 (击) *v.* to attack.

    勢 (势) *n.* posture. MdnC: 姿勢 (*zī shì* 姿势).

16. 噤 *v.* to close the mouth, keep silent. MdnC: 閉口 (*bì kǒu* 闭口).

    趨 (趋) *v.* to walk fast. MdnC: 快步走 (*kuài bù zǒu*).

    述 *v.* to tell. MdnC: 講 (*jiǎng* 讲).

    肺肝 *n.* lung and liver.

    鑄 (铸) 造 *v.* to cast, found, forge.

崇禎末，流賊張獻忠出沒蘄、黃、潛、桐間。[17] 史公以鳳廬道奉檄守禦。[18] 每有警，輒數月不就寢，使將士更休，而自坐幄幕

chóng zhēn mò　liú zéi zhāng xiàn zhōng chū mò qí　huáng　qián tóng jiān　　shǐ gōng yǐ fèng lú dào fèng xí shǒu yù　　měi yǒu jǐng zhé shù yuè bù jiù qǐn　　shǐ jiàng shì gēng xiū　　ér　zì　zuò wò mù

崇禎末年，流竄的叛军张献忠在蕲春、黄冈、潜山、桐城之间出没。[17] 史公以凤庐道员的身份奉命防守抵御(叛军)。[18] 每当有警报，(史公)就几个月不去睡觉，让其他将领士兵轮流休息，而自己坐在

外。¹⁹擇健卒十人，令二人蹲踞，而背倚之，
wài　　zé jiàn zú shí rén　　lìng èr rén dūn jù　　ér bèi yǐ zhī

漏鼓移，則番代。²⁰每寒夜起立，振衣裳，
lòu gǔ yí　　zé fān dài　　měi hán yè qǐ lì　　zhèn yī shāng

甲上冰霜迸落，鏗然有聲。²¹或勸以少休，
jiǎ shàng bīng shuāng bèng luò kēng rán yǒu shēng huò quàn yǐ shāo xiū

公曰：「吾上恐負朝廷，下恐愧吾師也。」²²
gōng yuē　　wú shàng kǒng fù cháo tíng　　xià kǒng kuì wú shī yě

帐篷外。¹⁹（史公）选了十个矫健的士兵，命令他们每两个人蹲坐着，背靠着背，更漏、更鼓一变，就（与其他组）轮番替换。²⁰每到寒冷的夜晚，（史公）站起来，抖一抖衣裳，铠甲上的冰霜就掉落下来，发出响亮的声音。²¹有人劝说（史公）稍微休息一下，史公说："我对上怕辜负了朝廷，对下怕面愧对我的老师。"²²

17. 崇禎 (祯) (family name 姓, Zhū 朱; given name 名, Yóujiǎn 由檢; era name 年號, Chóngzhēn 崇禎; temple name 廟號, Sīzōng 思宗; r. 1627–1644), Emperor Si 明思宗, the last emperor of the Ming dynasty.

末 *n.* ending period. Here it refers to the ending period of Chongzhen reign of the Ming dynasty. MdnC: 末年 (*mò nián*).

流 *v.* to flow. Here it means "to flee hither and thither" 流竄 (*liú cuàn* 流窜).

賊 (贼) *n.* bandits, traitors. Here it refers to rebel forces 叛軍 (*pàn jūn* 叛军).

張獻忠 (张献忠) (family name 姓, Zhāng 張; given name 名, Xiànzhōng 獻忠; style 字, Bǐngwú 秉吾; literary name 號, Jìngxuān 敬軒; 1606–1647), one of the leaders of the rebel forces during the late Ming dynasty. Zhang Xianzhong established the Great Western Court 大西 in Sichuan Province in 1644 and then was defeated by the Qing army in 1646.

出沒 (没 mò) *v.* to appear and disappear, haunt.

蘄 (蕲) place name in present-day Qichun 蘄春, Hubei Province.

黃 (黄) place name in present-day Huanggang 黄冈, Hubei Province.

潛 (潜) place name in present-day Qianshan 潛山, Anhui Province.

桐 place name in present-day Tongcheng 桐城, Anhui Province.

18. 以 *coverb.* with. See L2 Grammar Note 1 ②.

鳳廬 (凤庐) covers present-day Chuzhou 滁州 and present-day Hefei 合肥, Anhui Province.

道 *n.* regional governor, prefect. MdnC: 道員 (*dào yuán* 道员).

奉 *v.* to receive with respect. MdnC: 奉命 (*fèng mìng*).

檄 *n.* a call to arms.

守 *v.* to guard. MdnC: 防守 (*fáng shǒu*).

禦 (御) *v.* to resist. MdnC: 抵禦 (*dǐ yù* 抵御).

19. 警 *n.* alarm, alert. MdnC: 警報 (*jǐng bào* 警报).

輒 (辄) *adv.* always, every time. MdnC: 就 (*jiù*).

就 *v.* to go to, approach.

寢 (寝) *v.* to sleep, rest. MdnC: 睡覺 (*shuì jiào* 睡觉).

將 (将 jiàng) *n.* commander, general. MdnC: 將領 (*jiāng lǐng* 将领).

士 *n.* soldiers. MdnC: 士兵 (*shì bīng*).

更 (gēng) *v.* to change, alternate. MdnC: 輪流 (*lún liú* 轮流).

幄幕 *n.* tent. MdnC: 帳篷 (*zhàng péng* 帐篷).

20. 擇 (择) *v.* to select, choose. MdnC: 選 (*xuǎn* 选).

    健 *adj.* strong and vigorous. MdnC: 矯健 (*jiǎo jiàn* 矫健).

    卒 *n.* soldier, guard. MdnC: 士兵 (*shì bīng*).

    令 *v.* to order. MdnC: 命令 (*mìng lìng*).

    蹲 *v.* to squat.

    踞 *v.* to crouch, squat, sit. MdnC: 蹲坐 (*dūn zuò*).

    倚 *v.* to lean on. MdnC: 靠 (*kào*).

    漏 *n.* water clock, clepsydra. MdnC: 更漏 (*gēng lòu*).

    鼓 *n.* drum. Here it refers to signaling the time by drumming. MdnC: 更鼓 (*gēng gǔ*).

    移 *v.* to move. Here it means "the clock changes."

    番 *v.* to take turns. MdnC: 輪番 (*lún fān* 轮番).

    代 *v.* to replace. MdnC: 替換 (*tì huàn*).

21. 振 *v.* to shake. MdnC: 抖 (*dǒu*).

    甲 *n.* armor, shell. MdnC: 鎧甲 (*kǎi jiǎ* 铠甲).

    迸 *v.* to disperse, spout.

    鏗 (铿) 然 *adj.* loud and powerful (sound).

22. 或 *indefinite pron.* someone. MdnC: 有人 (*yǒu rén*). See L6 Grammar Note 4 ①.

    勸 (劝) *v.* to persuade, convince. MdnC: 勸説 (*quàn shuō* 劝说).

    少 (shāo) *adv.* used in the sense of 稍 (*shāo*), meaning "a little" 稍微 (*shāo wēi*).

    恐 *v.* to be afraid. MdnC: 怕 (*pà*).

    負 (负) *v.* to let down, disappoint. MdnC: 辜負 (*gū fù* 辜负).

    愧 *v.* to be ashamed, feel guilty. MdnC: 愧疚 (*kuì jiù*).

史公治兵，往來桐城，必躬造左公第，
shǐ gōng zhì bīng　wǎng lái tóng chéng　bì gōng zào zuǒ gōng dì

候太公、太母起居，拜夫人於堂上。 23
hòu tài gōng　　tài mǔ qǐ　jū　　bài fū　rén yú táng shàng

史可法带领军队，往来(经过)桐城。必定亲自到左公的宅第去(拜访)，问候太公和太母安好，在大堂上拜见左公的夫人。 23

23. 治 *v.* to manage, govern.

    躬 *adv.* personally, in person. MdnC: 親自 (*qīn zì* 亲自).

    造 *v.* to go to. MdnC: 到 (*dào*) ⋯⋯去 (*qù*).

    第 *n.* residence, dwelling. MdnC: 宅第 (*zhái dì*).

    候 *v.* to send one's regards to, extend greetings to. MdnC: 問候 (*wèn hòu* 问候).

    太公 *n.* a respectful form of address for someone else's father. Here it refers to Zuo Guangdou's father.

    太母 *n.* a respectful form of address for someone else's mother. Here it refers to Zuo Guangdou's mother.

    起居 *n.* daily life.

    拜 *v.* to pay a formal visit. MdnC: 拜見 (*bài jiàn* 拜见).

夫人 Zuo Guangdou's wife.

余宗老塗山， 左公甥也， 與先君子善，
yú zōng lǎo tú shān　zuǒ gōng shēng yě　yǔ xiān jūn zǐ shàn

謂獄中語乃親得之於史公云。 [24]
wèi yù zhōng yǔ nǎi qīn dé zhī yú shǐ gōng yún

我的族祖父方文(塗山)是左公的女婿。他与先父交好。(方文)说，(左公)在狱中说的话，是(他)亲自从史公那里听到的。[24]

《方望溪全集》，北京：中國書店 (1991), 116—117.

24. 宗老 *n.* elder members of the patriline.
　　塗 (涂) 山 or 方文 the brother of Fang Bao's grandfather. 塗 (涂) 山 is his literary name.
　　甥 *n.* nephew. Here it refers to Zuo Guangdou's son-in-law 女婿 (*nǚ xù*).
　　善 *v.* to be friendly with. MdnC: 交好 (*jiāo hǎo*).
　　親 (亲) *adv.* personally, in person. MdnC: 親自 (*qīn zì* 亲自).
　　云 *ending particle.* used to end an indirect quotation. See Grammar Note 1.

語法注釋 Grammar Note

1. 云　*ending particle.* As an ending particle, 云 means "it was said."

余宗老塗山，⋯⋯謂獄中語乃親得之於史公云。

[我的族祖父方涂山，⋯⋯说（左公）在狱中说的话，是（他）亲自从史公那里听到的。]

余登箕山，其上蓋有許由冢云。(L13)

[我登上箕山，据说山上可能有許由的墓。]

Literary Analysis

1. The biographical account describes various recognition scenes: in the monastery, Zuo recognizes Shi as an exceptional student, and in prison, Shi recognizes Zuo despite his changed circumstances. How does the theme of recognition relate to larger Confucian themes of recognizing men of talent?

2. Analyze parallels between the father-son relationship—one of the five cardinal Confucian bonds—and the teacher-student relationship portrayed here. How are they similar and dissimilar?

3. Loyalty to the fallen Ming dynasty was a major theme in literature of the early Qing. Discuss the theme of loyalty as it figures in this account. Consider loyalties to country, family, and teacher.

　　☞ *HTRCProse*, chapter 1, "An Anatomy of the Chinese Prose Form: An Overview," C1.3, and chapter 15, "Ming and Qing Occasional Prose: Letters and Funerary Inscriptions."

—RHS

課後練習 Exercises

一 給加點字注音 Give the pinyin romanization for each dotted word.

1. 炮烙 （____, ____） 2. 廡 （____） 3. 京畿 （____） 4. 逆閹 （____） 5. 斬 （____）

6. 崇禎 （____, ____） 7. 眥 （____） 8. 長鑱 （____） 9. 塗山 （____） 10. 桐 （____）

二 在括號中給句中加點的字注音，並選出正確的釋義 Give the pinyin romanization for each dotted word; then select the correct definition from the following list, and write it in the blank.

平庸　不明白　閉(闭)口　等　蹲坐　快步走　**信服**　火炬　靠　詢問(询问)

1. 小信未孚（fú） ___信服___　2. 叩之寺僧（　）_____　3. 倚墻而坐（　）_____

4. 諸兒碌碌（　）_____　5. 目光如炬（　）_____　6. 昧大義 （　）_____

7. 趨而走 　（　）_____　8. 無俟姦人構陷（　）_____

9. 令二人蹲踞（　）_____　10. 史噤不敢發聲（　）_____

三 選擇釋義並填空 Match each word in the left column with its correct definition in the middle column. Fill in each blank in the right column with an appropriate word from the left column.

謀謀劃(谋划)	領(领)	一日，風雪嚴寒，從數騎出，____行，入古寺。
微_____	舉(举)起	公閱畢，即解貂皮覆生，爲____户，叩之寺僧，則史公可法也。
掩_____	作勢(势)	
呈_____	**謀劃(谋划)**	及試，吏呼名至史公，公瞿然注視，____卷，即面____第一。
署_____	輪(轮)番	
更_____	到…去	一日使史____敝衣草屨，背筐，手長鑱，爲除不潔者，____入，微指左公處。
引_____	親(亲)身	
奮_____	微服	公辨其聲，而目不可開，乃____臂以指撥眥。
勢_____	替換(替换)	
禦_____	簽(签)	因摸地上刑械，作投擊____。
番_____	呈上	史公以鳳廬道奉檄守____。
代_____	關(关)	擇健卒十人，令二人蹲踞，而背倚之，漏鼓移，則____ ____。
躬_____	換	
造_____	防禦(御)	史公治兵，往來桐城，必____ ____左公第，候太公、太母起居，拜夫人於堂上。

四 請用給出的字填空 Fill in each blank with an appropriate word from the following list.

耳　且　然　焉　云　以　如

1. 吾諸兒碌碌，他日繼吾志事，惟此生＿＿＿。
2. 久之，聞左公被炮烙，旦夕＿＿＿死。持五十金，涕泣謀於禁卒，卒感＿＿＿。
3. 公辨其聲，而目不可開，乃奮臂＿＿＿指撥眥，目光＿＿＿炬。
4. 每寒夜起立，振衣裳，甲上冰霜迸落，鏗＿＿＿有聲。
5. 余宗老塗山，左公甥也，與先君子善，謂獄中語乃親得之於史公＿＿＿。

五 爲加點字選擇正確釋義，並根據釋義來翻譯句子 Match each dotted word with its correct modern Chinese equivalent by circling the latter. Then translate each sentence into modern Chinese.

1. 又何間焉?　　　　　　　　　　　　　ⓐ 爲什麽（为什么）　b. 憑什麽（凭什么）　c. 多少

現代文翻译：你又为什么要参与到这件事情里面？

＿＿＿＿＿＿＿＿＿＿＿＿＿＿＿＿＿＿＿＿＿＿＿＿＿＿＿＿＿＿＿＿＿＿＿＿＿

2. 一日，風雪嚴寒，從數騎出，微行，入古寺。　a. 跟從（从）　b. 使……跟從（从）　c. 從（从）前

現代文翻译：＿＿＿＿＿＿＿＿＿＿＿＿＿＿＿＿＿＿＿＿＿＿＿＿＿＿＿＿＿＿＿

3. 吾諸兒碌碌，他日繼吾志事，惟此生耳。　　　　　a. 罷（罢）了　b. 耳朵　c. 啊

現代文翻译：＿＿＿＿＿＿＿＿＿＿＿＿＿＿＿＿＿＿＿＿＿＿＿＿＿＿＿＿＿＿＿

4. 持五十金，涕泣謀於禁卒，卒感焉。　　　　　a. 於（于）之　b. 什麽（么）　c. 啊

現代文翻译：＿＿＿＿＿＿＿＿＿＿＿＿＿＿＿＿＿＿＿＿＿＿＿＿＿＿＿＿＿＿＿

5. 引入，微指左公處，則席地倚墻而坐，面額焦爛不可辨。　a. 座位　b. 宴席　c. 以……爲（为）席

現代文翻译：＿＿＿＿＿＿＿＿＿＿＿＿＿＿＿＿＿＿＿＿＿＿＿＿＿＿＿＿＿＿＿

6. 公辨其聲，而目不可開，乃奮臂以指撥眥，目光如炬。　a. 用　b. 來（来）　c. 因爲（为）

現代文翻译：＿＿＿＿＿＿＿＿＿＿＿＿＿＿＿＿＿＿＿＿＿＿＿＿＿＿＿＿＿＿＿

7. 老夫已矣，汝復輕身而昧大義，天下事誰可支拄者！　　a. 我　b. 你　c. 他

現代文翻译：＿＿＿＿＿＿＿＿＿＿＿＿＿＿＿＿＿＿＿＿＿＿＿＿＿＿＿＿＿＿＿

8. 或勸以少休，公曰："吾上恐負朝廷，下恐愧吾師也。"　　　　a. 有人 b. 或者 c. 有時（时）

现代文翻译：_____

單元練習

Unit Exercises

一、辨析加點字在不同句中注音和釋義的異同 Give the pinyin romanization for each dotted word, and then write in its correct definition.

1. 鄙　肉食者鄙，未能遠謀。　　　　　　　　（**bǐ**）<u>目光短淺</u>

越國以鄙遠，君知其難也。　　　　　（　　）＿＿＿＿＿＿＿

2. 載　夫學者載籍極博，猶考信六藝。　　　　（　　）＿＿＿＿＿＿＿

及至，西伯卒，武王載木主。　　　　（　　）＿＿＿＿＿＿＿

3. 叩　伯夷、叔齊叩馬而諫。　　　　　　　　　（　　）＿＿＿＿＿＿＿

叩之寺僧，則史公可法也。　　　　　（　　）＿＿＿＿＿＿＿

4. 號　故自號曰李赤。　　　　　　　　　　　　（　　）＿＿＿＿＿＿＿

其友號而救之。　　　　　　　　　　（　　）＿＿＿＿＿＿＿

5. 環　環堵蕭然，不蔽風日。　　　　　　　　　（　　）＿＿＿＿＿＿＿

持出，洗其汙，眾環之以至旦。　　　（　　）＿＿＿＿＿＿＿

6. 更　縣之吏更召巫師善呪術者守赤，赤自若也。（　　）＿＿＿＿＿＿＿

一日，使史更敝衣草屨。　　　　　　（　　）＿＿＿＿＿＿＿

7. 微　從數騎出，微行，入古寺。　　　　　　　（　　）＿＿＿＿＿＿＿

引入，微指左公處。　　　　　　　　（　　）＿＿＿＿＿＿＿

8. 如　夜，赤又如厠久。　　　　　　　　　　　（　　）＿＿＿＿＿＿＿

富貴如可求，雖執鞭之士，吾亦爲之。（　　）＿＿＿＿＿＿＿

二、用給出的字填空，並選擇正確的釋義 Fill in the blanks with words from list A, and then write in their modern Chinese equivalents from list B.

A. Words for Filling the Blanks　　　　　　　B. Modern Chinese Equivalents

沒	篤	吝	抵	伺		同情	不明	到⋯⋯去	歸(归)附　保護(护)
厭	悲	結	捍	昧		到	向往	爲(为)⋯⋯而死	專(专)心　縫補(缝补)
徇	慕	歸	**鄙**	造		在意	消失	監視(监视)	**目光短浅** 吃飽(饱)

1. 肉食者 ＿鄙＿，未能遠謀。　　　[目光短浅]　　2. 神農、虞、夏忽焉＿＿＿＿兮。　　　[　　　　]

3. 顏淵雖_____學。　　　[　　] 4. 余_____伯夷之意。　　　[　　]

5. 去_____他縣。　　　[　　] 6. 逆閹防_____甚嚴。　　　[　　]

7. 必躬_____左公第。　　　[　　] 8. 赤入廁，舉其袱_____門。　　[　　]

9. 我安適_____矣？　　　[　　] 10. 既醉而退，曾不_____情去留。[　　]

11. 短褐穿_____，簞瓢屢空。[　　] 12. 然回也屢空，糟糠不_____。　[　　]

13. 閑靜少言，不_____榮利。[　　] 14. 貪夫_____財，烈士_____名。[　　]

15. 汝復輕身而_____大義。[　　]

三、給加點字選擇正確的釋義，並選出與加點字用法相同的句子 Circle the letter of the correct definition (a, b, c, or d) for the dotted word in each boldfaced sentence. Then circle the letter of the sentence (A, B, C, or D) that employs the dotted word in the same way as the boldfaced sentence.

1. 臣之妻私臣。　　　a. 這(这)件事情 b. 他 ⓒ 的 d. 他們

　　A. 夫晉，何厭之有？　　　**B.** 不闕秦，將焉取之？

　　C. 肉食者謀之，又何間焉？　　Ⓓ 能面刺寡人之過者，受上賞。

2. 伯夷、叔齊恥之，義不食周粟。　a. 羞恥(耻) b. 以……爲恥(耻) c. 慚(惭)愧 d. 恨

　　A. 吾妻之美我者，私我也。　　　B. 不戰而屈人之兵，善之善者也。

　　C. 焉用亡鄭以陪鄰？　　　D. 博我以文，約我以禮。

3. 及餓且死，作歌。　　a. 將(将)要 b. 而且 c. 和 d. 但是

　　A. 以其無禮於晉，且貳於楚。　　B. 由也爲之，比及三年，可使有勇，且知方也。

　　C. 其友叫且言之。　　　D. 聞左公被炮烙，旦夕且死。

4. 或曰：“天道無親，常與善人。”　a. 或者 b. 有人 c. 有時(时) d. 有些

　　A. 方六七十，如五六十，求也爲之。　B. 或擇地而蹈之，時然後出言……

　　C. 抑固有厠鬼耶？　　　D. 親戚知其如此，或置酒而招之。

5. 太夫人在堂，安得有是？　a. 安靜 b. 安全 c. 怎麼(么) d. 哪裏(里)

　　A. 我安適歸焉？　　　B. 衣食所安，弗敢專也，必以分人。

　　C. 縱性情，安恣睢。　　D. 安見方六七十如五六十而非邦也者？

6. 他日繼吾志事，惟此生耳。　a. 聽(听) b. 耳朵 c. 罷(罢)了 d. 啊

　　A. 目可以見，耳可以聽。　　B. 能謗議於市朝，聞寡人之耳者，受下賞。

　　C. 目明而耳聰，不可學明矣。　　D. 人皆有之，賢者能勿喪耳。

7. 神農、虞、夏忽焉沒兮……　　a. 於(于)此 b. 然 c. 怎麼(么) d. 啊

A. 瞻之在前，忽焉在後。　　　　　B. 余甚惑焉。

C. 君子疾沒世而名不稱焉。　　　　D. 其友與俱遊者有姻焉。

8. **儻所謂天道，是邪非邪？**　　a. 是　b. 這(这)件事情　c. 對(对)　d. 他的

A. 是遵何德哉？　　　　　　　　B. 是其病心而爲是耶？

C. 太夫人在堂，安得有是？　　　D. 及至是非取與向背決不爲赤者，幾何人耶？

四、閱讀下面的段落，選擇正確的釋義 Read the following passage, and select the correct definition for each dotted word.

蝜蝂傳
柳宗元

蝜蝂者，善負小蟲也。行遇物，輒持取，卬其首負之。背愈重，雖困劇不止也。其背甚澀，物積因不散，卒躓仆不能起。人或憐之，爲去其負。苟能行，又持取如故。又好上高，極其力不已，至墜地死。

今世之嗜取者，遇貨不避，以厚其室，不知爲己累也，唯恐其不積。及其怠而躓也，黜棄之，遷徙之，亦以病矣。苟能起，又不艾。日思高其位、大其祿，而貪取滋甚，以近於危墜，觀前之死亡不知戒。雖其形魁然大者也，其名人也，而智則小蟲也。亦足哀夫！

《柳宗元集校注》，北京：中華書局 (2013), 1212–1213.

蝜蝂 (fù bǎn) a kind of small insect.
卬 (áng) v. to raise (one's head).　困劇 adj. very exhausted, tired.
澀 (sè) adj. rough, not smooth.　躓仆 (zhì pū) v. to fall.
墜 (zhuì) v. to fall down.　黜 (chù) v. to dismiss.
棄 v. to abandon.　艾 (yì) v. to stop, regret.
魁 (kuí) adj. big.

1. 善負小蟲也。　　a. 好　　　b. 善良　　　c. 擅長(擅长)
2. 善負小蟲也。　　a. 背　　　b. 拿　　　c. 辜負(负)
3. 輒持取。　　　　a. 但　　　b. 就　　　c. 車(车)
4. 雖困劇不止也。　a. 即使　　b. 但是　　c. 因爲(为)
5. 物積因不散。　　a. 多　　　b. 高　　　c. 積纍(积累)
6. 卒躓仆不能起。　a. 終於(终于)　b. 死去　c. 完結(结)

7. 人或憐之。	a. 或者	b. 有時(时)	c. 而
8. 極其力不已。	a. 停止	b. 自己	c. 已經(经)
9. 日思高其位。	a. 很高	b. 使……高	c. 高度
10. 大其祿。	a. 使……大	b. 大小	c. 以……爲(为)大

五、將下列句子翻譯成現代漢語 Translate the following sentences into modern Chinese.

1. 父死不葬，爰及干戈，可謂孝乎？以臣弑君，可謂仁乎？

現代文翻译：＿＿＿＿＿＿＿＿＿＿＿＿＿＿＿＿＿＿＿＿＿

2. 登彼西山兮，采其薇矣。以暴易暴兮，不知其非矣。

現代文翻译：＿＿＿＿＿＿＿＿＿＿＿＿＿＿＿＿＿＿＿＿＿

3. 歲寒，然後知松柏之後凋。

現代文翻译：＿＿＿＿＿＿＿＿＿＿＿＿＿＿＿＿＿＿＿＿＿

4. 豈以其重若彼，其輕若此哉？

現代文翻译：＿＿＿＿＿＿＿＿＿＿＿＿＿＿＿＿＿＿＿＿＿

5. 不戚戚於貧賤，不汲汲於富貴。

現代文翻译：＿＿＿＿＿＿＿＿＿＿＿＿＿＿＿＿＿＿＿＿＿

6. 今世皆知笑赤之惑也，及至是非取與向背決不爲赤者，幾何人耶？

現代文翻译：＿＿＿＿＿＿＿＿＿＿＿＿＿＿＿＿＿＿＿＿＿

7. 老夫已矣，汝復輕身而昧大義，天下事誰可支拄者！

現代文翻译：＿＿＿＿＿＿＿＿＿＿＿＿＿＿＿＿＿＿＿＿＿

8. 每寒夜起立，振衣裳，甲上冰霜迸落，鏗然有聲。

現代文翻译：＿＿＿＿＿＿＿＿＿＿＿＿＿＿＿＿＿＿＿＿＿

第十八課

曹丕《與吳質書》

"Letter to Wu Zhi" (Cao Pi)

Introduction

Cao Pi 曹丕 (courtesy name Zihuan 子桓; 187–226) was the first Wei emperor of the Three Kingdoms period. In 220, after forcing Emperor Xian of the Eastern Han to abdicate, Cao enthroned himself as Emperor Wen of Wei. Also an accomplished man of letters, Cao is well known for his pentasyllabic poetry and his "Discourse on Literature" 論文 ("Lùnwén" 论文), the earliest extant treatise on literary criticism.

"Letter to Wu Zhi" is representative of Cao Pi's epistolary writings. In 218, while collating several essays by his friend and minister Wu Zhi (177–230), Cao is struck by a sudden feeling of nostalgia for their time together. Prompted to write about their friendship and lament the transience of life, Cao composes a letter that his distinct lyrical style, elegant tone, and melodious cadences. A translation of this text is given in *HTRCProse*, chapter 7, "Han and Six Dynasties Epistolary Prose: Memorials and Letters," C7.8.

正文與簡體譯文 Text and Modern Chinese Translation

二月三日，丕白：歲月易得，別來行復
èr yuè sān rì　　pī bái　suì yuè yì dé　bié lái xíng fù

四年。¹ 三年不見，《東山》猶嘆其遠，況乃
sì nián　　sān nián bú jiàn　　dōng shān　yóu tàn qí yuǎn kuàng nǎi

過之，思何可支！² 雖書疏往返，未足解其勞
guò zhī　　sī hé kě zhī　　suī shū shū wǎng fǎn　wèi zú jiě qí láo

結。³
jié

二月三日，曹丕陈说：时间过得很快，分别又将四年了！¹三年不见，《东山》诗尚且感叹分别的时间长久，何况（我们的分别）又超过三年，思念之情怎么能承受得住！²即使有书信往来，却不足以解开郁结在心中的思念。³

1. 白 *v.* to speak. MdnC: 陳説 (*chén shuō* 陈说).
   歲 (岁) 月 *n.* years.
   別 *n.* separation. MdnC: 分別 (*fēn bié*).
   行 (xíng) *adv.* (to be) about. MdnC: 將 (*jiāng* 将).
   復 (复) *adv.* again. MdnC: 又 (*yòu*).
2. 《東 (东) 山》 a poem from "Airs of Bin" 豳風 ("Bīn fēng" 豳风) in the *Book of Poetry*. It says "自我不見，於今三年."
   猶 (犹) *adv.* still. MdnC: 尚 (*shàng*). See L3 Grammar Note 3 ①.

嘆 (叹) *v.* to sigh. MdnC: 感嘆 (*gǎn tàn* 感叹).

遠 (远) *adj.* far, remote. Here it means a long time. MdnC: 長久 (*cháng jiǔ* 长久).

況 (况) *conj.* let alone. MdnC: 何況 (*hé kuàng* 何况). See Grammar Note 1.

過 (过) *v.* to be more than. MdnC: 超過 (*chāo guò* 超过).

思 *n.* longing. MdnC: 思念 (*sī niàn*).

支 *v.* to hold, bear, endure. MdnC: 承受 (*chéng shòu*).

3. 雖 (虽) *conj.* even though. MdnC: 即使 (*jí shǐ*). See L4 Grammar Note 6.

書 (书) 疏 *n.* letter. MdnC: 書信 (*shū xìn* 书信).

往返 *v.* to move back and forth.

解 (*jiě*) *v.* to untie. MdnC: 解開 (*jiě kāi* 解开).

勞結 (劳结) *n.* worry, pent-up emotion. MdnC: 鬱結 (*yù jié* 郁结).

昔年疾疫，親故多離其災，徐、陳、應、
xī nián jí yì　qīn gù duō lí qí zāi　xú　chén　yìng

劉，一時俱逝，痛可言邪！ [4] 昔日遊處，行則
liú　yì shí jù shì　tòng kě yán yé　xī rì yóu chǔ　xíng zé

連輿，止則接席，何曾須臾相失。 [5] 每至觴酌
lián yú　zhǐ zé jiē xí　hé céng xū yú xiāng shī　měi zhì shāng zhuó

流行，絲竹並奏，酒酣耳熱，仰而賦詩，當
liú xíng　sī zhú bìng zòu　jiǔ hān ěr rè　yǎng ér fù shī　dāng

此之時，忽然不自知樂也。 [6] 謂百年已分，可
cǐ zhī shí　hū rán bù zì zhī lè yě　wèi bǎi nián jǐ fèn　kě

長共相保，何圖數年之間，零落略盡，言之
cháng gòng xiāng bǎo hé tú shù nián zhī jiān　líng luò lüè jìn　yán zhī

傷心。 [7] 頃撰其遺文，都爲一集，觀其姓名，
shāng xīn　qǐng zhuàn qí yí wén　dū wéi yì jí　guān qí xìng míng

已爲鬼錄。 [8] 追思昔遊，猶在心目，而此諸
yǐ wéi guǐ lù　zhuī sī xī yóu　yóu zài xīn mù　ér cǐ zhū

子，化爲糞壤，可復道哉！ [9]
zǐ　huà wéi fèn rǎng　kě fù dào zāi

建安二十二年的瘟疫，亲戚朋友很多都遭遇了这场灾难，徐幹、陈琳、应场、刘桢，一时间都去世了，心中的悲痛怎么可以言说呢！ [4] 以前一同交游相处，出行时就车连着车，停下来时就座位接着座位，哪里曾经片刻分离过啊！ [5] 每到饮酒传杯，弦乐器管乐器一同演奏，酒喝得高兴，仰头作诗，每当这个时候，并不知道快乐一会儿就过去了。 [6] （我们常）说百岁长寿是自己应得的，可长久在一起，相互保持（这份情谊），怎料想几年时间，（朋友）差不多都去世了，说起这件事情就让人伤心。 [7] 近来我编辑他们遗留下来的诗文，聚集成一部文集。看他们的名字，已经都在阴间的名录上了。 [8] 追忆从前的交游，还在心间眼前，可是这些好朋友，都已化成粪土了，怎还忍心再说呢！ [9]

4. 昔 *adj.* formerly, past.

　　疾 *n.* illness.

　　疫 *n.* pestilence. MdnC: 瘟疫 (*wēn yì*).

　　疾疫 refers to the pestilence in 217 CE. Five of the Seven Masters of Jian'an 建安七子 (*jiàn ān qī zǐ*) died in that year. See Culture Note 1.

　　親 (亲) *n.* relatives. MdnC: 親人 (*qīn rén* 亲人).

　　故 *adj.* old friends. MdnC: 朋友 (*péng you*).

　　離 (离) *v.* to leave. Here it is used in the sense of 罹 (*lí*), meaning "to suffer from" 遭遇 (*zāo yù*).

　　災 (灾) *n.* disaster. MdnC: 災難 (*zāi nàn* 灾难).

　　徐 or 徐幹 (style 字, Wěicháng 偉長; 171–218), one of the Seven Masters of Jian'an 建安七子.

　　陳 or 陳琳 (style 字, Kǒngzhāng 孔璋; ?–217), one of the Seven Masters of Jian'an 建安七子.

　　應 or 應瑒 (style 字, Délián 德璉; 177–217), one of the Seven Masters of Jian'an 建安七子.

　　劉 or 劉楨 (style 字, Gōnggàn 公幹; 180–217), one of the Seven Masters of Jian'an 建安七子.

　　俱 *adv.* all, completely. MdnC: 都 (*dōu*). See L24 Grammar Note 1 ②.

　　逝 *v.* to pass away. MdnC: 去世 (*qù shì*).

　　邪 (*yé*) *ending interrogative particle.* MdnC: 呢 (*ne*). See L11 Grammar Note 2.

5. 遊 (游) *v.* to socialize, spend leisurely time together. MdnC: 交遊 (*jiāo yóu* 交游).

　　處 (处 chǔ) *v.* to get along with. MdnC: 相處 (*xiāng chǔ* 相处).

　　連 (连) *v.* to connect.

　　輿 (舆) *n.* carriage. MdnC: 車 (*chē* 车).

　　接 *v.* to connect.

　　席 *n.* mat, seat. MdnC: 座位 (*zuò wèi*).

　　須 (须) 臾 *n.* for a moment, in an instant. MdnC: 片刻 (*piàn kè*).

　　失 *v.* to lose. Here it means "to separate (from each other)" 分離 (*fēn lí* 分离).

6. 觴 (觞) *n.* wine goblet. MdnC: 酒杯 (*jiǔ bēi*).

　　酌 *n.* wine goblet.

　　流行 *v.* to spread. Here it means "to hand over."

　　絲 (丝) *n.* silk, string. Here it refers to string instruments 弦樂器 (*xián yuè qì* 弦乐器).

　　竹 *n.* bamboo. Here it refers to wind instruments 管樂器 (*guǎn yuè qì* 管乐器).

　　並 (并) *adv.* both, together. MdnC: 一同 (*yì tóng*). See L24 Grammar Note 1 ⑤.

　　奏 *v.* to play, perform. MdnC: 演奏 (*yǎn zòu*).

　　酣 *adj.* tipsy.

　　仰 *v.* to look up.

　　賦 (赋) *v.* to compose (a verse or poem). MdnC: 作 (*zuò*).

　　忽然 *adv.* suddenly. Here it means "very fast."

7. 百年 a hundred years. Here it refers to longevity 長壽 (*cháng shòu* 长寿).

　　分 (fèn) *n.* what one deserves. MdnC: 應得的 (*yīng dé de* 应得的).

　　保 *v.* to keep. MdnC: 保持 (*bǎo chí*).

　　圖 (图) *v.* to expect. MdnC: 料想 (*liào xiǎng*).

　　零落 *adj.* withered and fallen. Here it refers to friends' deaths.

　　略 *adv.* almost. MdnC: 差不多 (*chà bù duō*).

　　盡 (尽 jìn) *adj.* exhausted.

8. 頃 (顷) *adv.* just now, recently. MdnC: 近來 (*jìn lái* 近来).

撰 *v.* to compose. Here it means "to edit or compile" 編輯 (*biān jí* 编辑).

遺 (遗) *v.* to leave behind. MdnC: 遺留 (*yí liú* 遗留).

都 (dū) *v.* to accumulate. MdnC: 聚集 (*jù jí*).

集 *n.* anthology.

鬼錄 (录) *n.* the list of the dead in the underworld 陰間 (*yīn jiān* 阴间).

9. 追思 *v.* to recall, recollect, look back. MdnC: 追憶 (*zhuī yì* 追忆).

諸 (诸) *adj.* all, every.

化 *v.* to transform.

糞 *n.* dung, manure.

壤 *n.* earth, dirt. MdnC: 土 (*tǔ*).

道 *v.* to say, tell.

觀古今文人， 類不護細行， 鮮能以名節
guān gǔ jīn wén rén　　lèi bú hù xì xíng　　xiǎn néng yǐ míng jié

自立。[10] 而偉長獨懷文抱質， 恬惔寡欲， 有箕
zì lì　　ér wěi cháng dú huái wén bào zhì　tián dàn guǎ yù　yǒu jī

山之志， 可謂彬彬君子者矣。[11] 著《中論》二
shān zhī zhì　　kě wèi bīn bīn jūn zǐ zhě yǐ　　zhù　zhōng lùn　èr

十餘篇， 成一家之言， 辭義典雅， 足傳于後，
shí yú piān　chéng yì jiā zhī yán　　cí yì diǎn yǎ　zú chuán yú hòu

此子爲不朽矣。[12] 德璉常斐然有述作之意， 其
cǐ zǐ wéi bù xiǔ yǐ　　dé liǎn cháng fěi rán yǒu shù zuò zhī yì　qí

才學足以著書， 美志不遂， 良可痛惜。[13] 間者
cái xué zú yǐ zhù shū　měi zhì bú suì　liáng kě tòng xī　jiàn zhě

歷覽諸子之文， 對之抆淚， 既痛逝者， 行自
lì lǎn zhū zǐ zhī wén　duì zhī wěn lèi　jì tòng shì zhě　xíng zì

念也。[14]
niàn yě

看古今的文人，大多不注意自己细小的行为，少有人能够靠名誉和节操来确立自己(的地位)。[10] 只有徐干有文采有品质，恬淡少欲望，有箕山许由的志向，可说是彬彬君子啊！[11] (徐干)著《中论》二十多篇，成就一家的言论，文辞意义典雅，足以传给后代，这个人(的精神和著作)将永远存在！[12] 应场文采斐然，常有写作的愿望。他的才学也足以让他著书。美好的志向没有实现，实在让人痛惜！[13] 近来我遍读他们的文章，对着文章擦着眼泪，既痛惜死去的朋友，又想到自己(生命短暂)。[14]

10. 類 (类) *adv.* mostly, approximately. MdnC: 大多 (*dà duō*).

護 (护) *v.* to protect. Here it means "to pay attention to" 注意 (*zhù yì*).

細 (细) *adj.* small, detailed, trivial.

行 (xíng) *n.* behavior, manner.

鮮 (鲜 xiǎn) *adj.* rare. MdnC: 少 (*shǎo*).

名 *n.* fame, reputation. MdnC: 名譽 (*míng yù* 名誉).

節 (节) *n.* moral principle. MdnC: 節操 (*jié cāo* 节操).

立 *v.* to stand, set up.

11. 偉長 (伟长) Xu Gan's 徐幹 style name.

獨 (独) *adv.* only.

懷 (怀) *v.* to carry.

文 *n.* literary talent. MdnC: 文采 (*wén cǎi*).

抱 *v.* to embrace. Here it means "to have."

質 (质) *n.* character, quality. MdnC: 品質 (*pǐn zhì* 品质).

恬惔 (淡) *adj.* indifferent to fame or gains.

寡 *adj.* few. MdnC: 少 (*shǎo*).

箕山 Ji Mountain, where Xu You 許由 lived as a hermit.

箕山之志 the aspiration to abandon fame or fortune.

彬彬 *adj.* refined and courteous.

12. 著 (zhù) *v.* to write (a book).

《中論》 (中论) Xu Gan's anthology on political issues.

成 *v.* to accomplish, achieve. MdnC: 成就 (*chéng jiù*).

家 *n.* school, field.

言 *n.* speech, opinion. MdnC: 言論 (*yán lùn* 言论).

辭 (辞) *n.* words, phrases. MdnC: 文辭 (*wén cí* 文辞).

義 (义) *n.* meaning. MdnC: 意義 (*yì yì* 意义).

典雅 *adj.* refined and elegant.

傳 (传 chuán) *v.* to pass along, transmit.

後 (后) *n.* later generation.

朽 *adj.* rotten, decayed.

不朽 *adj.* immortal.

13. 德璉 Ying Yang's 應瑒 style name.

斐 *adj.* colorful.

斐然 *adj.* striking and brilliant. Here it refers to Ying Yang's great talent for writing.

述 *v.* to narrate, state.

作 *v.* to compose.

美 *adj.* beautiful, good. MdnC: 美好 (*měi hǎo*).

志 *n.* aspiration, wish. MdnC: 志向 (*zhì xiàng*).

遂 *v.* to accomplish, achieve. MdnC: 實現 (*shí xiàn* 实现).

良 *adv.* indeed. MdnC: 實在 (*shí zài* 实在). See Grammar Note 3.

痛惜 *v.* to deeply regret.

14. 間 (jiàn) 者 *n.* recently. MdnC: 近來 (*jìn lái* 近来).

歷 (历) *adv.* all over. MdnC: 遍 (*biàn*).

覽 (览) *v.* to read, see. MdnC: 讀 (*dú* 读).

拭 *v.* to wipe. MdnC: 擦 (*cā*).

淚 (泪) *n.* tears.

逝 *v.* to pass away.

逝者 the dead.

行 (xíng) *adv.* also. MdnC: 又 (*yòu*).

念 *v.* to think of.

孔璋章表殊健，微爲繁富。[15]公幹有逸
kǒng zhāng zhāng biǎo shū jiàn wēi wéi fán fù　gōng gàn yǒu yì

氣，但未遒耳；其五言詩之善者，妙絕時
qì　dàn wèi qiú ěr　qí wǔ yán shī zhī shàn zhě　miào jué shí

人。[16]元瑜書記翩翩，致足樂也。[17]仲宣獨
rén　yuán yú shū jì piān piān　zhì zú lè yě　zhòng xuān dú

自善於辭賦，惜其體弱，不足起其文，至於
zì shàn yú cí fù　xī qí tǐ ruò　bù zú qǐ qí wén　zhì yú

所善，古人無以遠過。[18]昔伯牙絕絃於鍾期，
suǒ shàn　gǔ rén wú yǐ yuǎn guò　xī bó yá jué xián yú zhōng qī

仲尼覆醢於子路，痛知音之難遇，傷門人之
zhòng ní fù hǎi yú zǐ lù　tòng zhī yīn zhī nán yù　shāng mén rén zhī

莫逮。[19]諸子但爲未及古人，自一時之儁也。
mò dài　zhū zǐ dàn wéi wèi jí gǔ rén　zì yì shí zhī jùn yě

今之存者，已不逮矣。[20]後生可畏，來者難
jīn zhī cún zhě　yǐ bú dài yǐ　hòu shēng kě wèi　lái zhě nán

誣，然恐吾與足下不及見也。[21]
wū　rán kǒng wú yǔ zú xià bù jí jiàn yě

陈琳的章表写得非常雄健有力，(不过)稍微有些冗长(不够简洁)。[15]刘桢有飘逸的气质，只是不够遒劲有力；他五言诗中的好作品，写得极妙，超越同时其他人。[16]阮瑀的书札奏记文字优美，使人感到非常快乐啊！[17]王粲一个人擅长辞赋，可惜他的文章风格纤弱，不足以振作文章(的气势)。至于他擅长的部分，古人没有人能远远地超过他。[18]过去伯牙断掉琴弦，(因为)钟子期(过世了)；孔子翻倒所有的肉酱，(因为)子路(在卫国被杀了)；(伯牙是)痛惜知音难再遇见，(孔子是)伤心弟子没有人能及得上(子路)。[19]这些朋友只是还比不上古人，但终究都是一时才俊，现在活着的人，都不及他们。[20]将来的年轻人是令人敬畏的，后来人(我们)很难胡乱评说，但是恐怕我和您是来不及看到了。[21]

15. 孔璋 Chen Lin's 陳琳 style name.
　　章 *n.* official communication to the emperor to thank him for his kindness.
　　表 *n.* a memorial to the emperor concerning state affairs.
　　殊 *adv.* specially, really. MdnC: 非常 (*fēi cháng*).
　　健 *adj.* strong, powerful. MdnC: 雄健 (*xióng jiàn*).
　　微 *adv.* a little. MdnC: 稍微 (*shāo wēi*).
　　繁富 *adj.* complicated and numerous. Here it implies that Chen Lin's essays are not concise enough.
16. 公幹 Liu Zhen's 劉楨 style name.
　　逸 *adj.* free, uninhibited, aloof. MdnC: 飄逸 (*piāo yì*).

氣 (气) *n.* breath, air. Here it means "distinct quality" 氣質 (*qì zhì* 气质).

遒 *adj.* strong, forceful. MdnC: 遒勁 (*qiú jìn* 遒劲).

耳 *ending particle.* carries an exclamatory tone. MdnC: 罷了 (*bà le* 罢了). See L7 Grammar Note 4.

五言詩 (诗) pentasyllabic poetry.

善者 *n.* good ones, good poems.

妙 *adj.* excellent, clever, wonderful.

絕 (绝) *adv.* superbly, unsurpassed.

時 (时) 人 *n.* contemporaries.

17. 元瑜 or 阮瑀 (style 字, Yuányú 元瑜; ?–212), one of the Seven Masters of Jian'an 建安七子.

書 (书) *n.* official letters. MdnC: 書札 (*shū zhá* 书札).

記 (记) *n.* official dispatch sent to the emperor. MdnC: 奏記 (*zòu jì* 奏记).

翩翩 *adj.* beautiful, elegant.

致 *v.* to cause, let. MdnC: 使 (*shǐ*).

18. 仲宣 or 王粲 (style 字, Zhòngxuān 仲宣; 177–217), one of the Seven Masters of Jian'an 建安七子.

獨 (独) 自 *adv.* alone, only.

善 *v.* to be good at. MdnC: 擅長 (*shàn cháng* 擅长).

辭賦 (辞赋) or 賦 a literary genre, rhapsody.

惜 *v.* to be sad about.

體 (体) *n.* body. Here it refers to literary style 風格 (*fēng gé* 风格).

弱 *adj.* weak. MdnC: 纖弱 (*xiān ruò* 纤弱).

起 *v.* to rise, go up. Here it is used as a causative verb, 使······起, meaning "to make … rise." MdnC: 振作 (*zhèn zuò*). See L7 Grammar Note 1 ①.

過 (过) *v.* to surpass, be better than.

19. 伯牙 (family name 氏, Bó 伯; given name 名, Yá 牙), an official in the Jin state during the Spring and Autumn period. He is a famed player of the Chinese seven-string zither.

絕 (绝) *v.* to cut off, break. MdnC: 斷 (*duàn* 断).

絃 (弦) *n.* string on the musical instrument.

鍾期 or 鍾子期 (given name 名, Huī 徽; style 字, Zǐqī 子期), a woodcutter in the Chu state during the Spring and Autumn period known for his extraordinary music sensibility.

伯牙絕絃於鍾期 refers to the story that Bo Ya never played his musical instrument after Zhong Ziqi died. See Culture Note 2.

仲尼 Confucius's style name.

覆 *v.* to overturn, turn over. MdnC: 翻倒 (*fān dào*).

醢 *n.* meat pickle. MdnC: 肉醬 (*ròu jiàng*).

子路 Zhong You's 仲由 style name.

仲尼覆醢於子路 refers to the story that Confucius threw away all the meat pickle after Zhong You was executed by the Wei state. See Culture Note 3.

知音 *n.* a friend who is appreciative of others' talents.

門 (门) 人 *n.* disciple. MdnC: 弟子 (*dì zǐ*).

莫 *indefinite pron.* none, no one. MdnC: 沒有人 (*méi yǒu rén*). See L3 Grammar Note 2 ①.

逮 (dài) *v.* to reach, get to a point. MdnC: 及 (*jí*).

20. 但爲 (wéi) *adv.* only. MdnC: 只是 (*zhǐ shì*).

自 *adv.* certainly. MdnC: 當然 (*dāng rán* 当然).

雋 (隽/俊) *n.* a person of outstanding talents. MdnC: 才雋 (*cái jùn* 才俊).

存 *adj.* alive. MdnC: 活着 (*huó zhe*).

21. 後 (后) 生可畏 a quotation of Confucius from chapter 9 子罕 ("Zǐ hǎn") of the *Analects* 論語: "The young deserve to be respected. How could you know the generations to come will not be as good as today's?" 後生可畏，焉知來者不如今也.

後 (后) 生 *n.* young people, youth. MdnC: 年輕人 (*nián qīng rén* 年轻人).

畏 *v.* to fear. Here it means "to respect or be in awe of" 敬畏 (*jìng wèi*).

來 (来) 者 *n.* people of later generations.

誣 (诬) *v.* to defame, slander. Here it refers to making irresponsible remarks about the young people 胡亂評説 (*hú luàn píng shuō* 胡乱评说).

恐 *v.* to be afraid. MdnC: 恐怕 (*kǒng pà*).

足下 *n.* a formal way to address friends, you. MdnC: 您 (*nín*).

年行已長大，所懷萬端，時有所慮，至
nián xíng yǐ zhǎng dà suǒ huái wàn duān shí yǒu suǒ lǜ zhì

通夜不瞑，志意何時復類昔日？[22] 已成老翁，
tōng yè bù míng zhì yì hé shí fù lèi xī rì yǐ chéng lǎo wēng

但未白頭耳。光武言年三十餘，在兵中十
dàn wèi bái tóu ěr guāng wǔ yán nián sān shí yú zài bīng zhōng shí

歲，所更非一。[23] 吾德不及之，年與之齊
suì suǒ gēng fēi yī wú dé bù jí zhī nián yǔ zhī qí

矣。[24] 以犬羊之質，服虎豹之文，無眾星之
yǐ yǐ quǎn yáng zhī zhì fú hǔ bào zhī wén wú zhòng xīng zhī

明，假日月之光，動見瞻觀，何時易乎？[25]
míng jiǎ rì yuè zhī guāng dòng jiàn zhān guān hé shí yì hū

恐永不復得爲昔日遊也。少壯真當努力，年
kǒng yǒng bú fù dé wéi xī rì yóu yě shào zhuàng zhēn dāng nǔ lì nián

一過往，何可攀援！古人思炳燭夜遊，良有
yí guò wǎng hé kě pān yuán gǔ rén sī bǐng zhú yè yóu liáng yǒu

以也。[26]
yǐ yě

年纪已经增大了，所想的事情极多，时常有所思虑，以至于整夜都睡不着，志向和意趣什么时候能再像从前(那样)呢？[22](我)已经变成老头儿了，只是头发还没白罢了！汉光武帝曾经说，年纪三十多，在军队中十年，所经历的不只是一件事(而已)。[23]我德行不及他，年龄和他相同啊！[24](我)以犬羊(般的低)素质，(表面)却披着虎豹(般的)花纹(处在太子之位上)，没有众多星星闪亮(的才能)，借着(我父亲曹操)日月(般)的光芒(登上高位)。我的行动一直被人注意着，(这种情形)什么时候才能改变啊！[25]恐怕永远不能再像从前那样游玩了！年轻时真应该努力，年纪一过去了，怎能挽留得住呢！古人想晚上拿着蜡烛去游玩，确实有原因啊！[26]

22. 年行 (xíng) *n.* age. MdnC: 年紀 (*nián jì* 年纪).

　　懷 (怀) *v.* to cherish the memory of. MdnC: 想 (*xiǎng*).

　　萬 (万) 端 *adj.* multifarious. MdnC: 極多 (*jí duō* 极多).

　　時 (时) *adv.* often. MdnC: 時常 (*shí cháng* 时常).

　　慮 (虑) *v.* to consider, think of.

　　通 *adj.* through, whole. MdnC: 整 (*zhěng*).

　　瞑 *v.* to shut (one's eyes).

　　志 *n.* aspiration, wish. MdnC: 志向 (*zhì xiàng*).

　　意 *n.* intent, purpose. MdnC: 意趣 (*yì qù*).

　　類 *v.* to be like. MdnC: 像 (*xiàng*).

23. 翁 *n.* old man.

　　光武 or 漢光武帝 (ancestral name 姓, Liú 劉; given name 名, Xiù 秀; style 字, Wénshū 文叔; posthumous name 謚, Guāngwǔ 光武; 5 BCE –57 CE), the first emperor of the Eastern Han dynasty.

　　兵 *n.* soldier. Here it refers to troops in general 軍隊 (*jūn duì* 军队).

　　歲 (岁) *n.* year. MdnC: 年 (*nián*).

　　更 (gēng) *v.* to go through, experience. MdnC: 經歷 (*jīng lì* 经历).

24. 德 *n.* moral integrity. MdnC: 德行 (*dé xíng*).

　　齊 (齐) *adj.* equal, same.

25. 犬 *n.* dog.

　　羊 *n.* sheep.

　　質 (质) *n.* quality, accomplishment. MdnC: 素質 (*sù zhì* 素质).

　　犬羊之質 (质) the author's humble self-comparison with dogs and sheep to emphasize his insufficient talents and abilities.

　　服 *v.* to wear. MdnC: 披 (*pī*).

　　虎 *n.* tiger.

　　豹 *n.* leopard.

　　文 *n.* natural markings on animals.

　　虎豹之文 natural markings of tigers and leopards. Here it refers to the cultural and ritual trappings bestowed on the author as the crown prince.

　　假 (jiǎ) *v.* to borrow. MdnC: 借 (*jiè*).

　　動 (动) *n.* behavior. MdnC: 行動 (*xíng dòng* 行动).

　　見 (见 jiàn) *particle.* by. MdnC: 被 (*bèi*). See Grammar Note 2.

　　瞻 *v.* to look, gaze.

　　觀 (观 guān) *v.* to look at, watch.

　　易 *v.* to change. MdnC: 改變 (*gǎi bàn* 改变).

26. 恐 *v.* to be afraid. MdnC: 恐怕 (*kǒng pà*).

　　少 (shào) 壯 (壮) *n.* the young and vigorous 年輕人 (*nián qīng* 年轻人).

　　年 *n.* age. MdnC: 年紀 (*nián jì* 年纪).

　　攀援 *v.* climb, support. Here it means "to retain" 挽留 (*wǎn liú*).

　　炳 *v.* to hold, grasp. MdnC: 拿 (*ná*).

　　燭 (烛) *n.* candle. MdnC: 蠟燭 (*là zhú* 蜡烛).

　　良 *adv.* indeed. MdnC: 確實 (*què shí* 确实). See Grammar Note 3.

以 *n.* reason, cause. MdnC: 原因 (*yuán yīn*). See Grammar Note 4 ⑥.

項何以自娛？ 頗復有所述造不？ 東望於
qǐng hé yǐ zì yú   pō fù yǒu suǒ shù zào fǒu   dōng wàng wū

邑， 裁書敍心。 丕白。 [27]
yì   cái shū xù xīn   pī bái

近来您用什么来自娱自
乐啊？又有什么著述
吗？向东望心中<u>忧郁烦
闷</u>，写信来<u>叙述</u>自己的
心情。曹丕陈说。[27]

《文選》，上海：上海古籍出版社 (1986)，1896–1898.

27. 項 (顷) *adv.* just now, recently. MdnC: 近來 (*jìn lái* 近来).

娛 (娱) *v.* to entertain, amuse. MdnC: 娛樂 (*yú lè* 娱乐).

頗 (颇) *adv.* very. MdnC: 很 (*hěn*).

述造 *v.* to write, produce. MdnC: 著述 (*zhù shù*).

不 (fǒu) *particle.* or not? See Grammar Note 5 ②.

於邑 (*wū yì*) *adj.* depressed, irritated. MdnC: 憂鬱煩悶 (*yōu yù fán mèn* 忧郁烦闷).

裁 *v.* to cut out.

裁書 (书) to write a letter. Paper used by ancient Chinese was often rolled. Thus, a person needed to cut off a piece of paper from a roll when writing a letter.

敍 (叙) *v.* to tell, express. MdnC: 敍述 (*xù shù* 叙述).

文化常識 Culture Notes

1. 建安七子 The Seven Masters of the Jian'an (196–220) were Kong Rong 孔融 (style 字, Wénjǔ 文舉; 153–208), Chen Lin 陳琳, Wang Can 王粲, Xu Gan 徐幹, Ruan Yu 阮瑀, Ying Yang 應瑒, and Liu Zhen 劉楨. This title is traced to Cao Pi's 曹丕 "Discourse on Literature" 論文 and has been widely used by later generations. These seven masters, together with the Three Caos, generally represent the apex of literary achievement during the Jian'an period.

2. 伯牙絕絃 is a story from *Master Lie* 列子 (*Liè zǐ*) that tells of the great friendship between the lute player Bo Ya 伯牙 and the woodcutter Zhong Ziqi 鍾子期. Bo Ya is known as an excellent player of the seven-string lute in his period. Once he was thinking of climbing Tai Mount 泰山 while he was playing his lute. Zhong Ziqi heard the music and noted that he seemed to have seen Tai Mount. After a while, Bo Ya thought of flowing water while playing, and Zhong Ziqi said that he seemed to have seen the river and the sea. Later, Zhong Ziqi died, and Bo Ya was so sad that he destroyed his lute and never played music again.

3. 孔子覆醢 is a story originally from the chapter titled "Tan Gong, I" 檀弓上 ("Tán gōng shàng") in the *Book of Rites* 禮記. 醢 literally means "minced meat" but can also denote an extremely gruesome capital punishment in ancient China: the chopping of the dead body into meat pickle. The story goes that Confucius's disciple Zilu 子路 was executed by the Hai 醢 torture in the Wei state. Confucius heard it and felt so sad that he threw away all his meat pickle and never ate any again for the rest of his life.

語法注釋 Grammar Notes

1. 況   *conj.* let alone. MdnC: 何況 (*hé kuàng* 何况).
(况)

三年不見，《東山》猶嘆其遠，況乃過之，思何可支！

[三年不见，《东山》尚且感叹分别的时间太长，何况（我们的分别）还超过了三年，思念 之情怎么能够承受得住！]

2. 見   **jiàn** *particle.* a passive voice indicator: by. MdnC: 被 (*bèi*).
(见)

以犬羊之質，服虎豹之文，無眾星之明，假日月之光，動見瞻觀，何時易乎？

[（我）凭着犬羊的素质，却穿着虎豹的花纹，没有众多星星闪亮，却借着日月的光，我的行动一直被人注意着，（这种情形）什么时候才能改变啊！]

3. 良   *adv.* indeed. MdnC: 實在 (*shí zài* 实在), 確實 (*què shí* 确实).

美志不遂，良可痛惜。

[美好的志向没有实现，实在让人痛惜啊！]

古人思炳燭夜遊，良有以也。

[古人想晚上拿着蜡烛去游玩，确实是有原因的啊！]

4. 以   Six uses of 以 are explained in this book. In addition to the use below, see 以①②③④ in L2 Grammar Note 1 and 以⑤ in L10 Grammar Note 2.

⑥ *n.* reason, cause. MdnC: 原因 (*yuán yīn*).

古人思炳燭夜遊，良有以也。

[古人想晚上拿着蜡烛去游玩，确实是有原因的啊！]

5. 不   ① **bù** *adv.* not. MdnC: 不 (*bù*), 没有 (*méi yǒu*).

美志不遂，良可痛惜。

[美好的志向没有实现，实在让人痛惜啊！]

小大之獄，雖不能察，必以情。(L1)

[各种讼诉案，即使不能一一考察，一定会根据事情（来判断）。]

② **fǒu** *negative particle.* Written as 否, it is used in alternative questions, meaning "or not?"

頗復有所述造不？

[又有什么著述没有？]

Literary Analysis

While Cao Pi's epistolary outpouring of emotion has moved countless hearts across generations, the discerning insight demonstrated in his literary criticism—the very first of its kind—mesmerizes every curious mind engaged in the study of Chinese literary history. Readers are invariably touched by Cao's fond appreciation of the beauty of human creation and his heartrending regret over the transience of physical existence. While hard to imagine, the same sentimental Cao Pi who wept over his deceased friends' beautiful letters just two years later became the first emperor of the Wei state (220–265). Nonetheless, the strong, direct feelings expressed by his seemingly simple words remain convincingly genuine and sincere.

Cao's pithy assessment of the literary achievements of the "worthies" of his time focuses on *qi* 氣 (an important topic in his "Discourse on Literature")—that is, the idiosyncratic life force and verve of personality radiating from written work. By comparing their accomplishments with those of ancient literary masters as well as talents still to come, Cao hints, ever so lightly, at the issue of immortality through writing (another important topic in his "Discourse"). He is not sure he can emulate the worthies of the past and present, especially as he considers the deplorable approach of "old age" (though still in his early thirties) and the helplessness and loneliness created by the passing away of dear friends from the good old days.

—XL

課後練習 Exercises

一 給加點字注音 Give the pinyin romanization for each dotted word.

1. 觴酌 (____, ____) 2. 酣 (____) 3. 鬼錄 (____) 4. 德璉 (____) 5. 斐然 (____)

6. 糞壤 (____, ____) 7. 醢 (____) 8. 孔璋 (____) 9. 元瑜 (____) 10. 不暝 (____)

二 在括號中給句中加點的字注音，並選出正確的釋義 Give the pinyin romanization for each dotted word; then select the correct definition from the following list, and write it in the blank.

相處(处)   實現(实现)   近來(来)   拿   才雋(俊)

經歷(经历)   車(车)   **信服**   倒掉   擦

1. 小信未孚（ fú ）　信服 2. 行則連輿 (　) _____ 3. 昔日遊處 (　) _____

4. 對之抆淚 (　) _____ 5. 美志不遂 (　) _____ 6. 所更非一 (　) _____

7. 頃撰其遺文 (　) _____ 8. 仲尼覆醢於子路 (　) _____

9. 自一時之雋也 (　) _____ 10. 古人思炳燭夜遊 (　) _____

三 選擇釋義並填空 Match each word in the left column with its correct definition in the middle column. Fill in each blank in the right column with an appropriate word from the left column.

謀謀劃(谋划)	素質(质)	歲月易得，別來____復四年。
行_____	接	雖書疏往返，未足____其勞結。
解_____	遒勁(劲)	昔日遊處，行則____輿，止則接____，何曾須臾相
連_____	**謀劃(谋划)**	失！
席_____	敘(叙)述	
類_____	注意	

護_____　　借
鮮_____　　座位
逸_____　　相同
遒_____　　被
質_____　　大多
服_____　　少
假_____　　解開(开)
齊_____　　飄逸
見_____　　將(将)
敘_____　　披

觀古今文人，____不____細行，____能以名節自立。

公幹有____气，但未____耳；其五言詩之善者，妙絕時人。

吾德不及之，年與之____矣。以犬羊之____，____虎豹之文，無眾星之明，____日月之光，動____瞻觀，何時易乎？

東望於邑，裁書____心。

四　請用給出的字填空 Fill in each blank with an appropriate word from the following list (some words may be used more than once).

猶(犹)　　況(况)　　以　　然　　何　　不　　良

1. 三年____見，《東山》____嘆其遠，____乃過之，思____可支！
2. 當此之時，忽____ ____自知樂也。
3. 德璉常斐____有述作之意，其才學足____著書，美志____遂，____可痛惜。
4. 少壯真當努力，年一過往，____可攀援！古人思炳燭夜遊，____有____也。

五　爲加點字選擇正確釋義，並根據釋義來翻譯句子 Match each dotted word with its correct modern Chinese equivalent by circling the latter. Then translate each sentence into modern Chinese.

1. 又何間爲？　　　　　　　　　　　ⓐ爲什麼(为什么) b. 憑什麼(凭什么) c. 多少

現代文翻译：你又为什么要参与到这件事情里面？
_____

2. 三年不見，《東山》猶嘆其遠，況乃過之，思何可支！　　a. 情況(况) b. 何況(况) c. 而且

現代文翻译：_____

3. 觀古今文人，類不護細行，鮮能以名節自立。　　　a. 憑藉(凭借) b. 認爲(认为) c. 原因

現代文翻译：_____

4. 德璉常斐然有述作之意，其才學足以著書，美志不遂，良可痛惜。a. 然而 b. 好 c. 實(实)在

現代文翻译：_____

5. 諸子但爲未及古人，自一時之雋也，今之存者，已不逮矣。　　a. 但是　b. 只是　c. 爲(为)了

現代文翻译：_____

6. 古人思秉燭夜遊，良有以也。　　a. 憑藉(凭借)　b. 用　c. 原因

現代文翻译：_____

7. 頃何以自娛？頗復有所述造不？　　a. 没有　b. 不是　c. 不能

現代文翻译：_____

第十九課

蘇轍《上樞密韓太尉書》

"Letter Presented to Military Affairs Commissioner and Defender-in-Chief Han Qi"
(Su Zhe)

Introduction

Su Zhe 蘇轍 (courtesy names Ziyou 子由 and Tongshu 同書; 1039–1112) was a statesman in the Northern Song dynasty and one of the Eight Masters of Prose of Tang and Song 唐宋八大家 (see L16 Culture Note 1). Su Zhe; his father, Su Xun 蘇洵 (1009–1066); and his brother, Su Shi 蘇軾 (1037–1101), are all renowned for their literary achievements and often referred to as the Three Sus 三蘇 (*Sānsū* 三苏).

Su Zhe writes this letter in 1057 shortly after passing the imperial service examination and becoming a Presented Scholar 進士 (*jìnshì* 进士). Addressed to the eminent statesman Han Qi 韓琦 (1008–1075), its main purpose is to request a meeting, but instead of making an explicit request, Su describes how a literary work can nourish his vital breath 氣 (*qì* 气) or creative energy by allowing it to explore "the world's extraordinary tales and grand spectacles." He then compares seeing Han to beholding "the great sights of all under Heaven," subtly expressing his desire to meet. This indirectness of expression attests to Su Zhe's virtuosity in prose structuring. A translation of this text is given in *HTRCProse*, chapter 12, "Tang and Song Occasional Prose: Prefaces and Epistolary Writing," C12.6.

正文與簡體譯文 Text and Modern Chinese Translation

太尉執事：轍生好爲文，思之至深。[1] 以
tài wèi zhí shì　zhé shēng hào wéi wén　sī zhī zhì shēn　　　yǐ

爲文者氣之所形，然文不可以學而能，氣可
wéi wén zhě qì zhī suǒ xíng　rán wén bù kě yǐ xué ér néng　qì kě

以養而致。[2] 孟子曰：「我善養吾浩然之
yǐ yǎng ér zhì　　mèng zǐ yuē　　wǒ shàn yǎng wú hào rán zhī

氣。」[3] 今觀其文章，寬厚宏博，充乎天地之
qì　　　　jīn guān qí wén zhāng　kuān hòu hóng bó　chōng hū tiān dì zhī

間，稱其氣之小大。[4] 太史公行天下，周覽四
jiān　　chèn qí qì zhī xiǎo dà　　tài shǐ gōng xíng tiān xià　zhōu lǎn sì

海名山大川，與燕、趙間豪俊交游，故其文
hǎi míng shān dà chuān　yǔ yān　zhào jiān háo jùn jiāo yóu　gù qí wén

韩太尉先生：我生性喜欢写文章，（对写作）想得非常深入。[1]（我）认为文章是气所形成的，但文章不可以只通过学习就能写好，气是可以通过培养而得到的。[2] 孟子说："我善于培养我的浩然之气。"[3] 现在看孟子的文章，宽阔厚重宏伟博大，充满于天地之间，和他的气大小相称。[4] 太史公司马迁走天下，到处游览四海、名山、

疎蕩，頗有奇氣。⁵此二子者，豈嘗執筆學爲
shū dàng　　pō yǒu qí qì　　　cǐ èr zǐ zhě　　qǐ cháng zhí bǐ xué wéi

如此之文哉？⁶其氣充乎其中而溢乎其貌，動
rú cǐ zhī wén zāi　　qí qì chōng hū qí zhōng ér yì hū qí mào　　dòng

乎其言而見乎其文，而不自知也。⁷
hū qí yán ér xiàn hū qí wén　　　ér bù zì zhī yě

大河，与燕赵之地的豪杰们交往，所以他的文字疏放不受拘束，很有奇气。⁵这两个人，难道曾经拿笔学习写这样的文章吗？⁶他们的气充满着文章而自然地洋溢在外表，从而改变了他们的语言，体现在他们的文章中，但他们自己不知道。⁷

1. 太尉 defender-in-chief, military commander in ancient China.

   執 (执) 事 an honorific placed after one's title or position.

   生 *n.* birth. Here it means "nature or disposition" 生性 (*shēng xìng*).

   文 *n.* essay. MdnC: 文章 (*wén zhāng*).

   至 *adv.* extremely. MdnC: 非常 (*fēi cháng*).

2. 以爲 (为 wéi) *v.* to think. MdnC: 認爲 (*rèn wéi* 认为).

   文者 *n.* essay. MdnC: 文章 (*wén zhāng*).

   氣 (气) *n.* air.

   形 *v.* to form.

   然 *conj.* however, but. MdnC: 但是 (*dàn shì*). See L5 Grammar Note 2 ①.

   養 (养) *n.* to nourish, develop, cultivate. MdnC: 培養 (*péi yǎng* 培养).

   致 *v.* to reach, get. MdnC: 得到 (*dé dào*).

3. 孟子 a quotation from chapter 3, "Gongsun Chou, I" 公孫丑上 ("Gōngsūn Chǒu Shàng" 公孙丑上), of the *Mencius*.

   浩然 *adj.* flood-like.

4. 寬 (宽) *adj.* wide, spacious. MdnC: 寬闊 (*kuān kuò* 宽阔).

   厚 *adj.* thick, profound. MdnC: 厚重 (*hòu zhòng*).

   宏 *adj.* grand, vast. MdnC: 宏偉 (*hóng wěi* 宏伟).

   博 *adj.* broad, vast. MdnC: 博大 (*bó dà*).

   充 *v.* to fill up. MdnC: 充滿 (*chōng mǎn* 充满).

   乎 *prep.* at, in. MdnC: 在 (*zài*). See L6 Grammar Note 2 ③.

   稱 (称 chèn) *v.* to match. MdnC: 相稱 (*xiāng chèn* 相称).

5. 太史公 grand historian. See also L13 note 9.

   周 *adv.* completely, around. MdnC: 到處 (*dào chù* 到处).

   覽 (览) *v.* to view, look at. MdnC: 遊覽 (*yóu lǎn* 游览).

   川 *n.* river. MdnC: 河 (*hé*).

   燕 (yān) one of the seven states in the Warring States period. It includes most of present-day Beijing and the northern part of Hebei Province.

   趙 (赵) one of the seven states in the Warring States period. It includes the southern part of present-day Hebei Province, the central part of present-day Shanxi Province, and the northeastern corner of present-day Shaanxi Province.

豪俊 *n.* people who have exceptional abilities, outstanding people. MdnC: 豪傑 (*háo jié* 豪杰).

交游 *v.* to socialize. MdnC: 交往 (*jiāo wǎng*).

疎 (疏) *adj.* sparse. Here it means "unrestrained or unconventional" 疏放 (*shū fàng*).

蕩 (荡) *adj.* unrestrained. MdnC: 不拘束 (*bù jū shù*).

頗 (颇) *adv.* very. MdnC: 很 (*hěn*).

奇 *adj.* extraordinary.

6. 豈 (岂) *interrogative particle.* MdnC: 難道 (*nán dào* 难道). See L8 Grammar Note 4.

嘗 (尝) *adv.* once. MdnC: 曾經 (*céng jīng* 曾经).

執 (执) *v.* to hold in one's hand, carry. MdnC: 拿 (*ná*).

7. 溢 *v.* to overflow. MdnC: 洋溢 (*yáng yì*).

貌 *n.* appearance. MdnC: 外表 (*wài biǎo*).

動 (动) *v.* to make something change. MdnC: 改變 (*gǎi biàn* 改变).

見 (见) *v.* to see. Here it is used in the sense of 現 (*xiàn* 现), meaning "to appear or be present" 顯現 (*xiǎn xiàn* 显现).

轍生十有九年矣。其居家所與游者，不
zhé shēng shí yǒu jiǔ nián yǐ　　qí jū jiā suǒ yǔ yóu zhě　bú

過其鄰里鄉黨之人；所見不過數百里之間，
guò qí lín lǐ xiāng dǎng zhī rén　　suǒ jiàn bú guò shù bǎi lǐ zhī jiān

無高山大野可登覽以自廣。百氏之書雖無
wú gāo shān dà yě kě dēng lǎn yǐ zì guǎng　bǎi shì zhī shū suī wú

所不讀，然皆古人之陳跡，不足以激發其
suǒ bù dú　rán jiē gǔ rén zhī chén jì　bù zú yǐ jī fā qí

志氣。[8] 恐遂汩沒，故決然捨去，求天下奇
zhì qì　kǒng suì gǔ mò　gù jué rán shě qù　qiú tiān xià qí

聞壯觀，以知天地之廣大。[9] 過秦、漢之[a]
wén zhuàng guān yǐ zhī tiān dì zhī guǎng dà　guò qín　hàn zhī

故都，恣觀終南、嵩、華之[b]高，北顧黃河
gù dū　zì guān zhōng nán sōng　huà zhī　gāo　běi gù huáng hé

之[b]奔流，慨然想見古之豪傑。[10]
zhī　bēn liú　kǎi rán xiǎng jiàn gǔ zhī háo jié

苏辙我出生十九年了。我在家时交往的人，只是我的邻居和家乡的人。我见到的地方只有数百里之间，没有高山旷野可以攀登游览来开阔自己(的眼界)。诸子百家的书，即使没有没读过的，但都是古人过去的事迹，不足以激发我的志气。[8]我担心自己就此被埋没，所以决然地离开了(家)，去追求天下新奇的见闻，壮美的景观，来知道天地广大。[9]我经过秦朝、汉朝的故都，尽情观赏着终南山、嵩山、华山的高大雄伟，向北去看黄河奔流，感慨地想起了古代的英雄豪杰。[10]

8. 生 *n.* birth. MdnC: 出生 (*chū shēng*).

其 *possessive pron.* his. Here it refers to Su Zhe. See L2 Grammar Note 5 ②.

游 *v.* to socialize with. MdnC: 交往 (*jiāo wǎng*).

鄰 (邻) 里 *n.* neighborhood. MdnC: 鄰居 (*lín jū* 邻居).

鄉黨 (乡党) *n.* hometown. MdnC: 家鄉 (*jiā xiāng* 家乡).

野 *n.* wilderness. MdnC: 曠野 (*kuàng yě* 旷野).

以 *conj.* in order to. MdnC: 來 (*lái* 来). See L2 Grammar Note 1 ③.

廣 (广) *v.* broaden. MdnC: 開闊 (*kāi kuò* 开阔).

百氏 refers to the one hundred schools of thought before the Qin dynasty. MdnC: 諸子百家 (*zhū zǐ bǎi jiā* 诸子百家). See L2 Culture Note 2 for 氏.

雖 (虽) *conj.* even though. MdnC: 即使 (*jí shǐ*). See L4 Grammar Note 6.

陳 (陈) *adj.* old, of the past. MdnC: 過去的 (*guò qù de* 过去的).

跡 (迹) *n.* track, trace, footprint. MdnC: 事跡 (*shì jì* 事迹).

足 *adj.* enough. 不足以 means "not enough to."

激發 (发 *fā*) *v.* to stimulate, evoke.

志氣 (气) *n.* aspiration, ambition.

9. 恐 *v.* to be afraid. MdnC: 擔心 (*dān xīn* 担心).

遂 *adv.* then, from then on. MdnC: 就此 (*jiù cǐ*).

汩 *v.* to run swiftly (as water). 汩沒 (没 *mò*) means "to cover up, bury, or neglect" 埋沒 (*mái mò* 埋没).

決 (决) 然 *adv.* resolutely, determinedly.

捨 (舍) *v.* to give up.

去 *v.* to leave. MdnC: 離開 (*lí kāi* 离开).

聞 (闻) *n.* what is heard. MdnC: 見聞 (*jiàn wén* 见闻).

壯 (壮) *adj.* big, grand, magnificent. MdnC: 壯美 (*zhuàng měi* 壮美).

觀 (观 *guān*) *n.* view, sight. MdnC: 景觀 (*jǐng guān* 景观).

10. 秦 Qin dynasty (221–207 BCE), capital 都城: 咸陽 (*xián yáng* 咸阳), in present-day Xianyang, Shaanxi Province.

漢 (汉) Western Han dynasty 西漢 (206 BCE–8 CE), capital 都城: 長安 (*cháng ān* 长安), in present-day Xi'an 西安, Shaanxi Province.

Eastern Han dynasty 東漢 (25–220 CE), capitals 都城: 洛陽 (*luò yáng* 洛阳, 25–190), in present-day Luoyang, Henan Province; 長安 (*cháng ān* 长安, 190–196), in present-day Xi'an, Shaanxi Province; and 許都 (*xǔ dū* 许都, 196–220), in present-day Xuchang 許昌, Henan Province.

故都 (*dū*) *n.* former capital, ancient capital.

恣 *adv.* without constraint. MdnC: 盡情 (*jìn qíng* 尽情).

觀 (观 *guān*) *v.* to view, see, enjoy. MdnC: 觀賞 (*guān shǎng* 观赏).

終 (终) 南 (山) Zhongnan Mountains, also known as Taiyi Mountains 太乙山. This generally refers to the middle part of the Qin Mountains 秦嶺, in present-day Shaanxi Province.

嵩 (山) Mount Song, known as the Central Mountain 中嶽 (*zhōng yuè* 中岳) of the Five Great Mountains 五嶽 (*wǔ yuè* 五岳). It is located in the central part of present-day Henan Province.

華 (华 *huà* 山) Mount Hua, known as the Western Mountain 西嶽 (*xī yuè* 西岳), one of the Five Great Mountains 五嶽 (*wǔ yuè* 五岳). It is located to the east of the present-day city of Xi'an 西安, Shaanxi Province.

之 ᵦ *particle.* a nominative marker. See L2 Grammar Note 2 ⑤.

北 *n.* north. Here it is used as an adverb, meaning "northward" 向北 (*xiàng běi*).

顧 (顾) *v.* to see, watch. MdnC: 看 (*kàn*).

黃河 the Yellow River.

奔流 *v.* to flow at a great speed.

慨然 *adv.* with deep feeling.

豪傑 (杰) *n.* extraordinary people.

至京師仰觀天子宮闕之壯，與倉廩、府
zhì jīng shī yǎng guān tiān zǐ gōng què zhī zhuàng yǔ cāng lǐn fǔ

庫、城池、苑囿之富且大也，而後知天下之
kù chéng chí yuàn yòu zhī fù qiě dà yě ér hòu zhī tiān xià zhī

巨麗。[11] 見翰林歐陽公，聽其議論之宏辯，
jù lì jiàn hàn lín ōu yáng gōng tīng qí yì lùn zhī hóng biàn

觀其容貌之秀偉，與其門人賢士大夫遊，而
guān qí róng mào zhī xiù wěi yǔ qí mén rén xián shì dà fū yóu ér

後知天下之文章聚乎此也。[12]
hòu zhī tiān xià zhī wén zhāng jù hū cǐ yě

到了汴京我仰視着天子壯美的宮殿和富庶广大的粮仓、府库、城墙、护城河、皇家园林，然后知道天下广阔富丽。[11] 我见到翰林学士欧阳修，听到他的议论宏大善辩，看他容貌秀美(身材)魁伟，并与他的弟子，贤士和大夫们往来，然后知道天下的文章都聚集在这里啊！[12]

11. 京師 (师) *n.* the capital of the country—namely, 汴京 (*biàn jīng*) or 東京汴梁 (*dōng jīng biàn liáng*) in the Northern Song dynasty. It is in present-day Kaifeng 開封, Henan Province.

仰 *v.* to look up.

闕 (阙 *què*) *n.* watchtowers in front of the palace gates.

宮 (宫) 闕 *n.* imperial palace. MdnC: 宮殿 (*gōng diàn* 宫殿).

之 *particle.* a nominative marker. See L2 Grammar Note 2 ⑤.

倉廩 (仓廪) *n.* granary. MdnC: 糧倉 (*liáng cāng* 粮仓).

府庫 (库) *n.* government storehouse to store treasures and weapons.

城 *n.* city wall. MdnC: 城墙 (*chéng qiáng* 城墙).

池 *n.* moat. MdnC: 護城河 (*hù chéng hé* 护城河).

苑囿 *n.* garden, park. It refers to the imperial garden here.

巨 *adj.* gigantic, enormous.

麗 (丽) *adj.* beautiful.

12. 翰林 scholars in the Hanlin Academy. See Culture Note 1.

歐陽公 or 歐陽脩 (欧阳修) (family name 姓, Ōuyáng 歐陽; given name 名, Xiū 脩; style 字, Yǒngshū 永叔; literary name 號, Liùyī jūshì 六一居士; 1007–1072), one of the dominant figures of Northern Song literature and politics. He is a literary titan excelling in a variety of genres and is one of the Eight Masters of Prose of Tang and Song 唐宋八大家 (see L16 Culture Note 1). He is the famed compiler of *The New History of the Tang Dynasty* 新唐書 (*Xīn Táng shū* 新唐书).

辯 (辩) *adj.* persuasive, eloquent. MdnC: 善辯 (*shàn biàn* 善辩).

秀 *adj.* refined, elegant, graceful. MdnC: 秀美 (*xiù měi*).

偉 (伟) *adj.* big, great. MdnC: 魁偉 (*kuí wěi* 魁伟).

門 (门) 人 *n.* disciple, student. MdnC: 弟子 (*dì zǐ*).

賢 (贤) 士 *n.* able and virtuous gentleman.

大夫 *n.* senior officials.

聚 *v.* to gather. MdnC: 聚集 (*jù jí*).

太尉以ₐ才略冠天下，天下之所恃以ᵇ無
tài wèi yǐ cái lüè guàn tiān xià tiān xià zhī suǒ shì yǐ wú

太尉您凭借才能谋略而名冠天下，老百姓都依

憂，四夷之所憚以ᵦ不敢發，入則周公、召
yōu　　sì yí zhī suǒ dàn yǐ　　bù gǎn fā　　rù zé zhōu gōng shào

公，出則方叔、召虎。¹³而轍也未之見焉。¹⁴
gōng　　chū zé fāng shū　　shào hǔ　　ér zhé yě wèi zhī jiàn yān

且夫人之學也，不志其大，雖多而何爲？¹⁵
qiě fú rén zhī xué yě　　bú zhì qí dà　　suī duō ér hé wéi

轍之來也，於山見終南、嵩、華之高，於水
zhé zhī lái yě　　yú shān jiàn zhōng nán　sōng huà zhī gāo　　yú shuǐ

見黃河之大且深，於人見歐陽公。而猶以爲
jiàn huáng hé zhī dà qiě shēn　　yú rén jiàn ōu yáng gōng　　ér yóu yǐ wéi

未見太尉也。¹⁶故願得觀ₐ賢人之光耀，聞一
wèi jiàn tài wèi yě　　gù yuàn dé guān xián rén zhī guāng yào wén yī

言以自壯，然後可以盡天下之大觀ᵦ而無憾
yán yǐ zì zhuàng　　rán hòu kě yǐ jìn tiān xià zhī dà guān ér wú hàn

者矣。¹⁷
zhě yǐ

靠您，所以没有忧虑；四方异族忌惮您，所以不敢发兵；在朝廷，您就是周公、召公(那样的贤臣)，出征时您就是方叔、召虎(那样的猛将)。¹³可苏辙(我到现在)也没见到您啊！¹⁴况且人的学问，没有大志向，即使学得多又有什么用呢？¹⁵我(这次)来，于山，我看到了终南山、嵩山、华山高大雄伟；于水，我看到黄河宏大深广；于人，我拜见了欧阳公，但我仍以为没有拜见太尉(很遗憾)！¹⁶所以希望能够看到贤人的风采，听到您的话来壮大自己，然后可以看尽天下的壮美景象而没有遗憾了！¹⁷

13. 以ₐ *coverb.* by means of. MdnC: 憑藉 (*píng jiè* 凭借). See L2 Grammar Note 1 ②.

才 *n.* ability, talent. MdnC: 才能 (*cái néng*).

略 *n.* plan, strategy. MdnC: 謀略 (*móu lüè* 谋略).

冠 (guàn) *v.* to be the best, above all the others.

恃 *v.* to rely on, depend on. MdnC: 依靠 (*yī kào*).

以ᵦ *conj.* and thereby. MdnC: 而 (*ér*). See L2 Grammar Note 1 ③.

憂 (忧) *n.* worry, concern. MdnC: 擔憂 (*dān yōu* 担忧).

夷 *n.* a derogatory term for non-Han tribal people living to the northeastern part of China proper.

四夷 Four Barbarians. See Culture Note 2.

憚 (惮 dàn) *v.* to fear, be afraid. MdnC: 忌憚 (*jì dàn* 忌惮).

發 (发 fā) *v.* to send out. Here it means "to send/dispatch troops" 發兵 (*fā bīng* 发兵).

入 *v.* to enter. Here it refers to "at court" 在朝庭 (*zài cháo tíng*).

周公 or 周公旦 (ancestral name 姓, Jī 姬; given name 名, Dàn 旦; posthumous name 謚, Wén 文; ?–1032? BCE), also known as Duke Wen of Zhou 周文公. He is the fourth son of King Wen of Zhou 周文王 (1152–1056 BCE), and he played an important role in helping his brother, King Wu of Zhou 周武王 (?–1043 BCE), to build the Western Zhou.

召公 (ancestral name 姓, Jī 姬; given name 名, Shì 奭; ?–1032? BCE), also known as 召伯 and 召康公. He is a member of the royal family of the Zhou dynasty. As a contemporary of Duke Wen of Zhou 周公旦, Duke Shao also assisted King Wu of Zhou 周武王 in building the Western Zhou.

出 *v.* to go out. Here it refers to going on an expedition 出征 (*chū zhēng*).

方叔 (ancestral name 姓, Jī 姬), a minister in the reign of King Xuan of Zhou 周宣王 (?–782 BCE). He is known for a series of victories over the armies of minorities.

召虎 (ancestral name 姓, Jī 姬; family name 氏, Shào 召; given name 名, Hǔ 虎; posthumous name 謚, Mù 穆), also known as 召伯虎 and 召穆公. He is a descendant of 召公奭 and is famous for assisting King Xuan of Zhou 周宣王 and defeating the so-called Huai Barbarians 淮夷.

14. 未之見 the normal word order should be 未見之 in the Song time.

   焉 *ending particle*. MdnC: 啊 (*a*). See L2 Grammar Note 3 ②.

15. 且夫 (fú) *conj.* besides, furthermore. MdnC: 況且 (*kuàng qiě* 况且). See L13 Grammar Note 2 ②.

   學 (学) *n.* learning, study. MdnC: 學問 (*xué wèn* 学问).

   志 *n.* purpose, will. Here it is used as a verb, meaning "to have purpose" 有志向 (*yǒu zhì xiàng*).

16. 之 *particle*. a nominative marker. See L2 Grammar Note 2 ⑤.

   猶 (犹) *adv.* still, yet. MdnC: 仍 (*réng*). See L3 Grammar Note 3 ①.

   以爲 (为 wéi) *v.* to consider, think.

17. 願 (愿) *v.* to be willing to, like to. MdnC: 希望 (*xī wàng*).

   觀ₐ (观 guān) *v.* to view, see, enjoy. MdnC: 看 (*kàn*).

   光耀 *adj.* brilliant and glorious demeanor. MdnC: 風采 (*fēng cǎi* 风采).

   壯 (壮) *adj.* strong. Here it is used as a causative verb, 使……壯, meaning "to strengthen" 壯大 (*zhuàng dà* 壮大). See L7 Grammar Note 1 ②.

   觀ᵦ (观 guān) *n.* view, sight. MdnC: 景象 (*jǐng xiàng*).

   憾 *n.* regret. MdnC: 遺憾 (*yí hàn* 遗憾).

轍年少，未能通習吏事。¹⁸嚮之來非有
zhé nián shào   wèi néng tōng xí lì shì   xiàng zhī lái fēi yǒu

取於斗升之祿，偶然得之，非其所樂。¹⁹然
qǔ yú dǒu shēng zhī lù   ǒu rán dé zhī   fēi qí suǒ lè   rán

幸得賜歸待選，使得優游數年之間，將歸益
xìng dé cì guī dài xuǎn   shǐ dé yōu yóu shù nián zhī jiān   jiāng guī yì

治其文，且學爲政。²⁰太尉苟以爲可教而
zhì qí wén   qiě xué wéi zhèng   tài wèi gǒu yǐ wéi kě jiào ér

辱教之，又幸矣！²¹
rǔ jiào zhī   yòu xìng yǐ

苏辙年纪很轻，还不能通晓做官的事情。¹⁸先前来(京城)，不是要获取微薄的薪水，偶然间得到了，也不是我所高兴的事情。¹⁹但幸运地得到恩赐还乡,等待(吏部)选拔，使我可以有几年悠闲的时光，将用到更好地研究文章，学习处理政务上。²⁰太尉如果认为我还可以教导，而且(愿)屈尊来教我，(那我就)更幸运了！²¹

蘇轍《欒城集》，上海：上海古籍出版社 (2009), 477–478.

18. 通 *v.* to understand thoroughly, be proficient in. MdnC: 通曉 (*tōng xiǎo* 通晓).

   習 (习) *v.* to be used to, be familiar with.

   吏 *n.* functionaries, low-level officials. MdnC: 官員 (*guān yuán* 官员).

19. 嚮 (向) *adv.* earlier, previously, formerly. MdnC: 先前 (*xiān qián*).

   取 *v.* to obtain, get. MdnC: 獲取 (*huò qǔ* 获取).

   斗升 *measure word*. measurement capacity in ancient China. 一斗 equals 十升. Here it refers to (a) meager (salary) 微薄 (*wēi bó*).

祿 (禄) *n.* (official's) emolument. MdnC: 薪水 (*xīn shuǐ*).

20. 幸 *adv.* luckily, fortunately. MdnC: 幸運 (*xìng yùn* 幸运).

賜 (赐) *v.* (an emperor) bestows something. MdnC: 恩賜 (*ēn cì* 恩赐).

歸 (归) *v.* to return (to one's hometown). MdnC: 還鄉 (*huán xiāng* 还乡).

待 *v.* to wait for. MdnC: 等待 (*děng dài*).

選 (选) *v.* to select, elect. MdnC: 選拔 (*xuǎn bá* 选拔).

優遊 (优游) *v.* to be leisurely and carefree. MdnC: 悠閑 (*yōu xián* 悠闲).

益 *adv.* more, further. MdnC: 更加 (*gèng jiā*).

治 *v.* to work on, study. MdnC: 研究 (*yán jiū*).

爲 (为 *wéi*) *v.* to manage, do. MdnC: 處理 (*chù lǐ* 处理).

政 *n.* administrative affairs. MdnC: 政務 (*zhèng wù* 政务).

21. 苟 *conj.* if. MdnC: 如果 (*rú guǒ*). See Grammar Note 1 ①.

教 (jiào) *v.* to teach, instruct. MdnC: 教導 (*jiào dǎo* 教导).

辱 *v.* to humble oneself to do something. MdnC: 屈尊 (*qū zūn*).

文化常識 Culture Notes

1. 翰林 or 翰林學士 Hanlin or Hanlin Bachelor is an official post. Hanlins belong to the Hanlin Academy 翰林學士院 (*Hàn lín xué shì yuàn*) or 翰林院, an institution first founded in the Tang dynasty to recruit talent in such fields as literature, calligraphy, painting, and medicine. During the reign of Emperor Xuan of the Tang 唐玄宗 (r. 713–756), Hanlins began to engage in secretarial work for the emperor. Gradually the Hanlin Academy took on more administrative responsibilities and eventually became an official branch of the court during the Northern Song dynasty. During this period, the selection of Hanlin members was closely associated with imperial examinations 科舉 (*kē jǔ* 科举). In the Ming and Qing dynasties, the Hanlin Academy took charge of writing official documents and editing historical works. It also provided counsel for emperors. Generally speaking, the post-Tang Hanlin Academy is composed of scholar-officials enjoying superior social status.

2. 四夷 Four Barbarians is a derogatory general term for four major tribal minorities living in the border regions of ancient China: Eastern Yi 東夷 (*dōng yí* 东夷), Western Rong 西戎 (*xī róng*), Southern Man 南蠻 (*nán mán* 南蛮), and Northern Di 北狄 (*běi dí*). The words *Yi, Rong, Man,* and *Di* are all derogatory.

語法注釋 Grammar Note

1. 苟 ① *conj.* if. MdnC: 如果 (*rú guǒ*), 假若 (*jiǎ ruò*).

太尉苟以爲可教而辱教之，又幸矣！

[太尉如果认为我还可以教导，而且（愿意）屈尊来教我，（那我就）更幸运了！]

② *adv.* unscrupulously. MdnC: 苟且 (*gǒu qiě*).

生亦我所欲，所欲有甚於生者，故不爲苟得也。（L7）

[生命是我想要的，但我想要的东西还有超过了生命的，所以不能苟且活着。]

Literary Analysis

1. The form of address used in epistolary writings usually sheds light on the social relationship between the addresser and addressee. This is particularly true of premodern Chinese epistolary writings. In this letter, Su Zhe places the honorific "執事" (literally meaning "staffers in charge") after the official title of his addressee, Han Qi, to convey his profound respect for and deference to Han, the most powerful military official in the land at the time. Compare this letter's opening with that of Cao Pi's letter in the preceding lesson and ponder the absence of the addressee's name in Cao's letter. What does that absence tell us about the addresser-addressee relationship?

2. This letter is best known for its innovative exposition on how to cultivate cosmic-moral vital energy (*qi* 氣) as a means of achieving literary greatness. But did Su Zhe write this letter primarily to share his view on literary creativity?

3. Like Han Yu's "A Prose Farewell to Dong Shaonan" (lesson 26), this letter exemplifies the art of indirection employed in the greatest communicative writings by Tang-Song masters of ancient-style prose. How would you distinguish the modes of indirect expression used in these two texts? 👉 *HTRCProse*, C1.2, C11.2, and C12.6, for detailed literary analyses of these two texts.

—ZC

課後練習 Exercises

一 給加點字注音 Give the pinyin romanization for each dotted word.

1. 轍 （＿＿） 2. 太尉 （＿＿） 3. 闕 （＿＿） 4. 苑囿 （＿＿, ＿＿） 5. 倉廩 （＿＿, ＿＿）

6. 嵩 （＿＿） 7. 華山 （＿＿） 8. 夷 （＿＿） 9. 宮闕 （＿＿, ＿＿） 10. 泪沒 （＿＿, ＿＿）

二 在括號中給句中加點的字注音，並選出正確的釋義 Give the pinyin romanization for each dotted word; then select the correct definition from the following list, and write it in the blank.

依靠　　屈尊　　顯現（显现）　　相稱（称）　　薪水　　**信服**　　洋溢　　盡（尽）情　　忌憚（惮）

1. 小信未孚（fú） ＿＿**信服**＿＿ 2. 稱其氣之小大（ ） ＿＿＿＿＿ 3. 溢乎其貌（ ） ＿＿＿＿＿

4. 恣觀 （ ） ＿＿＿＿＿ 5. 天下之所恃 （ ） ＿＿＿＿＿ 6. 斗升之祿（ ） ＿＿＿＿＿

7. 見乎其文（ ） ＿＿＿＿＿ 8. 四夷之所憚 （ ） ＿＿＿＿＿ 9. 辱教之 （ ） ＿＿＿＿＿

三 選擇釋義並填空 Match each word in the left column with its correct definition in the middle column. Fill in each blank in the right column with an appropriate word from the left column.

謀謀劃（谋划）　　改變（变）　　太史公行天下，周＿＿四海名山大川。
充＿＿＿＿＿　　事跡（迹）
覽＿＿＿＿＿　　恩賜（赐）

動＿＿＿＿＿　　　研究
通＿＿＿＿＿　　　**謀劃**（谋划）
跡＿＿＿＿＿　　　等待
待＿＿＿＿＿　　　遊覽（游览）
治＿＿＿＿＿　　　通曉（晓）
賜＿＿＿＿＿　　　充滿（满）

其氣＿＿乎其中而溢乎其貌，＿＿乎其言而見乎其文，而不自知也。

百氏之書，雖無所不讀，然皆古人陳＿＿＿，不足以激發其志氣。

轍年少，未能＿＿＿習吏事。

然幸得＿＿＿歸＿＿＿選，便得優遊數年之間，將歸益＿＿＿其文，且學爲政。

四　請用給出的字填空 Fill in each blank with an appropriate word from the following list.

雖（虽）　以　爲（为）　焉　之　且　然　夫

1. 文不可＿＿＿學而能，氣可以養而致。　2. 百氏之書＿＿＿無所不讀，＿＿＿皆古人之陳跡。

3. 而轍也未＿＿＿見＿＿＿。　　　　　　4. ＿＿＿＿＿＿人之學也，不志其大，雖多而何＿＿＿？

五　爲加點字選擇正確釋義，並根據釋義來翻譯句子 Match each dotted word with its correct modern Chinese equivalent by circling the latter. Then translate each sentence into modern Chinese.

1. 又何間焉？　　　　　　　　　　ⓐ爲什麼（为什么）　b. 憑什麼（凭什么）　c. 多少

現代文翻译：你又为什么要参与到这件事情里面？

＿＿＿＿＿＿＿＿＿＿＿＿＿＿＿＿＿＿＿＿＿＿＿＿＿

2. 此二子者，豈嘗執筆學爲如此之文哉？　　　a. 嘗試（尝试）b. 曾經（经）c. 品嘗（尝）

現代文翻译：＿＿＿＿＿＿＿＿＿＿＿＿＿＿＿＿＿＿＿＿＿

3. 所見不過數百里之間，無高山大野可登覽以自廣。　a. 以⋯⋯爲廣（广）　b. 使⋯⋯廣（广）　c. 大

現代文翻译：＿＿＿＿＿＿＿＿＿＿＿＿＿＿＿＿＿＿＿＿＿

4. 太尉以才略冠天下，天下之所恃以無憂，四夷之所憚以不敢發。

　　　　　　　　　　　　　　　　　a. 而　b. 憑藉（凭借）　c. 認爲（认为）

現代文翻译：＿＿＿＿＿＿＿＿＿＿＿＿＿＿＿＿＿＿＿＿＿

5. 太尉苟以爲可教而辱教之，又幸矣！　　　　　　a. 如果　b. 苟且　c. 不

現代文翻译：＿＿＿＿＿＿＿＿＿＿＿＿＿＿＿＿＿＿＿＿＿

馬守真《寄王百穀書》

"Letter to Wang Zhideng (Baigu)" (Ma Shouzhen)

Introduction

This lesson features a brief letter written by the famous late-Ming courtesan Ma Shouzhen 馬守真 (courtesy name Xianglan 湘蘭; 1548–1605) to her beloved patron-lover Wang Zhideng 王穉登 (courtesy name Baigu 百穀; 1535–1612). Ma Shouzhen is one of the Eight Beauties of Qinhuai (the renowned pleasure quarters in present-day Nanjing) 秦淮八艷 (Qínhuái bāyàn), known for her paintings of orchids and bamboo and for her collection of poems, *Collected Works of Xianglan* 湘蘭集 (*Xiānglán jí*).

正文與簡體譯文 Text and Modern Chinese Translation

別後妾頃刻在懷， 即寤寐未忘知己。[1]
bié hòu qiè qǐng kè zài huái   jí wù mèi wèi wàng zhī jǐ

遙憶故人， 再續舊好， 恨各一天涯， 中心
yáo yì gù rén   zài xù jiù hǎo   hèn gè yī tiān yá   zhōng xīn

鬱結， 不能朝夕繼見， 聯枕論心。[2] 又兼秋
yù jié   bù néng zhāo xī jì jiàn   lián zhěn lùn xīn   yòu jiān qiū

水盈窗， 寒蛩破夢， 此情此景， 真妾銷魂
shuǐ yíng chuāng hán qióng pò mèng cǐ qíng cǐ jǐng   zhēn qiè xiāo hún

時哉![3] 何日既見君子， 了卻相思宿債， 作
shí zāi   hé rì jì jiàn jūn zǐ   liǎo què xiāng sī sù zhài   zuò

人間世未有之歡乎![4] 長江險塹， 莫能匍匐，
rén jiān shì wèi yǒu zhī huān hū   cháng jiāng xiǎn qiàn mò néng pú fú

八行相訊， 神與書馳。[5]
bā háng xiāng xùn shén yǔ shū chí

趙世傑輯《古今女史》卷八，明崇禎刻本

离别后，我就在想念你，任何时候都不忘你这个知己。[1]回忆故人，想再继续旧时的情谊。可遗憾（我们）天各一方，（我为此）心中郁结，不能（与你）早晚一直见面，谈论心中所想。[2] 再加上（想着我们一起听）秋雨落满窗户，睡梦中（一起被）深秋的蟋蟀叫声惊醒，这样的情景，是我（最幸福）销魂的时刻啊![3] 什么时候才能再见你，了结我的相思旧债，再继续人间未有的欢乐（时光）啊![4] 长江险要的天堑（隔开我们，我）不能渡过，（只能写）信来询问（你的消息），而我的心神与这封书信一同前往。[5]

1. 妾 *n.* concubine. Here it is a humble title used by a woman to refer to herself.

頃 (顷) 刻 *adv.* instantly, in no time.

懷 (怀) *v.* to think of, miss. MdnC: 想念 (*xiǎng niàn*).

即 *adv.* in other words.

寤寐 *adv.* at any time. 寤寐 is a word from the first poem, " 'Guan Guan,' Cry the Ospreys" 關雎 ("Guān jū" 关雎), in the *Book of Poetry*. 寤 means "to wake up," and 寐 means "to be asleep." They are used together to refer to the time awake or asleep.

知己 *n.* a friend who knows and understands you well.

2. 遙憶 (遥忆) *v.* to recall. MdnC: 回憶 (*huí yì* 回忆).

續 (续) *v.* to continue.

舊 (旧) 好 *n.* old friendship.

恨 *v.* to regret. MdnC: 遺憾 (*yí hàn* 遗憾).

天涯 *n.* end of the world.

鬱結 *n.* worry.

繼 (继) *adv.* continually. MdnC: 一直 (*yì zhí*).

聯 (联) *v.* to connect.

枕 *n.* pillow.

3. 兼 *adv.* in addition, moreover.

水 *n.* water. Here 秋水 refers to the rain in the fall.

盈 *v.* to be full of. MdnC: 溢滿 (*yì mǎn* 溢满).

蛩 *n.* cricket. MdnC: 蟋蟀 (*xī shuài*). 寒蛩 refers to crickets in the late fall.

破 *v.* to break. Here it means "to wake up." MdnC: 驚醒 (*jīng xǐng* 惊醒).

銷 (销) 魂 *adj.* extremely excited or happy.

時 (时) *n.* moment. MdnC: 時刻 (*shí kè* 时刻).

4. 了卻 (销) *v.* to solve, settle. MdnC: 了結 (*liǎo jié* 了结).

宿 (sù) *adj.* old, long-standing. MdnC: 舊 (*jiù* 旧).

債 (债) *n.* debt, loan. Here it refers to the favor to be repaid 情債 (*qíng zhài* 情债).

5. 長 (长) 江 the Yangtze River.

險 (险) *adj.* dangerous. MdnC: 險要 (*xiǎn yào* 险要).

塹 (堑) *n.* moat, trench.

莫 *adv.* do not. See 莫 ② in L37 Grammar Note 1.

匍匐 *v.* to crawl. Here it means "to cross (the Yangtze River)" 渡過 (*dù guò* 渡过).

八行 (háng) *n.* eight lines, referring to a letter 信 (*xìn*).

訊 (讯) *v.* to ask, inquire. MdnC: 詢問 (*xún wèn* 询问).

馳 (驰) *v.* to go quickly. MdnC: 前往 (*qián wǎng*).

Literary Analysis

Compare this female-authored letter with the four male-authored letters in this unit. Do you observe any differences in theme, form, diction, and voice between these two types of letters? For more female-authored letters, see *HTRCProse*, C15.1, Gu Ruopu 顧若璞, "Letter to My Younger Brother" 與弟 ("Yǔ dì" 与弟), and C15.7, Wang Duanshu 王端淑, "Letter to Madame Feng" 柬馮夫人 ("Jiǎn Féng fūrén" 柬冯夫人).

—ZC

課後練習　Exercises

一　給加點字注音　Give the pinyin romanization for each dotted word.

1. 寤寐（＿＿＿,＿＿＿）2. 八行（＿＿＿）3. 險塹（＿＿＿）4. 匍匐（＿＿＿,＿＿＿）

二　在括號中給句中加點的字注音，並選出正確的釋義　Give the pinyin romanization for each dotted word; then select the correct definition from the following list, and write it in the blank.

險(险)要　　**信服**　　詢問(询问)　　蟋蟀　　舊(旧)　　溢滿(满)

1. 小信未孚（ **fú** ）　**信服**　　2. 秋水盈窗（　）＿＿＿＿＿　　3. 寒蛩破夢（　）＿＿＿＿＿

4. 相思宿債（　）＿＿＿＿＿　　5. 長江險塹（　）＿＿＿＿＿　　6. 八行相訊（　）＿＿＿＿＿

三　選擇釋義並填空　Match each word in the left column with its correct definition in the middle column. Fill in each blank in the right column with an appropriate word from the left column.

謀謀劃(谋划)	時(时)刻	別後妄頃刻＿＿＿懷，即寤寐未忘知己。
懷＿＿＿＿＿＿	一直	遙憶故人，再續舊好，＿＿＿各一天涯，中心鬱結，
恨＿＿＿＿＿＿	驚(惊)醒	不能朝夕＿＿＿見，聯枕論心。
繼＿＿＿＿＿＿	前往	又兼秋水盈窗，寒蛩＿＿＿夢，此情此景，真妄銷魂
破＿＿＿＿＿＿	**謀劃(谋划)**	＿＿＿哉！
時＿＿＿＿＿＿	想念	長江險塹，莫能匍匐，八行相訊，神與書＿＿＿。
馳＿＿＿＿＿＿	遺(遗)憾	

四　請用給出的字填空　Fill in each blank with an appropriate word from the following list.

乎　　何　　莫　　之　　既

1. ＿＿＿日＿＿＿見君子，了卻相思宿債，作人間世未有＿＿＿歡＿＿＿!
2. 長江險塹，＿＿＿能匍匐，八行相訊，神與書馳。

五　爲加點字選擇正確釋義，並根據釋義來翻譯句子　Match each dotted word with its correct modern Chinese equivalent by circling the latter. Then translate each sentence into modern Chinese.

1. 又何閒焉？　　　　　　　　　　　　ⓐ爲什麼(为什么)　b.憑什麼(凭什么)　c.多少

現代文翻译：你又为什么要参与到这件事情里面？

2. 別後妾頃刻在懷，即寤寐未忘知己。　　　　　　　a. 立刻　b. 即使　c. 就是

现代文翻译：_____

3. 何日既見君子，了卻相思宿債，作人間世未有之歡乎！

　　　　　　　　　　　　　　a. 怎麼（么）　b. 曾經（经）　c. 爲什麼（为什么）

现代文翻译：_____

4. 長江險塹，莫能匍匐，八行相訊，神與書馳。　　　　a. 没有人　b. 不要　c. 就

现代文翻译：_____

第二十一課

夏完淳《獄中上母書》

"Letter to My Mothers, From Prison" (Xia Wanchun)

Introduction

The Ming poet Xia Wanchun 夏完淳 (1631–1647) wrote this letter to his formal mother, née Sheng, in 1647. His father, Xia Yunyi 夏允彝 (1596–1645), a prominent figure in the Jiangnan region, counted among his friends Zhang Pu 張溥 (1602–1641), leader of the Fu Society, and Chen Zilong 陳子龍 (1608–1647), a famous Ming poet whose writing appears in lesson 31. Xia Wanchun's reputation for literary achievement began in his teens; his prose was deeply influenced by his early teacher, Chen Zilong.

Together with his father and Chen Zilong, Xia Wanchun fought the Manchus after their conquest of China in 1644. Even after his father's suicide (following a defeat), Xia Wanchun fought on with Chen Zilong, joining Wu Yi's anti-Manchu force in the Lake Tai area. In 1647, he was captured and interrogated by Hong Chengchou 洪承疇 (1593–1665), a former Ming official who had surrendered to the Qing court. Xia refused to surrender to the Qing, condemning Hong's disloyalty to the Ming dynasty. Soon after, Xia was executed in Nanjing at the age of seventeen.

Before his execution, Xia Wanchun wrote this profoundly touching letter of farewell to his mother. In it, he explains why he had to be separated from her and then, in his parting words, thanks her for raising him, suggests arrangements for his own family, and reaffirms the worthiness of dying for a noble cause. A translation of this text is given in *HTRCProse*, chapter 15, "Ming and Qing Occasional Prose: Letters and Funerary Inscriptions," C15.5.

正文與簡體譯文 Text and Modern Chinese Translation

不孝完淳，今日死矣。以身殉父，不得
bú xiào wán chún　jīn rì sǐ yǐ　yǐ shēn xùn fù　bù dé

以身報母矣。¹痛自嚴君見背，兩易春秋，冤
yǐ shēn bào mǔ yǐ　　tòng zì yán jūn jiàn bèi　liǎng yì chūn qiū　yuān

酷日深，艱辛歷盡。²本圖復見天日，以報大
kù rì shēn　jiān xīn lì jìn　　běn tú fù jiàn tiān rì　　yǐ bào dà

仇，卹死榮生，告成黃土。³奈天不佑我，鍾
chóu　xù sǐ róng shēng　gào chéng huáng tǔ　nài tiān bú yòu wǒ　zhōng

不孝子完淳今天要死去
了，用身體為父親而死，
不能再用身體報答母親
了！¹自從父親去世，
（我）非常悲痛，兩年了，
冤仇悲痛日日加深，經歷
盡了艱難與辛苦。²本來
（我）圖謀重見天日，來報
大仇，使死去的人得到撫
恤，活著的人得到榮耀，

虐明朝。⁴ 一旅纔興， 便成齏粉。⁵ 去年之舉，
nüè mímg cháo   yì lǚ cái xīng   biàn chéng jī fěn   qù nián zhī jǔ

淳已自分必死， 誰知不死， 死於今日也！⁶
chún yǐ zì fèn bì sǐ   shuí zhī bù sǐ   sǐ yú jīn rì yě

斤斤延此二年之命， 菽水之養， 無一日焉。⁷
jīn jīn yán cǐ èr nián zhī mìng   shū shuǐ zhī yǎng   wú yí rì yān

致慈君托迹於空門， 生母寄生於別姓， 一門
zhì cí jūn tuō jì yú kōng mén shēng mǔ jì shēng yú bié xìng   yì mén

漂泊， 生不得相依， 死不得相問。⁸ 淳今日
piāo bó   shēng bù dé xiāng yī   sǐ bù dé xiāng wèn   chún jīn rì

又溘然先從九京， 不孝之罪， 上通於天。⁹
yòu kè rán xiān cóng jiǔ jīng   bú xiào zhī zuì   shàng tōng yú tiān

把成功(的消息)报告给去世(的父亲)。³ 无奈上天不保佑我，集中(很多)灾难，加到了明朝之上。⁴ 军队才刚刚建成，就(被清军打败)，化成齑粉。⁵ 去年的举动，我已料想到自己必死，谁知竟没有死，死在了今天！⁶ 仅延续了两年的生命，没有一天(报答)母亲的供养(之恩)啊！⁷ (因为我)致使母亲躲藏在寺庙，生母陆氏寄居在别人家中。(我们)一家人都漂泊着，活着的时候不能相互依靠，死去时不能互相安慰。⁸ 我今天又突然先赴九泉，不孝大罪，上天都知道了！⁹

1. 不孝 literary meaning "not filial." It is used by sons to humbly refer to themselves after their parents have died.

以 *coverb.* with. MdnC: 用 (*yòng*). See L2 Grammar Note 1 ②.

殉 *v.* to die for a cause. MdnC: 爲 (*wèi* 为) ……而死 (*ér sǐ*).

報 (报) *v.* to repay. MdnC: 報答 (*bào dá* 报答).

2. 痛 *n.* sorrow. MdnC: 悲痛 (*bēi tòng*).

嚴 (严) 君 a respectful way to address one's own father. MdnC: 父親 (*fù qīn* 父亲).

見 (见 jiàn) 背 a euphemistic term, meaning "to pass away." MdnC: 去世 (*qù shì*).

易 *v.* to change.

春秋 spring and autumn—namely, a year.

冤 *n.* rancor. MdnC: 冤仇 (*yuān chóu*).

酷 *adj.* cruel. Here it refers to the grief that the author suffered 悲痛 (*bēi tòng*).

日 *adv.* day by day. MdnC: 一天天 (*yì tiān tiān*).

深 *adj.* deep. Here it is a verb, meaning "to deepen" 加深 (*jiā shēn*).

艱 (艰) *n.* difficulty. MdnC: 艱難 (*jiān nán* 艰难).

辛 *n.* suffering. MdnC: 辛苦 (*xīn kǔ*).

歷 (历) *v.* to experience (difficulty), undergo. MdnC: 經歷 (*jīng lì* 经历).

盡 (尽) *adv.* thoroughly, exhaustively.

3. 本 *adv.* originally. MdnC: 本來 (*běn lái* 本来).

圖 (图) *v.* to plan, seek. MdnC: 圖謀 (*tú móu* 图谋).

復 (复) *adv.* again. MdnC: 重 (*chóng*).

報 (报) *v.* to avenge, revenge. MdnC: 報仇 (*bào chóu* 报仇).

仇 *n.* enmity.

卹 (恤) *n.* compensation. MdnC: 撫卹 (*fǔ xǔ* 抚恤). Here it is used as a causative verb, 使……卹, meaning "to make ... receive compensation." See L7 Grammar Note 1 ③.

榮 (荣) *n.* glory, honor. MdnC: 榮耀 (*róng yào* 荣耀). Here it is used as a causative verb, 使……榮, meaning "to make ... gain glory or honor." See L7 Grammar Note 1 ③.

告 *v.* to report, tell. MdnC: 報告 (*bào gào* 报告).

成 *n.* success, victory. MdnC: 成功 (*chéng gōng*).

黃土 *n.* yellow earth. Here it refers to the tombs of Xia's dead father and ancestors.

4. 奈 *adv.* nothing can be done now that…. MdnC: 無奈 (*wú nài* 无奈). See Grammar Note 2.

佑 *v.* to bless, help, protect. MdnC: 保佑 (*bǎo yòu*).

鍾 (钟) *v.* to concentrate, accumulate. MdnC: 集中 (*jí zhōng*).

虐 *adj.* cruel, tyrannical. Here it refers to disasters and difficulties 災難 (*zāi nàn* 灾难).

明朝 (cháo) the Ming dynasty (1368–1644).

5. 旅 *n.* a battalion of roughly five hundred soldiers. Here it refers to troops raised and led by the Southern Ming general Wu Yi 吳易 (?–1646). Xia Wanchun joined Wu's troops and became a staff officer there.

纔 (才) *adv.* just.

興 (兴 xīng) *v.* to rise, thrive. Here it means "to be built" 建成 (*jiàn chéng*).

成 *v.* to become.

齏 (齑) *adj.* minced. 齏 (齑) 粉 means "broken pieces or powder." Here it refers to the defeat of Wu Yi's army by the Qing army in 1646.

6. 舉 (举) *n.* action, behavior. MdnC: 舉動 (*jǔ dòng* 举动). 去年之舉 (举) refers to Xia Wanchun's joining Wu Yi's anti-Qing army.

分 (fèn) *v.* to expect, presume, think. MdnC: 料想 (*liào xiǎng*).

7. 斤斤 *adv.* clearly. Here it means "only" 僅僅 (*jǐn jǐn* 仅仅).

延 *v.* to extend. MdnC: 延續 (*yán xù* 延续).

菽 *n.* beans and peas. 菽水 means "poor and simple meals." Here it refers to parents' support.

養 (养) *v.* to raise, support. MdnC: 供養 (*gòng yǎng* 供养).

焉 *ending particle.* MdnC: 啊 (*a*). See L2 Grammar Note 3 ②.

8. 致 *v.* to cause, bring about, result in. MdnC: 致使 (*zhì shǐ*).

慈君 refers to Xia Wanchun's formal mother, Shengshi 盛氏.

託 (托) 迹 refers to the fact that Xia Wanchun's legal mother had to take refuge in the Buddhist temple.
　託 (托) is a verb, meaning "to entrust," and 迹 means "traces or footprints."

空門 (门) *n.* Buddhism. Here it refers to the Buddhist temple 寺廟 (*sì miào* 寺庙).

生母 refers to Xia Wanchun's birth mother, Lushi 陸氏.

寄生 *v.* to depend on others to survive. Here it means "to live or stay (in someone's home)" 寄居 (*jì jū*).

別姓 *n.* someone else's surname.

門 (门) *n.* household, family.

漂泊 *v.* to float, wander. Here it refers to the fact that the entire Xia family drifted apart.

依 *v.* to depend on, rely on. MdnC: 依靠 (*yī kào*).

問 (问) *v.* to inquire. MdnC: 安慰 (*ān wèi*).

9. 溘然 *adv.* suddenly. MdnC: 突然 (*tū rán*).

從 (从) *v.* to follow.

九京 or 九泉 Nine Springs. It refers to the underworld.

嗚呼！ 雙慈在堂， 下有妹女， 門祚衰
wū hū　shuāng cí zài táng　xià yǒu mèi nǔ　mén zuò shuāi

薄， 終鮮兄弟。¹⁰ 淳一死不足惜， 哀哀八口，
báo　zhōng xiǎn xiōng dì　chún yì sǐ bù zú xī　āi āi bā kǒu

何以為生！¹¹ 雖然， 已矣！ 淳之身， 父之所
hé yǐ wéi shēng　suī rán　yǐ yǐ　chún zhī shēn　fù zhī suǒ

遺； 淳之身， 君之所用。¹² 為父為君， 死亦
yí　chún zhī shēn　jūn zhī suǒ yòng　wèi fù wèi jūn　sǐ yì

何負於雙慈！¹³ 但慈君推乾就溼， 教禮習詩，
hé fù yú shuāng cí　dàn cí jūn tuī gān jiù shī　jiāo lǐ xí shī

十五年如一日；嫡母慈惠， 千古所難。¹⁴ 大
shí wǔ nián rú yí rì　dí mǔ cí huì　qiān gǔ suǒ nán　dà

恩未酬， 令人痛絕。¹⁵ 慈君託之義融女兄，
ēn wèi chóu　lìng rén tòng jué　cí jūn tuō zhī yì róng nǔ xiōng

生母託之昭南女弟。¹⁶
shēng mǔ tuō zhī zhāo nán nǔ dì

哎，两位母亲都健在，下面还有妹妹女儿。家运衰败，一直都没有兄弟。¹⁰我死了不足怜惜，（但我悲痛）这八口人，怎么活下去啊！¹¹即使这样，罢了。我的身体，是父亲遗留下的；我的身体，是为皇帝所用的。¹²为了父亲，为了皇帝，我死去又怎么会辜负两位母亲呢！¹³但母亲您（从前）把我放到干的床上睡，而自己睡湿床，教我礼仪（教我）学习诗歌，十五年如一日。母亲慈爱和恩惠，千百年来都难有啊！¹⁴大恩还没有报答，令人痛心极了！¹⁵母亲就托付给义融姐了，我的生母就托付给昭南妹了。¹⁶

10. 嗚 (呜) 呼 *exclamatory word*. alas. MdnC: 哎 (*ài*).

雙 (双) *adj.* two, both, a set of two. MdnC: 兩 (*liǎng* 两).

慈 *n.* maternal love. Here it means "mother" 母親 (*mǔ qīn* 母亲).

在堂 in the hall, which metaphorically means that the mothers are still alive. MdnC: 健在 (*jiàn zài*).

祚 *n.* blessing. MdnC: 福氣 (*fú qì* 福气).

門 (门) 祚 *n.* family's fortune. MdnC: 家運 (*jiā yùn* 家运).

衰 *v.* to decline, wane. MdnC: 衰敗 (*shuāi bài* 衰败).

薄 *adj.* weak, poor.

鮮 (鲜 xiǎn) *adv.* hardly.

11. 惜 *v.* to feel pity for (somebody). MdnC: 憐惜 (*lián xī* 怜惜).

哀哀 *adv.* with grief, mournfully. MdnC: 悲痛 (*bēi tòng*).

何以 how? MdnC: 怎麼 (*zěn me* 怎么). See L1 Grammar Note 3 ③.

為 (为 wéi) 生 *v.* to make a living, survive. MdnC: 活下去 (*huó xià qù*).

12. 雖 (虽) 然 *conj.* even so. MdnC: 即使這樣 (*jí shǐ zhè yàng* 即使这样).

已 *v.* to be over, stop. MdnC: 罷了 (*bà le* 罢了). See Grammar Note 1 ②.

遺 (遗) *v.* to leave behind, bequeath. MdnC: 遺留 (*yí liú* 遗留).

君 *n.* emperor. MdnC: 皇帝 (*huáng dì*).

13. 負 (负) *v.* to fail to live up to. MdnC: 辜負 (*gū fù* 辜负).

14. 推 *v.* to push, push forward.

乾 (干 gān) *adj.* dry. Here it refers to a dry place to sleep.

就 *v.* to approach, draw close to.

溼 (湿) *adj.* wet. Here it refers to a wet bed.

推乾就溼 refers to the kind acts of Xia Wanchun's formal mother, such as "moving him to a dry place while she herself slept on the wet bed."

禮 (礼) *n.* rite. MdnC: 禮儀 (*lǐ yí* 礼仪).

習 (习) *v.* to learn. MdnC: 學習 (*xué xí* 学习).

嫡母 *n.* address of the legal mother by children of concubines.

慈 *adj.* kind, loving. MdnC: 慈愛 (*cí ài*).

惠 *n.* favor. MdnC: 恩惠 (*ēn huì*).

難 (难 nán) *adj.* hard, difficult. Here it means "hard to have" 難有 (*nán yǒu* 难有).

15. 恩 *n.* favor.

酬 *v.* to repay. MdnC: 報答 (*bào dá* 报答).

絕 (绝) *adv.* extremely. MdnC: 極 (*jí* 极).

16. 之 *particle*. added syllable, no meaning in itself. See L1 Grammar Note 2 ④.

義 (义) 融 literary name of Xia Wanchun's older sister, Xia Shuji 夏淑吉.

女兄 older sister. MdnC: 姐 (*jiě*).

昭南 literary name of Xia Wanchun's younger sister, Xia Huiji 夏惠吉.

女弟 younger sister. MdnC: 妹 (*mèi*).

淳死之後，　新婦遺腹得雄，　便以爲家
chún sǐ zhī hòu　　xīn fù yí fù dé xióng　　biàn yǐ wéi jiā

門之幸；　如其不然，　萬勿置後。¹⁷會稽大望，
mén zhī xìng　　rú qí bù rán　　wàn wù zhì hòu　　kuài jī dà wàng

至今而零極矣。¹⁸節義文章，　如我父子者幾
zhì jīn ér líng jí yǐ　　jié yì wén zhāng　　rú wǒ fù zǐ zhě jǐ

人哉！¹⁹立一不肖後，　如西銘先生，　爲ₐ人所
rén zāi　　lì yī bú xiào hòu　　rú xī míng xiān shēng　　wéi rén suǒ

詬笑，　何如不立之爲ᵦ愈耶！²⁰嗚呼！大造茫
gòu xiào　　hé rú bú lì zhī wéi　　yù yé　　wū hū　　dà zào máng

茫，　總歸無後，　有一日中興再造，　則廟食千
máng　zǒng guī wú hòu　　yǒu yí rì zhōng xīng zài zào　　zé miào shí qiān

秋，　豈止麥飯豚蹄不爲餒鬼而已哉！²¹若有
qiū　　qǐ zhǐ mài fàn tún tí bù wéi něi guǐ ér yǐ zāi　　ruò yǒu

妄言立後者，　淳且與先文忠在冥冥誅殛頑
wàng yán lì hòu zhě chún qiě yǔ xiān wén zhōng zài míng míng zhū jí wán

嚚，　決不肯捨！²²
yín　　jué bù kěn shě

我死了之后，（如果）妻子生了一个儿子，就是我们家的幸运；如果不是，千万不要立后嗣。¹⁷会稽的大望族，到现在凋零到了极点。¹⁸操守、正义、文章，像我们父子这样的人有几个啊！¹⁹如果像西铭先生那样，立一个不肖后嗣，被人家诟病耻笑，还不如不立后嗣更好啊！²⁰哎，天地广大无边，（家族）最终趋向于无后啊！（如）有一天（明朝）能够中兴再建，那么（我们）在庙中长久地享受祭祀，又怎么会只是麦饭猪蹄（这样粗糙的食物）而不至于成为饿鬼而已呢？²¹如果有人胡说要立后嗣，我和先父将要在阴间诛杀这顽固愚蠢的人，绝对不会放弃！²²

17. 新婦 (妇) *n.* new wife. MdnC: 妻子 (*qī zǐ*).

    遺 (遗) 腹 *n.* a posthumous birth.

    雄 *n.* male. Here it refers to a son 兒子 (*ér zi*).

    家門 (门) *n.* family, clan. MdnC: 家族 (*jiā zú*).

    幸 *n.* good luck. MdnC: 幸運 (*xìng yùn* 幸运).

    然 *pron.* like this. See L8 Grammar Note 5 ③.

    萬 (万) *number.* ten thousand. Here it means "by no means" 千萬 (*qiān wàn* 千万).

    勿 *adv.* do not. MdnC: 不 (*bù*).

    置 *v.* to set up, establish. MdnC: 立 (*lì*).

    後 (后) *n.* descendant, heir. MdnC: 後嗣 (*hòu sì* 后嗣).

18. 會 (会 kuài) 稽 place name in present-day Shaoxing 紹興, Zhejiang Province.

    望 *adj.* respected, admired, prestigious. Here it refers to a distinguished family or clan of high repute 望族 (*wàng zú*).

    零 *number.* zero. Here it is a verb, meaning "to wane or be in decline" 凋零 (*diāo líng*).

    極 (极) *n.* extreme. MdnC: 極點 (*jí diǎn* 极点).

19. 節 (节) *n.* moral character, virtue. MdnC: 操守 (*cāo shǒu*).

    義 (义) *n.* righteousness. MdnC: 正義 (*zhèng yì* 正义).

20. 肖 (xiào) *adj.* similar, like. MdnC: 相似 (*xiāng sì*). 不肖 means "unlikely or unworthy."

    西銘先生 張溥 (family name 姓, Zhāng 張; given name 名, Pǔ 溥; style 字, Qiándù 乾度/Tiānrú 天如; literary name 號, Xīmíng 西銘; 1602–1641), one of the leading figures of the Restoration Society 復社 (*Fù shè* 复社) in the late Ming.

    立一不肖後，如西銘先生 refers to Zhang Pu's story of setting up an heir. Zhang had no sons. One year after he died, Qian Qianyi 錢謙益 (1582–1664), the leading figure of the late Ming literary circle, set up an heir for him. Later, Qian Qianyi surrendered to the Qing army. Thus, scholars thought that it was detrimental to Zhang Pu's reputation.

    爲 a (为 wéi) *particle.* a passive voice indicator: by. MdnC: 被 (*bèi*). See Grammar Note 3 ⑤.

    詬 (诟) *v.* to criticize severely. MdnC: 詬病 (*gòu bìng* 诟病).

    笑 *v.* to ridicule, sneer at. MdnC: 恥笑 (*chǐ xiào* 耻笑).

    何如 how? what is it like? MdnC: 怎麼樣 (*zěn me yàng* 怎么样). See L6 Grammar Note 3 ④.

    爲 b (为 wéi) *v.* to be. See L9 Grammar Note 1 ③.

    愈 *adj.* better. MdnC: 更好 (*gèng hǎo*).

21. 造 *n.* fortune. MdnC: 造化 (*zào huà*). 大造 means "heaven and earth" 天地 (*tiān dì*).

    茫茫 *adj.* boundless, vast.

    歸 (归) *v.* to return to, tend to, incline to. MdnC: 趨向 (*qū xiàng* 趋向).

    無後 (无后) no successors, no descendants.

    中興 (兴 xīng) *n.* resurgence of a country.

    造 *v.* to make, build, construct. MdnC: 建立 (*jiàn lì*).

    廟 (庙) 食 temple sacrifice. It refers to the situation in which people who had great merits were enshrined in the temple after their death and were able to enjoy sacrifices offered by their descendants.

    千秋 *n.* a thousand years, a long time.

    豈 (岂) *interrogative particle.* MdnC: 怎麼 (*zěn me* 怎么). See L8 Grammar Note 4.

止 used in the sense of 只 (*zhǐ*), meaning "only."

麥 (麦) *n.* wheat, grain. 麥飯 (麦饭) means "grain meals."

豚 *n.* small pigs. MdnC: 豬 (*zhū* 猪).

蹄 *n.* foot, hoof.

麥飯豚蹄 refers to meals that are simple and coarse 粗糙 (*cū cāo*).

餒 (馁) *adj.* hungry. MdnC: 餓 (*è* 饿).

而已 *ending particle.* nothing more. See Grammar Note 1 ③.

22. 妄 *adv.* frivolously, carelessly, rashly. MdnC: 胡亂 (*hú luàn*).

言 *v.* to say, tell. MdnC: 説 (*shuō* 说).

且 *adv.* about to, will. MdnC: 將要 (*jiāng yào* 将要). See L13 Grammar Note 2 ③.

先 *adj.* previous, dead.

文忠 (公) or 夏允彝 (given name 名, Yǔnyí 允彝; style 字, Yízhòng 彝仲; literary name 號, Yuángōng 瑗公; posthumous name 諡, Wénzhōng 文忠; 1596–1645), Xia Wanchun's father, a famous poet in the late Ming.

冥 *adj.* dim. 冥冥 here means "underworld" 陰間 (*yīn jiān* 阴间).

誅 (诛) 殛 *v.* to kill. MdnC: 誅殺 (*zhū shā* 诛杀).

頑 (顽) *v.* stubborn, obstinate. MdnC: 頑固 (*wán gù* 顽固).

嚚 (yín) *adj.* thick-headed. MdnC: 愚蠢 (*yú chǔn*).

捨 (舍) *v.* to give up, abandon. MdnC: 放棄 (*fàng qì* 放弃).

兵戈天地， 淳死後， 亂且未有定期。 [23]
bīng gē tiān dì   chún sǐ hòu   luàn qiě wèi yǒu dìng qī

雙慈善保玉體， 無以淳爲念。 [24] 二十年後，
shuāng cí shàn bǎo yù tǐ   wú yǐ chún wéi niàn   èr shí nián hòu

淳且與先文忠爲北塞之舉矣。 [25] 勿悲， 勿
chún qiě yǔ xiān wén zhōng wéi běi sài zhī jǔ yǐ   wù bēi   wù

悲。 相託之言， 慎勿相負！ [26]
bēi   xiāng tuō zhī yán   shèn wù xiāng fù

战争遍布天地之间。我死后，战乱还没有确定的日期(结束)。[23] 两位母亲好好保重身体，不要想念我。[24] (如果死后我和父亲再度为人)二十年后，我和父亲还要在北方要塞击败清军。[25] 不要悲伤！不要悲伤！我嘱托的话，一定不要违背。[26]

23. 戈 *n.* spear. MdnC: 矛 (*máo*). 兵戈 means "weapon." Here it refers to war 戰爭 (*zhàn zhēng* 战争).

亂 (乱) *n.* chaos, disorder. Here it refers to the chaos caused by war 戰亂 (*zhàn luàn* 战乱).

定 *adj.* fixed. MdnC: 確定 (*què dìng* 确定).

期 *n.* date. MdnC: 日期 (*rì qī*).

24. 保 *v.* to take care of (oneself). MdnC: 保重 (*bǎo zhòng*).

玉體 (体) literally means "jade body." A respectful way to say "your health."

念 *v.* to think of. Here it is used as a noun, meaning "the person to think of or miss."

以我爲 (为 *wéi*) 念 think about me. See L2 Grammar Note 1 ④.

25. 塞 (sài) *n.* frontier, fortress. MdnC: 要塞 (*yào sài*). 北塞 refers to frontiers in the north.

舉 (举) *n.* undertaking, enterprise. MdnC: 舉動 (*jǔ dòng* 举动).

爲 (为 *wéi*) 北塞之舉 (举) means to defeat the Qing army in the north.

26. 勿 *adv.* do not. MdnC: 不要 (*bú yào*).

託 (托) *v.* to entrust. MdnC: 囑托 (*zhǔ tuō* 嘱托).

負 (负) *v.* to disregard, betray. MdnC: 違背 (*wéi bèi* 违背).

武功甥將來大器，家事盡以委之。²⁷ 寒
wǔ gōng shēng jiāng lái dà qì　　jiā shì jìn yǐ wěi zhī　　　hán

食盂蘭，一杯清酒，一盞寒燈，不至作若敖
shí yú lán　　yì bēi qīng jiǔ　　yì zhǎn hán dēng　　bú zhì zuò ruò áo

之鬼，則吾願畢矣。²⁸ 新婦結褵二年，賢孝
zhī guǐ　　zé wú yuàn bì yǐ　　　xīn fù jié lí èr nián　　xián xiào

素著，武功甥好爲我善待之。²⁹ 亦武功渭陽
sù zhù　　wǔ gōng shēng hǎo wèi wǒ shàn dài zhī　　yì wǔ gōng wèi yáng

情也。³⁰ 語無倫次，將死言善。痛哉，痛
qíng yě　　yǔ wú lún cì　　jiāng sǐ yán shàn　　tòng zāi　　tòng

哉！³¹
zāi

武功外甥将来(必成)大器，家里的事可以都委托给他。²⁷寒食节、盂兰节，一杯清酒，一盏寒灯(来供奉我，使我)不至于成为无人祭祀的饿鬼，那么我的愿望就完成了。²⁸妻子(与我)成婚两年，贤惠孝顺，素来为人所知，武功外甥好好替我善待她。²⁹也是(我和)武功的舅甥情谊啊！³⁰(我写得)语无伦次，(但都是我)将死前的心里话。悲痛啊！(心里太)悲痛了！³¹

27. 武功 name of Xia Shuji's 夏淑吉 son.

   甥 *n.* nephew. MdnC: 外甥 (*wài shēng*).

   器 *n.* talent. MdnC: 才幹 (*cái gàn* 才干). 大器 means "a person of great talents."

   盡 (尽 *jìn*) *adv.* all. MdnC: 都 (*dōu*).

   委 *v.* to entrust, trust. MdnC: 委托 (*wěi tuō*).

28. 寒食 (節) Cold Food (Festival), a traditional Chinese holiday that occurs one or two days before Tomb-Sweeping Day (*Qīng míng* 清明) in each lunar year.

   盂蘭 (節) Ghost (Festival), also known as Middle Moon (Festival) 中元 (節), is a traditional Buddhist festival that is held on July 15 in each lunar year.

   盞 (盏) measure word of lamp.

   若敖 (氏) a family clan of the Chu state in the Spring and Autumn period.

   若敖之鬼 refers to a family clan that has no descendants to perform sacrifices to the ancestors.

   願 (愿) *n.* will, wish. MdnC: 願望 (*yuàn wàng* 愿望).

   畢 (毕) *v.* to complete, finish. MdnC: 完成 (*wán chéng*).

29. 結褵 (结缡) *v.* to marry. MdnC: 成婚 (*chéng hūn*). 褵 (缡) means "a bridal veil."

   賢 (贤) *adj.* virtuous, good. MdnC: 賢惠 (*xián huì* 贤惠).

   孝 *adj.* filial. MdnC: 孝順 (*xiào shun* 孝顺).

   素 *adv.* normally, usually. MdnC: 平素 (*píng sù*).

   著 (*zhù*) *adj.* obvious, known.

   善待 *v.* to be kind to.

30. 渭陽 (阳) 情 an allusion to the poem "Weiyang" 渭陽 ("Wèi yáng") in the *Book of Poetry*, praising the bond between uncle and nephew 舅甥情誼 (*jiù shēng qíng yì* 舅甥情谊).

31. 倫 (伦) *n.* logic, order.

次 *n.* sequence, order.

將 (将 *jiāng*) *adv.* will, about to.

將死言善　a quotation of Confucius from chapter 8 泰伯 ("Tài Bó") of the *Analects*. "When a man is about to die, his words are good" 人之將死，其言也善.

人生孰無死，貴得死所耳。³² 父得爲忠
rén shēng shú wú sǐ　guì dé sǐ suǒ ěr　fù dé wéi zhōng

臣，子得爲孝子，含笑歸太虛，了我分內
chén　zǐ dé wéi xiào zǐ　hán xiào guī tài xū　liǎo wǒ fèn nèi

事。³³ 大道本無生，視身若敝屣，但爲氣所
shì　dà dào běn wú shēng　shì shēn ruò bì xǐ.　dàn wéi qì suǒ

激，緣悟天人理。³⁴ 惡夢十七年，報仇在來
jī　yuán wù tiān rén lǐ　è mèng shí qī nián　bào chóu zài lái

世。³⁵ 神遊天地間，可以無愧矣！³⁶
shì　shén yóu tiān dì jiān　kě yǐ wú kuì yǐ

《夏完淳集箋校》，上海：上海古籍出版社 (1991)，413–414.

谁的人生能没有死！可贵的是要死得其所。³² 父亲能够成为忠臣，儿子能够成为孝子，含着笑归天，了结我分内的事情。³³ 大道本来就是从无生发(再归于无，所以)我把自己的身体看成是破草鞋(一样的)。³⁴ 只是我被正气所激励，由此领悟到天人的道理。这十七年(象一场)恶梦，报仇只能等到来世。³⁵ 我的魂魄在天地之间游荡，可没有愧疚了！³⁶

32. 孰 *interrogative pron.* who? MdnC: 誰 (*shuí* 谁). See L4 Grammar Note 1.

貴 (贵) *adj.* valuable. MdnC: 可貴 (*kě guì* 可贵).

死所 it is a worthy death. MdnC: 死得其所 (*sǐ dé qí suǒ*).

33. 含 *v.* to contain. 含笑 means "to have a smile on one's face."

太虛 *n.* heaven.

了 (*liǎo*) *v.* to complete, finish. MdnC: 了結 (*liǎo jié* 了结).

分 (*fèn*) *n.* duty, assignment, job.

34. 視 (视) *v.* to regard, think.

敝 *adj.* tattered, ragged. MdnC: 破 (*pò*).

屣 *n.* straw sandals. MdnC: 草鞋 (*cǎo xié*).

35. 但 *adv.* only. MdnC: 只是 (*zhǐ shì*). See L31 Grammar Note 2.

爲 (为 *wéi*) *particle.* by. MdnC: 被 (*bèi*). See Grammar Note 3 ⑤

氣 (气) *n.* air. Here it means "righteousness" 正氣 (*zhèng qì* 正气).

激 *v.* to urge, encourage, impel. MdnC: 激勵 (*jī lì* 激励).

緣 (缘) *adv.* thereupon. MdnC: 由此 (*yóu cǐ*).

悟 *v.* to realize, comprehend. MdnC: 領悟 (*lǐng wù* 领悟).

天人 *n.* heaven and human.

理 *n.* principle. MdnC: 道理 (*dào lǐ*).

惡 (恶 *è*) 夢 (梦) *n.* nightmare.

報 (报) 仇 *v.* to avenge, revenge.

來 (来) 世 *n.* next life.

36. 神 *n.* spirit, soul. MdnC: 魂魄 (*hún pò*).
　　愧 *n.* regrets. MdnC: 愧疚 (*kuì jiù*).

語法注釋 Grammar Notes

1. 已　① *adv.* already. MdnC: 已經 (*yǐ jīng* 已经).

去年之舉，醇已自分必死，誰知不死，死於今日也！

　　[去年的举动，我已经料想到我必然要死的，谁知道却没有死，死在了今天。]

今之存者，已不逮矣。（L18）

　　[现在活着的人，都已经不及他们了。]

② *v.* to end, stop. MdnC: 停止 (*tíng zhǐ*), 完 (*wán*), 罷了 (*bà le* 罢了).

雖然，已矣。

　　[即使这样，罢了！]

距闉，有三月而後已。（L11）

　　[堆积攻城用的土山，又要三个月之后才能完。]

③ 而已/而已矣/則已 *ending particle.* nothing more. MdnC: 罷了 (*bà le* 罢了). See L11 Grammar Note 1 ②.

有一日中興再造，則廟食千秋，豈止麥飯豚蹄，不爲餒鬼而已哉？

　　[（如果）有一天（明朝）能够中兴再建，那么（我们）在庙中长久的享受祭祀，难道只是麦饭猪蹄，不至于成为饿鬼罢了吗？]

天下之亂物具此而已矣。(L12)

　　[天下的祸乱之事，都在这里罢了。]

2. 奈　*adv.* nothing can be done now that…. MdnC: 無奈 (*wú nài* 无奈).

奈天不佑我，鍾虐明朝。

　　[无奈上天不保佑我，集中（很多）灾难，加到了明朝之上。！]

3. 爲　Five uses of 爲 are explained in this book. In addition to the use below, see 爲① in L2
（为）　Grammar Note 6, 爲② in L7 Grammar Note 5, 爲③ in L9 Grammar Note 1, and 爲④ in L11 Grammar Note 4.

⑤ **wéi** *particle.* a passive voice indicator: by. MdnC: 被 (*bèi*).

立一不肖後，如西銘先生，爲人所詬笑……

　　[像西铭先生那样，立一个不肖子嗣，被人所诟骂笑话……]

Literary Analysis

1. Describe the tone of the letter. Do you think Xia Wanchun feels confident? Ambivalent? Justified? What makes you think so?
2. Xia Wanchun asserts that he is dying for a purpose. What does he consider the purpose of his death?

Do you agree that his death will achieve this purpose? Why or why not?

3. Analyze Xia Wanchun's relationships with his family members. Whom does he respect and seek to emulate? Whom does he tenderly love? About whom is he most concerned? Connect your observations to what you know about Confucian family structures.

☞ *HTRCProse*, chapter 15, "Ming and Qing Occasional Prose: Letters and Funerary Inscriptions."

—RHS

課後練習 Exercises

一 給加點字注音 Give the pinyin romanization for each dotted word.

1. 淳 (＿＿) 2. 齏 (＿＿) 3. 盂蘭 (＿＿, ＿＿) 4. 誅殛 (＿＿, ＿＿) 5. 門祚 (＿＿)
6. 荻 (＿＿) 7. 溘 (＿＿) 8. 餒鬼 (＿＿, ＿＿) 9. 頑嚚 (＿＿, ＿＿)

二 在括號中給句中加點的字注音，並選出正確的釋義 Give the pinyin romanization for each dotted word; then select the correct definition from the following list, and write it in the blank.

詬(诟)病　少　料想　興(兴)起　撫卹(抚恤)　**信服**　爲(为)……而死　要塞

1. 小信未孚（ **fú** ）　**信服**　2. 以身殉父 （ ）＿＿＿　3. 卹死榮生 （ ）＿＿＿
4. 一旅纔興 （ ）＿＿＿　5. 終鮮兄弟 （ ）＿＿＿　6. 自分必死 （ ）＿＿＿
7. 北塞之舉 （ ）＿＿＿　8. 詬笑 （ ）＿＿＿

三 選擇釋義並填空 Match each word in the left column with its correct definition in the middle column. Fill in each blank in the right column with an appropriate word from the left column.

謀謀劃(谋划)	胡説(说)	冤＿＿日深，艱辛＿＿盡。
酷＿＿	報答(报答)	致慈君＿＿迹於空門，生母寄生於別姓，一門漂泊，生不得相依，死不得相＿＿。
歷＿＿	安慰	大恩未＿＿，令人痛＿＿。
託＿＿	極(极)	立一不＿＿後，如西銘先生，爲人所詬笑，何如不立之爲＿＿耶？
問＿＿	更好	有一日中興再＿＿，則廟食千秋，豈止麥飯豚蹄，不爲餒鬼而已哉？若有＿＿言立後者，淳且與先文忠在冥冥誅殛頑嚚，決不肯捨！
酬＿＿	建立	相託之言，慎勿相＿＿。
絕＿＿	**謀劃(谋划)**	武功甥將來大＿＿，家事盡以委之。寒食盂蘭，一杯清酒，一盞寒燈，不至作若敖之鬼，則吾願＿＿矣。
肖＿＿	才干	
愈＿＿	托付	
造＿＿	經歷(经历)	
妄＿＿	完成	
器＿＿	相似	
負＿＿	慘(惨)痛	
畢＿＿	違(违)背	

四 請用給出的字填空 Fill in each blank with an appropriate word from the following list.

已　而已　焉　則(则)　之　何以　爲(为)　然

1. 菽水＿＿養，無一日＿＿。　　　2. 哀哀八口，＿＿ ＿＿爲生？雖＿＿，＿＿矣。
3. 有一日中興再造，＿＿廟食千秋，豈止麥飯豚蹄，不＿＿ 餒鬼＿＿ ＿＿哉？

五 爲加點字選擇正確釋義，並根據釋義來翻譯句子 Match each dotted word with its correct modern Chinese equivalent by circling the latter. Then translate each sentence into modern Chinese.

1. 又何間焉?　　　　　　　　　ⓐ 爲什麼(为什么)　b. 憑什麼(凭什么)　c. 多少

現代文翻譯：你又为什么要参与到这件事情里面？

＿＿＿＿＿＿＿＿＿＿＿＿＿＿＿＿＿＿＿＿

2. 不孝淳今日死矣，以身殉父，不得以身報母矣。　　a. 因爲(为)　b. 用　c. 來(来)

現代文翻譯：＿＿＿＿＿＿＿＿＿＿＿＿＿＿＿＿

3. 本圖復見天日，以報大仇，卹死榮生，告成黃土。　a. 使……榮耀(荣耀)　b. 茂盛　c. 光榮(荣)

現代文翻譯：＿＿＿＿＿＿＿＿＿＿＿＿＿＿＿＿

4. 去年之舉，淳已自分必死，誰知不死，死於今日也。　a. 已經(经)　b. 既然　c. 罷(罢)了

現代文翻譯：＿＿＿＿＿＿＿＿＿＿＿＿＿＿＿＿

5. 立一不肖後，如西銘先生，爲人所詬笑，何如不立之爲愈耶！　a. 做　b. 爲(为)了　c. 被

現代文翻譯：＿＿＿＿＿＿＿＿＿＿＿＿＿＿＿＿

6. 有一日中興再造，則廟食千秋，豈止麥飯豚蹄，不爲餒鬼而已哉！

　　　　　　　　　　　　　　a. 已經(经)　b. 既然　c. 罷(罢)了

現代文翻譯：＿＿＿＿＿＿＿＿＿＿＿＿＿＿＿＿

7. 新婦結褵二年，賢孝素著，武功甥爲我善待之。　　a. 替　b. 做　c. 被

現代文翻譯：＿＿＿＿＿＿＿＿＿＿＿＿＿＿＿＿

第二十二課

鄭燮《濰縣署中與舍弟墨第二書》

"Second Letter to My Younger Cousin Mo,
Written from My Official Residence in Wei County"
(Zheng Xie)

Introduction

Zheng Xie 鄭燮 (courtesy name Kerou 克柔; pseudonyms Banqiao 板橋 and Banqiao daoren 板橋道人; 1693–1766) achieved fame as a writer, calligrapher, and painter during the Kangxi, Yongzheng, and Qianlong reigns, and was one of the Eight Eccentrics of Yangzhou 揚州八怪 (*Yángzhōu bāguài* 扬州八怪).

    This letter is the second in a series of letters Zheng Xie wrote to his cousin Zheng Mo after Xie was appointed magistrate of Wei County in 1746 and entrusted the care of his son Zheng Lin to his cousin. Not wanting his son spoiled, Zheng Xie often wrote to Zheng Mo about how to teach him. This is one of the most famous Chinese family letters on parenting.

正文與簡體譯文 Text and Modern Chinese Translation

余五十二歲始得一子，豈有不愛之理！[1]
yú wǔ shí èr suì shǐ dé yì zǐ   qǐ yǒu bú ài zhī lǐ

然愛之必以其道，雖嬉戲頑耍，務令忠厚悱
rán ài zhī bì yǐ qí dào   suī xī xì wán shuǎ wù lìng zhōng hòu fěi

惻，毋爲刻急也。[2]
cè   wú wéi kè jí yě

我五十二岁才得到了一个儿子，难道会有不爱他的道理吗！[1]但是爱他必须要依据一定的规则，即使游戏玩耍，也务必使他忠厚，不要让他苛刻急躁。[2]

1. 始 *adv.* then, only then. MdnC: 才 (*cái*).
   豈 (岂) *interrogative particle.* MdnC: 難道 (*nán dào* 难道). See L8 Grammar Note 4.
   理 *n.* reason. MdnC: 道理 (*dào lǐ*).
2. 然 *conj.* however. MdnC: 但是 (*dàn shì*). See L5 Grammar Note 2 ①.
   以 *coverb.* by means of. MdnC: 依據 (*yī jù* 依据). See L2 Grammar Note 1 ②.
   道 *n.* way, principle. MdnC: 規則 (*guī zé* 规则).
   雖 (虽) *conj.* even though. MdnC: 即使 (*jí shǐ*). See L4 Grammar Note 6.
   嬉戲 (戏) *v.* to play. MdnC: 游戲 (*yóu xì* 游戏).
   務 (务) *v.* to be sure to, must, should. MdnC: 務必 (*wù bì* 务必).

令 *v.* to make. MdnC: 使 (*shǐ*). See Grammar Note 1.

忠厚 *n.* honest and generous.

悱惻 (恻) *adj.* sad, sorrowful.

毋 *adv.* don't. MdnC: 不要 (*bú yào*).

刻 *adj.* harsh, mean. MdnC: 苛刻 (*kē kè*).

急 *adj.* anxious, impatient. MdnC: 急躁 (*jí zào*).

平生最不喜籠中養鳥，我圖娛悦，彼在
píng shēng zuì bù xǐ lóng zhōng yǎng niǎo wǒ tú yú yuè   bǐ zài

因牢，何情何理，而必屈物之性以適吾性
qiú láo   hé qíng hé lǐ   ér bì qū wù zhī xìng yǐ shì wú xìng

乎！³至於髮系蜻蜓，綫縛螃蟹，爲小兒頑
hū   zhì yú fà jì qīng tíng   xiàn fù páng xiè   wéi xiǎo ér wán

具，不過一時片刻便摺拉而死。⁴夫天地生
jù   bú guò yī shí piàn kè biàn zhé lā ér sǐ   fú tiān dì shēng

物，化育劬勞，一蟻一蟲，皆本陰陽五行之
wù   huà yù qú láo   yì yǐ yì chóng   jiē běn yīn yáng wǔ xíng zhī

氣絪縕而出。⁵上帝亦心心愛念。而萬物之性
qì yīn yūn ér chū   shàng dì yì xīn xīn ài niàn   ér wàn wù zhī xìng

人爲貴，吾輩竟不能體天之心以爲心，萬物
rén wéi guì   wú bèi jìng bù néng tǐ tiān zhī xīn yǐ wéi xīn   wàn wù

將何所托命乎？⁶蛇蚖、蜈蚣、豺狼、虎豹，
jiāng hé suǒ tuō mìng hū   shé wán   wú gōng   chái láng   hǔ bào

蟲之最毒者也，然天既生之，我何得而殺
chóng zhī zuì dú zhě yě   rán tiān jì shēng zhī   wǒ hé dé ér shā

之？⁷若必欲盡殺，天地又何必生？亦惟驅之
zhī   ruò bì yù jìn shā   tiān dì yòu hé bì shēng   yì wéi qū zhī

使遠，避之使不相害而已。⁸蜘蛛結網，於人
shǐ yuǎn   bì zhī shǐ bù xiāng hài ér yǐ   zhī zhū jié wǎng   yú rén

何罪，或謂其夜間咒月，令人墙傾壁倒，遂
hé zuì   huò wèi qí yè jiān zhòu yuè   lìng rén qiáng qīng bì dǎo   suì

擊殺無遺。⁹此等說話，出於何經何典，而遂
jī shā wú yí   cǐ děng shuō huà   chū yú hé jīng hé diǎn   ér suì

(我)平生最不喜欢用笼子养鸟。我谋求(自己)娱悦，(可)鸟在牢笼里。怎样的人情道理，必须使它屈服来适应我的性情！³至于用头发系蜻蜓，用线捆螃蟹，做成小孩子的玩具，不过一会儿，(蜻蜓螃蟹)就会被折断而死。⁴天地万物，都是辛苦养育的。一只蚂蚁、一只小虫，都是从阴阳五行之气生成而来的。⁵上天也是一心爱念(万物)。而万物之中人最为宝贵，我们竟然不能体谅上天的用心，把它当作自己的心意，万物怎能把生命托付(给我们)啊！⁶毒蛇、蜈蚣、豺狼、虎豹、是动物中最毒的。但上天既然把它们生出来，我为什么要杀了它们呢？⁷如果一定要全都杀掉，天地又何必把它们生出来！也只是把它们驱赶走，使它们远离，躲避开，使(它们)不(与人)互相伤害罢了！⁸蜘蛛结网，对人来说，有什么罪过呢！有人说它夜间诅咒月亮，让墙壁倾斜倒

以此殘物之命，可乎哉？可乎哉？ [10]
yǐ cǐ cán wù zhī mìng　kě hū zāi　kě hū zāi

下，于是把它们全部击杀。[9]这样的言论，出自什么经典？而据此来<u>残害</u>其他生物的性命，可以吗？可以吗？ [10]

3. 平生 *n.* all one's life.

籠 (笼) *n.* cage.

圖 (图) *v.* to seek. MdnC: 謀求 (*móu qiú* 谋求).

娛悅 (娱悦) *v.* to entertain, amuse.

彼 *demonstrative pron.* that. See L14 Grammar Note 2 ①. Here it refers to birds in a cage.

囚牢 *n.* jail, prison. Here it refers to a birdcage.

何 *interrogative pron.* what? MdnC: 什麼 (*shén me* 什么). See L1 Grammar Note 3 ①.

情 *n.* reason. MdnC: 人情 (*rén qíng*).

屈 *v.* to surrender. MdnC: 屈服 (*qū fú*). Here it used as a causative verb, 使 (*shǐ*)······屈服 (*qū fú*), meaning "to make … surrender." See L7 Grammar Note 1 ①.

性 *n.* nature. MdnC: 本性 (*běn xìng*).

以 *conj.* in order to. MdnC: 來 (*lái* 来). See L2 Grammar Note 1 ③.

適 (适) *v.* to adapt, adjust, fit. MdnC: 適應 (*shì yìng* 适应).

4. 髮 (发) *n.* hair. MdnC: 頭髮 (*tóu fà* 头发).

系 (jì) *v.* to bind, tie.

蜻蜓 *n.* dragonfly.

綫 (线) *n.* thread.

縛 (缚) *v.* to tie. MdnC: 捆 (*kǔn*).

螃蟹 *n.* crab.

頑 (顽) 具 *n.* toys. MdnC: 玩具 (*wán jù*).

一時 (时) *n.* a short period, a short moment. MdnC: 一會兒 (*yí huìr* 一会儿).

片刻 *n.* a short moment.

摺拉 *v.* to break off. MdnC: 折斷 (*zhé duàn* 折断).

5. 夫 (fú) *initial particle.* no meaning in itself. See L2 Grammar Note 4 ①.

生物 *n.* living creatures.

化育 *v.* to generate (living creatures).

劬 *adj.* hardworking. MdnC: 勤勞 (*qín láo* 勤劳).

蟻 (蚁) *n.* ant. MdnC: 螞蟻 (*mǎ yǐ* 蚂蚁).

蟲 (虫) *n.* bug, insect.

陰陽 (阴阳) yin and yang, the two opposite yet complementary cosmic principles.

五行 (xíng) five elements.

絪縕 (絪缊) the state of interaction between yin and yang.

6. 上帝 *n.* god. Here it refers to god on high 上天 (*shàng tiān*).

貴 (贵) *adj.* valuable. MdnC: 寶貴 (*bǎo guì* 宝贵).

輩 (辈) *n.* generation.

竟 *adv.* unexpectedly, to one's surprise. MdnC: 竟然 (*jìng rán*).

體 (体) *v.* to understand, be considerate of. MdnC: 體諒 (*tǐ liàng* 体谅).

心 *n.* intention, motivation. MdnC: 用心 (*yòng xīn*).

托 *v.* to entrust. MdnC: 托付 (*tuō fù*).

7. 蛇 *n.* snake.

蚖 *n.* a poisonous snake.

蜈蚣 *n.* centipede.

豺 *n.* jackal.

狼 *n.* wolf.

虎 *n.* tiger.

豹 *n.* leopard.

蟲 (虫) *n.* animal. MdnC: 動物 (*dòng wù* 动物).

8. 盡 (尽) *adv.* totally, thoroughly. MdnC: 都 (*dōu*).

惟 *adv.* only. MdnC: 只是 (*zhǐ shì*). See Grammar Note 2 ②.

驅 (驱) *v.* to expel, drive away. MdnC: 驅趕 (*qū gǎn* 驱赶).

避 *v.* to avoid, escape. MdnC: 躲避 (*duǒ bì*).

9. 蜘蛛 *n.* spider.

結 (结) *v.* to knot.

網 (网) *n.* web, net.

罪 *n.* crime, guilt. MdnC: 罪過 (*zuì guò* 罪过).

或 *indefinite pron.* someone. MdnC: 有人 (*yǒu rén*). See L6 Grammar Note 4 ①.

咒 *v.* to curse. MdnC: 詛咒 (*zǔ zhòu* 诅咒).

傾 (倾) *v.* to incline, lean. MdnC: 傾斜 (*qīng xié* 倾斜).

倒 (倒) *v.* to fall over, collapse. MdnC: 倒下 (*dǎo xià*).

遂 *conj.* then, consequently. MdnC: 於是 (*yú shì* 于是).

擊殺 (击杀) *v.* to attack and kill.

遺 (遗) *v.* to omit, neglect. MdnC: 遺漏 (*yí lòu* 遗漏).

10. 說話 (说话) *v.* to speak. Here it refers to the talk about spiders. MdnC: 言論 (*yán lùn* 言论).

經 (经) *n.* classics.

典 *n.* canon.

殘 (残) *v.* to injure, kill. MdnC: 殘害 (*cán hài* 残害).

我不在家，兒子便是你管束。要須長其
wǒ bú zài jiā　　ér zi biàn shì nǐ guǎn shù　　yào xū zhǎng qí

忠厚之情，驅其殘忍之性，不得以爲猶子而
zhōng hòu zhī qíng qū qí cán rěn zhī xìng　　bù dé yǐ wéi yóu zǐ　ér

姑縱惜也。¹¹ 家人兒女，總是天地間一般人，
gū zòng xī yě　　jiā rén ér nǚ　　zǒng shì tiān dì jiān yì bān rén

當一般愛惜，不可使吾兒凌虐他。¹² 凡魚飧
dāng yì bān ài xī　　bù kě shǐ wú ér líng nüè tā　　fán yú sūn

果餅，宜均分散給，大家歡嬉跳躍。¹³ 若吾
guǒ bǐng　　yí jūn fēn sàn gěi　　dà jiā huān xī tiào yuè　　ruò wú

我不在家，儿子就由你来管束。必须要增长他忠厚的性情，驱离他残忍的性情，不能以为他是你侄子，就姑息放纵怜惜他。¹¹ 仆人子女，总是天地间一样的人，应当一样爱惜他们，不可以让我儿子欺凌虐待他。¹² 凡是鱼肉、饭食、水果、糕饼，应该平均分给(大家)，让大家都开心得跳起来。¹³ 如果我

兒坐食好物， 令家人子遠立而望， 不得一沾
ér zuò shí hǎo wù　　lìng jiā rén zǐ yuǎn lì ér wàng　　bù dé yì zhān

唇齒； 其父母見而憐之， 無可如何， 呼之
chún chǐ　　qí fù mǔ jiàn ér lián zhī　　wú kě rú hé　　hū zhī

使去， 豈非割心剜肉乎！ [14]
shǐ qù　　qǐ fēi gē xīn wān ròu hū

儿子坐着吃好东西，让仆人的孩子远远站着，望（着他吃，自己）不能够吃，他的父母见到了怜惜他，却没办法怎么样（我儿子），叫他让他离开，难道这不是割人家的心头的肉吗？[14]

11. 管束 v. to discipline.
須 (须) v. must, have to. MdnC: 必須 (bì xū 必须).
長 (长 zhǎng) v. to grow. Here is it used as a causative verb, 使……長, meaning "to increase" 增長 (zēng zhǎng 增长). See L7 Grammar Note 1 ①.
殘 (残) 忍 adj. cruel, ruthless.
猶 (犹) 子 n. nephew. MdnC: 侄子 (zhí zi).
姑 v. to tolerate. MdnC: 姑息 (gū xī).
縱 (纵) v. to indulge. MdnC: 放縱 (fàng zòng 放纵).
惜 v. to cherish. MdnC: 憐惜 (lián xī 怜惜).

12. 家人 n. family members. Here it refers to servants 僕人 (pú rén 仆人).
凌 v. to bully and humiliate. MdnC: 欺凌 (qī líng).
虐 v. to abuse, mistreat. MdnC: 虐待 (nüè dài).

13. 凡 adv. in general, overall. MdnC: 凡是 (fán shì). See L10 Grammar Note 4.
飧 n. cooked food, supper. MdnC: 飯食 (fàn shí 饭食).
宜 v. should, ought to. MdnC: 應該 (yīng gāi 应该).
均 adj. even, equal. MdnC: 平均 (píng jūn).

14. 沾 v. to touch.
唇齒 (齿) n. lip and tooth. 一沾唇齒 (齿) means "to eat."
如何 how is it? MdnC: 怎麼樣 (zěn me yàng 怎么样). See L6 Grammar Note 3 ④.
呼 v. to call. MdnC: 叫 (jiào).
去 v. to leave. MdnC: 離開 (lí kāi 离开).
豈 (岂) interrogative particle. MdnC: 難道 (nán dào 难道). See L8 Grammar Note 4.
割 v. to cut.
剜 v. to cut out, pick out.

夫讀書中舉中進士作官， 此是小事， 第一
fú dú shū zhòng jǔ zhòng jìn shì zuò guān　cǐ shì xiǎo shì　　dì yī

要明理作個好人。 [15] 可將此書讀與郭嫂、 饒嫂
yào míng lǐ zuò gè hǎo rén　　kě jiāng cǐ shū dú yǔ guō sǎo　　ráo sǎo

聽， 使二婦人知愛子之道在此不在彼也。 [16]
tīng　　shǐ èr fù rén zhī ài zǐ zhī dào zài cǐ bú zài bǐ yě

（一个人）读书，考中举人，考中进士，做官，这都是小事，第一要明白事理，做个好人。[15] 可以将这封书信读给（你）郭嫂和饶嫂听，使她们两人知道爱儿子的道理在这里不在那里。[16]

郑燮《鄭板橋文集》，成都：巴蜀書社 (1997), 14–15.

15. 中 (zhòng) *v.* to hit (the target). MdnC: 考中 (*kǎo zhòng*).

　　舉 (举) or 擧 (举) 人 a successful candidate in the imperial examinations at the provincial level in the Ming and Qing dynasties.

　　進 (进) 士 Presented Scholar, the highest degree awarded in the imperial examinations.

16. 書 (书) *n.* letter. MdnC: 書信 (*shū xìn* 书信).

　　嫂 *n.* older brother's wife, sister-in-law.

　　彼 *pron.* used with 此 to make a contrast between two ways of taking care of children. 此 refers to "要明理作个好人," while 彼 refers to previous actions used to take care of children. See L14 Grammar Note 2 ②.

語法注釋 Grammar Notes

1. 令　　*v.* to make, cause. 令 and 使 are used to make a causative structure. MdnC: 使 (*shǐ*), 讓 (*ràng* 让).　See L7 Grammar Note 1 on causative construction.

　　　　　雖嬉戲玩耍，務令忠厚悱惻，毋爲刻急也。

　　　　　[即使游戏玩耍，务必使（他）不如忠厚，不要让他苛刻急躁。]

　　　　　或謂其夜間咒月，令人墻傾壁倒，遂擊殺無遺。

　　　　　[有人说它夜间诅咒月亮，让人家的墙壁倾斜倒下，于是击杀它们，没有遗漏。]

2. 惟　　Two uses of 惟/唯 are explained in this book.　In addition to the use below, see 惟/唯 ① in
/唯　　L2 Grammar Note 7.

　　　　　② *adv.* only. MdnC: 只是 (*zhǐ shì*).

　　　　　亦惟驅之使遠，避之使不相害而已。

　　　　　[也只是把他们驱赶走，使它们远离，躲避开，使（它们）不（与人）互相伤害罢了！]

Literary Analysis

1. What values do you think the letter is trying to instill? It ends by asserting that the most important thing is "to be a good person." What does Zheng Xie mean by this? In his opinion, are human beings born good? Or must they become good through a process of education?

2. The letter addresses several hierarchical relationships: between adults and children, between human beings and animals, and between masters and servants. In each case, what are the ethical responsibilities of those in power?

3. Zheng Xie suggests that hierarchical relationships can go awry because of either cruelty or excessive leniency. What are the risks of each?

　　☞ *HTRCProse*, chapter 15, "Ming and Qing Occasional Prose: Letters and Funerary Inscriptions."

—RHS

課後練習 Exercises

一　給加點字注音　Give the pinyin romanization for each dotted word.

1. 蟻（＿＿＿）　2. 蚖（＿＿＿）　3. 絪縕（＿＿＿, ＿＿＿）　4. 蜈蚣（＿＿＿, ＿＿＿）

5. 豺（＿＿＿）　6. 饒（＿＿＿）　7. 悱惻（＿＿＿, ＿＿＿）　8. 剟　（＿＿＿）

二　在括號中給句中加點的字注音，並選出正確的釋義　Give the pinyin romanization for each dotted word; then select the correct definition from the following list, and write it in the blank.

勤勞(劳)　折斷(断)　詛(诅)咒　不要　飯(饭)食　**信服**　驅趕(驱赶)　務(务)必

1. 小信未孚　　（ fú ）　**信服**　　　2. 務令忠厚悱惻　　（　）＿＿＿＿＿＿

3. 毋爲刻急　　　　（　）＿＿＿＿＿　4. 化育劬勞　　　　（　）＿＿＿＿＿＿

5. 摺拉而死　　　　（　）＿＿＿＿＿　6. 或謂其夜間咒月　（　）＿＿＿＿＿＿

7. 魚飧果餅　　　　（　）＿＿＿＿＿　8. 驅之使遠　　　　（　）＿＿＿＿＿＿

三　選擇釋義並填空　Match each word in the left column with its correct definition in the middle column. Fill in each blank in the right column with an appropriate word from the left column.

謀謀劃(谋划)	急躁	然愛之必以其＿＿＿，雖嬉戲頑耍，務令忠厚悱惻，毋爲＿＿＿＿也。
道＿＿＿＿	系住	
刻＿＿＿＿	罪過(过)	至於髮＿＿＿蜻蜓，綫＿＿＿螃蟹，爲小兒頑具，不過一時片刻便摺拉而死。
急＿＿＿＿	**謀劃(谋划)**	
系＿＿＿＿	遺(遗)漏	
縛＿＿＿＿	姑息	蜘蛛結網，於人何＿＿＿，或謂其夜間咒月，令人墙傾壁倒，遂擊殺無＿＿＿。
罪＿＿＿＿	規則(规则)	
遺＿＿＿＿	放縱(纵)	要須長其忠厚之情，驅其殘忍之性，不得以爲猶子而＿＿＿＿＿惜也。
姑＿＿＿＿	苛刻	
縱＿＿＿＿	捆住	

四　請用給出的字填空　Fill in each blank with an appropriate word from the following list (some words may be used more than once).

惟　令　豈(岂)　而已　然　彼　以　爲(为)　何

1. 余五十二歲始得一子，＿＿＿有不愛之理！＿＿＿愛之必＿＿＿其道，雖嬉戲頑耍，務＿＿＿忠厚悱惻，毋＿＿＿刻急也。

2. 平生最不喜籠中養鳥，我圖娛悅，＿＿＿在囚牢，＿＿＿情＿＿＿理，而必屈物之性以適吾性乎！

3. 亦＿＿＿驅之使遠，避之使不相害＿＿＿＿＿。

4. 可將此信讀與郭嫂、饒嫂聽，使二婦人知愛子之道在此不在＿＿＿也。

五 爲加點字選擇正確釋義，並根據釋義來翻譯句子 Match each dotted word with its correct modern Chinese equivalent by circling the latter. Then translate each sentence into modern Chinese.

1. 又何間焉？　　　　　　　　　　　　　　　ⓐ爲什麽（为什么）b.憑什麽（凭什么）c.多少

现代文翻译：你又为什么要参与到这件事情里面？

＿＿＿＿＿＿＿＿＿＿＿＿＿＿＿＿＿＿＿＿＿＿＿＿＿＿＿＿＿＿

2. 平生最不喜籠中養鳥，我圖娛樂，彼在囚牢，何情何理，而必屈物之性以適吾性乎！

　　　　　　　　　　　　　　　　　　　　a. 屈服　b. 使……屈服　c. 委屈

现代文翻译：＿＿＿＿＿＿＿＿＿＿＿＿＿＿＿＿＿＿＿＿＿＿＿＿＿＿

3. 然天既生之，我何得而殺之？　　　　　　　　a. 但是　b. 所以　c. 自然

现代文翻译：＿＿＿＿＿＿＿＿＿＿＿＿＿＿＿＿＿＿＿＿＿＿＿＿＿＿

4. 亦惟驅之使遠，避之使不相害而已。　　　　　a. 但是　b. 只是　c. 難（难）道

现代文翻译：＿＿＿＿＿＿＿＿＿＿＿＿＿＿＿＿＿＿＿＿＿＿＿＿＿＿

5. 蜘蛛結網，於人何罪，或謂其夜間咒月，令人墙傾壁倒，遂擊殺無遺。

　　　　　　　　　　　　　　　　　　　　　　a. 使　b. 命令　c. 下令

现代文翻译：＿＿＿＿＿＿＿＿＿＿＿＿＿＿＿＿＿＿＿＿＿＿＿＿＿＿

6. 凡魚飧果餅，宜均分散給，大家歡嬉跳躍。　　a. 平凡　b. 總（总）共　c. 凡是

现代文翻译：＿＿＿＿＿＿＿＿＿＿＿＿＿＿＿＿＿＿＿＿＿＿＿＿＿＿

7. 可將此信讀與郭嫂、饒嫂聽，使二婦人知愛子之道在此不在彼也。

　　　　　　　　　　　　　　　　　　　　　　a. 他　b. 那里　c. 饒（饶）嫂

现代文翻译：＿＿＿＿＿＿＿＿＿＿＿＿＿＿＿＿＿＿＿＿＿＿＿＿＿＿

單元練習

Unit Exercises

一、辨析加點字在不同句中注音和釋義的異同 Give the pinyin romanization for each dotted word, and then write in its correct definition.

1. 鄙　肉食者鄙，未能遠謀。　　　　　　（ **bǐ** ）<u>目光短淺</u>

　　　越國以鄙遠，君知其難也。　　　　　（　　）_____

2. 處　昔日遊處，行則連輿，止則接席。　（　　）_____

　　　引入，微指左公處。　　　　　　　　（　　）_____

3. 更　光武言年三十餘，在兵中十歲，所更非一。（　　）_____

　　　縣之吏更召巫師善呪術者守赤。　　　（　　）_____

4. 稱　今觀其文章……，稱其氣之小大。　（　　）_____

　　　君子疾沒世而名不稱焉？　　　　　　（　　）_____

5. 觀　恣觀終南、嵩、華之高。　　　　　（　　）_____

　　　求天下奇聞壯觀。　　　　　　　　　（　　）_____

6. 召　入則周公、召公，出則方叔、召虎。（　　）_____

　　　縣之吏更召巫師善呪術者守赤。　　　（　　）_____

7. 分　淳已自分必死。　　　　　　　　　（　　）_____

　　　周與胡蝶，則必有分矣。　　　　　　（　　）_____

8. 沒　恐遂汩沒，故決然捨去。　　　　　（　　）_____

　　　君子疾沒世而名不稱焉？　　　　　　（　　）_____

二、用給出的字填空，並選擇正確的釋義 Fill in the blanks with words from list A, and then write in their modern Chinese equivalents from list B.

A. Words for Filling the Blanks　　　　　　B. Modern Chinese Equivalents

憚	塞	殘	娛	告		借	屈尊	近來(来)	殘(残)害	通曉(晓)
恣	通	頃	避	祚		欺凌	躲避	福氣(气)	盡(尽)情	報(报)告
支	凌	辱	**鄙**	假		要塞	承受	娛樂(娱乐)	**目光短淺**	忌憚(惮)

1. 肉食者 ___鄙___，未能遠謀。　[**目光短淺**]　　2. _____撰其遺文，都爲一集。　[　　　　]

3. 思何可_____。 [   ]   4. _____日月之光。 [   ]

5. 頃何以自_____? [   ]   6. _____觀終南、嵩、華之高。 [   ]

7. 四夷之所_____以不敢發。 [   ]   8. 轍年少，未能_____習吏事。 [   ]

9. 卹死榮生，_____成黃土。 [   ]   10. 太尉苟以爲可教而_____教之。 [   ]

11. 門_____衰薄，終鮮兄弟。 [   ]   12. 淳且與先文忠爲北_____之舉。 [   ]

13. 遂以此_____物之命。 [   ]   14. 不可使吾兒_____虐他。 [   ]

15. _____之使不相害而已。 [   ]

三、給加點字選擇正確的釋義，並選出與加點字用法相同的句子 Circle the letter of the correct definition (a, b, c, or d) for the dotted word in each boldfaced sentence. Then circle the letter of the sentence (A, B, C, or D) that employs the dotted word in the same way as the boldfaced sentence.

1. 臣之妻私臣   a. 這(这)件事情 b. 他 (c) 的 d. 他們
   A. 夫晉，何厭之有？   B. 不闕秦，將焉取之？
   C. 肉食者謀之，又何間焉？   (D) 能面刺寡人之過者，受上賞。

2. 美志不遂，良可痛惜。   a. 確實(确实) b. 好 c. 賢(贤)良 d. 丈夫
   A. 良人者，所仰望而終身也。   B. 與其妾訕其良人。
   C. 古人思炳燭夜遊，良有以也。   D. 吾將瞷良人之所之也。

3. 立一不肖後，如西銘先生，爲人所詬笑。 a. 認爲(认为) b. 做 c. 是 d. 被
   A. 但爲氣所激，緣悟天人理   B. 以爲文者氣之所形
   C. 淳且與先文忠爲北塞之舉   D. 此子爲不朽矣。

4. 雖然，已矣。   a. 已經(经) b. 罷了 c. 所以 d. 不得已
   A. 今之存者，已不逮矣。   B. 天下之亂物具此而已矣。
   C. 年行已長大。   D. 去年之舉，淳已自分必死。

5. 務令忠厚悱惻。   a. 命令 b. 使 c. 指令 d. 小令
   A. 令初下，群臣進諫。   B. 慢令致期謂之賊。
   C. 乃下令。   D. 或謂其夜間咒月，令人墻傾壁倒。

6. 然文不可以學而能。   a. 而且 b. 但是 c. 因此 d. 的樣(样)子
   A. 德璉常斐然有述作之意。   B. 慨然想見古之豪傑。
   C. 當此之時，忽然不自知樂也。   D. 然恐吾與足下不及見也。

7. 太尉以才略冠天下。   a. 憑藉(凭借) b. 來(来) c. 原因 d. 認爲(认为)
   A. 天下之所恃以無憂。   B. 古人思炳燭夜遊，良有以也。

C. 觀古今文人……鮮能以名節自立。　　D. 其才學足以著書。

四、閱讀下面的段落，選擇正確的釋義 Read the following passage, and select the correct definition for each dotted word in the following list.

《答李翊書》節選
韓愈

　　六月二十六日，愈白：李生足下：生之書辭甚高，而其問何下而恭也！能如是，誰不欲告生以其道。道德之歸也有日矣，況其外之文乎？抑愈所謂望孔子之門牆而不入于其宮者，焉足以知是且非邪？雖然，不可不爲生言之。……

　　有志乎古者希矣！志乎古必遺乎今。吾誠樂而悲之。亟稱其人，所以勸之，非敢褒其可褒而貶其可貶也。問於愈者多矣，念生之言不志乎利，聊相爲言之。愈白。

《韓昌黎文集校注》，上海：上海古籍出版社 (1986), 169–171.

韓愈 or 愈 (768–824).　　李翊 a person's name.
下 *adj.* humble.　　恭 *adj.* courteous.　　亟 (jí) *adv.* urgently.
褒 *v.* to praise.　　貶 (贬) *v.* to criticize.　　聊 *adv.* for the time being.

1. 愈白。　　　　　　　　　a. 白色　　　　b. 説(凭借)　　c. 明白
2. 生之書辭甚高。　　　　　a. 文辭(辞)　　b. 告別　　　　c. 躲開(开)
3. 能如是。　　　　　　　　a. 比　　　　　b. 如果　　　　c. 像
4. 況其外之文乎？　　　　　a. 情況(况)　　b. 況(况)且　　c. 比如
5. 抑愈所谓……　　　　　　a. 抑制　　　　b. 壓(压)抑　　c. 抑或
6. 焉足以知是且非邪？　　　a. 怎麽(么)　　b. 難(难)道　　c. 因此
7. 焉足以知是且非邪？　　　a. 將要　　　　b. 和　　　　　c. 姑且
8. 有志乎古者希矣。　　　　a. 少　　　　　b. 希望　　　　c. 珍惜
9. 吾誠樂而悲之。　　　　　a. 誠實(诚实)　b. 確實(确实)　c. 誠懇(诚恳)
10. 念生之言不志乎利。　　　a. 想　　　　　b. 讀(读)　　　c. 念頭(头)

五、將下列句子翻譯成現代漢語 Translate the following sentences into modern Chinese.

1. 每至觴酌流行，絲竹並奏，酒酣耳熱，仰而賦詩，當此之時，忽然不自知樂也。

現代文翻译：_____

2. 昔伯牙絕絃於鐘期，仲尼覆醢於子路，痛知音之難遇，傷門人之莫逮。

現代文翻译：＿＿＿＿＿＿＿＿＿＿＿＿＿＿＿＿＿＿＿＿＿＿＿＿＿＿＿

3. 以犬羊之質，服虎豹之文，無衆星之明，假日月之光，動見瞻觀，何時易乎？

現代文翻译：＿＿＿＿＿＿＿＿＿＿＿＿＿＿＿＿＿＿＿＿＿＿＿＿＿＿＿

4. 恐遂泪沒，故決然捨去，求天下奇聞壯觀，以知天地之廣大。

現代文翻译：＿＿＿＿＿＿＿＿＿＿＿＿＿＿＿＿＿＿＿＿＿＿＿＿＿＿＿

5. 故願得觀賢人之光耀，聞一言以自壯，然後可以盡天下之大觀而無憾者矣。

現代文翻译：＿＿＿＿＿＿＿＿＿＿＿＿＿＿＿＿＿＿＿＿＿＿＿＿＿＿＿

6. 奈天不佑我，鍾虐明朝。一旅纔興，便成齏粉。

現代文翻译：＿＿＿＿＿＿＿＿＿＿＿＿＿＿＿＿＿＿＿＿＿＿＿＿＿＿＿

7. 嗚呼！大造茫茫，總歸無後，有一日中興再造，則廟食千秋，豈止麥飯豚蹄，不爲餒鬼而已哉？

現代文翻译：＿＿＿＿＿＿＿＿＿＿＿＿＿＿＿＿＿＿＿＿＿＿＿＿＿＿＿

8. 而萬物之性人爲貴，吾輩竟不能體天之心以爲心，萬物將何所托命乎？

現代文翻译：＿＿＿＿＿＿＿＿＿＿＿＿＿＿＿＿＿＿＿＿＿＿＿＿＿＿＿

王羲之《蘭亭集序》

"Preface to the Poems of the Orchid Pavilion Gathering" (Wang Xizhi)

Introduction

The "Preface to the Poems of the Orchid Pavilion Gathering" is a literary and calligraphic work by the eminent Eastern Jin calligrapher Wang Xizhi 王羲之 (courtesy name Yishao 逸少；303–361), a native of Langya 琅琊 (present-day Linyi 臨沂, Shandong Province). He is revered as "the sage of calligraphy" for his great achievements in all major scripts—clerical, running, and cursive.

In early March 353, Wang Xizhi, Xie An 謝安 (320–385), and other literati gathered at the Lanting (Orchid Pavilion) to drink wine and write poems. In his preface to the collection of poems composed on that occasion, Wang describes the scenic Lanting landscape and the banquet's delights before succumbing to melancholia over the impermanence of life.

This preface is acclaimed as a prose masterpiece with its lucid and spontaneous style, enhanced by parallel phrasing and subtle allusions.

正文與簡體譯文 Text and Modern Chinese Translation

永和九年， 歲在癸丑， 暮春之初， 會a
yǒng hé jiǔ nián　　suì zài guǐ chǒu　mù chūn zhī chū　huì

于會b稽山陰之蘭亭， 脩禊事也。[1]羣賢畢
yú kuài　jī shān yīn zhī lán tíng　xiū xì shì yě　　qún xián bì

至， 少長咸集。[2]此地有崇山峻領， 茂林脩
zhì　　shào zhǎng xián jí　cǐ dì yǒu chóng shān jùn lǐng　mào lín xiū

竹； 又有清流激湍， 暎帶左右， 引以爲流
zhú　　yòu yǒu qīng liú jī tuān　yìng dài zuǒ yòu　　yǐn yǐ wéi liú

觴曲水。[3]列坐其次， 雖無絲竹管弦之盛，
shāng qū shuǐ　liè zuò qí cì　　suī wú sī zhú guǎn xián zhī shèng

一觴一詠， 亦足以暢敍幽情。[4]
yì shāng yì yǒng　　yì zú yǐ chàng xù yōu qíng

晋穆帝永和九年，即癸丑这一年，三月初，（我们）会集在会稽山北面的兰亭做禊事。[1]诸多贤人全到了，年少的年长的都聚集（在这里）。[2]这个地方有高山峻岭，有茂密的树林，高高的竹子；又有清澈的小溪，急速流动的湍流，辉映着左右四周，引来（溪水）作为漂浮酒杯的曲水。[3]（大家）排列坐在曲水的旁边，即使没有各种乐器（演奏的）盛况，一边喝酒一边吟咏作诗，也是足以来尽情述说深藏的情怀的！[4]

1. 永和 one of the reign titles 年號 (*nián hào* 年号) of Emperor Mu of Jin 晉穆帝 (r. 345–361). 永和 is from 345 to 356. 永和九年 is 353.

   歲 (岁) *n.* year.

   癸丑 the year 353. See L2 Culture Note 1 for the traditional Chinese calendrical system 天干地支.

   暮 *adj.* late. 暮春 means "late spring or lunar March."

   會ₐ (会 *huì*) *v.* to meet. MdnC: 會集 (*huì jí* 会集).

   會_b (会 *kuài*) 稽山 in the south of present-day Shaoxing 紹興, Zhejiang Province.

   陰 (阴) *n.* the north side of a mountain or the south side of a river.

   脩 (修) *v.* to perform (the ceremony).

   禊 *n.* used in the sense of 禊 (*xì*), a ceremony of purification in each spring or autumn season.

2. 羣 (群) *adj.* many. MdnC: 諸多 (*zhū duō* 诸多).

   賢 (贤) *n.* virtuous people. MdnC: 賢人 (*xián rén* 贤人).

   畢 (毕) *adv.* completely. MdnC: 全 (*quán*).

   至 *v.* to arrive. MdnC: 到 (*dào*).

   少 (*shào*) *n.* the young. MdnC: 少年 (*shào nián*).

   長 (长 *zhǎng*) *n.* the old. MdnC: 長者 (*zhǎng zhě*).

   咸 *adv.* all. MdnC: 都 (*dōu*).

   集 *v.* to gather. MdnC: 聚集 (*jù jí*).

3. 崇 *adj.* high. MdnC: 高 (*gāo*).

   峻 *adj.* steep and high. MdnC: 峻峭 (*jùn qiào*).

   領 (领) *v.* to lead. Here it is used as a noun in the sense of 嶺 (*lǐng* 岭), meaning "mountains" 山嶺 (*shān lǐng* 山岭).

   茂 *adj.* dense, luxuriant. MdnC: 茂密 (*mào mì*).

   林 *n.* woods, forest. MdnC: 樹林 (*shù lín* 树林).

   脩 (修) *adj.* tall. MdnC: 高 (*gāo*).

   竹 *n.* bamboo.

   清 *adj.* clear. MdnC: 清澈 (*qīng chè*).

   流 *v.* to flow. Here it means "stream" 小溪 (*xiǎo xī*).

   激 *v.* to dash, referring to water. Here it is used as an adjective, meaning "running or rapid" 急 (*jí*).

   湍 *adj.* rapidly running (water). Here it is used to mean "rapids" 湍流 (*tuān liú*).

   暎帶 (映带) *v.* to shine, reflect. MdnC: 輝映 (*huī yìng* 辉映).

   引 *v.* to channel (water).

   以爲 (为 *wéi*) or 以 (溪水) 爲 (曲水) to channel (the water) as (a winding brook). See L2 Grammar Note 1 ④.

   流 *v.* to flow. Here it means "floating (goblets)" 漂浮 (*piāo fú*).

   觴 (觞) *n.* wine goblet. MdnC: 酒杯 (*jiǔ bēi*).

   曲 (qū) 水 *n.* winding flow of water.

4. 列 *v.* to line up. MdnC: 排列 (*pái liè*).

   次 *n.* next in sequence. Here it refers to the edge of a brook.

   雖 (虽) *conj.* even though. MdnC: 即使 (*jí shǐ*). See L4 Grammar Note 6.

   絲 (丝) *n.* silk. Here it refers to string instruments.

   竹 *n.* bamboo. Here it refers to woodwind instruments.

   管 *n.* tube, pipe. Here it refers to wind instruments.

弦 *n.* string. Here it refers to string instruments.

絲竹管弦 refers to traditional Chinese musical instruments in general 樂器 (*yuè qì* 乐器).

盛 *adj.* spectacular, grand. MdnC: 盛況 (*shèng kuàng* 盛况).

詠 (咏) *v.* to sing (a poem/song), chant. MdnC: 吟詠 (*yín yǒng* 吟咏).

暢 (畅) *adv.* joyfully, uninhibitedly. MdnC: 盡情 (*jìn qíng* 尽情).

叙 *v.* to narrate, express. MdnC: 述説 (*shù shuō* 述说).

幽 *adj.* deep, hidden. MdnC: 深藏 (*shēn cáng*).

是日也， 天朗氣清， 惠風和暢； 仰觀宇
shì rì yě　tiān lǎng qì qīng　huì fēng hé chàng yǎng guān yǔ

宙之大， 俯察品類之盛。⁵所以遊目騁懷， 足
zhòu zhī dà　fǔ chá pǐn lèi zhī shèng　suǒ yǐ yóu mù chěng huái　zú

以極視聽之娛， 信可樂也。⁶
yǐ jí shì tīng zhī yú　xìn kě lè yě

这一天，天气晴朗，空气清新，暖风和煦(让人感到)舒畅。抬头仰望宇宙浩大，低头俯看观察万事万物的繁盛。⁵用来随意观看，放开胸怀，足以极尽视觉听觉上的欢娱(享受)，实在很快乐啊！⁶

5. 是 *demonstrative pron.* this. MdnC: 這 (*zhè* 这). See L3 Grammar Note 1 ①.

朗 *adj.* clear and bright. MdnC: 晴朗 (*qíng lǎng*).

惠風 (风) *n.* breeze. MdnC: 暖風 (*nuǎn fēng* 暖风).

和 *n.* gentle, warm. MdnC: 和煦 (*hé xù*).

暢 (畅) *adj.* joyful, happy. MdnC: 舒暢 (*shū chàng* 舒畅).

仰 *v.* to look up.

宇宙 *n.* the universe.

俯 *v.* to lower one's eyes.

察 *v.* to observe, watch. MdnC: 觀察 (*guān chá* 观察).

品類 (类) *n.* category, group. Here it refers to all kinds of things.

盛 *adj.* prosperous, spectacular. MdnC: 繁盛 (*fán shèng* 繁盛).

6. 所以 to use. MdnC: 用來 (*yòng lái* 用来).

遊 (游) 目 *v.* to look around freely.

騁 (骋) *v.* to give free rein to (one's mind/feelings). MdnC: 放開 (*fàng kāi* 放开).

懷 (怀) *n.* bosom. MdnC: 胸懷 (*xiōng huái* 胸怀).

極 (极) *v.* to reach far, attain. MdnC: 極盡 (*jí jìn* 极尽).

視 (视) *n.* vision, sight. MdnC: 視覺 (*shì jué* 视觉).

聽 (听) *n.* hearing. MdnC: 聽覺 (*tīng jué* 听觉).

娛 *n.* joy, entertainment, pleasure. MdnC: 歡娛 (*huān yú* 欢娱).

信 *adv.* indeed. MdnC: 實在 (*shí zài* 实在).

夫人之相與， 俯仰一世， 或取諸懷抱，
fú rén zhī xiāng yǔ　fǔ yǎng yí shì　huò qǔ zhū huái bào

人和人的相处，低头抬头之间就是人的一生。

悟言一室之内， 或因寄所託， 放浪形骸之
wù yán yí shì zhī nèi　　huò yīn jì suǒ tuō　　fàng làng xíng hái zhī

外。[7] 雖趣舍萬殊， 静躁不同， 當其欣於所
wài　　suī qū shě wàn shū　　jìng zào bù tóng　　dāng qí xīn yú suǒ

遇， 暫得於己， 快然自足， 不知老之將至。[8]
yù　　zàn dé yú jǐ　　yàng rán zì zú　　bù zhī lǎo zhī jiàng zhì

及其所之既倦， 情隨事遷， 感慨係之矣。[9]
jí qí suǒ zhī jì juàn　　qíng suí shì qiān　　gǎn kǎi xì zhī yǐ

向之所欣， 俛仰之間以[a]爲陳迹， 猶不能不
xiàng zhī suǒ xīn　　fǔ yǎng zhī jiān yǐ　　wéi chén jì　　yóu bù néng bù

以[b]之興懷；況脩短隨化， 終期於盡。[10] 古
yǐ　　zhī xīng huái　　kuàng xiū duǎn suí huà　　zhōng qī yú jìn　　gǔ

人云：「死生亦大矣。」豈不痛哉！[11]
rén yún　　sǐ shēng yì dà yǐ　　qǐ bú tòng zāi!

有人从自己的胸怀抱负中获取（智慧），在室内与人畅谈；有人顺着自己的喜好，寄托自己的精神，放荡不羁地生活。[7] 即使人趋向舍弃各有不同，安静躁动各不相同，当人遇到让自己欣喜的东西或时刻时，都会有暂时的自得，感到高兴满足，却不知道衰老将要来到！[8] 等到他对所得到的厌倦了，感觉随着事物变化而变化，感慨（也）附着其中。[9] 从前所欣喜的事物，低头抬头间很快就被当成了旧日的痕迹，尚且不能不因它而引发（自己的）情怀；何况（人生命的）长短都是由自然造化决定的，（每个人）最终（都）预期（自己会走向生命的）尽头。[10] 古人说："死生是件大事啊！"这怎能不让人感到悲痛呢！[11]

7. 與 (与 yǔ) *v.* to get along with.

　相與 (与 yǔ) *v.* to get along or socialize. MdnC: 相處 (*xiāng chǔ* 相处).

　俯仰 a short moment.

　世 *n.* lifetime, generation. MdnC: 一生 (*yì shēng*).

　或 *indefinite pron.* someone. MdnC: 有人 (*yǒu rén*). See L6 Grammar Note 4 ①.

　諸 (诸) *particle.* contraction of 之於 (*zhī yú*), meaning "from." MdnC: 從 (从 *cóng*) ......中 (*zhōng*). See L8 Grammar Note 3.

　抱 *n.* ambition, aspiration. MdnC: 抱負 (*bào fù* 抱负).

　悟 *v.* to understand. Here it is used in the sense of 晤 (*wù*), meaning "to meet or talk face to face."

　因 *v.* to follow from. MdnC: 順着 (*shùn zhe* 顺着).

　寄 *v.* to place (hope) in, find (spiritual support) in something. MdnC: 寄託 (*jì tuō*).

　託 *v.* to entrust, rely on. 所託 here refers to what one treasures.

　放浪 *v.* to behave in an unrestrained manner. MdnC: 放蕩不羈 (*fàng dàng bù jī* 放荡不羁).

　骸 *n.* body, skeleton. 形骸 means "human body."

8. 趣 (qū) used in the sense of 趨 (*qū* 趋), meaning "to walk fast, tend, or incline."

舍 (shě) *v.* to give up, quit.

趣舍 *v.* to lean forward or to abandon.

殊 *adj.* different. MdnC: 不同 (*bù tóng*).

静 *adj.* quiet. MdnC: 安静 (*ān jìng*).

躁 *adj.* impatient, rash. MdnC: 躁動 (*zào dòng* 躁动).

欣 *v.* to be happy, be delighted. MdnC: 欣喜 (*xīn xǐ*).

遇 *v.* to meet, encounter. MdnC: 遇到 (*yù dào*).

暫 (暂) *adv.* temporarily. MdnC: 暫時 (*zàn shí* 暂时).

快然 *adj.* unhappy. Here 快 should be a scribal error of 快, meaning "happy."

老 *adj.* old. Here it means "senescence or old age." MdnC: 衰老 (*shuāi lǎo*).

9. 之 *v.* to go, reach. MdnC: 到 (*dào*). See L7 Grammar Note 2 ⑦.

倦 *v.* to be tired of. MdnC: 厭倦 (*yàn juàn* 厌倦).

情 *n.* feeling. MdnC: 感覺 (*gǎn jué* 感觉).

遷 (迁) *v.* to change, move. MdnC: 變化 (*biàn huà* 变化).

感慨 *v.* to sigh with emotion.

係 (系) *v.* to bind, attach. MdnC: 附著 (*fù zhuó* 附着).

10. 向 *adj.* previously, formerly. MdnC: 從前 (*cóng qián* 从前).

俛 (俯) *v.* to lower one's head.

以 ₐ 爲 (为) or 以……爲…… to regard … as…. MdnC: 把 (*bǎ*) ……當作 (*dāng zuò* 当作). See L2 Grammar Note 1 ④.

陳 (陈) *adj.* old. MdnC: 舊 (*jiù* 旧).

迹 *n.* traces of the past. MdnC: 痕跡 (*hén jì* 痕迹).

猶 (犹) *adv.* still, yet. MdnC: 尚且 (*shàng qiě*). See L3 Grammar Note 3 ①.

以 ᵦ *prep.* for the sake of, because of. MdnC: 因 (*yīn*). See L2 Grammar Note 1 ①.

興 (兴 xīng) *v.* to rise, start. MdnC: 引發 (*yǐn fā* 引发).

懷 (怀) *n.* feeling, mind. MdnC: 情懷 (*qíng huái* 情怀).

況 (况) *conj.* let alone. MdnC: 何況 (*hé kuàng* 何况). See L18 Grammar Note 1.

脩 (修) *adj.* long. MdnC: 長 (*cháng* 长).

随 *v.* to follow.

化 *n.* nature. MdnC: 造化 (*zào huà*).

期 *v.* to expect. MdnC: 預期 (*yù qī* 预期).

盡 (尽 jìn) *n.* the end. MdnC: 盡頭 (*jìn tóu* 尽头).

11. 古人云 a quotation of Zhuangzi from chapter 5 德充符 ("Dé chōng fú") of the *Zhuangzi*.

豈 (岂) *interrogative particle.* MdnC: 怎麼 (*zěn me* 怎么). See L8 Grammar Note 4.

每攬昔人興感之由， 若合一契， 未嘗不
měi lǎn xī rén xīng gǎn zhī yóu　　ruò hé yí qì　　wèi cháng bù

臨文嗟悼， 不能喻之於懷。¹² 固知一死生爲虛
lín wén jiē dào　　bù néng yù zhī yú huái　　gù zhī yī sǐ shēng wéi xū

誕， 齊彭殤爲妄作。¹³ 後之視今， 亦由今之視
dàn qí péng shāng wéi wàng zuò　　hòu zhī shì jīn　　yì yóu jīn zhī shì

每当看到过去的人引发感慨的原因，如果(和我的感慨)符合得像一张符契，(我)面对这样的文章没有一次不嗟叹悲伤，不能明白(自己如此感慨的原因)。¹² 本

昔，悲夫！¹⁴ 故列叙時人，錄其所述，雖世殊
xī bēi fú　　 gù liè xù shí rén　 lù qí suǒ shù　 suī shì shū

事異，所以興懷，其致一也。¹⁵ 後之攬者，亦
shì yì　 suǒ yǐ xīng huái　 qí zhì yī yě　　　 hòu zhī lǎn zhě　　 yì

將有感於斯文。¹⁶
jiāng yǒu gǎn yú sī wén

《王羲之書法類編．蘭亭序八種》，天津：天津人民美術出版社 (2013), 2–3.

来就知道把死和生看作相同是虚妄荒诞的，把长寿和短命看作相同是荒唐的言论。¹³ 后人看现在的人也就像现在的人看过去的人，可悲啊！¹⁴ 因此一一排列记叙当时的人，记录他们所写的诗篇，即使世界不同了，事情不同了，(但)引发(人们)感怀的原因，其情致是一样的。¹⁵ 后来观看的人，也将感慨于这篇文章的。¹⁶

12. 攬 (揽) *v.* used in the sense of 覽 (*lǎn* 览), meaning "to look at or read" 看 (*kàn*).

　　昔 *adj.* formerly, past. MdnC: 過去 (*guò qù* 过去).

　　由 *n.* reason, cause. MdnC: 原因 (*yuán yīn*).

　　合 *v.* to fit, agree, match. MdnC: 符合 (*fú hé*).

　　契 *n.* deed in ancient China. Normally a deed was divided into two pieces, and each party would hold one piece as proof of the transaction. MdnC: 符契 (*fú qì*).

　　未嘗 (尝) not once. See Grammar Note 1.

　　臨 (临) *v.* to face, read. MdnC: 面對 (*miàn duì* 面对).

　　嗟 *v.* to sigh. MdnC: 嗟嘆 (*jiē tàn* 嗟叹).

　　悼 *v.* to grieve, lament. MdnC: 悲傷 (*bēi shāng* 悲伤).

　　喻 *v.* to understand. MdnC: 明白 (*míng bái*).

13. 固 *adv.* originally. MdnC: 本來 (*běn lái* 本来).

　　一 *number.* one. Here it is used as a putative verb, 以……爲一, meaning "to regard … as the same." See L14 Grammar Note 1 ②.

　　爲 (为 *wéi*) *v.* to be. MdnC: 是 (*shì*). See L9 Grammar Note 1 ③.

　　虛 *adj.* false, unfounded. MdnC: 虛妄 (*xū wàng*).

　　誕 (诞) *adj.* absurd. MdnC: 荒誕 (*huāng dàn* 荒诞).

　　齊 (齐) *adj.* even, equal, same. MdnC: 同樣 (*tóng yàng* 同样). Here it is used as a putative verb, 以……爲齊, meaning "to regard … as the same." See L14 Grammar Note 1 ①.

　　彭 or 彭祖 a legendary man of longevity, living for eight hundred years. Here it refers to long life 長壽 (*cháng shòu* 长寿).

　　殤 (殇) *v.* to die young. MdnC: 短命 (*duǎn mìng*).

　　妄 *adj.* absurd, foolish. MdnC: 荒唐 (*huāng táng*).

　　作 *n.* work. Here it means "talk" 言論 (*yán lùn* 言论).

14. 後 (后) *n.* later. Here it means "later generation."

　　之 *particle.* a nominative marker. See L2 Grammar Note 2 ⑤.

　　視 (视) *v.* to look at. MdnC: 看 (*kàn*).

亦 *adv.* also. MdnC: 也 (*yě*). See L5 Grammar Note 1 ①.

由 *n.* reason. Here it is used in the sense of 猶 (*yóu* 犹), meaning "(is) like" 就像 (*jiù xiàng*). See L3 Grammar Note 3 ② for 猶.

悲夫 (*fú*) *exclamatory word.* alas.

15. 列 *v.* to list, arrange in order. MdnC: 排列 (*pái liè*).

叙 *v.* to narrate, recount. MdnC: 記敘 (*jì xù* 记叙).

錄 (录) *v.* to write down, record. MdnC: 記錄 (*jì lù* 记录).

述 *v.* to narrate, give account of.

殊 *adj.* different. MdnC: 不同 (*bù tóng*).

異 (异) *adj.* different. MdnC: 不同 (*bù tóng*).

所以 the reason for.

致 *n.* intent, interest. MdnC: 情致 (*qíng zhì*).

16. 感 *v.* to sigh with emotion. MdnC: 感慨 (*gǎn kǎi*).

斯 *demonstrative pron.* this. MdnC: 這 (*zhè* 这). See L5 Grammar Note 3 ①.

語法注釋 Grammar Note

1. 嘗
(尝)
① *adv.* once, a marker of past tense. MdnC: 曾經 (*céng jīng* 曾经).

先君子嘗言，鄉先輩左忠毅公視學京畿。(L17)

[先父曾经说过，同乡先辈左忠毅公（光斗）视察京城地区的学政。]

此二子者，豈嘗執筆學爲如此之文哉？ (L19)

[这两个人，难道曾经拿着笔学习写这样的文章吗？]

② 未嘗不 double negative. Using 未 and 不 together turns the structure into a positive one. MdnC: 没有一次不 (*méi yǒu yí cì bù*).

每攬昔人興感之由，若合一契，未嘗不臨文嗟悼，不能喻之於懷。

[每当看到过去的人引发感慨的原因，如果（和我的感慨）符合的像一张符契，面对这样的文章没有一次不嗟叹悲伤，不能明白（自己感慨的原因）。]

Literary Analysis

As the author says, the elements in his work that "stir feelings" (*xīnggǎn* 興感 or *xīng huái* 興懷) can be seen in numerous writings before it. It is not what he says but how he says it that will—he assures himself—touch the hearts of future readers. In that perfect day, just as one is "looking up" 仰 (*yǎng*) and "looking down" 俯 (*fǔ*) across one's life (*fǔ yǎng yìshì* 俯仰一世 or *fǔ yǎng zhījiān* 俯仰之間), he looks up and down to fully enjoy 極 (*jí*) the abundance of myriad things. Then, suddenly, thoughts set in that all of this will end with his physical existence and eventually be no more. A melancholy brooding ensues. The sudden realization of life's brevity juxtaposed with the unfathomable enormity of the universe (*yǔ zhòu zhī dà* 宇宙之大)—what he sees "looking up"—seems to unleash his lament.

But it is also possible that precisely this cosmic understanding, gained through the same "looking up," lends him new insight into the existential situation of a human being. Partly due to the volatile transitional particle *gù* 固, the potential meanings of which range from "certainly" to "that being said" or even "although," the author's reflection on the Zhuangzian equalization of life and death invites conflicting interpretations. Put in context, his musing reads as much an inquisitive rethinking of the thoughts that once troubled Zhuangzi as a challenge to Daoist understanding. Whatever the case, this piece is first and foremost the spontaneous outpouring of feelings from a sensitive soul. Traces of philosophical contemplation may be detected in the solace the author allows himself at the end—that posterity will see him the same way he sees the ancients, Zhuangzi included. By bringing both past and future into this intense conversation about the meaning of existence, a transient being triumphs over the tyranny of time.

—XL

課後練習 Exercises

一 給加點字注音 Give the pinyin romanization for each dotted word.

1. 會稽 （＿＿＿, ＿＿＿）　2. 癸 （＿＿＿）　3. 脩禊 （＿＿＿）　4. 形骸 （＿＿＿）

5. 趣舍 （＿＿＿, ＿＿＿）　6. 快 （＿＿＿）　7. 彭殤 （＿＿＿）　8. 曲水 （＿＿＿）

二 在括號中給句中加點的字注音，並選出正確的釋義 Give the pinyin romanization for each dotted word; then select the correct definition from the following list, and write it in the blank.

輝映(辉映)　躁動(躁动)　引發(发)　荒誕(诞)　盡情(尽情)
峻峭　放開(开)　**信服**　湍流　嗟嘆(叹)

1. 小信未孚 （ **fú** ） ＿＿**信服**＿＿　2. 崇山峻領 （　） ＿＿＿＿　3. 清流激湍 （　） ＿＿＿＿

4. 暎帶左右 （　） ＿＿＿＿　5. 暢叙幽情 （　） ＿＿＿＿　6. 遊目騁懷 （　） ＿＿＿＿

7. 靜躁不同 （　） ＿＿＿＿　8. 興感之由 （　） ＿＿＿＿　9. 臨文嗟悼 （　） ＿＿＿＿

10. 一死生爲虚誕 （　） ＿＿＿＿

三 選擇釋義並填空 Match each word in the left column with its correct definition in the middle column. Fill in each blank in the right column with an appropriate word from the left column.

謀謀劃(谋划)	吟詠(咏)
畢＿＿＿＿	實(实)在
咸＿＿＿＿	胸懷(怀)
盛＿＿＿＿	**謀劃(谋划)**
詠＿＿＿＿	變(变)化
叙＿＿＿＿	舒暢
朗＿＿＿＿	附着
暢＿＿＿＿	原因
懷＿＿＿＿	符合

群賢＿＿＿至，少長＿＿＿集。

雖無絲竹管弦之＿＿＿，一觴一＿＿＿，亦足以暢＿＿＿幽情。

天＿＿＿氣清，惠風和＿＿＿，仰觀宇宙之大，俯察品類之盛，所以遊目騁＿＿＿，足以極視聽之娛，＿＿＿可樂也。

及其所之既＿＿＿，情隨事＿＿＿，感慨＿＿＿之矣。

信＿＿＿＿＿　全　　　　　　　　每攬昔人興感之＿＿＿，若＿＿＿一契，未嘗不＿＿＿文
倦＿＿＿＿＿　面對(对)　　　　嗟＿＿＿，不能喻之於＿＿＿。
遷＿＿＿＿＿　悲傷(伤)
係＿＿＿＿＿　盛況(况)
由＿＿＿＿＿　晴朗
合＿＿＿＿＿　述說(说)
臨＿＿＿＿＿　都
悼＿＿＿＿＿　厭(厌)倦

四 請用給出的字填空 Fill in each blank with an appropriate word from the following list (some words may be used more than once).

猶(犹)　況(况)　以　夫　嘗(尝)　不　或

1. 引＿＿＿＿爲流觴曲水，列坐其次。

2. ＿＿＿＿人之相與，俯仰一世，＿＿＿＿取諸懷抱，悟言一室之內，＿＿＿＿因寄所託，放浪形骸之外。

3. 向之所欣，俛仰之間＿＿＿＿爲陳迹，＿＿＿＿＿＿＿＿能＿＿＿＿＿＿＿＿之興懷；＿＿＿＿脩短隨化，終期於盡。

4. 每攬昔人興感之由，若合一契，未＿＿＿＿＿＿＿＿臨文嗟悼，不能喻之於懷。

五 为加點字選擇正確釋義，並根據釋義來翻譯句子 Match each dotted word with its correct modern Chinese equivalent by circling the latter. Then translate each sentence into modern Chinese.

1. 又何間焉?　　　　　　　　　(a) 爲什麼(为什么) b. 憑什麼(凭什么) c. 多少

現代文翻译：你又为什么要参与到这件事情里面？

＿＿＿＿＿＿＿＿＿＿＿＿＿＿＿＿＿＿＿＿＿＿＿＿＿＿＿

2. 是日也，天朗氣清，惠風和暢。　　a. 這(这) b. 對(对) c. 是的

現代文翻译：＿＿＿＿＿＿＿＿＿＿＿＿＿＿＿＿＿＿＿＿＿＿

3. 或取諸懷抱，悟言一室之內。　　a. 之於(于) b. 各个 c. 諸(诸)侯

現代文翻译：＿＿＿＿＿＿＿＿＿＿＿＿＿＿＿＿＿＿＿＿＿＿

4. 及其所之既倦，情隨事遷，感慨係之矣。　a. 的 b. 他 c. 到

現代文翻译：＿＿＿＿＿＿＿＿＿＿＿＿＿＿＿＿＿＿＿＿＿＿

5. 況脩短隨化，終期於盡。 　　　　　　　　　a. 情況（況）b. 何況（況）c. 而且

現代文翻译：＿＿＿＿＿＿＿＿＿＿＿＿＿＿＿＿＿＿＿＿＿＿＿＿＿

6. 固知一死生爲虛誕，齊彭殤爲妄作。　　　a. 以……爲齊（为齐）b. 齊國（齐国）c. 整齊（齐）

現代文翻译：＿＿＿＿＿＿＿＿＿＿＿＿＿＿＿＿＿＿＿＿＿＿＿＿＿

<h1 style="text-align:center">第二十四課</h1>

<h1 style="text-align:center">陶淵明《桃花源記》</h1>

"An Account of the Peach Blossom Spring" (Tao Yuanming)

Introduction

An introduction to Tao Yuanming's life appears in lesson 15. This text is the preface Tao wrote for his poem "Peach Blossom Spring" 桃花源詩 ("Táohuāyuán shī" 桃花源诗), an auxiliary prose work that has become far more famous and influential than the poem itself. It tells the story of an unnamed fisherman who strays into groves of blossoming peach trees and discovers a utopia: a farming village isolated from historical time and the vicissitudes of the outside world. In this village, everyone lives in a natural state of contentment, undisturbed by social norms or government regulations. Contrasting the peaceful and unfettered life of the Peach Blossom Spring with the social chaos of his time, Tao expresses a strong wish to withdraw from the chaotic and treacherous political world.

正文與簡體譯文 Text and Modern Chinese Translation

晋太元中，武陵人捕魚爲業；緣溪行，
jìn tài yuán zhōng　　wǔ líng rén bǔ yú wéi yè　　yuán xī xíng

忘路之遠近。¹ 忽逢桃花林夾岸，數百步中
wàng lù zhī yuǎn jìn　　hū féng táo huā lín jiā àn　　shù bǎi bù zhōng

無雜樹，芳華鮮美，落英繽紛。² 漁人甚異
wú zá shù　　fāng huá xiān měi　　luò yīng bīn fēn　　yú rén shèn yì

之。復前行，欲窮其林。³
zhī　　fù qián xíng　　yù qióng qí lín

东晋太元年间，有个武陵人以捕鱼为职业。（一天他划着小船）沿着小溪走，忘记了路程的远近。¹ 忽然遇见一片桃花林长在岸的两边，（长达）几百步的（桃花林）中没有别的树，芬芳的桃花鲜艳美丽，花瓣纷纷落下。² 渔人感到非常奇怪，又往前走了一段，想走到树林的尽头去。³

1. 晋 (晋) the Jin dynasty. Here it refers to the Eastern Jin (317–420).
   太元 one of the reign titles 年號 (*nián hào* 年号) of Emperor Xiaowu of Jin 晉孝武帝 (r. 372–396). 太元 is from 376 to 396.
   武陵 place name in present-day Changde 常德 (*cháng dé*), Hunan Province.
   捕 *v.* to hunt.
   業 (业) *n.* job. MdnC: 職業 (*zhí yè* 职业).
   緣 (缘) *prep.* along. MdnC: 沿着 (*yán zhe*).

行 *v.* to walk forward. Here it refers to moving forward by boat.

溪 *n.* brook, creek.

路 *n.* road, way. Here it means "distance" 路程 (*lù chéng*).

2. 忽 *adv.* all of a sudden. MdnC: 忽然 (*hū rán*).

逢 *v.* to meet, encounter. MdnC: 遇見 (*yù jiàn* 遇见).

桃 *n.* peach.

夾 (夹 *jiā*) 岸 on both banks.

數 (数 *shù*) *adj.* several. MdnC: 幾 (*jǐ* 几).

步 *n.* steps. It is a measurement of length in ancient China. Three hundred steps equal one *li* 里.

雜 (杂) *adj.* various, mixed, miscellaneous. Here it means "different."

芳 *adj.* fragrant. MdnC: 芬芳 (*fēn fāng*).

華 (华) *n.* flower. MdnC: 花 (*huā*).

鮮 (鲜 *xiān*) *adj.* bright. MdnC: 鮮艷 (*xiān yàn* 鲜艳).

英 *n.* flower. MdnC: 花 (*huā*).

繽紛 (缤纷) *adj.* in profusion. Here it refers to a profusion of petals 花瓣 (*huā bàn*).

3. 漁 (渔) 人 *n.* fisherman.

異 (异) *adj.* strange. MdnC: 奇怪 (*qí guài*). Here it is used as a putative verb, 以……爲異, meaning "to think that something is odd." See L14 Grammar Note 1 ①.

窮 (穷) *adj.* poor. Here it is used as a verb, meaning "to go to the end of" 到盡頭 (*dào jìn tóu* 到尽头).

林盡水源， 便得一山。 山有小口，髣
lín jìn shuǐ yuán　　biàn dé yì shān　　shān yǒu xiǎo kǒu　　fǎng

髴若有光。 便捨船， 從口入。⁴初極狹， 纔
fú ruò yǒu guāng biàn shě chuán　cóng kǒu rù　　　chū jí xiá　　cái

通人。 復行數十步， 豁然開朗。⁵土地平曠，
tōng rén　　　fù xíng shǔ shí bù　　huò rán kāi lǎng　　tǔ dì píng kuàng

屋舍儼然。 有良田、 美池、 桑竹之屬。⁶阡
wū shè yǎn rán　yǒu liáng tián　měi chí　sāng zhú zhī shǔ　qiān

陌交通， 雞犬相聞。⁷其中往來種作， 男女
mò jiāo tōng　　jī quǎn xiāng wén　qí zhōng wǎng lái zhòng zuò nán nǚ

衣著悉如外人。⁸黃髮垂髫並怡然自樂。⁹
yī zhuó xī rú wài rén　huáng fà chuí tiáo bìng yí rán zì lè

树林的尽头是溪水的源头，出现一座山。山有个小洞口，里面好像有光。(渔夫)舍弃了船，从洞口进去。⁴开始时路非常窄，仅能通过一个人。又走了几十步，突然就开阔明亮了。⁵土地平坦空阔，房屋整齐。里面有肥沃的田地、美丽的池塘、桑树竹子之类的(树木)。⁶田间小路交错相通，鸡叫声狗叫声到处都能听见。⁷人们在其中来来往往耕种劳作，男人和女人的衣着穿戴都和外面的人一样。⁸老人和孩子都自得其乐。⁹

4. 盡 (尽 *jìn*) *n.* end. MdnC: 盡頭 (*jìn tóu* 尽头).

源 *n.* source. MdnC: 源頭 (*yuán tóu* 源头).

髣髴 or 仿佛 *v.* to seem, be like. MdnC: 好像 (*hǎo xiàng*).

捨 (舍) *v.* to give up, abandon. MdnC: 捨棄 (*shě qì* 舍弃).

5. 初 *adv.* in the beginning. MdnC: 開始 (*kāi shǐ* 开始).

極 (极) *adv.* very, extremely. MdnC: 非常 (*fēi cháng*).

狹 (狭) *adj.* narrow. MdnC: 窄 (*zhǎi*).

纔 (才) *adv.* only. MdnC: 僅僅 (*jǐn jǐn* 仅仅).

豁然 *adj.* broad, wide-open. MdnC: 開闊 (*kāi kuò* 开阔).

開 (开) 朗 *adj.* bright and broad.

6. 曠 (旷) *adj.* broad, wide. MdnC: 空闊 (*kōng kuò* 空阔).

舍 (shè) *n.* house, cottage.

儼 (俨) 然 *adj.* neatly arranged. MdnC: 整齊 (*zhěng qí* 整齐).

良 *adj.* good. Here it means "fertile (farmland)" 肥沃 (*féi wò*).

池 *n.* pond. MdnC: 池塘 (*chí táng*).

桑竹 *n.* mulberry tree and bamboo.

屬 (属 shǔ) *n.* category, group. MdnC: 類 (*lèi* 类).

7. 阡陌 *n.* cross paths in the farmlands. MdnC: 田間小路 (*tián jiān xiǎo lù* 田间小路). 阡 means "longitudinal path between fields," and 陌 means "latitudinal path between fields."

交 *v.* to crisscross. MdnC: 交錯 (*jiāo cuò* 交错).

通 *v.* to be connected, be linked. MdnC: 相通 (*xiāng tōng*).

聞 (闻) *v.* to hear. MdnC: 聽見 (*tīng jiàn* 听见).

8. 種 (种) *v.* to till, cultivate. MdnC: 耕種 (*gēng zhòng* 耕种).

作 *v.* to work, labor over. MdnC: 勞作 (*láo zuò* 劳作)

著 (着 zhuó) *v.* to attach, wear. 衣著 (着 zhuó) means "apparel."

悉 *adv.* all. MdnC: 都 (*dōu*). See Grammar Note 1 ④.

9. 髮 (发 fà) *n.* hair. 黃髮 (发) means "yellow hair." Here it refers to old people.

髫 *n.* children's hair style in ancient China. Here 垂髫 refers to children.

怡然 *adj.* pleased, relaxed, at ease.

見漁人，乃大驚。問所從來，具答之。[10]
jiàn yú rén　　nǎi dà jīng　　wèn suǒ cóng lái　　jù dá zhī

便要還家，爲設酒殺雞作食。[11] 村中聞有此
biàn yāo huán jiā　　wèi shè jiǔ shā jī zuò shí　　　cūn zhōng wén yǒu cǐ

人，咸來問訊。[12] 自云先世避秦時亂，率妻
rén　xián lái wèn xùn　　　zì yún xiān shì bì qín shí luàn　　shuài qī

子邑人，來此絕境，不復出焉，遂與外人
zǐ　yì rén　　lái cǐ jué jìng　　bú fù chū yān　　suì yǔ wài rén

間隔。[13] 問今是何世，乃不知有漢，無論魏
jiàn gé　　　wèn jīn shì hé shì　　nǎi bù zhī yǒu hàn　　wú lùn wèi

晉。[14] 此人一一爲具言所聞，皆歎惋。[15] 餘
jìn　　　cǐ rén yī yī　wèi jù yán suǒ wén　　jiē tàn wǎn　　　yú

里面的人见到渔夫大吃一惊。问他从哪里来，(渔夫)都回答了。[10] 于是邀请(渔夫)回家，为他摆酒杀鸡做饭(来招待他)。[11] 村中人听说有这个人，都跑来打听消息。[12] 他们自己说，祖先躲避秦时的战乱，率领妻子孩子和同乡来到这个与世隔绝的地方，不再出去，于是与外面的人隔绝了。[13] 问渔人现在是什么朝代，他们竟不知道有汉朝，

人各復延至其家，皆出酒食。¹⁶停數日，辭
rén gè fù yán zhì qí jiā　jiē chū jiǔ shí　tíng shù rì　cí

去。此中人語云：「不足爲外人道也。」¹⁷
qù　cǐ zhōng rén yǔ yún　　bù zú wèi wài rén dào yě

更不用说魏晋了。¹⁴渔夫把自己听到的都对他们详细说了。（他们）都慨叹惋惜。¹⁵其余的人又各自邀请他去自己家，都拿出酒饭（招待他）。¹⁶停留了几天，（渔人要）告辞离去。桃花源中人对他说："（我们的事）不值得对外面的人说。"¹⁷

10. 驚 (惊) *v.* to be surprised. MdnC: 吃驚 (*chī jīng* 吃惊).
   具 used in the sense of 俱 (*jù*), meaning "all or completely" 全都 (*quán dōu*). See Grammar Note 1 ②.

11. 要 (yāo) *v.* to ask. Here it is used in the sense of 邀 (*yāo*), meaning "to invite" 邀請 (*yāo qǐng* 邀请).
   還 (还 huán) *v.* to return, go (home). MdnC: 回 (*huí*).
   爲 (为 wèi) *prep.* for. See L7 Grammar Note 5 ②.
   設 (设) *v.* to arrange, set up.

12. 聞 (闻) *v.* to hear. MdnC: 聽說 (*tīng shuō* 听说).
   咸 *adv.* all, completely. MdnC: 都 (*dōu*). See Grammar Note 1 ①.
   訊 (讯) *n.* news, information. MdnC: 消息 (*xiāo xi*).

13. 云 *v.* to say. MdnC: 說 (*shuō* 说).
   先世 *n.* ancestry. MdnC: 祖先 (*zǔ xiān*).
   避 *v.* to hide, escape, avoid. MdnC: 躲避 (*duǒ bì*).
   秦 the Qin dynasty (221–207 BCE).
   亂 (乱) *n.* chaos. MdnC: 戰亂 (*zhàn luàn* 战乱).
   率 *v.* to lead, head. MdnC: 率領 (*shuài lǐng* 率领).
   妻子 *n.* wife and children. MdnC: 妻子孩子 (*qī zǐ hái zi*).
   邑 *n.* a large city in ancient China. 邑人 refers to people from the same town 同鄉 (*tóng xiāng* 同乡).
   絕 (绝) *adj.* isolated. MdnC: 隔絕 (*gé jué* 隔绝).
   境 *n.* area, region. MdnC: 地方 (*dì fāng*).
   焉 *pron.* from here. MdnC: 從這裏 (*cóng zhè lǐ* 从这里). See L1 Grammar Note 4 ①.
   間 (间) 隔 *v.* to be separate, be isolated. MdnC: 隔絕 (*gé jué* 隔绝).

14. 世 *n.* era, generation. Here it refers to the present dynasty. MdnC: 朝代 (*cháo dài*).
   乃 *adv.* unexpectedly, to one's surprise. MdnC: 竟然 (*jìng rán*).
   漢 (汉) the Han dynasty (206 BCE–220 CE).
   無論 (无论) not to mention. MdnC: 不用說 (*bú yòng shuō* 不用说).
   魏 or 曹魏 the Wei dynasty (220–265).
   晉 (晋) the Jin dynasty (266–420).

15. 歎 (叹) *v.* to sigh. MdnC: 慨嘆 (*kǎi tàn* 慨叹).
   惋 *v.* to regret. MdnC: 惋惜 (*wǎn xī*).

16. 餘 (余) *adj.* remaining, left. 餘 (余) 人 means "other people."
   延 *v.* to extend. Here it means "to invite" 邀請 (*yāo qǐng* 邀请).

17. 停 *v.* to stop over, stay. MdnC: 停留 (*tíng liú*).
　　辭 (辞) *v.* to take leave, bid farewell. MdnC: 告辭 (*gào cí* 告辞).
　　足 *adj.* enough. Here it means "worth" 值得 (*zhí dé*).
　　爲 (为 *wèi*) *prep.* to, for. MdnC: 對 (*duì* 对). See L7 Grammar Note 5 ②.
　　道 *v.* to talk, tell. MdnC: 説 (*shuō* 说).

既出， 得其船， 便扶向路， 處處誌
jì chū　　dé qí chuán　　biàn fú xiàng lù　　chù chù zhì

之。¹⁸ 及郡下， 詣太守説如此。¹⁹ 太守卽遣
zhī　　　jí jùn xià　　yì tài shǒu shuō rú cǐ　　tài shǒu jí qiǎn

人隨其往， 尋向所誌， 遂迷， 不復得路。²⁰
rén suí qí wǎng　xún xiàng suǒ zhì　　suì mí　　bú fù dé lù

(渔人)已经出了(桃花源)，找到了他的小船，于是沿着从前来的路，处处做标记。¹⁸到了武陵郡，(渔人)拜见太守，说了桃花源的事情。¹⁹太守立刻派人跟随他前往寻找从前做的标记，最终迷路了，找不到去桃花源的路。²⁰

18. 既 *adv.* already. MdnC: 已經 (*yǐ jīng* 已经). See L1 Grammar Note 5.
　　扶 *v.* to go along with. MdnC: 沿着 (*yán zhe*).
　　向 *adj.* previously, formerly. MdnC: 從前 (*cóng qián* 从前).
　　誌 (志) *v.* to mark, sign. MdnC: 做標記 (*zuò biāo jì* 做标记).
19. 及 *v.* to arrive, get to. MdnC: 到 (*dào*).
　　郡 *n.* county. Here it refers to Wuling 武陵.
　　詣 (诣) *v.* to pay a formal visit to. MdnC: 拜見 (*bài jiàn* 拜见).
　　太守 *n.* head of a prefecture, governor.
20. 卽 (即) *adj.* quickly, immediately. MdnC: 立刻 (*lì kè*).
　　遣 *v.* to send. MdnC: 派遣 (*pài qiǎn*).
　　隨 (随) *v.* to go after, follow. MdnC: 跟隨 (*gēn suí* 跟随).
　　尋 (寻) *v.* to search, look for. MdnC: 尋找 (*xún zhǎo* 寻找).
　　遂 *adv.* eventually, finally. MdnC: 終於 (*zhōng yú* 终于).
　　迷 *v.* to get lost. MdnC: 迷路 (*mí lù*).

南陽劉子驥， 高尚士也。 聞之， 欣然
nán yáng liú zǐ jì　　gāo shàng shì yě　　wén zhī　　xīn rán

規往， 未果， 尋病終。 後遂無問津者。²¹
guī wǎng　　wèi guǒ　　xún bìng zhōng hòu suì wú wèn jīn zhě

《陶淵明集》，北京：中華書局 (1995), 165–166.

南阳的刘子骥，是品德高尚的人。听说了这件事情后，高兴地计划前往，(但)没有实现。(刘子骥)不久就病死了。后来再也没有要探访(桃花源)的人了！²¹

21. 南陽 (阳) place name in present-day Nanyang 南陽, Henan Province.
　　劉子驥 (given name 名, Línzhī 驥之; style 字, Zǐ jì 子驥; 376–396), a person in the Eastern Jin dynasty.

高尚 *adj.* dignified and noble demeanor.

欣然 *adv.* joyfully. MdnC: 高興地 (*gāo xìng de* 高兴地).

規 (规) *v.* to plan. MdnC: 計劃 (*jì huà* 计划).

果 *n.* achievement, result. MdnC: 實現 (*shí xiàn* 实现).

尋 (寻) *adv.* immediately, soon after. MdnC: 不久 (*bù jiǔ*).

終 (终) *v.* to end. Here it means "to die" 死 (*sǐ*).

津 *n.* ferry. MdnC: 渡口 (*dù kǒu*).

問 (问) 津 *v.* to ask for directions. Here it means "to look for or explore" 探訪 (*tàn fǎng* 探访).

語法注釋 Grammar Note

1. 咸、具(俱)、皆、悉、並　*adv.* all, completely. MdnC: 都 (*dōu*), 全都 (*quán dōu*).

　①　咸 *adv.* all. MdnC: 都 (*dōu*).

　　　村中聞有此人，咸來聞訊。

　　　　　[村中人听说有这么个人，都跑来打听消息。]

　　　群賢畢至，少長咸集。（L22）

　　　　　[诸位贤人全到了，年少的年长的都聚集（在这里）。]

　②　具(俱) *adv.* all, completely. MdnC: 全都 (*quán dōu*).

　　　此人一一爲具言所聞。

　　　　　[这个人把自己听到的事情全都为他们详细言说。]

　③　皆 *adv.* all, completely. MdnC: 都 (*dōu*), 全都 (*quán dōu*).

　　　皆歎惋。

　　　　　[（他们）都慨叹惋惜。]

　④　悉 *adv.* all. MdnC: 都 (*dōu*).

　　　其中往來種作，男女衣著悉如外人。

　　　　　[人们在其中来来往往耕种劳作，男人和女人的衣着穿戴都和外面的人一样。]

　⑤　並(并) *adv.* both, together. MdnC: 都 (*dōu*).

　　　黃髮垂髫並怡然自樂。

　　　　　[老人和孩子都自得其乐。]

Literary Analysis

Unlike those utopian "no-place" islands or their oriental counterpart Shangri-La, the peaceful small world under Tao Yuanming's pen is devoid of mysterious quietude and otherworldliness. In the eyes of the intruding fisherman, the common men and women in the Peach Blossom Spring function "in exactly the same way" as people outside. Indeed, the forefathers of the villagers chose to come to this place not to pursue an ethereal better life but simply to run away from trouble. In this world—still "mundane" yet totally secluded from its "dusty" other—time has stopped. Hence, there is no knowledge of Han or Wei and Jin—or of the conflicts and wars closely associated with those troubling dynasty names.

The pristine yet self-sufficient and self-contented community recalls the ideal country Laozi envisions in the *Dao De Jing*. The crowing rooster and barking dog conspicuously heard in the Peach Blossom Spring undoubtedly come from Laozi's chapter 80. (The rooster and dog are heard again fifteen hundred years later in Lu Xun's "The Good Story," another version of the ideal country tinged with the rosy hue of the Peach Blossom Spring.) Just as the residents in Laozi's "small state" do not want to know about, or be known by, people on the other side of the fence, the villagers in the Peach Blossom Spring beseech the fisherman not to disclose their existence. Their concern turns out to be unnecessary: the ending of the story provides yet another lesson informed with Laozi's, or even Zhuangzi's, wisdom— namely, that the Peach Blossom Spring is not to be sought but only encountered by accident.

—XL

課後練習 Exercises

一 給加點字注音 Give the pinyin romanization for each dotted word.

1. 繽紛 （＿＿, ＿＿） 2. 髣髴 （＿＿, ＿＿） 3. 邑 （＿＿） 4. 髫 （＿＿） 5. 驥 （＿＿）

二 在括號中給句中加點的字注音，並選出正確的釋義 Give the pinyin romanization for each dotted word; then select the correct definition from the following list, and write it in the blank.

僅僅(仅)　　類(类)　　邀請(请)　　拜見(见)　　沿着
做標記(标记)　　**信服**　　渡口　　整齊(齐)

1. 小信未孚 （**fú**）　**信服**　　2. 緣溪行 （　）＿＿＿＿　　3. 便要還家 （　）＿＿＿＿

4. 屋舍儼然 （　）＿＿＿＿　　5. 纔通人 （　）＿＿＿＿　　6. 桑竹之屬 （　）＿＿＿＿

7. 處處誌之 （　）＿＿＿＿　　8. 詣太守 （　）＿＿＿＿　　9. 無問津者 （　）＿＿＿＿

三 選擇釋義並填空 Match each word in the left column with its correct definition in the middle column. Fill in each blank in the right column with an appropriate word from the left column.

謀謀劃 (谋划)	派遣	忽逢桃花林夾岸，數百步中無雜樹，芳華鮮美，落
英＿＿＿＿	沿着	＿＿＿繽紛。漁人甚異之。復前行，欲＿＿＿其林。
窮＿＿＿＿	計劃(计划)	
狹＿＿＿＿	消息	初極＿＿＿，纔通人。
具＿＿＿＿	**謀劃 (谋划)**	
訊＿＿＿＿	不久	村中聞有此人，咸來問＿＿＿。
延＿＿＿＿	從(从)前	此人一一爲＿＿＿言所聞，皆嘆惋。餘人各復＿＿＿
扶＿＿＿＿	迷路	至其家，皆出酒食。
向＿＿＿＿	邀請(请)	既出，得其船，便＿＿＿路，處處誌之 。
遣＿＿＿＿	窄	

迷＿＿＿＿＿＿ 詳細(详细)　　　　太守即＿＿＿人隨其往，尋向所誌，遂＿＿＿，不復得
規＿＿＿＿＿＿ 到盡頭(尽头)　　　路。
尋＿＿＿＿＿＿ 花
　　　　　　　　　　　　　　　　聞之，欣然＿＿＿往。未果，＿＿＿病終。

四　請用給出的字填空 Fill in each blank with an appropriate word from the following list.

並(并)　　所　　具　　皆　　然　　咸

1. 土地平曠，屋舍儼＿＿＿。　　2. 黃髮垂髫＿＿＿怡然自樂。　3. 問＿＿＿從來，＿＿＿答之。
4. 村中聞有此人，＿＿＿來問訊。5. 此人一一為＿＿＿言所聞，＿＿＿歎惋。

五　為加點字選擇正確釋義，並根據釋義來翻譯句子 Match each dotted word with its correct modern Chinese equivalent by circling the latter. Then translate each sentence into modern Chinese.

1. 又何間焉?　　　　　　　　　　　ⓐ為什麼(为什么) b. 憑什麼(凭什么) c. 多少

現代文翻譯：你又为什么要参与到这件事情里面？

＿＿＿＿＿＿＿＿＿＿＿＿＿＿＿＿＿＿＿＿＿＿＿

2. 漁人甚異之。　　　　　　　　　a. 以……為異(为异) b. 不同 c. 奇異(异)

現代文翻譯：＿＿＿＿＿＿＿＿＿＿＿＿＿＿＿＿＿＿＿＿＿

3. 其中往來種作，男女衣著悉如外人。　　　　　a. 熟悉 b. 像 c. 都

現代文翻譯：＿＿＿＿＿＿＿＿＿＿＿＿＿＿＿＿＿＿＿＿＿

4. 自云先世避秦時亂，率妻子邑人來此絕境，不復出焉，遂與外人間隔。
　　　　　　　　　　　　　　　　　　a. 啊 b. 於(于)之 c. 於(于)是

現代文翻譯：＿＿＿＿＿＿＿＿＿＿＿＿＿＿＿＿＿＿＿＿＿

5. 此中人語云：「不足為外人道也。」　　　　a. 對(对) b. 因為(为) c. 認為(认为)

現代文翻譯：＿＿＿＿＿＿＿＿＿＿＿＿＿＿＿＿＿＿＿＿＿

第二十五課

李白《春夜宴從弟桃花園序》

"The Spring Feast at Peach Blossom Garden with My Younger Cousins"
(Li Bai)

Introduction

Li Bai (701–762) and Du Fu 杜甫 (712–770), together embodying the poetic genius of the High Tang, are often paired (Li-Du 李杜) as China's two greatest poets. While Du is revered as the sage-poet 詩聖 (*shīshèng* 诗圣) for projecting a grand, somber Confucian vision in his poetry, Li has endeared himself to posterity as the immortal-poet 詩仙 (*shīxiān* 诗仙) who transcends worldly bondage, assumes the role of a free-roaming cosmic spirit, and creates a dazzling world of imagination.

This composition accompanied a collection, now lost, of poems Li and his cousins composed at a springtime feast. Like Wang Xizhi in his "Preface to the Poems of the Orchid Pavilion Gathering" (lesson 23), Li depicts the joys of a wine and poetry-writing gathering, a beautiful scene in nature, and an awareness of human transience. But the tones of the two prefaces are markedly different. Wang's preface turns from joyful to melancholy as the author is suddenly gripped by sorrow over the evanescence of all joys. In contrast, Li begins by acknowledging human transience but follows with a burst of joie de vivre that continues to the very end. In form, however, the two prefaces are noticeably similar. If Wang's preface represents a prototype of parallel prose, Li's preface furnishes an example of mature parallel prose, marked by its use of alternate-line parallelism. A translation of this text is given in *HTRCProse*, chapter 12, "Tang and Song Occasional Prose: Prefaces and Epistolary Writing," C12.1.

👉 *HTRCProse*, chapter 12, "Tang and Song Occasional Prose: Prefaces and Epistolary Writing," for further comments on this preface and chapter 9, "Six Dynasties Parallel Prose: Descriptive and Expository," for an analysis of the parallel prose form.

正文與簡體譯文 Text and Modern Chinese Translation

夫天地者， 萬物之逆旅也； 光陰者， 百
fú tiān dì zhě　wàn wù zhī nì lǚ yě　guāng yīn zhě bǎi

代之過客也。¹ 而浮生若夢， 爲歡幾何？² 古
dài zhī guò kè yě　ér fú shēng ruò mèng　wéi huān jǐ hé　gǔ

人秉燭夜遊， 良有以也。³ 況陽春召我以烟
rén bǐng zhú yè yóu　liáng yǒu yǐ yě　kuàng yáng chūn zhào wǒ yǐ yān

天地是万物的客舍；白天和黑夜，是世世代代时间的过客。¹而短暂的人生就像一场梦，欢乐的时候能有多少呢？²古人晚上拿着蜡烛去游玩，确实有原因啊！³何况温暖的春天用美丽的

景，大塊假我以文章。⁴會桃花之芳園，序
jǐng　　dà kuài jiǎ wǒ yǐ wén zhāng　　huì táo huā zhī fāng yuán　xù

天倫之樂事。⁵羣季俊秀，皆爲惠連。⁶吾人
tiān lún zhī lè shì　　qún jì jùn xiù　　jiē wéi huì lián　　wú rén

詠歌，獨慚康樂。⁷幽賞未已，高談轉清。⁸
yǒng gē　　dú cán kāng lè　　yōu shǎng wèi yǐ　gāo tán zhuǎn qīng

開瓊筵以坐花，飛羽觴而醉月，不有佳詠，
kāi qióng yán yǐ zuò huā　　fēi yǔ shāng ér zuì yuè　　bù yǒu jiā yǒng

何伸雅懷？⁹如詩不成，罰依金谷酒數。¹⁰
hé shēn yǎ huái　　rú shī bù chéng　　fá yī jīn gǔ jiǔ shù

《李白集校注》，上海：上海古籍出版社 (1980), 1590.

景象来召唤我，大自然把各种美好借给我。⁴（我们）相聚在桃花飘香的园子里，一同叙说兄弟间快乐的事！⁵贤弟们都有才华，都可成为谢惠连（那样的才子）。⁶我吟咏作诗，只惭愧自己不如谢灵运。⁷幽闲地欣赏（着园中的美景），还没赏完，高谈阔论（已）转向清雅（的话题）。⁸摆开美好的筵席，坐在花中，飞快地（举起）酒杯，醉倒在月下。没有好诗，怎么来抒发高雅的情怀呢！⁹如果诗没作成，依照金谷园罚酒的数目来惩罚。¹⁰

1. 夫 (fú) *initial particle*. See L2 Grammar Note 4 ①.

   ……者……也 an equivalent of the verb to be in English construction. What appears before 者 is the subject, and what appears after it is the predicate. See L4 Grammar Note 3 ③.

   逆 *v.* to welcome, receive.

   旅 *n.* traveler, guest.

   逆旅 *n.* originally means "to welcome the traveler and let them stay." Here it refers to a travel lodge 客舍 (*kè shè*).

   光陰 (阴) *n.* daytime and dark night. It refers to time.

   代 *n.* era, generation.

   百代 a hundred generations. It refers to a long time.

   過 (过) 客 *n.* passing traveler.

2. 浮 *adj.* floating, transient. MdnC: 短暫 (*duǎn zàn* 短暂).

   生 *n.* human life. MdnC: 人生 (*rén shēng*).

   夢 (梦) *n.* dream.

   爲 (为 wéi) *v.* to do, have. See L2 Grammar Note 6 ①.

   歡 (欢) *n.* joy, pleasure. MdnC: 歡樂 (*huān lè* 欢乐).

   幾 (几) 何 how many? how much? MdnC: 多少 (*duō shǎo*). See L3 Grammar Note 7.

3. 秉 *v.* to hold, grasp. MdnC: 拿 (*ná*).

   燭 (烛) *n.* candle. MdnC: 蠟燭 (*là zhú* 蜡烛).

   良 *adv.* indeed. MdnC: 確實 (*què shí* 确实). See L18 Grammar Note 3.

   以 *n.* reason, cause. MdnC: 原因 (*yuán yīn*). See L18 Grammar Note 4 ⑥.

4. 況 (况) *conj.* let alone. MdnC: 何況 (*hé kuàng* 何况). See L18 Grammar Note 1.

   陽 (阳) *adj.* warm, sunny. MdnC: 温暖 (*wēn nuǎn*).

召 (*zhào*) *v.* to summon. MdnC: 召喚 (*zhào huàn* 召唤).

以 *coverb.* with. MdnC: 用 (*yòng*). See L2 Grammar Note 1 ②.

烟 *n.* haze, mist, smoke. 烟景 means "beautiful scenery."

大塊 (块) *n.* the earth, nature. MdnC: 大自然 (*dà zì rán*).

假 (*jiǎ*) *v.* to provide, lend. MdnC: 借給 (*jiè gěi* 借给).

文章 *n.* miscellaneous colors and patterns. Here it refers to various beautiful images, colors, sounds, etc. in nature.

5. 會 (会) *v.* to gather, get together. MdnC: 相聚 (*xiāng jù*).

芳 *adj.* fragrant. MdnC: 香 (*xiāng*).

序 *n.* preface. Here it is used in the sense of 叙 (*xù*), meaning to "narrate or recount" 叙说 (*xù shuō* 叙说).

倫 (伦) *n.* human relations.

天倫 (伦) *n.* the bond among family members. Here it refers to brotherhood.

6. 群 *n.* many, group.

季 *n.* the youngest of brothers. Here it refers to "younger brothers" 賢弟 (*xián dì* 贤弟).

俊秀 *adj.* talented and excellent.

惠連 or 謝惠連 (406–433), a famous poet and scholar in the (Liu) Song dynasty.

7. 吾人 *pron.* I. MdnC: 我 (*wǒ*).

詠 (咏) *v.* to sing (a poem/song), chant. MdnC: 吟詠 (*yín yǒng* 吟咏).

歌 *v.* to sing (a song).

獨 (独) *adv.* only.

慚 (惭) *v.* to be ashamed. MdnC: 慚愧 (*cán kuì* 惭愧).

康樂 or 謝靈運 (385–433), a famous landscape poet in the Jin and (Liu) Song dynasties.

8. 幽 *adj.* quiet and leisurely. MdnC: 幽閑 (*yōu xián* 幽闲).

賞 (赏) *v.* to enjoy, appreciate. MdnC: 欣賞 (*xīn shǎng* 欣赏).

已 *v.* to stop, end. See L21 Grammar Note 1 ②.

高談 (谈) *v.* to talk to one's heart's content, talk unrestrainedly.

轉 (转) *v.* to turn, change into.

清 *adj.* pure. MdnC: 清雅 (*qīng yǎ*).

9. 瓊 (琼) *adj.* elegant, beautiful. MdnC: 美好 (*měi hǎo*).

筵 *n.* bamboo mat. Here it refers to a banquet or feast 筵席 (*yán xí*).

以 *conj.* used here to denote a purpose. MdnC: 來 (*lái* 来). See L2 Grammar Note 1 ③.

飛 (飞) *adv.* fast, quickly. MdnC: 飛快 (*fēi kuài* 飞快).

羽觴 (觞) *n.* ancient Chinese goblet that has wings on both sides. MdnC: 酒杯 (*jiǔ bēi*).

醉 *v.* to be drunk.

佳 *adj.* good, excellent, fine. MdnC: 好 (*hǎo*).

詠 (咏) *n.* poem. MdnC: 詩 (*shī* 诗).

伸 *v.* to express, state. MdnC: 抒發 (*shū fā* 抒发).

雅 *adj.* elegant. MdnC: 高雅 (*gāo yǎ*).

懷 (怀) *n.* feeling. MdnC: 情懷 (*qíng huái* 情怀).

10. 罰 (罚) *v.* to punish. MdnC: 懲罰 (*chéng fá* 惩罚).

依 *v.* according to. MdnC: 依照 (*yī zhào*).

金谷園 (园) Golden Valley Villa, in present-day Luoyang 洛陽, Henan Province, was built by Shi Chong 石崇 (249–300) of the Western Jin dynasty. There Shi often held feasts and composed the "Preface to Golden Valley Poems" 金谷詩序 ("Jīngǔ Shī Xù" 金谷诗序). In that preface, he wrote that anyone who could not compose a poem was punished by having to drink three *dou* of wine (遂 各賦詩以敘中懷，或不能者，罰酒三斗).

數 (数 shù) *n*. number. MdnC: 數目 (*shù mù* 数目).

Literary Analysis

Apart from their thematic affinities noted in the introduction, this text readily lends itself to formal comparison with Wang Xizhi's "Preface to the Poems of the Orchid Pavilion Gathering" (lesson 23). If Wang's preface gives us a good example of aggregative patterning, Li's preface introduces us to the art of parallel patterning.

👉 *HTRCProse*, chapter 1, "An Anatomy of the Chinese Prose Form: An Overview," and C9.3–4 for detailed analyses of these two major forms of textual patterning.

—ZC

課後練習 Exercises

一 在括號中給句中加點的字注音，並選出正確的釋義 Give the pinyin romanization for each dotted word; then select the correct definition from the following list, and write it in the blank.

懲罰 (惩罚)　　召喚 (唤)　　拿　　筵席　　借給 (给)　　酒杯　　**信服**

1. 小信未孚　　　　（ **fú** ）　 **信服**　　 2. 陽春召我以烟景　　（　）＿＿＿＿

3. 秉燭夜遊　　　（　）＿＿＿＿　　 4. 大塊假我以文章　　（　）＿＿＿＿

5. 開瓊筵以坐花　（　）＿＿＿＿　　 6. 罰依金谷酒數　　　（　）＿＿＿＿

7. 飛羽觴而醉月　（　）＿＿＿＿

二 選擇釋義並填空 Match each word in the left column with its correct definition in the middle column. Fill in each blank in the right column with an appropriate word from the left column (some words may be used more than once).

<u>謀謀劃 (谋划)</u>　　叙説 (叙说)　　　　而＿＿生若夢，爲＿＿幾何？

浮＿＿＿＿　　　　幽閑 (幽闲)　　　　古人秉燭夜遊，＿＿有以也。

歡＿＿＿＿　　　　清雅　　　　　　　＿＿桃花之＿＿園，＿＿天倫之樂事。

良＿＿＿＿　　　　吟詠 (咏)　　　　　吾人＿＿歌，獨＿＿康樂。

會＿＿＿＿　　　　美好

芳＿＿＿＿　　　　飛 (飞) 快　　　　　＿＿賞未已，高談轉＿＿。

序＿＿＿＿　　　　**謀劃 (谋划)**

詠_____	飄浮	開____筵以坐花，____羽觴而醉月，不有佳____，
慚_____	抒發(发)	何____ ____懷。
幽_____	確實(确实)	
清_____	相聚	
瓊_____	香	
飛_____	高雅	
伸_____	歡樂(欢乐)	
雅_____	慚(惭)愧	

三 請用給出的字填空 Fill in each blank with an appropriate word from the following list (some words may be used more than once).

良　夫　者　也　之　何　以　爲(为)

1. ____天地____，萬物____逆旅____；光陰____，百代____過客____。
2. 古人秉燭夜遊，____有____也。　　　　3. 而浮生若夢，____歡幾____？

四 爲加點字選擇正確釋義，並根據釋義來翻譯句子 Match each dotted word with its correct modern Chinese equivalent by circling the latter. Then translate each sentence into modern Chinese.

1. 又何間焉？　　　　　　　　　　　ⓐ.爲什麼(为什么) b.憑什麼(凭什么) c.多少

現代文翻译：你又为什么要参与到这件事情里面？

_____

2. 而浮生若夢，爲歡幾何？　　　　　a.幾個(几个) b.多少 c.什麼(什么)

現代文翻译：_____

3. 況陽春召我以烟景，大塊假我以文章。　　a.情況(况) b.何況(况) c.而且

現代文翻译：_____

4. 群季俊秀，皆爲惠連；吾人詠歌，獨慚康樂。　　a.做 b.爲(为)了 c.被

現代文翻译：_____

5. 幽賞未已，高談轉清。　　　　　　a.已經(经) b.既然 c.停止

現代文翻译：_____

6. 開筵席以坐花，飛羽觴而醉月。　　　　　　　a. 來（来）b. 原因 c. 而且

现代文翻译：_____

7. 不有佳詠，何伸雅懷？　　　　　　　　　　　a. 否 b. 不是 c. 没

现代文翻译：_____

第二十六課

韓愈《送董邵南序》

"A Prose Farewell to Dong Shaonan" (Han Yu)

Introduction

The renowned writer and Confucian thinker of the mid-Tang Han Yu 韓愈 (courtesy name Tuizhi 退之; 768–824). along with Liu Zongyuan (see lesson 16), set the standard for the Ancient Prose Movement 古文運動. , Han also heads the list of the Eight Prose Masters of Tang and Song 唐宋八大家 (see L16 Culture Note 1).

The prose farewell 序 (*xù*), as a popular prose genre, dates to the early Tang. Writing in the Yuanhe 元和 years (805–820) of Tang emperor Xianzong 唐憲宗, Tan addresses his farewell to his friend Dong Shaonan. Frustrated with repeated career setbacks and failures in the imperial examinations, Dong has decided to seek patronage from military governors in the Yan and Zhao regions north of the Yellow River. To Han, Dong's departure is a de facto defection from the imperial court to separatist local lords, and he writes this prose farewell to subtly dissuade his friend from pursuing this course.

In just over one hundred words, this classic work of Tang ancient-style prose introduces many twists and turns and accomplishes what would be impossible for a lesser writer; yet Han subtly, yet unmistakably, conveys his opposition to Dong's departure with all the politeness and sympathy required of a prose farewell. A translation of this text is given in *HTRCProse*, chapter 11, "Tang and Song Occasional Prose: Accounts of Places, Things, and Events," C11.2.

正文與簡體譯文 Text and Modern Chinese Translation

燕趙古稱多感慨悲歌之士。¹董生舉進
yān zhào gǔ chēng duō gǎn kǎi bēi gē zhī shì dǒng shēng jǔ jìn

士，連不得志於有司。²懷抱利器，鬱鬱適
shì lián bù dé zhì yú yǒu sī huái bào lì qì yù yù shì

茲土，吾知其必有合也。³董生勉乎哉！⁴夫
zī tǔ wú zhī qí bì yǒu hé yě dǒng shēng miǎn hū zāi fú

以子之不遇時，苟慕義彊仁者皆愛惜焉。⁵
yǐ zǐ zhī bú yù shí gǒu mù yì qiǎng rén zhě jiē ài xī yān

矧燕趙之士出乎其性者哉？⁶
shěn yān zhào zhī shì chū hū qí xìng zhě zāi

燕赵之地，据说自古就多有用悲壮的歌声来抒发(内心悲愤的)人。¹董生被举荐(参加)进士考试，在主考官那里却接连不能实现自己的志愿。²(董生)身怀才能，(却)郁闷得去这个地方。我知道您一定会有所遇合！³董先生努力吧！⁴你这样没有遇到好的时机，如果

（遇到的）是仰慕正
义，勉力实行仁政的
人，（一定会）爱惜
（你这样的人才）啊！[5]
何况是燕赵之地的
人，（追求仁义）是出
自他们的本性啊！[6]

1. 燕 (yān) one of the seven states in the Warring States period. It includes most of present-day Beijing and the northern part of Hebei Province.

   趙 (赵) one of the seven states in the Warring States period. It includes the southern part of present-day Hebei Province, central part of present-day Shanxi Province, and northeastern corner of present-day Shaanxi Province.

   稱 (称 chēng) v. to say. Here it means "it is said" 據説 (jù shuō 据说).

   感慨 v. to sigh deeply, lament.

   悲 adj. sad. MdnC: 悲壯 (bēi zhuàng 悲壮).

2. 舉 (举) v. to recommend. MdnC: 舉薦 (jǔ jiàn 举荐). Here it means "to be recommended."

   進 (进) 士 n. Presented Scholar, a coveted degree in imperial examinations. Here it refers to Dong's participation in imperial examinations to obtain this degree.

   連 (连) adv. continuously. MdnC: 接連 (jiē lián 接连).

   志 n. will, ambition. MdnC: 志願 (zhì yuàn 志愿).

   有司 n. official. Here it refers to examination officials 主考官 (zhǔ kǎo guān).

3. 懷 (怀) 抱 v. to cherish, embrace, carry.

   利器 n. sharp weapon or tool. Here it refers to talents 才能 (cái néng).

   鬱鬱 (郁) adj. depressed.

   適 (适) v. to go to, get to. MdnC: 去 (qù).

   茲 demonstrative pron. this. MdnC: 這 (zhè 这). See Grammar Note 1.

   土 n. land, region. Here it refers the Yan and Zhao region.

   合 v. to get along well with. MdnC: 遇合 (yù hé).

4. 勉 v. to try hard, make an effort. MdnC: 努力 (nǔ lì).

   乎 particle. a suffix with no meaning. See L3 Grammar Note 4 ①.

5. 之 particle. a nominative marker. See L2 Grammar Note 2 ⑤.

   遇 v. to meet. MdnC: 遇到 (yù dào).

   時 (时) n. opportunity, chance. MdnC: 時機 (shí jī 时机).

   苟 conj. if. MdnC: 如果 (rú guǒ). See L19 Grammar Note 1 ①.

   慕 v. to admire, long for. MdnC: 仰慕 (yǎng mù).

   義 (义) n. righteousness. MdnC: 正義 (zhèng yì 正义).

   彊 (qiǎng) v. used in the sense of 強 (qiǎng 强), meaning "to do one's utmost" 勉力 (miǎn lì).

   仁 n. benevolence.

   愛 (爱) 惜 v. to cherish.

   焉 ending particle. MdnC: 啊 (a). See L2 Grammar Note 3 ②.

6. 矧 conj. let alone. MdnC: 何況 (hé kuàng 何况).

   乎 prep. from. See L6 Grammar Note 2 ③.

性 *n.* human nature. MdnC: 本性 (*běn xìng*).

然吾嘗聞： 風俗與化移易，吾惡知其今
rán wú cháng wén　fēng sú yǔ huà yí yì　wú wū zhī qí jīn

不異於古所云邪？ [7] 聊以吾子之行卜之也。 [8]
bú yì yú gǔ suǒ yún yé　liáo yǐ wú zǐ zhī xíng bǔ zhī yě

董生勉乎哉！
dǒng shēng miǎn hū zāi!

但是我曾经听人说：风俗跟随着教化改变。我怎么知道那里现在（的风俗）是否与古人所说的不同呢？ [7] 姑且拿先生的行程来测定一下吧！ [8] 董先生，努力吧！

7. 然 *conj.* however. MdnC: 但是 (*dàn shì*). See L5 Grammar Note 2 ①.
　嘗 (尝) *adv.* ever, once. MdnC: 曾經 (*céng jīng* 曾经). See L23 Grammar Note 1 ①.
　風 (风) 俗 *n.* custom.
　與 (与 *yǔ*) *v.* to follow. MdnC: 跟隨 (*gēn suí* 跟随).
　化 *v.* to influence, transform. MdnC: 教化 (*jiào huà*).
　移易 *v.* to change, transform. MdnC: 改變 (*gǎi biàn* 改变).
　惡 (恶 *wū*) *interrogative particle.* how come? MdnC: 怎麼 (*zěn me* 怎么). See L12 Grammar Note 2 ①.
　異 (异) *adj.* different. MdnC: 不同 (*bù tóng*).
　云 *v.* to say. MdnC: 說 (*shuō* 说).
　邪 (*yé*) *ending interrogative particle.* MdnC: 呢 (*ne*). See L11 Grammar Note 2.
8. 聊 *adv.* for the moment, tentatively. MdnC: 姑且 (*gū qiě*).
　以 *coverb.* to use. MdnC: 拿 (*ná*). See L2 Grammar Note 1 ②.
　卜 (*bǔ*) *v.* to predict. Here it means "to test or evaluate" 測定 (*cè dìng* 测定).

吾因子有所感矣： 為我弔望諸君之墓，
wú yīn zǐ yǒu suǒ gǎn yǐ　wèi wǒ diào wàng zhū jūn zhī mù

而觀於其市復有昔時屠狗者乎？ [9] 為我謝曰：
ér guān yú qí shì fù yǒu xī shí tú gǒu zhě hū　wèi wǒ xiè yuē

明天子在上， 可以出而仕矣！ [10]
míng tiān zǐ zài shàng　kě yǐ chū ér shì yǐ

《韓昌黎文集校注》，上海：上海古籍出版社 (1986), 247–248.

我因您的事情很有感触：为我凭吊望诸君乐毅的墓，然后看看当地的集市，还有像过去（高渐离一样）屠狗的人吗？ [9] 为我告诉他们说：现在是英明的皇帝在上面（执政），你们可以出来做官了！ [10]

9. 因 *prep.* because of.
　感 *v.* to be touched by. MdnC: 感觸 (*gǎn chù* 感触).
　為 (为 *wèi*) *prep.* for. See L7 Grammar Note 5 ②.
　弔 (吊) *v.* to mourn. Here it means "to pay homage to the dead" 憑弔 (*píng diào* 凭吊).
　望諸 (诸) 君 or 樂毅 (Yue Yi), a famous military leader of the Yan state during the reign of King
　　Zhao of Yan 燕昭王 (r. 313–279 BCE) in the Warring States period. After King Zhao of Yan died,

Yue Yi left the Yan state and went to the Zhao state, where he received the title Lord of Zhujun 望諸君.

墓 *n.* tomb.

觀 (观) *v.* to watch, see.

市 *n.* market. MdnC: 集市 (*jí shì*).

復 (复) *adv.* still. MdnC: 還 (*hái* 还).

昔時 (时) in former times. MdnC: 過去 (*guò qù* 过去).

屠 *v.* to butcher.

屠狗者 a person who butchers dogs. It refers to Gao Jianli 高漸離 of the Yan state in the Warring States period. Gao was a good friend of Jing Ke 荊軻 (?–227 BCE), who attempted but failed to assassinate King Zheng of Qin 秦王政 (later the first Emperor of Qin 秦始皇). Before Jing Ke left on his assassination mission, Gao once performed a song of farewell.

乎 *ending particle.* MdnC: 嗎 (*ma* 吗). See L6 Grammar Note 2 ②.

10. 謝 (谢) *v.* tell. MdnC: 告訴 (*gào sù* 告诉).

明 *adj.* wise and enlightened. MdnC: 英明 (*yīng míng*).

天子 *n.* emperor. Here it refers to Emperor Xian of Tang 唐憲宗 (r. 805–820).

仕 *v.* to serve in the government, be an official. MdnC: 做官 (*zuò guān*).

語法注釋 Grammar Note

1. 茲   *demonstrative pron.* this. MdnC: 這 (*zhè* 这).

懷抱利器，鬱鬱適茲土，吾知其必有合也。

[（董先生）身懷才能，（却）郁闷得到这个地方去。我知道您一定会有所遇合！]

Literary Analysis

Brevity of expression was promoted as a key trait by Tang dynasty advocates of ancient-style prose, among whom Han Yu was a leader. Brevity in this context stands in contrast to the duplication required in the great stylistic alternative, parallel prose, in which nearly all statements are formulated in couplets of redundant parallel members (parallel in syntax and meaning) or equally balanced antithetical statements. Parallel prose ends up producing language that essentially says everything twice and thereby resorts to allusive and periphrastic language to provide an elegant appearance that belies the essential redundancy of exposition. Ancient-prose stylists had no patience with such elegance, viewing it as artificial and a misdirection of a writer's attention to verbal ornamentation at the expense of the substance of what was being said.

But advocates of ancient-style prose were not content simply to abandon the second member of each parallel utterance. They also prized the cultivation of a generally choppy and abrupt prose rhythm, marked by short phrases, phrases of unequal length, and heavy use of grammatical particles, interjections, rhetorical questions, and injunctions, all of which are found in this lesson's text.

At a higher level, making a virtue of brevity often led to meaning being conveyed through indirection, with key points unsaid or said only implicitly, the better to induce the reader to pause and ponder the implications of the abbreviated delivery. (In the following dynasty, the Song, ancient-style writers actually competed with each other to complete a prose composition in the fewest characters.) Han Yu's "Prose Farewell to Dong Shaonan" became a model for this kind of brevity through indirection. Consisting of three short sections, the farewell conveys a meaning that is the inverse of its ostensible encouragement. Despite Han's repeated injunctions, Dong is on the verge of leaving the capital after failing the examinations to embark on a new course and seek his fortune in the northern region known in ancient times as a haven for men of stalwart principle who could not bend to the corrupt ways of the world. However, what the farewell ends up suggesting is that Dong's abandonment of the capital and the chance for an official career there is the worst choice he could make. The ingenious turning point in the farewell is the second section, in which Han Yu introduces the unexpected thought that perhaps the ancient land of heroes is no longer what it used to be. This prepares the way for a related thought in the final section: that the ancient tradition of withdrawal from public life and service has itself become outmoded. The justification for such withdrawal no longer holds, Han Yu suggests, because the current ruler is not the kind who forces men of principle into proud withdrawal. The farewell, written to dissuade Dong Shaonan from his chosen course, is cleverly disguised as an ostensible commendation of that choice.

—RE

課後練習 Exercises

一　在括號中給句中加點的字注音，並選出正確的釋義 Give the pinyin romanization for each dotted word; then select the correct definition from the following list, and write it in the blank.

仰慕　　憑弔(凭吊)　　測(测)定　　勉力　　據説(据说)　　**信服**

1. 小信未孚　　　　　(fú)　　<u>信服</u>　　　2. 燕趙古稱多慷慨悲歌之士 (　)　_____

3. 慕義彊仁者　　　(　)　_____　　4. 以吾子之行卜之　　　　(　)　_____

5. 慕義彊仁者　　　(　)　_____　　6. 爲我弔望諸君之墓　　　(　)　_____

二　選擇釋義並填空 Match each word in the left column with its correct definition in the middle column. Fill in each blank in the right column with an appropriate word from the left column.

謀謀劃(谋划)	英明	董生____進士，____不得____於有司。
舉_____	感觸(触)	懷抱利器，鬱鬱適茲土，吾知其必有____也。
連_____	告訴(诉)	吾因子有所____矣。
志_____	**謀劃(谋划)**	爲我____曰：____天子在上，可以出而____矣。
合_____	做官	
感_____	遇合	
謝_____	舉薦(举荐)	
明_____	志願(愿)	
仕_____	連續(连续)	

三 請用給出的字填空 Fill in each blank with an appropriate word from the following list (some words may be used more than once).

邪　茲　嘗(尝)　苟　然　惡(恶)　以　爲(为)

1. 懷抱利器，鬱鬱適＿＿＿土，吾知其必有合也。
2. 夫＿＿＿子之不遇時，＿＿＿慕義彊仁者皆愛惜焉。
3. ＿＿＿吾＿＿＿聞：風俗與化移易，吾＿＿＿知其今不異於古所云＿＿＿？
4. ＿＿＿我謝曰：明天子在上，可＿＿＿出而仕矣。

四 爲加點字選擇正確釋義，並根據釋義來翻譯句子 Match each dotted word with its correct modern Chinese equivalent by circling the latter. Then translate each sentence into modern Chinese.

1. 又何間焉?　　　　　　　　　ⓐ爲什麼(为什么) b. 憑什麼(凭什么) c. 多少

現代文翻譯：你又为什么要参与到这件事情里面？

＿＿＿＿＿＿＿＿＿＿＿＿＿＿＿＿＿＿＿＿＿＿＿

2. 懷抱利器，鬱鬱適茲土,吾知其必有合也。　　a. 滋生 b. 這(这) c. 它

現代文翻譯：＿＿＿＿＿＿＿＿＿＿＿＿＿＿＿＿＿＿

3. 夫以子之不遇時，苟慕義彊仁者皆愛惜焉。　　a. 如果 b. 苟且 c. 難(难)道

現代文翻譯：＿＿＿＿＿＿＿＿＿＿＿＿＿＿＿＿＿＿

4. 矧燕趙之士出乎其性者哉?　　a. 情況(况) b. 何況(况) c. 而且

現代文翻譯：＿＿＿＿＿＿＿＿＿＿＿＿＿＿＿＿＿＿

5. 風俗與化移易,吾惡知其今不異於古所云邪?　　a. 怎麼(怎么) b. 憎恨 c. 惡(恶)行

現代文翻譯：＿＿＿＿＿＿＿＿＿＿＿＿＿＿＿＿＿＿

6. 爲我弔望諸君之墓,而觀於其市復有昔時屠狗者乎?　　a. 做 b. 因爲(为) c. 替

現代文翻譯：＿＿＿＿＿＿＿＿＿＿＿＿＿＿＿＿＿＿

第二十七課

李清照《打馬圖經序》

"Preface to a Handbook for 'Capture the Horse'" (Li Qingzhao)

Introduction

Li Qingzhao 李清照 (literary name, Yi'an Jushi 易安居士; 1084–1155) remains China's most famous female poet. Although she left behind a sizable collection of poetic works, only a few of her prose writings have survived. This lesson features the preface to her illustrated handbook on Capture the Horse, a popular game during the Song dynasty thought to involve some sort of gambling. Fond of the game herself, Li produced, in addition to this handbook, two poems ("A Rhapsody on 'Capture the Horse'" 打馬賦 and "A *Ci* Poem on 'Capture the Horse'" 打馬圖經命詞).

　　In this preface, Li tells of her reasons for composing the handbook and introduces various methods she devised for winning the game. The work has been praised for its clear exposition, elegant phrasing, and aesthetic appeal. A translation of this text is given in *HTRCProse*, chapter 12, "Tang and Song Occasional Prose: Prefaces and Epistolary Writing," C12.3.

正文與簡體譯文 Text and Modern Chinese Translation

慧則通， 通則無所不達； 專則精， 精則
huì zé tōng　　tōng zé wú suǒ bù dá　　zhuān zé jīng　　jīng zé

無所不妙。[1] 故庖丁之 a 解牛， 郢人之 a 運斤，
wú suǒ bù miào　　gù páo dīng zhī　jiě niú　　yǐng rén zhī　yùn jīn

師曠之 b 聽， 離婁之 b 視，[2] 大至於堯舜之 b
shī kuàng zhī　tīng　　lí lóu zhī　shì　　dà zhì yú yáo shùn zhī

仁， 桀紂之 b 惡， 小至於擲豆起蠅， 巾角拂
rén　　jié zhòu zhī　è　　xiǎo zhì yú zhì dòu qǐ yíng　　jīn jiǎo fú

棋， 皆臻至理者何？ 妙而已。[3]
qí　　jiē zhēn zhì lǐ zhě hé　　miào ér yǐ

（人如果）聰慧就會（思路）通暢，思路通暢就沒有到達不了的境地；（做事）專注就會變得精通，精通就沒什麼不能了解的妙处了。[1]因此庖丁（轻松地）肢解一头牛，郢人（的朋友）挥动斧头（帮他去除鼻子上的灰尘），师旷（超凡）的听觉，离娄（强大）的视力，大到尧舜的仁政，桀纣的恶行，小到扔豆子捉苍蝇、用手巾角或头巾角弹棋子，（这些）都达到了极高的境地，为什么呢？（知道其中的）妙处罢了！[3]

1. 慧 *adj.* intelligent. MdnC: 聰慧 (*cōng huì* 聪慧).
　　通 *adj.* open, clear. MdnC: 通暢 (*tōng chàng* 通畅).

達 (达) *v.* to reach. MdnC: 到達 (*dào dá* 到达).

專 (专) *adj.* fully concentrated on, focused. MdnC: 專注 (*zhuān zhù* 专注).

精 *adj.* proficient. MdnC: 精通 (*jīng tōng*).

妙 *n.* subtlety. MdnC: 妙處 (*miào chù* 妙处).

2. 庖丁 Cook Ding, a fictional character from chapter 3 養生主 of the *Zhuangzi*. 庖 means "cook," and 丁 is the name. 庖丁 is a butcher who is very skilled at cutting up a cow.

之 ₐ *particle.* a nominative marker. See L2 Grammar Note 2 ⑤.

解 *v.* to cut up, dismember. MdnC: 肢解 (*zhī jiě*).

郢 place name, the capitol of the Chu state in the Spring and Autumn period.

運 (运) *v.* to wield. MdnC: 揮動 (*huī dòng* 挥动).

斤 *n.* axe. MdnC: 斧頭 (*fǔ tóu* 斧头).

郢人之運斤 a story from chapter 24, "Xu Wugui"徐無鬼, of the *Zhuangzi*. It tells of a Ying person 郢人 who had a little mud on the top of his nose and asked an artisan for help. The artisan 匠石 (Shi 石 is the name) wielded an axe so well that he immediately cut the dirt off without hurting the nose of the Ying person.

師曠 (师旷) Master Kuang, a musical official of the Jin state in the Spring and Autumn period. He is famous for his remarkable hearing. See also L3 note 12 for 師.

之 ᵦ *particle.* a possessive marker. MdnC: 的 (*de*). See L1 Grammar Note 2 ②.

聽 (听) *n.* hearing. MdnC: 聽覺 (*tīng jué* 听觉).

離婁 (离娄) a person in the period of Yellow Emperor 黃帝 (2717?–2599 BCE) who is known for having powerful vision.

視 (视) *n.* vision. MdnC: 視力 (*shì lì* 视力).

3. 堯 (尧) a legendary sage-king. See Yao's brief biography in L13 note 3.

舜 a legendary sage who succeeded Yao. See Shun's brief biography in L13 note 3.

仁 *n.* benevolence.

桀 or 夏桀 (ancestral name 姓, Sì 姒; family name 氏, Xiàhòu 夏后; given name 名, Guǐ 癸; posthumous name 謚, Jié 桀; r. 1652?–1600 BCE), the last king of the Xia dynasty. Jie 桀 is the derogatory posthumous title given to denounce his tyranny.

紂 (纣) See King Zhou of Shang's brief biography in L13 note 19.

惡 (恶 è) *n.* evil, vice, wickedness. MdnC: 惡行 (*è xíng* 恶行).

擲 (掷) *v.* to throw, pitch. MdnC: 扔 (*rēng*).

起 *v.* to get up. Here it means "to catch (a fly with one's bare hands)" 捉 (*zhuō*).

蠅 (蝇) *n.* fly.

擲豆起蠅 (掷豆起蝇) a story from chapter 4 of *The Sequel to Miscellaneous Morsels from Youyang* 酉陽雜俎續集 (*Yǒuyáng zázǔ xùjí* 酉阳杂俎续集) by Duan Chengshi 段成式 (803?–863). It tells of Zhang Fen 張芬, who showed at a banquet how easily he could catch flies with his bare hands after seeing a guest successfully hitting flies with beans.

巾 *n.* towel.

拂 *v.* to flick.

巾角拂棋 a story from chapter 21, "Skill and Art"巧藝 ("Qiǎo yì" 巧艺), of *A New Account of the Tales of the World* 世說新語 (*Shìshuō xīnyǔ* 世说新语). It tells that Cao Pi 曹丕 (see Cao Pi's brief biography in lesson 18) was able to use the corner of a handkerchief to flick chess pieces without a miss. One guest of Cao Pi's said that he could do even better. Then the guest used a corner of his cloth scarf to flick chess pieces.

臻 *v.* reach. MdnC: 達到 (*dá dào* 达到).

至理 *n.* the best.

而已 *ending particle.* nothing more. MdnC: 罷了 (*bà le* 罢了). See L21 Grammar Note 1 ③.

後世之人，不惟學聖人之道不到聖處；
hòu shì zhī rén　bù wéi xué shèng rén zhī dào　bú dào shèng chù

雖嬉戲之事，亦不得其依稀彷彿而遂止者多
suī xī xì zhī shì　yì bú dé qí yī xī fǎng fú ér suì zhǐ zhě duō

矣。夫博者無他，爭先術耳，故專者能之。⁴
yǐ　fú bó zhě wú tā　zhēng xiān shù ěr　gù zhuān zhě néng zhī

予性喜博，凡所謂博者皆耽之，晝夜每忘寢
yú xìng xǐ bó　fán suǒ wèi bó zhě jiē dān zhī　zhòu yè měi wàng qǐn

食。且平生多寡未嘗不進者何？精而已。⁵
shí　qiě píng shēng duō guǎ wèi cháng bù jìn zhě hé　jīng ér yǐ

后世的人，不只是学圣人之道学不到圣人的境地，即使是游戏，也大多不能达到(差不多的境地)就停止了。赌博游戏没什么特别之处，(找到)争先的办法罢了！所以专注的人能做好。⁴我天性喜欢赌博，凡是所说的赌博游戏都沉溺其中，白天晚上每每忘记睡觉吃饭。而且我平生赌多赌少，没有不赢的时候，为什么呢？精通罢了！⁵

4. 惟 *adv.* only. See L22 Grammar Note 2 ②.

聖 (圣) 人 *n.* sage.

嬉戲 (戏) *v.* to play. MdnC: 游戲 (*yuó xì* 游戏).

依稀 *adj.* vague, unclear.

仿佛 *adj.* similar, seemingly.

博 *v.* to gamble. 博者 means "the playing of a gambling game."

爭 (争) 先 *v.* to try to be the first to do (things).

術 (术) *n.* method, techniques. MdnC: 辦法 (*bàn fǎ* 办法).

5. 凡 *adv.* overall, in general. MdnC: 凡是 (*fán shì*). See L10 Grammar Note 4.

耽 *v.* to indulge in. MdnC: 沉溺 (*chén nì*).

晝 (昼) *n.* daytime.

寢 (寝) *v.* to sleep.

未嘗 (尝) never yet. See L23 Grammar Note 1 ②.

進 (进) *v.* to enter. Here it means "to win" 贏 (*yíng* 赢).

自南渡來，流離遷徙，盡散博具，故罕
zì nán dù lái　liú lí qiān xǐ　jìn sàn bó jù　gù hǎn

爲之，然實未嘗忘於胸中也。⁶今年冬十月
wéi zhī　rán shí wèi cháng wàng yú xiōng zhōng yě jīn nián dōng shí yuè

朔，聞淮上警報，江浙之人，自東走西，自
shuò　wén huái shàng jǐng bào jiāng zhè zhī rén　zì dōng zǒu xī　zì

自从南渡以来，我流离失所，赌博的工具都(在迁徙的途中)散落了，因此很少做这件事了。但是心中确实从未忘记过。⁶今年冬天十月初一，听到淮河上的

南走北；居山林者謀入城市，居城市者謀入
nán zǒu běi　　jū shān lín zhě móu rù chéng shì　　jū chéng shì zhě móu rù

山林，旁午絡繹，莫不失所。[7]易安居士亦自
shān lín　　bàng wǔ luò yì　　mò bù shī suǒ　　yì ān jū shì yì zì

臨安沂流，涉嚴灘之險，抵金華，卜居陳氏
lín ān sù liú　　shè yán tān zhī xiǎn　　dǐ jīn huá　　bǔ jū chén shì

第。[8]乍釋ₐ舟楫而見軒窗，意頗釋ᵦ然。更
dì　　zhà shì　　zhōu jí ér jiàn xuān chuāng　　yì pō shì rán　　gēng

長燭明，奈此良夜乎？于是博奕之事講矣。[9]
cháng zhú míng nài cǐ liáng yè hū　　yú shì bó yì zhī shì jiǎng yǐ

警报，江浙的人，从东跑到西，从南跑到北；住在山林里的人要进城市，住在城市的人要进山林，交错纵横，络绎不绝，没有人能不失去自己的家。[7]我也从临安(沿着钱塘江)逆流而上，经过严陵濑的险滩，到了金华，选择住在陈氏的宅第。[8](我)刚刚下船，见到房间的窗户，心里很释然。夜很长，烛火很亮，(我要怎么)打发这么美好的夜晚呢？于是就来讲讲博弈的事情。[9]

6. 南渡 South Migration, referring to the historical event when the imperial family of the Song dynasty fled from the capital to the south between 1127 and 1130.

流離 (离) *v.* to become homeless and wander around.

遷 (迁) 徙 *v.* to migrate, move.

具 *n.* tool. MdnC: 工具 (*gōng jù*).

罕 *adv.* rarely, seldom. MdnC: 很少 (*hěn shǎo*).

然 *conj.* however. MdnC: 但是 (*dàn shì*). See L5 Grammar Note 2 ①.

7. 朔 *n.* first day of a lunar month.

淮 the Huai River, originating in present-day Henan Province and flowing through Henan, Anhui, and Jiangsu Provinces.

警報 (警报) *n.* alarm.

江浙 the area of present-day Jiangsu and Zhejiang Provinces.

謀 (谋) *v.* to plan.

旁 (*bàng*) 午 *adv.* across and athwart. MdnC: 縱橫交錯 (*zòng héng jiāo cuò* 纵横交错).

絡繹 (络绎) *adv.* continuously connected.

莫 *indefinite pron.* none, no one. MdnC: 沒有人 (*méi yǒu rén*). See L3 Grammar Note 2 ①.

8. 易安居士 Li Qingzhao's literary name.

臨 (临) 安 place name in present-day Hangzhou, Zhejiang Province.

沂 (溯) *v.* to go upstream. MdnC: 逆流而上 (*nì liú ér shàng*).

流 *n.* current, stream. Here it refers to the Qiantang River 錢塘江 in Zhejiang Province.

涉 *v.* to ford, wade through.

嚴灘 (严滩) Yan Rapids, normally called 嚴陵瀬 (*Yánlíng lài*), in present-day Tonglu County 桐廬, Zhejiang Province. It is said that Yan Guang 嚴光, a renowned recluse in the Eastern Han dynasty, used to go fishing in this place. On the way from Lin'an 臨安 to Jinhua 金華, Li Qingzhao passed this place and wrote a poem entitled "Setting Off from Yan Rapids at Night" 夜發嚴灘 ("Yèfā Yántān" 夜发严滩).

險 (险) *n.* narrow pass.

抵 *v.* reach, arrive. MdnC: 到 (*dào*).

金華 (华) place name in present-day Jinhua, Zhejiang Province.

卜 (*bǔ*) *v.* to select. MdnC: 選擇 (*xuǎn zé* 选择).

第 *n.* residence, dwelling. MdnC: 宅第 (*zhái dì*).

9. 乍 *adv.* just. MdnC: 剛剛 (*gāng gāng* 刚刚).

釋ₐ (释) *v.* to release. Here it means "to get off (the boat)."

舟楫 *n.* boat and oar. Here it refers to a boat.

軒窗 (轩窗) *n.* windows. Here it refers to a room or house.

釋ᵦ 然 *adj.* released, relaxed. See L5 Grammar Note 2 ② for 然.

更 (*gēng*) *n.* clock. Here it refers to the night.

奈 *v.* to deal with. MdnC: 打發 (*dǎ fā* 打发).

博弈 *n.* gambling and chess playing.

講 (讲) *v.* to talk about, discuss.

且長行、葉子、博塞、彈棋，近世無
qiě cháng xíng　yè zǐ　bó sāi　tán qí　jìn shì wú

傳。¹⁰ 若打揭、大小豬窩、族鬼、胡畫、數
chuán　ruò dǎ jiē　dà xiǎo zhū wō　zú guǐ　hú huà　shǔ

倉、睹快之類，皆鄙俚不經見。¹¹ 藏酒、摴
cāng　dǔ kuài zhī lèi　jiē bǐ lǐ bù jīng jiàn　cáng jiǔ　chū

蒲、雙蹙融，近漸廢絕。¹² 選仙、加減、插
pú　shuāng cù róng　jìn jiàn fèi jué　xuǎn xiān　jiā jiǎn　chā

關火，質魯任命，無所施人智巧。¹³ 大小象
guān huǒ　zhì lǔ rèn mìng　wú suǒ shī rén zhì qiǎo　dà xiǎo xiàng

戲、奕棋，又惟可容二人。獨采選、打馬，
xì　yì qí　yòu wéi kě róng èr rén　dú cǎi xuǎn　dǎ mǎ

特爲閨房雅戲。¹⁴ 嘗恨采選叢繁，勞於檢閱，
tè wèi guī fáng yǎ xì　cháng hèn cǎi xuǎn cóng fán　láo yú jiǎn yuè

故能通者少，難遇勍敵；打馬簡要，而苦無
gù néng tōng zhě shǎo　nán yù qíng dí　dǎ mǎ jiǎn yào　ér kǔ wú

文采。¹⁵
wén cǎi

长行、叶子、博塞、弹棋，这些是没有流传下来的游戏。¹⁰打揭、大小猪窝、族鬼、胡画、数仓、睹快这类游戏，都很粗俗，（我这里）不常见。¹¹藏酒、摴蒲、双蹙融，近来渐渐没人玩儿了。¹²选仙、加减、插关火，（这些游戏）简单粗笨，完全靠运气，没有办法运用智慧和技巧。¹³大小象棋、围棋，又只允许两个人（玩）。只有采选、打马，是特别适合闺房中玩的雅致游戏。¹⁴（我）曾经不喜欢采选的繁杂，要经常翻检查看，所以精通的人少，很难遇到劲敌。打马很简单，但是苦于缺少花样。¹⁵

10. 且 *initial particle.* used at the beginning of a sentence to introduce a statement, no meaning in itself. See also 夫 (fú) in L2 Grammar Note 4 ①.

   長 (长 cháng) 行 (xíng) *n.* a gambling game prevalent in the Tang dynasty.

   葉 (叶) 子 *n.* gambling cards.

   博塞 (sāi) *n.* also called 格五, a chess game in ancient China.

   彈 (弹 tán) 棋 *n.* an ancient Chinese chess game that started in the Han dynasty.

   是 *demonstrative pron.* these (referring to games). See L3 Grammar Note 1 ①.

   傳 (传 chuán) *v.* to transmit, hand down. MdnC: 流傳 (liú chuán 流传).

11. 打揭、大小豬窩 (猪窝)、族鬼、胡畫 (画)、數 (数 shǔ) 倉 (仓)、睹快 *n.* gambling game names.

   鄙俚 *adj.* low, vulgar, rustic. MdnC: 粗俗 (cū sú).

   經 (经) 見 (见 jiàn) *adj.* common, usual. MdnC: 常見 (cháng jiàn 常见).

12. 藏酒、摴蒲、雙 (双) 蠥融 *n.* gambling game names.

   廢絕 (废绝) *v.* to terminate.

13. 選 (选) 仙、加減、插關 (关) 火 *n.* gambling game names.

   質 (质) *adj.* basic.

   魯 (鲁) *adj.* stupid, vulgar. MdnC: 粗笨 (cū bèn).

   任 (rèn) 命 *adj.* accepting of one's fate.

   施 *v.* to act. MdnC: 運用 (yùn yòng 运用).

   智 *n.* wisdom. MdnC: 智慧 (zhì huì).

   巧 *n.* skills. MdnC: 技巧 (jì qiǎo).

14. 象戲 (戏) *n.* Chinese chess. MdnC: 象棋 (xiàng qí).

   弈棋 *n.* go game. MdnC: 圍棋 (wéi qí 围棋).

   惟 *adv.* only. See L22 Grammar Note 2 ②.

   容 *v.* to allow. MdnC: 允許 (yún xǔ 允许).

   采選 (选) *n.* an ancient Chinese game that first appeared in the Tang dynasty.

   特爲 (为 wèi) *adv.* specially, for a special purpose.

   閨 (闺) 房 *n.* boudoir.

   雅 *adj.* refined and elegant. MdnC: 雅致 (yǎ zhì).

15. 恨 *v.* to disfavor, dislike.

   叢 (丛) 繁 *adj.* complicated, multifarious. MdnC: 繁雜 (fán zá 繁杂).

   勞 (劳) *v.* to labor over.

   檢閱 (检阅) *v.* to review, look over. MdnC: 翻檢 (fān jiǎn 翻检).

   通 *v.* to be proficient in. MdnC: 精通 (jīng tōng).

   勍敵 (敌) *n.* a well-matched and powerful opponent. MdnC: 勁敵 (jìn dí 劲敌).

   簡 (简) 要 *adj.* concise, simple.

   苦 *v.* to suffer from.

   文采 *n.* literary talent. Here it refers to the pattern and design of the game 花樣 (huā yàng 花样).

按打馬世有兩種： 一種一將十馬者， 謂
àn dǎ mǎ shì yǒu liǎng zhǒng　　yì zhǒng yí jiàng shí mǎ zhě　　wèi

之關西馬； 一種無將二十馬者， 謂之依經
zhī guān xī mǎ　　yì zhǒng wú jiàng èr shí mǎ zhě　　wèi zhī yī jīng

打马一般有两种(玩法)：一种是一个将棋子和十个马棋子，叫关西马；一种是没有将棋子，有二十个马

馬。 流行既久，　各有圖經凡例可考。　行移賞
mǎ　　liú xíng jì jiǔ　　gè yǒu tú jīng fán lì kě kǎo　　xíng yí shǎng

罰，　互有同異。 [16] 又宣和間人取兩種馬，　參
fá　　hù yǒu tóng yì　　yòu xuān hé jiān rén qǔ liǎng zhǒng mǎ　cān

雜加減，　大約交加僥倖，　古意盡矣。 所謂宣
zá jiā jiǎn　　dà yuē jiāo jiā jiǎo xìng　　gǔ yì jìn yǐ　　suǒ wèi xuān

和馬者是也。 [17] 予獨愛依經馬，　因取其賞罰互
hé mǎ zhě shì yě　　yú dú ài yī jīng mǎ　　yīn qǔ qí shǎng fá hù

度，　每事作數語，　隨事附見，　使兒輩圖之。 [18]
dù　　měi shì zuò shù yǔ　　suí shì fù jiàn　　shǐ ér bèi tú zhī

不獨施之博徒，　實足貽諸好事，　使千萬世
bù dú shī zhī bó tú　　shí zú yí zhū hǎo shì　　shǐ qiān wàn shì

後，　知命辭打馬，　始自易安居士是也。 [19] 時
hòu　　zhī mìng cí dǎ mǎ　　shǐ zì yì ān jū shì shì yě　　shí

紹興四年十一月二十四日，　易安室序。 [20]
shào xīng sì nián shí yī yuè èr shí sì rì　　yì ān shì xù

《李清照集箋注》，上海：上海古籍出版社 (2013)，366—367.

棋子，叫依经马。（这两种玩法）流行很久了，各有图谱凡例可参考。规则赏罚，也互有相同和不同的地方。[16] 宣和年间，有人取这两种打马玩法，将两者参杂加减，大概增加了些侥幸的成分，原来打马的意趣都没了，这就是所谓的宣和马。[17] 我只喜欢依经马，于是取来这个游戏赏罚的规则，在每一条规则上写几句，在规则后附上自己的见解，让子侄后辈（给）规则画上图例。[18]（这《打马图经》）不但可以用在赌博上，确实还留下了好处，让千秋后代的人都知道用文辞（来写）打马游戏的，是从我易安居士开始的！[19] 绍兴四年十一月二十四日，易安居士作序。[20]

16. 按 *n.* note, comment. Normally 按 indicates that the author's comment starts here.

　　將 (将 *jiàng*) *n.* general.

　　圖經 (图经) *n.* illustrated handbook. MdnC: 圖譜 (*tú pǔ* 图谱).

　　凡例 *n.* explanatory notes, guide to a book.

　　考 *v.* to consult. MdnC: 參考 (*cān kǎo* 参考).

　　行移 *n.* notices issued by the government. Here it refers to the rules of a game 規則 (*guī zé* 规则).

　　賞罰 (赏罚) *n.* reward and punishment.

17. 宣和 era name of Emperor Hui of the Song (1119–1125).

　　參雜 (参杂) *v.* to mix.

　　大約 (约) *adv.* probably.

　　交加 *v.* to mingle. Here it means "to increase" 增加 (*zēng jiān*).

　　僥幸 *n.* good luck.

　　古意 *n.* the charm of the traditional game.

18. 度 *n.* rule. MdnC: 規則 (*guī zé* 规则).

隨 *adj.* following.

附 *v.* to attach.

見 (见) *n.* opinions. MdnC: 見解 (*jiàn jiě* 见解).

兒輩 (儿辈) *n.* younger generation, son and nephew. MdnC: 後輩 (*hòu bèi* 后辈).

圖 (图) *v.* to draw.

19. 博徒 *n.* gambler. Here it refers to a gambling game.

實 (实) 足 *adv.* completely, fully.

貽 (贻) *v.* to leave behind. MdnC: 留 (*liú*).

命 *v.* to use.

辭 *n.* expression.

20. 紹興 (绍兴) era name of Emperor Gao of the Song (1131–1162). 紹興四年 is 1134.

Literary Analysis

Only 139 characters long, the preface is a mine of information. It presents vivid snapshots of wartime life, people's suffering, and the joys of temporary peace, all while providing detailed instructions on how to play Capture the Horse and explaining the unique method Li invented. Her elucidations of "慧、通、达" and "专、精、妙" have taken on broad significance well beyond the game, as her preface is extensively cited by later literati. For a translation and discussion of this preface, see *HTRCProse*, chapter 12, "Tang and Song Occasional Prose: Prefaces and Epistolary Writing," C12.3.

—ZC

課後練習 Exercises

一 給加點字注音 Give the pinyin romanization for each dotted word.

1. 旁午 (____, ____) 2. 絡繹 (____, ____) 3. 庖 (____) 4. 郢 (____) 5. 桀 (____)
6. 摴蒲 (____, ____) 7. 麞融 (____, ____) 8. 勍 (____) 9. 淮 (____) 10. 朔 (____)

二 在括號中給句中加點的字注音，並選出正確的釋義 Give the pinyin romanization for each dotted word; then select the correct definition from the following list, and write it in the blank.

流傳(传)　達(达)到　粗笨　很少　逆流而上　打發(发)　留　信服　選擇(选择)

1. 小信未孚 (fú) ___信服___ 2. 奈此良夜乎 ( ) _____ 3. 故罕爲之 ( ) _____
4. 近世無傳 ( ) _____ 5. 自臨安泝流 ( ) _____ 6. 質魯任命 ( ) _____
7. 皆臻至理 ( ) _____ 8. 卜居陳氏第 ( ) _____ 9. 貽諸好事 ( ) _____

三 選擇釋義並填空 Match each word in the left column with its correct definition in the middle column. Fill in each blank in the right column with an appropriate word from the left column (some words may be used more than once).

謀謀劃(谋划)	揮動(挥动)
精＿＿＿＿	規則(规则)
解＿＿＿＿	到
運＿＿＿＿	贏(赢)
擲＿＿＿＿	沉溺
起＿＿＿＿	剛剛(刚)
耽＿＿＿＿	**謀劃(谋划)**
進＿＿＿＿	精通
抵＿＿＿＿	肢解
乍＿＿＿＿	捉
度＿＿＿＿	扔

專則＿＿＿，＿＿＿則無所不妙。

故庖丁之＿＿＿牛，郢人之＿＿＿斤，師曠之聽，離妻之視，大至於堯舜之仁，桀紂之惡，小至於＿＿＿豆＿＿＿蠅，巾角拂棋，皆臻至理者何？

予性喜博，凡所謂博者皆＿＿＿之，晝夜每忘寢食。且平生多寡未嘗不＿＿＿者何？精而已。

易安居士亦自臨安泝流，涉嚴灘之險，＿＿＿金華，卜居陳氏第。＿＿＿釋舟楫而見軒窗，意頗釋然。

予獨愛依經馬，因取其賞罰互＿＿＿，每事作數語，隨事附見，使兒輩圖之。

四 請用給出的字填空 Fill in each blank with an appropriate word from the following list (some words may be used more than once).

凡　者　而　已　然　何

1. 皆臻至理者＿＿＿？妙＿＿＿＿＿＿。

2. 予性喜博，＿＿＿所謂博者皆耽之。

3. 且平生多寡未嘗不進＿＿＿何？精＿＿＿已。

4. 乍釋舟楫而見軒窗，意頗釋＿＿＿。

五 爲加點字選擇正確釋義，並根據釋義來翻譯句子 Match each dotted word with its correct modern Chinese equivalent by circling the latter. Then translate each sentence into modern Chinese.

1. 又何間焉？　　　　ⓐ爲什麼(为什么) b. 憑什麼(凭什么) c. 多少

現代文翻譯：你又为什么要参与到这件事情里面？
＿＿＿＿＿＿＿＿＿＿＿＿＿＿＿＿＿＿＿＿＿＿＿

2. 慧則通，通則無所不達；專則精，精則無所不妙。　　a. 就 b. 多少 c. 什麼(什么)

現代文翻譯：＿＿＿＿＿＿＿＿＿＿＿＿＿＿＿＿＿＿＿

3. 後世之人，不惟學聖人之道不到聖處；雖嬉戲之事，亦不得其依稀彷彿而遂止者多矣。

a. 但是 b. 即使 c. 而且

現代文翻譯：＿＿＿＿＿＿＿＿＿＿＿＿＿＿＿＿＿＿＿

4. 居山林者謀入城市，居城市者謀入山林，旁午絡繹，莫不失所。　　a. 没有人 b. 不要 c. 被

现代文翻译：＿＿＿＿＿＿＿＿＿＿＿＿＿＿＿＿＿＿＿＿＿＿＿＿＿＿

5. 嘗恨采選叢繁，勞於檢閱，故能通者少，難遇勍敵；打馬簡要，而苦無文采。

a. 品嘗（尝）b. 既然 c. 曾經（曾经）

现代文翻译：＿＿＿＿＿＿＿＿＿＿＿＿＿＿＿＿＿＿＿＿＿＿＿＿＿＿

第二十八課

商景蘭《未焚集序》

"Preface to *The Collection of Unburned Poems*" (Shang Jinglan)

Introduction

Shang Jinglan 商景兰 (courtesy name Meisheng 眉生; 1605–1676), a renowned woman writer of the late Ming and early Qing, prepared this preface for a collection of poems written by her deceased daughter Qi Deqiong 祁德琼. Shang herself was a prominent figure in the cohort of women poets living in Shaoxing, Zhejiang Province. At the age of sixteen, she was married to Qi Biaojia 祁彪佳 (1602–1645), a famous prose writer and playwright. This happy marriage, hailed in its time as that of "a golden boy and a jade girl," came to a tragic end in 1645.

   With the fall of the Ming dynasty in 1644, the Manchu court soon summoned Qi Biaojia for service. Defiant, Qi rejected the summons and drowned himself in a pond beside his home. From this point on, Shang Jinglan taught and reared their children alone, yet never ceased to write. She also inspired other women within and beyond the Qi clan to write, thus forming the famed Shaoxing group of women poets, which included her three daughters and two daughters-in-law as well as other female talents from central Zhejiang.

   This preface affords a glimpse into the creative activities of a young woman within the Qi family compound, tinged with her mother's sorrowful recollection.

正文與簡體譯文 Text and Modern Chinese Translation

吾女德瓊之長逝也，蓋十有二年矣。生
wú nǚ dé qióng zhī cháng shì yě　gài shí yǒu èr nián yǐ　shēng

平吟詠十不存一二。每一念及，輒爲惘然。
píng yín yǒng shí bù cún yī èr　měi yí niàn jí　zhé wéi wǎng rán

今春吾婿鄂叔，集其遺詩，得六十六首，將
jīn chūn wú xù è shū　jí qí yí shī　dé liù shí liù shǒu　jiāng

付棗梨，因持示予，並請予序。[1] 予撫卷嘆
fù zǎo lí　yīn chí shì yú　bìng qǐng yú xù　yú fǔ juàn tàn

息，摘其警句，令諸女孫向月下朗吟，覺昔
xī　zhāi qí jǐng jù　lìng zhū nǚ sūn xiàng yuè xià lǎng yín　jué xī

時詠絮頌椒風度，恍在目前，不禁涕淚交
shí yǒng xù sòng jiāo fēng dù　huǎng zài mù qián　bù jīn tì lèi jiāo

我的女儿德琼逝去很久了，大概有十二年了。她生平时吟咏（创作的诗篇），十首里不能留存一二，每想到这，总感到惘然。今年春天，我的女婿（王）鄂叔收集了她遗留的诗稿，有六十六首，将要交付印刷出版。于是他拿着稿子给我看，并请我给文集作序。[1] 我抚摸着书卷长叹着，摘选其中的警句，让孙女们在月下朗读吟咏，觉得从前（德琼）吟诗颂椒时的风度，恍惚就

墮。 [2]

duò

在眼前，禁不住眼泪掉下来。[2]

1. 蓋 (盖) *adv.* probably. See L13 Grammar Note 1.

吟詠 (咏) *v.* to recite (poems). Here it means "to write (poems)."

輒 (辄) *adv.* always.

惘然 *adj.* perplexed.

婿 *n.* son-in-law. MdnC: 女婿 (*nǚ xù*).

鄂叔 or 王鄂叔 Shang Jinglan's son-in-law, Qi Deqiong's husband.

付 *v.* to give, hand over. MdnC: 交付 (*jiāo fù*).

棗 (枣) 梨 wooden printing tools. Here it refers to publishing.

2. 嘆 (叹) 息 *v.* to sigh.

警句 *n.* aphorism.

女孫 (孙) *n.* granddaughter. MdnC: 孫女 (*sūn nǚ* 孙女).

昔時 (时) *adv.* in former times. MdnC: 從前 (*cóng qián* 从前).

詠 (咏) 絮 an allusion to chapter 2, "Speech and Word" 言語 ("Yányǔ" 言语), of *A New Account of the Tales of the World* 世說新語. The story tells of Xie Daoyun 謝道韞, a talented woman in the Eastern Jin dynasty, who described snow with this line: 未若柳絮因風起 (it is better to compare snow to catkins flying in the wind). Later 詠絮 became a poetic appellation for talented women.

頌 (颂) 椒 an ancient custom. People perform sacrificial services for their ancestors on the first day of the lunar year with pepper wine and cypress wine 椒柏酒, or they offer the wine to parents to celebrate their birthdays.

恍 *adv.* seemingly. MdnC: 恍惚 (*huǎng hū*).

墮 *v.* to fall. MdnC: 掉 (*diào*).

夫自先忠敏棄世以來，恃子若女，相依
fú zì xiān zhōng mǐn qì shì yǐ lái   shì zǐ ruò nǚ   xiāng yī

膝下，或對雪聯吟，或看花索句，聊藉風
xī xià   huò duì xuě lián yín   huò kàn huā suǒ jù   liáo jiè fēng

雅，以卒桑榆。[3] 今幼子見背，弱女云亡，即
yǎ   yǐ zú sāng yú   jīn yòu zǐ jiàn bèi   ruò nǚ yún wáng   jí

香奩麗句，亦僅存片羽。予復何心，能無悲
xiāng lián lì jù   yì jǐn cún piàn yǔ   yú fù hé xīn   néng wú bēi

悼？[4] 且吾女自幼工詩，每得句，即爲先忠敏
dào   qiě wú nǚ zì yòu gōng shī   měi dé jù   jí wéi xiān zhōng mǐn

所稱賞。今既從先忠敏遊地下，想夜臺中
suǒ chēng shǎng jīn jì cóng xiān zhōng mǐn yóu dì xià xiǎng yè tái zhōng

定多佳什。[5] 而未亡人尚延視息，勿獲相從。
dìng duō jiā shí   ér wèi wáng rén shàng yán shì xī wù huò xiāng cóng

自从先夫去世以来，（只有）母亲的儿子和女儿，相依在我身边，（我们）有时对着雪景联句，有时看着花开思索佳句，暂且借助这些风雅的事情，来度过我的晚年。[3] 现在我的小儿子去世了，柔弱的女儿也去世了，即使是她闺阁时所作的佳句，也只有少量留存下来。除了悲悼，我还能有什么样的心思啊！[4] 而且我的女儿从小就擅长写诗，每次得到佳句，就会被父亲所赞赏。现在她已经跟从父亲到了地下，想来地下一定有很多（他们的）佳作。[5]

是益增吾痛也。 年老多病， 言不能文， 漫書
shì yì zēng wú tòng yě　　nián lǎo duō bìng　yán bùnéng wén　màn shū

數言， 以誌哀感云爾。⁶甲寅二月朔， 眉生氏
shù yán　　yǐ zhì āi gǎn yún ěr　　jiǎ yín èr yuè shuò　méi shēng shì

題。 ⁷
tí

可是我还活着，不能跟着他们离去。这更增加我的痛苦。我现在年老多病，说话不能成文，随意写下几句，来记录心中哀痛的感想之类的。⁶甲寅年二月初一，眉生氏题。⁷

《祁彪佳集》，北京：中華書局 (1960), 297.

3. 忠敏　Qi Biaojia's posthumous name.

棄 (弃) 世 *v.* to pass away, die.

恃 *n.* mother.

若 *conj.* and.

膝下 at the knees. Here it refers to closeness to the mother.

或 *adv.* sometimes. See L15 Grammar Note 4 ②.

聯 (联) 吟 or 聯句 an ancient way to collectively compose a poem, usually at a banquet. Each poet takes a turn composing and chanting one line, and eventually they combine all their lines into one poem.

索 *v.* to seek.

聊 *adv.* for a moment. MdnC: 暫且 (*zàn qiě* 暂且).

藉 (jiè) *v.* to get the help from. MdnC: 藉助 (*jiè zhù* 借助).

以 *conj.* in order to. See L2 Grammar Note 1 ③.

卒 *v.* to finish.

桑榆 *n.* old age. MdnC: 晚年 (*wǎn nián*).

4. 見 (见 jiàn) 背 *v.* to pass away. MdnC: 去世 (*qù shì*). See also L21 note 2.

云亡 *v.* to pass away.

香奩 (奁) *n.* women's makeup bag. Here it refers to a boudoir 閨閣 (*guī gé* 闺阁).

麗 (丽) 句 *n.* beautiful poetic line. MdnC: 佳句 (*jiā jù*).

片 *adj.* a few. MdnC: 少量 (*shǎo liàng*).

羽 *n.* feather. Here it refers to poems.

悲悼 *v.* to grieve over.

5. 工 *v.* to be good at. MdnC: 擅長 (*shàn cháng* 擅长).

爲 (为 wéi) *particle.* by. MdnC: 被 (*bèi*). See L21 Grammar Note 3 ⑤.

夜臺 (台) *n.* tomb. Here it refers to the underworld.

什 (shí) *n.* writings. MdnC: 作品 (*zuò pǐn*).

6. 未亡人 *n.* a title that widows use to refer to themselves.

延 *v.* to stretch, extend.

視 (视) 息 *n.* vision and breath, referring to human life.

勿 *adv.* don't.

益 *adv.* more, further.

漫 *adv.* freely. MdnC: 隨意 (*suí yì*).

誌 (志) *v.* to write down, record. MdnC: 記錄 (*jì lù* 记录).

云爾 (尔) *particle.* like so. See Grammar Note 1 ③.

7. 甲寅 the thirteenth year of Emperor Kangxi (r. 1661–1722) of the Qing, 1674.
朔 *n.* the first day of the lunar month.

語法注釋 Grammar Note

1. 爾　Three uses of 爾 are explained in this book. In addition to the use below, see 爾①② in L6 Grammar Note 1.

③ *particle.* used at the end of the sentence together with 云, meaning "like this or like so."

年老多病，言不能文，漫書數言，以誌哀感云爾。

[我现在年老多病，说话不能成文，随意写下几句，来记录心中哀痛的感想这类的话。]

Literary Analysis

This short preface is a tour de force of prose structuring. Read it again sentence by sentence, identify the times and places anchoring each, and by so doing, sort out the multiple layers of recollection. Consider how the author interweaves all these memory fragments into a seamless whole.

—ZC

課後練習 Exercises

一 給加點字注音 Give the pinyin romanization for each dotted word.

1. 棗梨 （____, ____）　2. 惘然 （____）　3. 輒 （____）　4. 鄂 （____）
5. 桑榆 （____, ____）　6. 香奩 （____）　7. 寅 （____）　8. 恃 （____）

二 在括號中給句中加點的字注音，並選出正確的釋義 Give the pinyin romanization for each dotted word; then select the correct definition from the following list, and write it in the blank.

記錄(记录)　掉　暫(暂)且　交付　擅長(长)　隨意
少量　作品　恍惚　藉(借)助　女婿　**信服**

1. 小信未孚（ fú ）　**信服**　2. 吾婿鄂叔（　）_____　3. 以付棗梨（　）_____
4. 恍在目前（　）_____　5. 涕淚交墮（　）_____　6. 聊藉風雅（　）_____
7. 聊藉風雅（　）_____　8. 僅存片羽（　）_____　9. 自幼工詩（　）_____
10. 定多佳什（　）_____　11. 漫書數語（　）_____　12. 以誌哀感（　）_____

三 請用給出的字填空 Fill in each blank with an appropriate word from the following list (some words may be used more than once).

勿　云　爲(为)　蓋(盖)　或　爾(尔)　若

1. 吾女德瓊之長逝也，＿＿＿十有二年矣。
2. 每一念及，輒＿＿＿悯然。
3. 夫自先忠敏棄世以來，恃子＿＿＿女，相依膝下，＿＿＿對雪聯吟，＿＿＿看花索句，聊藉風雅，以卒桑榆。
4. 而未亡人尚延視息，＿＿＿獲相從。
5. 年老多病，言不能文，漫書數言，以誌哀感＿＿＿＿＿＿。

四 爲加點字選擇正確釋義，並根據釋義來翻譯句子 Match each dotted word with its correct modern Chinese equivalent by circling the latter. Then translate each sentence into modern Chinese.

1. 又何間焉?　　　　　　　　　　(a.)爲什麼(为什么)　b. 憑什麼(凭什么)　c.多少

現代文翻譯：你又为什么要参与到这件事情里面？
_____

2. 吾女德瓊之長逝也，蓋十有二年矣。　　　　a.可能　b.建造　c.何不

現代文翻譯：_____

3. 恃子若女，相依膝下。　　　　　　　　　　a.假若　b.和　c.至於(于)

現代文翻譯：_____

4. 或對雪聯吟，或看花索句，聊藉風雅，以卒桑榆。　　a.有人　b.或者　c.有時(时)

現代文翻譯：_____

5. 且吾女自幼工詩，每得句，即爲先忠敏所稱賞。　　a.做　b.爲(为)了　c.被

現代文翻譯：_____

6. 而未亡人尚延視息，勿獲相從。　　　　　　a.匆匆　b.不能　c.不要

現代文翻譯：_____

7. 年老多病，言不能文，漫書數言，以誌哀感云爾。　　　　　a. 來（来）b. 原因 c. 而且

现代文翻译：＿＿＿＿＿＿＿＿＿＿＿＿＿＿＿＿＿＿＿＿＿＿＿＿＿＿＿

單元練習

Unit Exercises

一、辨析加點字在不同句中注音和釋義的異同 Give the pinyin romanization for each dotted word, and then write in its correct definition.

1. 鄙   肉食者鄙，未能遠謀。   （ **bǐ** ）<u>目光短淺</u>

       越國以鄙遠，君知其難也。   （   ）_____

2. 會   會于會稽山陰之蘭亭。   （   ）_____

       會桃花之芳園。   （   ）_____

3. 異   雖世殊事異，所以興懷，其致一也。（   ）_____

       漁人甚異之。   （   ）_____

4. 由   每攬昔人興感之由。   （   ）_____

       亦由今之視昔。   （   ）_____

5. 數   數百步中無雜樹。   （   ）_____

       罰依金谷酒數。   （   ）_____

6. 尋   尋向所誌。   （   ）_____

       尋病終。   （   ）_____

7. 舉   董生舉進士。   （   ）_____

       去年之舉，淳已自分必死。   （   ）_____

二、用給出的字填空，並選擇正確的釋義 Fill in the blanks with words from list A, and then write in their modern Chinese equivalents from list B.

A. Words for Filling the Blanks   B. Modern Chinese Equivalents

騁 悼 訊 假 慕   消息 變(变)化 沿着   拜見(见) 悲傷(伤)
仕 業 延 伸 聊   借   抒發(发) 放開(开) 邀請(请) 做官
遷 緣 詣 鄙   仰慕 姑且   職業(职业) **目光短淺**

1. 肉食者 ___鄙，未能遠謀。   [目光短淺]   2. 臨文嗟_____。   [   ]

3. 遊目_____懷。   [   ]   4. 情隨事_____。   [   ]

5. _____溪行。   [   ]   6. 武陵人捕魚爲_____。   [   ]

7. 咸來問_____。   [   ]   8. 餘人各復_____至其家。   [   ]

9. ＿＿＿太守說如此。 [　　　] 10. 大塊＿＿＿我以文章。 [　　　]

11. 何＿＿＿雅懷？ [　　　] 12. ＿＿＿以吾子之行卜之。 [　　　]

13. 苟＿＿＿義彊仁者皆愛惜。 [　　　] 14. 可以出而＿＿＿矣。 [　　　]

三、給加點字選擇正確的釋義，並選出與加點字用法相同的句子 Circle the letter of the correct definition (a, b, c, or d) for the dotted word in each boldfaced sentence. Then circle the letter of the sentence (A, B, C, or D) that employs the dotted word in the same way as the boldfaced sentence.

1. 臣之妻私臣。　　　　　　　　　a. 這(这)件事情 b. 他 ⓒ 的 d. 他們

   A. 夫晉，何厭之有？　　　　　　**B.** 不闕秦，將焉取之？

   C. 肉食者謀之，又何間焉？　　　Ⓓ 能面刺寡人之過者，受上賞。

2. 或取諸懷抱，悟言一室之內。　　a. 之於(于) b. 各 c. 每 d. 全

   A. 宗廟會同，非諸侯而何？　　　B. 吾諸兒碌碌。

   C. 性猶湍水也，決諸東方則東流。　D. 而此諸子，化爲糞壤。

3. 一死生爲虛誕，齊彭殤爲妄作。　a. 認爲(认为) b. 替 c. 是 d. 被

   A. 但爲氣所激，緣悟天人理。　　B. 以爲文者氣之所形。

   C. 淳且與先文忠爲北塞之舉。　　D. 此子爲不朽矣。

4. 漁人甚異之。　　　　　　　　　a. 以……爲異(为异) b. 使……異(异) c. 不同 d. 奇怪

   A. 一日，風雪嚴寒，從數騎出。　B. 吾惡知其今不異於古所云邪？

   C. 酣觴賦詩，以樂其志。　　　　D. 一死生爲虛誕，齊彭殤爲妄作。

5. 村中聞有此人，咸來問訊。　　　a. 少數(数) b. 大部分 c. 咸陽(阳) d. 全都

   A. 或取諸懷抱，悟言一室之內。　B. 其中往來種作，男女衣著悉如外人。

   C. 初極狹，纔通人。　　　　　　D. 見漁人，乃大驚。

6. 率妻子邑人來此絕境，不復出焉。 a. 啊 b. 什麼(么) c. 怎麼(么) d. 於(于)之

   A. 朝濟而夕設版焉。　　　　　　B. 必知亂之所自起，焉能治之。

   C. 苟慕義彊仁者皆愛惜焉。　　　D. 焉用亡鄭以倍鄰？

7. 矧燕趙之士出乎其性者哉？　　　a. 雖(凭借)然 b. 即使 c. 何況(况) d. 但是

   A. 夫天地者，萬物之逆旅也。　　B. 苟慕義彊仁者皆愛惜焉。

   C. 然吾嘗聞：……．　　　　　　D. 況脩短隨化，終期於盡。

四、閱讀下面的段落，選擇正確的釋義　Read the following passage, and select the correct definition for each dotted word in the following list.

《歸去來兮辭》序
陶淵明

　　余家貧，耕植不足以自給。幼稚盈室，缾無儲粟，生生所資，未見其術。親故多勸余爲長吏，脫然有懷，求之靡途。會有四方之事，諸侯以惠愛爲德，家叔以余貧苦，遂見用爲小邑。于時風波未靜，心憚遠役。彭澤去家百里，公田之利，足以爲酒，故便求之。及少日，眷然有歸歟之情。何則？質性自然，非矯勵所得。飢凍雖切，違己交病。嘗從人事，皆口腹自役。於是悵然慷慨，深愧平生之志。猶望一稔，當斂裳宵逝。尋程氏妹喪于武昌，情在駿奔，自免去職。仲秋至冬，在官八十餘日。因事順心，命篇曰《歸去來兮》。乙巳歲十一月也。

《陶淵明集》，北京：中華書局 (1995), 159.

給 (给 jǐ) *v.* to supply.　幼稚 *n.* children, kids.　盈 *v.* to be filled with.
缾 (瓶) *n.* jar, bottle.　儲 (储) *v.* to store.　脫然 *adj.* easily.
役 *v.* to serve, work.　彭澤 place name.　眷 *v.* to care for.
矯勵 (矫励) *v.* to rectify.　奔 *v.* to mourn.

1. 親故多勸余爲長吏。　　　a. 舊(旧)　　　b. 所以　　　c. 朋友
2. 家叔以余貧苦。　　　　　a. 用　　　　　b. 因爲(为)　　c. 而
3. 遂見用爲小邑。　　　　　a. 做　　　　　b. 被　　　　　c. 因爲(为)
4. 彭澤去家百里。　　　　　a. 離開(离开)　b. 走去　　　　c. 距離(离)
5. 嘗從人事。　　　　　　　a. 品嘗(尝)　　b. 常常　　　　c. 曾經(经)
6. 深愧平生之志。　　　　　a. 愧疚　　　　b. 遺(遗)憾　　c. 害怕
7. 猶望一稔。　　　　　　　a. 像　　　　　b. 仍然　　　　c. 猶(犹)豫
8. 尋程氏妹喪於武昌。　　　a. 不久　　　　b. 找　　　　　c. 去

五、將下列句子翻譯成現代漢語　Translate the following sentences into modern Chinese.

1. 夫人之相與，俯仰一世，或取諸懷抱，悟言一室之內，或因寄所託，放浪形骸之外。

現代文翻譯：＿＿＿＿＿＿＿＿＿＿＿＿＿＿＿＿＿＿＿＿＿＿＿＿＿＿＿＿＿＿＿

2. 向之所欣，俛仰之間以爲陳迹，猶不能不以之興懷；況脩短隨化，終期於盡。

現代文翻譯：＿＿＿＿＿＿＿＿＿＿＿＿＿＿＿＿＿＿＿＿＿＿＿＿＿＿＿＿＿＿＿

3. 問今是何世，乃不知有漢，無論魏晉。

現代文翻译：_____

4. 既出，得其船，便扶向路，處處誌之。

現代文翻译：_____

5. 況陽春召我以烟景，大塊假我以文章。

現代文翻译：_____

6. 開瓊筵以坐花，飛羽觴而醉月，不有佳詠，何伸雅懷。

現代文翻译：_____

7. 夫以子之不遇時，苟慕義彊仁者皆愛惜焉。

現代文翻译：_____

8. 爲我弔望諸君之墓，而觀於其市復有昔時屠狗者乎？

現代文翻译：_____

第二十九課

韓愈《原道》（上）

"On the Origin of the Way" (I) (Han Yu)

Introduction

A biographical note on Han Yu appears in lesson 26. Of all his expository essays, this is arguably the best known—praised for mounting a counteroffensive against ascendant Buddhism and Daoism and for reviving the great Confucian tradition in a new vein known as neo-Confucianism. Han begins the essay by redefining the foundational concepts of benevolence and righteousness 仁義 (*rényì* 仁义), as well as the Way and its power 道德 (*dàodé*), through unflattering contrastive references to Daoist, Mohist, and Buddhist views. To buttress his claim for Confucianism's superiority, he goes on to credit revered Confucian sages with establishing a civilized society marked by well-differentiated roles and duties for rulers, officials, and common people. These are the highlights of the essay's first half, covered in this lesson. A translation of this text is given in *HTRCProse*, chapter 10, "Tang and Song Expository Prose: The Practice of Persuasion," C10.1.

正文與簡體譯文 Text and Modern Chinese Translation

博愛之 _a 謂仁，行而宜之 _b 之 _a 謂義；由
bó ài zhī   wèi rén   xíng ér yí zhī   zhī   wèi yì   yóu

是而之 _c 焉之 _a 謂道，足乎己，無待於外之 _a
shì ér zhī   yān zhī   wèi dào   zú hū jǐ   wú dài yú wài zhī

謂德。¹ 仁與義，爲定名，道與德，爲虛位：
wèi dé   rén yǔ yì   wéi dìng míng   dào yǔ dé   wéi xū wèi

故道有君子小人，而德有凶有吉。²
gù dào yǒu jūn zǐ xiǎo rén   ér dé yǒu xiōng yǒu jí

广泛地爱人叫做仁，适宜恰当地实行仁叫做义；从仁义（出发）而继续往前走叫做道，充实自己，不依赖外物，叫做德。¹ 仁和义，是固定的名称，道和德，是空名：所以道有君子和小人（的差别），而德有凶恶和美好（的不同）。²

1. 博 *adj.* large, wide, extensive. MdnC: 廣泛 (*guǎng fàn* 广泛).

   之 _a *particle.* a nominative marker. See L2 Grammar Note 2 ⑤.

   仁 *n.* benevolence, virtue, and morality.

   行 (xíng) *v.* to put into practice. MdnC: 實行 (*shí xíng* 实行).

   宜 *adv.* properly, appropriately. MdnC: 適宜 (*shì yí* 适宜).

   之 _b *demonstrative pron.* It refers to 仁. See L1 Grammar Note 2 ①.

   義 (义) *n.* righteousness.

   由 *prep.* from. MdnC: 從 (*cóng* 从).

是 *demonstrative pron.* It refers to 仁義. See L3 Grammar Note 1 ①.

之 c *v.* to go, reach. MdnC: 往 (*wǎng*). See L7 Grammar Note 2 ⑦.

焉 *demonstrative pron.* equivalent of 之. It refers to 仁義. See L6 Grammar Note 5 ⑤.

道 *n.* way, path.

足 *adj.* enough, complete. Here it is used as a causative verb, 使……足, meaning "to enrich" 充實 (*chōng shí* 充实). See L7 Grammar Note 1 ②.

乎 *prep.* a variant of 於 (*yú* 于). See L6 Grammar Note 2 ③.

待 *v.* to wait for, depend on, rely on. MdnC: 依賴 (*yī lài* 依赖).

外 *n.* outside.

德 *n.* virtuous character.

2. 定 *adj.* fixed. MdnC: 固定 (*gù dìng*).

虛位 *n.* empty seat. Here it refers to the empty name, a name without substance 空名 (*kōng míng*).

君子 *n.* man of virtue.

小人 *n.* a mean person.

凶 *adj.* evil. MdnC: 惡 (*è* 恶).

吉 *adj.* good. MdnC: 美好 (*měi hǎo*).

老子之小仁義，非毀之也，其見者小也。
lǎo zǐ zhī xiǎo rén yì　fēi huǐ zhī yě　qí jiàn zhě xiǎo yě

坐井而觀天，曰「天小」者，非天小也。[3]
zuò jǐng ér guān tiān　yuē　tiān xiǎo　zhě　fēi tiān xiǎo yě

彼以煦煦爲仁，孑孑爲義，其小之也則宜。[4]
bǐ yǐ xù xù wéi rén　jié jié wéi yì　qí xiǎo zhī yě zé yí

其所謂道 a，道 b 其所道，非吾所謂道也。其
qí suǒ wèi dào　dào　qí suǒ dào　fēi wú suǒ wèi dào yě　qí

所謂德 a，德 b 其所德，非吾所謂德也。[5] 凡
suǒ wèi dé　dé　qí suǒ dé　fēi wú suǒ wèi dé yě　fán

吾所謂道德云者，合仁與義言之也，天下之
wú suǒ wèi dào dé yún zhě　hé rén yǔ yì yán zhī yě　tiān xià zhī

公言也。[6] 老子之所謂道德云者，去仁與義言
gōng yán yě　lǎo zǐ zhī suǒ wèi dào dé yún zhě　qù rén yǔ yì yán

之也，一人之私言也。[7]
zhī yě　yì rén zhī sī yán yě

老子輕視仁义，并不是要詆毀仁义，而是他的見识少。坐在井里面看天，说"天很小"的话，不是天(真的)小！[3] 他把小恩小惠当作仁，把谨小慎微当作义，那么他轻视仁义也是合适的。[4] 老子所说的道，是把他说的道当作道，不是我所说的道。他所说的德，是把他说的德当作德，不是我所说的德。[5] 凡是我所说的道德之类的话，是结合了仁和义来说的，是天下的公论。[6] 老子所说的道德这类的话，背离了仁和义，是他个人的言论。[7]

3. 老子 (family name 姓, Lǐ 李; given name 名, Ěr 耳; style 字, Bóyáng 伯陽; 571?–? BCE), a Chinese philosopher in the Spring and Autumn period. He is known as the founder of Daoism and the author of *Classic of Way and Virtue* 道德經 (*Dào dé jīng* 道德经).

小 *adj.* small. Here it is used as a putative verb, 以……爲小, meaning "to belittle" 輕視 (*qīng shì* 轻视). See L14 Grammar Note 1 ①.

毀 (毁) *v.* to destroy. MdnC: 詆毀 (*dǐ huǐ* 诋毁).

見 (见) 者 *n.* understanding, knowledge, experience. MdnC: 見識 (*jiàn shí* 见识).

4. 彼 *demonstrative pron.* that, referring to 老子. MdnC: 他 (*tā*). See L14 Grammar Note 2 ①.

以……爲 (为 *wéi*) …… to regard … as…. MdnC: 把 (*bǎ*) ……當作 (*dāng zuò* 当作). See L2 Grammar Note 1 ④.

煦煦 *adj.* kind and gentle. Here it refers to favor and kindness 恩惠 (*ēn huì*).

孑孑 *adj.* small. Here it means "overcautiousness" 謹小慎微 (*jǐn xiǎo shèn wēi* 谨小慎微).

5. 道 ₐ *n.* way, truth.

道 ᵦ *v.* used as a putative verb here, 以……爲道, meaning "to deem … as the way" 把 (*bǎ*) ……當作道 (*dāng zuò dào* 当作道). See L14 Grammar Note 1 ②.

其所道 means "what he called the way"— namely, 其所謂道.

德 ₐ *n.* morality.

德 ᵦ *v.* used as a putative verb here, 以……爲德, meaning "to deem something as the moral" 把 (*bǎ*) ……當作德 (*dāng zuò dé* 当作德). See L14 Grammar Note 1 ②.

6. 云 *ending particle.* 云 means "it was said." See L17 Grammar Note 1.

合 *v.* to combine, put together. MdnC: 結合 (*jié hé* 结合).

公言 *n.* public opinion. MdnC: 公論 (*gōng lùn* 公论).

7. 去 *v.* to leave, be away from. MdnC: 背離 (*bèi lí* 背离).

私 *adj.* private, personal. MdnC: 個人 (*gè rén* 个人).

周道衰， 孔子沒， 火於秦， 黃老于漢，
zhōu dào shuāi kǒng zǐ mò   huǒ yú qín   huáng lǎo yú hàn

佛于晉、 魏、 梁、 隋之間。⁸其言道德仁義
fó yú jìn   wèi   liáng suí zhī jiān   qí yán dào dé rén yì

者， 不入于楊， 則入于墨； 不入于老， 則入
zhě bú rù yú yáng zé rù yú mò   bú rù yú lǎo   zé rù

于佛。 入于彼， 必出於此。⁹入者主之， 出者
yú fó   rù yú bǐ   bì chū yú cǐ   rù zhě zhǔ zhī   chū zhě

奴之。 入者附之， 出者汙之。¹⁰噫！ 後之人其
nú zhī   rù zhě fù zhī   chū zhě wū zhī   yī   hòu zhī rén qí

欲聞仁義道德之說， 孰從而聽之？ ¹¹老者曰：
yù wén rén yì dào dé zhī shuō   shú cóng ér tīng zhī   lǎo zhě yuē

「孔子， 吾師之弟子也。」 佛者曰： 「孔
kǒng zǐ   wú shī zhī dì zǐ yě   fó zhě yuē   kǒng

子， 吾師之弟子也。」 ¹²爲孔子者， 習聞其
zǐ   wú shī zhī dì zǐ yě   wéi kǒng zǐ zhě   xí wén qí

周道衰落，孔子去世，秦代焚書坑儒，黃老之術在汉代(兴起)，佛教(兴起)于晋朝、北魏、梁代、隋朝之间。⁸那些讨论道德仁义的人，不是归于杨朱学派，就是归入墨家学派。不是归于老子的学说，就是归入佛教的理论，归入到了那一家，必然就离开这一家。⁹尊崇归入的学派，贬低远离的学派。附和归入的学派，污蔑远离的学派。¹⁰哎！后来人想要知道仁义道德的学说，要选哪一家来听呢？¹¹尊崇老子的人说："孔子是我们老师的弟子。"尊崇佛教的人说："孔子是

説，樂其誕而自小也，亦曰：「吾師亦嘗師
shuō　lè qí dàn ér zì xiǎo yě　yì yuē　　wú shī yì cháng shī

之」云爾。¹³ 不惟舉之於其口，而又筆之於其
zhī　yún ěr　　bù wéi jǔ zhī yú qí kǒu　ér yòu bǐ zhī yú qí

書。¹⁴ 噫！後之人雖欲聞仁義道德之説，其孰
shū　　yī　hòu zhī rén suī yù wén rén yì dào dé zhī shuō　qí shú

從而求之？¹⁵ 甚矣！人之ₐ好怪也。不求其
cóng ér qiú zhī　　shèn yǐ　rén zhī　hào guài yě　bù qiú qí

端，不訊其末，惟怪之ᵦ欲聞。¹⁶
duān　bú xùn qí mò　wéi guài zhī　yù wén

我们老师的弟子。"¹²
尊崇孔子的人，常听这
种理论，乐于(接受)它
的荒诞而轻视自己，也
说："我的老师曾师从
他们"之类的话。¹³ 不
只在嘴里讨论，而且把
这些记录到书里。¹⁴
哎！后来人即使想知道
仁义道德的学说，那么
选哪一个来探求呢？¹⁵
太过分了！人们喜好怪
诞(的言论)，不去探求
它的开端，不去考察它
的结果，只是想要听闻
怪诞(的言论)！¹⁶

8. 周 the Western Zhou dynasty (1046?–771 BCE).

　　衰 *v.* to decline. MdnC: 衰落 (*shuāi luò*).

　　沒 (没 mò) *v.* to die. MdnC: 死 (*sǐ*).

　　火 *n.* fire, referring to the burning of the books in the Qin dynasty 焚書坑儒 (*fén shū kēng rú* 焚书坑儒).

　　秦 the Qin dynasty (221–207 BCE).

　　黃老 refers to a syncretic Daoist tradition that rose in the second century BCE, named after the Yellow Emperor 黃帝 (*Huáng dì*) and Laozi 老子.

　　漢 (汉) the Han dynasty (206 BCE–220 CE).

　　佛 Buddhism.

　　晉 (晋) the Han dynasty (206 BCE–220 CE).

　　魏 or 北魏 the Wei dynasty (386–534).

　　梁 the Liang dynasty (503–557).

　　隋 the Sui dynasty (581–618).

9. 楊 (杨) or 楊朱 (395?–335? BCE), a philosopher in the Warring States period.

　　墨 or 墨家 the Mohist school. See lesson 12 for a brief note on the Mohism.

　　彼……此 used together to make a contrast between this and that. See L14 Grammar Note 2 ②.

10. 主 *n.* host, owner. Here it is used as a putative verb, 以……爲主, meaning "to revere" 尊崇 (*zūn chóng*). See L14 Grammar Note 1 ②.

　　奴 *n.* slave, servant. Here it is used as a putative verb, 以……爲奴, meaning "to belittle" 貶低 (*biǎn dī* 贬低). See L14 Grammar Note 1 ②.

　　附 *v.* to echo. MdnC: 附和 (*fù hè*).

　　汙 (污) *v.* to smear. MdnC: 污蔑 (*wū miè*).

11. 噫 *exclamatory word.* alas. MdnC: 唉 (*ài*).

　　孰 *interrogative pron.* who? which? See L4 Grammar Note 1 ①.

12. 老者 the follower of Laozi.

　　弟子 *n.* disciple.

佛者 followers of Buddha.

13. 爲 (为 wéi) *v.* to do. Here it means "to revere" 尊崇 (*zūn chóng*).

　　習 (习) *v.* to become familiar with, be used to.

　　樂 (乐 lè) *v.* to take delight in. MdnC: 樂於 (*lè yú* 乐于).

　　誕 (诞) *adj.* absurd. MdnC: 荒誕 (*huāng dàn* 荒诞).

　　小 *adj.* small. Here it is used as a putative verb, 以……爲小, meaning "to belittle" 輕視 (*qīng shì* 轻视). See L14 Grammar Note 1 ①.

　　師 (师) *n.* teacher. Here it is used as a putative verb, 以……爲師, meaning "to study under" 師從 (*shī cóng* 师从). See L14 Grammar Note 1 ②.

　　云爾 (尔) *particle.* like so. See L28 Grammar Note 1 ③.

14. 惟 *adv.* only. MdnC: 只 (*zhǐ*). See L22 Grammar Note 2 ②.

　　舉 (举) *v.* to talk. MdnC: 談論 (*tán lùn* 谈论).

　　筆 (笔) *v.* to write. MdnC: 記錄 (*jì lù* 记录).

15. 其 *adv.* used to suggest a tentative tone. MdnC: 那麽 (*nà me* 那么). See L2 Grammar Note 5 ③.

16. 甚 (shèn) *adv.* extremely. MdnC: 過分 (*guò fèn* 过分).

　　之 _a *particle.* a nominative marker. See L2 Grammar Note 2 ⑤.

　　好 (hào) *v.* to like, desire. MdnC: 喜好 (*xǐ hào*).

　　怪 *adj.* strange, bizarre. MdnC: 怪誕 (*guài dàn* 怪诞).

　　端 *n.* beginning. MdnC: 開端 (*kāi duān* 开端).

　　訊 (讯) *v.* to inquire, ask, examine. MdnC: 考察 (*kǎo chá*).

　　末 *n.* the end, last stage. MdnC: 結果 (*jié guǒ* 结果).

　　之 _b *particle.* marks the inversion of objects and has no meaning. See L2 Grammar Note 2 ⑥.

古之爲民者四， 今之爲民者六。古之教
gǔ zhī wéi mín zhě sì　 jīn zhī wéi mín zhě liù　 gǔ zhī jiào

者處其一， 今之教者處其三。 [17] 農之家一，
zhě chǔ qí yī　 jīn zhī jiào zhě chǔ qí sān　 nóng zhī jiā yī

而食粟之家六。工之家一， 而用器之家六。
ér shí sù zhī jiā liù　 gōng zhī jiā yī　 ér yòng qì zhī jiā liù

賈之家一， 而資焉之家六。 [18] 奈之何民不窮
gǔ zhī jiā yī　 ér zī yān zhī jiā liù　 nài zhī hé mín bù qióng

且盜也！ [19]
qiě dào yě

古时候老百姓有四类，现在老百姓有六类。古时候教育（别人）的人占（四类）中的一类，现在教育别人的人占六类中的三类。[17] 务农的人家有一户，但吃粮食的人家有六户。做手工的人家有一户，但（需要）用具的人家有六户。经商的人家有一户，而靠他们供给的人家有六户。[18] 怎么才能让老百姓不因为贫穷而去偷盗啊！[19]

17. 四 *number.* four. Here it refers to four classes of people: officials 士 (*shì*), farmers 農 (*nóng* 农), craftsmen 工 (*gōng*), and merchants 賈 (*gǔ* 贾).

　　六 *number.* six. Here it refers to the previous four groups together with Buddhists and Daoists.

　　教 (jiào) *v.* to teach, instruct.

　　處 (chǔ) *v.* to occupy. MdnC: 佔 (*zhàn* 占).

農 (农) *n.* agriculture. MdnC: 務農 (*wù nóng* 务农).

粟 *n.* grain. Here it refers to food 糧食 (*liáng shí* 粮食).

18. 工 *n.* craftsman.

用器 *n.* utensils. MdnC: 用具 (*yòng jù*).

賈 (贾 *gǔ*) *v.* to sell or buy. Here it refers to doing business 經商 (*jīng shāng* 经商).

資 (资) *v.* to supply. MdnC: 供給 (*gòng jǐ* 供给).

焉 *demonstrative pron.* by those. See L1 Grammar Note 4 ①.

19. 奈······何 how to deal with? See Grammar Note 1.

之 *demonstrative pron.* those. See L1 Grammar Note 2 ①.

盜 *v.* to steal. MdnC: 偷盜 (*tōu dào*).

古之時，人之害多矣。有聖人者立，然
gǔ zhī shí rén zhī hài duō yǐ yǒu shèng rén zhě lì rán

後教之以相生養之道。²⁰爲之君，爲之師，驅
hòu jiāo zhī yǐ xiāng shēng yǎng zhī dào wéi zhī jūn wéi zhī shī qū

其蟲蛇禽獸而處之中土。²¹寒，然后爲之衣。
qí chóng shé qín shòu ér chǔ zhī zhōng tǔ hán rán hòu wéi zhī yī

飢，然后爲之食。木處而顛，土處而病也，
jī rán hòu wéi zhī shí mù chǔ ér diān tǔ chǔ ér bìng yě

然后爲之宮室。²²爲之工，以贍其器用。爲之
rán hòu wéi zhī gōng shì wéi zhī gōng yǐ shàn qí qì yòng wéi zhī

賈，以通其有無。²³爲之醫藥，以濟其夭死。
gǔ yǐ tōng qí yǒu wú wéi zhī yī yào yǐ jì qí yāo sǐ

爲之葬埋祭祀，以長其恩愛。²⁴爲之禮，以次
wéi zhī zàng mái jì sì yǐ cháng qí ēn ài wéi zhī lǐ yǐ cì

其先後。爲之樂，以宣其湮鬱。²⁵爲之政，以
qí xiān hòu wéi zhī yuè yǐ xuān qí yān yù wéi zhī zhèng yǐ

率其怠勌。爲之刑，以鋤其強梗。²⁶相欺也，
shuài qí dài juàn wéi zhī xíng yǐ chú qí qiáng gěng xiāng qī yě

爲之符璽、斗斛、權衡以信之。²⁷相奪也，爲
wéi zhī fú xǐ dǒu hú quán héng yǐ xìn zhī xiāng duó yě wéi

之城郭、甲兵以守之。²⁸害至而爲之備，患生
zhī chéng guō jiǎ bīng yǐ shǒu zhī hài zhì ér wéi zhī bèi huàn shēng

而爲之防。²⁹今其言曰：「聖人不死，大盜不
ér wèi zhī fáng jīn qí yán yuē shèng rén bù sǐ dà dào bù

古时候人们的灾祸很多。圣人出现了，然后教人们相互生养的方法。²⁰(圣人)当他们的君王，当他们的老师，驱走虫蛇禽兽，把他们安顿在中原。²¹天冷了然后教他们做衣服；饿了然后教他们种粮食。住在树上容易跌落，住在野地里容易生病，然后教他们建房屋。²²圣人教他们手工，来供给他们用具。教他们经商，来交换他们没有的东西。²³圣人教他们医病制药，来救治年少时死去的人。教他们丧葬掩埋祭祀，来增强人与人之间的恩爱感情。²⁴圣人教他们礼仪，来(区分)先后(尊卑)的次序。教他们音乐，来宣泄心中的郁闷。²⁵圣人教他们管理政事，来带领怠惰懒散的人。教他们刑罚，来铲除强暴之徒。²⁶(对)相互欺骗(的人)，圣人教他们做符信印玺、斗斛、秤锤秤杆来使他们相信(对

止；剖斗折衡，而民不爭。」嗚呼！其亦不
zhǐ　pōu dǒu zhé héng　ér mín bù zhēng　　wū hū　　qí yì bù

思而已矣！³⁰如古之無聖人，人之類滅久矣。
sī ér yǐ yǐ　　rú gǔ zhī wú shèng rén　　rén zhī lèi miè jiǔ yǐ

何也？無羽毛鱗介以居寒熱也，無爪牙以爭
hé yě　　wú yǔ máo lín jiè yǐ jū hán rè yě　　wú zhǎo yá yǐ zhēng

食也。³¹
shí yě

方)。²⁷(对)相互抢夺的人，教他们(建造)内外城墙、铠甲和军队来守护自己。²⁸灾害来了就教他们防备，祸患发生了就教他们预防。²⁹现在有话说："圣人不死，大盗就不会消失；(只有)打破斗斛折断秤杆，老百姓(才)不会争夺。"天啊！这也是没有思考(就说出来的话)罢了！³⁰如果古代没有圣人，人类已经灭亡很久了！为什么？因为人没有(动物的)羽毛鳞甲来适应寒冷或炎热(的地方)，没有(动物的)爪牙来争夺食物啊！³¹

20. 害 *n.* disaster. MdnC: 災禍 (*zāi huò* 灾祸).

　　立 *v.* to stand, establish. Here it means "to appear" 出現 (*chū xiàn* 出现).

　　以 *coverb.* with. See L2 Grammar Note 1 ②.

　　生養 (养) *v.* to live and grow.

21. 君 *n.* king. MdnC: 君王 (*jūn wáng*).

　　驅 (驱) *v.* to drive away. MdnC: 驅走 (*qū zǒu* 驱走).

　　蟲 (虫) 蛇 *n.* insect and snake.

　　禽獸 (兽) *n.* birds and beasts.

　　處 (chǔ) *v.* to settle. MdnC: 安頓 (*ān dùn* 安顿).

　　中土 *n.* central plains. MdnC: 中原 (*zhōng yuán*).

22. 飢 (饥) *adj.* hungry. MdnC: 餓 (*è* 饿).

　　木 *n.* tree, woods. MdnC: 樹 (*shù* 树).

　　處 (chǔ) *v.* to stay, live. MdnC: 住 (*zhù*).

　　顛 (颠) *v.* to fall, drop down. MdnC: 跌落 (*diē luò*).

　　土 *n.* earth. Here it refers to uncultivated land 野地 (*yě dì*).

　　宮室 *n.* buildings, houses. MdnC: 房屋 (*fáng wū*).

23. 贍 (赡) *v.* to supply. MdnC: 供給 (*gòng jǐ* 供给).

　　器用 *n.* utensils. MdnC: 用具 (*yòng jù*).

　　通 *v.* to exchange. MdnC: 交換 (*jiāo huàn* 交换).

24. 醫 (医) *v.* to heal, cure.

　　濟 (济) *v.* to help, aid. MdnC: 救治 (*jiù zhì*).

　　夭 *v.* to die young.

　　葬 *n.* funeral. MdnC: 喪葬 (*sāng zàng* 丧葬).

　　埋 *v.* to bury. MdnC: 掩埋 (*yǎn mái*).

祭祀 *n.* sacrifices.

長 (长 cháng) *adj.* long. Here it is used as a causative verb, 使……長, meaning "to increase" 增強 (*zēng qiáng* 增强). See L7 Grammar Note 1 ②.

25. 禮 (礼) *n.* rules of propriety, rituals. MdnC: 禮儀 (*lǐ yí* 礼仪).

次 *n.* order, sequence. MdnC: 次序 (*cì xù*).

樂 (乐 yuè) *n.* music. MdnC: 音樂 (*yīn yuè* 音乐).

宣 *v.* to release (one's emotion). MdnC: 宣泄 (*xuān xiè*).

湮鬱 (郁) *adj.* depressed. MdnC: 鬱悶 (*yù mèn* 郁闷).

26. 政 *n.* government. MdnC: 政事 (*zhèng shì*).

率 (shuài) *v.* to lead, guide. MdnC: 帶領 (*dài lǐng* 带领).

怠 *adj.* lazy, idle. MdnC: 怠惰 (*dài duò*).

勌 (倦) *adj.* lazy, indolent. MdnC: 懶散 (*lǎn sǎn* 懒散).

刑 *n.* penalty, punishment. MdnC: 刑罰 (*xíng fá* 刑罚).

鋤 (锄) *v.* to eradicate, eliminate. MdnC: 鏟除 (*chǎn chú* 铲除).

強 (强) 梗 *adj.* violent, brutal. MdnC: 強暴 (*qiáng bào* 强暴).

27. 欺 *v.* to cheat, deceive. MdnC: 欺騙 (*qī piàn* 欺骗).

符 *n.* tally. MdnC: 符信 (*fú xìn*).

璽 (玺) *n.* seal. MdnC: 印璽 (*yìn xǐ* 印玺).

斗 (dǒu) *n.* a Chinese measure of capacity.

斛 *n.* an ancient Chinese measure of capacity, which equals ten *dous* 斗.

權 (权) *n.* balance weight. MdnC: 秤錘 (*chèng chuí* 秤锤).

衡 *n.* balance beam. MdnC: 秤桿 (*chèng gǎn* 秤杆).

信 *v.* trust, believe. Here it is used as a causative verb, 使……信, meaning "to make … trust" 使 (*shǐ*) ……相信 (*xiāng xìn*). See L7 Grammar Note 1 ①.

28. 奪 (夺) *v.* to snatch, seize. MdnC: 搶奪 (*qiǎng duó* 抢夺).

郭 *n.* a wall built outside of the city.

甲 *n.* armor, shell. MdnC: 鎧甲 (*kǎi jiǎ* 铠甲).

守 *v.* defense. MdnC: 守護 (*shǒu hù* 守护).

29. 備 *v.* to guard against, prepare for. MdnC: 防備 (*fáng bèi* 防备).

患 *n.* calamity, trouble. MdnC: 禍患 (*huò huàn* 祸患).

防 *v.* to prevent, guard against. MdnC: 預防 (*yù fáng* 预防).

30. 今其言 a quotation from chapter 10, "Open the Box" 胠篋 ("Qū qiè"), of the *Zhuangzi*.

盜 *n.* robber, outlaw.

剖 *v.* to cut, break.

折 (zhé) *v.* to break off. MdnC: 折斷 (*zhé duàn* 折断).

而已 *ending particle.* nothing more. MdnC: 罷了 (*bà le* 罢了). See L21 Grammar Note 1 ③.

31. 類 (类) *n.* category, group.

滅 (灭) *v.* to die out. MdnC: 滅亡 (*miè wáng* 灭亡).

羽毛 *n.* feather and fur.

鱗 (鳞) 介 *n.* scale and shell.

爪 (zhǎo) 牙 *n.* claw and teeth.

是故： 君者， 出令者也； 臣者， 行君之
shì gù　　jūn zhě　　chū lìng zhě yě　　chén zhě　　xíng jūn zhī

令而致之民者也； 民者， 出粟米麻絲， 作器
lìng ér zhì zhī mín zhě yě　　mín zhě　　chū sù mǐ má sī　　zuò qì

皿， 通貨財， 以事其上者也。³² 君不出令， 則
mǐn　　tōng huò cái　　yǐ shì qí shàng zhě yě　　jūn bù chū lìng　　zé

失其所以爲君。 臣不行君之令而致之民， 則
shī qí suǒ yǐ wéi jūn　　chén bù xíng jūn zhī lìng ér zhì zhī mín　　zé

失其所以爲臣。 民不出粟米麻絲， 作器皿，
shī qí suǒ yǐ wéi chén　　mín bù chū sù mǐ má sī　　zuò qì mǐn

通貨財， 以事其上， 則誅。³³ 今其法曰：「必
tōng huò cái　　yǐ shì qí shàng　　zé zhū　　jīn qí fǎ yuē　　bì

棄而君臣， 去而父子， 禁而相生養之道。」
qì ěr jūn chén　　qù ěr fù zǐ　　jìn ěr xiāng shēng yǎng zhī dào

以求其所謂清淨寂滅者。³⁴ 嗚呼！ 其亦幸而出
yǐ qiú qí suǒ wèi qīng jìng jì miè zhě　　wū hū　　qí yì xìng ér chū

於三代之後， 不見黜於禹、 湯、 文、 武、 周
yú sān dài zhī hòu　　bú jiàn chù yú yǔ　　tāng　　wén　　wǔ　　zhōu

公、 孔子也； 其亦不幸而不出於三代之前，
gōng　　kǒng zǐ yě　　qí yì bú xìng ér bù chū yú sān dài zhī qián

不見正於禹、 湯、 文、 武、 周公、 孔子也。³⁵
bú jiàn zhèng yú yǔ　　tāng　　wén　　wǔ　　zhōu gōng kǒng zǐ yě

因此，君王是发布命令的人；大臣是执行君王的命令并把命令送达到老百姓那里的人；老百姓是生产粟米麻丝，制作工具器皿，交换货物钱财，来供奉他们的君王的人。³² 君王不发布命令，就会失去他作为君王的权力。大臣不执行君王的命令并送达到老百姓那里，就失掉他作为臣子的职责。老百姓不出产粟米麻丝，制作器皿，交换货财，来供奉君王，就要受到惩罚。³³ 现在佛法说："必须抛弃你的君臣关系，背离你的父子关系，禁止你的生养之道。"来求得所说的清净寂灭的境界。³⁴ 哎！他们很幸运，出现在夏商周三代之后，不会被夏禹、商汤王、周文王、周武王、周公和孔子贬斥；他们也很不幸，没有出现在三代之前，没有被夏禹、商汤王、周文王、周武王、周公和孔子矫正。³⁵

《韓昌黎文集校注》，上海：上海古籍出版社 (1986), 12–16.

32. 是故 for this reason. MdnC: 因此 (*yīn cǐ*). See L3 Grammar Note 1 ③.
　　令 *n.* order. MdnC: 命令 (*mìng lìng*).
　　行 (xíng) *v.* to carry out, enact. MdnC: 執行 (*zhí xíng* 执行).
　　致 *v.* to deliver. MdnC: 送達 (*sòng dá* 送达).
　　麻絲 (丝) *n.* hemp and silk.
　　皿 *n.* containers.
　　貨 (货) *n.* commodity, merchandise. MdnC: 貨物 (*huò wù* 货物).
　　財 (财) *n.* money, cash. MdnC: 錢財 (*qián cái* 钱财).
　　事 *v.* to serve for. MdnC: 供奉 (*gòng fèng*).
33. 誅 (诛) *v.* to punish. MdnC: 懲罰 (*chéng fá* 惩罚).
34. 其 *personal pron.* it. Here it refers to Buddhism. See L2 Grammar Note 5 ①.

棄 (弃) *v.* to abandon, forsake. MdnC: 拋棄 (*pāo qì* 抛弃).

而 *pron.* used in the sense of 爾 (*ěr* 尔); second-person pronoun: you. MdnC: 你 (*nǐ*).

去 *v.* to leave, be away from. MdnC: 背離 (*bèi lí* 背离).

禁 (*jìn*) *v.* to stop, forbid. MdnC: 禁止 (*jìn zhǐ*).

清淨寂滅 Buddhist doctrine of purity and nirvāna.

35. 幸 *adj.* lucky, fortunate. MdnC: 幸運 (*xìng yùn* 幸运).

三代 the Xia, Shang, andZhou dynasties.

見 (见 *jiàn*) *particle.* by. MdnC: 被 (*bèi*). See L18 Grammar Note 2.

黜 *v.* to dismiss, denounce. MdnC: 貶斥 (*biǎn chì* 贬斥).

湯 or 商湯 (ancestral name 姓, Zǐ 子; given name 名, Lǚ 履; 1670 ?–1587 BCE), the founder of the Shang dynasty.

周公 or 周公旦 See 周公's brief biography in L19 note 13.

正 *v.* to rectify. MdnC: 矯正 (*jiǎo zhèng* 矫正).

語法注釋 Grammar Note

1. 奈 ⋯⋯ 何   how does one deal with? how come? MdnC: 對 (*duì* 对) ⋯⋯ 怎麼樣 (*zěn me yàng* 怎么样)，怎麼才能 (*zěn me cái néng* 怎么才能).

奈之何民不窮且盜也！

［对那些（老百姓）怎么样老百姓才能不会因为贫穷而去偷盗啊！］

Literary Analysis

1. In his essay, Han Yu presents several different types of people: "gentlemen of noble worth" 君子 and "small-minded men" 小人 in the first passage; "Laozi" 老子 and "I" 吾 in the second passage; Daoists 老者, Buddhists 佛者, and Confucians 孔子者 in the third passage; the four and six classes of people in the fourth passage; "rulers" 君, "ministers" 臣, and "people" 民 in the sixth passage; and so on. What do these various groupings suggest about Han Yu's values and his understanding of Chinese society and culture? In what ways can you see this same logic of breaking larger concepts or structures (human society, history, etc.) into smaller constituent parts employed elsewhere throughout Han's argument?

2. The first half of Han's essay is broken down into six distinct passages. First, identify and summarize in a short phrase or sentence the key argument or theme of each passage. Then consider how Han links these discrete passages together to form a coherent whole. For example, how does each passage end or begin? In what ways does his diction or argument in a particular passage echo that of an earlier passage or foreshadow a later one?

3. Based on his rhetorical moves in this composition, against what or whom do you think Han was arguing? Speculate why Han chose to use the *yuan* 原 (origin-tracing) genre—a genre believed to have been created by Han himself—to argue that the old (i.e., Confucian) Way is best?

☞ *HTRCProse*, chapter 10, "Tang and Song Expository Prose: The Practice of Persuasion," for further comments.

—AKD

課後練習 Exercises

一　給加點字注音　Give the pinyin romanization for each dotted word.

1. 煦煦 (＿＿，＿＿)　2. 祭祀 (＿＿，＿＿)　3. 符璽 (＿＿，＿＿)　4. 噫 (＿＿)

5. 孑孑 (＿＿，＿＿)　6. 斗斛 (＿＿，＿＿)　7. 鱗介 (＿＿，＿＿)　8. 皿 (＿＿)

二　在括號中給句中加點的字注音，並選出正確的釋義　Give the pinyin romanization for each dotted word; then select the correct definition from the following list, and write it in the blank.

污蔑　經(经)商　貶(贬)斥　懶(懒)散　供給(给)
死　跌落　荒誕(诞)　**信服**　糧(粮)食

1. 小信未孚（**fú**）　**信服**　2. 孔子沒 (　) ＿＿＿＿　3. 樂其誕而自小 (　) ＿＿＿＿

4. 出者汙之 (　) ＿＿＿＿　5. 食粟 (　) ＿＿＿＿　6. 賈之家一 (　) ＿＿＿＿

7. 木處而顛 (　) ＿＿＿＿　8. 見黜 (　) ＿＿＿＿　9. 贍其器用 (　) ＿＿＿＿

10. 率其怠勩 (　) ＿＿＿＿

三　選擇釋義並填空　Match each word in the left column with its correct definition in the middle column. Fill in each blank in the right column with an appropriate word from the left column.

謀謀劃(谋划)	附和
宜＿＿＿＿	開(开)端
待＿＿＿＿	供給(给)
附＿＿＿＿	**謀劃(谋划)**
舉＿＿＿＿	考察
筆＿＿＿＿	救治
端＿＿＿＿	帶領(领)
訊＿＿＿＿	適(适)宜
資＿＿＿＿	鏟(铲)除
濟＿＿＿＿	談論(谈论)
宣＿＿＿＿	依賴
率＿＿＿＿	送達(达)
鋤＿＿＿＿	記錄(记录)
致＿＿＿＿	宣泄

博愛之謂仁，行而＿＿＿之之謂義，由是而之焉之謂道，足乎己，無＿＿＿於外之謂德。

入者＿＿＿之，出者汙之。

不惟＿＿＿之於其口，而又＿＿＿之於其書。

不求其＿＿＿，不＿＿＿其末。

賈之家一，而＿＿＿焉之家六。

爲之醫藥，以＿＿＿其夭死。

爲之樂，以＿＿＿其湮鬱。爲之政，以＿＿＿其怠勩。爲之刑，以＿＿＿其強梗。

臣者，行君之令而＿＿＿之民者也。

四　請用給出的字填空　Fill in each blank with an appropriate word from the following list.

焉　彼　此　惟　則(则)　者　凡

1. ____吾所謂道德云____，合仁與義言之也，天下之公言也。

2. 其言道德仁義者，不入于楊，____入于墨。　　3. 入于____，必出于____。

4. 不____舉之於其口，而又筆之於其書。　　5. 賈之家一，而資____之家六。

五　爲加點字選擇正確釋義，並根據釋義來翻譯句子 Match each dotted word with its correct modern Chinese equivalent by circling the latter. Then translate each sentence into modern Chinese.

1. 又何間焉?　　　　　　　　　　　ⓐ爲什麼(为什么)　b. 憑什麼(凭什么)　c. 多少

現代文翻译：你又为什么要参与到这件事情里面？

_____

2. 博愛之謂仁，行而宜之之謂義，由是而之焉之謂道，足乎己，無待於外之謂德。

a. 怎麼(么)　b. 仁義(义)　c. 在此

現代文翻译：_____

3. 彼以煦煦爲仁，孑孑爲義，其小之也則宜。　　　a. 使……小　b. 大小　c. 以……爲(为)小

現代文翻译：_____

4. 老子之所謂道德云者，去仁與義言之也，一人之私言也。　a. 之類(类)　b. 白雲(云)　c. 説(说)

現代文翻译：_____

5. 後之人其欲聞仁義道德之説，孰從而求之?　　　a. 誰(谁)　b. 熟悉　c. 哪裏(哪里)

現代文翻译：_____

6. 奈之何民不窮且盜也!　　　a. 爲什麼(为什么)　b. 對(对)……怎麼樣(怎么样)　c. 何不

現代文翻译：_____

7. 其亦幸而出於三代之後，不見黜於禹、湯、文、武、周公、孔子也。

a. 看見(见)　b. 出現(现)　c. 被

現代文翻译：_____

第三十課

韓愈《原道》（下）

"On the Origin of the Way" (II) (Han Yu)

Introduction

In this second half of his essay, Han Yu launches an all-out attack on Buddhist and Daoist personal ethics and societal principles, blaming them for all the collapses of the ethico-sociopolitical order in China's past. He even issues an open call, whether literal or metaphorical, to disrobe Buddhist monks and make them unbelievers, burn their scriptures, turn their monasteries into farmhouses, and reeducate them with Confucian teachings. Han makes every effort to trace the transmission of the Confucian Way, extending from legendary King Yao 堯, King Shun 舜, and King Yu 禹, through King Tang 湯 of Shang and the Zhou Kings of Wen 文 and Wu 武, as well as Duke Zhou 周公, to Confucius and Mencius while subtly placing himself as the next in line in this grand lineage of Confucian sages. This lineage is to be inherited by Cheng Yi 程頤 (1033–1107), Zhu Xi 朱熹 (1130–1200), and other Song thinkers as a mainstay of Song neo-Confucianism.

正文與簡體譯文 Text and Modern Chinese Translation

帝之與王， 其號名殊， 其所以爲聖一
dì zhī yǔ wáng　　qí hào míng shū　　qí suǒ yǐ wéi shèng yī

也。[1]夏葛而冬裘， 渴飲而飢食， 其事殊， 其
yě　　xià gé ér dōng qiú　　kě yǐn ér jī shí　　qí shì shū　　qí

所以爲智一也。[2]今其言曰：「曷不爲太古之
suǒ yǐ wéi zhì yī yě　　jīn qí yán yuē　　hé bù wéi tài gǔ zhī

無事？」[3]是亦責冬之ₐ裘者曰： 「曷不爲葛
wú shì　　shì yì zé dōng zhī qiú zhě yuē　　hé bù wéi gé

之ᵦ之ᵪ易也？」責飢之ₐ食者曰： 「曷不爲
zhī zhī yì yě　　zé jī zhī shí zhě yuē　　hé bù wéi

飲之ᵦ之ᵪ易也？」[4]《傳》曰：「古之欲明ₐ
yǐn zhī zhī yì yě　　zhuàn yuē　　gǔ zhī yù míng

明ᵦ德於天下者， 先治其國； 欲治其國者， 先
míng dé yú tiān xià zhě　　xiān zhì qí guó　　yù zhì qí guó zhě　　xiān

五帝和三王，他们的名号不同，他们成为圣人的原因是一样的。[1]夏天穿葛衣，冬天穿裘衣，渴了饮水，饿了吃东西，这些事情不同，但成为人类智慧的原因是一样的。[2]现在道家的言论称："为什么不实行太古时不做事(那样的无为而治呢)？"[3]这就(像)责怪冬天穿裘衣的人说："为什么不穿葛衣？那么容易！"责怪饿了就吃的人说："为什么不喝水？那么容易！"[4]《礼记》说："古时人想发扬美德，

齊其家；欲齊其家者，先修其身；欲修其身
qí qí jiā　　yù qí qí jiā zhě　　xiān xiū qí shēn　　yù xiū qí shēn

者，先正其心；欲正其心者，先誠其意。」[5]
zhě　　xiān zhèng qí xīn　　yù zhèng qí xīn zhě　　xiān chéng qí yì

然則，古之所謂正心而誠意者，將以有爲
rán zé　　gǔ zhī suǒ wèi zhèng xīn ér chéng yì zhě jiāng yǐ yǒu wéi

也。[6]今也欲治其心，而外天下國家，滅其
yě　　jīn yě yù zhì qí xīn　　ér wài tiān xià guó jiā　　miè qí

天常：子焉而不父 [a]其父 [b]，臣焉而不君 [a]其
tiān cháng　　zǐ yān ér bú fù　qí fù　　chén yān ér bù jūn　qí

君 [b]，民焉而不事 [a]其事 [b]。[7]孔子之 [a]作《春
jūn　　mín yān ér bú shì　qí shì　　kǒng zǐ zhī　zuò　chūn

秋》也，諸侯用夷 [a]禮，則夷 [b]之 [b]；進於中
qiū　yě　　zhū hóu yòng yí　lǐ　　zé yí　zhī　　jìn yú zhōng

國 [a]，則中國 [b]之。[8]《經》曰：「夷狄之有
guó　　zé zhōng guó zhī　　jīng　yuē　　yí dí zhī yǒu

君，不如諸夏之亡！」[9]《詩》曰：「戎狄是
jūn　　bù rú zhū xià zhī wú　　shī　yuē　　róng dí shì

膺，荊舒是懲。」[10]今也，舉夷狄之法，而加
yīng　jīng shū shì chéng　　jīn yě　　jǔ yí dí zhī fǎ　　ér jiā

之先王之教之上，幾何其不胥而爲夷也！[11]
zhī xiān wáng zhī jiào zhī shàng jǐ hé qí bù xū ér wéi yí yě

先要治理他的国家；想
治理国家，先要管理他
的家庭；想管理家庭，
先要修养自身；想修养
自身，先要端正他的心
思；想端正心思，先要
使自己的意念真诚。」[5]
既然如此，那么古人所
说的端正心意有诚意，
要以此来有所作为。[6]
现在人也要修养心性，
却把天下国家的事情当
作外物（抛弃），灭绝天
理伦常：做儿子的不把
自己的父亲当作父亲，
做臣子的不把自己的君
王当作君王，老百姓啊
不把自己该做的事情当
作事情。[7]孔子作《春
秋》时，诸侯用夷人的
礼仪，就把他们当作夷
人；采用了中原的礼
仪，就把他们当作中原
人。[8]《论语》："夷狄
有君王，还不如中原各
国没有君王呢！"[9]《诗
经》："抵抗戎狄，惩
罚楚国舒国。"[10]现在
推举夷狄之法，把它加
在先王的教化之上，那
么多少人不都成为夷人
了吗？[11]

1. 帝 n. emperor. Here it refers to the five emperors listed in the chapter titled "Five Emperors" 五帝 ("Wǔ dì") in *Grand Scribe's Records*: Huangdi 黃帝, Zhuan Xu 顓頊, Di Ku 帝嚳, Yao 堯, and Shun 舜. See King Yao's and King Shun's brief biographies in L13 note 3.

　王 *n.* king. Here it refers to the first kings of the three dynasties: King Yu 禹 of the Xia, King Tang 湯 of the Shang, and King Wen 文 and King Wu 武 of the Zhou. See King Yu's brief biography in L13 note 4, King Wen's brief biography in L13 note 18, and King Wu's brief biography in L13 note 19.

　號 (号 hào) *n.* title. MdnC: 名號 (*míng hào* 名号).

　殊 *adj.* different. MdnC: 不同 (*bù tóng*).

2. 葛 (gé) *n. Pueraria lobata.* Here it refers to summer clothes.

　裘 *n.* fur coat.

智 *n.* wisdom. MdnC: 智慧 (*zhì huì*).

3. 其 *personal pron.* it. Here 其 refers to Daoism. See L2 Grammar Note 5 ①.

曷 *initial interrogative particle.* why? MdnC: 爲什麼 (*wèi shén me* 为什么). See Grammar Note 1.

爲 (为 *wéi*) *v.* to carry out, enact. MdnC: 實行 (*shí xíng* 实行).

太古 *n.* remote antiquity.

之 *particle.* a nominative marker. See L2 Grammar Note 2 ⑤.

4. 是 *demonstrative pron.* this. It refers to Daoist opinions. See L3 Grammar Note 1 ①.

責 (责) *v.* to blame. MdnC: 責怪 (*zé guài* 责怪).

之 ₐ *particle.* a possessive marker. MdnC: 的 (*de*). See L1 Grammar Note 2 ②.

葛 *v.* to wear clothes.

之 ♭ *particle.* an added syllable with no meaning in itself. See L1 Grammar Note 2 ④.

之 c *demonstrative pron.* this. See L1 Grammar Note 2 ①.

5. 傳 (传 *zhuàn*) *n.* annotation on Confucian classics. Here it refers to the *Book of Rites* 禮記, and the following quote is from its chapter titled "Great Learning" 大學 ("Dà xué" 大学).

之 *particle.* an added syllable with no meaning in itself. See L1 Grammar Note 2 ④.

明 ₐ *adj.* clear. Here it is used as a causative verb, 使⋯⋯明, meaning "to make clear or illuminate" 發揚 (*fā yang* 发扬). See L7 Grammar Note 1 ②.

明 ♭ *adj.* bright, luminous. MdnC: 光明 (*guāng míng*).

德 *n.* morality. MdnC: 品德 (*pǐn dé*).

治 *v.* to govern. MdnC: 治理 (*zhì lǐ*).

齊 (齐 *qí*) *adj.* even, neat. Here it is used as a causative verb, 使⋯⋯齊, meaning "to make neat or to manage" 管理 (*guǎn lǐ*). See L7 Grammar Note 1 ②.

修 *v.* to cultivate. MdnC: 修養 (*xiū yǎng* 修养).

正 *adj.* correct. Here it is used as a causative verb, 使⋯⋯正, meaning "to rectify" 端正 (*duān zhèng*). See L7 Grammar Note 1 ②.

誠 (诚) *adj.* sincere. Here it is used as a causative verb, 使⋯⋯誠, meaning "to make sincere" 使 (*shǐ*) ⋯⋯真誠 (*zhēn chéng* 真诚). See L7 Grammar Note 1 ②.

6. 然則 (则) if it is so, then.... MdnC: 既然如此，那麼 (*jì rán rú cǐ nà me* 那么). See L10 Grammar Note 1.

爲 (为 *wéi*) *v.* to behave, act. MdnC: 作爲 (*zuò wéi* 作为).

7. 外 *adj.* external, foreign. Here it is used as a putative verb, 以⋯⋯爲外, meaning "to think of … as external things" 把 (*bǎ*) ⋯⋯當作外物 (*dāng zuò wài wù* 当作外物). See L14 Grammar Note 1 ①.

滅 (灭) *v.* to exterminate. MdnC: 滅絕 (*miè jué* 灭绝).

天 *n.* heaven. Here it means "moral principles or morality" 天理 (*tiān lǐ*).

常 *adj.* common. Here it means "proper human relationship" 倫常 (*lún cháng* 伦常).

焉 *particle.* used as a pause in the middle of the sentence. MdnC: 啊 (*a*). See Grammar Note 3 ⑦.

父 ₐ *n.* father. Here it is used as a putative verb, 以⋯⋯爲父, meaning "to think of … as father" 把 (*bǎ*) ⋯⋯當作父親 (*dāng zuò fù qīn* 当作父亲). See L14 Grammar Note 1 ②.

父 ♭ *n.* father. MdnC: 父親 (*fù qīn* 父亲).

8. 之 ₐ *particle.* a nominative marker. See L2 Grammar Note 2 ⑤.

《春秋》 *Spring and Autumn Annals.*

諸 (诸) 侯 *n.* dukes, lords.

夷 ₐ *n.* ancient people who lived to the northeast of China but who were not were Chinese; barbarians.

禮 (礼) *n.* rules of propriety, ritual. MdnC: 禮儀 (*lǐ yí* 礼仪).

夷 ♭ *v.* 以……爲夷, meaning "to regard … as barbarian" 把 (*bǎ*) ……當作夷人 (*dāng zuò yí rén* 当作夷人). See L14 Grammar Note 1 ②.

之 ♭ *personal pron.* them, referring to dukes or lords. See L1 Grammar Note 2 ③.

進 (进) *v.* to make progress, advance.

中國 (国) ₐ *n.* central plains.

9. 經 (经) *n.* classics. This is a quotation of Confucius from chapter 3 八佾 ("Bā yì") of the *Analects*.

夷狄 *n.* barbarians. See L19 Culture Note 2.

諸 (诸) 夏 *n.* all states in central areas.

亡 (*wú*) used in the sense of 無 (*wú* 无), meaning "to not have" 没有 (*méi yǒu*).

10. 《詩》 (诗) *Book of Poetry* 詩經. This is a quotation from "Deep Palace" 閟宮 ("Bì gōng") of the "Hymns of Lu" 魯頌 ("Lǔ sòng" 鲁颂) in the *Book of Poetry*.

戎 *n.* barbarians. See L19 Culture Note 2.

是 *particle.* marking the inversion of the object. See Grammar Note 2 ⑤.

膺 *v.* to confront, attack. MdnC: 抵抗 (*dǐ kàng*).

荊 the Chu state in the Zhou dynasty.

舒 the Shu state, which was conquered by the Xu state 徐 in the Spring and Autumn period.

懲 (惩) *v.* to punish. MdnC: 懲罰 (*chéng fá* 惩罚).

11. 舉 (举) *v.* to raise up. Here it means "to praise highly" 推崇 (*tuī tóng*).

教 (jiào) *n.* teaching. MdnC: 教化 (*jiào huà*).

幾 (几 jǐ) 何 how many? MdnC: 多少 (*duō shǎo*). See L3 Grammar Note 7.

其 *adv.* used to suggest a tentative tone. MdnC: 那麼 (*nà me* 那么). See L2 Grammar Note 5 ③.

胥 *adv.* all. MdnC: 都 (*dōu*).

夫所謂先王之教者，何也？博愛之謂
fú suǒ wèi xiān wáng zhī jiào zhě　hé yě　bó ài zhī wèi

仁，行而宜之之謂義，由是而之焉之謂道，
rén　xíng ér yí zhī zhī wèi yì　yóu shì ér zhī yān zhī wèi dào

足乎己，無待於外之謂德。其文，《詩》、
zú hū jǐ　wú dài yú wài zhī wèi dé　qí wén　shī

《書》、《易》、《春秋》；其法，禮、
shū　yì　chūn qiū　qí fǎ　lǐ

樂、刑、政；其民，士、農、工、賈；其
yuè　xíng　zhèng　qí mín　shì　nóng　gōng　gǔ　qí

位，君臣、父子、師友、賓主、昆弟、夫
wèi　jūn chén　fù zǐ　shī yǒu　bīn zhǔ　kūn dì　fū

婦；其服，麻絲；其居，宮室；其食，粟
fù　qí fú　má sī　qí jū　gōng shì　qí shí　sù

所谓先王的教化是什么呢？广泛地爱人叫做仁，适宜恰当地实行仁叫做义；从仁义继续往前叫做道，充实自己不依赖外物，叫做德。先王的文字有《诗经》、《尚书》、《易经》、《春秋》；先王的治理方法有礼仪、音乐、刑罚、政令；先王的百姓有士人、农民、工人、商人；先王时的人伦地位有君臣、父子、师友、宾主、兄弟、夫妇；先王时的衣服是麻布丝绸的；先王时的住所是房屋；先王时的食

米、果蔬、魚肉。其爲道易明，而其爲教易
mǐ　guǒ shū　yú ròu　　qí wéi dào yì míng　　ér qí wéi jiào yì

行也。¹² 是故以之爲己，則順而祥；以之爲
xíng yě　　　shì gù yǐ zhī wéi jǐ　　zé shùn ér xiáng　　yǐ zhī wéi

人，則愛而公；以之爲心，則和而平；以之
rén　zé ài ér gōng　　yǐ zhī wéi xīn　　zé hé ér píng　　yǐ zhī

爲天下國家，無所處而不當。¹³ 是故生則得其
wéi tiān xià guó jiā　wú suǒ chǔ ér bú dàng　　shì gù shēng zé dé qí

情，死則盡其常；郊焉而天神假，廟焉而人
qíng　sǐ zé jìn qí cháng　jiāo yān ér tiān shén gé　miào yān ér rén

鬼饗。¹⁴ 曰：「斯道也，何道也？」曰：「斯
guǐ xiǎng　　yuē　　　sī dào yě　　hé dào yě　　yuē　　sī

吾所謂道也，非向所謂老與佛之道也。」¹⁵ 堯
wú suǒ wèi dào yě　　fēi xiàng suǒ wèi lǎo yǔ fú zhī dào yě　　yáo

以是傳之舜，舜以是傳之禹，禹以是傳之湯，
yǐ shì chuán zhī shùn　shùn yǐ shì chuán zhī yǔ　　yǔ yǐ shì chuán zhī tāng

湯以是傳之文、武、周公，文、武、周公傳
tāng yǐ shì chuán zhī wén　wǔ　zhōu gōng　　wén　wǔ　zhōu gōng chuán

之孔子，孔子傳之孟軻，軻之死，不得其傳
zhī kǒng zǐ　　kǒng zǐ chuán zhī mèng kē　kē zhī sǐ　　bù dé qí chuán

焉。荀與揚也，擇焉而不精，語焉而不詳。¹⁶
yān　　xún yǔ yáng yě　　zé yān ér bù jīng　　yǔ yān ér bù xiáng

由周公而上，上而爲君，故其事行；由周公
yóu zhōu gōng ér shàng shàng ér wéi jūn　gù qí shì xíng　yóu zhōu gōng

而下，下而爲臣，故其説長。¹⁷
ér xià　　xià ér wéi chén　gù qí shuō cháng

物是粟米、水果、蔬菜、鱼肉。先王制定的道理容易明白，而他的教化容易实行。¹² 因此用先王之道来教育自己就平顺吉祥；用先王之道教育别人就博爱公正；用先王之道来修养内心就平和安定；用先王之道来治理天下国家，没有处理得不适当的地方。¹³ 因此活着就得到人与人之间的情谊，死去就完结人和人之间的伦常；郊祀祭天时天神来到，庙里祭祖时祖先的魂灵来享用（祭品）。¹⁴ 有人问："这道是什么道？"（我）说："这是我所说的道，不是先前所说的老子和佛教的道。"¹⁵ 尧把这道传给舜，舜把它传给禹，禹把它传给商汤王，商汤王把它传给周文王、周武王和周公，周文王、周武王和周公传给孔子，孔子传给孟轲，孟轲死后，就不能传了。荀子和扬雄，选择了一些，但不精当，谈到了一些，但不详细。¹⁶ 从周公往上（得道的人）都在上做君王，所以他们的道能实行；从周公往下，得道的人都在下面做臣子，因此他们的学说能够（流传）长久。¹⁷

12. 文 *n.* word, text. MdnC: 文字 (*wén zì*).
　　《書》 (书) *Book of History* 尚書.
　　《易》 *Book of Changes* 易經.

士 *n.* scholar, elite.

農 (农) *n.* farmer.

賈 (贾 *gǔ*) *n.* merchant. MdnC: 商人 (*shāng rén*).

位 *n.* seat, position. MdnC: 地位 (*dì wèi*).

賓 (宾) 主 *n.* guest and host.

昆 *n.* elder brother. MdnC: 兄 (*xiōng*).

居 *n.* dwelling. MdnC: 住所 (*zhù suǒ*).

13. 以 *coverb.* to use. MdnC: 用 (*yòng*). See L2 Grammar Note 1 ②.

之 *demonstrative pron.* refers to the teaching of former kings. See L1 Grammar Note 2 ①.

順 (顺) *adj.* smooth. MdnC: 平順 (*píng shun* 平顺).

祥 *adj.* lucky. MdnC: 吉祥 (*jí xiáng*).

公 *adj.* fair. MdnC: 公正 (*gōng zhèng*).

處 (处 *chǔ*) *v.* to deal with, manage. MdnC: 處理 (*chǔ lǐ* 处理).

當 (当 *dàng*) *adj.* proper. MdnC: 適當 (*shì dàng* 适当).

14. 情 *n.* love, friendship. MdnC: 情誼 (*qíng yì*).

盡 (尽 *jìn*) *v.* to complete, finish. MdnC: 完結 (*wán jié* 完结).

郊 *n.* suburbs. Since the ancient worship of heaven and earth often took place in the southern suburbs, it was also called 郊祀 (*jiāo sì*).

焉 *particle.* used as a pause in the middle of the sentence. See Grammar Note 3 ⑦.

假 *v.* used in the sense of 格 (*gé*), meaning "to arrive" 到 (*dào*).

廟 (庙) *n.* the temple at which to worship ancestors. Here it refers to ancestral worship 祭祖 (*jì zǔ*).

人鬼 *n.* humans and ghosts. Here it refers to ancestors' spirits.

饗 (飨) *n.* banquet. Here it is used in the sense of 享 (*xiǎng*), meaning "to enjoy" 享用 (*xiǎng yòng*).

15. 斯 *demonstrative pron.* this. MdnC: 這 (*zhè* 这). See L5 Grammar Note 3 ①.

向 *adv.* earlier, previously, formerly. MdnC: 先前 (*xiān qián*).

16. 是 *demonstrative pron.* this. MdnC: 這 (*zhè* 这). See L3 Grammar Note 1 ①.

傳 (传 *chuán*) *v.* to transmit.

荀 or 荀況 (fl. 313?–238? BCE).

揚 or 揚雄 (style 字, Zǐyún 子雲; 53 BCE–18 CE), a philosopher and poet in the Western Han dynasty.

擇 (择) *v.* to choose, select. MdnC: 選擇 (*xuǎn zé* 选择).

焉 *demonstrative pron.* refers to the 道 that the author mentioned. See L6 Grammar Note 5 ⑤.

精 *adj.* precise, essential, appropriate. MdnC: 精當 (*jīng dàng* 精当).

語 (语) *v.* to talk about, mention. MdnC: 談到 (*tán dào* 谈到).

詳 (详) *adj.* in details. MdnC: 詳細 (*xiáng xì* 详细).

17. 說 (说) *n.* doctrine, idea, thought. MdnC: 學說 (*xué shuō* 学说).

然則，如之何而可也？曰：「不塞不流，
rán zé　　rú zhī hé ér kě yě　　yuē　　　bú sè bù liú

不止不行。」¹⁸ 人ₐ其ₐ人ᵦ，火其ₐ書，廬
bù zhǐ bù xíng　　　　　rén qí rén　　huǒ qí shū　lú

既然这样，那么怎样才可以(让儒道继续)呢？我认为："不堵塞(佛老之道)，(儒道就)不能流传；不禁止佛老之

其 _a 居，明先王之 _a 道 _a 以道 _b 之 _b，鰥寡孤獨
qí jū míng xiān wáng zhī dào yǐ dǎo zhī guān guǎ gū dú

廢疾者有養也：其 _b 亦庶乎其 _c 可也！ [19]
fèi jí zhě yǒu yǎng yě qí yì shù hū qí kě yě

《韓昌黎文集校注》，上海：上海古籍出版社 (1986), 17–19.

道，儒道就不能实行。"[18] 使和尚道士成为普通人，烧毁佛道的经书，把他们的寺庙变成民居，发扬先王之道来引导老百姓，让独居老人与孤儿、残疾人、病人都有供养：也就差不多可以了！[19]

18. 如之何 or 如何 how come? how? MdnC: 怎麼樣 (*zěn me yàng* 怎么样). See Grammar Note 4.

塞 (*sè*) *v.* to block. 堵塞 (*dǔ sè*).

流 *v.* to spread, circulate. MdnC: 流傳 (*liú chuán* 流传).

止 *v.* to stop. MdnC: 禁止 (*jìn zhǐ*).

19. 人 *n.* human being. Here it is used as a causative verb, 使……人, meaning "to make … human (again)." See L7 Grammar Note 1 ③.

其 _a *demonstrative pron.* those. See L6 Grammar Note 6 ④.

其 _a 人 _b refers to Buddhist followers 和尚 (*hé shàng*) and Daoist followers 道士 (*dào shì*).

火 *n.* fire. Here it is used as a verb, meaning "to burn" 燒毀 (*shāo huǐ* 烧毁).

廬 (庐) *n.* hut, cottage. MdnC: 民居 (*mín jū*). Here it is used as a causative verb, 使……廬, meaning "to make … change into huts." See L7 Grammar Note 1 ③.

居 *n.* dwelling. Here it refers to Buddhist and Daoist temples.

明 *adj.* clear. Here it is used as a causative verb, 使……明, meaning "to make clear or illuminate" 發揚 (*fā yang* 发扬). See L7 Grammar Note 1 ②.

之 _a *particle.* a possessive marker. MdnC: 的 (*de*). See L1 Grammar Note 2 ②.

道 _b *v.* used in the sense of 導 (*dǎo* 导), meaning "to guide" 引導 (*yǐn dǎo* 引导).

之 _b *personal pron.* them, referring to common people. See L1 Grammar Note 2 ③.

鰥 *n.* widower.

寡 *n.* widow.

孤 *n.* orphan.

獨 *n.* old people without children.

廢 *n.* people with disabilities. MdnC: 殘疾 (*cán jí* 残疾).

疾 *n.* sick people. MdnC: 病人 (*bìng rén*).

養 (养) *v.* to take care, raise, supply. MdnC: 供養 (*gòng yǎng* 供养).

其 _b *demonstrative pron.* those, referring to previous actions. See L6 Grammar Note 6 ④.

庶乎 *adv.* almost. MdnC: 差不多 (*chà bù duō*).

其 _c *adv.* used to suggest a tentative tone. See L2 Grammar Note 5 ③.

語法注釋 Grammar Notes

1. 曷 *initial interrogative particle.* a variant of 何. what? why? how? MdnC: 什麼 (*shén me* 什么), 爲什麼 (*wèi shén me* 为什么), 怎麼 (*zěn me* 怎么).

曷不爲太古之無事？
.

[为什么不实行太古时候那样的无为而治呢？]

2. 是　Five uses of 是 are explained in this book. In addition to the use below, see 是①②③ in L3 Grammar Note 1 and 是④ in L14 Grammar Note 4.

⑤ *particle.* marking the inversion of objects; it has no meaning in itself.

《詩》曰：「戎狄是膺，荊舒是懲。」
　　　　　　　　　.　　　　　　.

[《诗经》说："抵抗戎狄，惩罚楚国舒国。"]

3. 焉　Seven uses of 焉 are explained in this book. In addition to the use below, see 焉① in L1 Grammar Note 4, 焉②③ in L2 Grammar Note 3, 焉④ in L5 Grammar Note 4, 焉⑤ in L6 Grammar Note 5, and 焉⑥ in L12 Grammar Note 1.

⑦ *particle.* used as a pause in the middle of sentence; it has no meaning in itself.

子焉而不父其父，臣焉而不君其君，民焉而不事其事。
　.　　　　　　　　　.　　　　　　　　　.

[儿子不把父亲当作父亲，臣子不把君王当作君王，老百姓啊不把该做的事情当作事情。]

郊焉而天神假，廟焉而人鬼饗。
　.　　　　　　　.

[郊祀祭天时天神来到，庙里祭祖时祖先的魂灵来享用(祭品)。]

4. 如之何　what about it? how about it? MdnC: 怎麼樣 (*zěn me yàng* 怎么样)，怎麼辦 (*zěn me bàn* 怎么办).

然則，如之何而可也？
　.　　.　.　.

[既然这样，那么怎么办才可以呢？]
　　　.　.

Literary Analysis

1. Han Yu relies on canonical texts, historical evidence, and common opinion to establish the authority of his definition of the Way in Chinese culture. How does each cited source contribute to the authority of his definition? Are there differences in the kinds of authority these sources seem to grant?

2. What distinctions does Han draw between humans and nonhumans in his essay? What role do these distinctions play in his larger argument?

3. What distinctions does Han make between Chinese and non-Chinese? What defines someone as Chinese? Which traits does he suggest are irrelevant?

4. Han clearly criticizes both Buddhists and Daoists in this work, but does he critique them in the same way? How do you explain differences in how Han treats these two traditions?

5. Han repeats individual words or phrases throughout the composition. What rhetorical function does this repetition serve? Consider in particular these three examples: (1) the fifth passage in lesson 26, where 爲之 is repeated seventeen times; (2) this lesson's first passage, where the question 曷不爲 is repeated three times in succession; and (3) this lesson's second passage, where 其 is repeated nine times. Do the repeated words always mean the same thing in these examples?

☞ *HTRCProse*, chapter 10, "Tang and Song Expository Prose: The Practice of Persuasion."

—AKD

課後練習 Exercises

一 給加點字注音 Give the pinyin romanization for each dotted word.

1. 葛（＿＿）2. 裘（＿＿）3. 戎狄（＿＿,＿＿）4. 荊（＿＿）5. 夷（＿＿）
6. 軻（＿＿）7. 苟（＿＿）8. 鰥寡孤獨（＿＿, ＿＿,＿＿, ＿＿）

二 在括號中給句中加點的字注音，並選出正確的釋義 Give the pinyin romanization for each dotted word; then select the correct definition from the following list, and write it in the blank.

堵塞　　享用　　病人　　懲罰(惩罚)　　到　　抵抗　　**信服**　　都

1. **小信未孚（fú）　信服**　2. 戎狄是膺　（　）＿＿＿＿　3. 荊舒是懲　（　）＿＿＿＿
4. 不塞不流（　）＿＿＿＿　5. 鰥寡孤獨疾（　）＿＿＿＿　6. 廟焉而鬼饗（　）＿＿＿＿
7. 幾何其不胥爲夷也（　）＿＿＿＿　8. 郊焉而天神假（　）＿＿＿＿

三 選擇釋義並填空 Match each word in the left column with its correct definition in the middle column. Fill in each blank in the right column with an appropriate word from the left column (some words may be used more than once).

謀謀劃(谋划)	端正
責＿＿＿＿	修養(养)
治＿＿＿＿	推崇
齊＿＿＿＿	**謀劃(谋划)**
修＿＿＿＿	吉祥
正＿＿＿＿	選擇(选择)
誠＿＿＿＿	詳細(详细)
舉＿＿＿＿	禁止
祥＿＿＿＿	流傳(传)
公＿＿＿＿	供養(养)
擇＿＿＿＿	燒毀(烧毁)
詳＿＿＿＿	管理
流＿＿＿＿	責(责)怪
止＿＿＿＿	真誠(诚)
火＿＿＿＿	治理
養＿＿＿＿	公正

是亦＿＿＿冬之裘者曰：「曷不爲葛之之易也？」

古之欲明明德於天下者，先＿＿＿其國；欲＿＿＿其國者，先＿＿＿其家；欲＿＿＿其家者，先＿＿＿其身；欲＿＿＿其身者，先＿＿＿其心；欲＿＿＿其心者，先＿＿＿其意。

＿＿＿夷狄之法，而加之先王之教之上，幾何其不胥而爲夷也！

是故以之爲己，則順而＿＿＿；以之爲人，則愛而＿＿＿；以之爲心，則和而平。

荀與揚也，＿＿＿焉而不精，語焉而不＿＿＿。

曰：「不塞不＿＿＿，不＿＿＿不行。」

人其人，＿＿＿其書，廬其居，明先王之道以道之，鰥寡孤獨疾者有＿＿＿也：亦庶乎其可也！

四 請用給出的字填空 Fill in each blank with an appropriate word from the following list.

曷　　如　　焉　　爲(为)　　何　　其

1. 今其言曰：「＿＿＿不爲太古之無事？」 2. 子＿＿＿而不父其父，臣焉 而不君＿＿＿君。

3. 幾＿＿＿其不胥而＿＿＿夷也!　　　　　　4. 然則，＿＿＿之何而可也?

五　爲加點字選擇正確釋義，並根據釋義來翻譯句子 Match each dotted word with its correct modern Chinese equivalent by circling the latter. Then translate each sentence into modern Chinese.

1. 又何間焉?　　　　　　　　　　　(a.)爲什麼(为什么) b. 憑什麼(凭什么) c. 多少

現代文翻译：你又为什么要参与到这件事情里面？

＿＿＿＿＿＿＿＿＿＿＿＿＿＿＿＿＿＿＿＿＿＿＿＿＿＿＿＿＿＿＿＿

2. 是亦責冬之裘者曰：「曷不爲葛之之易也?」　　a. 爲什麼(为什么) b. 什麼(什么) c. 誰(谁)

現代文翻译：＿＿＿＿＿＿＿＿＿＿＿＿＿＿＿＿＿＿＿＿＿＿＿＿＿＿＿＿

3. 古之欲明明德於天下者，先治其國。　　　　a. 明亮 b. 以……爲(为)明 c. 使……明

現代文翻译：＿＿＿＿＿＿＿＿＿＿＿＿＿＿＿＿＿＿＿＿＿＿＿＿＿＿＿＿

4. 子焉而不父其父，臣焉 而不君其君，民焉而不事其事。

　　　　　　　　a. 父親(亲) b. 以……爲(为)父 c. 使……成爲(为)父親(亲)

現代文翻译：＿＿＿＿＿＿＿＿＿＿＿＿＿＿＿＿＿＿＿＿＿＿＿＿＿＿＿＿

5. 今也，举夷狄之法，而加之先王之教之上，幾何其不胥爲夷也!

　　　　　　　　　　　　　a. 那麼(那么) b. 他 c. 這(这)

現代文翻译：＿＿＿＿＿＿＿＿＿＿＿＿＿＿＿＿＿＿＿＿＿＿＿＿＿＿＿＿

6. 荀與揚也，擇焉而不精，語焉而不詳。　　　　a. 啊 b. 之 c. ……的樣(样)子

現代文翻译：＿＿＿＿＿＿＿＿＿＿＿＿＿＿＿＿＿＿＿＿＿＿＿＿＿＿＿＿

7. 然則，如之何而可也?　　　　a. 怎麼辦(怎么办) b. 什麼(什么) c. 爲什麼(为什么)

現代文翻译：＿＿＿＿＿＿＿＿＿＿＿＿＿＿＿＿＿＿＿＿＿＿＿＿＿＿＿＿

第三十一課

陳子龍《君子疾沒世而名不稱焉》

"A Superior Man Detests Dying Without Achieving Renown"
(Chen Zilong)

Introduction

Chen Zilong 陳子龍 (courtesy names Renzhong 人中 and Wozi 臥子; 1608–1647), was a famous scholar, poet, and Ming loyalist of the late Ming dynasty. A staunch anti-Manchu fighter, he resolutely refused to surrender to the Qing and committed suicide by drowning himself in a river. With this noble death, he attained the ideal of a Confucian gentleman earning everlasting renown through great moral deeds, as he himself had set forth in the famed eight-legged essay we will read in this lesson. On the merits of this essay, Chen passed the civil service examination and obtained the Presented Scholar degree in the tenth year of Chongzhen (1637). A translation of this text is given in *HTRCProse*, chapter 14, "Ming and Qing Eight-Legged Essays," C14.1.

The eight-legged essay was the most important and famous component of the civil service examinations from the second half of the fifteenth century to the beginning of the twentieth century. Although candidates were required to compose in other genres as well, it was their performance on the eight-legged essay that was pivotal to their success. The genre is known for its extremely stringent requirements in both form and content.

The standard structure of the eight-legged essay consists of "Breaking open the topic" 破題 (*pòtí* 破题), "Developing the topic" 承題 (*chéngtí* 承题), "Beginning discussion" 起講 (*qǐjiǎng* 起讲), and "Grand conclusion" 大結 (*dàjié* 大结) in four sets: "Initial legs" 起股 (*qǐgǔ*), "Middle legs" 中股 (*zhōnggǔ*), "Penultimate legs" 後股 (*hòugǔ* 后股), and "Last legs" 束股 (*shùgǔ*). The "Initial legs" are two sets of sentences (a pair of legs) that observe strict formal parallelism, just as the following three do. In this standard structure, the total number of legs is eight—hence the name *eight-legged essay*. In actual compositions, however, writers could produce essays with six, ten, or as many as sixteen legs.

The topics of the eight-legged essay were phrases, sentences, or passages drawn from the so-called Four Books of the Confucian canon: the *Great Learning* 大學 (*Dàxué* 大学), *Doctrine of the Mean* 中庸 (*Zhōngyōng*), *Analects* 論語 (*Lúnyǔ* 论语), and *Mencius* 孟子 (*Mèngzǐ*). Writers were required to follow the exegesis of the Four Books by the Zhu Xi 朱熹 (1130–1200) school, whose philosophy has often been referred to as neo-Confucianism or the Learning of the Way 道學 (*dàoxué* 道学). They could not, however, repeat the phrasing of the court-sanctioned commentaries. Conveying and elaborating on their understanding of the commentaries, they were supposed to "speak on behalf of a sage" 代聖人立言 (*dài shèngrén lìyán* 代圣人立言) by adopting the persona of the Confucian sage in the argumentation.

正文與簡體譯文 Text and Modern Chinese Translation

【破題】無後世之名，聖人之所憂也。[1]
wú hòu shì zhī míng　shèng rén zhī suǒ yōu yě

【承題】夫一時之名不必有也，後世之名不可無
fú yì shí zhī míng bú bì yǒu yě　hòu shì zhī míng bù kě wú

也。故君子不求名，而又不得不疾乎此。[2]
yě　gù jūn zǐ bù qiú míng　ér yòu bù dé bù jí hū cǐ

在后世没有名声，是圣人所担忧的事情。[1]

（对君子而言）一时的名声不必有，（但）在后世的名声不可没有。所以君子不追求名声，却又不得不对此表示担心。[2]

1. 破題 (题) breaking open the topic, the first section of the eight-legged essay. It identifies the meaning of the designated topic.

後 (后) 世 n. later generation, posterity.

名 n. reputation, fame, renown. MdnC: 名聲 (míng shēng 名声).

聖 (圣) 人 n. sage.

憂 (忧) v. to worry. MdnC: 擔憂 (dān yōu 担忧).

2. 承題 (题) developing the topic, the second section of the eight-legged essay. It supplements the first section by further explaining the thesis.

疾 v. to be anxious for. MdnC: 擔心 (dān xīn 担心).

乎 prep. at, for, about. MdnC: 對 (duì 对). See L6 Grammar Note 2 ③.

此 pron. this. It refers to the situation of having no posthumous reputation.

【起講】夫子若曰：好名者，人之恆情也。[3]故下
fū zǐ ruò yuē　hào míng zhě　rén zhī héng qíng yě　gù xià

士求名，人亦不得以爲躁，但我恨其急一時
shì qiú míng　rén yì bù dé yǐ wéi zào　dàn wǒ hèn qí jí yí shí

之名，而非千秋萬世之名耳。[4]若君子則知所
zhī míng　ér fēi qiān qiū wàn shì zhī míng ěr　ruò jūn zǐ zé zhī suǒ

以審處於此矣。[5]
yǐ shěn chǔ yú cǐ yǐ

夫子大致说过：喜好名声是人之常情。[3] 所以下等人士追求名声，人们也不能认为他太急躁了，但我很遗憾他只是急于一时的名声，而不是千秋万代的名声罢了。[4] 至于君子就知道怎么慎重处理这件事情了。[5]

3. 起講 (讲) beginning discussion, the third section of eight-legged essay. It requires the writer to step into the persona of the ancient sage and start speaking in his voice. In addition, the section usually lays out the issues to be elaborated on later and sets the stage for the core—namely, the eight-legged sections.

夫子 n. master. Here it should refer to Confucius.

若 adv. probably. MdnC: 大致 (dà zhì).

好 (hào) v. to like, desire. MdnC: 喜好 (xǐ hào).

恆 (恒) adj. regular, constant. MdnC: 常 (cháng).

4. 下士 n. a gentleman of the lowest kind.

亦 *adv.* also. MdnC: 也 (*yě*). See L5 Grammar Note 1 ①.

以爲 (为 *wéi*) or 以……爲…… to regard … as…. MdnC: 認爲 (*rèn wéi* 认为). See L2 Grammar Note 1 ④.

躁 *adj.* impetuous, rash. MdnC: 急躁 (*jí zào*).

恨 *v.* to regret. MdnC: 遺憾 (*yí hàn* 遗憾).

急 *v.* to worry.

千秋 a thousand years.

萬 (万) 世 ten thousand generations.

耳 *ending particle.* MdnC: 罷了 (*bà le* 罢了). See L7 Grammar Note 4.

5. 若 *conj.* about. MdnC: 至於 (*zhì yú* 至于). See L14 Grammar Note 3 ③.

審 (审) *v.* to examine carefully, investigate. Here it is used as an adverb, meaning "cautiously or carefully" 慎重 (*shèng zhòng*).

處 (处 *chǔ*) *v.* to deal with, manage. MdnC: 處理 (*chǔ lǐ* 处理).

【起股】以爲ₐ一時之名， 自我爲之， 而其權在
　　　　　yǐ wéi　yì shí zhī míng　　zì wǒ wéi zhī　　ér qí quán zài

人， 苟我之聰明才力注乎名,則有名， 而皆
rén　　gǒu wǒ zhī cōng míng cái lì zhù hū míng zé yǒu míng　　ér jiē

倚人以爲ᵦ重， 盛與衰我不得而知之， 此名ₐ
yǐ rén　yǐ wéi　zhòng　shèng yǔ shuāi wǒ bù dé ér zhī zhī　　cǐ míng

而名ᵦ者也； ⁶
ér míng　zhě yě

(我)认为一时的名声，由我做成，但(决定的)权力在别人。如果我把自己的聪明才力都专注在名声上，就会得到名声。但这名声都要倚靠别人以(我)为重，(这是可持久的)盛名、还是(很快就)衰败(的名声)，我不得而知。这是为了名声而求名的人。⁶

6. 起股 initial legs (also called 起比) is the fourth section of the essay. It usually focuses on one aspect of the central thesis onto which the subsequent legs can be built.

以爲ₐ (为 *wéi*) *v.* to think. MdnC: 認爲 (*rèn wéi* 认为).

自 *prep.* from, by. MdnC: 由 (*yóu*). See Grammar Note 1 ①.

權 (权) *n.* power. MdnC: 權力 (*quán lì* 权力).

人 *n.* others. MdnC: 別人 (*bié rén*).

苟 *conj.* if. MdnC: 如果 (*rú guǒ*). See L19 Grammar Note 1 ①.

注 *v.* to pour, concentrate. MdnC: 專注 (*zhuān zhù* 专注).

倚 *v.* to rely on, depend on. MdnC: 倚靠 (*yǐ kào*).

以爲ᵦ (为 *wéi*) or 以 (我) 爲…… to think of me as…. See L2 Grammar Note 1 ④.

重 *adj.* important. MdnC: 重要 (*zhòng yào*).

盛 *adj.* flourishing, prosperous.

衰 *v.* to decline, wane.

名ₐ *n.* reputation, renown. Here it is used as an adverb, meaning "for reputation" 爲了名聲 (*wèi le míng shēng* 为了名声).

名ᵦ *n.* reputation, renown. Here it is used as a verb, meaning "to attain reputation" 求名 (*qiú míng*).

千秋萬世之名， 自人爲之， 而其權在
qiān qiū wàn shì zhī míng　zì rén wéi zhī　ér qí quán zài

我， 苟我之聰明才力注乎名，未必有名， 而
wǒ　gǒu wǒ zhī cōng míng cái lì zhù hū míng wèi bì yǒu míng　ér

常修己以自立， 高與下我將得而定之， 此名
cháng xiū jǐ yǐ zì lì　gāo yǔ xià wǒ jiāng dé ér dìng zhī　cǐ míng

而實者也。 [7]
ér shí zhě yě

（流传）千秋万代的名声，由别人来促成，但（决定的）权利在于我自己。如果我的聪明才力，专注在名声上，不一定会有好名声。但我常常自我修养来确立自己，高尚还是低下，我将能自己来确定。这是为了名声而得到了实质（内涵）的人。[7]

7. 修 v. to cultivate. MdnC: 修養 (xiū yǎng 修养).
　　定 v. to determine. MdnC: 確定 (què dìng 确定).
　　實 (实) n. substance, truth. MdnC: 實質 (shí zhì 实质).

【中股】名而名者， 無之在於未沒世之前， 君子
míng ér míng zhě　wú zhī zài yú wèi mò shì zhī qián　jūn zǐ

豈可以徒疾乎？ [8]
qǐ kě yǐ tú jí hū

名而實者， 無之在於既沒世之後， 君子
míng ér shí zhě　wú zhī zài yú jì mò shì zhī hòu　jūn zǐ

豈得而不疾乎？ [9]
qǐ dé ér bù jí hū

为名而求名的人，（如果）在没去世之前，没有得到名声，君子怎么可能只有遗憾呢？ [8]
为名而得实的人，（如果）在已经去世之后还没有名声，君子怎么能不遗憾呢！ [9]

8. 中股 middle legs (also called 中比) is the fifth section of the essay. It often carries the most substantial portion of the argument.
　　豈 (岂) interrogative particle. MdnC: 怎麼 (zěn me 怎么). See L8 Grammar Note 4.
　　徒 adv. only, merely. MdnC: 只有 (zhǐ yǒu).
9. 既 adv. already. MdnC: 已經 (yǐ jīng 已经). See L1 Grammar Note 5.

【後股】人之生也， 有愛有憎， 故有幸而有名
rén zhī shēng yě　yǒu ài yǒu zēng　gù yǒu xìng ér yǒu míng

者， 有不幸而無名者， 至於身沒之後， 與其
zhě　yǒu bú xìng ér wú míng zhě　zhì yú shēn mò zhī hòu　yǔ qí

人不相接， 則不可曰愛憎之所爲也， 而寂寂
rén bù xiāng jiē　zé bù kě yuē ài zēng zhī suǒ wéi yě　ér jì jì

者竟如斯， 則將何以自異於里巷之子耶？ [10]
zhě jìng rú sī　zé jiāng hé yǐ zì yì yú lǐ xiàng zhī zǐ yé

人的一生中有时被人喜爱有时被人憎恶。因此有人幸运而留名，也有人不幸而无名。至于去世之后，与后来的人不相互接触，则不能说（留名或无名）是由后来人的喜爱或憎恶造成的。但是安静孤独的人竟然会像这样（没有名

人之生也，有失勢有得勢，故有幸而無名者，
rén zhī shēng yě　yǒu shī shì yǒu dé shì　　gù yǒu xìng ér wú míng zhě

又有不幸而有名者，至於身沒之後，與其時
yòu yǒu bú xìng ér yǒu míng zhě　zhì yú shēn mò zhī hòu　yǔ qí shí

不相及，則又有非得勢失勢之可論矣，而泯
bù xiāng jí　　zé yòu yǒu fēi dé shì shī shì zhī kě lùn yǐ　　ér mǐn

泯者遂如斯，則又何以自別於草木之儔耶？
mǐn zhě suì rú sī　　zé yòu hé yǐ zì bié yú cǎo mù zhī chóu yé

声），那么将怎么让自己与街巷里的人有所不同呢？ [10] 人的一生也有失去权势、得到权势的时候。所以有人幸运却没有名声，又有人不幸却有名声。至于身死之后，与当时不相关联，那么又有了不是得势或者失势（可决定后世留名的）论断。而名声不显的人就像这样，那么又怎么让自己与草木之类有所区别呢？ [11]

10. 後 (后) 股 last legs (also called 後比) is the sixth section of the essay. It is often substantial because it typically serves to extend the reasoning of the middle legs.

憎 *n.* hate. MdnC: 憎惡 (*zēng wù* 憎恶).

幸 *adj.* lucky, fortunate. MdnC: 幸運 (*xìng yùn* 幸运).

接 *v.* to connect, contact. MdnC: 接觸 (*jiē chù* 接触).

寂寂 *adj.* quiet, alone.

竟 *adv.* unexpectedly, to one's surprise. MdnC: 竟然 (*jìng rán*).

斯 *demonstrative pron.* this. MdnC: 這樣 (*zhè yàng* 这样). See L5 Grammar Note 3 ①.

何以 how? MdnC: 怎麼 (*zěn me* 怎么). See L1 Grammar Note 3 ③.

異 (异) *adj.* different. MdnC: 不同 (*bù tóng*).

里巷 *n.* streets and alleys. MdnC: 街巷 (*jiē xiàng*).

11. 勢 (势) *n.* power or influence.

及 *adj.* relevant. MdnC: 關聯 (*guān lián* 关联).

泯泯 *adj.* obscure.

遂 *adv.* then, from then on. MdnC: 就 (*jiù*).

別 *v.* to distinguish. MdnC: 區別 (*qū bié* 区别).

儔 (俦) *n.* category, kind. MdnC: 類 (*lèi* 类).

【束股】人之貴乎榮名者，貴其有益生之樂也；
rén zhī guì hū róng míng zhě　guì qí yǒu yì shēng zhī lè　yě

君子之貴榮名者，貴其有不死之業也。死
jūn zǐ zhī guì róng míng zhě　guì qí yǒu bù sǐ zhī yè　yě　　sǐ

而無聞，則其死可悲矣；死而可悲，則其生
ér wú wén　zé qí sǐ kě bēi yǐ　　sǐ ér kě bēi　zé qí shēng

更可悲矣。是以君子抗節礪行，惟恐不及
gèng kě bēi yǐ　　shì yǐ jūn zǐ kàng jié lì xíng　wéi kǒng bù jí

普通人看重美名，是看重它有增加人生快乐的（功用）；君子看重美名，是看重它是不朽的功业。 [12] 人死了却没有闻名于世，那么他的死是可悲的；死得很可悲，那么他的人生就更可悲了！因此君子坚守自己的节操，磨砺自己

耳。¹³人之以爲沒世之名者，是我身後之計
ěr　　rén zhī yǐ wéi mò shì zhī míng zhě　　shì wǒ shēn hòu zhī jì

也；君子以爲沒世之名者，是我大生之事
yě　　jūn zǐ yǐ wéi mò shì zhī míng zhě　　shì wǒ dà shēng zhī shì

也。¹⁴死而無聞，則其死不及憂矣；死不及
yě　　sǐ ér wú wén　　zé qí sǐ bù jí yōu yǐ　　sǐ bù jí

憂，則其生大可憂矣。是以君子趨事赴功，
yōu　　zé qí shēng dà kě yōu yǐ　　shì yǐ jūn zǐ qū shì fù gōng

惟日不足耳。¹⁵
wéi rì bù zú ěr

的行为，就怕自己达不到啊！¹³普通人认为去世后的名声，是我死后的计划；君子认为去世后的名声，是我人生的大事。¹⁴人死了却没有闻名于世，那么他的死也不值得担忧；到死都不值得担忧，那么这样的人生就非常让人担忧了。因此君子创立事业，追求功业，只怕时间不够啊！¹⁵

12. 束股 last legs, the seventh section of the essay. It serves to extend the reasoning of the previous six legs and put an end to the discussion.

貴 (贵) *adj.* distinguished, valuable. Here it is used as a putative verb, 以……爲貴, meaning "to attach importance to" 看重 (*kàn zhòng*). See L14 Grammar Note 1 ①.

榮 (荣) *n.* glory, honor.

榮 (荣) 名 *n.* good reputation. MdnC: 美名 (*měi míng*).

益 *v.* to increase. MdnC: 增加 (*zēng jiā*).

不死 *adj.* immortal. MdnC: 不朽 (*bù xiǔ*).

業 (业) *n.* achievement, accomplishment. MdnC: 功業 (*gōng yè* 功业).

13. 聞 *v.* to be known. MdnC: 聞名 (*wén míng* 闻名).

悲 *adj.* sad, lamentable.

是以 therefore, so. MdnC: 因此 (*yīn cǐ*). See L3 Grammar Note 1 ③.

抗 *v.* to resist. Here it means "to uphold" 堅守 (*jiān shǒu* 坚守).

節 (节) *n.* principle, moral principle. MdnC: 節操 (*jié cāo* 节操).

礪 (砺) *v.* to sharpen. MdnC: 磨礪 (*mó lì* 磨砺).

行 *n.* behavior, conduct. MdnC: 行爲 (*xíng wéi* 行为).

惟 *adv.* only. MdnC: 只 (*zhǐ*). See L22 Grammar Note 2 ②.

恐 *v.* to fear. MdnC: 怕 (*pà*).

及 *v.* to reach, get to. MdnC: 達到 (*dá dào* 达到).

14. 計 (计) *n.* plan. MdnC: 計劃 (*jì huà* 计划).

15. 趨 (趋) *v.* to hasten, hurry.

赴 *v.* to go to.

功 *n.* achievement, accomplishment. MdnC: 功業 (*gōng yè* 功业).

趨 (趋) 事赴功 means "to establish a career and strive for achievements."

日 *n.* time. MdnC: 時間 (*shí jiān* 时间).

【大結】人但見君子之爲人也，譽之而不喜，毀
rén dàn jiàn jūn zǐ zhī wéi rén yě　　yù zhī ér bù xǐ　　huǐ

世人只看见君子的为人：称赞他，（君子）没

之而不懼，以爲君子之忘名也如此， 而不知
zhī ér bù jù   yǐ wéi jūn zǐ zhī wàng míng yě rú cǐ   ér bù zhī

有所其不忘也；不大言以欺人，不奇行以駭
yǒu suǒ qí bù wàng yě   bù dà yán yǐ qī rén   bù qí xíng yǐ hài

俗，以爲君子之遠名也如此， 而不知有所甚
sú   yǐ wéi jūn zǐ zhī yuǎn míng yě rú cǐ   ér bù zhī yǒu suǒ shèn

不遠也。¹⁶蓋有大於此者而已，有久於此者
bù yuǎn yě   gài yǒu dà yú cǐ zhě ér yǐ   yǒu jiǔ yú cǐ zhě

而已。¹⁷若夫營營於旦夕之間，是求速盡者
ér yǐ   ruò fú yíng yíng yú dàn xī zhī jiān   shì qiú sù jìn zhě

也，好名者豈如是乎？¹⁸
yě   hào míng zhě qǐ rú shì hū

《欽定四書文校注》，武漢：武漢大學出版社 (2009), 481.

有多高興，詆毀他，君子也不害怕。（由此世人）认为君子就这样忘记了自己名声，却不知道君子从来不会忘记（要身后留名）。君子不用大话来欺骗世人，不用奇怪的行为来惊骇世人，由此世人认为君子就这样远离自己名声，却不知道君子从来离自己的名声都不远。¹⁶可能有些事情比这些（普通人看到的）更重要，有些事情比这些（普通人以为的持续）更长久罢了。¹⁷至于追求一天（成名），是想要快速求得名声的人，（真正）求名的人怎会这样呢？¹⁸

16. 大結 (结) grand conclusion, the eighth and final section. It sums up the previous analysis and offers a broad perspective that both reiterates and elevates the central argument.

但 *adv.* only. MdnC: 只 (*zhǐ*). See Grammar Note 2.

譽 (誉) *v.* to praise. MdnC: 稱贊 (*chēn zàn* 称赞).

喜 *v.* to be happy about. MdnC: 高興 (*gāo xìng* 高兴).

毀 (毁) *v.* to slander, defame. MdnC: 詆毀 (*dǐ huǐ* 诋毁).

懼 (惧) *v.* to be afraid of. MdnC: 害怕 (*hài pà*).

大言 *n.* exaggeration. MdnC: 大話 (*dà huà* 大话).

欺 *v.* to cheat, deceive. MdnC: 欺騙 (*qī piàn* 欺骗).

奇 *adj.* strange, weird.

駭 (骇) *v.* to astonish, astound. MdnC: 驚駭 (*jīng hài* 惊骇).

俗 *n.* common people. MdnC: 世人 (*shì rén*).

甚 (*shèn*) *adv.* extremely, very.

遠 (远) *v.* to be away from. MdnC: 遠離 (*yuǎn lí* 远离).

17. 蓋 (盖) *adv.* probably. MdnC: 可能 (*kě néng*). See L13 Grammar Note 1.

而已 *ending particle.* nothing more. MdnC: 罷了 (*bà le* 罢了). See L21 Grammar Note 1 ③.

18. 若夫 *conj.* as for, about. MdnC: 至於 (*zhì yú* 至于). See L36 Grammar Note 1.

營營 (营) *v.* to pursue, rush for. MdnC: 追求 (*zhuī qiú*).

旦夕 *n.* morning and evening, a short period.

速 *adj.* fast. MdnC: 快 (*kuài*).

盡 (尽 *jìn*) *v.* to complete, finish.

語法注釋 Grammar Notes

1. 自 ① *prep.* from, by. MdnC: 由 (*yóu*), 從 (*cóng* 从).

以爲一時之名，自我爲之，而其權在人……

[（我）认为一时的名声，由我完成，（但决定的）权力在别人……]

有朋自遠方來，不亦樂乎？(L5)

[有朋友从远方来了，不是很快乐吗？]

② *pron.* self. MdnC: 自己 (*zì jǐ*).

而常修己以自立……

[而经常自我修养来确立自己……]

窺鏡而自視，又弗如遠甚。(L4)

[照照镜子看了看自己，更觉得自己不如徐公美。]

2. 但 *adv.* only. MdnC: 只 (*zhǐ*), 只是 (*zhǐ shì*).

人但見君子之爲人也……

[人们只看到君子做人……]

公幹有逸氣，但未遒耳。(L18)

[刘桢有飘逸的气质，只是不够遒劲有力。]

但爲氣所激，緣悟天人理。(L21)

[只是我被正气所激励，由此领悟到天人的道理。]

Literary Analysis

1. Chen Zilong's "A Superior Man Detests Dying Without Achieving Renown" is considered an exemplary eight-legged essay. How does his essay meet those stringent formal requirements? Can you identify its eight legs and other structural parts? What do you think are the features and functions of the different parts?

2. What are the rhetorical components Chen uses for the central thesis of the essay? How does he manage to create contrasts among them and build a layered argument? How do you evaluate his rhetorical strategies?

3. The topic of an eight-legged essay comes from a Confucian canonical text—in this case, a statement made by Confucius in the *Analects*. How well do you think Chen embodies the voice of Confucius? Given that the eight-legged essay was the most important part of the civil service examinations for most of the late imperial period, what are the ideological implications of the essay?

👉 *HTRCProse*, chapter 14, "Ming and Qing Eight-Legged Essays" for further comments on Chen Zilong's prose writings. See also the analysis of Chen's same essay in *HTRCProse*, chapter 1, "An Anatomy of the Chinese Prose Form: An Overview," C1.8.

—ML

課後練習 Exercises

一　在括號中給句中加點的字注音，並選出正確的釋義 Give the pinyin romanization for each dotted word; then select the correct definition from the following list, and write it in the blank.

磨礪(砺)　　急躁　　憎惡(恶)　　類(类)　　驚駭(惊骇)
擔(担)心　　處(处)理　　**信服**　　倚靠

1. 小信未孚　　　　　(**fú**) <u>　信服　</u>　　2. 君子疾沒世而名不稱焉　(　) <u>　　　　　</u>

3. 人亦不得以爲躁人　(　) <u>　　　　　</u>　　4. 若君子則知所以審處於此　(　) <u>　　　　　</u>

5. 皆倚人爲重　　　　(　) <u>　　　　　</u>　　6. 人之生也有愛有憎　　　(　) <u>　　　　　</u>

7. 草木之儔　　　　　(　) <u>　　　　　</u>　　8. 君子抗節礪行　　　　　(　) <u>　　　　　</u>

9. 不奇行以駭俗　　　(　) <u>　　　　　</u>

二　選擇釋義並填空 Match each word in the left column with its correct definition in the middle column. Fill in each blank in the right column with an appropriate word from the left column.

謀<u>謀劃(谋划)</u>　　　慎重

憂<u>　　　　</u>　　　增加

恆<u>　　　　</u>　　　專(专)注

恨<u>　　　　</u>　　　堅(坚)守

審<u>　　　　</u>　　　**謀劃(谋划)**

注<u>　　　　</u>　　　稱贊(称赞)

益<u>　　　　</u>　　　害怕

業<u>　　　　</u>　　　擔憂(担忧)

抗<u>　　　　</u>　　　詆毀(诋毁)

及<u>　　　　</u>　　　常

譽<u>　　　　</u>　　　遺憾(遗憾)

懼<u>　　　　</u>　　　功業(业)

毀<u>　　　　</u>　　　達(达)到

無後世之名，聖人之所<u>　　</u>也。

夫子若曰：“好名者，人之<u>　　</u>情也。”

但我<u>　　</u>其急一時之名，而非千秋萬世之名耳。若君子則知所以<u>　　</u>處於此矣。

苟我之聰明才力<u>　　</u>乎名，則有名。

君子之貴乎榮名者，貴其有<u>　　</u>生之樂也；君子之貴乎榮名者，貴其有不死之<u>　　</u>也。

是以君子<u>　　</u>節礪行，唯恐不<u>　　</u>耳。

人但見君子之爲人也，<u>　　</u>之而不喜，<u>　　</u>之而不<u>　　</u>也。

三　請用給出的字填空 Fill in each blank with an appropriate word from the following list (some words may be used more than once).

斯　何　自　以　苟　若　惟　耶　夫

1. <u>　　</u>爲一時之名，<u>　　</u>我爲之，而其權在人，<u>　　</u>我之聰明才力，注乎名則有名，而皆倚人以爲重，盛與衰我不得而知之，此名而名者也。

2. 而寂寂者竟如<u>　　</u>，則將<u>　　</u>以<u>　　</u>異於里巷之子<u>　　</u>？

3. 是<u>　　</u>君子趨事赴功，<u>　　</u>日不足耳。

4. <u>　　</u><u>　　</u>營營於旦夕之間，是求速盡者也，好名者豈如是乎？

四　爲加點字選擇正確釋義，並根據釋義來翻譯句子 Match each dotted word with its correct modern Chinese equivalent by circling the latter. Then translate each sentence into modern Chinese.

1. 又何間焉?　　　　　　　　　　　　　　ⓐ.爲什麼（为什么）b. 憑什麼（凭什么）c. 多少

現代文翻譯：你又为什么要参与到这件事情里面？

_____

2. 若君子則知所以審處於此矣。　　　　　　　a. 好像 b. 至於（于）c. 你

現代文翻譯：_____

3. 苟我之聰明才力注乎名，則有名。　　　　　a. 如果 b. 但是 c. 而且

現代文翻譯：_____

4. 名而名者，無之在於未沒世之前，君子豈可以徒疾乎?

　　　　　　　　　　　　　a. 爲什麼（为什么）b. 怎麼（么）c. 什麼（什么）

現代文翻譯：_____

5. 人之貴乎榮名者，貴其有益生之樂也。　a. 使……貴（贵）重 b. 以……爲貴（为贵）c. 貴（贵）重

現代文翻譯：_____

6. 人但見君子之爲人也，譽之而不喜，毀之而不懼，以爲君子之忘名也如此。

　　　　　　　　　　　　　　　　　　　　　a. 但是 b. 而且 c. 只

現代文翻譯：_____

7. 若夫營營於旦夕之間，是求速盡者也，好名者豈如是乎?　a. 至於（于）b. 所以 c. 可是

現代文翻譯：_____

第三十二課

黃宗羲《原君》

"On the Origin of Rulership" (Huang Zongxi)

Introduction

Huang Zongxi 黃宗羲 (courtesy name Taichong 太沖; pseudonyms Nanlei 南雷 and Lizhou 梨洲; 1610–1695) stands as one of the three great thinkers (with Gu Yanwu 顧炎武 [1613–1682] and Wang Fuzhi 王夫之 [1619–1692]) of the late Ming and early Qing. Huang was a prolific writer, producing over fifty titles filling more than three hundred volumes, and his research spanned the Confucian classics, history, philosophy, geography, astronomy, the Chinese calendar, and other fields.

This essay is the first segment of his famous work *Awaiting the Visit of an Enlightened Emperor in Times of Hardship* 明夷待訪錄 (*Míngyí dàifǎnglù*), written in the first year of Qing Kangxi's reign (1662). In the Chinese title, *Míngyí* 明夷 refers to the thirty-sixth hexagram in the *Book of Changes* 周易 (*Zhōuyì*) and may also be translated as "frustration." The next phrase, *dàifǎng* 待訪, means "awaiting the visit of an enlightened emperor." Huang uses the essay to explore the origin of emperorship and the inherent responsibilities of an emperor. Building on the words of Mencius—"To a state, the people are the most important, the state is secondary, and the ruler is the least important"—Huang relentlessly condemns the misconduct of later emperors and sets forth an emperor's ineluctable responsibility to the people. The essay follows a tight logical structure that undergirds a sustained, step-by-step process of comparative analysis.

正文與簡體譯文 Text and Modern Chinese Translation

有生之初，人各自私也，人各自利也，
yǒu shēng zhī chū　rén gè zì sī yě　rén gè zì lì yě

天下有公利而莫或興之，有公害而莫或除
tiān xià yǒu gōng lì ér mò huò xīng zhī　yǒu gōng hài ér mò huò chú

之。[1] 有人者出，不以一己之利爲利，而使
zhī　　yǒu rén zhě chū　bù yǐ yì jǐ zhī lì wéi lì　ér shǐ

天下受其利，不以一己之害爲害，而使天下
tiān xià shòu qí lì　bù yǐ yì jǐ zhī hài wéi hài　ér shǐ tiān xià

釋其害，此其人之勤勞必千萬於天下之人。[2]
shì qí hài　cǐ qí rén zhī qín láo bì qiān wàn yú tiān xià zhī rén

有生命开始，每个人都是自私的，每个人都是自利的，天下有对公众有利的事情，却没人把它稍微建立起来，有对公众有害的事情，也没人除掉它。[1] 有个人出现了，他不把自己的利益当作利益，而是使天下都得到他的利益，不把自己的灾祸当作灾祸，而使天下都能够避开灾

夫以千萬倍之勤勞而己又不享其利，必非天
fú　yǐ qiān wàn bèi zhī qín láo ér　jǐ yòu bù xiǎng qí lì　　bì fēi tiān

下之人情所欲居也。³故古之人君，量而不
xià zhī rén qíng suǒ yù jū yě　　gù gǔ zhī rén jūn　　liáng ér bú

欲入者，許由、務光是也；入而又去之者，
yù rù zhě　　xǔ yóu　　wù guāng shì yě　　rù ér yòu qù zhī zhě

堯、舜是也；初不欲入而不得去者，禹是
yáo　　shùn shì yě　　chū bú yù rù　ér bù dé qù zhě　　yǔ shì

也。豈古之人有所異哉？⁴好逸惡勞，亦猶
yě　　qǐ gǔ zhī rén yǒu suǒ yì zāi　　hào yì wù láo　　yì yóu

夫人之情也。⁵
fú rén zhī qíng yě.

祸。这个人的勤劳必然是天下人的千万倍。²千万倍的勤劳努力，而自己又不享受勤劳带来的利益，这必然不是天下人心里想做的。³所以古代的君王，考量之后不想就位的人，是许由、务光；就位了而又离开的人，是尧、舜；开始不想就位而最后又不能离开的，是禹。难道古代人有什么不同吗？⁴喜好安逸，厌恶劳作，也就是人之常情啊！⁵

1. 生 *n.* being. MdnC: 生命 (*shēng mìng*).

   各 *adj.* every, each. MdnC: 每個 (*měi gè* 每个).

   自私 *adj.* selfish, self-centered.

   自利 *adj.* self-interest.

   公 *adj.* public. MdnC: 公眾 (*gōng zhòng* 公众).

   利 *n.* interest, profit, benefit. MdnC: 利益 (*lì yì*).

   莫 *indefinite pron.* none. MdnC: 沒有人 (*méi yǒu rén*). See L3 Grammar Note 2 ①.

   或 *adv.* a bit, a little. MdnC: 稍微 (*shāo wēi*). See Grammar Note 1 ③.

   興 (兴 *xīng*) *v.* to rise, prosper. MdnC: 建立 (*jiàn lì*).

   除 *v.* to remove, get rid of, eliminate. MdnC: 除掉 (*chú diào*).

2. 以……爲 (为 *wéi*) …… to think of something as…. See L2 Grammar Note 1 ④.

   一己 oneself. MdnC: 自己 (*zì jǐ*).

   受 *v.* to receive, get. MdnC: 得到 (*dé dào*).

   害 *n.* disaster. MdnC: 災禍 (*zāi huò* 灾祸).

   釋 (释) *v.* to release, get rid of. Here it means "to avoid or keep from" 避開 (*bì kāi* 避开).

3. 夫 (fú) *initial particle.* See L2 Grammar Note 4 ①.

   享 *v.* to enjoy. MdnC: 享受 (*xiǎng shòu*).

   情 *n.* feelings, thoughts.

   居 *v.* to occupy (the position).

4. 人君 *n.* emperor. MdnC: 君王 (*jūn wáng*).

   量 (*liáng*) *v.* to evaluate, consider. MdnC: 考量 (*kǎo liáng*).

   入 *v.* to enter. Here it means to take a position 就位 (*jiù wèi*).

   許 (许) 由 See Xu You's brief biography in L13 note 7.

   務 (务) 光 See Wu Guang's brief biography in L13 note 8.

   堯 (尧) See Yao's brief biography in L13 note 3.

   舜 See Shun's brief biography in L13 note 3.

禹 See Yu's brief biography in L13 note 4.

豈 (岂) *interrogative particle.* MdnC: 難道 (*nán dào* 难道). See L8 Grammar Note 4.

5. 逸 *adj.* free, easy, and comfortable. MdnC: 安逸 (*ān yì*).

惡 (恶 wù) *v.* to dislike, hate. MdnC: 厭惡 (*yàn wù* 厌恶).

勞 (劳) *n.* work, labor. MdnC: 勞作 (*láo zuò* 劳作).

後之爲人君者不然，以爲天下利害之權
hòu zhī wéi rén jūn zhě bù rán　　yǐ wéi tiān xià lì hài zhī quán

皆出於我，我以天下之利盡歸於己，以天下
jiē chū yú wǒ　　wǒ yǐ tiān xià zhī lì jìn guī yú jǐ　　yǐ tiān xià

之害盡歸於人，亦無不可。使天下之人不敢
zhī hài jìn guī yú rén　　yì wú bù kě　　shǐ tiān xià zhī rén bù gǎn

自私，不敢自利，以我之大私爲天下之大
zì sī　　bù gǎn zì lì　　yǐ wǒ zhī dà sī wéi tiān xià zhī dà

公。[6] 始而慙焉，久而安焉，視天下爲莫大
gōng　　shǐ ér cán yān　　jiǔ ér ān yān　　shì tiān xià wéi mò dà

之產業，傳之子孫，受享無窮，漢高帝所謂
zhī chǎn yè　　chuán zhī zǐ sūn　　shòu xiǎng wú qióng　　hàn gāo dì suǒ wèi

「某業所就，孰與仲多」者，其逐利之情不
mǒu yè suǒ jiù　　shú yǔ zhòng duō　　zhě　　qí zhú lì zhī qíng bù

覺溢之於辭矣。[7] 此無他，古者以天下爲 a
jué yì zhī yú cí yǐ　　cǐ wú tā　　gǔ zhě yǐ tiān xià wéi

主，君爲 a 客，凡君之所畢世而經營者，爲 b
zhǔ　　jūn wéi　　kè　　fán jūn zhī suǒ bì shì é jīng yíng zhě　　wèi

天下也。今也以君爲主，天下爲客，凡天下
tiān xià yě　　jīn yě yǐ jūn wéi zhǔ　　tiān xià wéi kè　　fán tiān xià

之無地而得安寧者，爲君也。[8] 是以其未得
zhī wú dì ér dé ān níng zhě　　wèi jūn yě　　shì yǐ qí wèi dé

之也，屠毒天下之肝腦，離散天下之子女，
zhī yě　　tú dú tiān xià zhī gān nǎo　　lí sàn tiān xià zhī zǐ nǚ

以博我一人之產業，曾不慘然！曰「我固爲
yǐ bó wǒ yì rén zhī chǎn yè　　zēng bù cǎn rán　　yuē　　wǒ gù wèi

子孫創業也」。[9] 其既得之也，敲剝天下之
zǐ sūn chuàng yè yě　　qí jì dé zhī yě　　qiāo bō tiān xià zhī

后来为人君王的人就不这样了，（他们）认为（决定）天下利益祸患的权力都出于我，我把天下的利益都归于自己，把天下的祸患都归于别人，也没什么不可以的。让天下的人都不敢自私，不敢自利，把我个人的私利当作天下的公利。[6] 开始时还对这种做法感到惭愧，时间久了就安心了！他们认为天下是自己最大的产业，传给子孙，享受无穷无尽（的利益）。汉高祖所说的"我的产业所达到的成就，和我二哥比，谁的更多"这种话，（让他）追逐利益的心思不知不觉在言辞中流露出来。[7] 没有其他（的原因），古时把天下当作主要的，君王是次要的，君王用毕生来努力经营，是为了天下人啊！现在把君王当作主要的，天下是次要的。天下没有一个地方能够得到安宁，是为了君王啊！[8] 因此，他没有得到天下时，就残害天下人，使天下的子女离散，来换取我一个人的产业，竟不觉得悲痛！说："我本来就是为了子孙创业。"[9] 等他已经得到了天下，敲诈

骨髓，離散天下之子女，以奉我一人之淫
gǔ suǐ　　lí sàn tiān xià zhī　zǐ nǚ　　　yǐ fèng wǒ yì rén zhī yín

樂，視爲當然，曰「此我產業之花息也」。10
lè　　shì wéi dāng rán　　yuē　cǐ wǒ chǎn yè zhī huā xī yě

然則爲天下之大害者，君而已矣。向使無
rán zé wéi tiān xià zhī　dà hài zhě　　jūn ér yǐ yǐ　　xiàng shǐ wú

君，人各得自私也，人各得自利也。嗚呼！
jūn　　rén gè dé zì sī yě　　　rén gè dé zì lì yě　　　wū hū

豈設君之道固如是乎！11
qǐ shè jūn zhī dào gù rú shì hū

剥夺天下人的骨髓，使天下人子女离散，来供奉我一个人淫乐，（把这）视作理所当然，说："这是我产业的利息啊！"10 既然如此，制造天下大祸害的人，就是君王！假使没有君王，每个人都自私，每个人都自利。哎！难道设立君王的道理本来是像这样的吗？11

6. 然 *pron.* like this. MdnC: 這樣 (*zhè yàng* 这样). See L8 Grammar Note 5 ③.

以爲 (为 *wéi*) *v.* to think, regard. MdnC: 認爲 (*rèn wéi* 认为).

權 (权) *n.* power, authority. MdnC: 权力 (*quán lì*).

盡 (尽 *jìn*) *adv.* totally, thoroughly. MdnC: 都 (*dōu*).

歸 (归) *v.* belong to.

7. 慙 (惭) *adj.* ashamed. MdnC: 慚愧 (*cán kuì* 惭愧).

爲 *demonstrative pron.* for this (behavior). MdnC: 對這 (*duì zhè* 对这). See L1 Grammar Note 4 ①.

安 *adj.* feeling relieved, at ease. MdnC: 安心 (*ān xīn*).

視 (视) *v.* to regard, think. MdnC: 認爲 (*rèn wéi* 认为).

莫大 *adj.* greatest. MdnC: 最大 (*zuì dà*).

產業 (产业) *n.* property, estate.

傳 (传 *chuán*) *v.* to hand down.

無窮 (无穷) *adv.* endlessly.

漢高帝 or 漢高祖 (family name 姓, Liú 劉; given name 名, Bāng 邦; style 字, Jì 季; posthumous name 謚, Gāo Huángdì 高皇帝; r. 202–195 BCE), Emperor Gao, the founder and the first emperor of the Han dynasty.

漢高帝所謂 a quotation of Emperor Gao of the Han from "Biography of Emperor Gao" 高祖本紀 ("Gāo zǔ běn jì" 高祖本纪) in *Grand Scribe's Records*.

某 *pron.* someone. Here it refers to Emperor Gao of the Han himself.

就 *v.* to achieve. MdnC: 成就 (*chéng jiù*).

孰 *interrogative pron.* who? Which? See L4 Grammar Note 1 ① for 孰與 (与).

仲 *n.* middle, second. Here it refers to the second brother of Emperor Gao of the Han.

逐 *v.* to pursue, chase. MdnC: 追逐 (*zhuī zhú*).

不覺 (觉 *jué*) *adv.* unconsciously.

溢 *v.* to overflow. MdnC: 流露 (*liú lù*).

辭 (辞) *n.* words. MdnC: 言辭 (*yán cí* 言辞).

8. 以……爲 ₐ(为 *wéi*) …… to regard… as…. See L2 Grammar Note 1 ④.

主 *adj.* primary. MdnC: 主要 (*zhǔ yào*).

客 *adj.* secondary. MdnC: 次要 (*cì yào*).

凡 *adv.* in general, overall. See L10 Grammar Note 4.

畢 (毕) *adv.* completely.

經營 (经营) *v.* to engage, operate, manage.

爲ᵦ (为 *wèi*) *prep.* for. See L7 Grammar Note 5 ②.

安寧 (宁) *n.* peace.

9. 屠毒 *n.* poison. Here it is used as a causative verb, 使……遭受屠毒, meaning "to kill" 殘害 (*cán hài* 残害). See L7 Grammar Note 1 ③.

肝腦 (脑) *n.* liver and brain. Here it stands for people.

離 (离) 散 *adj.* scattered, separate. Here it is used as a causative verb, 使……離 (离) 散. See L7 Grammar Note 1 ②.

以 *conj.* in order to. MdnC: 來 (*lái* 来). See L2 Grammar Note 1 ③.

博 *v.* to exchange, get in return. MdnC: 換取 (*huàn qǔ* 换取).

曾 (*zēng*) *adv.* just, even. MdnC: 竟 (*jìng*). See L15 Grammar Note 1.

慘 (惨) 然 *adj.* sad, grieved. MdnC: 悲痛 (*bēi tòng*).

固 *adv.* originally. MdnC: 本來 (*běn lái* 本来).

10. 敲 *v.* to extort. MdnC: 敲詐 (*qiāo zhà* 敲诈).

剝 (剥) *v.* to exploit. MdnC: 剝削 (*bō xuē* 剥削).

骨髓 *n.* marrow.

奉 *v.* to supply. MdnC: 供奉 (*gòng fèng*).

淫樂 (乐) *n.* debauchery.

花息 *n.* interest. MdnC: 利息 (*lì xī*).

11. 然則 (则) if it is so, then…. See L10 Grammar Note 1.

向使 *conj.* if, supposing. MdnC: 假使 (*jiǎ shǐ*). See Grammar Note 2.

設 (设) *v.* to set up, establish. MdnC: 設立 (*shè lì* 设立).

古者天下之人愛戴其君，比之如父，擬
gǔ zhě tiān xià zhī rén ài dài qí jūn　　bǐ zhī rú fù　　nǐ

之如天，誠不爲過也。¹² 今也天下之人怨惡
zhī rú tiān　　chéng bù wéi guò yě　　　jīn yě tiān xià zhī rén yuàn wù

其君，視之如寇讎，名之爲獨夫，固其所
qí jūn　　shì zhī rú kòu chou　　míng zhī wéi dú fū　　gù qí suǒ

也。¹³ 而小儒規規焉以君臣之義無所逃於天
yě　　　ér xiǎo rú guī guī yān yǐ jūn chén zhī yì wú suǒ táo yú tiān

地之間，至桀、紂之暴，猶謂湯、武不當誅
dì zhī jiān　　zhì jié　　zhòu zhī bào　　yóu wèi tāng　　wǔ bù dāng zhū

之，而妄傳伯夷、叔齊無稽之事，使兆人萬
zhī　　　ér wàng chuán bó yí　　shū qí wú jī zhī shì　　shǐ zhào rén wàn

姓崩潰之血肉，曾不異夫腐鼠。¹⁴ 豈天地之
xìng bēng kuì zhī xuè ròu　　zēng bù yì fú fǔ shǔ　　　qí tiān dì zhī

古时候天下人爱戴他们的君王，把君王比作父亲，把君王比拟为青天，确实不过分！¹² 现在天下人怨恨厌恶他们的君王，把君王看成仇敌一样，把他叫做"独夫"，这本来就是他(应得的)结果。¹³ 但是小儒们见识短浅，认为君臣之间的伦理关系存在天地之间，不能逃避。甚至对夏桀、商纣的暴政，还说商汤和周武不应当诛杀他们，而且乱传伯夷、叔齐的没有考证过的事。那么千千万万的老百姓死去的身体，竟然和腐烂的老鼠没有不同吗！¹⁴ 难道

大，於兆人萬姓之中，獨私其一人一姓
dà　　yú zhào rén wàn xìng zhī zhōng dú sī　qí yì rén yí xìng

乎？ [15] 是故武王聖人也，孟子之言，聖人之
hū　　shì gù wǔ wáng shèng rén yě　mèng zǐ zhī yán　shèng rén zhī

言也。 [16] 後世之君，欲以如父如天之空名禁
yán yě　　hòu shì zhī jūn　yù yǐ rú fù rú tiān zhī kōng míng jìn

人之窺伺者，皆不便於其言，至廢孟子而不
rén zhī kuī　sì　zhě　jiē bú biàn yú　qí yán　zhì fèi mèng zǐ ér bú

立，非導源於小儒乎！ [17]
lì　　fēi dǎo yuán yú xiǎo rú hū

天下这么大，在千千万万的老百姓中，只能偏爱君王一人一姓吗？ [15] 因此，周武王是圣人啊！孟子的（民贵君轻）言论，是圣人之言啊！ [16] 后世的君王，想用像父亲像青天这样的空名来禁止别人窥探（自己），都觉得孟子的言论对自己不利，于是废掉了孟子（的牌位）不再祭祀他，这难道不是来源于小儒们（的见识短浅）吗？ [17]

12. 愛 (爱) 戴 *v.* to love and hold in esteem.
　　比 *v.* to compare.
　　擬 (拟) *v.* to compare, liken to.
　　誠 (诚) *adv.* indeed. MdnC: 確實 (*què shí* 确实).
　　過 (过) *adv.* too much, overly. MdnC: 過分 (*guò fèn* 过分).

13. 寇 *n.* enemy. MdnC: 敵人 (*dí rén* 敌人).
　　讎 (仇) *n.* enemy, rival.
　　獨 (独) 夫 *n.* bad ruler, autocrat.
　　所 *n.* result. MdnC: 結果 (*jié guǒ* 结果).

14. 儒 *n.* Confucian scholar. MdnC: 儒生 (*rú shēng*).
　　小儒 refers to those short-sighted scholars.
　　規規 (规) *adj.* short-sighted. MdnC: 見識短淺 (*jiàn shí duǎn qiǎn* 见识短浅).
　　焉 *particle.* used as an emotive particle. See L5 Grammar Note 4 ④.
　　以 *v.* to think, regard. MdnC: 認爲 (*rèn wéi* 认为). See L10 Grammar Note 2 ⑤.
　　義 (义) *n.* principle, law.
　　逃 *v.* to escape, run away from. MdnC: 逃避 (*táo bì*).
　　桀 or 夏桀 See King Jie of Xia's brief biography in L27 note 3.
　　紂 (纣) or 商紂王 See King Zhou of Shang's brief biography in L13 note 19.
　　湯 or 商湯 (ancestral name 姓, Zǐ 子; given name 名, Lǚ 履; 1670?–1587 BCE), the founder of the Shang dynasty.
　　武 or 周武王 See King Wu of Zhou's brief biography in L13 note 19.
　　誅 (诛) *v.* to kill. MdnC: 誅殺 (*zhū shā* 诛杀).
　　妄 *adv.* wantonly, carelessly, rashly. MdnC: 胡亂 (*hú luàn*).
　　稽 *v.* to investigate, examine. MdnC: 考證 (*kǎo zhèng* 考证).
　　兆 *number.* million. MdnC: 百萬 (*bǎi wàn* 百万).
　　兆人萬姓 refers to millions of people.
　　崩潰 (溃) *v.* to collapse.
　　血 (xuè) 肉 *n.* blood and flesh. Here it refers to the human body.
　　曾 (zēng) *adv.* just, even. MdnC: 竟 (*jìng*). See L15 Grammar Note 1.

腐 *adj.* rotten. MdnC: 腐爛 (*fǔ làn* 腐烂).

15. 獨 (独) *adv.* only.

　　私 *adj.* private. Here it is used as verb, meaning "to be partial to" 偏愛 (*piān ài* 偏爱).

16. 聖人 *n.* sage.

　　孟子之言 refers to Mencius's words "the people are the most important, the state is the next, and the ruler is the least important" 民爲貴，社稷次之，君爲輕 in chapter 7 盡心下 ("Jìn xīn xià" 尽心下) of the *Mencius*.

17. 空 (kōng) *adj.* empty.

　　禁 (jìn) *v.* to restrict, forbid. MdnC: 禁止 (*jìn zhǐ*).

　　窺 (窥) 伺 *v.* to spy on, watch. MdnC: 窺探 (*kuī tàn* 窥探).

　　便 *adj.* convenient, of value, useful. MdnC: 利 (*lì*).

　　廢 (废) *v.* to terminate, discard.

　　廢 (废) 孟子而不立 refers to the story in which Zhu Yuanzhang 朱元璋 (the first emperor of the Ming dynasty; r. 1368–1398) gave an order to remove Mencius's tablet from Confucius's temples.

　　導 (导) 源 *v.* to originate from, derive from. MdnC: 來源 (*lái yuán* 来源).

雖然，使後之爲君者，果能保此產業，
suī rán　shǐ hòu zhī wéi jūn zhě　guǒ néng bǎo cǐ chǎn yè

傳之無窮，亦無怪乎其私之也。[18] 既以產業視
chuán zhī wú qióng　yì wú guài hū qí sī zhī yě　　jì yǐ chǎn yè shì

之ₐ，人之ᵦ欲得產業，誰不如我？[19] 攝緘縢，
zhī　rén zhī　yù dé chǎn yè　shuí bù rú wǒ　　shè jiān téng

固扃鐍，一人之。智力不能勝天下欲得之ₐ者
gù jiōng jué　yì rén zhī　zhì lì bù néng shèng tiān xià yù dé zhī zhě

之ᵦ眾，遠者數世，近者及身，其血肉之ᵦ崩
zhī zhòng　yuǎn zhě shù shì　jìn zhě jí shēn　qí xuè ròu zhī bēng kuì

潰在其子孫矣。[20] 昔人願世世無生帝王家，而
kuì zài qí zǐ sūn yǐ　xī rén yuàn shì shì wú shēng dì wáng jiā　ér

毅宗之語公主，亦曰：「若何爲生我家！」[21]
yì zōng zhī yǔ gōng zhǔ　yì yuē　　ruò hé wéi shēng wǒ jiā

痛哉斯言！回思創業時，其欲得天下之心，
tòng zāi sī yán　huí sī chuàng yè shí　qí yù dé tiān xià zhī xīn

有不廢然摧沮者乎！[22]
yǒu bú fèi rán cuī jǔ zhě hū

即使这样，假使后来作为君王的人，果然能够保有这些产业，一直传给后代，那也不怪他们将天下据为己有。[18] 既然把天下当产业来看，别人也想要得到这些产业，谁不像我（一样）呢？[19] （所以）拉紧绳子，加固锁头，一个人的智力不能胜过众多想得到天下的人，远的不过几代，近的就到自己了，他们血肉崩溃，就发生在他子孙上。[20] 南朝的宋顺帝愿以后世世代代不要生在帝王家，而明毅宗崇祯对长平公主也说："你为什么生在我家！"[21] 这话真是让人痛心啊！回头想想创业的时候，他们想要得到天下的雄心，有不感到沮丧失望的吗！[22]

18. 使 *conj.* if, supposing. MdnC: 假使 (*jiǎ shǐ*).

　　果 *adv.* really. MdnC: 果然 (*guǒ rán*).

　　保 *v.* to keep, preserve. MdnC: 保有 (*bǎo yǒu*).

私 *adj.* private. Here it is used as a causative verb, 使……私, meaning "to appropriate … as one's own" 據爲已有 (*jù wéi jǐ yǒu* 据为己有). See L7 Grammar Note 1 ②.

19. 之 ₐ *personal pron.* it. 之 refers to the sovereign, monarch. See L1 Grammar Note 2 ③.

之 ♭ *particle.* a nominative marker. See L2 Grammar Note 2 ⑤.

20. 攝 (摄) *v.* to pull, drag, draw. MdnC: 拉 (*lā*).

緘 (缄) *n.* rope, cord. MdnC: 繩子 (*shéng zi* 绳子).

縢 *n.* rope, cord. MdnC: 繩子 (*shéng zi* 绳子).

固 *adj.* solid, sturdy. Here it is used as a causative verb, 使……固, meaning "to solidify" 加固 (*jiā gù*). See L7 Grammar Note 1 ②.

扃 *n.* door bar, latch.

鐍 *n.* lock, hasp.

扃鐍 means locks 鎖頭 (*suǒ tóu* 锁头).

之 ꜀ *particle.* a possessive marker. See L1 Grammar Note 2 ②.

衆 (众) *pron.* many. MdnC: 衆多 (*zhòng duō* 众多).

數 (数 shù) 世 *n.* several generations. MdnC: 幾代 (*jǐ dài* 几代).

崩潰 (溃) *v.* to collapse, fall apart.

21. 昔人 refers to Emperor Shun of the Song 宋順帝 (r. 477–479) in the Six Dynasties. He was the last emperor of the Liu Song dynasty. According to the account given in chapter 135 of *Comprehensive Mirror in Aid of Governance* 資治通鑒 (*Zī zhì tōng jiàn* 资治通鉴), before he was forced out of the palace, he cried and wished that he had never beeen born into a royal family.

明毅宗 or 崇禎 (family name 姓, Zhū 朱; given name 名, Yuójiǎn 由檢; era name 年號, Chóngzhēn 崇禎; temple name 廟號, Sīzōng/ Yìzōng 思宗/毅宗; r. 1627–1644), the last emperor of the Ming dynasty.

公主 *n.* princess. Here it refers to Princess Changpin 長平公主 (1629?–1646), the second daughter of Emperor Chongzhen.

若 *pron.* you. MdnC: 你 (*nǐ*). See Grammar Note 3 ④.

何爲 (为 wéi) why? MdnC: 爲什麼 (*wèi shén me* 为什么).

毅宗之語 a quotation from chapter 121 of *History of the Ming Dynasty* 明史.

22. 廢 (废) 然 *adv.* frustrated and disappointed. MdnC: 沮喪失望 (*jǔ sàng shī wàng* 沮丧失望).

摧沮 *adj.* frustrated and depressed. MdnC: 沮喪 (*jǔ sàng* 沮丧).

是故明乎爲君之職分，則唐、虞之世，
shì gù míng hū wéi jūn zhī zhí fèn　zé táng　yú zhī shì

人人能讓，許由、務光非絕塵也；不明乎爲
rén rén néng ràng　xǔ yóu　wù guāng fēi jué chén yě　bù míng hū wéi

君之職分，則市井之間，人人可欲，許由、
jūn zhī zhí fèn　zé shì jǐng zhī jiān　rén rén kě yù　xǔ yóu

務光所以曠後世而不聞也。²³然君之職分難
wù guāng suǒ yǐ kuàng hòu shì ér bù wén yě　rán jūn zhī zhí fèn nán

明，以俄頃淫樂不易無窮之悲，雖愚者亦明
míng　yǐ é qīng yín lè bú yì wú qióng zhī bēi　suī yú zhě yì míng

因此，明白作为君王的职责，那么唐尧、虞舜的时代，人人都能让出（君王的位子），许由、务光也不是超越世俗的；如果不明白作为君王的职责，那么在市井之间，人人都可以想要君王之位，因此许由、务光在后代不存在了也没听说了。²³ 虽然君王的职责难以明了，（但）

之矣。[24]
zhī yǐ

用片刻的淫乐享受，不值得换来无穷的悲哀，即使愚蠢的人也明白这个道理啊！[24]

《黃宗羲全集》第一冊，杭州：浙江古籍出版社 (1985), 2–3.

23. 明 *v.* to make clear, understand. MdnC: 明白 (*míng bái*).

職 (职) 分 *n.* duty. MdnC: 職責 (*zhí zé* 职责).

唐 唐堯 (尧) or 堯 (尧) See L13 note 3.

虞 虞舜 or 舜 See L13 note 2 and note 3.

讓 (让) *v.* to give away, yield.

絕 (绝) *v.* to go beyond, stand aloof from. MdnC: 超越 (*chāo yuè*).

塵 (尘) *n.* the mundane world. MdnC: 塵俗 (*chén sú* 尘俗).

市井 *n.* market and street.

曠 (旷) *v.* to be absent.

聞 (闻) *v.* to hear. MdnC: 聽說 (*tīng shuō* 听说).

24. 俄頃 (顷) *n.* a short moment. MdnC: 片刻 (*piàn kè*).

易 *v.* to exchange. MdnC: 換 (*huàn* 换).

愚 *adj.* silly, foolish. MdnC: 愚蠢 (*yú chǔn*).

語法注釋 Grammar Notes

1. 或　Four uses of 或 are explained in this book. In addition to the use below, see 或① in L6 Grammar Note 4, 或② in L15 Grammar Note 4, and 或④ in L36 Grammar Note 2.

③ *adv.* a little, a bit, slightly. MdnC: 稍微 (*shāo wēi*).

天下有公利而莫或興之，有公害而莫或除之。

[天下有对公众有利的事，却没人把它稍微建立起来，有对公众有害的事，也没人除掉它。]

2. 向使／使　*conj.* if, supposing. MdnC: 假使 (*jiǎ shǐ*).

向使無君，人各得自私也，人各得自利也。

[假使没有君王，每个人都能得到自己的私利，每个人都得到自己的利益。]

使後之爲君者，果能保此産業，傳之無窮，亦無怪乎其私之也。

[假使后来作为君王的人，果然能够保有这些产业，一直传给后代，那也不怪他们将天下据为己有。]

3. 若　Four uses of 若 are explained in this book. In addition to the use below, see 若①② in L4 Grammar Note 4 and 若③ in L14 Grammar Note 3.

④ *pron.* second-person pronoun: you. MdnC: 你 (*nǐ*).

若何爲生我家！

[你为什么生在我的家里？]

Literary Analysis

In many ways, this essay may be seen as the Chinese equivalent of a Western Enlightenment manifesto: it dismisses any ruler's claim to divine mandate, sanctions the killing of despots, and proclaims the sacred *collective* rights of the people (rather than the individual's rights emphasized by Enlightenment thinkers).

Huang develops a highly coherent theory of rule akin to the notion of governance *for* and, to a lesser extent, *of* the people. To him, such rulership is not a utopian ideal but actually its ultimate origin. He begins the essay by stressing that venerated sages of high antiquity all came from the common people and became eminent rulers only because they rose above self-interest and worked tirelessly to serve the interests of all. To emphasize their all-too-human (as opposed to divine) character, Huang cites many instances of sage figures yielding their rule because the hardships and self-sacrifice were too great. In later times, however, this for-the-people ethos was jettisoned and replaced with ever more shameless and oppressive for-the-ruler heads. To Huang, that such pernicious despots could thrive was in no small measure due to the petty Confucians 小儒 (*xiǎorú*), who granted them heavenly legitimacy and simultaneously eliminated the high Confucian sanction on dethroning and killing evil rulers (exemplified by King Wen of Zhou's killing of the last Shang king and Mencius's explicit endorsement). Huang concludes the essay by showing how this perversion of Confucianism could haunt the ruler, as evidenced by the pitiable lament of the last Ming emperor—under whose reign Huang lived for thirty-four years—-that his daughter had been born into an imperial family and that he had to kill her before hanging himself.

Though he stopped short of calling for the abolition of monarchy, Huang is undoubtedly an iconoclastic thinker. To fully grasp his antitradition stance, compare his comment on Boyi and Shuqi with Confucius's and Xima Qian's praise of these two historical figures (lessons 13 and 14). Compare also his "uncomplimentary," human accounts of Yao and Shun with Han Yu's veneration of these two cardinal Confucian sages (lesson 26).

This essay is a tour de force of repetitive patterning. How would you compare its patterning with that in lesson 4 (a narrative text) and lesson 31 (an eight-legged essay)? See *HTRCProse*, chapter 1, "An Anatomy of the Chinese Prose Form: An Overview," C1.4, for further comments on repetitive patterning.

—ZC

課後練習 Exercises

一 給加點字注音 Give the pinyin romanization for each dotted word.

1. 緘縢 （＿＿，＿＿）　2. 寇讎 （＿＿，＿＿）　3. 桀 （＿＿）　4. 扃鐍 （＿＿，＿＿）

二 在括號中給句中加點的字注音，並選出正確的釋義 Give the pinyin romanization for each dotted word; then select the correct definition from the following list, and write it in the blank.

誅殺(诛杀)　　百萬(万)　　拉　　慚(惭)愧　　建立　　**信服**　　厭惡(厌恶)　　考量　　考核

1. 小信未孚（ fú ） 　信服　　2. 莫或興之（　）＿＿＿＿　3. 量而不欲入（　）＿＿＿＿

4. 始而慙焉（　）＿＿＿＿　5. 好逸惡勞（　）＿＿＿＿　6. 不當誅之　（　）＿＿＿＿

7. 無稽之事（　）＿＿＿＿　8. 兆人萬姓（　）＿＿＿＿　9. 攝緘縢　　（　）＿＿＿＿

三　選擇釋義並填空 Match each word in the left column with its correct definition in the middle column. Fill in each blank in the right column with an appropriate word from the left column.

謀<u>謀劃(谋划)</u>　　安逸

公＿＿＿＿＿　　剝(剥)削

釋＿＿＿＿＿　　追逐

享＿＿＿＿＿　　換(换)取

逸＿＿＿＿＿　　敲詐(诈)

勞＿＿＿＿＿　　超越

就＿＿＿＿＿　　**謀劃(谋划)**

逐＿＿＿＿＿　　設(设)立

溢＿＿＿＿＿　　成就

博＿＿＿＿＿　　勞(劳)作

敲＿＿＿＿＿　　沮喪(丧)失望

剝＿＿＿＿＿　　流露

奉＿＿＿＿＿　　讓(让)位

設＿＿＿＿＿　　避開(开)

固＿＿＿＿＿　　塵(尘)俗

廢＿＿＿＿＿　　公衆(众)

讓＿＿＿＿＿　　供奉

絕＿＿＿＿＿　　享受

塵＿＿＿＿＿　　加固

天下有＿＿＿利而莫或興之，有＿＿＿害而莫或除之。

不以一己之害爲害，而使天下＿＿＿其害，此其人之勤勞必千萬於天下之人。

夫以千萬倍之勤勞而己又不＿＿＿其利，必非天下之人情所欲居也。

好＿＿＿惡勞，亦猶夫人之情也。

漢高帝所謂「某業所＿＿＿，孰與仲多」者，其＿＿＿利之情＿＿＿之於辭矣。

是以其未得之也，屠毒天下之肝腦，離散天下之子女，以＿＿＿我一人之產業，曾不慘然！

其既得之也，＿＿＿＿＿天下之骨髓，離散天下之子女，以＿＿＿我一人之淫樂，視爲當然，曰「此我一人之花息也。」

嗚呼！豈＿＿＿君之道固如是乎！

攝緘縢，＿＿＿扃鐍，一人之智力不能勝天下欲得之者之衆。

回思創業時，其欲得天下之心，有不＿＿＿然摧沮者乎！

是故明乎爲君之職分，則唐、虞之世，人人能＿＿＿，許由、務光非＿＿＿＿＿也。

四　請用給出的字填空 Fill in each blank with an appropriate word from the following list (some words may be used more than once).

或　　如　　使　　以　　然　　莫　　者

1. 天下有公利而＿＿＿＿＿＿興之，有公害而＿＿＿＿＿＿除之。

2. 有人＿＿＿出，不＿＿＿一己之利爲利，而＿＿＿天下受其利；不＿＿＿一己之害爲害，而＿＿＿天下釋其害。此其人之勤勞必千萬於天下之人。

3. 後之爲人君＿＿＿不＿＿＿，＿＿＿爲天下之權皆出於我，我＿＿＿天下之利盡歸於己，＿＿＿天下之害盡歸於人，亦無不可。

4. 古＿＿＿天下之人愛戴其君，比之＿＿＿父，擬之＿＿＿天，誠不爲過也。

五 爲加點字選擇正確釋義，並根據釋義來翻譯句子 Match each dotted word with its correct modern Chinese equivalent by circling the latter. Then translate each sentence into modern Chinese.

1. 又何間焉？　　　　　　　　　ⓐ 爲什麼（为什么）b. 憑什麼（凭什么）c. 多少

現代文翻譯：你又为什么要参与到这件事情里面？

＿＿＿＿＿＿＿＿＿＿＿＿＿＿＿＿＿＿＿＿＿＿＿

2. 天下有公利而莫或興之，有公害而莫或除之。　　a. 或許（许）b. 稍微 c. 有人

現代文翻譯：＿＿＿＿＿＿＿＿＿＿＿＿＿＿＿＿＿＿

3. 好逸惡勞，亦猶夫人之情也。　　　　a. 猶（犹）豫 b. 還（还）c. 就像

現代文翻譯：＿＿＿＿＿＿＿＿＿＿＿＿＿＿＿＿＿＿

4. 後之爲人君者不然，以爲天下之權皆出於我。　a. 這樣（这样）b. 的樣（样）子 c. 對（对）

現代文翻譯：＿＿＿＿＿＿＿＿＿＿＿＿＿＿＿＿＿＿

5. 始而慙焉，久而安焉。　　　　　a. 怎麼（么）b. 的樣（样）子 c. 於（于）之

現代文翻譯：＿＿＿＿＿＿＿＿＿＿＿＿＿＿＿＿＿＿

6. 向使無君，人各得自私也，人各得自利也。　　　a. 假使 b. 而且 c. 因此

現代文翻譯：＿＿＿＿＿＿＿＿＿＿＿＿＿＿＿＿＿＿

7. 若何爲生我家！　　　　　　a. 如果 b. 你 c. 爲什麼（为什么）

現代文翻譯：＿＿＿＿＿＿＿＿＿＿＿＿＿＿＿＿＿＿

第三十三課

梁啓超《少年中國説》（節選）

"Young China," Excerpt (Liang Qichao)

Introduction

"Young China" was written by Liang Qichao 梁啟超 (courtesy name Zhuo Ru 卓如; aka Master of the Studio Drinking Ice 飲冰室主; 1873–1929), one of the foremost leaders of the Wuxu Reform 戊戌維新 (*Wùxū wéixīn* 戊戌维新) of 1898, a national movement to reform China's government using Western constitutional monarchy as a model. When Empress Dowager Cixi suppressed this movement, Liang fled to Japan, where he continued to advocate a constitutional monarchy for China and later supported the New Culture Movement (1915–1923) and the May 4th Movement (1919). An extremely prolific writer, Liang left a huge body of political writings and scholarly works in history, bibliography, literature, and calligraphy, among other areas. They have been assembled in *Collected Works from the Studio Drinking Ice* 飲冰室合集 (*Yǐnbīng shì héjí* 饮冰室合集).

In "Young China," written after the failure of the Wuxu Reform, Liang repudiates the idea of China as an aging, decrepit empire and projects instead his fervently optimistic, even utopian vision of a youthful China in an effort to lift the spirits of a downtrodden nation. He declares that China is still very young with its best days ahead and encourages the Chinese people to shoulder the significant task of building this new and aspiring China.

This essay is noted for its rich metaphors, varying sentence lengths, alternation of patterned and nonpatterned segments, and use of new, modern vocabulary. It offers us a glimpse of the transition from traditional to modern Chinese prose.

正文與簡體譯文 Text and Modern Chinese Translation

日本人之稱我中國也，一則曰老大帝
rì běn rén zhī chēng wǒ zhōng guó yě　yī zé yuē lǎo dà dì

國，再則曰老大帝國。[1] 是語也，蓋襲譯歐
guó　zài zé yuē lǎo dà dì guó　　shì yǔ yě　　gài xí yì ōu

西人之言也。[2] 嗚呼！我中國其果老大矣乎？
xī rén zhī yán yě　　wū hū　　wǒ zhōng guó qí guǒ lǎo dà yǐ hū

梁啟超曰：惡！是何言！是何言！吾心目中
liáng qǐ chāo yuē　wū　　shì hé yán　　shì hé yán　　wú xīn mù zhōng

日本人称呼我中国，一称我们老大帝国，再称我们老大帝国。[1] 这个称呼，可能是因袭欧洲西方人翻译的话。[2] 哎，我们中国果真是老大吗？梁启超说："不！这是什么话！这是什么话！我心中有一个少年中国！"[3]

有一少年中國在！[3]
yǒu yī shào nián zhōng guó zài

1. 日本 *n.* Japan.
   則 (则) a word to mark a subparagraph.
   老大 *adj.* very old.
   帝國 (国) *n.* empire.
2. 是 *demonstrative pron.* this. MdnC: 這 (*zhè* 这). See L3 Grammar Note 1 ①.
   蓋 (盖) *adv.* probably. MdnC: 可能 (*kě néng*). See L13 Grammar Note 1.
   襲 (袭) *v.* to follow, copy. MdnC: 因襲 (*yīn xí* 因袭).
   譯 (译) *n.* translation. MdnC: 翻譯 (*fān yì* 翻译).
   歐 (欧) *n.* Europe. MdnC: 歐洲 (*ōu zhōu* 欧洲).
   西人 *n.* Westerner. MdnC: 西方人 (*xī fāng rén*).
3. 其 *personal pron.* 其 refers to China. See L2 Grammar Note 5 ①.
   果 *adv.* really. MdnC: 果真 (*guǒ zhēn*).
   惡 (恶 *wū*) *exclamatory word.* See Grammar Note 1 ②.

欲言國之老少，請先言人之老少。老年
yù yán guó zhī lǎo shào　qǐng xiān yán rén zhī lǎo shào　lǎo nián

人常思既往，少年人常思將來。惟思既往也，
rén cháng sī jì wǎng　shào nián rén cháng sī jiāng lái　wéi sī jì wǎng yě

故生留戀心；惟思將來也，故生希望心。[4]惟
gù shēng liú liàn xīn　wéi sī jiāng lái yě　gù shēng xī wàng xīn　wéi

留戀也，故保守；惟希望也，故進取。惟保
liú liàn yě　gù bǎo shǒu　wéi xī wàng yě　gù jìn qǔ　wéi bǎo

守也，故永舊；惟進取也，故日新。[5]
shǒu yě　gù yǒng jiù　wéi jìn qǔ yě　gù rì xīn

想要说国家的老和少，请先说人的老少。老年人常思念过去，少年人常向往将来。只有思念过去，才会产生留恋的心思；只有向往将来，才能产生希望的心愿。[4]心中留恋，（人就）保守；心怀希望，人就进取。因为保守，人就永远陈旧；因为进取，才会每天更新。[5]

4. 既往 *n.* past. MdnC: 過去 (*guò qù* 过去).
   惟 *adv.* only. MdnC: 只有 (*zhǐ yǒu*). See L22 Grammar Note 2 ②.
   留戀 (恋) *n.* nostalgia.
5. 保守 *adj.* conservative, prudent.
   進 (进) 取 *adj.* aggressive, aspiring.
   永 *adv.* forever. MdnC: 永遠 (*yǒng yuǎn* 永远).
   舊 (旧) *adj.* old, out-of-date. MdnC: 陳舊 (*chén jiù* 陈旧).
   日 *adv.* every day. MdnC: 每天 (*měi tiān*).
   新 *adj.* new, fresh, updated. MdnC: 更新 (*gēng xīn*).

⋯⋯⋯

梁啓超曰：我中國其果老大矣乎？是今
liáng qǐ chāo yuē　wǒ zhōng guó qí guǒ lǎo dà yǐ hū　shì jīn

日全地球之一大問題也。如其老大也，則是
rì quán dì qiú zhī yí dà wèn tí yě　rú qí lǎo dà yě　zé shì

中國爲過去之國，即地球上昔本有此國，而
zhōng guó wéi guò qù zhī guó　jí dì qiú shàng xī běn yǒu cǐ guó　ér

今漸漸滅，他日之命運殆將盡也。[6]如其非老
jīn jiàn sī miè　tā rì zhī mìng yùn dài jiāng jìn yě　rú qí fēi lǎo

大也，則是中國爲未來之國，即地球上昔未
dà yě　zé shì zhōng guó wéi wèi lái zhī guó　jí dì qiú shàng xī wèi

現此國，而今漸發達，他日之前程且方長
xiàn cǐ guó　ér jīn jiàn fā dá　tā rì zhī qián chéng qiě fāng cháng

也。[7]欲斷今日之中國爲老大耶？爲少年耶？
yě　yù duàn jīn rì zhī zhōng guó wéi lǎo dà yé　wéi shào nián yé

則不可不先明「國」字之意義。夫國也者，
zé bù kě bù xiān míng guó zì zhī yì yì　fú guó yě zhě

何物也？有土地，有人民，以居於其土地之人
hé wù yě　yǒu tǔ dì　yǒu rén mín　yǐ jū yú qí tǔ dì zhī rén

民，而治其所居之土地之事，自制法律而自守
mín　ér zhì qí suǒ jū zhī tǔ dì zhī shì　zì zhì fǎ lǜ ér zì shǒu

之；有主權，有服從，人人皆主權者，人人
zhī　yǒu zhǔ quán　yǒu fú cóng　rén rén jiē zhǔ quán zhě　rén rén

皆服從者。[8]夫如是，斯謂之完全成立之國，
jiē fú cóng zhě　fú rú shì　sī wèi zhī wán quán chéng lì zhī guó

地球上之有完全成立之國也，自百年以來
dì qiú shàng zhī yǒu wán quán chéng lì zhī guó yě　zì bǎi nián yǐ lái

也。[9]完全成立者，壯年之事也。未能完全成
yě wán quán chéng lì zhě　zhuàng nián zhī shì yě wèi néng wán quán chéng

立而漸進於完全成立者，少年之事也。故吾
lì ér jiàn jìn yú wán quán chéng lì zhě　shào nián zhī shì yě　gù wú

得一言以斷之曰：歐洲列邦在今日爲壯年
dé yì yán yǐ duàn zhī yuē　ōu zhōu liè bāng zài jīn rì wéi zhuàng nián

梁启超说：我们中国果真是老大帝国吗？这是今天地球上的一个大问题。如果中国是老大帝国，那么这个中国就是过去的国家，就是地球上过去本来有这个国家，但现在渐渐消亡了，以后的命运差不多将要完结了。[6]如果中国不是老大帝国，那么这个中国就是未来的国家，就是地球上过去没有出现的国家，现在渐渐发达起来，以后的前程还正长呢！[7]想要判断今天的中国是老大帝国呢？是少年中国呢？那么不可以不先明了了"国"字的意义。国家是什么东西呢？有土地，有人民，让居住在其土地上的人民，治理他们居住的土地上的事情，自己制定法律，自己遵守它；有主权，有服从，每个人都是有主权的人，每个人都服从(法律)。[8]如果这样，那么可以称它是完全成立的国家，地球上有完全成立的国家，是近百年以来的(事情)。[9]完全成立的国家，是壮年。未能完全成立，而是渐渐地进步成为完全成立地国家，这是少年的事情。所以我用一句话来判断

國，而我中國在今日爲少年國。 [10]

guó　ér wǒ zhōng guó zài jīn rì wéi shào nián guó

它：今天欧洲各国是
壮年国家，而我中国
在今天是少年国家。 [10]

6. 則 (则) *conj.* then. MdnC: 那麼 (*nà me* 那么). See L11 Grammar Note 1 ①.

　即 *adv.* namely.

　昔 *n.* past.

　本 *adv.* originally. MdnC: 本來 (*běn* 本来).

　漸滅 (灭) *v.* to disappear. MdnC: 消亡 (*xiāo wáng*).

　他日 *n.* some day. Here it refers to the future.

　殆 *adv.* almost. MdnC: 差不多 (*chà bù duō*).

　盡 (尽 *jìn*) *v.* to complete, finish. MdnC: 完結 (*wán jié* 完结).

7. 發達 (发达) *v.* to develop, advance.

　方 *adv.* just. MdnC: 正 (*zhèng*).

8. 斷 (断) *v.* to judge. MdnC: 判斷 (*pàn duàn* 判断).

　以 *coverb.* to use. See L2 Grammar Note 1 ②.

　治 *v.* to govern, manage. MdnC: 治理 (*zhì lǐ*).

　制 *v.* to make, draft. MdnC: 製定 (*zhì dìng* 制定).

　守 *v.* to abide by, comply with. MdnC: 遵守 (*zūn shǒu*).

　主權 (权) *n.* sovereignty.

9. 斯 *conj.* then. MdnC: 則 (*zé* 则). See L5 Grammar Note 3 ②.

10. 壯 (壮) 年 *n.* prime of one's life.

　列 *adj.* each. MdnC: 各 (*gè*).

　邦 *n.* state. MdnC: 國家 (*guó jiā* 国家).

······

梁啓超曰：造成今日之老大中國者，則中
liáng qǐ chāo yuē　zào chéng jīn rì zhī lǎo dà zhōng guó zhě zé zhōng

國老朽之冤業也。製出將來之少年中國者，則
guó lǎo xiǔ zhī yuān yè yě　zhì chū jiāng lái zhī shào nián zhōng guó zhě　zé

中國少年之責任也。 [11]······故今日之責任，不
zhōng guó shào nián zhī zé rèn yě　　gù jīn rì zhī zé rèn　bú

在他人，而全在我少年。少年智則國智，少年
zài tā rén　ér quán zài wǒ shào nián　shào nián zhì zé guó zhì　shào nián

富則國富；少年強則國強，少年獨立則國獨
fù zé guó fù　shào nián qiáng zé guó qiáng　shào nián dú lì zé guó dú

立；少年自由則國自由；少年進步則國進步；
lì　shào nián zì yóu zé guó zì yóu　shào nián jìn bù zé guó jìn bù

梁启超说：造成今天
衰老中国的原因，是
中国衰老腐朽(的人)
的罪孽。制出将来的
少年中国，是中国少
年人的责任。 [11] ······
所以今天的责任，不
在别人，全在我少
年。少年人有智慧，
那么国家就有智慧；
少年人富有，国家就
富有；少年人强壮，
国家就强壮；少年人
独立，国家就独立；
少年人自由，国家就

少年勝於歐洲，則國勝於歐洲；少年雄於地
shào nián shèng yú ōu zhōu zé guó shèng yú ōu zhōu shào nián xióng yú dì

球，則國雄於地球。[12]
qiú　　zé guó xióng yú dì qiú

自由；少年人进步，国家就进步；少年人胜过欧洲，国家就胜过欧洲，少年人在地球上是杰出的，国家在地球上就杰出。[12]

11. 朽 *adj.* old, decayed. MdnC: 腐朽 (*fǔ xiǔ*).
　　冤業 (业) *n.* guilt, crime. MdnC: 罪孽 (*zuì niè*).

12. 雄 *adj.* strong, outstanding. MdnC: 傑出 (*jié chū* 杰出).

红日初升，其道大光。河出伏流，一瀉汪
hóng rì chū shēng　qí dào dà guāng　hé chū fú liú　yí xiè wāng

洋。[13] 潛龍騰淵，鱗爪飛揚。[14] 乳虎嘯谷，百
yáng　qián lóng téng yuān　lín zhǎo fēi yáng　rǔ hǔ xiào gǔ　bǎi

獸震惶。[15] 鷹隼試翼，風塵吸張。[16] 奇花初胎，
shòu zhèn huáng　yīng sǔn shì yì　fēng chén xī zhāng　qí huā chū tāi

喬喬皇皇。[17] 干將發硎，有作其芒。[18] 天戴其
yù yù huáng huáng　gān jiāng fā xíng　yǒu zuò qí máng　tiān dài qí

蒼，地履其黃。[19] 縱有千古，橫有八荒。前途
cāng　dì lǚ qí huáng　zòng yǒu qiān gǔ　héng yǒu bā huāng　qián tú

似海，來日方長。[20] 美哉我少年中國，與天不
sì hǎi　lái rì fāng cháng　měi zāi wǒ shào nián zhōng guó　yǔ tiān bù

老！壯哉我中國少年，與國無疆！[21]
lǎo　zhuàng zāi wǒ zhōng guó shào nián yǔ guó wú jiāng

《飲冰室合集》，北京：中華書局 (1989), 7–12.

红色的太阳刚升起，道路上满是霞光。黄河从地下潜伏的水流中流出，一泻千里。[13] 潜伏的巨龙从深潭中飞腾而出，龙鳞龙爪在空中飞扬。[14] 初生的幼虎在山谷中吼叫，野兽们都感到震惊惶恐。[15] 鹰隼准备起飞，风和尘土四处飞扬。[16] 奇花开始孕育(花蕾)，明艳美丽。[17] 干将宝剑刚在磨刀石上磨好，发出光芒。[18] 我们少年头顶着苍茫的青天，脚踩着黄土大地。[19] 从纵向看，有千年的历史，从横向看，有四面八方(的土地)。我们少年的前途像大海一样宽广，未来的日子正长！[20] 美好啊！我少年中国，和天一样不会衰老！雄壮啊！我中国少年，和国家一样万寿无疆！[21]

13. 其道大光 a quotation from the chapter titled Yi 益 ("Yì") in the *Book of Changes*, meaning "the way is so bright."
　　河 *n.* river. Here it refers to the Yellow River 黄河 (*huáng hé* 黄河).
　　伏 *adj.* hidden, concealed. MdnC: 潛伏 (*qián fú* 潜伏).
　　流 *n.* stream.

瀉 (泻) *v.* to pour down, flow.

汪洋 *adj.* vast, boundless.

14. 潛 (潜) *v.* to hide, conceal. MdnC: 潛伏 (*qián fú* 潜伏).

龍 (龙) *n.* dragon.

騰 (腾) *v.* to fly, rise. MdnC: 飛騰 (*fēi téng* 飞腾).

淵 (渊) *n.* deep pool, abyss. MdnC: 深潭 (*shēn tán*).

鱗 (鳞) *n.* scales.

爪 (*zhǎo*) *n.* claws.

飛揚 (飞扬) *v.* to fly, rise.

15. 乳 *adj.* newborn. MdnC: 初生 (*chū shēng*).

嘯 (啸) *v.* to roar, howl. MdnC: 吼叫 (*hǒu jiào*).

獸 (兽) *n.* wild animals. MdnC: 野獸 (*yě shòu* 野兽).

震 *v.* to fear, be shocked. MdnC: 震驚 (*zhèn jīng* 震惊).

惶 *v.* to fear. MdnC: 惶恐 (*huáng kǒng*).

16. 鷹 (鹰) 隼 *n.* eagle and falcon.

試 (试) 翼 *v.* to prepare for flying.

吸 *v.* to contract. MdnC: 收縮 (*shōu suō* 收缩).

張 (张) *v.* to expand. MdnC: 擴張 (*kuò zhāng* 扩张).

17. 奇 *adj.* fantastic, marvelous.

胎 *n.* fetus. Here it is used as a verb, meaning "to gestate" 孕育 (*yùn yù*).

喬喬皇皇 *adj.* extremely beautiful. This is a quotation of Yang Xiong's 揚雄 (53 BCE–18 CE) words "物登明堂，喬喬皇皇" in chapter 2 of his *Great Mystery* 太玄經 (*Tài xuán jīng* 太玄经).

18. 干將 (*gān jiāng*) a swordsmith in the Spring and Autumn period. Here it refers to the renowned sword.

硎 *n.* whetstone. MdnC: 磨刀石 (*mó dāo zhí*).

發 (发 *fā*) 硎 *v.* to sharpen (a knife) from a whetstone. This phrase comes from Cook Ding's 庖丁 words "刀刃若新发于硎" in chapter 3 養生主 ("Yǎngshēng zhǔ" 养生主) of the *Zhuangzi*.

作 *v.* to shine, emanate. MdnC: 發出 (*fā chū* 发出).

芒 *n.* ray, glitter. MdnC: 光芒 (*guāng máng*).

19. 戴 *v.* to wear on the head. MdnC: 頂着 (*dǐng zhe* 顶着).

蒼 (苍) *adj.* vast, boundless. MdnC: 蒼芒 (*cāng máng* 苍芒).

履 *v.* to step on. MdnC: 踩 (*cǎi*).

20. 縱 (纵) *adj.* vertical. MdnC: 縱向 (*zòng xiàng* 纵向).

橫 (横) *adj.* horizontal. MdnC: 橫向 (*héng xiàng*).

八荒 or 八方 eight directions: east, west, north, south, southeast, southwest, northeast, and northwest. Later it refers to places in all directions—namely, everywhere.

來 (来) *adj.* coming, next. MdnC: 未來 (*wèi lái* 未来).

21. 壯 (壮) *adj.* grand and powerful. MdnC: 雄壯 (*xióng zhuàng* 雄壮).

疆 *n.* boundary, limit. 無 (无) 疆 means "boundless or without limit."

語法注釋 Grammar Note

1. 惡　Two uses of 惡 are explained in this book. In addition to the use below, see 惡①in L12
(恶)　Grammar Note 2.

② **wū** *particle*. to express an exclamation of surprise.

> 梁啟超曰：惡！是何言！是何言！
>
> ［梁启超说：　哦不！这是什么话！这是什么话！？］

Literary Analysis

This essay is known as one of the most elegantly written political essays. The passage below focuses on Liang's powerful intellectual argument; others, not excerpted here, are exceptional for their lyrical expression, interweaving historical images and scenes drawn from both Chinese and Western sources. Liang's argument is straightforward and hardly needs further explanation, but note how he adroitly uses repetitive patterning to present and amplify it. Identify the types of repetitive patterning and their different functions—to sharpen contrast, build rhetorical force, or something else.

☞ *HTRCProse*, chapter 1, "An Anatomy of the Chinese Prose Form: An Overview," C1.4, for further comments on repetitive patterning.

—ZC

課後練習 Exercises

一 給加點字注音 Give the pinyin romanization for each dotted word.

1. 鱗爪 （＿＿, ＿＿）　2. 隼 （＿＿）　3. 喬喬皇皇 （＿＿,＿＿）　4. 干將 （＿＿,＿＿）

二 在括號中給句中加點的字注音，並選出正確的釋義 Give the pinyin romanization for each dotted word; then select the correct definition from the following list, and write it in the blank.

差不多　消亡　惶恐　稱(称)呼　踩　因襲(袭)　**信服**　腐朽　吼叫

1. 小信未孚（**fú**）　__信服__　2. 稱我中國 （　）　＿＿＿　3. 今漸漸滅 （　）　＿＿＿

4. 乳虎嘯谷 （　）　＿＿＿　5. 老朽之冤業（　）　＿＿＿　6. 百獸震惶（　）　＿＿＿

7. 殆將盡也（　）　＿＿＿　8. 地履其黃 （　）　＿＿＿　9. 襲譯 （　）　＿＿＿

三 選擇釋義並填空 Match each word in the left column with its correct definition in the middle column. Fill in each blank in the right column with an appropriate word from the left column (some words maybe used more than once).

謀謀劃(谋划)	判斷(断)	是語也，蓋襲＿＿歐西人之言也。
譯＿＿＿＿	初生	
斷＿＿＿＿	震驚(惊)	少年＿＿於地球，則國＿＿於地球。
邦＿＿＿＿	**謀劃(谋划)**	
雄＿＿＿＿	飛騰(飞腾)	故吾得一言以＿＿之曰：歐洲列＿＿在今日爲壯年
伏＿＿＿＿	頂(顶)着	國，而我中國在今日爲少年國。

騰_____　潛(潜)伏　　　　河出____流，一瀉汪洋。潛龍____淵，鱗爪飛揚。
乳_____　光芒　　　　　____虎嘯谷，百獸____惶。
震_____　翻譯(译)
芒_____　國(国)家　　　　干將發硎，有作其____。　天____其蒼，地履其黃。
戴_____　傑(杰)出

四 請用給出的字填空 Fill in each blank with an appropriate word from the following list.

則(则)　　惡(恶)　　惟　　如

1. 日本人之稱我中國也，一____曰老大帝國。　　2. 梁啟超曰：____！是何言！

3. ____其非老大也，則是中國爲未來之國。　　4. ____保守也，故永舊。

五 爲加點字選擇正確釋義，並根據釋義來翻譯句子 Match each dotted word with its correct modern Chinese equivalent by circling the latter. Then translate each sentence into modern Chinese.

1. 又何間焉?　　　　　　　　(a.)爲什麼(为什么) b. 憑什麼(凭什么) c. 多少

現代文翻譯：你又为什么要参与到这件事情里面？

_____

2. 是語也，蓋襲譯歐西人之言也。　　　　　　a. 因此 b. 而且 c. 可能

現代文翻譯：_____

3. 惟思既往也，故生留戀心；惟思將來也，故生希望心。　　a. 但是 b. 只有 c. 難(难)道

現代文翻譯：_____

4. 夫如是，斯謂之完全成立之國，地球上之有完全成立之國也，自百年以來也。

　　　　　　　　　　　　　　　　　a. 則(则) b. 因此 c. 但是

現代文翻譯：_____

5. 少年强則國强，少年獨立則國獨立。　　　　a. 可是 b. 如果 c. 那麼(么)

現代文翻譯：_____

第三十四課

呂碧城《興女權貴有堅忍之志》

"Acquiring Women's Rights and Status Requires Perseverance and Patience" (Lü Bicheng)

Introduction

Lü Bicheng 呂碧城 (courtesy name Dunfu 遁夫; 1883–1943), whose extraordinary talents brought her distinction in the early decades of the twentieth century, is widely known as China's first woman newspaper contributor and editor, first high-profile advocate of women's rights, and first accomplished female writer of political essays.

"Acquiring Women's Rights and Status Requires Perseverance and Patience" was published in 1904 in *Ta Kung Pao* 大公報, the oldest Chinese newspaper, where Lü was working as an apprentice editor. This and other essays she wrote ushered in incessant movements and struggles for women's rights in the twentieth century, contributing to a rapid and profound transformation of traditional Chinese society.

正文與簡體譯文 Text and Modern Chinese Translation

登山者，不可畏路徑之崎嶇；涉海者，
dēng shān zhě　　bù kě wèi lù jìng zhī qí qū　　shè hǎi zhě

不可畏風波之險惡；創偉業者，不可畏事體
bù kě wèi fēng bō zhī xiǎn è　　chuàng wěi yè zhě　　bù kě wèi shì tǐ

之艱難。[1]竊維中國人心渙散，志氣不堅，發
zhī jiān nán　　qiè wéi zhōng guó rén xīn huàn sàn　　zhì qì bù jiān　　fā

一言輒模棱，舉一事類團沙。[2]或空言無補，
yì yán zhé mó léng　　jǔ yí shì lèi tuán shā　　huò kōng yán wú bǔ

或有始無終，或事已垂成，往往因頑固之阻
huò yǒu shǐ wú zhōng　　huò shì yǐ chuí chéng wǎng wǎng yīn wán gù zhī zǔ

撓，而意興頹敗，致使功廢半途，為後世之
náo　　ér yì xìng tuí bài　　zhì shǐ gōng fèi bàn tú　　wéi hòu shì zhī

遺憾。[3]我女子不幸而生於支那，憔悴於壓制
yí hàn　　wǒ nǚ zǐ bù xìng ér shēng yú zhī nà　　qiáo cuì yú yā zhì

之下，呻吟於桎梏之中，久無復生人趣。[4]豈
zhī xià　　shēn yín yú zhì gù zhī zhōng　　jiǔ wú fù shēng rén qù　　qǐ

登山的人，不可畏懼路途崎岖；渡海的人，不可畏懼风波险恶；创立伟大事业的人，不可畏惧世事艰难。[1]私下觉得中国人人心涣散，志气不坚定，说句话就模棱两可，做件事大抵像一团散沙。[2]有些人说空话，对事情没什么帮助，有些人做事有始无终，有些人做事已接近成功，往往因为遭到顽固的阻挠，而变得兴致败坏，致使功业在进行一半时停止，成为后世的遗憾。[3]我们女子很不幸生在中国，在(男权)压制下变得憔悴，在(礼教)的桎梏中呻吟，久久不能再有人生

知<u>物極則反</u>，忽而有男女平權之倡，此又不
zhī wù jí zé fǎn　　hū ér yǒu nán nǚ píng quán zhī chàng cǐ yòu bù

幸中之大幸也。⁵
xìng zhōng zhī dàxìng yě

的乐趣。⁴谁知物极必反，忽然出现了男女权利平等的倡议，这又是不幸中的大幸啊！⁵

1. 畏 *v.* to be afraid of. MdnC: 畏懼 (*wèi jù* 畏惧).

   崎嶇 (岖) *adj.* rugged, rough.

   涉 *v.* to wade, cross. MdnC: 渡 (*dù*).

2. 竊 (窃) *adv.* privately (a humble expression). MdnC: 私下 (*sī xià*).

   維 (维) *particle.* used to introduce the subject; it has no meaning in itself. See L2 Grammar Note 7 ①.

   渙 (涣) 散 *adj.* slack, divided.

   志氣 (气) *n.* aspiration, ambition.

   堅 (坚) *adj.* firm. MdnC: 堅定 (*jiān dìng* 坚定).

   輒 (辄) *adv.* every time, always.

   模棱 *adj.* ambiguous.

   類 (类) *adv.* probably.

3. 或 *indefinite pron.* someone. See L6 Grammar Note 4 ①.

   有始无终 to start something but fail to carry it through.

   垂 *adv.* close to, approximately.

   頑 (顽) 固 *adj.* stubborn.

   意興 (兴) *n.* interest, enthusiasm. MdnC: 興致 (*xìng zhì* 兴致).

   頹敗 (颓败) *v.* to decay, decline. MdnC: 敗壞 (*bài huài* 败坏).

   廢 (废) *v.* to terminate, stop.

4. 支那 ancient name of China. It came from the Sanskrit word *Cīna* and was originally used in both China and Japan during the ancient time. The Chinese came to regard the name as derogatory after World War II.

   憔悴 *adj.* haggard, worn out.

   呻吟 *v.* to moan, groan.

   桎梏 *n.* shackle.

5. 極 (极) *n.* extreme. MdnC: 極點 (*jí diǎn* 极点).

   反 *adj.* opposite.

   物極 (极) 則反 or 物極必反 things will turn opposite when they reach the extreme.

   平權 (权) *n.* equal rights.

   倡 *n.* proposal, initiative. MdnC: 倡議 (*chàng yì* 倡议).

夫女權一事，在外國則爲舊例，在<u>中國</u>
fú nǚ quán yí shì　　zài wài guó zé wéi jiù lì　zài zhōng guó

則屬創舉；外國則視爲公理，<u>中國</u>則視爲背
zé shǔ chuàng jǔ　wài guó zé shì wéi gōng lǐ　zhōng guó zé shì wéi bèi

逆。⁶蓋彼頑固之輩，據<u>惟我獨尊</u>之見，已深
nì　　gài bǐ wán gù zhī bèi　jù wéi wǒ dú zūn zhī jiàn　yǐ shēn

女权这件事，在外国是旧例，在中国就属于创举；在外国就被视为公理，在中国就被视为叛逆。⁶可能那些顽固的人，唯我独尊的见解，已经深深印入他们的脑

印入腦筋，牢不可破，詎能以二三書生之筆
yìn rù nǎo jīn　　láo bù kě pò　　jù néng yǐ èr sān shū shēng zhī bǐ

墨爭哉！[7]雖然，剛刃可折，不可使曲；匹夫
mò zhēng zāi　suī rán　gāng rèn kě zhé　bù kě shǐ qū　pǐ fū

可殺，志不可奪。[8]彼強權者，亦視吾有牛馬
kě shā　zhì bù kě duó　bǐ qiáng quán zhě　yì shì wú yǒu niú mǎ

馴伏之性，故被以羈軛耳。若我有自立之性
xún fú zhī xìng　gù pī yǐ jī è ěr　ruò wǒ yǒu zì lì zhī xìng

質，彼雖有極強之壓力，適足以激吾自立之
zhì　bǐ suī yǒu jí qiáng zhī yā lì　shì zú yǐ jī wú zì lì zhī

志氣，增吾自立之進步，亦何慮乎？[9]夫以二
zhì qì　zēng wú zì lì zhī jìn bù　yì hé lǜ hū　fú yǐ èr

萬萬之生靈，五千年之冤獄，雖必待彼蒼降
wàn wàn zhī shēng líng wǔ qiān nián zhī yuan yù　suī bì dài bǐ cāng jiàng

一絕世偉人，大聲急呼，特立獨行，爲之倡
yī jué shì wěi rén　dà shēng jí hū　tè lì dú xíng　wèi zhī chàng

率；終須我女子痛除舊習，各自維新，人人
shuài　zhōng xū wǒ nǚ zǐ tòng chú jiù xí　gè zì wéi xīn　rén rén

有獨立之思想，人人有自主之魄力，然後可
yǒu dú lì zhī sī xiǎng　rén rén yǒu zì zhǔ zhī pò lì　rán hòu kě

以眾志成城，雖無尺寸之柄，自能奏奇功於
yǐ zhòng zhì chéng chéng suī wú chǐ cùn zhī bǐng　zì néng zòu qí gōng yú

無形，獲最後之戰勝。[10]
wú xíng　huò zuì hòu zhī zhàn shèng

中，牢不可破，岂能用两三篇书生的文章(和他们)争论！[7]即使这样，刚刃可以被折断，却不可以被弯曲；普通人可以被杀，但志气不可被夺走。[8]那些握有强权的人，也把我(们)看作是有驯服天性的牛和马，所以给我们加上束缚。如果我们有自立的性格，他们即使有极强的压制力，刚好足以激发我的志气，增强我自立的(能力，让我)进步，有什么可担忧的呢？[9]二万万的人民，五千年的冤狱，即使必须等待苍天降下一个绝世伟人，大声疾呼，特立独行，作为人民的引导，也终究需要我们女子痛除旧习，革新自己，人人有独立的思想，人人有自主的魄力，然后可以众志成城，即使没有微小的权力，也自然能够无形之中取得成功，获得最后的胜利。[10]

6. 舊 (旧) 例 *n.* old rules.
　創舉 (创举) *n.* new creation, pioneering work.
　背逆 *n.* rebellion, betrayal. MdnC: 叛逆 (*pàn nì*).
7. 彼 *demonstrative pron.* those. MdnC: 那些 (*nà xiē*). See L14 Grammar Note 2 ①.
　輩 (辈) *n.* people of the same group or class.
　據 (据) *prep.* according to. MdnC: 根據 (*gēng jù* 根据).
　惟 (唯) 我獨 (独) 尊 extremely conceited, overweening. See L22 Grammar Note 2 ② for 惟.
　見 (见 *jiàn*) *n.* opinion, view. MdnC: 見解 (*jiàn jiě* 见解).
　腦 (脑) 筋 *n.* brain.
　牢不可破 *adj.* unbreakable.

詎 (诅) *particle.* an equivalent of 豈 (*qǐ* 岂, see L8 Grammar Note 4), meaning "how come?"

筆 (笔) 墨 *n.* brush and ink, referring to essays. MdnC: 文章 (*wén zhāng*).

爭 (争) *v.* to argue, debate. MdnC: 爭論 (*zhēng lùn* 争论).

8. 雖 (虽) 然 even so.

剛 (刚) 刃 *n.* hard blade.

折 (zhé) *v.* to break off. MdnC: 折斷 (*zhé duàn* 折断).

曲 (qū) *adj.* bent. MdnC: 彎曲 (*wān qū* 弯曲).

匹夫 *n.* ordinary man.

志 *n.* ambition, aspiration. MdnC: 志氣 (*zhì qì* 志气).

9. 馴 (驯) 服 *adj.* tame.

被 (pī) *v.* to put on.

羈軛 (羁轭) *n.* halter, yoke. Here it refers to restraint, restriction 束縛 (*shù fù* 束缚).

適 (适) *adv.* just. MdnC: 剛好 (*gāng hǎo* 刚好).

激 *v.* to stimulate. MdnC: 激發 (*jī fā* 激发).

慮 (虑) *n.* concern, worry. MdnC: 擔憂 (*dān yōu* 担忧).

10. 生靈 (灵) *n.* the people. MdnC: 人民 (*rén mín*).

冤獄 (狱) *n.* injustice.

彼蒼 (苍) *n.* blue sky, heaven. MdnC: 蒼天 (*cāng tiān* 苍天).

降 *v.* to drop, grant.

絕 (绝) 世 *adj.* incomparable, best.

大聲 (声) 急呼 or 大聲疾呼 *v.* to loudly appeal to the public.

特立獨 (独) 行 *adj.* unconventional, unique.

倡率 (shuài) *n.* guidance. MdnC: 引導 (*yǐn dǎo* 引导).

痛 *adv.* painstakingly.

維 (维) 新 *v.* to reform, innovate. MdnC: 革新 (*gé xīn*).

眾 (众) 志成城 when people are united, they become extremely strong. 志 means "a person's will"; here 城 means "city wall." Literally, the phrase means that when people with the same will are united, they will become unbreakable like the city wall.

尺寸之柄 *n.* tiny power. 尺寸 means "a little"; here 柄 means "power."

奏 *v.* to achieve. MdnC: 取得 (*qǔ dé*).

奇 *adj.* unusual, incredible.

但今之興女權者，較創國家、奪疆土爲
dàn jīn zhī xīng nǚ quán zhě　jiào chuàng guó jiā　duó jiāng tǔ wéi

尤難。創國業者，猶眾人之所共聞也，歷史
yóu ná　chuàng guó yè zhě　yóu zhòng rén zhī suǒ gòng wén yě　lì shǐ

之所共見也。若女權，則我中國閉關自守，
zhī suǒ gòng jiàn yě　ruò nǚ quán　zé wǒ zhōng guó bì guān zì shǒu

數千年來從無一人發此問題，爲眾人耳所未
shù qiān nián lái cóng wú yì rén fā cǐ wèn tí　wéi zhòng rén ěr suǒ wèi

但今天兴起女权，与创立国家，争夺疆土比较，是尤其困难的。创立国家这件事，还是大家共同听闻的，历史共同见证的。至于女权，我中国闭关自守，数千年来从没有一个人提出这个问题，是大家闻所未闻，见所未见的事

聞，目所未見。[11] 男子聞之， 固叱爲怪異矣；
wén　　mù suǒ wèi jiàn　　　nán zǐ wén zhī　　　gù chì wéi guài yì yǐ

即女子受壓制之教育， 既成習慣， 乍語以此
jí nǔ　zǐ shòu yā zhì zhī jiào yù　　jì chéng xí guàn　　zhà yǔ yǐ cǐ

二字， 亦必茫然不解。[12] 是必須先爲之易舊腦
èr zì　　　yì bì máng rán bù jiě　　　shì bì xū xiān wèi zhī　yì jiù nǎo

筋， 造新魄力， 然後再爲之出闇世界， 闢新
jīn　　zào xīn pò lì　　rán hòu zài wèi zhī chū àn shì jiè　　　pì xīn

乾坤， 豈非較之創國尤難乎？[13] 而女權之興，
qián kūn　qǐ fēi jiào zhī chuàng guó yóu nán hū　　ér nǔ quán zhī xīng

雖較創國爲難， 若告厥成功之日， 則其功較
suī jiào chuàng guó wéi nán　ruò gào jué chéng gōng zhī rì zé qí gōng jiào

創國獨偉， 其利益較皇祚獨重， 其幸福且將
chuàng guó dú wěi　qí lì yì jiào huáng zuò dú zhòng qí xìng fú qiě jiāng

永久享受而無窮。[14]
yǒng jiǔ xiǎng shòu ér wú qióng

情。[11]男子听到女权，当然会呵斥其为怪异之说；就是女子（长期）接受（被）压制的教育，已经成习惯了，突然用这两个字和她们交谈，她们也必然茫然不解。[12]必须先为她们换掉旧的脑筋，创造新的魄力，然后再帮她们走出昏暗的世界，开辟新的乾坤，岂不是比创立国家还要难吗？[13]而女权的兴起，即使比创建国家更难，但如果有一天宣告成功了，它的功绩与创建国家相比特别伟大，它的利益和皇位相比特别重要，它（带来的）幸福将是永久的，可以享受无穷的！[14]

11. 疆土 *n.* territory.
尤 *adv.* especially, particularly. MdnC: 尤其 (*yóu qí*).
見 (见 *jiàn*) *v.* to witness. MdnC: 見證 (*jiàn zhèng* 见证).
若 *conj.* as for, about. MdnC: 至於 (*zhì yú* 至于). See L14 Grammar Note 3 ③.
閉關 (闭关) 自守 to close the gates of one's country and not communicate with all the foreign countries.

12. 固 *adv.* of course. MdnC: 當然 (*dāng rán* 当然).
叱 *v.* to scold, shout at. MdnC: 呵斥 (*hē chì*).
怪異 (较) *adj.* weird, odd.
乍 *adv.* suddenly. MdnC: 忽然 (*hū rán* 当然).
茫然不解 *v.* to have no idea.

13. 易 *v.* to change. MdnC: 換掉 (*huàn diào* 换掉).
闇 (暗) *adj.* dark. MdnC: 昏暗 (*hūn àn*).
闢 (辟) *v.* to open, start. MdnC: 開闢 (*kāi pì* 开辟).
乾坤 *n.* heaven and earth, universe.

14. 厥 *pron.* its. MdnC: 它的 (*tā de*).
獨 (独) *adv.* very. MdnC: 特別 (*tè bié*).
皇祚 *n.* imperial throne. MdnC: 皇位 (*huáng wèi*).

自丁酉、 戊戌以來， 女學始萌芽於上
zì dīng yǒu　　wù xū yǐ lái　　　nǔ xué shǐ méng yá yú shàng

自从丁酉年、戊戌年以来，女学在上海开始萌

海，駸駸乎頗有進步。¹⁵迨至今日，則女學校
hǎi qīn qīn hū pō yǒu jìn bù   dài zhì jīn rì zé nǔ xué xiào

立矣，女學會開矣，女報館設矣，女子遊學
lì yǐ nǔ xué huì kāi yǐ nǔ bào guǎn shè yǐ nǔ zǐ yóu xué

之風行矣。此不過草創伊始，爲日未久，故
zhī fēng xíng yǐ cǐ bú guò cǎo chuàng yī shǐ wéi rì wèi jiǔ gù

尚待改良，徐圖精進。¹⁶然行之日久，我女子
shàng dài gǎi liáng xú tú jīng jìn rán xíng zhī rì jiǔ wǒ nǔ zǐ

豈不能實收回其固有權利乎？今欲求持久，
qǐ bù néng shí shōu huí qí gù yǒu quán lì hū Jīn yù qiú chí jiǔ

則力有不足，且頑固諸輩，復壓制阻擾之，
zé lì yǒu bù zú qiě wán gù zhū bèi fù yā zhì zǔ rǎo zhī

其何以能成此宏功，償此大願哉？¹⁷則曰「貴
qí hé yǐ néng chéng cǐ hóng gōng cháng cǐ dà yuàn zāi zé yuē guì

有堅忍之志」而已。使吾二萬萬同胞，各具
yǒu jiān rěn zhī zhì ér yǐ shǐ wú èr wàn wàn tóng bāo gè jù

百折不撓之定見，則阻力愈大，進步愈速。¹⁸
bǎi zhé bù náo zhī dìng jiàn zé zǔ lì yù dà jìn bù yù sù

芽，迅猛地(发展)很有进步。¹⁵等到今天，女子学校建立了，女子学会开放了，女子报馆设立了，女子游学之风盛行了。这不过是刚开始的草创(阶段)，时间不久，所以还需要改良，慢慢地谋求进步。¹⁶但是盛行的日子长了，我们女子难道不能真正地收回我们固有地权利吗？现在想要谋求长久，但是能力还有不足，而且顽固的人，又压制阻挠扰乱我们的努力，那怎么才能成就这宏伟的功业，实现这个伟大的愿望呢？¹⁷由此说"贵有坚忍之志"。使我们两万万的同胞，都具有百折不挠的精神，那么(遇到的)阻力越大，(我们的)进步也越快。¹⁸

15. 丁酉 the year 1897. See L2 Culture Note 1.
    戊戌 the year 1898.
    萌芽 v. to sprout, germinate.
    駸駸 (骎) 乎 adv. quickly, swiftly. MdnC: 迅猛地 (xùn měng de). See L3 Grammar Note 4 ① for 乎.
16. 迨至 adv. by the time when. MdnC: 等到 (děng dào).
    學會 (学会) n. association, institute.
    報館 (报馆) n. newspaper office.
    遊學 (游学) v. to study in some other place, study abroad.
    行 v. to become popular, be prevalent. MdnC: 盛行 (shèng xíng).
    草創 (创) v. to start (a business, enterprise, etc.).
    伊始 adv. at the beginning.
    改良 v. to improve, reform.
    徐 adv. slowly. MdnC: 慢慢地 (màn màn de).
    圖 (图) v. to plan, pursue. MdnC: 謀求 (móu qiú 谋求).
    精進 (进) v. to advance.
17. 實 (实) adv. really, truly. MdnC: 真正地 (zhēn zhèng de).
    諸 (诸) adj. many.

何以 by what? how come? See L1 Grammar Note 3 ③.

宏 *adj.* grand, great.

償 (偿) *v.* to achieve. MdnC: 實現 (*shí xiàn* 实现).

18. 百折不撓 (挠) *adj.* a phrase used to describe a person who does not bend even after one hundred setbacks, indomitable.

定見 (见 jiàn) *n.* definite opinion, firm view.

速 *adj.* fast, speedy. MdnC: 快 (*kuài*).

處此黑闇世界，野蠻之輩甚多，迂儒之
chǔ cǐ hēi àn shì jiè　yě mán zhī bèi shèn duō　yū rú zhī

習未改，訾詆謗誹，自所不免。而事之有益
xí wèi gǎi　zī dǐ bàng fěi　zì suǒ bù miǎn　ér shì zhī yǒu yì

於眾生，無害於國家者，我女流必人人皆視
yú zhòng shēng wú hài yú guó jiā zhě　wǒ nǔ liú bì rén rén jiē shì

爲應盡之責任，寧冒萬死而不辭。[19] 雖能糜其
wéi yīng jìn zhī zé rèn　nìng mào wàn sǐ ér bù cí　ssuī néng mí qí

身，而不能奪其志；雖能阻其事，而不能緘
shēn　ér bù néng duó qí zhì　suī néng zǔ qí shì　ér bù néng jiān

其口；雖能毀其名，而不能餒其氣。竭力爲
qí kǒu　suī néng huǐ qí míng　ér bù néng něi qí qì　jié lì wéi

之，今日不成，明日爲之；明日不成，後日
zhī　jīn rì bù chéng　míng rì wéi zhī　míng rì bù chéng　hòu rì

爲之，鞠躬盡瘁，死而後已。[20] 果能如此，而
wéi zhī　jū gōng jìn cuì　sǐ ér hòu yǐ　guǒ néng rú cǐ　ér

終不獲與男子同趨於文明教化之途，爲平等
zhōng bú huò yǔ nán zǐ tóng qū yú wén míng jiào huà zhī tú　wéi píng děng

自由之人者，則余未之信也。若有其志而不
zì yóu zhī rén zhě　zé yú wèi zhī xìn yě　ruò yǒu qí zhì ér bù

思達其願，勤厥始而不免怠厥終者，則貽同
sī dá qí yuàn　qín jué shǐ ér bù miǎn dài jué zhōng zhě zé yí tóng

志之羞，與頑固以口實。[21] 所謂勝則王侯，敗
zhì zhī xiū　yǔ wán gù yǐ kǒu shí　suǒ wèi shèng zé wáng hóu bài

則賊寇，遭後世之唾罵，反不若今日之不興
zé zéi kòu　zāo hòu shì zhī tuò mà　fǎn bú ruò jīn rì zhī bù xīng

处在这黑暗的世界，野蛮的人很多，迂腐儒生的习气不改，(我们遇到)非议诽谤，是在所难免的。可这件事对老百姓有益，对国家无害，我们女人必须人人都把它视为应尽的责任，宁可万死不辞。[19] 即使(这黑暗世界)能摧残我们的身体，却不能夺走我们的志气；即使能阻挠我们的事业，却不能使我们闭口不言；即使能毁掉我们的名声，却不能让我们气馁。竭力去做这件事，今天不成功，明天(继续)去做；明天不成功，后天继续，鞠躬尽瘁，死而后已。[20] 果然能够这样，最终却不能获得途径，与男子一样趋向文明教化，做平等自由的人，这样的结果我不相信。如果有这样的志气，却不想(怎样)达成愿望，在事情开始时很努力，在事情最后不免变得懒惰，那么就给同志留下耻辱，给顽固的人(攻击我们的)借口。[21] 所谓胜利的人就成为王侯，失败的人就

此女學，不倡此女權之爲妙也。與其蜷伏哀
cǐ nǔ xué　　bú chàng cǐ nǔ quán zhī wéi miào yě　yǔ qí quán fú āi

鳴，何如登高痛哭？[22] 近世哲學家曰，二十世
míng　　hé rú dēng gāo tòng kū　　jìn shì zhé xué jiā yuē　èr shí shì

紀爲女權發達之時代，是爲二百兆女子禍福
jì wéi nǔ quán fā dá zhī shí dài　　shì wéi èr bǎi zhào nǔ zǐ huò fú

轉移之大關鍵哉！時不可失，海內同志，諸
zhuǎn yí zhī dà guān jiàn zāi　shí bù kě shī　　hǎi nèi tóng zhì　zhū

君子，其共勉之哉！[23]
jūn zǐ　　qí gòng miǎn zhī zāi

成为贼寇，遭到后世之人的唾骂，（如担心这样的结果，那么我们）倒不如今天不兴起女学，不倡议女权才好。与其蜷伏（在角落）哀鸣，不如登到高处去痛哭啊！[22] 近代有哲学家说，二十世纪是女权发展的时代，是两亿女子祸福转移的关键时候。时机不能失去，海内的同志们，各位君子，还是共同努力吧！[23]

《呂碧城詩文箋注》，上海：上海古籍出版社 (1985), 141–143.

19. 迂 *adj.* pedantic. MdnC: 迂腐 (*yū fǔ*).

儒 *n.* scholar.

訾詆 (诋) *v.* to slander, defame. MdnC: 非議 (*fēi yì* 非议).

謗誹 (谤诽) or 誹謗 *v.* to slander.

寧 (宁 nìng) *adv.* (would) rather. MdnC: 寧可 (*nìng kě* 宁可).

冒 *v.* to risk, contend with.

萬死不辭 (万死不辞) even when facing great dangers, one will not give up their duty.

20. 糜 *v.* to smash. Here it means "to destroy" 摧殘 (*cuī cán* 摧残).

緘 (缄) *v.* to close, seal. MdnC: 閉口 (*bì kǒu* 闭口).

餒 (馁) *adj.* hungry, used here as a causative verb, 使……餒, meaning "to make … discouraged."

鞠躬盡瘁，死而後已 a phrase from "Later Memorial on Expedition" 后出師表 ("Hòu Chūshī Biǎo" 后出师表) by 諸葛亮 (181–234), describing how he would devote himself to the Northern Expedition until the end of his life. Later the phrase has been used to describe a person who exerts his utmost to perform an assigned duty even at the cost of his life.

21. 趨 (趋) *v.* to run, tend to. MdnC: 趨向 (*qū xiàng* 趋向).

達 (达) *v.* to reach, accomplish. MdnC: 達成 (*dá chéng* 达成).

勤 *adj.* hardworking, industrious. MdnC: 努力 (*nǔ lì*).

怠 *adj.* idle. MdnC: 懶惰 (*lǎn duò* 懒惰).

貽 (贻) *v.* to give, leave behind. MdnC: 留 (*liú*).

羞 *n.* shame, disgrace. MdnC: 恥辱 (*chǐ rǔ* 耻辱).

口實 (实) *n.* excuse, pretext. MdnC: 借口 (*jiè kǒu*).

22. 王侯 *n.* the nobility.

賊 (贼) 寇 *n.* robber.

唾罵 (骂) *v.* to spit on and curse.

蜷伏 *v.* to curl up.

哀鳴 (鸣) *v.* to wail.

23. 哲學 (学) 家 *n.* philosopher.

兆 *number.* million. 二百兆 means "two hundred million" 兩億 (*liǎng yì* 两亿).

禍 (祸) 福 *n.* disaster and happiness.

時 (时) *n.* opportunity, chance. MdnC: 時機 (*shí jī* 时机).

海內 *adv.* throughout the entire country.

勉 *v.* to endeavor, try hard. MdnC: 努力 (*nǔ lì*).

Literary Analysis

Premodern Chinese women have left behind far more poetry than prose. With the rise of print culture, the Ming-Qing witnessed the brisk publication and circulation of poetry collections by female writers, but in prose, women were far less successful in breaking down gender barriers. Most prose genres, deeply intertwined with sociopolitical and cultural activities in the public arena, were off-limits to premodern women writers. Thus excluded, women concentrated their prose in two genres of a more private nature: letters and prefaces (often to books for circulation among family and friends), as shown by lessons 20, 27, and 28.

With the advent of the twentieth century, Chinese women began to break through traditional restraints and participate in a wider cultural and political life. As their world broadened, the scope of their prose did as well. Lü Bicheng presents a perfect case in point: arguably the most prominent female activist and writer in the early twentieth century, she was lionized as a female literary knight-errant (*wénxiá* 文俠), alongside the female martial knight-errant (*wǔxiá* 武俠), anti-Manchu martyr Qi Jin 秋瑾. The essay introduced here illustrates Lü's power both as a women's rights advocate and as a writer.

While many Chinese women were struggling to unshackle themselves from bound feet, Lü was already articulating ideas and ideals of women's rights that can still inspire today. Her accomplishment in prose art is no less astounding. She was the first woman to write and publish influential political essays, yet she did not show the slightest sign of a novice's uncertainty and timidity. Instead, she took her world by storm, assuming a transhistorical position and absolutely authoritative voice—not unlike national political leader Liang Qichao did (see lesson 33)—proclaiming the critical significance of women's liberation and charting the course for achieving that grand goal. The force of her argument is greatly amplified by her masterly use of prose cadence, diction, and varied textual patterning. Compare this essay with Liang's in lesson 33; chances are you will find yourself more deeply impressed with her work.

—ZC

課後練習　Exercises

一　給加點字注音　Give the pinyin romanization for each dotted word.

1. 憔悴 （＿＿＿, ＿＿＿）　2. 桎梏 （＿＿＿, ＿＿＿）　3. 覊軛 （＿＿＿, ＿＿＿）　4. 皇祚 （＿＿＿）

二　在括號中給句中加點的字注音，並選出正確的釋義　Give the pinyin romanization for each dotted word; then select the correct definition from the following list, and write it in the blank.

閉(闭)口　　它的　　懶(懒)惰　　**信服**　　迅猛　　摧殘(残)

1. 小信未孚（fú）　<u>信服</u>　**2.** 告厥成功　（　）_____　**3.** 駸駸乎（　）_____

4. 怠厥終　（　）_____　**5.** 糜其身　（　）_____　**6.** 緘其口（　）_____

三　選擇釋義並填空 Match each word in the left column with its correct definition in the middle column. Fill in each blank in the right column with an appropriate word from the left column.

謀謀劃(谋划)	實現(实现)	____海者，不可畏風波之險惡。
涉_____	迂腐	男子聞之，固____爲怪異矣。
叱_____	呵斥	其何以能成此宏功，____此大願哉？
償_____	**謀劃(谋划)**	處此黑闇世界，野蠻之輩甚多，____儒之習未改。
迂_____	渡	

四　爲加點字選擇正確釋義，並根據釋義來翻譯句子 Match each dotted word with its correct modern Chinese equivalent by circling the latter. Then translate each sentence into modern Chinese.

1. 又何間焉？　　　　　　　　　　a. 爲什麼(为什么)　b. 憑什麼(凭什么)　c. 多少

現代文翻譯：你又爲什麼要參與到這件事情裡面？

_____

2. 或空言無補，或有始無終，或事已垂成，往往因頑固之阻撓，而意興頹敗。

　　　　　　　　　　　　　　　　　　a. 或者　b. 有人　c. 可能

現代文翻譯：_____

3. 蓋彼頑固之輩，據惟我獨尊之見，已深印入腦筋，牢不可破，詎能以二三書生之筆墨爭哉！

　　　　　　　　　　　　　　　　　　a. 但是　b. 只有　c. 難(难)道

現代文翻譯：_____

4. 其何以能成此宏功，償此大願哉？　　a. 怎麼(么)　b. 爲什麼(为什么)　c. 則(则)

現代文翻譯：_____

單元練習

Unit Exercises

一、辨析加點字在不同句中注音和釋義的異同 Give the pinyin romanization for each dotted word and then write in its correct definition.

1. 鄙　**肉食者鄙，未能遠謀。**　　　　　（**bǐ**）<u>目光短浅</u>

　　　越國以鄙遠，君知其難也。　　　　（　）＿＿＿＿＿

2. 假　郊焉而天神假，廟焉而人鬼饗。　（　）＿＿＿＿＿

　　　假日月之光。　　　　　　　　　　（　）＿＿＿＿＿

3. 塞　不塞不流，不止不行。　　　　　　（　）＿＿＿＿＿

　　　淳且與先文忠爲北塞之舉矣。　　　（　）＿＿＿＿＿

4. 疾　鰥寡孤獨廢疾者有養也。　　　　　（　）＿＿＿＿＿

　　　君子疾沒世而名不稱焉。　　　　　（　）＿＿＿＿＿

5. 公　以之爲人，則愛而公。　　　　　　（　）＿＿＿＿＿

　　　天下有公利而莫或興之。　　　　　（　）＿＿＿＿＿

6. 汙　入者附之，出者汙之。　　　　　　（　）＿＿＿＿＿

　　　持出，洗其汙，衆環之以至旦。　　（　）＿＿＿＿＿

7. 殆　知彼知己者，百戰不殆。　　　　　（　）＿＿＿＿＿

　　　他日之命運殆將盡也。　　　　　　（　）＿＿＿＿＿

二、用給出的字填空，並選擇正確的釋義 Fill in the blanks with words from list A and then write in their modern Chinese equivalents from list B.

A. Words for Filling the Blanks

B. Modern Chinese Equivalents

奴	毀	昆	駭	妄
恨	順	常	固	作
折	譽	潛	**鄙**	就

加固	胡亂(乱)	詆毀(诋毁)	倫(伦)常	平順(顺)
兄	發(发)出	驚駭(惊骇)	貶(贬)低	遺(遗)憾
成就	潛(潜)伏	稱贊(称赞)	**目光短浅**	折斷(断)

1. 肉食者 ＿鄙，未能遠謀。　　[目光短浅]

2. 老子之小仁義，非＿＿＿之也。　[　　]

3. 入者主之，出者＿＿＿之。　[　　]

4. 剖斗＿＿＿衡。　　　　　　　　[　　]

5. 外天下國家，滅其天＿＿＿。　[　　]

6. 父子、師友、賓主、＿＿＿弟。[　　]

7. 以之爲己，則＿＿＿而詳。　[　　]

8. 但我＿＿＿其急一時之名。　　　[　　]

9. 不奇行以＿＿俗。 [　　　] 　　10. ＿＿之而不喜，毀之而不懼。 [　　　]

11. ＿＿龍騰淵，鱗爪飛揚。 [　　　] 　　12. ＿＿傳伯夷、叔齊無稽之事。 [　　　]

13. 攝緘縢，＿＿扄鐍。 [　　　] 　　14. 某業所＿＿，孰與仲多？ [　　　]

15. 干將發硎，有＿＿其芒。 [　　　]

三、給加點字選擇正確的釋義，並選出與加點字用法相同的句子 Circle the letter of the correct definition (a, b, c, or d) for the dotted word in each boldfaced sentence. Then circle the letter of the sentence (A, B, C, or D) that employs the dotted word in the same way as the boldfaced sentence.

1. 臣之妻私臣。　　　　　a. 這(这)件事情 b. 他 ⓒ 的 d. 他們

　　A. 夫晉，何厭之有？　　　　B. 不闕秦，將焉取之？

　　C. 肉食者謀之，又何間焉？　　Ⓓ 能面刺寡人之過者，受上賞。

2. 博愛之謂仁，行而宜之之謂義，由是而之焉之謂道。

　　　　　　　　　　　a. 於(于)之 b. 之(仁義) c. 啊 d. 然

　　A. 賈之家一，而資焉之家六。　　B. 子焉而不父其父，臣焉而不君其君。

　　C. 君子疾沒世而名不稱焉。　　D. 擇焉而不精，語焉而不詳。

3. 其亦幸而出於三代之後，不見黜於禹、湯、文、武、周公、孔子也。

　　　　　　　　　　　a. 被 b. 見識(见识) c. 看 d. 出現(现)

　　A. 人但見君子之為人也。　　B. 老子之小仁義，非毀之也，其見者小也。

　　C. 見漁人，乃大驚。　　D. 立一不肖後，如西銘先生，為人所詬笑。

4. 天下有公利而莫或興之。　　a. 或者 b. 有人 c. 有時(时) d. 稍微

　　A. 有公害莫或除之。　　B. 予嘗求古仁人之心，或異二者之為。

　　C. 或擇地而蹈之，時然後出言……　　D. 親戚知其如此，或置酒而招之。

5. 若何為生我家！　　　a. 像 b. 如果 c. 你 d. 比得上

　　A. 好名者豈如是乎？　　B. 棄而君臣，去而父子。

　　C. 夫子若曰：好名者，人之恆情也。　　D. 其旁出堡塢，有若門焉。

6. 子焉而不父其父。　　　a. 父親(亲) b. 以……為(为)父 c. 使……成父親(亲) d. 夫

　　A. 諸侯用夷禮，則夷之。　　B. 古之欲明明德於天下者。

　　C. 人其人，火其書。　　D. 先天下之憂而憂。

7. 今也，舉夷狄之法，而加之先王之教之上，幾何其不胥為夷也！

　　　　　　　　　　　a. 他 b. 這(这) c. 那麼(那么) d. ……的

A. 其亦幸而出於三代之後。　　B. 人其人，火其書。

C. 若壅其口，其與能幾何？　　D. 其友與俱遊者有姻焉。

8. 後之爲人君者不然，以爲天下之權皆出於我。

a. 雖(虽)然　b. 這樣(这样)　c. 對(对)　d. ……的樣(样)子

A. 然則，如之何而可也？　　B. 曰："是不然。"

C. 雖至天下之爲盜賊者亦然。　　D. 適莽蒼者三飡而反，腹猶果然。

四、閱讀下面的段落，選擇正確的釋義 Read the following passage, and select the correct definition for each dotted word in the following list.

師説
韓愈

古之學者必有師。師者，所以傳道、受業、解惑也。人非生而知之者，孰能無惑？惑而不從師，其爲惑也終不解矣。

生乎吾前，其聞道也，固先乎吾，吾從而師之；生乎吾後，其聞道也，亦先乎吾，吾從而師之。吾師道也，夫庸知其年之先後生於吾乎？是故無貴、無賤、無長、無少，道之所存，師之所存也。

嗟乎！師道之不傳也久矣！欲人之無惑也難矣！古之聖人，其出人也遠矣，猶且從師而問焉；今之衆人，其下聖人也亦遠矣，而恥學於師。是故聖益聖，愚益愚，聖人之所以爲聖，愚人之所以爲愚，其皆出於此乎？

愛其子，擇師而教之，於其身也，則恥師焉，惑矣！彼童子之師，授之書而習其句讀者也，非吾所謂傳其道、解其惑者也。句讀之不知，惑之不解，或師焉，或不焉，小學而大遺，吾未見其明也。

……

李氏子蟠，年十七，好古文，六藝經傳，皆通習之，不拘於時，請學於余。余嘉其能行古道，作《師説》以貽之。

《韓昌黎文集校注》，上海：上海古籍出版社 (1986), 42–44.

1. 古之學者必有師。　　a. ……的事　　b. ……的原因　　c. ……的人
2. 孰能無惑？　　a. 熟練(练)　　b. 怎麼(么)　　c. 誰(谁)
3. 生乎吾前。　　a. 於(于)　　b. 嗎(吗)　　c. 對(对)
4. 其聞道也。　　a. 聞(闻)名　　b. 知道　　c. 問(问)
5 吾從而師之。　　a. 使……師(师)　　b. 以……爲師(为师)　　c. 老師(师)

6. 其出人也遠矣。　　　a. 出去　　　b. 超出　　　c. 跳出

7. 猶且從師而問焉。　　a. 於（于）之　　b. 啊　　　c. 然

8. 恥學於師。　　　　　a. 使……恥（耻）　b. 以……爲恥（为耻）　c. 羞恥（耻）

9. 是故聖益聖，愚益愚。　a. 好處（处）　　b. 利益　　　c. 更加

10. 彼童子之師。　　　　a. 那些　　　b. 你　　　c. 這（这）

五、將下列句子翻譯成現代漢語 Translate the following sentences into modern Chinese.

1. 博愛之謂仁，行而宜之之謂義，由是而之焉之謂道，足乎己，無待於外之謂德。

現代文翻译：＿＿＿＿＿＿＿＿＿＿＿＿＿＿＿＿＿＿＿＿＿＿＿＿＿＿＿

2. 老子之所謂道德云者，去仁與義言之也，一人之私言也。

現代文翻译：＿＿＿＿＿＿＿＿＿＿＿＿＿＿＿＿＿＿＿＿＿＿＿＿＿＿＿

3. 孔子之作《春秋》也，諸侯用夷禮，則夷之；進於中國，則中國之。

現代文翻译：＿＿＿＿＿＿＿＿＿＿＿＿＿＿＿＿＿＿＿＿＿＿＿＿＿＿＿

4. 是故生則得其情，死則盡其常；郊焉而天神假，廟焉而人鬼饗。

現代文翻译：＿＿＿＿＿＿＿＿＿＿＿＿＿＿＿＿＿＿＿＿＿＿＿＿＿＿＿

5. 名而名者，無之在於未沒世之前，君子豈可以徒疾乎？

現代文翻译：＿＿＿＿＿＿＿＿＿＿＿＿＿＿＿＿＿＿＿＿＿＿＿＿＿＿＿

6. 若夫營營於旦夕之間，是求速盡者也，好名者豈如是乎？

現代文翻译：＿＿＿＿＿＿＿＿＿＿＿＿＿＿＿＿＿＿＿＿＿＿＿＿＿＿＿

7. 是以其未得之也，屠毒天下之肝腦，離散天下之子女，以博我一人之產業，曾不慘然！

現代文翻译：＿＿＿＿＿＿＿＿＿＿＿＿＿＿＿＿＿＿＿＿＿＿＿＿＿＿＿

8. 後世之君，欲以如父如天之空名禁人之窺伺者，皆不便於其言，至廢孟子而不立，非導源於小儒乎！

現代文翻译：＿＿＿＿＿＿＿＿＿＿＿＿＿＿＿＿＿＿＿＿＿＿＿＿＿＿＿

柳宗元《小石城山記》

"A Record of Little Stone Ramparts Hill" (Liu Zongyuan)

Introduction

A brief biographical note on the great mid-Tang writer Liu Zongyuan appears in lesson 16. "A Record of Little Stone Ramparts Hill" is the last piece in his *Eight Records of Yongzhou* 永州八記 (*Yǒngzhōu bājì* 永州八记), written during his exile to Yongzhou in present-day Guangxi Province. In this composition, Liu conveys the sense of wonder he felt on discovering a rocky hill's hidden beauty and compels us to join him in questioning why the Creator would place such a spectacular landscape in a remote region visited only by downtrodden exiles like himself. This combination of visual feast, philosophical musing, and personal lyricism is the hallmark of Liu's travel accounts. A translation of this text is given in *HTRCProse*, chapter 11, "Tang and Song Occasional Prose: Accounts of Places, Things, and Events," C11.1.

正文與簡體譯文 Text and Modern Chinese Translation

自西山道口徑北， 逾黃茅嶺而下， 有二
zì xī shān dào kǒu jìng běi　yú huáng máo lǐng ér xià　yǒu èr

道：[1]其一西出， 尋之無所得；[2]其一少北而
dào　qí yī xī chū　xún zhī wú suǒ dé　qí yī shāo běi ér

東， 不過四十丈， 土斷而川分， 有積石橫當
dōng　bú guò sì shí zhàng　tǔ duàn ér chuān fēn　yǒu jī shí héng dǎng

其垠。[3]其上爲睥睨、梁欐之形， 其旁出堡
qí yín　qí shàng wéi pì nì　liáng lì zhī xíng　qí páng chū bǎo

塢， 有若門焉。[4]窺之[a]正黑， 投以小石， 洞
wù　yǒu ruò mén yān　kuī zhī　zhèng hēi　tóu yǐ xiǎo shí　dòng

然有水聲， 其響之[b]激越， 良久乃已。[5]環之
rán yǒu shuǐ shēng　qí xiǎng zhī　jī yuè　liáng jiǔ nǎi yǐ　huán zhī

可上， 望甚遠， 無土壤而生嘉樹美箭， 益奇
kě shàng　wàng shèn yuǎn　wú tǔ rǎng ér shēng jiā shù měi jiàn　yì qí

而堅， 其疏數偃仰， 類智者所施設也。[6]
ér jiān　qí shū cù yǎn yǎng　lèi zhì zhě suǒ shī shè yě

从(永州城外)西山路口直接向北，越过黄茅岭往下，有两条路：[1]一条路向西延伸，探寻它没什么(美景)；[2]一条路稍微向北后又向东去，不超过四十丈之后，土路断了，一条河(把路)分开，有堆积的石头横挡在路的尽头。[3]石头上是女墙、屋梁的形状，旁边凸出一个(天然的)小城堡，在那像有道门。[4]看它(里面)很黑，用一个小石头(往里)扔，清楚地(听到)有水声，水声很洪亮，很久才停止。[5]环绕小城堡(走一圈，发现)可以上去，(上面可以)望得很远。上面没有土壤却生

长出很好的树木和美丽的竹子，更（显得石头）奇特而坚硬。树木竹子（的分布是）稀疏细密，还是低头抬头，都好像是智者设计好的。[6]

1. 西山 Western Mount, in present-day Yongzhou 永州, Hunan Province.

   徑 (径) *adv.* directly. MdnC: 直接 (*zhí jiē*).

   北 *n.* north. Here it means "northwards" 向北 (*xiàng běi*).

   逾 *v.* to cross over. MdnC: 越過 (*yuè guò* 越过).

   黃茅嶺 (黄茅岭) Yellow Thatch Ridge, in present-day Lingling 零陵, Hunan Province.

2. 西 *n.* west. Here it means "westwards" 向西 (*xiàng xī*).

   出 *v.* to go out. Here it means "to extend or stretch" 延伸 (*yán shēn*).

   尋 (寻) *v.* to seek, explore. MdnC: 探求 (*tàn qiú*).

3. 少 (shāo) *adv.* used in the sense of 稍 (*shāo*), meaning "a little or a bit" 稍微 (*shāo wēi*).

   東 (东) *n.* east. Here it means "eastwards" 向東 (*xiàng dōng* 向东).

   丈 *measure word.* unit of length in ancient China.

   土 *n.* dirt, earth. Here it refers to a dirt road 土路 (*tǔ lù*).

   斷 (断) *v.* to break. Here it means "the road was broken."

   川 *n.* river. MdnC: 河 (*hé*).

   積 (积) *v.* to accumulate, pile up. MdnC: 堆積 (*duī jī* 堆积).

   橫 (héng) *adv.* horizontally.

   當 (当) used in the sense of 擋 (*dǎng* 挡), meaning "to block."

   垠 *n.* end (of the road), edge. MdnC: 盡頭 (*jìn tóu* 尽头).

4. 睥睨 *n.* also called a daughter's wall 女兒墙 (*nǚ ér qiáng* 女儿墙) or 女墙 (*nǚ qiáng* 女墙). It is a parapet or a low protective wall built above the normal city wall in ancient China.

   梁欐 *n.* roof beam 屋梁 (*wū liáng*).

   堡塢 (坞) *n.* castle and fort. Here it refers to a small castle naturally formed by rocks.

   若 *v.* to be like. MdnC: 像(*xiàng*). See L4 Grammar Note 4 ①.

   焉 *pron.* there. MdnC: 在那 (*zài nà*). See L1 Grammar Note 4 ①.

5. 窺 (窥) *v.* to watch, explore, spy on. MdnC: 看 (*kàn*).

   之 ₐ *personal pron.* it. 之 refers to 堡塢. See L1 Grammar Note 2 ③.

   正 (zhèng) *adv.* just.

   投 *v.* to throw. MdnC: 扔 (*rēng*).

   以 *coverb.* use. MdnC: 用 (*yòng*). See L2 Grammar Note 1 ②.

   洞然 *adv.* clearly.

   響 (响) *n.* sound. MdnC: 聲響 (*shēng xiǎng* 声响).

   之 ♭ *particle.* a nominative marker. See L2 Grammar Note 2 ⑤.

   激越 *adj.* loud and far-reaching (sound). MdnC: 洪亮 (*hóng liàng*).

   良 *adv.* very. MdnC: 很 (*hěn*).

   已 *v.* to stop. MdnC: 停止 (*tíng zhǐ*).

6. 環 (环) *v.* to circle round. MdnC: 環繞 (*huán rào* 环绕).

嘉 *adj.* good. MdnC: 好 (*hǎo*).

箭 *n.* arrow. Here it refers to bamboo 竹子 (*zhú zi*).

益 *adv.* more. MdnC: 更 (*gèng*).

奇 *adj.* strange, peculiar, unusual. MdnC: 奇特 (*qí tè*).

堅 (坚) *adj.* hard, solid. MdnC: 堅硬 (*jiān yìng* 坚硬).

疏 *adj.* sparse. MdnC: 稀疏 (*xī shū*).

數 (数 *cù*) *adj.* fine, meticulous. MdnC: 細密 (*xì mì* 细密).

僂 *v.* to bow down. MdnC: 低頭 (*dī tóu* 低头).

仰 *v.* to look up. MdnC: 擡頭 (*tái tóu* 抬头).

類 (类) *v.* to seem as if. MdnC: 好像 (*hǎo xiàng*).

智者 *n.* wise man.

施設 (设) *v.* to arrange, set up.

噫！吾疑造物者之有無久矣。[7] 及是，
yī　wú yí zào wù zhě zhī yǒu wú jiǔ yǐ　jí shì

愈以爲誠有。[8] 又怪其不爲之中州，而列是
yù yǐ wéi chéng yǒu　yòu guài qí bù wéi zhī zhōng zhōu ér liè shì

夷狄，更千百年不得一售其伎，是固勞而
yí dí　gēng qiān bǎi nián bù dé yí shòu qí jì　shì gù láo ér

無用。[9] 神者儻不宜如是，則其果無乎？[10]
wú yòng　shén zhě tǎng bù yí rú shì　zé qí guǒ wú hū

或曰：「以慰夫賢而辱於此者。」[11] 或曰：
huò yuē　yǐ wèi fú xián ér rǔ yú cǐ zhě　huò yuē

「其氣之靈，不爲偉人，而獨爲是物，故
qí qì zhī líng　bù wéi wěi rén　ér dú wéi shì wù　gù

楚之南少人而多石。」是二者，余未信之。[12]
chǔ zhī nán shǎo rén ér duō shí　shì èr zhě　yú wèi xìn zhī

《柳河東集》，上海：上海古籍出版社 (2008), 476–477.

唉！我怀疑造物者是有是无很久了！[7] 到了这里，我更认为是确实存在的。[8] 但我又感到奇怪，造物者（为什么）不把它建在中原地区，却摆在了偏远的地方，经历了千百年，也不能显露出它的奇景，这就是徒劳无用（的功夫啊）！[9] 造物神假若不应这样，那么造物者真的不存在吗？[10] 有人说："（造物者在这里造出奇景）来安慰那些贤德却被贬官到此的人。"[11] 有人说："此地的灵气，不成就伟人，而只是造就这种实物，所以楚地南边人比较少，但是石头比较多。"这两种说法，我都不信。[12]

7. 噫 *exclamatory word.* alas. MdnC: 唉 (*ài*).

　　疑 *v.* to doubt, question. MdnC: 懷疑 (*huái yí* 怀疑).

　　之 *particle.* a nominative marker. See L2 Grammar Note 2 ⑤.

　　造物者 *n.* the creator who makes all things in the universe.

8. 及 *v.* to reach, get to. MdnC: 到 (*dào*).

　　是 *demonstrative pron.* this (place). MdnC: 這裏 (*zhè lǐ* 这里). See L3 Grammar Note 1 ①.

　　愈 *adv.* more. MdnC: 更加 (*gèng jiā*).

　　以爲 (为 *wéi*) *v.* to regard something as. MdnC: 認爲 (*rèn wéi* 认为).

誠 (诚) *adv.* indeed. MdnC: 確實 (*què shí* 确实).

9. 怪 *adj.* strange. Here it used as a putative verb, 以……爲怪, meaning "to think something odd." See L14 Grammar Note 1 ①.

其 *personal pron.* 其 refers to 造物者. See L2 Grammar Note 5 ①.

爲 (为 *wéi*) *v.* to make, create. See L2 Grammar Note 6 ①.

中州 *n.* central plains. MdnC: 中原 (*zhōng yuán*).

列 *v.* to list, arrange. MdnC: 擺 (*bǎi* 摆).

夷狄 barbarians. See L19 Culture Note 2. Here it refers to remote and uncivilized areas.

更 (*gēng*) *v.* to go through, experience. MdnC: 經歷 (*jīng lì* 经历).

售 *v.* to sell. Here it means "to show or present" 顯露 (*xiǎn lù* 显露).

伎 *n.* ability, skill. Here it refers to extraordinary scenery 奇景 (*qí jǐng*).

勞 (劳) *adv.* in vain. MdnC: 徒勞 (*tú láo* 徒劳).

10. 神者 *n.* god, creator.

儻 (倘) *conj.* if, supposing. MdnC: 假若 (*jiǎ ruò*). See Grammar Note 1.

宜 *v.* should, ought to. MdnC: 應當 (*yīng dāng* 应当).

11. 或 *indefinite pron.* someone. MdnC: 有人 (*yǒu rén*). See L6 Grammar Note 4 ①.

以 *conj.* in order to. MdnC: 來 (*lái* 来). See L2 Grammar Note 1 ③.

慰 *v.* to console. MdnC: 安慰 (*ān wèi*).

夫 (*fú*) *demonstrative pron.* those. MdnC: 那些 (*nà xiē*). See L2 Grammar Note 4 ②.

賢 (贤) *adj.* virtuous. MdnC: 賢德 (*xián dé* 贤德).

辱 *adj.* humiliated. Here it refers to being demoted (to this place) 貶官 (*biǎn guān* 贬官).

12. 靈 (灵) *n.* spirit.

獨 (独) *adv.* only. MdnC: 只是 (*zhǐ shì*).

楚 refers to the area of present-day Hubei and Hunan Provinces.

語法注釋 Grammar Note

1. 儻   *conj.* also 倘, meaning "if." MdnC: 如果 (*rú guǒ*), 儻若 (*tǎng ruò* 倘若), 假若 (*jiǎ ruò*).
(倘)
> 神者儻不宜如是，則其果無乎？
>> [造物的神假若不应像这样，那么造物者果然是不存在的吗？]
> 余甚惑焉，儻所謂天道，是耶非耶？（L14）
>> [我非常困惑啊！倘若有所说的天道，（这是）对的呢？还是不对的呢？]

Literary Analysis

This is perhaps the best-known of Liu Zongyuan's *Eight Records of Yongzhou*. First-person accounts of his excursions into the surrounding landscape of his exile in Yongzhou (modern Lingling, in southern Hunan close to the Guangxi border), the records are admired for Liu's limpid descriptions of Yongzhou's mountain scenes as well as his deft weaving into these descriptions of his reflections on life and the fate of an official in exile.

A distinctive trait of this prose piece is its indeterminacy of meaning. Different readers are likely to interpret it in different ways, something quite rare in traditional Chinese prose. And there is little question that this is the author's deliberate intention rather than an unintended effect. Having stumbled upon a completely hidden spot of exceptional landscape beauty (Little Stone Ramparts Hill of the title), Liu ponders the question of how its presence in such an out-of-the-way locale bears on the question of whether the world was created by a divine intelligence, a question he tells us he has long pondered. He then mentions two contradictory inferences about the divine intelligence question that may be drawn from the Little Stone Ramparts Hill site (bringing us no closer to an answer). Finally, he offers two other explanations of the little spot of beauty and concludes by telling us that he believes neither of them! Does he really disbelieve them? Both of them? Then why record them? It seems the author wants to hint at an answer to his doubts about divine intelligence and about the reasons for the location of Little Stone Ramparts Hill, but does not want to do so directly and unambiguously. Such is the singularity and lasting fascination of this short prose record.

☞ *HTRCProse*, chapter 11, "Tang and Song Occasional Prose: Accounts of Places, Things, and Events."

—RE

課後練習 Exercises

一 給加點字注音 Give the pinyin romanization for each dotted word.

1. 睥睨 （＿＿, ＿＿） 2. 梁欐 （＿＿,＿＿） 3. 塢 （＿＿） 4. 箭 （＿＿） 5. 狄 （＿＿）

二 在括號中給句中加點的字注音，並選出正確的釋義 Give the pinyin romanization for each dotted word; then select the correct definition from the following list, and write it in the blank.

細(细)密　稍微　越過(过)　擋(挡)住　經歷(经历)　直接　**信服**　盡頭(尽头)

1. **小信未孚（fú）** 信服 2. 徑北（　） ＿＿＿ 3. 逾黃茅嶺而下（　） ＿＿＿
4. 少北而東（　） ＿＿＿ 5. 疏數（　） ＿＿＿ 6. 更千百年 （　） ＿＿＿
7. 有積石橫當其垠 （　） ＿＿＿ 8. 有積石橫當其垠 （　） ＿＿＿

三 選擇釋義並填空 Match each word in the left column with its correct definition in the middle column. Fill in each blank in the right column with an appropriate word from the left column.

謀謀劃(谋划) 擺(摆)　其一西出，＿＿之無所得；其一少北而東，不過四
尋＿＿＿ 好像　十丈，土＿＿而川分，有積石橫當其垠。
斷＿＿＿ 環繞(环绕)
窺＿＿＿ **謀劃(谋划)**　＿＿＿之正黑，投以小石，洞然有水聲。
環＿＿＿ 顯(显)露
嘉＿＿＿ 中斷(断)　＿＿＿之可上，望甚遠，無土壤而生＿＿樹美箭，益
類＿＿＿ 探求　奇而堅，其疏數偃仰，＿＿智者所施設也。

列_____　　　安慰　　　　　　又怪其不爲之中州，而____是夷狄，更千百年不得
售_____　　　好　　　　　　　一____其伎，是固勞而無用。
慰_____　　　看
辱_____　　　貶(贬)官　　　　　　或曰：「以____夫賢而____於此者。」

四　請用給出的字填空 Fill in each blank with an appropriate word from the following list.

焉　　以　　然　　是　　或　　之

1. 其旁出堡塢，有若門____。窺____正黑，投____小石，洞____有水聲。
2. 又怪其不爲之中州，而列____夷狄。　　3. ____曰：「以慰夫賢而辱於此者。」

五　爲加點字選擇正確釋義，並根據釋義來翻譯句子 Match each dotted word with its correct modern Chinese equivalent by circling the latter. Then translate each sentence into modern Chinese.

1. 又何間焉？　　　　　　　　　　　　ⓐ爲什麼(为什么)　b. 憑什麼(凭什么)　c. 多少

現代文翻譯：你又为什么要参与到这件事情里面？

_____

2. 其上爲睥睨、梁欐之形，其旁出堡塢，有若門焉。　　a. 爲什麼(为什么)　b. 在那　c. 啊

現代文翻譯：_____

3. 窺之正黑，投以小石，洞然有水聲，其響之激越，良久乃已。　　a. 然而　b. 好　c. 實(实)在

現代文翻譯：_____

4. 神者儻不宜如是，則其果無乎？　　　　　　　　a. 可能　b. 假若　c. 何不

現代文翻譯：_____

5. 或曰：「其氣之靈，不爲偉人，而獨爲是物，故楚之南少人而多石。」

　　　　　　　　　　　　　　　　　　　a. 或許(许)　b. 可能　c. 有人

現代文翻譯：_____

6. 是二者，余未信之。　　　a. 二人　b. 兩樣東西(两样东西)　c. 兩種說法(两种说法)

現代文翻譯：_____

第三十六課

范仲淹《岳陽樓記》

"Yueyang Tower Inscription" (Fan Zhongyan)

Introduction

"Yueyang Tower Inscription" was composed by the eminent early Northern Song official-scholar Fan Zhongyan 范仲淹 (courtesy name Xiwen 希文; posthumous title Wenzheng 文正; 989–1052) for the newly rebuilt Yueyang Tower in the sixth year of the Qingli reign (1046) of Song Emperor Renzong 宋仁宗. Apart from his political and military accomplishments, Fan Zhongyan scaled the heights of literary excellence in both *shi* and *ci* poetry as well as in prose.

Composed at the invitation of his friend Teng Zijing, governor of Baling, the inscription vividly captures the magnificent scenery around Dongting Lake through the change of seasons and describes how these changing scenes evoke myriad emotional responses from passing literati. Commenting on their responses, Fan declares that a true Confucian scholar-official should not be "pleased by external gains, nor saddened by one's own circumstances" 不以物喜，不以己悲. Moreover, he announces his personal goal of "being the first person to feel worried, before anyone else in the world does; being the last person to feel joy, after everyone else in the world does" 先天下人之憂而憂，後天下人之樂而樂. This statement has so touched readers of later times that it has become emblazoned in our memory of Fan as an inspiring Confucian moralist. A translation of this text is given in *HTRCProse*, chapter 11, "Tang and Song Occasional Prose: Accounts of Places, Things, and Events," C11.3.

正文與簡體譯文 Text and Modern Chinese Translation

慶曆四年春，　滕子京謫守巴陵郡。¹越明
qìng lì sì nián chūn　téng zǐ jīng zhé shǒu bā líng jùn　yuè míng

年，政通人和，百廢具興。²乃重修岳陽樓，
nián　zhèng tōng rén hé　bǎi fèi jù xīng　nǎi chóng xiū yuè yáng lóu

增其舊制，刻唐賢今人詩賦於其上。³屬予作
zēng qí jiù zhì　kè táng xián jīn rén shī fù yú qí shàng　zhǔ yú zuò

文以記之。⁴
wén yǐ jì zhī

庆历四年的春天，滕子京被贬官到巴陵郡做太守。¹过了第二年，政事顺利，人与人关系和谐，各项废止的事业都（重新）兴起了。²于是重新修缮了岳阳楼，扩大了旧时的规模，把唐代贤人和今人创作的诗赋刻在上面。³（滕子京）嘱托我写篇文章来记述这件事情。⁴

1. 慶曆 (庆历) a period in the reign of Emperor Renzong (r. 1022–1063) of the Northern Song dynasty 宋仁宗. It lasted from 1041 to1048. 慶曆四年 is 1044.

    滕子京 (family name 姓, Téng 滕; given name 名, Zōngliàng 宗諒; style 字, Zǐjīng 子京; 990–1047), who was awarded the Presented Scholar degree in the same year as Fan Zhongyan.

    謫 (谪) *v.* to be demoted. MdnC: 貶官 (*biǎn guān* 贬官).

    守 *v.* to become the prefect.

    巴陵郡 Baling County, in present-day Yueyang 岳陽, Hunan Province.

2. 越 *prep.* through. MdnC: 過 (*guò* 过).

    明年 next year.

    政 *n.* political affairs, administration. MdnC: 政事 (*zhèng shì*).

    通 *adj.* smooth. MdnC: 順利 (*shùn lì* 顺利).

    和 *adj.* harmonious. MdnC: 和諧 (*hé xié* 和谐).

    百 *number.* hundred. Here it means "all or every" 各 (*gè*).

    廢 (废) *v.* to abolish, abandon. MdnC: 廢止 (*fèi zhǐ* 废止).

    具 *adv.* all. MdnC: 都 (*dōu*). See L24 Grammar Note 1 ②.

    興 (兴 xīng) *v.* to rise, prosper. MdnC: 興起 (*xīng qǐ* 兴起).

3. 修 *v.* to repair. MdnC: 修繕 (*xiū shàn* 修缮).

    增 *v.* to increase, expand. MdnC: 擴大 (*kuò dà* 扩大).

    舊 (旧) *adj.* old, previous. MdnC: 舊時 (*jiù shí* 旧时).

    制 *n.* scale, structure. MdnC: 規模 (*guī mó* 规模).

    刻 *v.* to engrave.

    唐 the Tang dynasty (618–917).

    賢 (贤) *adj.* virtuous, good. Here it refers to the talented people.

4. 屬 (属) *v.* used in the sense of 囑 (*zhǔ* 嘱), meaning "to ask or require" 囑托 (*zhǔ tuō* 嘱托).

    記 (记) *v.* to produce a descriptive account. MdnC: 記述 (*jì shù* 记述).

予觀夫巴陵勝狀，在洞庭一湖。⁵銜遠
yú guān fú bā líng shèng zhuàng zài dòng tíng yī hú   xián yuǎn

山，吞長江，浩浩湯湯，橫無際涯；朝暉夕
shān tūn cháng jiāng hào hào shāng shāng héng wú jì yá zhāo huī xī

陰，氣象萬千。⁶此則岳陽樓之大觀也。前人
yīn, qì xiàng wàn qiān   cǐ zé yuè yáng lóu zhī dà guān yě qián rén

之述備矣。⁷然則北通巫峽，南極瀟湘，遷客
zhī shù bèi yǐ   rán zé běi tōng wū xiá nán jí xiāo xiāng qiān kè

騷人，多會於此，覽物之情，得無異乎？⁸
sāo rén duō huì yú cǐ lǎn wù zhī qíng dé wú yì hū

我观赏巴陵郡优美的景象，全在洞庭湖。⁵洞庭湖衔接着远处的山脉，吞吐着长江，浩浩荡荡，广阔得没有边际；早晨阳光照耀，傍晚天色昏暗，气象千变万化。⁶这就是岳阳楼的壮观景象！前人的记述很详尽了！⁷即使这样，洞庭湖向北通到巫峡，向南到达湘江，被贬官的人，诗人，多聚集在此，观看景物的心情，能没有不同吗？⁸

5. 觀 (观) *v.* to watch, observe. MdnC: 觀賞 (*guān shǎng* 观赏).

夫 *demonstrative pron.* that. MdnC: 那 (*nà*). See L2 Grammar Note 4 ②.

勝 (胜 *shèng*) *adj.* beautiful, wonderful. MdnC: 優美的 (*yōu měi de* 优美的).

狀 *n.* appearance, conditions. Here it means "view, scenery, or landscape" 景象 (*jǐng xiàng*).

洞庭 or 洞庭湖 Dongting Lake, in present-day Yueyang 岳陽, Hunan Province.

6. 銜 (衔) *v.* to hold in one's mouth. Here it means "to envelop or link up" 銜接 (*xián jiē* 衔接).

吞 *v.* to swallow. MdnC: 吞吐 (*tūn tǔ*).

湯湯 (汤汤 shāng shāng) *adj.* (water) flowing fast.

浩浩湯湯 (汤汤 shāng shāng) *adj.* vast and great (waves). MdnC: 浩蕩 (*hào dàng* 浩荡).

橫 (横 *héng*) *adj.* vast. MdnC: 廣闊 (*guǎng kuò* 广阔).

際 (际) *n.* border. MdnC: 邊際 (*biān jì* 边际).

涯 *n.* limit, border.

朝 (zhāo) *n.* morning. MdnC: 早晨 (*zǎo chén*).

暉 (晖) *n.* sunshine. Here it is used as a verb, meaning "to shine" 照耀 (*zhào yào*).

夕 *n.* evening. MdnC: 傍晚 (*bàng wǎn*).

陰 (阴) *adj.* dark. MdnC: 昏暗 (*hūn àn*).

氣 (气) 象 *n.* scene, image.

7. 大 *adj.* grand. MdnC: 壯觀 (*zhuàng guān* 壮观).

觀 (观) *n.* view, sight. MdnC: 景觀 (*jǐng guān* 景观).

述 *n.* description. MdnC: 記述 (*jì shù* 记述).

備 (备) *adj.* detailed, full. MdnC: 詳盡 (*xiáng jìn* 详尽).

8. 然則 *conj.* even like this, but…. MdnC: 雖然如此，但…… (*suī rán rú cǐ dàn*). See L10 Grammar Note 1.

北 *n.* north. Here it is an adverb, meaning "northwards" 向北 (*xiàng běi*).

通 *v.* to lead to.

巫峽 the Wu Gorge, also known as the Great Gorge 大峽. It is the second of the three gorges on the Yangtze River and extends about 45 km from Wushan 巫山縣 of Chongqing 重慶 to Badong 巴東, Hubei Province.

南 *n.* south. Here it is used as an adverb, meaning "southwards" 向南 (*xiàng nán*).

極 (极) *v.* to reach. MdnC: 到達 (*dào dá* 到达).

瀟 (潇) 湘 or 湘江 Xiang River. The Xiao branch 瀟水 joins the Xiang River in present-day Lingling 零陵, Hunan Province, and then flows into Dongting Lake.

遷 (迁) 客 *n.* officials who had been demoted to remote places.

騷 (骚) 人 *n.* poets.

會 (会) *v.* to meet, gather. MdnC: 聚集 (*jù jì*).

覽 (览) *v.* to watch, observe. MdnC: 觀看 (*guān kàn* 观看).

情 *n.* feeling, sentiment. MdnC: 心情 (*xīn qíng*).

若夫霪雨霏霏，連月不開，陰風怒號，
ruò fú yín yǔ fēi fēi　lián yuè bù kāi　yīn fēng nù háo

濁浪排空，日星隱耀，山嶽潛形，商旅不
zhuó làng pái kōng　rì xīng yǐn yào　shān yuè qián xíng　shāng lǚ bù

至于雨下个不停，连续几个月都不放晴，阴冷的风愤怒地吼叫着，浑浊的波浪冲击着天空。日月星辰隐藏了光辉，

行， 檣傾楫摧， 薄暮冥冥， 虎嘯猿啼；⁹登斯
xíng　qiáng qīng jí cuī　bó mù míng míng　hǔ xiào yuán tí　dēng sī

樓也， 則有去國懷鄉， 憂讒畏譏， 滿目蕭
lóu yě　zé yǒu qù guó huái xiāng　yōu chán wèi jī　mǎn mù xiāo

然， 感極而悲者矣！¹⁰
rán　gǎn jí ér bēi zhě yǐ

高山潛藏了形迹。商人不能前行，船的桅杆倒了，船桨断了。傍晚时分天色昏暗了，（只能听到）老虎的吼声和猿猴的啼叫。⁹（这时）登上这座楼，就会有（这样的）心情：离开国都思念家乡，担心（有人对皇帝进）逸言，害怕（有人）讥讽（自己），所以满眼望去都觉得萧条凄凉，感叹到了极点就感到悲伤。¹⁰

9. 若夫 *conj.* as for, about. MdnC: 至於 (*zhì yú* 至于). See Grammar Note 1.
   霪 (淫) *adj.* excessive. 霪 (淫) 雨 means "excessive rain."
   霏霏 *adj.* rainy or snowy.
   連 (连) *adj.* continuous. MdnC: 連續 (*lián xù* 连续).
   開 (开) *adj.* open. Here it means "to clear up" 放晴 (*fàng qíng*).
   號 (号 *háo*) *v.* to howl. MdnC: 吼叫 (*hǒu jiào*).
   濁 (浊) *adj.* muddy, turbid. MdnC: 渾濁 (*hún zhuó* 浑浊).
   排 *v.* to push, strike. MdnC: 衝擊 (*chōng jī* 冲击).
   隱 (隐) *v.* to hide, conceal. MdnC: 隱藏 (*yǐn cáng* 隐藏).
   耀 *n.* sunshine, radiance. MdnC: 光輝 (*guāng huī* 光辉).
   嶽 (岳) *n.* tall mountain.
   潛 (潜) *v.* to hide, conceal. MdnC: 潛藏 (*qián cáng* 潜藏).
   形 *n.* shape, trace. MdnC: 形跡 (*xíng jì* 形迹).
   商旅 *n.* traveling merchant. MdnC: 商人 (*shāng rén*).
   檣 (樯) *n.* mast. MdnC: 桅杆 (*wéi gān*).
   傾 (倾) *v.* to fall, collapse. MdnC: 倒 (*dǎo*).
   楫 *n.* oar, paddle. MdnC: 船槳 (*chuán jiǎng* 船桨).
   摧 *v.* to be broken. MdnC: 斷 (*duàn* 断).
   薄 (*bó*) *v.* to approach.
   暮 *n.* sunset, evening. 薄暮 means "at dusk or evening" 傍晚 (*bàng wǎn*).
   冥冥 *adj.* dark.
   嘯 (啸) *v.* to howl (as an animal). MdnC: 吼叫 (*hǒu jiào*).
   猿 (猨) *n.* gibbon. MdnC: 猿猴 (*yuán hóu*).
   啼 (嗁) *v.* to cry out. MdnC: 啼叫 (*tí jiào*).

10. 登 *v.* to climb up.
    斯 *demonstrative pron.* this. MdnC: 這 (*zhè* 这). See L5 Grammar Note 3 ①.
    有……者 there is the situation that.... See L8 Grammar Note 1 ⑥.
    去 *v.* to leave. MdnC: 離開 (*lí kāi* 离开).

國 (国) *n.* capital. MdnC: 國都 (*guó dū* 国都).

懷 (怀) *v.* to miss, long for. MdnC: 思念 (*sī niàn*).

鄉 (乡) *n.* hometown. MdnC: 家鄉 (*jiā xiāng* 家乡).

憂 (忧) *v.* to worry. MdnC: 擔心 (*dān xīn* 担心).

讒 (谗) *v.* to slander, defame. MdnC: 讒言 (*chán yán* 谗言).

畏 *v.* to fear, be afraid. MdnC: 害怕 (*hài pà*).

譏 (讥) *v.* to ridicule, vilify. MdnC: 譏諷 (*jī fěng* 讥讽).

蕭 (萧) 然 *adj.* bleak, desolate. MdnC: 凄涼 (*qī liáng*).

感 *v.* to sigh. MdnC: 感嘆 (*gǎn tào* 感叹).

極 (极) *n.* extreme. MdnC: 極點 (*jí diǎn* 极点).

悲 *adj.* sad. MdnC: 悲傷 (*bēi shāng* 悲伤).

至若春和景明，波瀾不驚，上下天光，
zhì ruò chūn hé jǐng míng　bō lán bù jīng　shàng xià tiān guāng

一碧萬頃，沙鷗翔集，錦鱗游泳，岸芷汀
yí bì wàn qǐng　shā ōu xiáng jí　jǐn lín yóu yǒng　àn zhǐ tīng

蘭，郁郁青青；¹¹而或長煙一空，皓月千
lán　yù yù qīng qīng　ér huò cháng yān yì kōng　hào yuè qiān

里，浮光躍金，静影沈璧；¹²漁歌互答，此
lǐ　fú guāng yuè jīn　jìng yǐng chén bì　yú gē hù dá　cǐ

樂何極！¹³登斯樓也，則有心曠神怡，寵辱
lè hé jí　dēng sī lóu yě　zé yǒu xīn kuàng shén yí　chǒng rǔ

偕忘，把酒臨風，其喜洋洋者矣。¹⁴
xié wàng　bǎ jiǔ lín fēng　qí xǐ yáng yáng zhě yǐ

至于春天和暖，阳光明媚，水波平静不动，上面的天空和下面的水光（连在一起），一片碧蓝，广阔无边。沙鸥一会飞翔一会停在一起，美丽的鱼在水中游动，岸上的小草，小洲上的兰花，芬芳茂盛。¹¹有时（湖上）大片的烟雾消失了，明亮的月光（照耀）千里，（水面上）浮动的月光闪着金光，安静的月影像沉浸在水中的玉璧。¹²渔人的歌声互相唱和，这种快乐哪有穷尽啊！¹³登上这座楼，就会有这样的情况：心胸开阔，精神愉快，荣耀和屈辱都忘记了，端着酒杯，面对春风，心里很高兴啊！¹⁴

11. 至若 *conj.* as for, about. MdnC: 至於 (*zhì yú* 至于). See Grammar Note 1.

和 (hé) *adj.* warm. MdnC: 和暖 (*hé nuǎn*).

景 *n.* sunshine. MdnC: 陽光 (*yáng guāng* 阳光).

明 *adj.* bright and beautiful. MdnC: 明媚 (*míng mèi*).

瀾 (澜) *n.* wave, ripple.

驚 (惊) *v.* to surprise. Here it means "to move."

碧 *n.* green jade. Here it refers to the light blue color.

頃 (顷) *measure word.* a unit of area that equals about 6.67 hectares.

沙鷗 (鸥) *n.* sand bird.

翔 *v.* to circle in the air. MdnC: 飛翔 (*fēi xiáng* 飞翔).

集 *v.* to perch on the tree.

錦 (锦) *n.* brocade. Here it means "beautiful" 美麗 (*měi lì* 美丽).

鱗 (鳞) *n.* fish scale. Here it refers to fish in the lake.

岸 *n.* bank, riverbank.

芷 *n.* sweet grass, angelica.

汀 *n.* islet. MdnC: 小洲 (*xiǎo zhōu*).

蘭 (兰) *n.* thoroughwort, eupatorium. MdnC: 蘭花 (*lán huā* 兰花).

郁郁 *adj.* fragrant and aromatic. MdnC: 芬芳 (*fēn fāng*).

青青 *adj.* lush. MdnC: 茂盛 (*mào shèng*).

12. 或 *adv.* sometimes. MdnC: 有時 (*yǒu shí* 有时). See L15 Grammar Note 4 ②.

煙 (烟) *n.* mist. MdnC: 烟霧 (*yān wù* 烟雾).

空 (*kōng*) *adj.* empty. Here it means "to disappear or vanish" 消失 (*xiāo shī*).

皓 *adj.* bright. MdnC: 明亮 (*míng liàng*).

浮 *adj.* floating. MdnC: 浮動 (*fú dòng* 浮动).

躍 (跃) *v.* to jump. Here it means "to shine" 閃 (*shǎng*).

金 *n.* gold. Here it refers to golden light 金光 (*jīn guāng*).

影 *n.* shadow.

沈 (沉 *chén*) *v.* to sink, submerge.

璧 *n.* jade disk. MdnC: 玉璧 (*yù bì*).

13. 漁 (渔) *n.* fishing. Here it refers to fishermen.

答 *v.* to answer. MdnC: 唱和 (*chàng hè*).

極 (极) *n.* extreme, end. MdnC: 窮盡 (*qióng jìn* 穷尽).

14. 旷 *adj.* open. MdnC: 開闊 (*kāi kuò* 开阔).

怡 *adj.* pleasant, happy. MdnC: 愉快 (*yú kuài*).

寵 (宠) *n.* favor. Here it means "honor or glory" 榮耀 (*róng yào* 荣耀).

辱 *n.* humiliation. MdnC: 屈辱 (*qū rǔ*).

偕 *adv.* all together.

把 *v.* to hold. MdnC: 端 (*duān*).

酒 *n.* wine cup. MdnC: 酒杯 (*jiǔ bēi*).

臨 (临) *v.* to face. MdnC: 面對 (*miàn duì* 面对).

洋洋 *adj.* happy.

嗟夫！予嘗求古仁人之心，或異二者之
jiē fú　　yú cháng qiú gǔ rén rén zhī xīn　　huò yì èr zhě zhī

為，何哉？ ¹⁵不以物喜，不以己悲。 ¹⁶居廟
wéi　hé zāi　　bù yǐ wù xǐ　　bù yǐ jǐ bēi　　jū miào

堂之高，則憂其民，處江湖之遠，則憂其
táng zhī gāo　zé yōu qí mín　chǔ jiāng hú zhī yuǎn　zé yōu qí

哎！我曾探求古代仁人的心理，或許和這兩種都不同，為什麼呢？ ¹⁵(他們)不因為外物(的好壞)或自己的(得失)高興或悲傷。 ¹⁶處在朝廷高位上，就擔心老百姓；處在邊遠地方，就

君。¹⁷ 是進亦憂，退亦憂。然則何時而樂
jūn　　shì jìn yì yōu　　tuì yì yōu　　rán zé hé shí ér　lè

耶？¹⁸ 其必曰「先天下之憂而憂，後天下之
yé　　qí bì yuē　xiān tiān xià zhī yōu ér yōu　　hòu tiān xià zhī

樂而樂」乎？¹⁹ 噫！微斯人，吾誰與歸？²⁰
lè ér lè　hū　　yī　　wēi sī rén　　wú shuí yǔ guī

時六年九月十五日。²¹
shí liù nián jiǔ yuè shí wǔ rì

《範文正公文集》，北京：中華書局 (1985), 19–20.

担心国君。¹⁷在朝廷做官也担心，被贬官到边远地区也担心。既然如此，那么什么时候才能高兴呢？¹⁸他们一定会说："在天下人担忧之前就担忧，在天下人快乐之后才快乐"吧！¹⁹哎！没有这种人啊！我和谁同路而归呢？²⁰时间是庆历六年九月十五日。²¹

15. 嗟夫 (fú) *exclamatory word.* oh! MdnC: 唉 (*ài*).

　　求 *v.* to explore. MdnC: 探求 (*tàn qiú*).

　　仁人 *n.* benevolent man.

　　或 *adv.* perhaps. MdnC: 或許 (*huò xǔ* 或许). See Grammar Note 2 ④.

　　爲 (为 *wéi*) *n.* action, behavior. Here it refers to the state of mind.

16. 以 *prep.* for the reason of. MdnC: 因爲 (*yīn wèi* 因为). See L2 Grammar Note 1 ①.

　　物 *n.* external circumstances. MdnC: 外物 (*wài wù*).

17. 居 *v.* to stay, occupy (the position). MdnC: 處在 (*chǔ zài* 处在).

　　廟 (庙) 堂 *n.* imperial court. MdnC: 朝廷 (*cháo tíng*).

　　高 *adj.* high, tall. Here it refers to high positions in court 高位 (*gāo wèi*).

　　憂 (忧) *v.* to worry. MdnC: 擔心 (*dān xīn* 担心).

　　民 *n.* common people.

　　江湖 *n.* river and lake. Here it refers to remote places 邊遠 (*biān yuǎn* 边远).

　　君 *n.* emperor, ruler.

18. 是 *demonstrative pron.* this. MdnC: 這 (*zhè* 这). See L3 Grammar Note 1 ①.

　　進 (进) *v.* to advance in one's career. Here it refers to 居廟堂之高.

　　退 *v.* to withdraw from the political world. Here it refers to 處江湖之遠.

19. 先 *adv.* earlier, before. Here it is used as a verb, meaning "to do something before everyone does" 在 (*zài*) ……之前 (*zhī qián*).

　　後 (后) *adv.* later, behind. Here it is used as a verb, meaning "to do something after everyone does" 在 (*zài*) ……之後 (*zhī hòu* 之后).

20. 噫 *exclamatory word.* alas. MdnC: 唉 (*ài*).

　　微 *adv.* no. MdnC: 没有 (*méi yǒu*).

　　歸 (归) *v.* to go with. MdnC: 同路 (*tóng lù*).

21. 時 (时) *n.* date.

　　六年 or 慶曆六年 the year 1046.

語法注釋 Grammar Notes

1. **若夫/至若** *conj.* as for, about. MdnC: 至於 (*zhì yú* 至于).

   若夫霪雨霏霏，連月不開……

   > [至于雨下个不停，连续几个月都不放晴 ……]

   至若春和景明，波瀾不驚……

   > [至于春天天气暖和，日光明媚，湖面平静无波……]

   若夫營營於旦夕之間，是求速盡者也，好名者豈如是乎？ (L31)

   > [至于一天到晚追求（名声），这是想快速求得名声的人，真正求名的人怎会这样
   > 呢？]

2. **或** Four uses of 或 are explained in this book. In addition to the use below, see 或① in L6 Grammar Note 4, 或② in L15 Grammar Note 4, and 或③ in L32 Grammar Note 1.

   ④ *adv.* perhaps, maybe. MdnC: 或許 (*huò xǔ* 或许).

   予嘗求古仁人之心，或異二者之爲，何哉？

   > [我曾经探求古时仁人的精神，或许不同于上面两种行为，为什么呢？]

Literary Analysis

It may be interesting to consider why this inscription for the reconstructed Yueyang Tower has become so remarkably famous. Surely much of its fame is due to Fan Zhongyan's very effective organizational strategy that leads to the concluding injunction. His exposition proceeds by successive implicit and explicit contradictions: starting with the circumstances that led to this inscription in the first section, he essentially tells us in the second that everything that might be said about the view from the tower has already been said. Immediately after, though, he rhetorically asks whether different passersby, depending on their situation, might nonetheless have very different reactions—different things to say.

This leads into the next two sections, in which Fan describes the scene experienced in two radically different and even antithetical ways; each depends on the viewer's circumstances, his state of mind, and the way he consequently perceives the river and anticipates his journey's continuation. Each experience of the scene is completely plausible and persuasive—however diametrically opposed. Having said it may be this and just as well that, Fan moves on to his powerful conclusion, in which he takes issue with and contravenes both preceding experiences of the scene in a culminating contradiction.

The conclusion involves a bit of authorial sleight of hand. The state of mind Fan advocates requires an almost impossible degree of self-denial and subjugation of the self to the larger interests of state, ruler, and common people. The ideal man he describes here is in a constant state of worry or anxiety over the condition of entities outside himself. The inspiration for this ideal, we're told, comes from "humane men of ancient times," but no man or written source is identified. We may well wonder if anyone who ever lived measures up to such a seemingly unattainable ideal. Certainly, it has never been formulated in so extreme and uncompromising a way—an important reason this inscription is so memorable.

☞ *HTRCProse,* chapter 11, "Tang and Song Occasional Prose: Accounts of Places, Things, and Events."

—RE

課後練習 Exercises

一 給加點字注音 Give the pinyin romanization for each dotted word.

1. 滕 (＿＿) 2. 浩浩湯湯 (＿＿, ＿＿) 3. 巫峽 (＿＿, ＿＿) 4. 芷 (＿＿)

5. 騷 (＿＿) 6. 檣傾楫摧 (＿＿, ＿＿) 7. 瀟湘 (＿＿, ＿＿) 8. 汀 (＿＿)

二 在括號中給句中加點的字注音，並選出正確的釋義 Give the pinyin romanization for each dotted word; then select the correct definition from the following list, and write it in the blank.

衔(衔)接　優(优)美　貶(贬)官　讒(谗)言
囑(嘱)托　潛(潜)藏　**信服**　吼叫　興(兴)起

1. 小信未孚（**fú**）　**信服**　2. 謫守巴陵（　）＿＿＿＿＿　3. 百廢具興（　）＿＿＿＿＿

4. 屬予作文（　）＿＿＿＿＿　5. 巴陵勝狀（　）＿＿＿＿＿　6. 衔遠山 （　）＿＿＿＿＿

7. 陰風怒號（　）＿＿＿＿＿　8. 山嶽潛形（　）＿＿＿＿＿　9. 憂讒畏譏（　）＿＿＿＿＿

三 選擇釋義並填空 Match each word in the left column with its correct definition in the middle column. Fill in each blank in the right column with an appropriate word from the left column.

謀謀劃(谋划)	渾濁(浑浊)	越明年，政＿＿人和，百廢具興。乃重修岳陽樓，增其舊＿＿，刻唐賢今人詩賦於其上，屬予作文以記之。
通＿＿＿＿＿	詳盡(详尽)	
制＿＿＿＿＿	遊覽(游览)	
暉＿＿＿＿＿	唱和	朝＿＿夕陰，氣象萬千。
備＿＿＿＿＿	**謀劃(谋划)**	前人之述＿＿矣。
濁＿＿＿＿＿	同路	
耀＿＿＿＿＿	規(规)模	若夫霪雨霏霏，連月不開，陰風怒號，＿＿浪排空，日星隱＿＿，山嶽潛形，商旅不行，檣傾楫＿＿，薄暮冥冥，虎嘯猿嘯。
摧＿＿＿＿＿	閃(闪)	
皓＿＿＿＿＿	沒(没)有	
躍＿＿＿＿＿	光輝(辉)	而或長煙一空，＿＿月千里，浮光＿＿金，靜影沈璧，漁歌互＿＿，此樂何極！
答＿＿＿＿＿	順(顺)利	
微＿＿＿＿＿	明亮	＿＿斯人，吾誰與＿＿？
歸＿＿＿＿＿	斷(断)	

四 請用給出的字填空 Fill in each blank with an appropriate word from the following list (some words may be used more than once).

或 以 之 若 然 則(則) 夫

1. 予觀＿＿巴陵勝狀，在洞庭一湖。

2. 前人＿＿述備矣，＿＿ ＿＿北通巫峽，南極瀟湘，遷客騷人，多會於此。

3. 至＿＿春和景明，波瀾不驚，上下天光，一碧萬頃。

4. 予嘗求古仁人＿＿心，＿＿異二者＿＿爲，何哉？

五 爲加點字選擇正確釋義，並根據釋義來翻譯句子 Match each dotted word with its correct modern Chinese equivalent by circling the latter. Then translate each sentence into modern Chinese.

1. 又何間焉?　　　　　　　　　　　ⓐ爲什麼(为什么) b. 憑什麼(凭什么) c. 多少

現代文翻译：你又为什么要参与到这件事情里面？

_____

2. 屬予作文以記之。　　　　　　　　　a. 來(来) b. 憑藉(凭借) c. 認爲(认为)

現代文翻译：_____

3. 然則北通巫峽，南極瀟湘，遷客騷人，多會於此，覽物之情，得無異乎？

　　　　　　　　　　　　　　　　a. 如果 b. 而且 c. 雖(虽) 然如此，但……

現代文翻译：_____

4. 至若春和景明，波瀾不驚，上下天光，一碧萬頃。　a. 至於(于) b. 好像 c. 如果

現代文翻译：_____

5. 不以物喜，不以己悲。　　　　　　a. 而 b. 因爲(为) c.認爲(认为)

現代文翻译：_____

6. 先天下之憂而憂，後天下之樂而樂。　　a. 祖先 b. 在……之前 c. 早先

現代文翻译：_____

7. 微斯人，吾誰與歸?　　　　　　　a. 和 b. 順從(顺从) c.贊(赞)同

現代文翻译：_____

第三十七課

張岱《陶庵夢憶》選篇

Selections from *The Dream Recollections of Tao'an* (Zhang Dai)

Introduction

Zhang Dai 張岱 (courtesy name Zongzi 宗子; aka Tao'an 陶庵; 1597–1679), distinguished prose writer of the late Ming/early Qing, is best known for his short familiar essays 小品文 (*xiǎopǐn wén*), most of which are collected in *The Dream Recollections of Tao'an* and *Dream Seeking at West Lake* 西湖夢尋 (*Xīhú mèngxún* 西湖梦寻).

    Zhang completed *The Dream Recollections of Tao'an* shortly after the fall of the Ming dynasty in 1644, but the work did not appear in print until the fortieth year of Qianlong's reign in the Qing dynasty (1755), about seventy-five years after Zhang's death. It is largely composed of accounts of daily activities, random thoughts, and observations of the lives and customs of late Ming people.

    In "Night Theater on the Gold Mountain," the first of the two essays presented in this lesson, Zhang reminisces about his overnight stay at the famed Jinshan Temple 金山寺 in Zhenjiang in the second year of the reign of Ming Emperor Chongzhen (1629). There, to the astonishment of the temple monks, Zhang gave an impromptu performance of a play about Han Shizhong's 韓世忠 (1090–1151) fight against invading Jin troops. The other essay, "Viewing Snow from the Heart of the Lake Pavilion," recounts the author's joyful experience of watching snow from the Huxin Pavilion. Zhang's essays ingeniously blend narrative, scenery, memory, and feelings into a dreamlike artistic vision, often in just a few hundred characters.

正文與簡體譯文 Text and Modern Chinese Translation

《金山夜戲》[1]
jīn shān yè xì

崇禎二年中秋後一日，余道鎮江往
chóng zhēn èr nián zhōng qiū hòu yī rì　yú dào zhèn jiāng wǎng

兖，日晡，至北固，艤舟江口。[2]月光倒囊
yǎn　rì bū　zhì běi gù　yǐ zhōu jiāng kǒu　yuè guāng dào náng

入水，江濤吞吐，露氣吸之，噀天爲白。[3]
rù shuǐ　jiāng tāo tūn tǔ　lù qì xī zhī　xùn tiān wéi bái

崇祯二年中秋后一天，我取道镇江，前往兖州。这天下午申时，到了北固，我在江口停船靠岸。[2]月光像囊中的水倒入江中，江上波涛吞吐，雾气(弥漫)吸收着

余大驚喜。移舟過金山寺，已二鼓矣，經
yú dà jīng xǐ　yí zhōu guò jīn shān sì　yǐ èr gǔ yǐ　jīng

龍王堂，入大殿，皆漆靜。⁴林下漏月光，
lóng wáng táng rù dà diàn　jiē qī jìng　lín xià lòu yuè guāng

疏疏如殘雪。⁵余呼小僕攜戲具，盛張燈火
shū shū rú cán xuě　yú hū xiǎo pú xié xì jù shèng zhāng dēng huǒ

大殿中，唱韓蘄王金山及長江大戰諸劇，
dà diàn zhōng chàng hán qí wáng jīn shān jí cháng jiāng dà zhàn zhū jù

鑼鼓喧填，一寺人皆起看。⁶有老僧以ₐ手
luó gǔ xuān tián　yí sì rén jiē qǐ kàn　yǒu lǎo sēng yǐ shǒu

背搬眼臀，翕然張口，呵欠與笑嚏俱至，
bèi sà yǎn yì　xī rán zhāng kǒu　hē qiàn yǔ xiào tì jù zhì

徐定睛，視爲何許人，以ᵦ何事何時至，皆
xú dìng jīng　shì wéi hé xǔ rén　yǐ　hé shì hé shí zhì　jiē

不敢問。⁷劇完將曙，解纜過江，山僧至山
bù gǎn wèn　jù wán jiāng shǔ　jiě lǎn guò jiāng　shān sēng zhì shān

腳，目送久之，不知是人、是怪、是鬼。⁸
jiǎo　mù sòng jiǔ zhī　bù zhī shì rén　shì guài　shì guǐ

《陶庵夢憶》，上海：上海古籍出版社 (1982), 4.

月光，喷薄到天上，天都变白了。³我很惊喜。移动小船，开过金山寺，已是晚上二更了。经过龙王堂，进入到大殿，都是一片漆黑寂静。⁴树林漏下的月光，疏疏落落，像残留的雪一样。⁵我叫仆人拿着演戏的道具，在大殿中大张灯火，唱了韩蕲王在金山和长江大战(金兵)几出戏。锣鼓喧天，金山寺里的人都起来看。⁶有老和尚用手背来揉眼睛，突然张开嘴，呵欠和笑声、喷嚏一起来了。慢慢地认真一看，看看是什么地方的人，因为什么事情，什么时候到的，都不敢问。⁷戏演完了，天快亮了，(我们)解开缆绳，上船过江。山上的和尚(跟着)到了山脚，目送我们很久，不知道我们是人、是妖怪、还是鬼。⁸

1. 金山 Golden Mount, in the northwestern part of present-day Zhenjiang 鎮江, Jiangsu Province.
   戲 n. theater, play.
2. 崇禎 (祯) the reign title of the last emperor of the Ming dynasty. 崇禎二年 is 1629. See L32 note 21 for 明毅宗 or 崇禎.
   中秋 Middle Autumn, the fifteenth day of the eighth month in the lunar calendar.
   道 n. road. Here it is used as a verb, meaning "to take to the road" 取道 (qǔ dào).
   鎮 (镇) 江 place name in present-day Zhenjiang 鎮江, Jiangsu Province.
   兗 (兖) or 兗州 in present-day Yanzhou, Shandong Province.
   晡 or 申時 (时) n. a time word in ancient China, about 3PM–5 PM.
   北固 place name in the northeastern part of present-day Zhenjiang 鎮江, Jiangsu Province.
   艤 (舣) v. to moor (a boat), anchor. MdnC: 停靠 (tíng kào).
   江口 n. estuary of the Yangtze River.
3. 倒 (dào) v. to pour.
   囊 n. bag.
   濤 (涛) n. wave, billow. MdnC: 波濤 (bō tāo 波涛).

吞吐 *v.* to swallow and spit, huff and puff.

露 *n.* dew. Here 露氣 (气) refers to mist on the river 霧氣 (*wù qì* 雾气).

吸 *v.* to absorb.

噀 *v.* to spit, sprinkle, spurt. MdnC: 噴薄 (*pēn bó* 喷薄).

4. 大 *adv.* very. MdnC: 很 (*hěn*).

移 *v.* to move.

金山寺 Golden Mount Temple.

鼓 *n.* drum. Here it refers to a drum used for marking time. 二鼓 is about 9 PM–11 PM.

經 (经) *v.* to pass through. MdnC: 經過 (*jīng guò* 经过).

龍 (龙) 王堂 Hall of the Dragon King.

殿 *n.* hall.

漆 *adj.* pitch-dark. MdnC: 漆黑 (*qī hēi*).

5. 漏 *v.* to leak, seep.

疏 *adj.* sparse. MdnC: 疏落 (*shū luò*).

殘 (残) *adj.* remnant, lingering. MdnC: 殘留 (*cán liú* 残留).

6. 呼 *v.* to call. MdnC: 叫 (*jiào*).

僕 (仆) *n.* servants. MdnC: 僕人 (*pú rén* 仆人).

攜 (携) *v.* carry. MdnC: 拿着 (*ná zhe*).

具 *n.* props. MdnC: 道具 (*dào jù*).

盛 (shèng) *adv.* to a high degree.

張 (张) *v.* to set up.

韓蘄王 or 韓世忠 (family name 姓, Hán 韓; given name 名, Shìzhōng 世忠; style 字, Liángchén 良臣; posthumous name 諡, Zhōngwǔ 忠武; 1089–1151), a major general of the Song dynasty in the Jin-Song wars.

諸 (诸) *adj.* various, all.

劇 (剧) *n.* drama, theater. MdnC: 戲 (*xì* 戏).

鑼 (锣) *n.* gong.

喧 *v.* to din.

填 *v.* to fill. Here it is used in the sense of 天 (*tiān*), meaning "sky."

7. 僧 *n.* monk. MdnC: 和尚 (*hé shàng*).

以 ₐ *coverb.* to use. MdnC: 用 (*yòng*). See L2 Grammar Note 1 ②.

手背 *n.* back of the hands.

搽 (sà) *v.* to rub. MdnC: 揉 (*róu*).

瞖 (翳) *n.* scar left after corneal lesions. Here 眼瞖 refers to eyes.

翕然 *adv.* suddenly. MdnC: 突然 (*tū rán*).

呵欠 *n.* yawn.

嚏 *n.* sneeze. MdnC: 噴嚏 (*pēn tì* 喷嚏).

俱 *adj.* all together. See L24 Grammar Note 1 ②.

徐 *adv.* slowly. MdnC: 慢慢地 (*màn màn de*).

定 *v.* to concentrate, focus.

定睛 *v.* to take a closer look.

許 (许) *n.* place. MdnC: 地方 (*dì fāng*).

以 ᵦ *prep.* for the reason of. MdnC: 因為 (*yīn wèi* 因为). See L2 Grammar Note 1 ①.

8. 曙 *n.* dawn. MdnC: 天亮 (*tiān liàng*).
   解 *v.* to untie.
   纜 (缆) *n.* cable. MdnC: 纜繩 (*lǎn sheng* 缆绳).
   山脚 *n.* the foot of a mountain.
   送 *v.* to watch (someone) leave.

《湖心亭看雪》[9]
hú xīn tíng kàn xuě

崇禎五年十二月，余住西湖。大雪三
chóng zhēn wǔ nián shí èr yuè　yú zhù xī hú　dà xuě sān

日，湖中人鳥聲俱絕。[10]
rì　hú zhōng rén niǎo shēng jù jué

崇禎五年十二月，我住在西湖。连下了三天大雪，湖中的人声和鸟声都没了。[10]

9. 湖心亭 Lake Heart Pavilion.
10. 崇禎五年 the year 1632.
    西湖 West Lake, in present-day Hangzhou 杭州, Zhejiang Province.
    絕 (绝) *v.* to cut off. Here it means "to disappear."

是日更定矣，余挐一小舟，擁毳衣
shì rì gēng dìng yǐ　yú ná yī xiǎo zhōu　yōng cuì yī

爐火，獨往湖心亭看雪。[11] 霧淞沆碭，天
lú huǒ　dú wǎng hú xīn tíng kàn xuě　wù sōng hàng dàng tiān

與雲、與山、與水，上下一白。[12] 湖上影
yǔ yún　yǔ shān　yǔ shuǐ　shàng xià yì bái　hú shàng yǐng

子，惟長堤一痕，湖心亭一點，與余舟一
zi　wéi cháng dī yì hén　hú xīn tíng yì diǎn　yǔ yú zhōu yí

芥，舟中人兩三粒而已。[13]
jiè　zhōu zhōng rén liǎng sān lì ér yǐ

这一天定更时，我划着一个小船，穿着皮毛做的衣服，带着炉火，独自前往湖心亭看雪。[11]雾淞白茫茫的一片，天和云、和山、和水、上上下下，全都是白色的。[12]湖上的影子，只有长堤的一抹痕迹，湖心亭的一点，和我的一叶小船，（以及）船上的两三个人罢了。[13]

11. 是 *demonstrative pron.* this. MdnC: 這 (*zhè* 这). See L3 Grammar Note 1 ①.
    更定 or 定更 The first time the drum is beaten to mark the time, about 8PM.
    挐 (拿) *v.* to pull out.
    擁 (拥) *v.* to embrace, hug. Here it means "to wear" 穿 (*chuān*).
    毳 *n.* hair of animals.
    毳衣 *n.* clothes made of fur.
    爐 (炉) 火 *n.* fire, ingle.
    獨 (独) *adv.* alone. MdnC: 獨自 (*dú zì* 独自).
12. 霧 (雾) 淞 *n.* rime ice.

沆碭 (砀) *adj.* a vast expanse of whiteness. MdnC: 白茫茫 (*bái máng máng*).

一 *adv.* all, completely. MdnC: 全 (*quán*).

13. 惟 *adv.* only. MdnC: 只有 (*zhǐ yǒu*). See L22 Grammar Note 2 ②.

堤 *n.* causeway, dike.

痕 *n.* trace, mark. MdnC: 痕跡 (*hén jì* 痕迹).

芥 *n.* grass.

粒 *measure word.* grain, small particle. Here it refers to how small human beings appear in the landscape.

到亭上，有兩人鋪氈對坐，一童子燒
dào tíng shàng yǒu liǎng rén pū zhān duì zuò　yì tóng zǐ shāo

酒爐正沸。¹⁴ 見余大喜，曰：「湖中焉得
jiǔ lú zhèng fèi　jiàn yú dà xǐ　yuē　hú zhōng yān dé

更有此人！」拉余同飲。¹⁵ 余強飲三大白
gèng yǒu cǐ rén　　lā yú tóng yǐn　yú qiǎng yǐn sān dà bái

而別。問其姓氏，是金陵人，客此。¹⁶
ér bié　wèn qí xìng shì　shì jīn líng rén　kè cǐ

到了亭子上，有两个人铺着毛毡面对面坐着，一个童子正在温酒，炉子正好滚沸。¹⁴（两人）看到我非常高兴，说："湖中怎么还会有您这样的人啊！"拉着我一同饮酒。¹⁵ 我尽力喝了三杯，然后和他们告别。问他们的姓氏，是金陵人士，客居在此。¹⁶

14. 鋪 (铺) *v.* to spread, unfold.

氈 (毡) *n.* felt. MdnC: 毛氈 (*máo zhān* 毛毡).

對 (对) *adv.* face to face.

童子 *n.* kid, child.

燒 (烧) 酒 *v.* to warm the wine.

沸 *v.* to boil. MdnC: 滚沸 (*gǔn fèi*).

15. 焉 *interrogative particle.* how? MdnC: 怎麽 (*zěn me* 怎么). See L2 Grammar Note 3 ③.

拉 *v.* to pull, drag.

飲 (饮) *v.* to drink (wine).

16. 強 (强 *qiǎng*) *v.* to push oneself, try one's best. MdnC: 盡力 (*jìn lì* 尽力).

大白 *n.* wine goblet.

金陵 place name in present-day Nanjing 南京, Jiangsu Province.

客 *n.* guest. Here it is used as a verb, meaning "to stay temporarily" 客居 (*kè jū*).

及下船，舟子喃喃曰：「莫説相公癡，
jí xià chuán zhōu zǐ nán nán yuē　mò shuō xiàng gōng chī

更有癡似相公者。」¹⁷
gèng yǒu chī sì xiàng gōng zhě

等到下了船，船夫小声嘀咕说："不要说相公您痴，还有和您一样痴的人！"¹⁷

《陶庵夢憶》，上海：上海古籍出版社 (1982), 28–29.

17. 舟子 *n.* boatman. MdnC: 船夫 (*chuán fū*).

喃喃 *v.* to whisper, mutter. MdnC: 嘀咕 (*dí gu*).

莫 *adv.* do not. MdnC: 不要 (*bú yào*). See Grammar Note 1 ②.

相公 *n.* an honorific title of literati.

癡 (痴) *v.* to be obsessed, crazy.

更 *adv.* still. MdnC: 還 (*hái* 还).

語法注釋 Grammar Note

1. 莫 Two uses of 莫 are explained in this book. In addition to the use below, see 莫① in L3 Grammar Note 2.

   ② *adv.* do not. MdnC: 不要 (*bú yào*).

   莫説相公癡，更有癡似相公者。

   [不要说相公您痴，还有像相公您一样痴的人啊！]

Literary Analysis

Zhang Dai's prose writings are exempla of the so-called lesser-grade prose. Originally a Buddhist word meaning "an abbreviated version" of a sutra, *lesser-grade* 小品 (*xiǎopǐn*) later evolved into a general term for short prose writings. In recent literary scholarship, however, it tends to refer to a Ming-Qing offshoot of occasional prose pioneered by the three Yuan brothers of the mid-Ming and perfected by Zhang Dai. Like Tang-Song prose masters, Zhang deploys words in the ancient style and avoids any kind of textual patterning. But unlike them, he does not search for grand moral or philosophical significance when viewing landscapes and human events (see lessons 31 and 32); instead, he finds joy in daily activities of no particular significance. His accounts of a nightly play performance and snow watching, featured in this lesson, are good cases in point.

Given this, it seems better to take the label *lesser-grade*, when applied to the prose of Zhang and other like-minded writers, as a reference to the pettiness of the subject matter. Zhang, however, more than makes up for this lack of thematic grandeur with his virtuosity in turning common occurrences into pleasurable objects of aesthetic perception and appreciation. Consider how he transmutes an ordinary temple visit into an unforgettable feast of the senses, culminating in a dream-like illusion. How rapidly and skillfully does he change the objects and angles of observation to create this amazing aesthetic effect? Consider also how he gives us a slow-motion, Monet-like visual treat in the second excerpt. How does he use the technique of size contrast to give a sense of dreamy unboundedness? Why does he insert conversations into this description: To make the quiet more keenly felt? To set off his supreme aesthetic sensibility? Or both and more?

☞ *HTRCProse*, chapter 16, "Ming and Qing Occasional Prose: Accounts of Places and People."

—ZC

課後練習 Exercises

一 給加點字注音 Give the pinyin romanization for each dotted word.

1. 奐 (____) 2. 晡 (____) 3. 崇禎 (____, ____) 4. 韓蘄王 (____, ____) 5. 嚏 (____)
6. 纜 (____) 7. 拏 (____) 8. 毳 (____) 9. 沈碭 (____, ____) 10. 氈 (____)

二 在括號中給句中加點的字注音，並選出正確的釋義 Give the pinyin romanization for each dotted word; then select the correct definition from the following list, and write it in the blank.

天亮　揉　停靠　毛氈(毡)　噴薄(喷薄)　盡(尽)力　**信服**　漆黑

1. **小信未孚（fú）　信服**　2. 艤舟江口（　）_____　3. 噀天爲白（　）_____
4. 皆漆靜　（　）_____　5. 掭眼瞖　（　）_____　6. 劇完將曙（　）_____
7. 鋪氈對坐（　）_____　8. 余強飲三大白二而別　（　）_____

三 選擇釋義並填空 Match each word in the left column with its correct definition in the middle column. Fill in each blank in the right column with an appropriate word from the left column (some words may be used more than once).

謀謀劃（谋划）　慢慢地
道_____　痕跡(迹)
疏_____　道具
殘_____　客居
攜_____　取道
具_____　嘀咕
徐_____　**謀劃（谋划）**
許_____　疏落
痕_____　地方
客_____　殘(残)留
喃_____　拿着

崇禎二年中秋後一日，余____鎮江往奐。

林下漏月光，____ ____如____雪。

余呼小僕____戲____，盛張燈火大殿中。

____定睛，視爲何____人，以何事何時至，皆不敢問。

湖上影子，惟長堤一____，湖心亭一點，與余舟一芥，舟中人兩三粒而已。

問其姓氏，是金陵人，____此。

及下舟，舟子____ ____曰："莫説相公癡，更有癡似相公者。"

四 請用給出的字填空 Fill in each blank with an appropriate word from the following list.

惟　而已　然　焉　之　何　以　爲(为)

1. 月光倒囊入水，江濤吞吐，露氣吸____，噀天____白。
2. 有老僧____手背掭眼瞖，翕____張口，呵欠與笑嚏俱至，徐定睛，視____ ____許人，以____事____時至，皆不敢問。
3. 見余大喜，曰："湖中____得更有此人！"
4. 湖上影子，____長堤一痕，湖心亭一點，與余舟一芥，舟中人兩三粒____ ____。

五 爲加點字選擇正確釋義，並根據釋義來翻譯句子 Match each dotted word with its correct modern Chinese equivalent by circling the latter. Then translate each sentence into modern Chinese.

1. 又何間焉?   ⓐ爲什麼(为什么) b.憑什麼(凭什么) c.多少

現代文翻译：你又为什么要参与到这件事情里面？

_____

2. 已二鼓矣，經龍王堂，入大殿，皆漆靜分。   a.已經(经) b.既然 c.罷(罢)

現代文翻译：_____

3. 徐定睛，視爲何許人，以何事何時至，皆不敢問。   a.因爲(为) b.用 c.來(来)

現代文翻译：_____

4. 是日更定矣，余拏一小舟，擁毳衣爐火，獨往湖心亭看雪。   a.這(这) b.是的 c.對(对)

現代文翻译：_____

5. 湖上影子，惟長堤一痕，湖心亭一點，與余舟一芥，舟中人兩三粒而已。

                                 a.已經(经) b.既然 c.罷(罢)了

現代文翻译：_____

6. 見余大喜，曰："湖中焉得更有此人！"   a.怎麼(么) b.啊 c.在此

現代文翻译：_____

第三十八課

薛福成《觀巴黎油畫記》

"The Record of a Visit to an Oil Painting Exhibition in Paris"
(Xue Fucheng)

Introduction

The late Qing diplomat Xue Fucheng 薛福成 (1838–1894) wrote "The Record of a Visit to an Oil Painting Exhibition in Paris" during a trip to France. In addition to serving as China's ambassador to four European countries (the United Kingdom, France, Italy, and Belgium) from 1889 to 1893, Xue was an ardent supporter of the Self-Strengthening Movement and an advocate for the development of domestic industry.

In this essay, Xue recounts his visit to the Wax Museum of Paris (*Musée Grévin*) and a gallery of oil paintings. He provides a detailed description of the famous *The Battle Between Prussia and France*, highlighting its technical virtuosity, artistic charm, and thematic significance as well as its profound aesthetic impact. A translation of this text is given in *HTRCProse*, chapter 16, "Ming and Qing Occasional Prose: Accounts of Places and People," C16.6.

正文與簡體譯文 Text and Modern Chinese Translation

光緒十六年春閏二月甲子，余遊巴黎蠟
guāng xù shí liù nián chūn rùn èr yuè jiǎ zǐ　yú yóu bā lí là

人館。[1] 見所製蠟人，悉仿生人，形體態度，
rén guǎn　jiàn suǒ zhì là rén　xī fǎng shēng rén　xíng tǐ tài dù

髮膚顏色，長短豐瘠，無不畢肖。[2] 自王公
fà fū yán sè　cháng duǎn fēng jí　wú bú bì xiào　zì wáng gōng

卿相以至工藝雜流，凡有名者，往往留像於
qīng xiàng yǐ zhì gōng yì zá liú　fán yǒu míng zhě wǎng wǎng liú xiàng yú

館，或立或臥，或坐或俯，或笑或哭，或飲
guǎn　huò lì huò wò　huò zuò huò fǔ　huò xiào huò kū　huò yǐn

或博，驟視之，無不驚爲生人者。[3] 余亟歎其
huò bó　zhòu shì zhī　wú bù jīng wéi shēng rén zhě　yú qì tàn qí

光绪十六年春，闰二月甲子这一天，我游览了巴黎蜡人馆。[1] 看到所制作的蜡人，全都仿照真人，形体神态、头发和皮肤的颜色，高矮胖瘦，没有不相似的。[2] 从王公大臣到手工艺人，各行各业，凡是有名气的人，往往都在馆中留有蜡像，有的站着，有的躺着，有的坐着，有的弯着腰，有的笑着，有的哭着，有的喝着酒，有的在

技之奇妙。⁴ 譯者稱：「西人絕技，尤莫逾
jì zhī qí miào　　 yì zhě chēng　　　 xī rén jué jì　　　 yóu mò yú

油畫，盍馳往油畫院，一觀普法交戰圖
yóu huà　　 hé chí wǎng yóu huà yuàn　 yì guān pǔ fǎ jiāo zhàn tú

乎？」⁵
hū

博弈游戏，猛然一看，无不惊叹他们像真人一样！³ 我多次赞叹这技艺奇妙。⁴ 翻译说："西方人的绝技，尤其没人能超越（的是）油画，（您）何不立刻去油画院，看一下普鲁士与法国交战的油画呢？"⁵

1. 光緒 (绪) the reign title of the ninth emperor of the Qing dynasty 清德宗 (r. 1875–1908). 光緒十六年 is 1890.

　閏 (闰) 二月 the leap second month. A leap month is added to the Chinese lunar calendar about every two to three years.

　遊 (游) v. to visit. MdnC: 遊覽 (yóu lǎn 游览).

　巴黎 Paris, France.

　蠟 (蜡) 人 n. wax figures.

　館 (馆) n. museum.

2. 製 (制) v. make. MdnC: 製作 (zhì zuò 制作).

　悉 adv. all. MdnC: 都 (dōu). See L24 Grammar Note 1 ④.

　仿 v. to imitate. MdnC: 仿照 (fǎng zhào).

　生人 n. real people. MdnC: 真人 (zhēn rén).

　形體 (体) n. body shape.

　態 (态) 度 n. demeanor. MdnC: 神態 (shén tài 神态).

　髮 (发 fà) n. hair. MdnC: 頭髮 (tóu fà 头发).

　膚 (肤) n. skin. MdnC: 皮膚 (pí fū 皮肤).

　長 (长) 短 adj. long and short. Here it means "tall and short" 高矮 (gāo ǎi).

　豐 (丰) adj. plump, fat. MdnC: 胖 (pàng).

　瘠 adj. slim, thin. MdnC: 瘦 (shòu).

　畢 (毕) adv. completely. MdnC: 全 (quán).

　肖 (xiào) adj. (looking) alike. MdnC: 相似 (xiāng sì).

3. 王公 n. princes and dukes. It generally refers to the nobility.

　卿相 n. ministers or high officials. MdnC: 大臣 (dà chén).

　以至 prep. up to. MdnC: 直到 (zhí dào).

　工藝 (艺) n. craft. Here it refers to craftsmen 手工藝人 (shǒu gōng yì rén 手工艺人).

　雜 (杂) 流 n. miscellaneous walks of life. MdnC: 各行各業 (gè háng gè yè 各行各业).

　凡 adv. in general, overall. MdnC: 凡是 (fán shì). See L10 Grammar Note 4.

　名 n. reputation. MdnC: 名氣 (míng qì 名气).

　像 n. wax figure. MdnC: 蠟像 (là xiàng 蜡像).

　或 indefinite pron. someone. MdnC: 有的人 (yǒu de rén). See L6 Grammar Note 4 ①.

　臥 v. to lie down. MdnC: 躺 (tǎng).

　俯 v. to bow, stoop. MdnC: 彎腰 (wān yāo 弯腰).

博 *v.* to play a game, gamble. MdnC: 博弈 (*bó yì*).

驟 (骤) *adv.* suddenly. MdnC: 猛然 (*měng rán*).

驚 (惊) *v.* to be surprised, be amazed. MdnC: 驚嘆 (*jīng tàn* 惊叹).

4. 亟 (亟) *adv.* repeatedly, again and again. MdnC: 多次 (*duō cì*).

嘆 (叹) *v.* to marvel at, praise. MdnC: 贊嘆 (*zàn tàn* 赞叹).

技 *n.* skill, artistry. MdnC: 技藝 (*jì yì* 技艺).

5. 譯 (译) 者 *n.* translator. MdnC: 翻譯 (*fān yì* 翻译).

稱 (称 chēng) *v.* to say. MdnC: 説 (*shuō* 说).

絕 (绝) 技 *n.* consummate skill.

尤 *adv.* especially, particularly. MdnC: 尤其 (*yóu qí*).

莫 *indefinite pron.* no one. MdnC: 没有人 (*méi yǒu rén*). See L3 Grammar Note 2 ①.

逾 *v.* to exceed. MdnC: 超越 (*chāo yuè*).

盍 *initial interrogative particle.* why not? MdnC: 何不 (*hé bù*). See L13 Grammar Note 3.

馳 (驰) *v.* go quickly.

普 or 普魯士 Prussia.

法 or 法國 France.

其法爲一大圓室，以巨幅懸之四壁，由
qí fǎ wéi yí dà yuán shì　　yǐ jù fú xuán zhī sì bì　　yóu

屋頂放光明入室。⁶人在室中，極目四望，則
wū dǐng fàng guāng míng rù shì rén zài shì zhōng　jí mù sì wàng　zé

見城堡、岡巒、溪澗、樹林，森然布列。⁷兩
jiàn chéng bǎo gāng luán　xī jiàn　shù lín　sēn rán bù liè　liǎng

軍人馬雜遝，馳者、伏者、奔者、追者、開
jūn rén mǎ zá tà　chí zhě　fú zhě　bēn zhě　zhuī zhě　kāi

槍者、燃礮者、搴大旗者、挽礮車者，絡繹
qiāng zhě　rán pào zhě　qiān dà qí zhě　wǎn pào chē zhě　luò yì

相屬。⁸每一巨彈墮地，則火光迸裂，煙燄迷
xiāng zhǔ　měi yí jù dàn duò dì　zé huǒ guāng bèng liè　yān yàn mí

漫，其被轟擊者，則斷壁危樓，或黔其廬，
màn　qí bèi hōng jī zhě　zé duàn bì wēi lóu　huò qián qí lú

或赭其垣。⁹而軍士之折臂斷足，血流殷地，
huò zhě qí yuán　ér jūn shì zhī zhé bì duàn zú　xuè liú yān dì

偃仰僵仆者，令人目不忍覩。¹⁰仰視天，則
yǎn yǎng jiāng pū zhě　lìng rén mù bù rěn dǔ　yǎng shì tiān　zé

明月斜挂，雲霞掩映；俯視地，則綠草如
míng yuè xié guà　yún xiá yǎn yìng　fǔ shì dì　zé lǜ cǎo rú

它的展出方式是在一大的圓形房間里，巨大的畫幅懸挂在四面墙上，從房間的頂部放進陽光。⁶人在展室的中間，放眼望去，就看到城堡、山岡、溪流、树林，密集分布排列着。⁷两支军队的人马纷乱拥挤，骑马奔驰的人、伏在地上的人、逃跑的人、追击的人、开枪的人、点燃火炮的人、拔取大旗的人、拉炮车的人，络绎不绝，相互连接(在一起)。⁸每一个巨大的炮弹落在地上，火光四射，烟雾火焰四处弥漫。被炮弹轰击的地方，(就剩下)断掉的墙壁和破损的楼房，或熏黑了房子，或烧红了墙壁。⁹而士兵手臂断了，脚断了，血流染

茵，川原無際。¹¹ 幾自疑身外卽戰場，而忘
yīn　　chuān yuán wú jì　　jī zì yí shēn wài jí zhàn chǎng　ér wàng

其在一室中者。迨以手捫之，始知其爲壁
qí　zài yí shì zhōng zhě　dài yǐ shǒu mén zhī　　shǐ zhī qí wéi bì

也，畫也，皆幻也。¹²
yě　　huà yě　　jiē huàn yě

红了地面。躺在地上的和倒在地上的(死伤)士兵，让人不忍心看。¹⁰抬头望，明月斜挂在天上，彩云映衬着；低头看，绿色的草地就像(铺在地上的)毯子一样，原野(广阔)没有边际。¹¹几乎怀疑自己之外就是战场，而忘记了是在一个房间中。等到用手触摸它，才知这是墙壁，是油画，(刚才所见的)都是虚幻。¹²

6. 法 *n.* way. Here it refers to the type of exhibition 展出方式 (*zhǎn chū fāng shì*).

圜 (圆) (*yuán*) *n.* circle. MdnC: 圓形 (*yuán xíng* 圆形).

幅 *n.* width of cloth or paper. Here it refers to the oil painting. MdnC: 畫幅 (*huà fú* 画幅).

懸 (悬) *v.* to hang up. MdnC: 懸挂 (*xuán guà* 悬挂).

7. 極 (极) 目 *v.* to look as far as one can.

城堡 *n.* castle.

岡巒 (冈峦) *n.* hills, mountains. MdnC: 山岡 (*shān gang* 山冈).

閒 (间) *n.* used in the sense of 澗 (*jiàn* 涧), meaning "creek."

森然 *adj.* dense. MdnC: 密集 (*mì jì*).

布 *v.* to distribute. MdnC: 分布 (*fēn bù*).

列 *v.* to put in order, arrange. MdnC: 排列 (*pái liè*).

8. 人馬 (马) *n.* forces, troop.

雜 (杂) 遝 *adj.* numerous and messy, massive and chaotic. MdnC: 紛亂 (*fēn luàn* 纷乱).

馳 (驰) *v.* to gallop. MdnC: 奔馳 (*bēn chí* 奔驰).

者 *auxiliary pron.* the ones who…. MdnC: ……的人 (*de rén*). See L1 Grammar Note 1 ①.

伏 *v.* to lie prostrate.

奔 *v.* to run, flee. MdnC: 逃跑 (*táo pǎo*).

追 *v.* to chase. MdnC: 追擊 (*zhuī jī* 追击).

燃 *v.* to light (fire). MdnC: 點燃 (*diǎn rán* 点燃).

礮 (炮) *n.* cannon.

搴 *v.* to seize. MdnC: 拔取 (*bá qǔ*).

挽 *v.* to pull, drag. MdnC: 拉 (*lā*).

礮車 (炮车) *n.* cannon cart.

絡繹 (络绎) *adj.* endless, in an endless stream.

屬 (属 zhǔ) *v.* to connect. MdnC: 連接 (*lián jiē* 连接).

9. 彈 (弹 dàn) *n.* shell. MdnC: 炮彈 (*pào dàn* 炮弹).

墮 (堕) *v.* to fall. MdnC: 落 (*luò*).

迸裂 *v.* to burst, split.

煙 (烟) *n.* smoke.

燄 (焰) *n.* flame. MdnC: 火燄 (*huǒ yàn* 火焰).

迷漫 or 彌 (弥) 漫 *v.* to fill (the air).

轟擊 (轰击) *v.* to bomb, bombard.

者 *auxiliary pron.* the place where…. MdnC: ……的地方 (*de dì fāng*). See L1 Grammar Note 1 ①.

斷 (断) *adj.* broken.

危 *adj.* dangerous, broken. MdnC: 破損 (*pò sǔn* 破损).

黔 *n.* black. Here it is used as a causative verb, 使……黔, meaning "to blacken" 熏黑 (*xūn hēi*). See L7 Grammar Note 1 ③.

盧 (庐) *n.* house. MdnC: 房子 (*fáng zi*).

赭 *n.* reddish brown. Here it is used as a causative verb, 使……赭, meaning "to burn into red" 燒紅 (*shāo hóng* 烧红). See L7 Grammar Note 1 ③.

垣 *n.* low wall. MdnC: 墙 (*qiáng* 墙).

10. 殷 (*yān*) *n.* reddish black. Here it is used as a causative verb, 使……殷, meaning "to dye … red" 染紅 (*rǎn hóng*). See L7 Grammar Note 1 ③.

偃仰 *v.* to lie down with one's face upward.

僵 *v.* to fall.

仆 (*pū*) *v.* to fall forward.

覩 (睹) *v.* to look at, watch. MdnC: 看 (*kàn*).

11. 仰 *v.* to look up. MdnC: 擡頭 (*tái tóu* 抬头).

霞 *n.* pink clouds. MdnC: 彩雲 (*cǎi yún* 彩云).

掩映 *v.* to set something off. MdnC: 映襯 (*yìng chèn* 映衬).

俯 *v.* to bow down. MdnC: 低頭 (*dī tóu* 低头).

茵 *n.* pad, seat pad. MdnC: 毯子 (*tǎn zi*).

川原 *n.* rivers and plains. Here it refers to flatlands. MdnC: 原野 (*yuán yě*).

際 (际) *n.* border. MdnC: 邊際 (*biān jì* 边际).

12. 幾 (几 *jǐ*) *adv.* almost. MdnC: 幾乎 (*jī hū* 几乎).

疑 *v.* to doubt. MdnC: 懷疑 (*huái yí* 怀疑).

迨 *conj.* until. MdnC: 等到 (*děng dào*).

以 *coverb.* to use. MdnC: 用 (*yòng*). See L2 Grammar Note 1 ②.

捫 (扪) *v.* to touch. MdnC: 觸摸 (*chù mō* 触摸).

始 *adv.* only then. MdnC: 才 (*cái*).

幻 *n.* illusion, imagination. MdnC: 虛幻 (*xū huàn*).

「余聞法人好勝，何以自繪敗狀，令人
yú wén fǎ rén hào shèng　hé yǐ　zì huì bài zhuàng lìng rén

喪氣若此？」[13] 譯者曰：「所以昭炯戒，激
sàng qì ruò cǐ　　yì zhě yuē　　suǒ yǐ zhāo jiǒng jiè　jī

衆憤，圖報復也。」則其意深長矣。[14]
zhòng fèn　tú bào fù yě　　zé qí yì shēn cháng yǐ

"我听说法国人好胜，为什么画自己失败的情景，让人看了如此丧气？"[13] 翻译说："这是为了昭示警示，激发民众的义愤，图谋报复。"那真是意义深远啊！[14]

13. 好勝 (胜) *adj.* eager to win, aggressive.

何以 how come? MdnC: 爲什麼 (*wèi shén me* 为什么). See L1 Grammar Note 3 ③.

繪 (绘) *v.* to paint. MdnC: 畫 (*huà* 画).

狀 (状) *n.* appearance. MdnC: 情景 (*qíng jǐng*).

喪氣 (丧气) *adj.* to feel disheartened.

14. 昭 (zhāo) *v.* to show. MdnC: 昭示 (*zhāo shì*).

炯 *adj.* bright, clear. MdnC: 明顯 (*míng xiǎn* 明显).

戒 *n.* warning, lesson. MdnC: 警示 (*jǐng shì*).

激 *v.* to stimulate, arouse. MdnC: 激發 (*jī fā* 激发).

眾 (众) *n.* people. MdnC: 民眾 (*mín zhòng* 民众).

憤 (愤) *n.* indignation. MdnC: 義憤 (*yì fèn* 义愤).

圖 (图) *v.* to plan, intend to. MdnC: 圖謀 (*tú móu* 图谋).

夫普法之戰，迄今雖爲陳迹，而其事信
fú pǔ fǎ zhī zhàn　　qì jīn suī wèi chén jì　　ér qí shì xìn

而有徵。¹⁵然則此畫果真邪？幻邪？幻者而同
ér yǒu zhēng　　rán zé cǐ huà guǒ zhēn yé　　huàn yé　　huàn zhě ér tóng

於真邪？真者而託於幻邪？¹⁶斯二者，蓋皆有
yú zhēn yé　　zhēn zhě ér tuō yú huàn yé　　sī èr zhě　　gài jiē yǒu

之。¹⁷
zhī

普法战争，到现在虽然已经成为陈迹，但这一事件是真实(发生过的)有证明的。¹⁵既然如此，那么这幅画果然是真的吗？还是虚构的？是虚构的油画符合真实的历史，还是真实的历史依托于虚构的油画(来展现)？¹⁶这两方面，可能都有吧！¹⁷

《庸庵文外編》卷四，影印本《庸庵全集（一）》，臺北：華文書局 (1971), 289.

15. 迄 *prep.* till. MdnC: 到 (*dào*).

信 *adj.* true. MdnC: 真實 (*zhēn shí* 真实).

徵 (征) *n.* evidence, proof. MdnC: 證明 (*zhèng míng* 证明).

16. 同 *v.* to be the same. MdnC: 符合 (*fú hé*).

託 (托) *v.* to rely on. MdnC: 依託 (*yī tuō*).

17. 蓋 *adv.* probably. MdnC: 可能 (*kě néng*). See L13 Grammar Note 1.

Literary Analysis

In this composition, Xue Fucheng writes about his impressions of Western mimetic art in two different media and modes. The wax figures astonish him with a verisimilitude that tricks him into fancying a face-to-face encounter with those historical personages. But this impression of static plastic art proves only a foretaste of what's to come. When seeing the oil painting *The Battle Between Prussia and France*, Xue is spellbound by a panoramic, dynamic battle scene, with all its gory sights and deafening cries. The mimetic power of this masterpiece is so mesmerizing that he feels himself beguiled into the picture as if on the battlefield himself. Interestingly, Xue's account seems to accomplish a comparable feat—to enthrall readers through the medium of words.

Xue's descriptive composition employs aggregative patterning, as he consistently and cumulatively organizes metrical binomes into four-character sentences. This gives the composition an elegant, slightly archaic feel. See *HTRCProse*, chapter 1, "An Anatomy of the Chinese Prose Form: An Overview," C1.5, for further comments on aggregative patterning.

—ZC

課後練習　Exercises

一　給加點字注音　Give the pinyin romanization for each dotted word.

1. 蠟　(＿＿＿)　2. 卿相　(＿＿＿)　3. 雜遝　(＿＿＿)　4. 髮膚　(＿＿＿, ＿＿＿)　5. 偃仰　(＿＿＿, ＿＿＿)

6. 礮　(＿＿＿)　7. 煙燄　(＿＿＿)　8. 奔者　(＿＿＿)　9. 絡繹　(＿＿＿, ＿＿＿)　10. 僵仆　(＿＿＿, ＿＿＿)

二　在括號中給句中加點的字注音，並選出正確的釋義　Give the pinyin romanization for each dotted word; then select the correct definition from the following list, and write it in the blank.

拔取　　使…變(变)紅　　觸(触)摸　　連(连)接
猛然　　證(证)明　　瘦　　昭示　　**信服**　　相似　　多次

1. 小信未孚　(**fú**)　**信服**　2. 長短丰瘠　(　)　＿＿＿＿＿＿　3. 無不畢肖　(　)　＿＿＿＿＿＿

4. 驟視之　(　)　＿＿＿＿＿　5. 余亟嘆其技　(　)　＿＿＿＿＿　6. 搴大旗者　(　)　＿＿＿＿＿

7. 絡繹相屬　(　)　＿＿＿＿＿　8. 或赭其垣　(　)　＿＿＿＿＿　9. 血流殷地　(　)　＿＿＿＿＿

10. 以手捫地　(　)　11. 昭炯戒　(　)　＿＿＿＿＿　12. 信而有徵　(　)　＿＿＿＿＿

三　選擇釋義並填空　Match each word in the left column with its correct definition in the middle column. Fill in each blank in the right column with an appropriate word from the left column.

謀謀劃(谋划)	落	見所製蠟人，悉＿＿＿生人。
仿＿＿＿＿＿	明顯(显)	譯者稱：「西人絕技，尤莫＿＿＿油畫。」
逾＿＿＿＿＿	懷(怀)疑	其法爲一大圓室，以巨幅＿＿＿之四壁。
懸＿＿＿＿＿	**謀劃(谋划)**	偃仰僵仆者，令人目不忍＿＿＿。
墮＿＿＿＿＿	符合	每一巨彈＿＿＿地，則火光迸裂，煙燄迷漫，其被轟擊
危＿＿＿＿＿	警示	者，則斷壁＿＿＿樓，或黔其廬，或赭其垣。
覿＿＿＿＿＿	依托	幾自＿＿＿身外卽戰場，而忘其在一室中者。＿＿＿以手
疑＿＿＿＿＿	等到	捫之，始知其爲壁也，畫也，皆幻也。
迨＿＿＿＿＿	懸(悬)挂	余聞法人好勝，何以自＿＿＿敗狀，令人喪氣若此？
繪＿＿＿＿＿	看	所以昭＿＿＿＿＿，激衆憤，圖報復也。
炯＿＿＿＿＿	破損(损)	幻者而＿＿＿於真邪？真者而＿＿＿於幻邪？
戒＿＿＿＿＿	仿照	
同＿＿＿＿＿	超越	
託＿＿＿＿＿	畫(画)	

四 請用給出的字填空 Fill in each blank with an appropriate word from the following list (some words may be used more than once).

凡　或　邪　則(则)　爲(为)　者

1. 自王公卿相以至工藝雜流，＿＿有名＿＿，往往留像於館，＿＿立＿＿臥，＿＿坐＿＿俯，＿＿笑＿＿哭，＿＿飲＿＿博，驟視之，無不驚＿＿生人＿＿。

2. 然＿＿此畫果真＿＿？幻＿＿？幻＿＿而同於真＿＿？真＿＿而託於幻＿＿？

五 爲加點字選擇正確釋義，並根據釋義來翻譯句子 Match each dotted word with its correct modern Chinese equivalent by circling the latter. Then translate each sentence into modern Chinese.

1. 又何間焉?　　　　　　ⓐ 爲什麼(为什么) b.憑什麼(凭什么) c.多少

現代文翻译：你又为什么要参与到这件事情里面？

＿＿＿＿＿＿＿＿＿＿＿＿＿＿＿＿＿＿＿＿＿＿

2. 見所製蠟人，悉仿生人。形體態度，髮膚顏色，長短豐瘠，無不畢肖。　a.休息 b.都 c.知道

現代文翻译：＿＿＿＿＿＿＿＿＿＿＿＿＿＿＿＿＿＿＿＿

3. 譯者稱："西人絕技，尤莫逾油畫，盍馳往油畫院，一觀普法交戰圖乎?"　a.大概 b.可能 c.何不

現代文翻译：＿＿＿＿＿＿＿＿＿＿＿＿＿＿＿＿＿＿＿＿

4. 每一巨彈墮地，則火光迸裂，煙燄迷漫，其被轟擊者，則斷壁危樓，或黔其廬，或赭其垣。　a.使……變(变)黑 b.貴(贵)州 c.黑色

現代文翻译：＿＿＿＿＿＿＿＿＿＿＿＿＿＿＿＿＿＿＿＿

5. "余聞法人好勝，何以自繪敗狀，令人喪氣若此?"　a.使 b.命令 c.下令

現代文翻译：＿＿＿＿＿＿＿＿＿＿＿＿＿＿＿＿＿＿＿＿

6. 然則此畫果真邪? 幻邪? 幻者而同於真邪? 真者而託於幻邪?　a.而且 b.但是 c.既然如此……那麼(么)

現代文翻译：＿＿＿＿＿＿＿＿＿＿＿＿＿＿＿＿＿＿＿＿

單元練習

Unit Exercises

一、辨析加點字在不同句中注音和釋義的異同 Give the pinyin romanization for each dotted word and then write in its correct definition.

1. 鄙　肉食者鄙，未能遠謀。　　　　（ bǐ ）目光短淺
　　　越國以鄙遠，君知其難也。　　　（　）＿＿＿＿＿

2. 數　其疏數偃仰，類智者所施設也。　（　）＿＿＿＿＿
　　　忽逢桃花林，數百步中無雜樹。　（　）＿＿＿＿＿

3. 屬　屬予作文以記之。　　　　　　　（　）＿＿＿＿＿
　　　絡繹相屬。　　　　　　　　　　（　）＿＿＿＿＿

4. 強　余強飲三大白而別。　　　　　　（　）＿＿＿＿＿
　　　少年強則國強。　　　　　　　　（　）＿＿＿＿＿

5. 殷　血流殷地。　　　　　　　　　　（　）＿＿＿＿＿
　　　武王已平殷亂。　　　　　　　　（　）＿＿＿＿＿

6. 勝　予觀夫巴陵勝狀，在洞庭一湖。　（　）＿＿＿＿＿
　　　余聞法人好勝。　　　　　　　　（　）＿＿＿＿＿

7. 更　更千百年不得一售其伎。　　　　（　）＿＿＿＿＿
　　　更有痴似相公者。　　　　　　　（　）＿＿＿＿＿

8. 逾　逾黃茅嶺而下。　　　　　　　　（　）＿＿＿＿＿
　　　西人絕技，尤莫逾油畫。　　　　（　）＿＿＿＿＿

二、用給出的字填空，並選擇正確的釋義 Fill in the blanks with words from list A, and then write in their modern Chinese equivalents from list B.

A. Words for Filling the Blanks

信　類　沸　布　答
陰　茵　曙　肖　覽
排　嘆　疏　鄙

B. Modern Chinese Equivalents

昏暗　滾沸　相似　衝擊(冲击)　真實(实)
唱和　天亮　毯子　觀(观)看　噴(喷)薄
好像　稀疏　分布　目光短淺

1. 肉食者 ＿＿鄙，未能遠謀。　**[目光短淺]**　　2. ＿＿＿數偃仰。　　　　　[　　　]
3. ＿＿＿智者所施設也。　　　[　　　]　　4. 朝暉夕＿＿＿。　　　　　[　　　]

5. ＿＿＿＿物之情，得無異乎？　[　　　]　　6. 濁浪＿＿＿＿空。　　　　　　　　　[　　　　]

7. 漁歌互＿＿＿＿。　　　　　　　[　　　]　　8. ＿＿＿＿天爲白。　　　　　　　　　[　　　　]

9. 劇完將＿＿＿＿。　　　　　　　[　　　]　　10. 一童子燒酒爐正＿＿＿＿。　　　[　　　　]

11. 長短豐瘠，無不畢＿＿＿＿。　[　　　]　　12. 森然＿＿＿＿列。　　　　　　　　[　　　　]

13. 綠草如＿＿＿＿。　　　　　　　[　　　]　　14. 其事＿＿＿＿而有徵。　　　　　　[　　　　]

三、給加點字選擇正確的釋義，並選出與加點字用法相同的句子 Circle letter of the correct definition (a, b, c, or d) for the dotted word in each boldfaced sentence. Then circle the letter of the sentence (A, B, C, or D) that employs the dotted word in the same way as the boldfaced sentence.

1. 臣之妻私臣　　　　　　　　　　a. 這(这)件事情　b. 他　ⓒ 的　d. 他們

　　A. 夫晉，何厭之有？　　　　　　B. 不闕秦，將焉取之？

　　C. 肉食者謀之，又何間焉？　　　Ⓓ 能面刺寡人之過者，受上賞。

2. 其旁出堡塢，有若門焉。　　　　a. 啊　b. 什麼(么)　c. 怎麼(么)　d. 於(于)之

　　A. 焉用亡鄭以陪鄰？　　　　　　B. 率妻子邑人來此絕境，不復出焉。

　　C. 必知亂之所自起，焉能治之。　D. 苟慕義彊仁者皆愛惜焉。

3. 不以物喜，不以己悲。　　　　　a. 憑藉(凭借)　b. 來(来)　c. 因爲(为)　d. 認爲(认为)

　　A. 天下之所恃以無憂。　　　　　B. 以爲文者氣之所形。

　　C. 古人思炳燭夜遊，良有以也。　D. 視爲何許人，以何事何時至，皆不敢問。

4. 微斯人，吾誰與歸？　　　　　　a. 和　b. 贊(赞)同　c. 嗎(吗)　d. 給與(给与)

　　A. 若壅其口，其與能幾何。　　　B. 唯求則非邦也與？

　　C. 秦伯說，與鄭人盟。　　　　　D. 失其所與，不知。

5. 是日更定矣。　　　　　　　　　a. 是　b. 這(这)　c. 對(对)　d. 他的

　　A. 是二者，余未信之。　　　　　B. 儻所謂天道，是邪非邪？

　　C. 目送久之，不知是人、是怪。　D. 問其姓氏，是金陵人。

6. 兩軍人馬雜遝，馳者、伏者……．　a. ……是……　b. ……的人　c. ……的原因

　　　　　　　　　　　　　　　　　　　　　　　　　　d. ……的東(东)西

　　A. 吾妻之美我者，私我也。　　　B. 類智者所施設也。

　　C. 是二者，余未信之。　　　　　D. 二者不可得兼，舍魚而取熊掌者也。

7. 投以小石，洞然有水聲。　　　　a. 而且　b. 但是　c. 這樣(这样)　d. 樣(样)子

　　A. 然鄭亡，子亦有不利焉？　　　B. 則見城堡、岡巒……森然布列。

　　C. 其勢則然也。　　　　　　　　D. 然則此畫果真邪？

四、閱讀下面的段落，選擇正確的釋義 Read the following passage and select the correct definition for each dotted word in the following list.

《鈷鉧潭記》
柳宗元

　　鈷鉧潭在西山西。其始蓋冉水自南奔注，抵山石，屈折東流；其顛委勢峻，盪擊益暴，齧其涯，故旁廣而中深，畢至石乃止。流沫成輪，然後徐行，其清而平者且十畝餘，有樹環焉，有泉懸焉。

　　其上有居者，以予之亟遊也，一旦款門來告曰：「不勝官租私券之委積，既芟山而更居，願以潭上田貿財以緩禍。」予樂而如其言。則崇其臺，延其檻，行其泉於高者而墜之潭，有聲潀然。尤與中秋觀月爲宜，於以見天之高，氣之迥。

　　孰使予樂居夷而忘故土者，非茲潭也歟？

《柳河東集》，上海：上海古籍出版社 (2008), 471–472.

鈷鉧 (gǔ mǔ) *n.* iron.　　　潭 creek.
冉水 the Ran Creek.　　　屈 a loanword of 曲 (*qū*).　　　顛委 upstream and downstream.
盪 (荡) *v.* to sweep.　　　齧 (啮 niè) *v.* to gnaw.　　　芟 (shān) *v.* to cut grass.

1. 其始蓋冉水自南奔注。　　　a. 可能　　b. 因爲 (为)　　c. 而且
2. 盪擊益暴。　　　　　　　　a. 好處 (处)　　b. 利益　　c. 更加
3. 畢至石乃止。　　　　　　　a. 完全　　b. 畢 (毕) 业　　c. 停
4. 然後徐行。　　　　　　　　a. 姓氏　　b. 才　　c. 慢慢地
5. 有樹環焉。　　　　　　　　a. 啊　　b. 於 (于) 此　　c. 因此
6. 有泉懸焉。　　　　　　　　a. 挂　　b. 危險 (险)　　c. 懸 (悬) 疑
7. 以予之亟遊也。　　　　　　a. 將要　　b. 多次　　c. 急切
8. 尤與中秋觀月爲宜。　　　　a. 應當 (应当)　　b. 合適 (适)　　c. 當 (当) 然
9. 孰使予樂居夷而忘故土？　　a. 熟悉　　b. 因爲 (为)　　c. 誰 (谁)
10. 非茲潭也歟？　　　　　　　a. 這 (这)　　b. 它　　c. 滋生

五、將下列句子翻譯成現代漢語 Translate the following sentences into modern Chinese.

1. 又怪其不爲之中州，而列是夷狄，更千百年不得一售其伎，是固勞而無用。

現代文翻译：_____

2. 或曰：“其氣之靈，不爲偉人，而獨爲是物，故楚之南少人而多石。”

現代文翻译：＿＿＿＿＿＿＿＿＿＿＿＿＿＿＿＿＿＿＿＿＿＿＿＿＿＿＿＿

3. 然則北通巫峽，南極瀟湘，遷客騷人，多會於此，覽物之情，得無異乎？

現代文翻译：＿＿＿＿＿＿＿＿＿＿＿＿＿＿＿＿＿＿＿＿＿＿＿＿＿＿＿＿

4. 登斯樓也，則有去國懷鄉，憂讒畏譏，滿目蕭然，感極而悲者矣！

現代文翻译：＿＿＿＿＿＿＿＿＿＿＿＿＿＿＿＿＿＿＿＿＿＿＿＿＿＿＿＿

5. 居廟堂之高，則憂其民，處江湖之遠，則憂其君。是進亦憂，退亦憂，然則何時而樂耶？

現代文翻译：＿＿＿＿＿＿＿＿＿＿＿＿＿＿＿＿＿＿＿＿＿＿＿＿＿＿＿＿

6. 有老僧以手背搔眼瞖，翕然張口，呵欠與笑嚏俱至，徐定睛，視爲何許人，以何事何時至，皆不敢問。

現代文翻译：＿＿＿＿＿＿＿＿＿＿＿＿＿＿＿＿＿＿＿＿＿＿＿＿＿＿＿＿

7. 每一巨彈墮地，則火光迸裂，煙燄迷漫，其被轟擊者，則斷壁危樓，或黔其廬，或赭其垣。

現代文翻译：＿＿＿＿＿＿＿＿＿＿＿＿＿＿＿＿＿＿＿＿＿＿＿＿＿＿＿＿

8. 譯者曰：“所以昭炯戒，激衆憤，圖報復也。”

現代文翻译：＿＿＿＿＿＿＿＿＿＿＿＿＿＿＿＿＿＿＿＿＿＿＿＿＿＿＿＿

語法點列表

Essentials of Classical Chinese Grammar Taught

GN   Grammar Notes
VN   Vocabulary Notes

1. Sentence Markers 語句標志

1.1 Declarative Sentence Markers 陳述句類

1.1.1 Sentence Structure Markers 句式標志

是② 是……也。	L3	GN 1
者② ……者也。	L4	GN 3
者③ ……者，……也。	L4	GN 3
爲③ ……，爲……。	L9	GN 1

1.1.2 Initial Particles 發語詞

夫①	L2	GN 4
唯/惟①	L2	GN 7
如③	L6	GN 3
至	L12	VN 8
且② 且夫	L13	GN 2
若③	L14	GN 3
且	L27	VN 10
按	L27	VN 16
若夫/至若	L36	GN 1

1.1.3 Ending Particles 句尾助詞

也① 也已/也已矣	L6	GN 7
也② 也者	L6	GN 7
耳	L7	GN 4
則② 則已	L11	GN 1
云	L17	GN 1
已③ 而已/而已矣	L21	GN 1
爾③	L28	GN 1

1.2 Interrogative Sentence Markers 疑問句類

1.2.1 Sentence Structure Markers 句式標志

何③ 何以	L1	GN 3
幾何	L3	GN 7
孰① A＋孰與＋B＋adjective?	L4	GN 1

孰② A＋與＋B 孰＋ adjective?	L4	GN 1
亦② 不亦……乎? (rhetorical question)	L5	GN 1
如④ 何如	L6	GN 3
奈……何	L29	GN 1
如之何	L30	GN 4

1.2.2 Initial Interrogative Particles 疑問發語詞

何①②	L1	GN 3
焉③	L2	GN 3
胡	L3	GN 6
何④	L4	GN 2
安	L6	GN 9
豈 (rhetorical question)	L8	GN 4
奚	L11	GN 3
惡① (wū)	L12	GN 2
盍	L13	GN 3
況 (rhetorical question)	L18	GN 1
矧 (rhetorical question)	L26	VN 6
曷	L30	GN 1

1.2.3 Ending Interrogative Particles 句尾疑問助詞

乎②	L6	GN 2
也② 也者	L6	GN 7
也③ 也與	L6	GN 7
與 (yú)	L7	GN 6
邪 (yé)	L11	GN 2
爲④ (wéi)	L11	GN 4
歟	L15	GN 3
耶	L16	GN 3
不② (fǒu)	L18	GN 5

1.3 Exclamatory Sentence Markers 感嘆句類

1.3.1 Exclamatory Words or Structure Markers 句式標志

于嗟	L13	VN 26
悲夫 (fú)	L14	VN 22
嗚呼	L21	VN 10
噫	L29	VN 11
惡② (wū)	L33	GN 1
嗟夫 (fú)	L36	VN 15

苟② L19 GN 1

奈 L21 GN 2

固 L23 VN 13

誠 L32 VN 12

或④ L36 GN 2

4.5 Scope 範圍

兼 L7 VN 6

獨 L7 VN 10

盡 (jìn) L8 VN 2

徧 L8 VN 5

凡 L10 GN 4

但爲 (wéi) L18 VN 20

惟/唯② L22 GN 2

畢 L23 VN 2

咸 L24 GN 1

具 (俱) L24 GN 1

皆 L24 GN 1

悉 L24 GN 1

並 L24 GN 1

但 L31 GN 2

5. Conjunctions 連詞

5.1 Coordinating 并列

然① L5 GN 2

如② L6 GN 3

且① L13 GN 2

抑 L16 GN 2

5.2 Subordinate 從屬

5.2.1 If Clauses 假設

若② L4 GN 5

苟① L19 GN 1

向使/使 L32 GN 2

儻 L35 GN 1

5.2.2 Then Clauses 那麼

斯② L5 GN 3

則① L11 GN 1

焉⑥ L12 GN 1

單元練習答案
Answers to Unit Exercises

Unit 1　一　1. 鄙 (*bǐ*) <u>目光短淺</u>; (*bǐ*) <u>把……當作邊疆</u>　2. 甚 (*shèn*) <u>超過</u>; (*shèn*) <u>厲害</u>

　　　　　　3. 朝 (*zhāo*) <u>早晨</u>; (*cháo*) <u>朝拜</u>　　　　4. 與 (*yǔ*) <u>交好</u>; (*yǔ*) <u>跟隨</u>; (*yù*) <u>和</u>

　　　　　　5. 師 (*shī*) <u>軍隊</u>; (*shī*) <u>少師</u>　　　　　6. 間 (*jiàn*) <u>參與</u>; (*jiàn*) <u>偶爾</u>

　　　二　1. 鄙 [目光短淺]　2. 徧 [遍及]　　3. 孚 [信服]　　4. 靡 [倒下]　　5. 賜 [恩惠]

　　　　　6. 闕 [損害]　　7. 易 [代替]　　8. 堪 [忍受]　　9. 阜 [增加]　　10. 悖 [相互衝突]

　　　　　11. 壅 [堵塞]　　12. 窺 [偷看]　　13. 私 [偏愛]　　14. 市 [集市]

　　　三　1. c, D　2. a, A　3. c, B　4. c, C　5. b, D　6. a, D　7. c, B

　　　四　1. b　　2. a　　3. b　　4. c　　5. a　　6. b　　7. a　　8. c　　9. b

　　　五　1. 衣服食物这些安养的东西，不敢独自享有，一定会分给别人。

　　　　　2. 第一次击鼓振作士气，第二次击鼓士气就衰落了，第三次击鼓士气就耗尽了。他们的士气耗尽了，我们的却很充沛，因此战胜他们。

　　　　　3. 如果让郑国灭亡对您有好处，那就冒昧地拿(这件事)来劳烦您的随从。

　　　　　4. 依靠他人的助力又去败坏他，不仁德；失掉我们的同盟之国，不明智；用攻击战乱代替和谐一致，不威武。

　　　　　5. 堵住老百姓的嘴，其后果之严重超过堵住河流。8 河流堵塞了，就会决堤，一定会伤到很多人。老百姓也是一样的。

　　　　　6. 老百姓心里担忧，然后用嘴说出来，这是想法成熟后的自然表现，怎么可以堵住呢？

　　　　　7. 我的妻子觉得我美，是她偏爱我；妾觉得我美，是她害怕我。客人觉得我美，是想有求于我。

　　　　　8. 能够在公共场合批评议论的人，传到我的耳朵里的，可以受到下等的赏赐。

Unit 2　一　1. 鄙 (*bǐ*) <u>目光短淺</u>; (*bǐ*) <u>把……當作邊疆</u>　2. 樂 (*lè*) <u>快樂</u>; (*yuè*) <u>音樂</u>

　　　　　　3. 威 (*wēi*) <u>威懾</u>; (*wēi*) <u>威嚴</u>　　　　4. 與 (*yǔ*) <u>給</u>; (*yǔ*) <u>贊同</u>

　　　　　　5. 方 (*fāng*) <u>方圓</u>; (*fāng*) <u>方向</u>　　　　6. 惡 (*è*) <u>惡政</u>; (*wù*) <u>厭惡</u>

　　　　　　7. 慢 (*màn*) <u>緩慢</u>; (*màn*) <u>怠慢</u>　　　　8. 乘 (*shèng*) <u>兵車</u>; (*chéng*) <u>乘坐</u>

　　　二　1. 鄙 [目光短淺]　2. 徧 [走遍]　　3. 吝 [吝嗇]　　4. 約 [約束]　　5. 俟 [等待]

　　　　　6. 處 [居住]　　7. 畔 [背叛]　　8. 信 [確實]　　9. 撰 [才能]　　10. 竭 [竭盡]

　　　　　11. 哂 [微笑]　　12. 慍 [生氣]　　13. 屏 [摒棄]　　14. 攝 [夾]　　15. 卒 [最後]

　　　三　1. c, D　2. a, C　3. c, A　4. d, B　5. b, D　6. b, B　7. c, B　8. b, D

　　　四　1. a　　2. c　　3. a　　4. c　　5. c　　6. c　　7. b　　8. a　　9. a　　10. b

　　　五　1. 别人不了解(我)，我也不生气，不也是一个有德行的君子吗？

　　　　　2. 夫子善于一步步地诱导学生，用文献典籍丰富我的知识，用礼来约束我的行为，使我想停止学习都不可能。

　　　　　3. 根据对老百姓有利的事，让他们得到利益，这不就是给人恩惠而不浪费吗? 选择老百姓可以劳作的事情让他们劳作，那么还有谁会怨恨呢? 想要仁德而得到仁德，那还有什么要贪图的？

　　　　　4. 有一千辆兵车的国家，夹在大国之间，给它加上（入侵的）军队，继续给它加上饥荒。3 我来治理这个国家的话，等到三年之后，就可以使这个国家的人民变得勇敢，而且知道方向。

　　　　　5. 使老百姓居住下来，不是凭借划定国家的疆界。稳固国防，不是依靠山河的险要。威慑天下，不是凭借兵器甲胄的坚固锋利。得到道义的人会有很多人帮助，失去道义就很少有人帮助。

　　　　　6. 优厚的俸禄，不分辨(是否合乎)礼义就接受了，这优厚的俸禄给我增加了什么好处呢？

　　　　　7. 最后到了东城外的坟墓间，丈夫走到祭拜的人前，乞讨他们剩下的食物。(食物)不够，丈夫又四下看看，到别的墓前(要)，这就是他吃饱喝足的方法。

　　　　　8. 现在，这水流，拍打它使它溅起来，可以使它高过额头；阻遏它，使它（往回）流，可以迫使它流上山。这难道是水的本性吗? 地势迫使它这样。

Unit 3　一　1. 鄙 (*bǐ*) <u>目光短淺</u>; (*bǐ*) <u>把……當作邊疆</u>　2. 適 (*shì*) <u>適應</u>; (*shì*) <u>去</u>

　　　　　　3. 勝 (*shēng*) <u>承受</u>; (*shèng*) <u>取勝</u>　　4. 與 (*yú*) <u>嗎</u>; (*yǔ*) <u>和</u>

　　　　　　5. 敵 (*dí*) <u>匹敵</u>; (*dí*) <u>敵手</u>　　　　　6. 惡 (*wù*) <u>厭惡</u>; (*è*) <u>不好</u>

7. 亡 (*wú*) 無；(*wáng*) 滅亡   8. 知 (*zhì*) 智慧；(*zhī*) 知道

二   1. 鄙 [目光短淺]   2. 拔 [遍及]   3. 安 [習慣]   4. 槍 [碰到]   5. 忿 [憤怒]
    6. 從 [放縱]   7. 宿 [隔夜]   8. 竊 [偷]   9. 施 [施行]   10. 培 [憑藉]
    11. 果 [飽]   12. 矯 [矯正]   13. 擒 [捉住]   14. 殆 [危險]

三   1. c, D   2. d, B   3. c, A   4. a, C   5. b, B   6. c, D   7. d, C

四   1. a   2. b   3. a   4. b   5. c   6. c   7. b   8. c   9. a

五   1. 大鵬鳥迁徙去南海時，(翅膀)拍打水面，(水浪達)三千里之高，盘旋着依着旋風向上飞到九万里
    的高空；離開時用六个月(飞到南海才)休息。
    2. 像野馬飞腾一样的雾气，(轻轻飘扬的)尘埃，都是生物的气息互相吹动的结果。
    3. 古时候圣明的君王认为人的本性不好，认为人性偏颇险恶而不端正，人们互相冲突混乱，社会不
    安定。因此(圣王)为人们建立礼义，制定法度，来矫正整饬人的喜好本性，使其变得端正，来驯服
    教化人的情性，从而引导他们。
    4. 那么可以看见东西的视力离不开眼睛，可以听到的听力离不开耳朵。眼睛的视力和耳朵的听
    力，不可通过学习而达到，是很清楚的。
    5. 所以擅长用兵的人，使敌人的军队屈服投降，不是通过与敌人作战(来实现的)。占领敌人的城
    池，不是通过进攻敌人的城池来实现的。毁掉敌人的国家，不是通过长时间与敌国作战来实现的。
    6. 了解对手了解自己，百战都没有危险；不了解对手，但了解自己，可能一场胜利，一场失败；不
    了解对手，不了解自己，每场战斗都会很危险。
    7. 圣人把治理天下作为自己的事业，必然知道(社会的)祸乱是从哪里产生的，于是才能够治理它；
    不知道祸乱从哪里产生的，就不能治理。
    8. 所以天下都相爱就安定了，都相互憎恨就祸乱了。

Unit 4

一   1. 鄙 (*bǐ*) 目光短淺；(*bǐ*) 把……當作邊疆   2. 載 (*zǎi*) 記錄；(*zài*) 載着
    3. 叩 (*kòu*) 勒住韁繩；(*kòu*) 詢問   4. 號 (*hào*) 稱呼；(*háo*) 大聲呼叫
    5. 環 (*huán*) 四周；(*huán*) 圍   6. 更 (*gèng*) 又；(*gēng*) 換
    7. 微 (*wēi*) 微服；(*wēi*) 稍微   8. 如 (*rú*) 去；(*rú*) 如果

二   1. 鄙 [目光短淺]   2. 沒 [消失]   3. 篤 [專心]   4. 悲 [同情]   5. 抵 [到]
    6. 伺 [監視]   7. 造 [到…去]   8. 捍 [保護]   9. 歸 [歸附]   10. 吝 [在意]
    11. 結 [縫補]   12. 厭 [吃飽]   13. 慕 [向往]   14. 徇 [爲……而死]   15. 昧 [不明]

三   1. c, D   2. b, A   3. a, D   4. b, B   5. c, D   6. c, D   7. b, A   8. c, D

四   1. c   2. b   3. b   4. a   5. c   6. a   7. b   8. a   9. b   10. a

五   1. 父亲去世不下葬，就开始战争，可以称作孝顺吗？凭臣子的身份去杀死国君，可以称作仁义吗？
    2. 登上那个西山呀！采摘它上面的野菜！用残暴(的臣子)来换残暴(的君王)啊！不知这是错误的！
    3. (到了)一年寒冷时，之后才会知道松树和柏树不会凋谢。
    4. 难道不是因为他们把(道德)看得那样重，把(富贵)看得这样轻吗？
    5. 不为贫穷和地位低下而忧愁，不为富有和地位高贵而心情急切。
    6. 现在世人都知道笑话李赤被迷惑(这件事)，至于(面对)是非、取与、向背时能不像李赤这样决断
    的人，有多少呢？
    7. 我已经完了，你又看轻自己，不明大义，天下的事情谁还能支撑啊！
    8. 每到寒冷的夜晚，(史公)站起来，抖一抖衣裳，铠甲上的冰霜就掉落下来，发出响亮的声音。

Unit 5

一   1. 鄙 (*bǐ*) 目光短淺；(*bǐ*) 把……當作邊疆   2. 處 (*chǔ*) 相處；(*chù*) 地方
    3. 更 (*gēng*) 經歷；(*gèng*) 又   4. 稱 (*chèn*) 相稱；(*chēng*) 稱道
    5. 觀 (*guān*) 觀賞；(*guàn*) 景觀   6. 召 (*shào*) 姓氏；(*zhào*) 召來
    7. 分 (*fèn*) 料想；(*fēn*) 不同   8. 沒 (*mò*) 淹沒；(*mò*) 死

二   1. 鄙 [目光短淺]   2. 頃 [近來]   3. 支 [承受]   4. 假 [借]   5. 娛 [娛樂]
    6. 恣 [盡情]   7. 憚 [忌憚]   8. 通 [通曉]   9. 告 [報告]   10. 辱 [屈尊]
    11. 祚 [福氣]   12. 塞 [要塞]   13. 殘 [殘害]   14. 凌 [欺凌]   15. 避 [躲避]

三   1. c, D   2. a, C   3. d, A   4. b, B   5. b, D   6. b, D   7. a, C

四   1. b   2. a   3. c   4. b   5. c   6. a   7. b   8. a   9. b   10. a

五　1. 每到饮酒传杯，弦乐器管乐器一同演奏，酒喝得高兴，仰头作诗，每当这个时候，并不知道快乐一会儿就过去了。

2. 过去伯牙断掉琴弦，(因为)钟子期(过世了)；孔子翻倒所有的肉酱，(因为)子路(在卫国被杀了)；(伯牙是)痛惜知音难再遇见，(孔子是)伤心弟子没有人能及得上(子路)。

3. (我)以犬羊(般的低)素质，(表面)却披着虎豹(般的)花纹(处在太子之位上)，没有众多星星闪亮(的才能)，借着(我父亲曹操)日月(般的)光芒(登上高位)。我的行动一直被人注意着，(这种情形)什么时候才能改变啊！

4. (我)担心自己就此被埋没了，所以决然地离开了(家)，去追求天下新奇的见闻，壮美的景观，来知道天地广大。

5. 所以我希望能够看到贤人的风采，听您一句话来壮大自己，然后就可以看尽天下的壮美景象而没有遗憾了！

6. 无奈上天不保佑我，集中(很多)灾难，加到了明朝之上。一只军队才刚刚建成，就(被清军打败)，化成齑粉。

7. 哎，天地广大无边，(家族)最终趋向于无后啊！(如)有一天(明朝)能够中兴再建，那么(我们)在庙中长久地享受祭祀，又怎么会只是麦饭猪蹄(这样粗糙的食物)而不至于成为饿鬼而已呢？

8. 而万物之中人最为宝贵，我们竟然不能体谅上天的用心，把它当作自己的心意，万物将怎样把生命托付(给我们)啊！

Unit 6

一　1. 鄙 (bǐ) 目光短淺；(bǐ) 把……當作邊疆　　2. 會 (kuài) 地名；(huì) 聚集
3. 異 (yì) 不同；(yì) 以……爲異　　4. 由 (yóu) 原因；(yóu) 就像
5. 數 (shù) 幾；(shù) 數目　　6. 尋 (xún) 尋找；(xún) 不久
7. 舉 (jǔ) 舉薦；(jǔ) 舉動

二　1. 鄙 [目光短淺]　2. 悼 [悲傷]　3. 騁 [放開]　4. 遷 [變化]　5. 緣 [沿着]
6. 業 [職業]　7. 訊 [消息]　8. 延 [邀請]　9. 詣 [拜見]　10. 假 [借]
11. 伸 [抒發]　12. 聊 [姑且]　13. 慕 [仰慕]　14. 仕 [做官]

三　1.c,D　2.a,C　3.c,D　4.a,D　5.d,B　6.d,A　7.c,D
四　1.c　2.b　3.a　4.c　5.c　6.b　7.b　8.a
五　1. 人和人的相处，低头抬头之间就是人的一生。有人从自己的胸怀抱负中获取(智慧)，在室内与人畅谈；有人顺着自己的喜好，寄托自己的精神，放荡不羁地生活。

2. 从前所欣喜的事物，低头抬头间很快就被当成了旧日的痕迹，尚且不能因它而引发(自己的)情怀；何况(人生命的)长短都是由自然造化决定的，(每个人)最终(都)预期(自己会走向生命的)尽头。

3. 问渔人现在是什么朝代，他们竟不知道有汉朝，更不用说魏晋两朝了。

4. (渔人)已经出了(桃花源)，找到了他的小船，于是沿着从前来的路，到处做标记。

5. 何况温暖的春天用美丽的景象来召唤我，大自然把各种美好借给我。

6. 摆开美好的筵席，坐在花中，飞快地(举起)酒杯，醉倒在月下。没有好诗，怎么来抒发高雅的情怀呢！

7. 以你这样没有遇到好的时机，如果(遇到的)是仰慕正义，勉力实行仁政的人，(一定会)爱惜(你这样的人才)啊！

8. 为我凭吊望诸君乐毅的墓，然后看看当地的集市，还有像过去(高渐离一样)屠狗的人吗？

Unit 7

一　1. 鄙 (bǐ) 目光短淺；(bǐ) 把……當作邊疆　　2. 假 (gé) 到；(jiǎ) 借
3. 塞 (sè) 堵塞；(sài) 要塞　　4. 疾 (jí) 病人；(jí) 擔心
5. 公 (gōng) 公正；(gōng) 公衆　　6. 汙 (wū) 污蔑；(wū) 髒
7. 殆 (dài) 危險；(dài) 差不多

二　1. 鄙 [目光短淺]　2. 毀 [詆毀]　3. 奴 [貶低]　4. 折 [折斷]　5. 常 [倫常]
6. 昆 [兄]　7. 順 [平順]　8. 恨 [遺憾]　9. 駭 [驚駭]　10. 譽 [稱贊]
11. 就 [成就]　12. 妄 [胡亂]　13. 固 [加固]　14. 潛 [潛伏]　15. 作 [發出]

三　1.c,D　2.b,D　3.a,D　4.d,A　5.c,B　6.b,A　7.c,C　8.b,C
四　1.c　2.c　3.a　4.b　5.b　6.b　7.a　8.b　9.c　10.a

五　1. 广泛地爱人叫做仁，适宜恰当地实行仁叫做义；从仁义(出发)而继续往前走叫做道，充实自己，不依赖外物，叫做德。

2. 老子所说的道德这类的话，背离了仁和义，是他个人的言论。

3. 孔子作《春秋》时，诸侯用夷人的礼仪，就把他们当作夷人(来看待)；采用了中原地区(的礼仪)，就把他们当作中原人。

4. 因此，活着就得到人与人之间的情谊，死去就完结人和人之间的伦常；郊祀祭天时天神来到，庙里祭祖时祖先的魂灵来享用(祭品)。

5. 为名而求名的人，(如果)在没去世之前，没有得到名声，君子怎么可能只有遗憾呢？

6. 至于追求一天(成名)，是想要快速求得名声的人，(真正)求名的人怎会这样呢？

7. 因此，他没有得到天下时，就残害天下人，使天下人的子女离散，来换取我一个人的产业，竟然还不觉得悲痛！

8. 后世的君王，想用像父亲像青天这样的空名来禁止别人窥探(自己)，都觉得孟子的言论对自己不利，于是废掉了孟子(的牌位)不再祭祀他，这难道不是来源于小儒们(的见识短浅)吗？

Unit 8　一　1. 鄙 (bǐ) 目光短淺；(bǐ) 把……當作邊疆　2. 數 (cù) 細密；(shù) 幾
3. 屬 (zhǔ) 囑托；(zhǔ) 連接　4. 強 (qiǎng) 盡力；(qiáng) 強大
5. 殷 (yān) 染紅；(yīn) 商朝　6. 更 (gēng) 經歷；(gèng) 還
7. 逾 (yú) 越過；(yú) 超越

二　1. 鄙 [目光短淺]　2. 疏 [稀疏]　3. 類 [好像]　4. 陰 [昏暗]　5. 覽 [觀看]
6. 排 [衝擊]　7. 答 [唱和]　8. 嚏 [噴薄]　9. 曙 [天亮]　10. 沸 [滾沸]
11. 肖 [相似]　12. 布 [分布]　13. 茵 [毯子]　14. 信 [真實]

三　1. c, D　2. d, B　3. c, D　4. a, C　5. b, A　6. b, B　7. d, B

四　1. a　2. c　3. a　4. c　5. b　6. a　7. b　8. b　9. c　10. a

五　1. (但我)又感到奇怪，造物者(为什么)不把它建在中原地区，却摆在了偏远的地方，经历了千百年，也不能显露出它的奇景，这本来就是徒劳无用(的功夫啊)！

2. 有人说：“此地的灵气，不成就伟人，而只是造就这种实物，所以楚地的南边人比较少，但是石头比较多。”

3. 虽然如此，但洞庭湖向北通到巫峡，向南尽头在湘江，被贬官的人，诗人，多聚集在此，观看景物的心情，能没有不同吗？

4. (这时)登上这座楼，就会有(这样的)心情：离开国都思念家乡，担心(有人对皇帝进)谗言，害怕(有人)讥讽(自己)，所以满眼望去都觉得萧条凄凉，感叹到了极点就感到悲伤。

5. 处在朝廷的高位上，就担心老百姓；处在边远的地方，就担心国君。这在朝廷做官也担心，被贬官到边远地区也担心。既然如此，那么什么时候才能高兴呢？

6. 有老和尚用手背来揉眼睛，突然张开嘴，呵欠和笑声、喷嚏一起来了。慢慢地认真一看，看看是什么地方的人，因为什么事情，什么时候到的，都不敢问。

7. 每一个巨大的炮弹落在地上，火光四射，烟雾火焰四处弥漫。被炮弹轰击的地方，(就剩下)断掉的墙壁和破损的楼房，或是熏黑了房子，或是烧红了墙壁。

8. 翻译说：“这是为了昭示明显的警示，激发民众的义愤，图谋报复。”